Lecture Notes in Computer Science 4834

Commenced Publication in 1973
Founding and Former Series Editors:
Gerhard Goos, Juris Hartmanis, and Jan van Leeuwen

T0223318

Renato Cerqueira Roy H. Campbell (Eds.)

Middleware 2007

ACM/IFIP/USENIX
8th International Middleware Conference
Newport Beach, CA, USA, November 26-30, 2007
Proceedings

 Springer

Volume Editors

Renato Cerqueira
PUC-Rio, Department of Informatics
Rua Marques de S. Vicente 225, 22453-900 Rio de Janeiro, Brazil
E-mail: rcerq@inf.puc-rio.br

Roy H. Campbell
University of Illinois at Urbana-Champaign
Department of Computer Science, Siebel Center for Computer Science
201 N. Goodwin Avenue MC-258, Urbana, IL 61801-2302, USA
E-mail: rhc@uiuc.edu

Library of Congress Control Number: 2007938898

CR Subject Classification (1998): C.2.4, D.4, C.2, D.1.3, D.3.2, D.2, H.2, H.4

LNCS Sublibrary: SL 2 – Programming and Software Engineering

ISSN   0302-9743
ISBN-10   3-540-76777-0 Springer Berlin Heidelberg New York
ISBN-13   978-3-540-76777-0 Springer Berlin Heidelberg New York

Springer is a part of Springer Science+Business Media

springer.com

© IFIP International Federation for Information Processing 2007
Printed in Germany

Typesetting: Camera-ready by author, data conversion by Scientific Publishing Services, Chennai, India
Printed on acid-free paper   SPIN: 12191420   06/3180   5 4 3 2 1 0

Preface

Nowadays, middleware technologies are the main infrastructure to support the development and execution of distributed systems, providing design abstractions, programming models and tools, frameworks, protocols, deployment mechanisms, and runtime services. Due to its broad scope, middleware research encompasses different research areas, such as distributed systems, operating systems, networking, multimedia systems, databases, programming languages, and software engineering.

This volume contains the proceedings of the Eighth Middleware Conference, held in Newport Beach, California, USA, November 26–30, 2007. Middleware is a series of conferences that started in 1998 with the aim of being the premier conference on middleware research and technology, where researchers from academia and industry can present and discuss the latest middleware results. The focus of the conference is the design, implementation, deployment, and evaluation of distributed systems platforms and architectures for future computing environments.

This year, we had 108 submissions from 25 different countries, among which the top 22 papers were selected for inclusion in the technical program of the conference. All papers were evaluated by at least three reviewers with respect to their originality, technical merit, presentation quality, and relevance to the conference themes. The selected papers present the latest results and breakthroughs on middleware research in areas including peer-to-peer computing, event-based and publish/subscribe architectures, mobile and ubiquitous systems, grid and cluster computing, sensor networks, component- and Web-based middleware, virtual machines, adaptive and autonomic systems, communication protocols and architectures, scalability, fault-tolerance, quality-of-service, resource management, multimedia streaming, and novel development paradigms and tools.

Middleware 2007 also featured an Experience Papers session, which consisted of papers with focus on applications and experience from the use of middleware. From the research paper submissions, four papers were invited to be presented in this session. Another eight papers were recommended for inclusion in the conference's Work-in-Progress Papers program.

Apart from the papers, the program included seven workshops, a doctoral symposium, invited talks, poster and demo presentations, and panels. We hope that the attendees enjoyed this year's Middleware Conference, gained new knowledge and insights from our program, participated in the presentations and discussions, and met others working on projects similar to theirs.

We would like to express our deepest appreciation to the authors of the submitted papers, to all Program Committee members for their diligence in the paper review and selection process, and to all external reviewers for their help in evaluating submissions. We would also like to thank ACM, IFIP, and USENIX for their technical sponsorship, and the corporate sponsors for their financial support. Finally, special thanks go to Nalini Venkatasubramanian and all the other Organizing Committee members for their hard work and effort to make Middleware 2007 a successful conference.

September 2007   Renato Cerqueira
                                                                 Roy H. Campbell

Organization

Middleware 2007 was organized under the auspices of IFIP TC6WG6.1 (International Federation for Information Processing, Technical Committee 6 [Communication Systems], Working Group 6.1 [Architecture and Protocols for Computer Networks]).

Executive Committee

Conference Chair	Nalini Venkatasubramanian (University of California, Irvine, USA)
Program Chairs	Roy H. Campbell (University of Illinois, Urbana Champaign, USA)
	Renato Cerqueira (PUC-Rio, Brazil)
Workshop Chairs	Radha Nandkumar (NCSA, USA)
	Baochun Li (University of Toronto, Canada)
Doctoral Symposium Chair	Qi Han (Colorado School of Mines, USA)
Industry Track Chair	Guruduth Banavar (IBM India Research Lab, India)
Work in Progress Chair	Edward Curry (Digital Enterprise Research Institute, Ireland)
Poster and Demo Chair	Valerie Issarny (INRIA, France)
Publicity Chair	Shivajit Mohapatra (Motorola Labs, USA)
Publicity in Europe	Paolo Bellavista (Università degli Studi di Bologna, Italy)
Local Arrangements Chair	Ray Klefstad (University of California, Irvine, USA)
Local Arrangements Committee	Sharad Mehrotra (University of California, Irvine, USA)
	Vana Kalogeraki (University of California, Riverside, USA)
	Deborah Nielsen (OCTANE@UCI, USA)
	Shellie Nazarenus (Calit2, USA)

Steering Committee

Gordon Blair (Chair)	Lancaster University, UK
Gustavo Alonso	ETH Zurich, Switzerland
Jan de Meer	SmartSpaceLab, Germany
Peter Honeyman	CITI, University of Michigan, USA
Hans-Arno Jacobsen	University of Toronto, Canada
Shanika Karunasekera	University of Melbourne, Australia

Elie Najm	ENST, France
Jean-Bernard Stefani	INRIA, France
Joe Sventek	University of Glasgow, UK
Maarten van Steen	Vrije Universiteit Amsterdam, Netherlands
Steve Vinoski	Verivue, USA

Program Committee

Gustavo Alonso	ETH Zurich, Switzerland
Cristiana Amza	University of Toronto, Canada
Jean Bacon	University of Cambridge, UK
Guruduth Banavar	IBM India Research Lab, India
Alberto Bartoli	University of Trieste, Italy
John Barton	IBM Almadem, USA
Christian Becker	University of Mannheim, Germany
Yolande Berbers	Katholieke Universiteit Leuven, Belgium
Gordon Blair	Lancaster University, UK
Jean-Pierre Briot	CNRS and University Paris 6, France
Andrew Campbell	Dartmouth College, USA
Walfredo Cirne	Google, USA
Clem Cole	USENIX, USA
Paolo Costa	Vrije Universiteit Amsterdam, Netherlands
Geoff Coulson	Lancaster University, UK
Jan de Meer	SmartSpaceLab, Germany
Fred Douglis	IBM T.J. Watson Research Center, USA
Naranker Dulay	Imperial College, UK
Markus Endler	PUC-Rio, Brazil
Pascal Felber	University of Neufchatel, Switzerland
Paulo Ferreira	INESC ID / Tech. Univ. of Lisbon, Portugal
Joni Fraga	Federal University of Santa Catarina, Brazil
Indranil Gupta	University of Illinois at Urbana-Champaign, USA
Valerie Issarny	INRIA, France
Hans-Arno Jacobsen	University of Toronto, Canada
Shanika Karunasekera	University of Melbourne, Australia
Bettina Kemme	McGill University, Canada
Fabio Kon	IME/USP, Brazil
Doug Lea	Oswego State University, USA
Rodger Lea	University of British Columbia, Canada
Satoshi Matsuoka	Tokyo Institute of Technology, Japan
Elie Najm	ENST, France
Priya Narasimhan	CMU, USA
Tamer Ozsu	University of Waterloo, Canada
Christian Perez	INRIA/IRISA, France
Gian Pietro Picco	University of Trento, Italy
Alexander Reinefeld	ZIB, Germany

Luis Rodrigues	University of Lisbon, Portugal
Antony Rowstron	Microsoft Research Cambridge, UK
Rick Schantz	BBN Technologies, USA
Douglas C. Schmidt	Vanderbilt University, USA
Jean-Bernard Stefani	INRIA, France
Joe Sventek	University of Glasgow, UK
Stefan Tai	IBM T.J. Watson Research Center, USA
Peter Triantafillou	University of Patras, Greece
Gregor von Laszewski	Argonne National Laboratory, USA

Referees

Ioannis Aekaterinidis	Danny Hughes	Anand Ranganathan
Hossam Afifi	Roberto Ierusalimschy	Thomas Röblitz
Eduardo Alchieri	Mathieu Jan	Kurt Rohloff
Nazareno Andrade	Björn Kolbeck	Claudia Roncancio
Zahid Anwar	Samuel Kounev	Paul Rubel
Michael Atighetchi	Avraham Leff	Gregor Schiele
Pedro Brandão	João Leitão	Matthias Schunter
Raphael Camargo	Guoli Li	Thorsten Schütt
Fernando Castor Filho	Jian Li	Sabina Serbu
Matteo Ceriotti	Antónia Lopes	Praveen Sharma
Lipo Chan	Paulo Mafra	Reza Sherafat
Ellick Chen	Renato Maia	Marc Shiely
Alex Cheung	Olivier Marin	Sriram Srinivasan
Lauro Costa	Thomas Mikalsen	Biplav Srivastava
Marco Danelutto	Hugo Miranda	Jan Stender
Khuzaima Daudjee	José Mocito	Niko Thio
Mike Dean	Monika Moser	Muhammad Umer
Alvaro Degas	Vinod Muthusamy	Luís Veiga
Mihai Dobrescu	Nanjangud Narendra	Jan Vitek
David Evans	Nikos Ntarmos	Qiang Wang
Daniel Fireman	Rafael Obelheiro	Michelle Wangham
Davide Frey	Marcelo Iury Oliveira	Matt Welsh
Matthew Gillen	José A. de Oliveira Neto	Alex Wun
Alfredo Goldman	Partha Pal	Eiko Yoneki
Minor Gordon	Sujay Parekh	Bechir Zalila
Paul Grace	Frédéric Peschanski	Charles Zhang
Irfan Hamid	Theoni Pitoura	Ning Zhang
Aaron Harwood	Stefan Plantikow	Chenfeng Zhou
Peter Honeyman	Michael Rabinovich	

Sponsoring Institutions

IFIP (International Federation for Information Processing)
http://www.ifip.org

Association for Computing Machinery
http://www.acm.org

 Advanced Computing Systems Association
http://www.usenix.org

Corporate Sponsors

    IBM Research
http://www.research.ibm.com

    BBN Technologies
http://www.bbn.com

OCTANe
http://www.octaneoc.org

Google
http://www.google.com

Table of Contents

Resource Management

Reliability and Fault Tolerance

Asynchronous Communication

R-OSGi: Distributed Applications Through Software Modularization

Jan S. Rellermeyer, Gustavo Alonso, and Timothy Roscoe

Department of Computer Science, ETH Zurich
8092 Zurich, Switzerland
{rellermeyer, alonso, troscoe}@inf.ethz.ch

Abstract. In this paper we take advantage of the concepts developed for centralized module management, such as dynamic loading and unloading of modules, and show how they can be used to support the development and deployment of distributed applications. We do so through R-OSGi, a distributed middleware platform that extends the centralized, industry-standard OSGi specification to support distributed module management. To the developer, R-OSGi looks like a conventional module management tool. However, at deployment time, R-OSGi can be used to turn the application into a distributed application by simply indicating where the different modules should be deployed. At run time, R-OSGi represents distributed failures as module insertion and withdrawal operations so that the logic to deal with failures is the same as that employed to deal with dependencies among software modules. In doing so, R-OSGi greatly simplifies the development of distributed applications with no performance cost. In the paper we describe R-OSGi and several use cases. We also show with extensive experiments that R-OSGi has a performance comparable or better than that of RMI or UPnP, both commonly used distribution mechanisms with far less functionality than R-OSGi.

1 Introduction

Modular design is a cornerstone of software engineering, and much effort has been invested in concepts and tools to manage modules and the dependencies among them. Nowadays, modularization pervades programming languages, development environments, and even system architectures. In particular, recent years have seen the emergence of "module management systems" which handle loading and unloading of modular program units at runtime, and dynamically creating and destroying bindings between services in different modules.

In this paper we explore using centralized module management as the basis for the design and deployment of distributed applications. Our work is based on the OSGi specification [1], a widely used module management API designed to work on a single system that we extend extend to work in a distributed setting.

R. Cerqueira and R.H. Campbell (Eds.): Middleware 2007, LNCS 4834, pp. 1–20, 2007.

The key insight is that the module boundaries instituted by centralized module management systems are generally well-suited to being repurposed as distribution boundaries. In the past, networked applications have typically distributed their functionality by interposing communication proxies at procedure calls or object method invocation, with mixed results. In particular, the issue of transparency has dogged distributed computing platforms based on these models: as Waldo et. al. [2] point out, a remote procedure invocation has fundamentally different semantics to a local call, and consequently fundamentally different exception handling code must be written by the programmer.

In contrast, module management systems like OSGi are designed to handle unloading of modules at any time, and include event notification functionality to enable programmers (indeed, to require them) to cleanly handle services disappearing without notice. We take advantage of this by representing communication-related failures as local module unloading events.

By doing so, we effectively turn software modules into the potential units of distribution. The result is *Remoting-OSGi* (R-OSGi), a distributed middleware platform that can transparently distribute parts of an application by simply distributing its software modules. R-OSGi is a middleware layer on top of OSGi. This matches the lightweight design of OSGi and allows us to use R-OSGi on any OSGi enabled application.

R-OSGi makes the following contributions:

1. *Seamless embedding in OSGi*: From the OSGi framework's point of view, local and remote services are indistinguishable. Existing OSGi applications can be distributed using R-OSGi without modification.
2. *Reliability*: The distribution of services does not add new failure patterns to an OSGi application. Developers deal with network-related errors in the same way they deal with errors caused by module interaction.
3. *Generality*: The middleware is not tailored to a subset of potential services. Every valid OSGi service is potentially accessible by remote peers.
4. *Portability*: The middleware runs Java VM implementations for typical resource-constrained mobile devices, such as PDAs or smartphones. The resource requirements of R-OSGi are by design modest.
5. *Adaptivity*: R-OSGi does not impose role assignments (e.g., client or server). The relation between modules is generally symmetric and so is the distributed application generated by R-OSGi.
6. *Efficiency*: R-OSGi is fast, its performance is comparable to the (highly optimized) Java 5 RMI implementation, and is two orders of magnitude faster than UPnP.

In the next section we discuss in more detail the relevance of module management systems for distributed applications, using OSGi as a case study. In Section 4 we discuss the architecture and design of R-OSGi, and describe the implementation in detail in Section 5. Section 6 presents performance results for R-OSGi, and Section 7 details several use cases including ubiquitous computing devices and a tool for refactoring a large, pre-existing OSGi-based application in Eclipse to run in a distributed setup. We conclude in Section 8.

2   Background

Models and frameworks for building distributed systems have a long history. The conventional approach is to make remote invocations identical to local procedure or method calls, as exemplified by Remote Procedure Calls (RPC) [3], Java Remote Method Invocation (RMI), the Common Object Request Broker Architecture (CORBA) [4], or the Distributed Component Object Model (DCOM) [5]. While providing a form of distribution transparency at the level of invocations, the application must nevertheless be manually factored into distributed components, and the large-scale structure of the application usually reflects this factoring. The same is generally true for analogous operating system-based approaches, such as Amoeba [6] or SOS [7].

Alternatively, centralized applications written in a component framework can be automatically factored into distributed components. Coign [8] partitions COM-based Windows applications into two parts that can be distributed in a client/server configuration. Coign instruments the code through binary rewriting, analyzes the dependencies between COM components and calculates a graph-cutting according to a cost metric for introducing network communication between the subgraphs. Similarly, JOrchestra [9] automatically partitions a program by rewriting bytecode to replace local methods with remote invocations, and object references with proxy references. In these approaches, the distribution is orthogonal to the original design, and occurs along object boundaries which were typically not designed with distribution in mind, giving rise to the kind of transparency and performance problems described in [2].

Recent centralized module management systems, e.g., MJ [10] and OSGi, in contrast to typical component frameworks, impose boundaries between modules which are explicit at the level of program code. This is done to better deal with dynamically loading, updating, and unloading of modules at runtime. We describe OSGi in more detail below, as it forms the basis of our system.

However, we note that to date, efforts to add distribution support to OSGi have either followed the OSGi specifications in providing protocol adapters to existing Jini [11] and Universal Plug and Play (UPnP) [12] infrastructures, or (as with the Newton Project [13]) introduce an additional component model for distribution independent of OSGi's module boundaries and based on an existing infrastructure like Jini. Both approaches are what might be termed "invasive": they require the application to be explicitly structured (or restructured) around the distribution model provided by Jini or UPnP, and hence the application must be factored in such a way as to conform to one of these component models. What is clearly missing is a way to have across remote OSGi instances without loosing the generality of the OSGi model, or, equivalently, to allow an OSGi application to be easily distributed along OSGi module boundaries. Filling this gap is the main result of this paper.

3   Overview of OSGi

Before discussing the design and implementation of R-OSGi, we briefly describe all the relevant aspects of the OSGi model. The OSGi specification is maintained by the OSGi Alliance (including vendors and users). OSGi is used in a number of systems (e.g., Eclipse [14]) and several open-source implementations exist, such as Apache Felix [15], Knopflerfish [16], and Concierge [17].

3.1   Basics of OSGi

OSGi is both (1) a programming model to develop Java applications from modular units (*bundles*) decoupled through *service interfaces*, and (2) a runtime infrastructure or *framework* for controlling the life cycle of bundles. Among other features, OSGi allows developers to dynamically manipulate bundles: new bundles can be added and existing bundles updated or removed all at runtime. OSGi maintains consistency across modules by keeping track of the dependencies between modules.

As in systems such as Tomcat [18], OSGi implements module management by using a separate class loader per bundle and disposing of the entire class loader when the bundle is unloaded. However, unlike Tomcat, where shared code has to be placed into the scope of a special *shared* class loader, all bundles loaded by an OSGi framework are allowed to define shared Java packages and interact through services.

3.2   OSGi Services

OSGi implements a centralized service-oriented architecture with loosely coupled *services* (Figure 1). In the OSGi model, any Java class can be published as a service to be used by other bundles in the system. Typically, a service includes an implementation (an instance of a class), one or more service interfaces under which the service is published, and a set of service properties. The OSGi framework maintains a *registry* of all services published in the system. Bundles can retrieve services by the name of their interface, and optionally use LDAP-style RFC 1960 [19] filter predicates on service properties for higher selectivity.

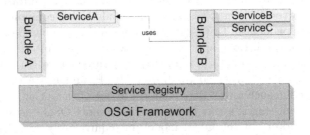

Fig. 1. OSGi Framework with Bundles and Services

Over the indirection of a service reference, a client bundle can bind to the service object and invoke operations on it from its own code. Since services might not be present or even disappear during the life cycle of the service's client, access to service objects must be mediated and controlled. OSGi does this by sending events whenever the state of a service changes. The typical pattern of service usage is to listen to such events and either disable parts of the requesting bundle when the requested service becomes unavailable or even trigger a halt of the whole bundle, if the presence of the service is required for correct operation of the bundle.

3.3   The OSGi Whiteboard Pattern

Besides services invoked from other bundles, OSGi services can also be used to simplify different variations of producer/consumer exchanges. Typically, the publish/subscribe pattern is used for this purpose: each event source maintains its own registry of subscribed listeners and delivers events to all subscribers as the events take place. The whiteboard pattern [20] used in OSGi simplifies this process. Instead of requiring each listener to subscribe to individual events and the source to hold the subscriptions, the OSGi *service registry* is used. Listeners register themselves under a specific listener service interface. Once this is done, the listener is not required to dynamically track all sources of events, instead, it has implicitly acquired a global subscription to all existing and future event sources. The OSGi registry is thus the whiteboard to which all listeners may subscribe. Event sources can retrieve all registered listeners whenever an event occurs. With such an approach, the coupling between listener and source is reduced to a minimum and the listener can place the subscription even if no source is currently present. It has been shown that the whiteboard pattern is often more efficient than traditional publish/subscribe in terms of code size and the total resulting number of classes [20].

4   The R-OSGi Approach

R-OSGi allows a centralized OSGi application to be transparently distributed at service boundaries by using proxies. Figure 2 shows a simplified example with one service provider (I) and one service consumer (J). To bundles on peer J, the R-OSGi proxy is indistinguishable from local OSGi services such as service A and B. The R-OSGi protocol on the proxy is used to make remote invocations to the original service, which is located on peer I, and events from I are transparently forwarded to J and occur as if they were issued by a local bundle. The only difference between local and remote services are additional properties that allow services aware of distribution to perform specialized operations, e.g., for system management.

R-OSGi uses four principal techniques to achieve the goal of transparency: (1) *dynamic proxy generation* at bind-time for cross-network invocation of services, (2) a *distributed Service Registry* based on SLP complementary to the

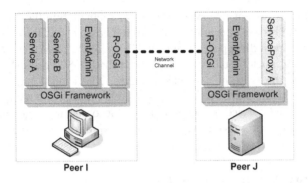

Fig. 2. Architectural Overview

centralized version in OSGi, (3) *mapping network and remote failures* to local module hotplug events, and (4) *type injection* to resolve distributed type system dependencies. We describe these in turn.

4.1 Dynamic Service Proxies

R-OSGi creates transparent client proxies for remote services on the fly. To a service client, these proxies behave as a local service and are also provided by locally-instantiated bundles. However, a proxy bundle redirects all service method calls to the original service residing on the remote machine and propagates the result of the method call back to the local client.

The approach of dynamically generating the proxy code at the client facilitates spontaneous interaction between services, but also reduces to a minimum the data (in the form of Java bytecode) that must be stored on the server or transferred over the network when a client binds to (or *fetches*) a service.

The typical information required to create a proxy for a particular service interface is determined by bytecode analysis of the original service when it is registered. When a client fetches the service interface, the service provider responds with the corresponding Java bytecode for the interface along with any serialized properties of the service.

From the interface bytecode, the client can then generate a full proxy for the service. No precompiled skeletons or stubs need to be provided by the implementor of the service, and no actual proxy code needs to be transferred. This is particularly useful in the case of *servers* running on resource-constrained devices, since the service provider bundle does not need to retain any code for the client proxy.

4.2 Service Registration and Location

OSGi is built around a centralized service registry. In order to transparently distribute OSGi applications, a distributed registry implementation is required. It is not possible to make a distributed service registry look like a local registry without changing the OSGi framework implementation. Thus, to avoid limiting the generality of the platform, R-OSGi works with a complementary service discovery protocol and builds proxies for remote services which then register their services with the conventional OSGi service registry. Hence, conventional OSGi bundles can be used (and distributed) in R-OSGi without modification.

OSGi uses an explicit binding model whereby the client bundle invokes (as a synchronous method call) the service registry, which hands over a set of *service references* in return. The request contains two arguments: the class name of the requested service and a filter expression which can, for instance, be used to distinguish between equivalent implementations of the same service type. Filters are based on the LDAP filter syntax (RFC 1960 [19]). A client in possession of a valid service reference can then attempt to establish a binding to the service, and afterwards invoke operations on it.

While the explicit binding model simplifies the handling of network and remote node failures in R-OSGi (see Section 4.3), the approach of building proxies for services introduces a potential scalability problem since in a large distributed system there might be a large number of nodes, and a large number of services. Each service proactively announcing its availability and the system generating proxies for every available service might increase network traffic, and tie up processing resources at the nodes.

R-OSGi's distributed service registry alleviates this problem by making service discovery (and thus the proxy generation) reactive. Bundles can register services of type `DiscoveryListener` and set properties to convey information about the service interfaces they are interested in, optionally including a filter string. Following the whiteboard pattern, R-OSGi keeps track of all registered listeners by observing service registration events from the local service registry. It initiates remote service discovery whenever there is an entity in the system that has announced a demand for a service.

Likewise, peers announce their offers of services to the network and allow remote access to them according to a locally-determined policy. Whenever a new service is registered with the local framework with properties that indicate it should be offered remotely, R-OSGi triggers registration of this service with the remote service discovery layer.

Explicit determination of which services to offer for remote access in this way can be performed by the application, at the cost of loss of transparency (since the application must set the required properties). Alternatively, a surrogate bundle separate from the application but residing on the same node can listen for local service registrations, and selectively re-export some services remotely without requiring the application itself to be distribution-aware.

4.3   Transparent Distribution

Transparently distributing programs designed for a single address space context has been a problematic concept. Waldo et. al. [2] provide a good summary of the main problems: networked systems are fundamentally different in behavior to centralized ones, and the semantics of an invocation are also fundamentally different. Consequently, the argument goes, it is unlikely that a centralized program will perform with acceptable performance, let alone correctly, when factored into distributed components. The basic problems here are communication latency and non-determinism, and unreliability (either due to message loss or partial failure of the nodes or network). These arguments are powerful and persuasive.

R-OSGi sidesteps these issues by intelligently exploiting the way that OSGi programs are already written – the assumption of unknown performance characteristics of cross-bundle calls. Furthermore, rather than masking distributed failures, R-OSGi exposes these events to application bundles, but in a form that the bundle is already designed to handle: the disappearance of service bundles through module unloading.

R-OSGi conceptually maps failures arising from the distribution of components to local hot-plug events. From the OSGi model, developers are used to guarding the code against the case that parts of the system are not available. Usually, this is done by listening to service events or using the OSGi *Service-Tracker*. In a purely local configuration, services can become unavailable when some entity in the system, in particular a user of the system, decides to stop or to uninstall the bundle that has provided the service. By mapping network malfunctions to these events that are already handled by the applications, we introduce no failure patterns that are not already possible in purely centralized situations.

For instance, if a service providing peer fails, we detect the breakdown of the network channel and the failure to reconnect. Having observed this, R-OSGi immediately uninstalls the proxy bundle. Even if the network operates without failures, the original service can throw exceptions. We serialize these exceptions and rethrow them in the proxy bundle to mime the exact behavior of the original service.

OSGi Services give no guarantee about execution time regardless of whether they are local or remote. Side effects of services such as threaded design or database accesses (e.g., a persistence service), can lead to an execution time that appears to be non-deterministic from the client point of view. A user might even decide to replace a fast implementation of a service by an extended but overall slower implementation and the client has to live with this situation. Furthermore, services are often event-driven and since events in OSGi are typically dispatched asynchronously, no assumptions about timing can be made. This is a considerable difference to plain objects, that are most often expected to execute methods within a very short time. A further difference between R-OSGi in comparison to systems like CORBA is that the granularity of distributed entities is much larger. In OSGi, services encapsulate whole functional units and the dependencies between services are typically restricted to semantical dependencies at the application level. Objects in contrast tend to have a larger number and often nested interconnections that make bad effects of the network more severe.

4.4   Type Injection

In OSGi, all code is modularized into bundles and imports of code from other bundles have to be explicitly declared in the bundle JAR manifest. Several implications arise in the context of proxy bundles. The service interface might use types in method parameters or return values that do not belong to the standard Java classes and cannot be assumed to be present at the client. This can either be the case if the type is declared by a class of the original service bundle, or because the package to where the class belongs was imported by the original service bundle. It has to be assured that the generated proxy is resolvable, i.e., it contains all the types that are used by methods of the service. R-OSGi thus has a special strategy to ensure type consistency for the service interface. Type injection is used to make service proxies self-contained.

When the (remotely accessible) service is registered, every type occurring in the service interface is observed by a static code analysis. If the type is contained in the service bundle and the package is declared to be exported by the service bundle, the corresponding class is added to the so-called *injection list*. Referenced types not contained in the service bundle are left out. In a second step, the transitive closure of all injections is formed, once again distinguishing between own and imported classes. The injections are saved with the service registration. Whenever a client fetches the service, the injections are transmitted in addition to the service interface and the service properties. During proxy generation, the injections are materialized and stored in the proxy bundle. The packages of all referenced classes not included in the injections are declared as imports of the proxy bundle. The packages of all injected classes are declared as exports to ensure type consistency within the framework. Classes from the packages *java.** and *org.osgi.** are excluded from the whole process since it is assumed that they belong to the execution environment. The result of the injection strategy is a minimal set of classes and package imports that make the service proxy self-contained and resolvable.

Beyond the described code analysis to determine the minimal set of injections, service registrations can be manually provided with classes that have to be injected into the bundle. This can be useful in particular cases, e.g., if an argument of a service method is an interface and the service provider wants to add an instantiable implementation of this interface.

5   Implementation

5.1   Distributed Service Registry

R-OSGi implements the distributed registry using the Service Location Protocol (SLP) [21,22,23] as the underlying mechanism. We discuss the choice of SLP over more apparently natural choices like Jini in this section. Rather than using a C-based daemon implementation of SLP like OpenSLP, we instead developed a pure Java implementation, jSLP [24]. jSLP implements all the mandatory features of the SLP protocol, plus most of the optional features, yet has a code footprint of only 55kBytes. We do not discuss jSLP further here for reasons of space; further information and complete source code can be found at [24].

SLP has several compelling features for R-OSGi: its adaptivity, the inherently distributed lookup process, and the similarity with OSGi in the naming of services. To use SLP as a fully decentralized service registry, we exploit the adaptive behavior of the SLP protocol. In SLP, when a dedicated *Directory Agent* is present, clients communicate exclusively with this central registry server. If no DA is present, the clients use multicast (as in SSDP [25]). Through this feature, R-OSGi implements a distributed SLP layer that can be used in a wide range of situations. In terms of naming, both OSGi and SLP identify a service by a single string. In OSGi, this is the fully qualified name of the interface under which the service has been registered. In SLP, the name is a service URL of the form `service:`*`serviceType:`*`//`*`URL`* where the service type is of the form *`abstractType:`*`concreteType`* By describing all OSGi services by the same abstract type `service:osgi` and using the fully qualified name of the interface as the concrete type, we have a bidirectional mapping between OSGi and SLP services. OSGi supports LDAPv2 filter predicates on service properties to allow more declarative and fine-granular services matching. This feature becomes particularly useful when the service registry is no longer a central but a large distributed one. With the choice of the SLP protocol that also supports LDAP filters over service attributes, R-OSGi leverages the power of expressive service predicate matching for the distributed case.

After a service is discovered, R-OSGi introduces an intermediate step before the actual service is delivered (i.e., imported into the local framework). This is important for security reasons as it allows users to, e.g., see the available remote services in a GUI before connecting to them. With such a step, R-OSGi matches the behavior of OSGi, which also uses an indirection over service references. R-OSGi also supports explicit connection to a remote peer if the application has *a priori* knowledge of the distribution of services in the system.

5.2   Network Channels and Message Transport

The communication structure of R-OSGi is purely message-based. For efficiency of parsing and handling, all messages are binary. Messages consist of a header that indicates the type of the message plus some common attributes, and a body with the parts specific to the message type.

Network channels in R-OSGi are by default persistent TCP connections using the TCP *keep-alive* option. As long as there is traffic within the timeout period, the connection is kept open. This reduces the overhead for the TCP handshake that would otherwise precede every call to a service. R-OSGi is nevertheless extensible. We have, for instance, implemented tunneling of R-OSGi messages through HTTP to support communication through firewalls.

When a connection through a network channel is established, the two peers exchange *symmetric leases* (Figure 3). A lease contains the names of the services that the peer offers as well as the event topics the peer is interested in. The latter is used in the context of remote events as discussed in Section 5.5. In R-OSGi,

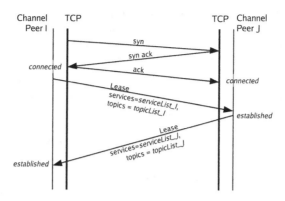

Fig. 3. R-OSGi Channel Establishment and symmetric leases

unlike in systems like Jini, a lease is more a contract between the two peers than a temporal limitation. Whenever changes to services or to subscriptions are announced through the lease, the peer that has issued the lease is obliged to invalidate the existing lease.

5.3   Proxy Generation

On the client side, the proxy is created through a *Proxy Generator*. The Proxy Generator is based on the *ASM* library [26], and it uses bytecode manipulation to create the service interface. First, an empty class is created that implements both the service interface as well as the OSGi specific interface (the *BundleActivator*). The OSGi specific parts, including the registration of the service with the local framework and retrieving the R-OSGi service, are implemented by emitting generic templates. Subsequently, every method of the service interface is visited and the corresponding method implementation created. Each method implementation delegates the method call to the network channel provided by R-OSGi and invokes the following method:

```
Object invokeMethod(final String serviceURL,
    final String methodSignature, final Object[] args)
    throws RemoteOSGiException;
```

The *serviceURL* is known at proxy generation time and hard-coded into the proxy, since every remote service gets its own proxy. The method signature is also a constant of each method implementation. The *args* array is built at runtime by aggregating the actual arguments.

The proxy-implementation of the service interface is packed into a JAR file together with the service interface. The required metadata is added to the manifest to turn the JAR file into a valid bundle. The service interface is then exported. This allows other bundles to import the interface if it is not yet known. Otherwise, the import statement is used and the newly created bundle is linked against the existing interface to preserve consistency within the framework. R-OSGi stores the generated bundle and installs it, which leads to a registration of the proxied service. Since the service is registered under the transmitted interface name, local bundles cannot distinguish between a proxied service and a local service, thereby preserving full location transparency.

5.4   Method Invocation

Every method invocation corresponding to a remote service is transformed into the *invokeMethod* call shown above and sent through the underlying R-OSGi channel. On the other side of the channel, the first step taken is to lookup the corresponding service. R-OSGi holds references to all services that are released for remote access in a HashMap to guarantee a quick lookup. On this service object, a reflective call of the original method is performed. However, the Java reflection API requires the formal method parameters for matching and these can differ from the types of the actual arguments. This is particularly true if one of the formal parameters is an interface or an abstract class. One option would be that for every method call, the whole type hierarchy of each of the arguments is used for matching. To avoid this overhead, the signature of the method is part of the transmitted message. R-OSGi uses the signature to unambiguously match the original method. If the reflective method call succeeds, the result value is packed into a response message and sent back. If an exception occurs, the exception object is serialized, packed into the response message, and thrown on the other side of the channel. This makes the syntactic behavior of the remote service indistinguishable from that of local services.

5.5   Remote Events

As in UPnP, R-OSGi implements both remote service invocation as well as an event based architecture. R-OSGi uses the OSGi concept of events as described in the R4 specification of the *EventAdmin* service. In R-OSGi, the EventAdmin service is implemented as a whiteboard pattern over the distributed service registry. A bundle registers for an event by registering an *EventHandler* service together with the property *event.topics* and the optional property *event.filter* stating a filter that is matched against the property set of occurring events. Topic strings of events follow a hierarchical structure and can be matched using wildcards. Bundles initially register the EventHandler in the local service registry. The subscription is announced to peers through a symmetric lease transmitted during the connection phase. On the other side of the channel, an EventHandler is registered locally for the stated topics and if any matching events are outstanding, they are sent back through the channel. To publish an event, bundles post it to the local *EventAdmin* service which then sends it to all registered listeners.

 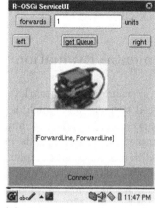

(a) connecting to service   (b) displaying a robot service

Fig. 4. ServiceUI for an R-OSGi-driven Lego Mindstorms Robot on a Zaurus PDA

5.6 Presentations

The fact that R-OSGi modules are treated as units for distribution offers unique opportunities to specialize some of these modules. One such specialization in R-OSGi is the idea of *presentations*. A presentation is a single class with an associated user interface that can be downloaded by the client rather than simply used remotely. Services can attach presentations by setting the property *service.user_interface* to the fully qualified name of a class implementing the interface *ServiceUIComponent*. Declared presentations are automatically injected into the proxy bundle and registered as services in a whiteboard fashion. On the client side, it is possible to run the optional R-OSGi *ServiceUI* bundle. This bundle displays the information about discovered services and allows the user to fetch these services. If the service has a presentation attached, the graphical component provides a Java AWT panel. This panel is displayed in a tabbed environment to allow the user to interact with multiple remote services.

We have used presentations for controlling smart devices. Figure 4 shows the screen of a PDA that connects to a Lego Mindstorms robot through R-OSGi. The software controlling the robot is developed using R-OSGi and contains a presentation with the user interface to control the robot. The PDA first connects to the *Robot Service* as a normal R-OSGi service (Figure 4.a). It then downloads the presentation with the robot controller interface which now runs locally and allows the PDA to become the robot controller. As the example shows, with R-OSGi presentations and the ServiceUI, it is possible to implement the idea of the universal remote control that can connect to any kind of (R-OSGi enabled) smart device and control it. The user interface for a service comes directly from the device and thus allows to connect to previously unknown devices without any need for configuration or installation of device drivers. Note as well that the demands on the developer are very small as it is only necessary that the user interface is designed as a module, something that it is likely to happen regardless of whether R-OSGi is used.

6 Experimental Evaluation

Since there is no standard benchmark for evaluating the performance of R-OSGi, we have adapted two suitable benchmarks from other areas.

The Javaparty/KaRMI [27] benchmark measures the performance of alternative RMI implementations. It calls various methods of a sample object using arguments of different size and complexity. We have implemented the Javaparty benchmark as an OSGi service which is transparently distributed by R-OSGi. For comparison, we have also implemented it as a service object which is distributed by RMI and as a UPnP service accessible through the Domoware UPnP service implementation [28] for OSGi. The benchmark client calls the different methods multiple times and determines the average invocation time from the accumulated runtime. Most of the arguments are instances of primitive types or primitive arrays with increasing length. We skipped the parts of the performance benchmarks that are specific to the KaRMI system and not relevant to R-OSGi.

The *WSTest* benchmark [29] measures the performance of web services. It was originally used to compare web service performance in Java and in .NET. The benchmark starts a number of agents that concurrently call one of four sample methods according to a predefined mix. The arguments of the method calls are complex objects. In the variant originally used by Sun and Microsoft, only one of the methods is called at once, concurrently by eight agents. Since UPnP is not able to use complex objects in service calls, we run this benchmark only for R-OSGi and RMI.

The benchmarks have been measured with the services running on an IBM R32 notebook with an 1.6 GHz Intel Pentium 4 Mobile CPU and with 512 MB RAM. The client was a Pentium 4, 3 GHz Desktop machine with 1 GB RAM. For the PDA tests a Sharp Zaurus 5500 with a StrongArm SA-1110 CPU running at 206 MHz and with 64 MB RAM has been used. In the notebook and the workstation, we use Sun J2SE 1.5 as the underlying VM. The Zaurus runs *cvm* [30], Sun's implementation of the CDC Personal Profile.

6.1 Service Binding

In a first experiment, we measured the *binding time*. In R-OSGi, this is the time spent to establish the connection, requesting the service, receiving the interface, and building the proxy. For RMI, this is the time needed to establish the connection and to download the stub from the codebase. The results are presented in Table 1. As the Table shows, R-OSGi performs better than RMI even though the client has more work to do. From our observations, the download of the stub is the source of the overhead in RMI. The differences between the two benchmarks are because the binding time depends on the complexity of the service and, in this case, this complexity is related to the number of service methods.

Table 1. Binding Time

Service	# Methods	Binding Time in μs	
		R-OSGi	RMI
JavaParty	7	147381	163702
WSTest	4	97147	168034

The benchmarks show that R-OSGi is more efficient in terms of binding time than RMI, an interesting result given the additional functionality that R-OSGi provides.

We have also tested how R-OSGi scales down to mobile devices by measuring the binding time for the Javaparty service on a Sharp Zaurus 5500 PDA with 802.11b wireless LAN. The measured binding time was 1585 milliseconds. This is a much higher overhead but comparable with the latency of such operations on mobile devices. Furthermore, this penalty has to be paid only once for each service.

6.2 Service Invocation

In a second experiment we compare the cost of invoking a remote service in R-OSGi, RMI, and UPnP using the Javaparty benchmark. Since UPnP does not support complex objects as arguments in service method calls, not all test methods of the benchmarks could be implemented for UPnP. The results are shown in Table 3. As the table shows, R-OSGi performs slightly better than RMI in many cases, especially when the arguments are complex objects. We also measured the round trip time in the test network which was 193 μs (+-7 μs). Compared with this value, the `ping()` method using R-OSGi has an overhead of only 1.5% whereas for RMI it is about 16%. Those tests that can be run with UPnP have an execution time two orders of magnitude larger than R-OSGi and RMI. The main reason is the high verbosity (resulting in higher network delays) and the expensive parsing of the XML involved.

A similar comparison was done using the WSTest benchmark (Table 2) where we measured both response time and throughput. R-OSGi has a lower response time per method and a higher throughput. We also tested the scalability of R-OSGi using this benchmark. The proposed setup of the WSTest specifications uses only eight agents. When, for instance, the echoVoid method is called by 80

Table 2. WSTest Benchmark Results

Test	R-OSGi		RMI	
	Resp.time (μs)	Throughput	Resp.time (μs)	Throughput
echoVoid	5799.109	1378.583	10914.879	732.583
echoStruct	11464.700	697.633	14067.500	568.533
echoList	12238.550	653.500	15390.130	519.767
echoSynthetic	2439.700	3275.567	3069.710	2604.667

Table 3. Javaparty Benchmark Results

Method invoked	Invocation Time in μs and STD		
	R-OSGi	RMI	UPnP
void ping()	195.813 ±0.52	225.18 ±0.738	87938.454 ±174.044
int ping()	214.633 ±0.479	227.98 ±0.645	87335 ±27.839
void ping(int)	216.838 ±0.43	227.172 ±0.789	87844.286 ±191.748
void ping(int, int)	227.043 ±0.427	228.885 ±0.509	88558.571 ±126.765
void ping(null)	202.974 ±0.393	228.031 ±0.472	-
void ping(Integer)	218.301 ±0.419	324.855 ±1.162	-
void ping(byte[1])	246.263 ±0.559	273.345 ±1.317	88770 ±122.241
void ping(byte[2])	246.237 ±0.425	273.656 ±0.54	88822.857 ±48.613
void ping(byte[4])	246.58 ±0.517	274.167 ±0.55	88832.857 ±40.958
void ping(byte[8])	247.94 ±0.51	274.41 ±0.514	88948.571 ±86.426
void ping(byte[16])	249.463 ±0.492	275.374 ±0.568	89088.571 ±39.071
void ping(byte[32])	252.988 ±0.514	277.174 ±0.681	89122.857 ±15.779
void ping(byte[64])	257.396 ±0.47	284.274 ±0.457	89055.714 ±19.166
void ping(byte[128])	270.142 ±0.704	295.539 ±0.591	89090 ±40.708
void ping(byte[256])	278.694 ±0.638	317.382 ±0.476	89162.857 ±38.439
void ping(byte[512])	337.612 ±0.818	363.596 ±0.692	89201.429 ±104.53
void ping(byte[1024])	429.258 ±0.966	457.977 ±0.947	89467.143 ±32.388
void ping(byte[2048])	532.447 ±1.031	582.424 ±1.19	89997.5 ±24.875
void ping(byte[4096])	692.89 ±1.072	718.177 ±1.158	91098.75 ±63.134
void ping(byte[8192])	1275.493 ±7.605	1095.5 ±2.291	98631.429 ±3185.514
void ping(byte[16384])	1903.204 ±11.198	1872.352 ±7.369	97718.571 ±36.027
void ping(byte[32768])	3941.772 ±65.534	3932.065 ±52.933	157588.571 ±93.263
void ping(float[1])	251.204 ±0.593	275.155 ±0.757	-
void ping(float[2])	252.204 ±0.574	276.011 ±0.5	-
void ping(float[4])	253.924 ±0.648	277.676 ±0.374	-
void ping(float[8])	256.831 ±0.526	279.994 ±0.796	-
void ping(float[16])	262.098 ±0.488	287.206 ±0.602	-
void ping(float[32])	273.858 ±0.5	297.677 ±0.662	-
void ping(float[64])	296.173 ±0.741	317.408 ±0.567	-
void ping(float[128])	344.244 ±0.701	369.27 ±2.416	-
void ping(float[256])	439.993 ±0.92	470.157 ±7.577	-
void ping(float[512])	551.247 ±1.21	605.09 ±9.467	-
void ping(float[1024])	723.892 ±1.592	749.488 ±3.622	-
void ping(float[2048])	1224.912 ±2.27	1251.543 ±10.059	-
void ping(float[4096])	1954.012 ±11.076	1945.257 ±38.723	-
void ping(float[8192])	4105.288 ±77.579	3982.534 ±59.839	-
void ping(float[16384])	8036.289 ±132.496	7916.875 ±132.722	-
void ping(float[32768])	13460.103 ±131.231	13839.062 ±104.921	-
void ping(DM(1024,1024))	918597.938 ±13063	923121.212 ±12276	-
void ping(DM(2048,2048))	3557125 ±16284	3614843.75 ±23682	-

concurrent agents, the response time for R-OSGi increases by only 5% whereas it increases by about 23% for RMI. This indicates that R-OSGi scales very well, even for large setups with massive distribution.

7   Use Cases

In this section we briefly present two use cases implemented with R-OSGi to illustrate its potential to distribute complex applications.

7.1   R-OSGi Deployment Tool

The first use case is a tool to help developers to distribute an application by *dragging and dropping* between a visualization of the modules of the application

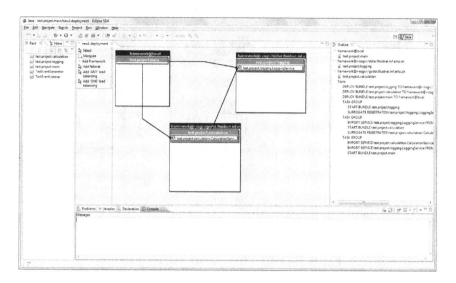

Fig. 5. Screenshot of the R-OSGi Deployment Tool

and a representation of the distributed nodes available. The tool has been written as an Eclipse *plugin* and provides an overview of all nodes running R-OSGi and where the application could be distributed. Through the R-OSGi capabilities to make explicit connections, the developer can add new OSGi nodes that are outside of the scope of service discovery. To distribute an application, the tool takes an ordinary OSGi application as input. It first analyzes the services and dependencies between the bundles. Then it graphically displays the architecture of the application as it would run on a single machine. The developer can then drag and drop bundles into the different available nodes. An example deployment with three bundles on two different nodes is shown in Figure 5. The tool visualizes all dependencies arising from this setup and gives the user an idea how many network communication is involved in a particular setup. Once the user commits a configuration, R-OSGi does all the work of deploying the bundles to the corresponding machines and creating surrogate registrations and discovery listeners. The result is the original application running in a distributed environment without requiring the developer to change a single line of code. The developer has full control on how the application is distributed. The tool is only intended to create static deployments. In the future, we will extend this tool to seamlessly introduce module replication, and allow the end-user to profit from fault-tolerance or load balancing by taking advantage of the distributed setup and the loose coupling of components.

7.2   R-OSGi Tea Machine

As an example of how to use R-OSGi with small devices, we have implemented a remote-controlled tea machine (along the lines of the Trojan Room coffee

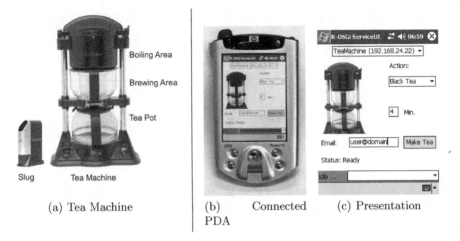

(a) Tea Machine   (b)   Connected   (c) Presentation
                   PDA

Fig. 6. R-OSGi-driven Smart Tea Machine

machine [31]). We took an off-the-shelf tea machine that is internally driven by an Atmel AT89C2051 microcontroller with 2KBytes flash and built a mobile controller for it using R-OSGi. Since the microcontroller is not powerful enough to run Java and R-OSGi, we added a serial port to the board and implemented a plain RS232 protocol to give out status messages and to control the brewing. The tea machine is connected to and controlled by an external LinkSys NSLU2 (*Slug*) embedded linux device.

The tea machine can be spontaneously remote-controlled by PDAs. When a user's PDA comes within range of the machine, it can download the corresponding R-OSGi presentation (Figure 6(c)) and then control the machine (Figure 6(b)). The controlling is done by method invocations on the service that is running on the Slug. This service interacts with the machine over the RS232 link. The status information received from the tea machine is transmitted to the presentation on the PDA as remote events. The current application allows notifications about the status of the tea machine to be sent per e-mail and also to a desktop machine by using R-OSGi over HTTP.

This use case demonstrates the potential of the concept of presentations. The current limitation of the approach is that the problem of different ratios and resolutions of the displays of mobile devices cannot be solved by using predefined AWT panels as R-OSGi does now. We will address this in future work and plan to extend R-OSGi's presentations to support a more declarative way of defining user interfaces that support adaptation to the end device.

8 Conclusions

R-OSGi allows distributed applications to be built using the same modularity features of OSGi, and allows existing OSGi applications to be transparently distributed along module boundaries. R-OSGi maps partial failures of the distributed application as a whole onto local module unload events, and represents traditional distributed systems support functions like service location as existing OSGi registration services. Experience has shown this novel approach avoids the problems typically encountered by transparent distribution systems, and we argue that R-OSGi does not present failure patterns to applications that could not occur in the centralized case.

While R-OSGi exploits OSGi's bundle concept to achieve this goal, it addresses significant further challenges. R-OSGi ensures consistency among shared classes by the use of type injection, and uses dynamic client proxy generation to allow even resource-constrained devices to provide services. R-OSGi is portable to all J2ME CDC profiles, is code compatible with Java back to Java 1.2, and runs entirely over a standard OSGi implementation. Despite these advantages, it is remarkably lightweight: R-OSGi has a file footprint of just 120 kBytes, slightly outperforms RMI in network tests, and is an order of magnitude faster than UPnP. Consequently, we argue that R-OSGi is an attractive approach to efficiently handle the complex structure of pervasive environments.

Acknowledgements

The work presented in this paper was supported (in part) by the National Competence Center in Research on Mobile Information and Communication Systems (NCCR-MICS), a center supported by the Swiss National Science Foundation under grant number 5005-67322.

References

1. OSGi Alliance: OSGi Service Platform - Release 4 (2005)
2. Waldo, J., Wyant, G., Wollrath, A., Kendall, S.: A Note on Distributed Computing. Technical Report SMLI TR-94-29, Sun Microsystems Labs (1994)
3. Birrell, A., Nelson, B.J.: Implementing remote procedure calls. ACM Transactions on Computer Systems 2(1), 39–59 (1984)
4. Object Management Group: The Common Object Request Broker: Architecture and Specification. 2nd edn. (1995)
5. Brown, N., Kindel, C.: Distributed Component Object Model Protocol – DCOM/1.0 (Expired Internet Draft). IETF (1998)
6. Mullender, S.J., van Rossum, G., Tanenbaum, A.S., van Renesse, R., van Staveren, H.: Amoeba: A Distributed Operating System for the 1990s. IEEE Computer 23(5), 44–53 (1990)
7. Shapiro, M., Gourbant, Y., Habert, S., Mosseri, L., Ruffin, M., Valot, C.: SOS: An Object-Oriented Operating System - Assessment and Perspectives. Computing Systems 2(4), 287–337 (1989)
8. Hunt, G.C., Scott, M.L.: The Coign Automatic Distributed Partitioning System. In: OSDI 1999. Proceedings of the 3rd Symposium on Operating Systems Design and Implementation (1999)

9. Tilevich, E., Smaragdakis, Y.: J-Orchestra: Automatic Java Application Partitioning. In: Magnusson, B. (ed.) ECOOP 2002. LNCS, vol. 2374, pp. 178–204. Springer, Heidelberg (2002)
10. Corwin, J., Bacon, D.F., Grove, D., Murthy, C.: MJ: A Rational Module System for Java and its Applications. In: OOPSLA 2003. Proceedings of the 18th Annual ACM SIGPLAN Conference on Object-Oriented Programming, Systems, Languages and Applications, pp. 241–254. ACM Press, New York (2003)
11. Waldo, J.: The Jini architecture for network-centric computing. Communications of the ACM 42(7), 76–82 (1999)
12. UPnP Forum: Universal Plug and Play Device Architecture (2000)
13. Paremus: The Newton Project (2006), http://newton.codecauldron.org
14. The Eclipse Foundation: Eclipse Project (2001), http://www.eclipse.org
15. Apache Foundation: Apache Felix (2005), http://incubator.apache.org/felix
16. Gatespace Telematics SA: Knopflerfish OSGi (2003), www.knopflerfish.org
17. Rellermeyer, J.S., Alonso, G.: Concierge: A Service Platform for Resource-Constrained Devices. In: Proceedings of the EuroSys 2007 Conference (2007)
18. Apache Foundation: Apache Tomcat (2006), http://tomcat.apache.org
19. Howes, T.: RFC 1960: A String Representation of LDAP Search Filters. IETF (1996)
20. Kriens, P., Hargrave, B.: Listeners considered harmful: The "whiteboard" pattern. Technical report, OSGi Alliance (2004)
21. Guttman, E.: Service Location Protocol: Automatic Discovery of IP Network Services. IEEE Internet Computing 3(4), 71–80 (1999)
22. Veizades, J., Guttman, E., Perkins, C.: RFC 2165: Service Location Protocol. IETF (1997)
23. Guttman, E., Perkins, C., Veizades, J.: RFC 2608: Service Location Protocol v2. IETF (1999)
24. Rellermeyer, J.S.: jSLP project, Java Service Location Protocol (2005), http://jslp.sourceforge.net
25. Goland, Y.Y., Cai, T., Leach, P., Gu, Y., Albright, S.: Simple Service Discovery Protocol (Expired Internet Draft). IETF (1999)
26. Bruneton, E., Lenglet, R., Coupaye, T.: ASM: A Code Manipulation Tool to Implement Adaptable Systems. Technical report, France Telecom R&D (2002)
27. Haumacher, B., Moschny, T., Philippsen, M.: The Javaparty Project (2005), http://www.ipd.uka.de/JavaParty
28. Demuru, M., Furfari, F., Lenzi, S.: The Domoware UPnP service for OSGi (2005), http://domoware.isti.cnr.it
29. Sun Microsystems: Web Service Preformance. Comparing Java 2 Enterprise Edition (J2EE platform) and.NET Framework (2004)
30. Sun Microsystems: J2me Personal Profile for Zaurus 2002, http://java.sun.com/developer/earlyAccess/pp4zaurus
31. The University of Cambridge Computer Laboratory: The Trojan Room Coffee Machine (1991), http://www.cl.cam.ac.uk/coffee/coffee.html

Argos, an Extensible Personal Application Server

Arne Munch-Ellingsen, Dan Peder Eriksen, and Anders Andersen

University of Tromsø, Norway

Abstract. Argos is a microkernel based, small-scale or personal middleware container that is extendible through deployment of system services. System services to support development of end user applications in sensor network, pervasive, context-aware and mobile setting have been developed and used to easily allow for application development of user application in this domain. Argos also gives enterprise container type support to user-centric application development, without the complexity and limitations enforced by enterprise containers.

Annotations, notifications, reflection, dependency injection and hot deployment are together used to create the Arogs run-time extensible and adaptable personal container.

1 Introduction

Traditional application servers support business applications and have a focus on scalability, integration, transaction management, safety and security [1]. Such enterprise application servers are well suited for enterprise applications that need this kind of system support. However, a large group of applications does not fit this model. Their demands are different and possibly highly specialized. One approach to create such applications is to start from scratch and integrate all needed services in each application. Typical such applications are found in embedded systems, in sensor networks, in context aware systems, and in personal or small-scale systems, often with the mobile phone or the laptop computer as the end user terminal.

Argos supports these kind of applications. Some requirements in these settings are similar to requirements that appear when developing enterprise applications. Examples include support for persistence (database), general web support (web server), and support for web service interface. Other requirements are domain specific or linked to the fact that such applications can be user-centric. One such important example is access to local resources (file system, sensors). Another observed aspect is that not all applications need the same system support: "one-size-does-not-fit-all". This observation led to the design and implementation of Argos, an expandable small-scale or personal application container with a minimal microkernel core[1].

---

[1] We will refer to the "microkernel core" as the "core" in the rest of the text.

R. Cerqueira and R.H. Campbell (Eds.): Middleware 2007, LNCS 4834, pp. 21–40, 2007.

The minimal Argos core can be extended for different application domains. The development of Argos applications should focus on the actual logic of the application and expect specialized support from the container at run-time. Argos supports rapid development of specialized applications in supported application domains. Argos is an extensible application server. Its minimal core supports life-cycle management and a few other core services. In a given setting this core is extended with system services implementing support needed by its applications. Such system services can provide persistence, bindings (to be able to bind to information sources), web services, and so on. The application programmer develops application components as Java objects (POJO, Plain Old Java Objects) [2]. Such components can specify application server and system component dependencies using annotations [3]. Examples are annotations specifying that a given method of the object should be invoked every 10th second (lifecycle) and that the current value of a given attribute of the object should be stored in a database (persistence).

The provided specialized application support makes it possible to create domain specific container configurations with Argos. Since Argos supports user-centric and small-scale systems, its users often refer to the Argos container as a personal container. In short, Argos is both a personal container and it can be used to create domain specific container configurations.

2   Argos Core

Argos is a container based middleware system and the Argos core is the minimum configuration that defines the Argos container. The Argos core defines a service and component model, including component lifecycle handling, implicit instrumentation (for monitoring and control) and a set of supported annotations. In the default configuration of Argos, a service is a collection of components, web pages (one possible presentation), desktop widgets (e.g. Yahoo! Widgets, another possible presentation), mobile applications (j2me or mobile cf .net applications), instrument panels (to monitor and control the service), and external wrappers (not discussed in this paper). An Argos component is a POJO class with additional meta information expressed using Argos supported annotations. The annotations are part of the default programming model offered to system services and user application programmers. The set of supported annotations can be increased through deployment of new system services. The Argos core container allows deployment of system services and user applications. System services are used to augment the intrinsic capabilities of the Argos core.

A system service implementation can be replaced with a different implementation providing the same kind of service. This can be used to replace a system service implementation with an improved implementation. It can also be used to replace the service with another implementation better supporting the current application needs and the current environment or setting of the application (adaptation).

User applications depend on the functionality of the Argos core and the deployed system services to create end user applications. The Argos core supports "Hot deployment" of system services and user applications. Argos deployment is described in more detail in section 3.

Figure 1 gives an overview of the Argos core with the default set of system services. It is of course possible to start Argos with no extra system services, but the default set of system services represents an often used configuration. Jetty [4] is an embedded web server, and Hibernate [5] and Derby [6] together provides persistence (Derby is a database and Hibernate is an object/relational persistence and query service). The web service system service provides web method (SOAP[7] and XML-RPC[8]) access to component methods. A more detailed description of the different system services will be given in section 4.

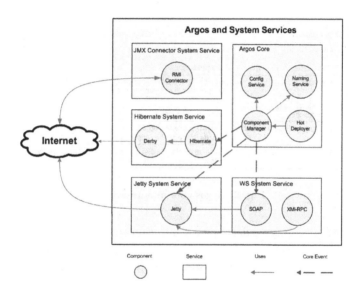

Fig. 1. Argos Core overview

The annotations supported by the Argos core are listed in figure 2.

The annotations that are supported by the Argos core are as the figure shows divided into the following categories:

Lifecycle. Annotations to control the component's lifecycle. They are used to annotate functionality performed in a timely manner (e.g. every 10th second), or when a component is created or destructed

Notification. Annotations to describe notifications and to handle sending and receiving of notifications (e.g this function will be performed when the given notification is received).

JMX related. Annotations to declare and describe instrumented methods and attributes.

Dependency injection	Description
@Component ("Name")	Inject reference to the component called "Name"
@NotificationSender	Inject reference to notification sender component
@ComponentMeta	Inject reference to my own meta information representation
@ServiceClassloader	Inject reference to the service class loader
@ServiceMeta	Inject reference to the service meta information representation. For example used to get reference to Hibernate session for this service.
Lifecycle	**Description**
@Init	Tag the initialization method of the component
@Execute(S)	Tag the execute method of the component. S is call interval
@Unload	Tag the initialization method of the component
Notification	**Description**
@NotificationInfo	Identifies a method that returnes an array of notification descriptions. The descriptions are used by JMX
@NotificationHandler	Identifies the method the container will call when a component has received a notification
JMX related	**Description**
@Description	Gives a textual description of the attribute. Used by JMX. The text is for example used in a JMX browser to describe a managed attribute
@Impact	Describe the impact type. Used by JMX. The type is for example used in a JMX browser to describe a managed methods type
@Instrument	Used to explicitly tell Argos to instrument this method
@InstrumentThisClassOnly	Used to instrument methods defined in this class and not methods defined in any super class
@Removeinstrumentation	Used to mark classes and methods telling Argos explicitly not to instrument the class or method

Fig. 2. Argos core annotations

Injection. Annotations for dependency injection (to get access to core and system service infrastructure). Dependency injection is a design pattern that decouples the client component from the system service implementation component [9,10].

Annotations in Argos are standard Java annotations. Using an annotation does not directly affect a component's semantics, but they do affect the way an Argos component is treated by the Argos container and the deployed system services, which can in turn affect the semantics of the instantiated component. Annotations in Argos are inspected reflectively at deploy time by the Argos core and by all the previously deployed system services.

The following example shows how the *Weather* service POJO component uses the @Init and @Execute annotations:

```
public class Weather {
    // Instruct container that this is the Weather components init method
    @Init public void init() {
        ...
    }
```

```
// Instruct container to call this method at 30s intervals
@Execute(30) public void execute() {
  ...
}
}
```

The Argos core uses reflection to identify the annotations supported by the Argos core and handles them appropriately when the service is deployed to the container. All annotations are handled before the component is started.

3   Argos Deployment

One of the main functions of the Argos core is to provide the ability to deploy system services and user applications. System services and applications must be presented to Argos in a Java archive file (jar) and the content of the jar file must follow the Argos deployment specification. Basically, the specification defines that deployment meta information needs to be included in a separate deployment descriptor (deploy.xml file) and that service content that is not POJO components needs to be added in designated folders in the jar file. In the deployment descriptor it is possible to express the following:

– Service name and version
– Service dependencies – references to other services that have to be deployed for this service to work properly
– List of components that the service contains (including possibility to express instantiating of multiple instances of the same POJO)
    – Component dependencies
    – Listen to properties, i.e. other components this component receives notifications from
    – Attribute configuration, i.e. start values for configurable attributes

Argos will store the meta information associated with a service in core objects. This meta information is available to system services using dependency injection annotations. Before any components are instantiated, all service dependencies are checked and validated, errors are logged and the service is not started if the dependencies are not met. The following example shows the deployment descriptor for the web service system service[2]:

```
<service name="!!Webservices" version="1.0">
  <depend on="!!Jetty6"/>
  <deploy>
    <component name="!!XML-RPC" class="argos.bangbang.xmlrpc.XmlRpc">
      <listen to="ComponentManager" />
    </component>
    <component name="!!Axis" class="argos.bangbang.axis.Axis">
      <listen to="ComponentManager" />
    </component>
  </deploy>
</service>
```

---

[2] System services in Argos is always deployed in jar files with names that starts with two exclamation marks (!!). This has also led to the convention that system service names starts with two exclamation marks.

System services (as the web service) can listen to notifications emitted by the Argos core (in this case, the core component *ComponentManager*). In this way they can perform their necessary actions associated to events emitted by the core. The web service system service will for example inspect all deployed components for @Webmethod annotations when the core emits the *SERVICE_STARTED* notification. If such annotations are found, their associated methods will be added as callable web methods (i.e. accessible through XML-RPC and SOAP calls).

4   System Services

A system service is a collection of components that augment the intrinsic functionality of the Argos core. System services are the pinnacle of Argos elasticity. Typically a system service consists of definitions for new annotations and components that semantically handle the functionality related to the new annotations. The web services system service is a good example. The general idea for this service is to make it easy for an application programmer to express that he wants to create a web service. The easiest way to express this would be to allow the application programmer to simply tag a method in a component's code in order to specify that the method shall be offered as a web method (similar to the WebMethod attribute in C#). It should be possible to use both XML-RPC and SOAP to invoke the newly created web method. The Argos web service, @Webmethod annotation allows the application programmer to do just that. If you tag a method in a component that is part of a service with the @Webmethod annotation, that method is automatically exposed as a web method by the Argos container (i.e. accessible through XML-RPC and SOAP calls).

The web service system service (!!Webservice) first defines the new annotation (@Webmethod). Secondly, it contains the necessary code to reflectively find all @Webmethod annotations in subsequently deployed user components. Thirdly, it interacts with the Argos core (using notifications and dependency injection) and the Jetty web server system service to create the glue between incoming web service calls and the appropriate method in the instantiated component. Figure 3 illustrates the concept. The figure shows the chain of events when a user application (UserApplication.jar) that depends on the web service and Jetty system services is deployed to the container. First (1) the Argos core emits the SERVICE_STARTED notification. The notification is received by the web service system service and it will use reflection (2) to find all (if any) @Webmethod annotations in all the deployed POJOs in the newly deployed user application. When it finds @Webmethod annotations it registers the web method with the Jetty system service (3). The web service system service uses dependency injection to access and update meta information about the user application.

Using annotations, notifications, reflection and dependency injection in this manner allows for dynamic deployable extensions to the Argos core.

The possibility to add system services makes it possible to create Argos configurations that fit specific needs. Although Argos in many ways resembles Enterprise Containers, the focus has been different. Enterprise containers need to be

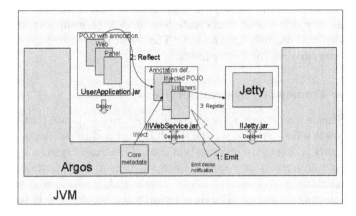

Fig. 3. Argos System Services

able to handle thousands of simultaneous requests to services that circle around legacy data. Our focus has been to provide a similar programming model for the creation of context aware, embedded or user-centric services that will be used by one or a handful of users. The design of Argos reflects that services are to be provided to a small number of simultaneous users. Argos allows deployed services to access the file system, open incoming and outgoing socket connections and to create threads. Enterprise systems usually do not allow such actions since it will make it extremely difficult to handle scaling and safety in a sensible manner (open connections to sockets or files and multiple threads makes it difficult to put components in a waiting pool). Argos components can with no restrictions behave in the same manner as POJOs running directly in a JVM. Argos adds expressive and powerful annotations to handle complicated tasks that are often needed when creating new services.

5   System Service Examples

System services can come in many shades. In the following subsections we will briefly describe a handful of system services that we have created at the time of writing.

The typical user application we have created uses sensors of some kind to gather context information. Sensors are often connected to a user's mobile phone. Typical sensors we have used are GPS, Step counters, temperature sensors, etc. In order to make it easy to use information from sensors in an Argos user application we have created a SMS system service, a Sensor system service and a TCP system service. The SMS service makes it possible to send and receive SMS message from a user application in Argos. The Sensor system service makes it possible to automatically connect new sensors to a users mobile phone (it also uses the SMS service for initial interaction with the phone's sensor framework client).

You will of course only deploy system services that your user application needs. In this way it is possible to create lean middleware support only for the features needed for your user applications. The result is an embedded or personal middleware system that suits your needs.

5.1   Sensor Framework System Service

The Argos Sensor framework actually consists of three separate parts. The first part is the Argos sensor system service which is deployed to the Argos container. The second part is a sensor configuration tool. The sensor system service handles incoming announcement requests from the sensor configuration tool. The sensor configuration tool is a standalone Java graphical tool used to describe the characteristics of a sensor. The description given by the user is transformed into a sensor configuration expressed as an XML document. When a sensor "announcement" is done from the tool, this description is transferred to the Argos Sensor framework system service. The sensor framework system service acts on the newly announced sensor configurations and handles all the sensor management needed to configure and start the sensor at the remote sensor location (i.e. connecting to the sensor, reading sensor data and transferring results back to the sensor framework system service. The third part of the sensor framework is a sensor host (remote) client program. The client program interacts with the Argos sensor system service to get the sensor configuration and download sensor specific plugins. The client program also automatically configures and starts the sensor and sends sensor data back to the Argos sensor system service as XML documents according to the Argos sensor data XML format. Currently we have only implemented a Windows Mobile 5.0 client program and a Java Windows client program. The Windows Mobile 5.0 client allows mobile phones with this operating system to act as Argos sensor framework clients. The Java Windows Client program allows Windows PCs to act as sensor framework clients (for example to manage USB or RS232 connected sensors). The typical scenario in the mobile setting is to connect Bluetooth or IR sensors to the mobile phone and send the collected sensor data to Argos using either a web service or TCP/IP interface. Once the Windows Mobile client program has been installed on the mobile phone, arbitrary Bluetooth or IR sensor may be connected to the phone. The installation, configuration and management of new sensors are done without touching the phone itself (i.e. remote management) [11].

5.2   TCP System Service

The Argos TCP/IP system service provides a tcp/ip communication abstraction for Argos user applications. It utilizes a scalable architecture based on the Java Non-Blocking IO libraries in order to provide a high performance connectivity framework that can support at least hundreds of simultaneous tcp/ip connections. The service is primarily suited for Argos user applications that need server functionality, but it also provides tcp/ip client connectivity. The client and server interface that is exposed to Argos applications is identical and based on a stream abstraction. Argos applications either read from the stream or write to the stream after a tcp/ip connection is established. The following illustrates usage of this service.

```
// Inject handler for the tcpService
@Component("!!TCPBinding") public TCPBinding tcpService;

// Use handler to create a server, connectionAccepted is called when clients connects
tcpService.addService(PORT, new ClientHandler());

// When clients connects, this method in the components ClientHandler interface
// is called. ClientHandler is an interface that is implemented by the component
// Note: read is blocking, write is non blocking

public void connectionAccepted(Connection con){
    TCPStream stream = con.getStream();
    byte[] buf = new byte[10];
    stream.read(buf);
    stream.write(buf);
}
```

5.3   Small Messaging Service (SMS) System Service

This service provides an easy to use abstraction (API) to send and receive SMS messages to/from mobile phones from Argos services. The following example shows how this system service is used to send a SMS message:

```
// Inject reference to SMS system service
@Component("!!SMSservice") public SMSservice smservice;
...
// Use the SMS system service to send an SMS
// The parameters are the phone number and the message
smservice.sendSMS("90914546", "How are you?");
...
```

This system service does not introduce any annotations. As the example shows, user applications can use dependency injection annotation, defined by the Argos core, to get a handler to the SMS system service component. This handler can then be used to send and receive SMS messages by invoking methods in the system service component.

5.4   Web System Services

Currently we have developed three web related system components. The web service system service component has already been described. A web server (Jetty) is also deployed as a system service in Argos and in addition, support for Axis (SOAP) is included as a separate system service component (in the web service system service). The following examples shows how a user application component creates a web method. The web method can be reached using SOAP or XML-RPC when the component is deployed in the Argos container.

```
public class Something {
  @WebMethod public String hello() {
    return "Hello, world!";
  }
}
```

5.5   TwoWay Notification System Service

The *Two Way system service* is a service that makes it easy to establish two way notification listening relationships, meaning that a service A listens to events submitted from service B and vice versa. The TwoWay system service lets either end establish the two way connection and avoids the problems of synchronizing the establishment of a two way connection between the two ends. This system service is useful when creating distributed services where user applications in different Argos containers need to cooperate. The following example shows how this system service is used to set up two way notification listening:

```
@Component("!!TwoWay") public TwoWay twoWay; // Inject reference

@ComponentMeta public ComponentMetaInfo meta; // Inject own meta info from core

@Init public void init() {
    ...
    // Set up mutual notification listening with the Manager component at host
    twoWay.setupTwoWay("Components:name=Manager", host, meta.getMyName());
    ...
}
```

5.6   Derby and Hibernate System Services

Support for persistence is handled by two system services components, the Derby and Hibernate system service components. Derby is an SQL database and Hibernate is an object to entity relationship transformation tool. We have also experimented with a separate persistence system service that makes it possible to use annotations to express that component attributes are to be stored in the embedded database. We are currently considering using *Hibernate Annotations* instead.

5.7   JMX Connector System Service

The *JMX Connector system service* opens an RMI port to the Argos MBean server. When the RMI port is open, the JMX Connector system service makes it possible for remote monitoring and management of the Argos container and its deployed system services and applications. We have also developed a JMX browser and service monitoring and management tool specific for the Argos container but any JMX compliant monitoring and management tool may be used. The special thing about the JMX browser (called Argus) is that it can use service specific instrument panels to give advanced (graphical) insight into Argos and its system services and user applications. Figure 4 shows Argus in use. The left side shows ordinary JMX browsing and the right side shows a user application specific instrument panel for the satellite ground station service. The telemetry input from a satellite ground station is visualized in a user application specific instrument panel. The satellite ground station monitoring service is not discussed in this paper.

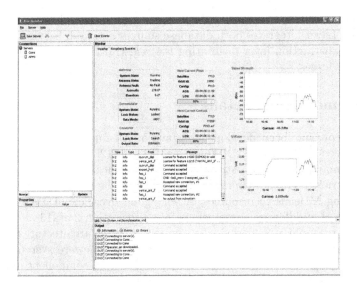

Fig. 4. Argus JMX monitoring and control tool

5.8   Service Management and Distribution System Service

The *service management and distribution system service* is a framework to provide distribution of system services and user applications in Argos. A service
provider creates a remote repository for their services and applications. These
services and applications then become available to their end users through the
service management and distribution system service. End users can download
new services and applications or update their existing services and applications
when an update is available.

The service management system service provides help in managing the container its deployed system services and applications. The end user can inspect
meta data associated with each service, and configure these to fit their own
needs. In addition, service management offers start, stop and updating (using
service distribution) of services and applications.

5.9   Transaction Management System Service

An experimental transaction system service for Argos has been developed. The
transaction system service supports flexible transaction processing by providing
the possibility to support an extensible number of transaction managers. The
current version of the experimental transaction system service uses two concurrently running transaction managers (DB-TM and WS-TM). The DB-TM
(Database Transaction Manager) supports traditional ACID transactions implementing a two-phase commit protocol. The WS-TM (Web Service Transaction
Manager) supports long-running transactions with relaxed atomicity following
a compensation-based scheme. Based on the requirements from the application,

one of them is selected to control the execution of an issued transaction. The Transaction Layer integrates both database sources and Web Services by implementing an abstraction layer facilitating the registration of, and the access to, the various sources.

6   Implementation Details

The Argos core has been developed in Java 5. All functionality in the Argos core is realized as a set of JMX DynamicMBeans [12]. JMX defines an architecture for management of distributed resources (local or remote). Resources must be instrumented to be manageable. In Argos, the instrumentation is done by associating MBeans to resources. A very good overview of JMX related to development of middleware containers is found in section 2 of [13].

The JMX technology also provides a component-based architecture that makes it easier to develop a monitored and manageable middleware system (as compared to starting from scratch). Argos extends the JMX component model with elements related to component and service metamodels, component lifecycle and component dependency handling.

The Argos core instantiates all system services and user applications with a DynamicMBean proxy associated to them. This means that all the major functionality in the Argos core, all Java classes in system services and all Java classes in user applications are instantiated with associated DynamicMBean proxies. This makes it possible to monitor and manage the Argos core, the system services and user applications through JMX.

System service or user application programmers are not exposed to JMX or MBeans, meaning that Java classes in system services and user applications does not have to implement any of the MBean interfaces. The component model exposed to application programmers is plain Java (with the possibility to add Argos core and system service specific annotations). Using the proxy pattern together with reflection and explicitly expressed meta-data is very powerful as it makes it possible to turn any java object into a DynamicMBean at run-time. The reflective inspection done by the DynamicProxy is the first of a series of reflective inspections performed on newly deployed components. The Argos core performs another inspection just prior to activating the new component. This run is done to collect information given by lifecycle annotations. In addition, potentially all deployed system services may inspect every newly deployed component to search for annotations that are part of that system services supported annotations (if any). The system service will also perform the actions (service) associated with the annotation. Dependency injection is just a special type of annotation and may be handled in all the reflective inspection passes (depending of what you would like to inject). Figure 5 illustrates the situation when a POJO has been deployed to the Argos container.

Since JMX and specifically MBeans are intentionally not exposed to the application program, the Argos container creates a dynamic MBean acting as a proxy

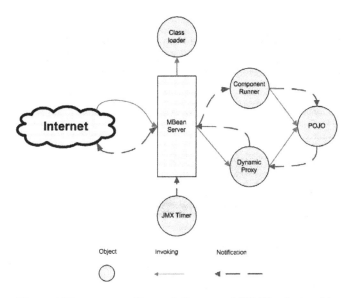

Fig. 5. MBean server, DynamicProxy and POJO relationship

to the POJO. The proxy MBean and the Component runner MBean handle all interaction between the MBean server and the POJO.

7 Example Applications

The Argos container has evolved as a result of needs/requirements that we have observed when developing software in the areas of:

- Applications related to sensor networks
- Context aware applications including usage of several types of sensors as context information sources
- Personal or small scale deployed services, i.e. services to one or a small number of persons
- Personalized services in a mobile phone setting, i.e. applications available using the mobile phone as end user terminal and sensors related to a person

Many of these applications follow the basic Input, Processing, Output pattern. The Sensor framework system services has been developed for Argos to make it easy to include sensors of different types as input sources for Argos applications. Currently, processing is usually performed in processing components, but we have ongoing work to include rule based processing as a separate system service. Output can easily be done to a database or to external endpoints through web services. Visualization of output can be done through GUI, Widgets or instrument panels. Some of the user applications that we have developed are briefly explained in the subsequent sections.

7.1   The Weather Service

This service consists of a very simple component that reads sensor data from weather instruments. The data is visualized in a service specific instrument panel. The instrument panel (viewed in the Argos JMX monitor) is shown in figure 6.

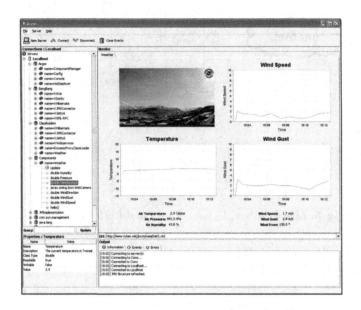

Fig. 6. The Weather service instrument panel

The weather service uses the *TCP system service* to bind to external weather sensors. The sensor values are stored in a database using the *Hibernate and Derby system service*. The service specific instrument panel is the only GUI for this service and the *JMX Connector system service* is used to make it possible to remotely connect to the Argos container that runs the weather service.

7.2   The XUfo Service

Automatically piloting of a flying radio controlled helicopter (called XUfo) using Bluetooth accellerometer and gyro sensors. The Argos components in this service read sensor data approximately every 10 ms, use Kalman filters [14] to adjust the readings and then compute control signals which are transferred back to the helicopter. The service also includes an instrument panel that visualizes the helicopter in a virtual 3D room. Figure 7 shows this instrument panel.

The XUfo service uses the *Sensor Framework system service* to connect to the Bluetooth sensor package on the helicopter (through a USB Bluetooth dongle). It also uses the Argos core notification annotations to bind the input and processing POJO components together (the input POJO emits notifications when new sensor readings are available).

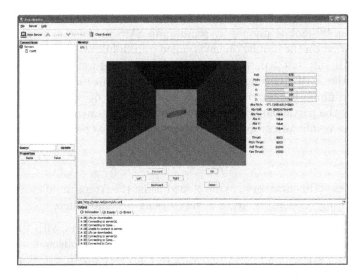

Fig. 7. XUfo service instrument panel

7.3   Lifestyle Services

Together with the Norwegian Center for Telemedicine we are developing a set of services that we have called "Lifestyle Services". In these services we are using sensors to read end user biometrics (for example Blood Glucose level, heart rate, activity level etc.). The service uses information from the sensors combined with a user profile and input from the end user to utilize behavioral change mechanisms in order to try to affect the end user's lifestyle. The sensors are connected to the end user's mobile phone. The Argos *Sensor Framework System Service* is used to connect sensors and to configure the transmission of sensor data from the mobile phone to the Argos container. Data from sensors is stored in a database using the *Hibernate and Derby system services* and is further processed using rules and processing components to calculate the interaction with the end user in order to attempt to change the end user's behavior.

7.4   Experience Sampling Service

The method called Experience Sampling Method(ESM) [15] aims at capturing immediate experiences from participants in a survey. Combining ESM with mobile technology gives the opportunity to design surveys that are to capture immediate experiences.

Using the features of Argos, a software tool for generating ESM based surveys has been designed and implemented. This tool, named esmDesk, is deployed in Argos as a user application and provides an experimenter with a graphical user interface where ESM based surveys can be created, modified and distributed to a set of mobile devices. Distribution of surveys, which are expressed in XML, is done using web services. When the experimenter has finished creating the survey using esmDesk, a set of participants is selected and esmDesk notifies the participants' mobile phones by sending an SMS message. The platform for running surveys on the mobile phone is called esmMobile and it receives the SMS message notifying that a new survey is available. Using web services esmMobile downloads the XML representation of the survey from esmDesk, interprets it and starts running the survey. After all the elements of the survey have been answered by the participant, answers are sent back to esmDesk, again using web services. The results are store in a database using Argos persistence support.

7.5   Others

Some other experimental services developed using the Argos middleware or some of the preceding versions of Argos is very briefly presented here:

Herding. The electronic shepherd system provides farmers with information describing the state of their animals. The information collected was used by a back-end system and generated various map views with associated animal alarms. GPS, temperature and motion sensors were used.

YPIV. Your Personal Infotainment Vault service will serve content to, for example, your mobile phone and to others that you decide to share content with. The content you manage in your YPIV can for example range from: Images, Music, Movies, Context information, PIM services, Ring tones, MMS content, Documents etc. The "sensors" in this service were radio station rippers and other content ingestion "sensors".

FiFamos. The main problem in a fish farm is that most of them are without supervision for a long time while they are exposed to changing weather conditions. FiFaMos is an advanced surveillance and alarm system for sea farms. GPS, camera, temperature, wind, wave, current, water quality and food level sensors were used.

8   Evaluation

Argos is evaluated by demonstrating that it matches the needs of the target application domains and by comparing it with other related projects.

8.1   Usage

In section 7 we have described some of the applications developed using Argos. Argos (including earlier versions of Argos called COMS and APMS) has been used to develop demonstrators internally at the lab and with external partners. Currently several projects of external partners have decided to use Argos in both research projects and in the development of prototypes and demonstrators of new services and products (including Norwegian Center of Telemedicine and Telenor R&I, Telenor is a Norwegian telecom company).

The core functionality of the Argos core (service and component model, lifecycle, notification, instrumentation and dependency injection) and functionality provided by deployed system services makes it easier to quickly develop new applications. The programmer can focus on the core functionality of the application.

The Weather application, the XUfo application and the Lifestyle applications described in section 7 all show how easy it is to integrate sensor data in an Argos application. The Argos core can be easily extended with new system services, and the Sensor framework system service (see section 5.1) matches some of the needs of these applications perfectly. In the Weather service the weather sensor data are collected, stored (see persistence provided by the Hibernate system service in section 5.6), and presented (see JMX Connector system service in section 5.7) with little effort from the application developer.

The XUfo application demonstrates that Argos can also be used in a (near real-time) control system. The efficiency of the Argos core and its notification support makes it possible to pilot a flying object with gyro and accellerometer sensors and a feedback loop through the Argos core that includes processing, visualization, and control signal computation (see figure 7).

The Experience Sampling application uses the persistence support provided by the Hibernate system service to easily store data collected from several respondents. The requirements of the Experience Sampling application also resulted in a new system service for SMS (Small Messaging Service). This system service are used in completely different applications that also includes mobile phones and SMS messaging (i.e. the Lifestyle service).

8.2   Related Work

Prism-MW [16] defines its setting as "programming-in-the-small-and-many". They claim to have a flexible, efficient, scalable and extensible platform for this setting of small, resource constrained, and highly mobile computing platforms. Flexibility is achieved in a similar way as in Argos by providing a core including a component model and events. However, the actual platform is very different. Connectors are an important part of the Prism-MW core and their task is to route events. Each component can be attached to any numbers of connectors, and each connector can serve any numbers of components. This flexibility is also used for system reconfigurability. Their focus on scalability and efficiency are not found in Argos and Argos extensibility can therefore not be compared to Prism-MW. In Prism-MW extensibility is provided by extending the core programming model (extending the connector class, the component class or the event class). Argos is extended by deploying new system-services at run-time. Hot deployment makes it possible to extend (and update) Argos at run-time. Argos provides more features for lifecycle support and system services and is aimed for different application domains.

JBoss [13] is a feature rich application server platform. Similar to Argos it has a core and is extended with system components to provide different system services. The difference here is that JBoss supports complex enterprise applications while Argos supports a completely different set of applications. Both the size (memory print and lines of codes) and the complexity of these two applications platforms differs a lot. We also argue that complexity for the application programmer is higher when using JBoss (or any other EJB application server) than using Argos. This is due to the focus on enterprise applications where more control is moved to the application server (obviously for efficiency and scaling, but also for safety and isolation). Another important difference is that in Argos, the programmer has access to local resources in the same way as any desktop application that is implemented using Java. This is important for many applications in the application domains targeted by Argos.

Gaia [17] and Mobile Gaia [18] is tied to the concept of Active Spaces where physical and computational infrastructure are merged into an integrated habitat. The focus is implicit support for resource awareness (discovery), multi-device interaction, context sensitivity, mobility, run-time adaption and user-centrism. This is very different from Argos. Argos could probably be used to develop this kind of platform by providing system services matching the functionality of Active Spaces. In Argos the term user-centric is used to describe applications and services accessing and using resources close to or related to the user (personal assets or private sensor data or similar). In Gaia this is used to describe the need of the application to adapt to the user (his context and preferences).

Another group of related platforms are MIDAS [19], JAGR [20], The Collective [21] and [22]. All of these platforms tries to solve the problem of (self) adaptive containers. In Argos it should be possible to add context aware system services that has similar approaches, but this is not part of Argos core.

9   Conclusions

The main contributions from the Argos project is that it gives useful (for this domain) enterprise container type support (e.g. component model, lifecycle support and persistence) to desktop and user-centric application development, without the complexity and limitations enforced by enterprise containers.

This grants developers of desktop and user-centric applications the advantage of tailored and advanced, flexible and extensible, middleware support. The result is the possibility to rapid develop feature rich applications that integrates and aggregates information from different sources and presents the results in different settings. Information sources can be sensors, user input, filesystem, databases, web services, and so on. The aggregated and processed data can in turn easily be presented as web pages, desktop widgets, web services, instrument panels or ordinary graphical user interfaces. The collected, aggregated and processed data can be easily persisted or propagated for further processing by other components.

The Argos middleware provides a leaner platform for development of desktop applications, demonstrators, prototypes and experimental middleware development than what would be the case if using for example the JBoss application container as a basis. The Argos core and default system services (Hibernate, Derby, Jetty, JMX Connector, web service) together counts 4,700 physical source code lines using SLOCCount[23]. In comparison, the JBoss microkernel alone counts 10,844 and a complete Jboss installation contains 630,443 physical source code lines using SLOCCount.

Currently the performance of Argos is beeing tested. Some preliminary tests have shown that the deployment time (including dependency testing) of new components grows linearly with the number of components deployed (tested up to 50,000 components). Tests have also shown that notifications are an efficient way to interact between components, Argos core, and system services. Dependency injection is not as efficient as notifications (probably because it uses reflection). The results have shown that usage of dependency injection takes three times longer than notifications. The most efficient way is ordinary method calls, but this differ from the two other approaches since it is not possible between components in different Argos containers.

The Argos middleware and Argus JMX monitor and all system services we have developed is stable and available under a BSD licence (open source software). More information about Argos can be found here:

`http://argos.cs.uit.no`

References

1. Andersen, A., Blair, G., Goebel, V., Karlsen, R., Stabell-Kulø, T., Yu, W.: Arctic beans: Configurable and re-configurable enterprise component architectures. IEEE Distributed Systems Online 2(7) (2001)
2. Gosling, J., Joy, B., Steele, G., Bracha, G.: The Java Language Specification, 3rd edn. Addison-Wesley, Reading (2005)
3. Sun Microsystems: Java annotations: Jsr 175, a metadata facility for the java programming language (2004), `http://www.jcp.org/en/jsr/detail?id=175`
4. Jetty: a full-featured web server implemented entirely in java (2007), `http://jetty.mortbay.org`
5. Hibernate: an object/relational persistence and query service (2007), `http://hibernate.org`
6. Derby: a relational database implemented entirely in java (2006), `http://db.apache.org/derby`
7. W3C: Simple object access protocol (soap) 1.1 (2000), `http://www.w3.org/TR/soap`
8. XML-RPC: remote procedure calling using http as the transport and xml as the encoding (1998), `http://www.xmlrpc.com`
9. Fowler, M.: Inversion of control containers and the dependency injection pattern (2004), `http://www.martinfowler.com/articles/injection.html`
10. Fowler, M.: Module assembly [programming]. Software, IEEE 21(2), 65–67 (2004)
11. OMA: Mobile device management protocols and mechanisms (2007), `http://www.openmobilealliance.org/tech/wg_committees/dm.html`
12. Sun Microsystems: Java management extensions (2006), `http://jcp.org/aboutJava/communityprocess/final/jsr003/index3.html`
13. Fleury, M., Reverbel, F.: The jboss extensible server. In: Endler, M., Schmidt, D.C. (eds.) Middleware 2003. LNCS, vol. 2672, pp. 344–373. Springer, Heidelberg (2003)
14. Kalman, R.E.: A new approach to linear filtering and prediction problems. Transactions of the ASME - Journal of basic Engineering 82, 34–45 (1960)
15. Conner, T.: Experience sampling resource page (2006), `http://psychiatry.uchc.edu/faculty/files/conner/ESM.htm`

16. Mikic-Rakic, M., Medvidovic, N.: Adaptable architectural middleware for programming-in-the-small-and-many. In: Endler, M., Schmidt, D. (eds.) Middleware 2003. ACM/IFIP/USENIX International Middleware Conference. Proceedings. Rio de Janeiro, Brazil. ACM. IFIP. Adv. Comput. Syst. Assoc., 16- 20 June, Springer, Berlin (2003)

17. Roman, M., Campbell, R.: A middleware-based application framework for active space applications. In: ACM/IFIP/USENIX International Middleware Conference, Rio de Janeiro, Brazil (2003)

18. Chetan, S., Al-Muhtadi, J., Campbell, R., Mickunas, M.D.: A middleware for enabling personal ubiquitous spaces. In: System Support for Ubiquitous Computing Workshop at the Sixth Annual Conference on Ubiquitous Computing, Nottingham, England (2004)

19. Popovici, A., Frei, A., Alonso, G.: A proactive middleware platform for mobile computing. In: Endler, M., Schmidt, D. (eds.) Middleware 2003. ACM/IFIP/USENIX International Middleware Conference, Springer, Berlin (2003)

20. Candea, G., Kiciman, E., Zhang, S., Keyani, P., Fox, A.: Jagr: an autonomous self-recovering application server. In: Parashar, M., Hariri, S., Raghavendra, C. (eds.) AMS 2003, Autonomic Computing Workshop: 5th Annual International Workshop on Active Middleware. Seattle, WA, USA. IBM. Nat. Sci. Found. Soc. Modeling & Simulation. IEEE. IEEE Comput. Soc. Arizona Center for Integrative Modeling & Simulation. Univ. Southern California. WINLAB, Rutgers Univ., June 25, 2003, IEEE Comput. Soc., Los Alamitos (2003)

21. Edward, C., Enda, R.: The collective: a common information service for self-managed middleware. In: Proceedings of the 4th workshop on Reflective and adaptive middleware systems, Grenoble, France, p. 1101528. ACM Press, New York (2005)

22. Gang, H., Tiancheng, L., Hong, M., Zizhan, Z., Zhao, L., Gang, F.: Towards autonomic computing middleware via reflection. In: COMPSAC 2004. Proceedings of the 28th Annual International Computer Software and Applications Conference, Hong Kong, China, September 28-29, 2003, IEEE Comput. Soc., Los Alamitos (2004)

23. Wheeler, D.: Sloccount, tools for counting physical source lines of code (sloc) (2007), http://www.dwheeler.com/sloccount

Compadres: A Lightweight Component Middleware Framework for Composing Distributed Real-Time Embedded Systems with Real-Time Java[*]

Jie Hu, Shruti Gorappa, Juan A. Colmenares[**], and Raymond Klefstad

Department of Electrical Engineering and Computer Science
University of California, Irvine, CA 92697, USA
{jieh, sgorappa, jcolmena, klefstad}@uci.edu

Abstract. Component frameworks simplify development of enterprise systems and enable code reuse, but most frameworks are unpredictable and hence unsuitable for embedded or real-time systems. Similarly, Java is increasingly being used to build embedded system software because of its portability and ease of use. The Real-Time Specification for Java (RTSJ) reduces the unpredictability in Java execution times by eliminating the need for a garbage collector. However, it introduces programming complexity that makes it difficult to build non-trivial applications. To bring the advantages of Java component development to DRE systems, while simultaneously simplifying the use of RTSJ, therefore, we have developed a new lightweight component model for RTSJ called *Compadres*. *Compadres* offers the following advantages: 1) Simple component definition in Java that abstracts away RTSJ memory management complexity; 2) System assembly from components by connecting ports that communicate through strongly-typed objects; 3) The *Compadres* compiler that automatically generates the scoped memory architecture for components, while the component framework handles communication between the components. To validate this work, we construct a non-trivial example application using the component framework, a simple real-time CORBA implementation. We then analyze the performance and efficiency of our component example versus a non-component example, RTZen. Our measurements show that our Compadres example built with components incurs only minor time overhead as compared to a comparable hand-coded example.

Keywords: Real-time Java, RTSJ, component framework, middleware.

[*] This material is based upon work supported by the National Science Foundation under Grant No. 0410218. Any opinions, findings, and conclusions or recommendations expressed in this material are those of the authors and do not necessarily reflect the views of the National Science Foundation.
[**] Also with the Applied Computing Institute, College of Engineering, University of Zulia.

R. Cerqueira and R.H. Campbell (Eds.): Middleware 2007, LNCS 4834, pp. 41–59, 2007.

1   Introduction

Distributed, real-time, embedded (DRE) systems pose significant challenges for software developers. As embedded systems, they typically have limited processing power and memory; as real-time systems, they have timing and predictability constraints; and as distributed systems, they must be able to communicate across heterogeneous platforms. Developing software that meets all of these constraints is costly and time-consuming: each application is typically custom-coded from scratch using C/C++ programming language. The limited space and processing power of DRE systems requires lean, specialized custom code, while the threading and memory control needed for real-time requirements requires highly-skilled programming.

By contrast, two existing technologies currently ease and speed development of non-DRE enterprise systems. First, component technology provides effective reusability for software applications for enterprise systems, allowing assembly of pre-coded, pre-tested subsystems into systems, saving both time and money for system development. Second, Java facilitates software development because not only is it relatively easy to use, eliminating complex memory management, but it also offers a large programmer base, library support, platform independence, and a better memory model that minimizes problems with buffer overruns and illegal references.

Unfortunately, the advantages of both component frameworks and the Java programming language have been unavailable to DRE systems developers. Current component frameworks incur too much memory overhead, decrease efficiency, and fail to support the real-time predictability requirements needed for DRE systems. Furthermore, Java cannot be used for real-time systems because its under-specified thread semantics and automatic memory management cause unpredictability.

In general, two complementary approaches have been proposed to reduce the unpredictability of Java– 1) the Real-Time Specification for Java (RTSJ) [1] and 2) real-time garbage collection [2,3]. Real-time garbage collectors (RTGCs) can be unsuitable for use in *hard* real-time systems because they cause an inherent minimum latency and large execution overhead [4]. It is also necessary to accurately predict parameters such as average and maximum allocation rates when using a RTGC. On the other hand, The RTSJ adds memory and thread models that enable predictability for real-time systems, but loses much of the ease of programming of Java. We have therefore developed a lightweight component model for RTSJ, called *Compadres*, that brings the advantages of Java component development to DRE systems, while simultaneously simplifying the use of RTSJ and providing real-time predictability. *Compadres* components are fine-grained object-oriented software artifacts that communicate via *ports*; applications can be developed by connecting these ports.

Compadres achieves ease of use, ease of testing, and a high level of reusability in the following ways:

– **Simple component definition in Java:** *Compadres* is a simple component model that hides the programming difficulty of the RTSJ scoped memory and threading model and yet is powerful enough to define most real-time systems.[1] The component implementations are separated from their threading model, allowing developers to implement the business code for the components using Java with some restrictions but without having to deal with the RTSJ memory management rules. Furthermore, any component may be used as an application process. This feature can also be used to convert a component into a stand-alone application. At a higher level, applications may be distributed in a network.

- **Automatic generation of scoped memory architecture:** The *Compadres* compiler (henceforth compiler) processes a user-defined component composition language file to generate the scoped memory architecture required for the application to run based on the RTSJ scope access rules. The compiler thus abstracts away the RTSJ memory management code from the user.
- **Simplified system assembly through composition of components:** *Compadres* provides hierarchical composition and extension; i.e., components may be incrementally composed into larger components. This feature facilitates incremental testing of components as well as final system testing.
- **Simple communication model:** Components are composed by connecting ports that communicate through strongly-typed objects, providing semantic checking at compile time.

The remainder of this paper is organized as follows: Section 2 presents the *Compadres* component model and describes how it abstracts RTSJ programming challenges. Section 3, presents a simple Real-time CORBA ORB built using *Compadres* and compare its performance to RTZen, our Real-time CORBA ORB for RTSJ [5]. Section 4 presents the related work and section 5 presents conclusions and future work.

2   The *Compadres* Component Framework for RTSJ

The process of developing an RTSJ application using *Compadres* is divided into two phases (see Fig. 1):

1. **Component Definition:** In this phase, the application programmer defines the components and their ports in an XML file following the *Component Definition Language* (CDL). The CDL file is compiled to generate the skeletons of the implementation classes of the components and the message handlers associated with the components' In ports. The programmer adds the implementation of the component and message handler classes using plain Java.
2. **Component Composition:** In this phase, composite components and connections among components are specified in an XML file according to the *Component Composition Language* (CCL) to form the application. The programmer uses the *Compadres* compiler to validate the CCL file and generate the RTSJ glue code needed to run the main application.

---

[1] The components may also use an RTSJ-safe library such as Javalution (http://javolution.org/).

Finally, the Java compiler is used for compiling the implementation classes of components and message handlers along with the generated RTSJ glue code to build the RTSJ application. The rest of the section describes in detail the phases for developing a *Compadres*-based RTSJ application.

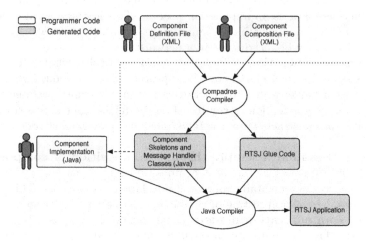

Fig. 1. Generation of a real-time Java application using the *Compadres* framework

2.1   Component Definition

The application programmer writes the CDL file in XML to define the components used in the application as well as the ports of each component. An example of a CDL file is presented in Listing 1.1. The definition of a component comprises the name of the component and the set of its ports. The definition of a port includes its name, its type, and the Java type of the message that is communicated through the port. Ports may be *input ports*, which receive messages or *output ports*, which send messages. Thus, the type of a port may be set to In or Out in the CDL file; the direction is specified in relation to the component itself. In particular, the port types and message types specified in the CDL file will be used to by the *Compadres* compiler to validate the CCL file.

The *Compadres* compiler parses the CCL file and generates the following Java skeleton classes for each component: 1) a component class and 2) one message handler class per In port. The component skeleton class extends the **Component** class, which contains the **addInPort()**, **addOutPort()**, and **_start()** methods. The **addInPort()** method associates a message handler class with the corresponding In port, and the **_start()** method is an empty method that may be implemented by the programmer to initialize the component. Each message handler skeleton class extends the **MessageHandler** class, which contains the **process()** method. The **process()** method accept one message object (of any Java datatype) as a parameter. When a message is sent to an In port, the corresponding **process()** method is called to handle the incoming message. The **process()** method of each message handler skeleton class is initially empty, so that the application programmer needs to implement it. The user may allocate objects using **new** in the implementation of component and message handler classes but does not need to determine which RTSJ memory region to use.

```
<Component>
    <ComponentName>Server</ComponentName>
        <Port>
        <PortName>DataOut</PortName>
        <PortType>Out</PortType>
        <MessageType>String</MessageType>
        </Port>
        <Port>
        <PortName>DataIn</PortName>
        <PortType>In</PortType>
        <MessageType>CustomType</MessageType>
        </Port>
</Component>

<Component>
    <ComponentName>Calculator</ComponentName>
    ....
</Component>
```

Listing 1.1. Component Definition Language file

2.2   Component Composition

A vital characteristic of *Compadres* components is that they are hierarchically *composable*. The Component Composition Language (CCL) file, written in XML format, allows programmers to construct an application from components. The CCL file is written once per application and defines the connections between components, thread priorities, and thread assignment to the components. The CCL decouples the definition of the individual components from their configuration and interaction, thereby enabling component reuse. The component implementations themselves are unaware of the runtime properties; the compiler handles the assignment of the components to memory regions and threads.

Connecting Components via Ports: Components are composed by connecting their appropriate ports, and the port connections are defined in the CCL file; Out ports must be connected to In ports, and the message types (obtained from the CDL file) must match exactly. However, *adapter* components may be introduced to connect two non-matching types.

Connection of ports must follow RTSJ scoping rules to ensure that the compiler can map these components into RTSJ scoped memory areas. In order to enforce the scoping rules, we designate ports as Internal or External in the CCL file. Hierarchically, components created inside another component are the children of that component; two or more components inside the same component are siblings of each other. Internal ports communicate a parent component with its child components; external ports communicate a child component with its parent or sibling components. Only sibling components can see the external ports of each other. Components can only exchange messages between their siblings and parent via external ports and between their own children via internal ports. Therefore, only the following port connections are allowed in the *Compadres* model: 1) internal port of the parent component to external port of the child component, 2) external ports of sibling components. When a component sends data from one of its Out ports, it relays the data to the In port(s) connected to it. When data arrives at an In port, the component that owns the port processes the data immediately in a new execution context and may generate outputs at its other ports.

A simple example of a hierarchical composition of five components is illustrated in Fig. 2. The components are constructed in three levels of scoped memory. Component A is the level-1 parent component. It has two child components, B and C, and is connected to them via internal ports. The component C in turn has two nested components, D and E.

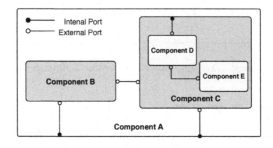

Fig. 2. Hierarchical composition of components via internal and external ports

The CCL file (example in Listing 1.2) contains application information under the following XML tags:

- ApplicationName: is the name of the application class to be generated.
- Component: specifies each component used in the application. This tag contains tags that indicate the name of the component class, name of the instance, its type (immortal or scoped), and its nesting level if the component is of type scoped. Component tags are nested to represent the parent-child relationship among components.
- Connection: contained in a Component tag, includes the list of ports of the component and their links with ports of other components.
- Port: represents a port of a component; it includes the name of the port and its attributes.
- PortAttributes: specifies the threading strategy (shared or dedicated), size of threadpool, and buffer size of each In port.
- Link: represents the end-point and type (internal or external) of a link between two component ports.
- RTSJAttributes: includes RTSJ memory pool attributes such as memory size in bytes and scope pool sizes.

```
<Application>
    <ApplicationName>MyApp</ApplicationName>
    <Component>
        <InstanceName>MyServer</InstanceName>
        <ClassName>Server</ClassName>
        <ComponentType>Immortal</ComponentType>
        <Connection>
            <!-- Define Ports -->
            <Port>
                <PortName>DataIn</PortName>
                <PortAttributes>
                    <BufferSize>5</BufferSize>
                    <Threadpool>Shared</Threadpool>
                    <MinThreadpoolSize>2</MinThreadpoolSize>
                    <MaxThreadpoolSize>10</MaxThreadpoolSize>
                </PortAttributes>
                <!-- Define connection to Out port of child-->
                <Link>
                    <PortType>Internal</PortType>
                    <ToComponent>Calculator</ToComponent>
                    <ToPort>DataOut</ToPort>
                </Link>
            </Port>
        </Connection>
        <Component>
            <InstanceName>MyCalculator</InstanceName>
            <ClassName>Calculator</ClassName>
            <ComponentType>Scoped</ComponentType>
            <ScopeLevel>1</ScopeLevel>
            <Connection>
                . . . .
            </Connection>
        </Component>
        . . . .
    </Component>

    <RTSJAttributes>
        <ImmortalSize>400000</ImmortalSize>
        <ScopedPool>
            <ScopeLevel>1</ScopeLevel>
            <ScopeSize>200000</ScopeSize>
            <PoolSize>3</PoolSize>
            . . . .
        </ScopedPool>
    </RTSJAttributes>
</Application>
```

Listing 1.2. Component Connection Language file

Any component, whether simple or composite, can be made into an application using the CCL file. In this phase the compiler serves two purposes: validation and glue code generation. First, it uses the CDL file to validate the CCL file for connections (to ensure that Out(In) ports are connected to In(Out) ports and there are no loops), RTSJ access rules, and message type matching. The connections are checked to ensure that each component's internal port is connected to the external ports of its children, and that the external ports of siblings are connected. This process ensures that message passing will not violate RTSJ memory access rules. The code generation tasks of the compiler in the component composition phase are: 1) allocating memory to components by analyzing the specified memory needs, 2) defining the RTSJ memory structure for the components, 3) generating glue code to create component instances and for component communication, and 4) generating the main application class that includes an empty _start() method that the programmer will need to implement.

In order to implement component ports, the compiler generates the code for managing the message buffer and threadpool associated with each In port, and the RTSJ glue code for connecting them to the MessageHandler of that port. The incoming messages at an In port are enqueued in its message buffer. The size of the message buffer is specified in the CCL file. Messages are assigned a priority in the send() method of the Out port. When a message arrives at an In port, a thread from the threadpool is assigned the priority of the incoming message and then calls the process() method of the corresponding MessageHandler. The number of threads in the pool is initialized to MinThreadpoolSize value and can go up to the MaxThreadpoolSize value, with both values specified in the CCL file. If these values are 0, the calling thread executes the process() method of the In port synchronously.

Structure of *Compadres* Component Applications: *Compadres* is a loosely coupled component model because a component can be 1) individually implemented and tested independent of the rest of the system, 2) incrementally deployed in a system, and 3) easily extracted from a system for reuse. Several components can be encapsulated to compose a new component. Composition and communication between components must follow the RTSJ memory access rules. Next, we briefly discuss the RTSJ memory structure and the restrictions it imposes on programming, and describe how the *Compadres* framework serves as an abstraction over the RTSJ memory model.

RTSJ Memory Structure [1]: An application's memory structure is constrained by the rules that govern memory access among the three types of memory regions defined in the RTSJ—heap, scoped, and immortal. Of these, the heap memory is garbage collected; therefore, *Compadres* components support only two types of RTSJ memory, scoped and immortal. *Scoped memory* is a region with a limited lifetime, which ends when there are no more threads executing in the region. Scoped memory can be of two types, linear-time, or variable-time: our memory model only uses linear-time or LTScopedMemory, which is allocated in a time proportional to its size and therefore predictable. ImmortalMemory is a fixed-sized area whose lifetime is the same as that of the JVM. Objects allocated in immortal memory, however, will never be garbage collected during the lifetime of the application. Scoped memory areas may be nested, producing a scoping structure called a scope stack. Since multiple memory areas can be entered from an existing memory area, this scope stack can form a tree-like structure. One key relationship is as follows: if scope B is entered from scope A, then A is considered the *parent* of B and B, the *child* of A (see Fig. 2). Two rules govern memory access among scopes. Code within a given scoped memory area X can reference memory in another region Y only if it can be guaranteed that the lifetime of the memory region Y is at least as long as that of the first region X. This lifetime can be guaranteed only if the requested object resides in an ancestor region (e.g., a parent or grandparent), immortal, or heap memory. Another important constraint is that a memory region can have only one parent, thereby preventing cycles in the scope stack (the *single parent rule*). The implication is that a single scope cannot have two or more threads from different parent scopes enter it. An important consequence of this restriction on scoping structure is that a real-time thread executing in a given region cannot access memory residing in a sibling region and vice versa. In the event that real-time threads in these two regions need to coordinate to perform some task, they will need to do so through memory stored in a common ancestor region. For example, in Fig. 3, a real-time thread in scope C cannot access scope B. They can only coordinate via objects stored in A or immortal memory. Table 1 depicts the complete access rules among scopes in Fig. 3.

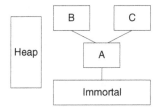

Fig. 3. Nested scopes

Table 1. Access rules for Fig. 3 assuming real-time threads are used. Note that if no-heap real-time threads are used, no references to the heap are permitted.

	to Heap	to Immortal	to A	to B	to C
from Heap	–	yes	no	no	no
from Immortal	yes	–	no	no	no
from A	yes	yes	–	no	no
from B	yes	yes	yes	–	no
from C	yes	yes	yes	no	–

Mapping Components to RTSJ Scopes: Each *Compadres* component is created in a separate (scoped or immortal) memory area. The RTSJ memory scopes in *Compadres* are hierarchical; thus, so are components– they may be nested inside other components. The outer memory area is the parent of the nested memory areas. The nested architecture follows the single parent rule, which ensures that each component has only one parent. The scope in which a component should be placed is based on 1) the lifetime of the component, and 2) its interaction with other components. The following rule determines the lifetime of each scope memory of component: *child components have a shorter lifetime than their parent since they are created in a scoped memory area with* *a depth greater than that of the parent component.* Therefore, scoped memory components that are triggered by other components and have shorter lifetime should be instantiated as their children.

One method to detect scoped memory regions for allocating objects from Java programs is to generate a directed acyclic graph based on object lifetimes and references and assign RTSJ memory scopes based on the depth of the object in the graph [6]. We use a similar approach, but at the level of components, rather than objects. As the lifetimes of scoped components are different, the scoped memory areas are not bound to components at compile-time, but at runtime. This memory can be reused after the scoped component is reclaimed. The *Compadres* component framework allows component instantiation at application runtime. Components are created in `LTScopedMemory`. Further optimization of component instantiation can be achieved by creating pools of scoped memory areas in immortal memory and reusing these areas at runtime. The size and number of scopes in the pools can be assigned in the CCL file under the `RTSJAttributes` tag (Listing 1.2).

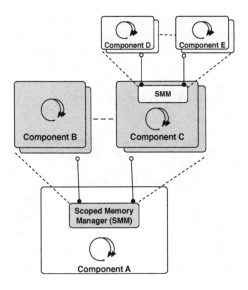

Fig. 4. Parent components communicate with their child components via scoped memory managers (SMMs)

Component Communication via Scoped Memory Managers: References to objects in different components are constrained by the RTSJ memory access rules described previously, but directly exchanging messages across ports may violate these restrictions. We solve this problem by using a *Scoped Memory Manager* (SMM), illustrated in Fig. 4. The SMM is used to connect an internal port of a component to the external port of its child component. In our framework, each parent component needs only one SMM to communicate with all its children. Each SMM of a parent component maintains a virtual proxy for every child component. Upon receiving a message intended for a child component, the SMM checks the proxies for the existing component or, if none are found, creates a new scoped memory component which should receive the message. After the messages are processed by the component, the scoped memory objects are reclaimed. To keep a child alive, the parent component requests a new child scoped memory component; and a `handle` is returned to the parent. The parent can kill the temporary component by calling `disconnect()` with the `handle`. This mechanism is implemented using the wedge thread pattern [7].

One of the most difficult aspects of application development using RTSJ is to implement the mechanisms to pass messages between objects in different scoped memory areas. We have identified three mechanisms to handle cross-scope method invocation and message passing:

- **Serialization:** The object is serialized and copied to a memory area that is accessible by the other scoped memory component.
- **Shared Object** [7]: The object shared by the components is created in a common ancestor memory area. Users need to identify the common ancestor memory area of the two child components and create the shared object in that memory area.
- **Handoff Pattern** [7]: A thread created in the source memory can access the destination memory through the memory area of their common ancestor.

The overhead of serialization causes it to be much less efficient than the handoff pattern. However, using the handoff pattern requires that developers know the scoped memory structure of applications. It also results in the component code becoming tightly coupled and difficult to reuse. The shared object approach is an efficient method but may lead to memory leaks if not implemented correctly. Moreover, users need to determine the common ancestor memory area for two threads, which involves tracing the threads at design time. Based on experience, we have found the shared object approach to be the most efficient and easiest to generate as part of the *Compadres* framework. Thereby, the *Compadres* framework reduces the programming effort by handling inter-component message passing transparently. This feature enables programmers to implement their logic inside each component using regular Java and hides the complexity of RTSJ scope access rules from them. The SMM of the parent component contains the message buffer of each external port of its child components. This message buffer serves as the shared object; therefore, the parents and its children can reference the messages from the buffer.

The *Compadres* framework creates a message pool per message type in the parent component's SMM (allocated in the parent component's memory area). To send a message, programmers get a message object from the pool by calling `getMessage()`, set the message data, and then send the message through the port via `send()`. The message is returned to the pool after it is processed by the receiver. This mechanism reuses objects, thus preventing the memory areas of parent components from being exhausted. The only restriction is that message objects should be RTSJ-safe – all the data contained in a message object must be allocated in the same memory area. Hence, *Compadres* is less restrictive than programming profiles such as the Ravenscar [8], which strictly disallow many features such as dynamic task allocation and dynamic priority assignment.

The shared object mechanism is inefficient in the case of message passing between components that do not have the same parent component but have a common ancestor, due to additional and expensive message copying. To optimize this type of communication, we relay the messages from the ancestral memory area using *shadow ports*. The *Compadres* framework provides a *shadow port* for a scoped component to communicate directly with its non-immediate ancestors without having to generate a message for its parent. For example, consider a three-level component structure in which component C needs to communicate with its grandparent A, but not with its parent B, illustrated in Fig. 5. In this case, programmers specifies the direct connection between components C and A. The compiler detects the need for a shadow port and generates the port connection that allows direct communication between C and A. The data structure for a regular port at B will not be generated and the message pool and buffer are created only in the memory area of component A.

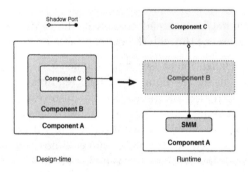

Fig. 5. The *shadow port* allows a child component to communicate with its ancestor directly rather than via its parent

3   Performance Results

We built and tested two examples using *Compadres*. The first example was designed to test *Compadres'* pure overhead for a simple round-trip co-located client-server request-reply. The second example was designed to test *Compadres'* usefulness in a more complete, real-world example of an ORB.

3.1   Overhead of the Framework

We first implemented a simple co-located client-server example and measured the round-trip time to send a client request message and receive a server reply message. The *Compadres* implementation of the example is illustrated in Fig. 6, and the programmer code is shown in Listings 7 and 8.

At application startup, an instance of an `ImmortalComponent` (IMC) and SMM are created in immortal memory, and the `_start()` method is called. The IMC creates an instance of a scoped memory component (`Client`) in a level-1 scoped memory region, `Client` ports are added, and the message handler `P2_Handler` is associated with the In port, `P2`. IMM sends a trigger message via `P1` instructing the `Client` to send a request message to the `Server`. When port `P2` receives this message, the `process()` method of `P2_Handler` is called and sends out a request message to the server via `Out` port `P3`. Since `Client` and `Server` are defined as siblings in the CCL file, the SMM creates the server component using `connect()` in sibling scoped memory region and sends the request message to the `Server`. This invokes the message handler for In port `P4`, which processes the request and sends a reply via `P5`. The reply message is received by the message buffer in SMM and routed to `Client` via `P6`.

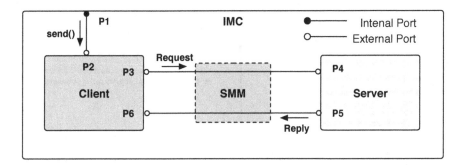

Fig. 6. The client-server scoped memory example

Testing Environment. This first example was tested on three platforms:

1. a non-real-time Pentium system: a 865 MHz Pentium III processor (Coppermine, 256KB Cache) with 512MB PC133 ECC SDRAM, running TimeSys Linux GPL 4.1 based on the Linux kernel 2.4.21, with the non-real-time Java Virtual Machine (JVM) Sun JDK 1.4 default garbage collector;
2. a real-time Pentium system: the same Pentium and OS above, with the RTSJ RI from TimeSys; and
3. a real-time Sun system: a Sun-Fire-V210 with a 1064 MHz UltraSPARC processor, running SunOS 5.0, with Sun's Mackinac[9].

Measurements. For all tests, measurements were based on steady state observations, where the system is run until the transitory effects of cold starts are eliminated before collecting the measured observations. We used the maximum of 10,000 observations as an estimate of a system's "worst case," a critical measurement for real-time systems that must be designed with the assumption that the system will always deliver the worst possible performance. A sample size at least this large was necessary to observe a reasonable estimate for the maximum

```
public class MyInteger {
    public int value = 0;
}

public class ImmortalComponent extends
    Component {
    // Compadres framework creates
    // ImmortalComponent in immortal memory
    public SMM smm = new SMM(...);
    //Define out-port
    // addOutPort(out-port name, SMM object,
    //   msg type, destination in-port name)
    public OutPort p1 = addOutPort("P1", smm
        , MyInteger.class, "MyClient_P2");
    public void _start(){
        // Get a message from the pool and
        // send it to the client component
        MyInteger m = (MyInteger) p1.
            getMessage();
        // Send trigger msg with priority 2
        p1.send(m, 2);
    }
}

public class Client extends Component {
    // addInPort(in-port name, SMM object,
    //   msg type, buffer size, threadpool
    //   strategy, min pool size, max pool
    //   size, message handler class)
    public InPort p2 = addInPort("P2", imc.
        smm, MyInteger.class, 10, 0, 1, 5,
        P2_MessageHandler.class);
    public OutPort p3 = addOutPort("P3",imc.
        smm,MyInteger.class,"MyServer_P3");
    public InPort p6 = addInPort("P6", imc.
        smm, MyInteger.class, 20, 0, 1, 5,
        P6_MessageHandler.class);
    public void _start() {
    }
}
```

```
public class Server extends Component {
    public InPort p4 = addInPort("P4", imc.
        smm, MyInteger.class, 20, 0, 1, 5,
        P4_MessageHandler.class);
    public OutPort p5 = addOutPort("P5",imc.
        smm,MyInteger.class,"MyClient_P6");
    public void _start(){}
}

public class P2_MessageHandler extends
    MessageHandler{
    public void process(Object data, SMM smm){
        //Get reference to out-port
        //   connected to server
        OutPort p3 = smm.getOutPort("P3");
        MyInteger i=(MyInteger)p3.getMessage();
        i.value = 3;
        // take timestamp ts_0
        . . . .
        p3.send(i, 3);
    }
}

public class P4_MessageHandler extends
    MessageHandler {
    public void process(Object data, SMM smm){
        // Get reference to out-port
        //   connected to client
        OutPort p5 = smm.getOutPort("P5");
        MyInteger i=(MyInteger)p5.getMessage();
        i.value = 4;
        p5.send(i, 3);
    }
}

public class P6_MessageHandler extends
    MessageHandler {
    public void process(Object data, SMM smm){
        // take timestamp ts_1
        . . .
    }
}
```

Fig. 7. Implementation classes of immortal and client components

Fig. 8. Implementation classes of server component and message handlers

latency because the maximum values tended to be extremely low-probability events. The range of the observations, i.e., jitter, was used as another measure of a system's predictability.

Results. Our framework is reasonably predictable on both Mackinac and Timesys RI, with jitter of $92\mu s$ and $55\mu s$ respectively, well within the 10ms described as typically acceptable for distributed real-time systems [10] The distribution of the round-trip latency values indicating maximum and minimum bounds is shown in Fig. 9, while Table 2 lists the jitter for each platform. The jitter on JDK1.4 is large, most likely caused by the garbage collector preempting the application threads. The jitter on Mackinac is larger than the jitter on Timesys RI; Timesys RI was installed on a real-time OS and Mackinac on SunOS 5.10. Although SunOS 5.10 provides some RT scheduling strategies, it is a non-real-time OS, allowing some system threads to preempt the application threads.

Table 2. Median and jitter of round-trip times on different platforms

Platform	Median (μs)	Jitter (μs)
Mackinac	99.58	92.17
RI	114.0	55.0
JDK1.4	56.43	317.27

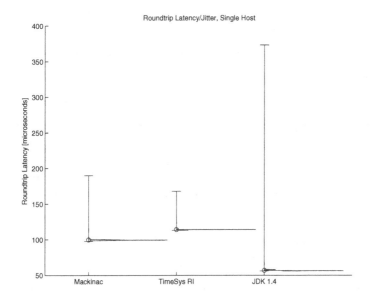

Fig. 9. Comparison of round-trip times of simple message passing

3.2   Constructing a Real-World Example: RT-CORBA

We use previous experience in building RTZen [5], an RTSJ implementation of RT-CORBA, to construct a simple RT-CORBA ORB using *Compadres*. CORBA exposes the ability to create and destroy CORBA components, such as POA and Transport, to the application. RTZen enables this by assigning scoped memory areas to these components. When the user creates (destroys) one of these components, the associated memory scope is created (freed). The design of the *Compadres* ORB is based on RTZen and is illustrated in Fig. 10. The *Compadres* CORBA client is a 3-level scoped structure. The level-1 memory contains an ORB component, which is allocated from immortal memory. Inside the ORB component is the Transport component, created in the level-2 scoped memory when a request message is received from the ORB component. When the client application makes a remote method call to the server, the ORB sends a message to the previously created Transport component. Upon receiving the message, the Transport creates a MessageProcessing component to generate the request in the level-3 scoped memory. After the MessageProcessing component obtains

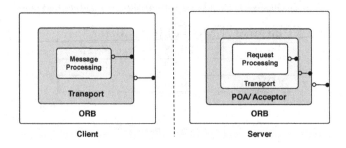

Fig. 10. Component structure of the *Compadres* ORB

the reply message from the server, it sends the result back to client application and destroys itself.

The *Compadres* CORBA server is a 4-level scoped structure. Similar to the client, the server-side application creates an ORB component in the level-1 immortal memory. A POA/Acceptor component is created by the ORB component in level-2 scoped memory. The POA/Acceptor component listens to and waits for client request messages. Once a client request message comes in, the POA component creates a Transport component in level-3 scoped memory to wait for client request messages. Once a message is received, a RequestProcessing component is created to process the client request in level-4 scoped memory. After processing the request and sending the reply back to the client, this component is destroyed.

With the hierarchical model of *Compadres*, it is easy for us to define and reuse components for the modules of CORBA. Although the Transport components of Client and Server are located in different memory levels and connected to different data processing components, we can reuse the Transport component at both the Client and Server. In addition, binding memory area with components at design time makes the memory hierarchical structure clearer and easier to maintain. Finally, the lifetime of each component matches the lifetime of each CORBA module.

3.3   Comparison of RT-CORBA with *Compadres* and RTZen

We compared our RT-CORBA ORB implementation using the *Compadres* framework's round-trip latency and jitter on a real-time platform with that of RTZen.[2] Both RTZen and the *Compadres* ORB demos were run on the same real-time platform, Timesys Linux and RI. Moreover, both server-side and client-side were run on single machine connected via loopback network. Since performance varied

---

[2] For the purposes of this experiment, the *Compadres* ORB can be considered to be functionally similar to RTZen; it includes marshalling and demarshalling, the most computationally-intensive modules of CORBA. The policy check mechanism has not been implemented, but it is not a computing intensive module and would not incur much overhead.

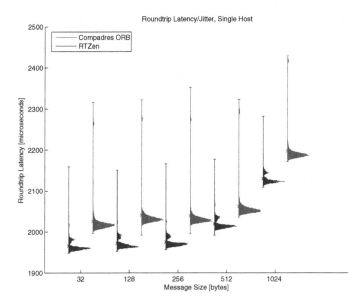

Fig. 11. Comparison of round-trip times of RTZen with the *Compadres* ORB for different message sizes

across different message sizes, we compared the two ORBs for the message size from 32 to 1024 bytes.

Both RTZen and the *Compadres* ORB are highly predictable, with the jitter value of 230μs and 300μs respectively. The *Compadres* ORB has a slightly larger jitter, likely caused by the scoped memory managers (SMMs). The distribution of the round-trip latency values is illustrated in Fig. 11, with the maximum and minimum bound indicated and with the 'x' representing the median latency. Again, the typical performance and predictability of both RTZen and the *Compadres* ORB are within 10ms, typically acceptable for distributed real-time systems [10]. In general, these jitter values are close to the expected values and highlight the predictability of RTSJ. Hence, our model demonstrates both predictability and low overhead.

4   Related Work

During the last decade several component-based real-time (CBRT) frameworks have been proposed [11,12,13,14]. However, none of these CBRT frameworks are based on RTSJ and, therefore, they do not deal with the complexities of the RTSJ's memory model. In the RTSJ domain, our previous work [15] was the first to bring together the ease-of-use of programming in Java with the real-time predictability of RTSJ using a component-based approach. *Compadres* compliments our previous work by providing a component model that supports the notion of ports and enables asynchronous communication. A similar RTSJ-based component framework is presented in [16]. It allows active and passive components to be created in individual scopes, uses a *Connector* component to specify the mode of connection between components, and allows creating and binding sub-components hierarchically.

Scoped Types and Aspects for real-time Java [17] presents an approach to reduce the programming complexity of RTSJ by allocating objects in scopes based on their types. This rule enables static checking and ensures that an assignment does not breach the program structure. However, it requires making minor changes to the virtual machine and uses aspects to separate real-time concerns from the Java code. Reflexes [18] is a an alterative to the RTSJ model; the authors use Java annotation to specify the object type as stable or dynamic, which allows the detection of illegal memory reference at compile time and eliminating runtime memory checks. However, it is very restrictive– it requires assigning one thread per reflex, prevents object reference across reflexes, and does not allow for memory hierarchy.

5   Conclusion

The RTSJ brings real-time performance to Java applications, but presents programming difficulties due to its memory model. We have presented *Compadres*, a component model that abstracts away the programming difficulty of RTSJ, while leveraging the advantages of component-based programming. In its current state, it provides predictability, RTSJ specification compliance, and reduces programming complexity. It provides a solid foundation for further research into implementations of real-time applications based on Java. Future work includes performance optimization of the component framework, developing a graphical user interface for connecting components, and code generation for transparently handling remote communication over a network.

Acknowledgements

The authors thank Susan Anderson Klefstad for help with revising the paper and Krishna Raman for his help with implementing the ORB demo. Juan A. Colmenares thanks the University of Zulia (LUZ) for supporting his participation in this research.

References

1. The Real-Time Specification for Java, http://www.rtsj.org
2. Bacon, D.F., Cheng, P., Rajan, V.T.: A real-time garbage collector with low overhead and consistent utilization. In: David, F. (ed.) POPL 2003: Proceedings of the 30th ACM SIGPLAN-SIGACT symposium on Principles of programming languages, pp. 285–298. ACM Press, New York (2003)

3. Sun Microsystems. Sun java real-time system 2.0
4. Pizlo, F., Vitek, J.: An emprical evaluation of memory management alternatives for real-time java. In: RTSS 2006. 27th IEEE International Real-Time Systems Symposium, pp. 35–46. IEEE Computer Society Press, Los Alamitos (2006)
5. Raman, K., Zhang, Y., Panahi, M., Colmenares, J.A., Klefstad, R., Harmon, T.: RTZen: highly predictable, Real-Time Java middleware for distributed and embedded systems. In: Proc. of the 6th Int'l Middleware Conference (December 2005)
6. Deters, M., Cytron, R.K.: Automated discovery of scoped memory regions for real-time java. In: ISMM 2002. Proceedings of the 3rd international symposium on Memory management, pp. 25–35. ACM Press, New York (2002)
7. Pizlo, F., Fox, J.M., Holmes, D., Vitek, J.: Real-time java scoped memory: Design patterns and semantics. In: ISORC 2004. Seventh IEEE International Symposium on Object-Oriented Real-Time Distributed Computing, pp. 101–110. IEEE Computer Society Press, Los Alamitos (2004)
8. Kwon, J., Wellings, A., King, S.: Ravenscar-java: a high-integrity profile for real-time java: Research articles. Concurr. Comput.: Pract. Exper. 17(5-6), 681–713 (2005)
9. Sun Microsystems. The Real-Time Java platform (June 2004)
10. Dibble, P.C.: Real-Time Java Platform Programming. Sun Microsystems Press (2002)
11. Stewart, D.B., Volpe, R.A., Khosla, P.K.: Design of dynamically reconfigurable real-time software using port-based objects. IEEE Transactions on Software Engineering 23(12) (December 1997)
12. (Kane) Kim, K.H.: Apis for real-time distributed object programming. IEEE Computer 33(6), 72–80 (2000)
13. Wang, S., Rho, S., Mai, Z., Bettati, R., Zhao, W.: Real-time component-based systems. In: Proc. 11th IEEE Real Time and Embedded Technology and Applications Symposium, pp. 428–437 (March 2005)
14. de Niz, D., Bhatia, G., Rajkumar, R.: Model-based development of embedded systems: The sysweaver approach. In: RTAS 2006. Proceedings of the 12th IEEE Real-Time and Embedded Technology and Applications Symposium, Washington, DC, USA, pp. 231–242. IEEE Computer Society, Los Alamitos (2006)
15. Colmenares, J.A., Gorappa, S., Panahi, M., Klefstad, R.: A Component Framework for Real-time Java. In: RTAS 2006. 12th IEEE Real-Time and Embedded Technology and Applications Symposium Work-in-Progress, IEEE Computer Society Press, Los Alamitos (2006)
16. Etienne, J.-P., Cordry, J., Bouzefrane, S.: Applying the CBSE paradigm in the real time specification for Java. In: JTRES 2006: Proceedings of the 4th international workshop on Java technologies for real-time and embedded systems, pp. 218–226. ACM Press, New York (2006)
17. Andreae, C., Coady, Y., Gibbs, C., Noble, J., Vitek, J., Zhao, T.: In: Thomas, D. (ed.) ECOOP 2006. LNCS, vol. 4067, Springer, Heidelberg (2006)
18. Spring, J.H., Pizlo, F., Guerraoui, R., Vitek, J.: Reflexes: abstractions for highly responsive systems. In: VEE 2007: Proceedings of the 3rd international conference on Virtual execution environments, pp. 191–201. ACM Press, New York (2007)

SIPHoc: Efficient SIP Middleware for Ad Hoc Networks

Patrick Stuedi, Marcel Bihr, Alain Remund, and Gustavo Alonso

Department of Computer Science, ETH Zurich
8092 Zurich, Switzerland
{stuedip, alonso}@inf.ethz.ch

Abstract. Mobile Ad Hoc Networks (MANETs) offer a flexible way to connect mobile devices to build complex infrastructures. A key issue in MANETs is session set up and management since, unlike in conventional networks, there is no centralized component to provide such a service. Yet, session set up is necessary to provide any form of communication beyond unreliable, single message communication. In this paper we describe SIPHoc, a middleware infrastructure for session set up and management in MANETs. SIPHoc provides the same interface as the SIP standard but its implementation is fully decentralized. Moreover, SIP session establishment to and from the Internet is possible as soon as a single node in the MANET has Internet access. The paper presents the architecture and implementation of SIPHoc and evaluates its performance. The experiments show that SIPHoc is message efficient and provides a low dial-to-ring delay. SIPHoc allows SIP based applications to be used in MANETs without modification. In the paper, this is demonstrated by showing how SIPHoc supports VoIP conversations within a MANET and between the MANET and end-points on the Internet.

1 Introduction

Multi hop, mobile ad-hoc networks (MANETs) offer the opportunity to extend networks beyond the reach of fixed infrastructures. They also allow to build complex distributed systems using mobile devices. A key problem with ad-hoc networks is that their very nature makes it difficult to implement any form of communication requiring *sessions* rather than just best-effort dissemination of independent packets.

Session establishment and management are key procedures in conventional networks. There is even a standard, the *Session Initiation Protocol* (SIP) [20], that is used as a signaling protocol in applications such as Internet conferencing, telephony, and instant messaging. Being able to use SIP in MANETs would be a significant step towards turning MANETs into seamless extensions of conventional networks. The difficulty in doing so lies on the highly centralized architecture of SIP and the need to provide a seamless session connection from the MANET to the Internet. Numerous attempts have been made at adapting SIP to MANETs [16,5,12] and there are studies on the cost of running SIP on MANETs [2]. Unfortunately, none of these proposals has been implemented and often they work only on either isolated MANETs or MANETs permanently connected to the Internet. Moreover, all existing solutions impose limitations on the network topology and/or the routing protocol.

R. Cerqueira and R.H. Campbell (Eds.): Middleware 2007, LNCS 4834, pp. 60–79, 2007.

In this paper we present SIPHoc, a middleware platform for session establishment and management in MANETs that does not suffer from any of the limitations of previous proposals and has been implemented. SIPHoc does not require any centralized components, is message efficient (through routing message piggyibacking), and independent of the routing protocol (currently, SIPHoc supports both AODV [18] and OLSR [4]). SIPHoc does not impose any topology, and allows seamless interaction with the Internet (by treating nodes connected to the Internet as *gateway services* and making this information known across the MANET as a distributed service). Unlike previous work, SIPHoc is compatible with the SIP standard.

To demonstrate the potential of SIPHoc and its feasibility, we have used SIPHoc to provide a *Voice-over-IP* (VoIP) solution that supports VoIP conversations within a MANET and between the MANET and end-points on the Internet. As far as we are aware, SIPHoc is the only platform that allows VoIP applications to run unchanged whether on the Internet or over a MANET. In the paper we also use the VoIP application to study the performance of SIPHoc and show that the resulting overhead is close to optimal and comparable to that of standard operations on MANETs.

2   Related Work and Contributions

The problem of running SIP on MANETs has many facets. In this section we describe SIP, the design constraints for SIPHoc, and how SIPHoc differs from related work.

2.1   SIP Overview

SIP is a protocol for session initiation and tear-down. SIP works by building an overlay network on top of a regular IP network using a set of SIP entities such as proxies and registrar servers. A *SIP proxy* is an intermediary entity primarily in charge of routing: its job is to ensure that a request is sent to another entity 'closer' to the targeted user. A *SIP registrar* is used by SIP applications to register their current location. A *SIP location service* is used by registrars to store user location information and by SIP proxies to query user location information.

A SIP application first registers with the system by communicating its *SIP user name* and its current location to a *registrar* (Figure 1a). The registrar to be used is either determined using DNS or it is statically configured (through the so called *outbound-proxy*). Registrars and proxies are logical entities and it is not uncommon to have them co-located on the same node. When the registrar hears from a node, it builds a *binding*, i.e., an association between a SIP user name and the corresponding contact address (typically an IP address or resolvable name).

To establish a session with another user whose current location is unknown, a *SIP INVITE message* is sent to the proxy/registrar (step 1, Figure 1b). The proxy responds with a *100 Trying message* (step 2). The 100 Trying response indicates that the INVITE message has been received and that the proxy is trying to route the INVITE message to the final destination. Since the outbound proxy/registrar does not know the location of user B, it uses a DNS server to locate the proxy of the destination node and forwards the INVITE message accordingly (steps 3 to 6). The receiving proxy/registrar uses the

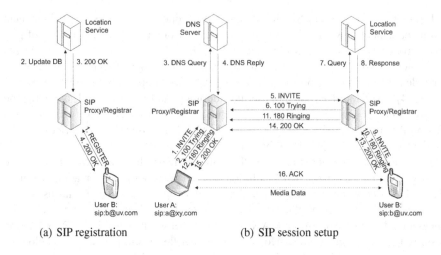

(a) SIP registration   (b) SIP session setup

Fig. 1. Basic SIP mechanism

previously registered binding information of the user to locate the destination (steps 7 and 8) and finally delivers the INVITE message to the intended recipient (step 9). The recipient responds with a *180 Ringing message*, which is routed back through the two proxies in the reverse direction (step 10 to 12). If user B decides to establish the session with user A, it responds with a *200 OK* (step 13 to 15). Finally, user A sends an ACK message to confirm the reception of the 200 OK message (step 16). At this stage, the two users have learned each others' contact address through the INVITE/200 OK messages and from then on they communicate directly, bypassing the two proxies.

2.2 SIP Compatibility, Decentralization and Message Efficiency

In a MANET, SIP must operate in a fully distributed manner while maintaining the same interface and procedures. This is a challenge because several of the problems caused by the decentralized nature of MANETS can be solved by ignoring SIP procedures. For instance, registrars can be eliminated if all applications pro-actively announce their contact addresses. This can be done using either a HELLO method [16] or REGISTER broadcast messages [12]. Such approaches create a significant message overhead and introduce incompatibilities with session mobility and tear-down. As an optimization, [12] suggests to use the Service Location Protocol (SLP) [9] to discover the SIP bindings. Unfortunately, SLP is also centralized and very inefficient in MANETs due to the heavy use of multicast [2]. Existing work to make SLP more efficient in MANETs is highly routing protocol specific [13].

In SIPHoc we strictly follow the SIP interface and message flow. We have tested the compatibility with SIP by running KPhone (sourceforge.net/projects/kphone), Twinkle (www.twinklephone.com), Jain SIP Communicator (snad.ncsl.nist.gov/proj/iptel) and Linphone (www.linphone.org) on top of SIPHoc without any modifications. SIPHoc addresses the lack of centralized registrars by using SLP to dynamically discover the SIP outbound proxy. However, the SLP service we use is adapted to MANETs: it only sends message by piggybacking them to the MANET routing messages. At the same time, SIPHoc does not depend on a particular routing protocol, rather new routing protocols can be easily incorporated as plug-ins to the platform.

2.3 Topology Independence

SIP relies on DNS to locate nodes (steps 3/4 in Figure 1b). A way to bypass the lack of a DNS infrastructure in MANETs is to restrict the network topology and assign specialized roles to given nodes [5]. This approach makes the endpoint discovery process easier and eliminates the need for (part of) the registrar since the position and communication paths to all nodes are known in advance. This approach does not introduce message overhead but imposes strong restrictions on the routing protocols. It is also very difficult to efficiently maintain a fixed routing topology in mobile settings. An alternative approach to restricted topologies is to form node clusters that act as DNS surrogates within the MANET [22,7]. However, electing and maintaining specialized nodes is difficult and expensive in MANETs. In fact, it has been shown [7] that in terms of transmitted messages, a fully distributed service discovery like the one used in SIPHoc outperforms the per-cluster approach, especially in mobile scenarios.

SIPHoc has been designed to be independent of the underlying network topology and, thus, it supports both static and mobile MANETs. As a result, SIPHoc avoids the problem of having to elect nodes for specialized tasks and replacing them when conditions change (e.g., when the node is switched off).

2.4 Connecting to and from the Internet

Connecting the MANET to the Internet poses several problems. First, the proxy does not know whether the target node is in the MANET or outside. Second, establishing sessions between nodes in and outside the MANET requires stable IP addresses. This can be done by using NAT [6] but it also requires additional mechanism like STUN [21]. If no NAT is available, extra mechanisms are needed to maintain consistent network addresses across connections of the MANET to the Internet.

A way to avoid such problems is to assume the MANET is permanently connected to the Internet. Then one can impose a fixed network topology leading to the gateway [3]. This approach does not work for establishing SIP sessions in MANETs not connected to the Internet and re-introduces the problems of fixed topologies. Fixed topologies can be avoided through dynamic gateway discovery [15]. There are also many proposals for routing traffic to the Internet from a MANET [23,19]. Unfortunately, all such proposals are routing protocol specific and cannot be generalized. Routing independent approaches exist [14] but require gateway nodes to be located according to a fixed hierarchy. A more flexible design without topology assumptions is described in [10]. Similarly, there are proposals based on IPv6 [15] and Mobile IP [10,23,19].

SIPHoc has been designed such that seamless and transparent communication with the Internet is available across the MANET as soon as one node in the MANET has Internet connectivity. To maintain generality and to be applicable today, SIPHoc does

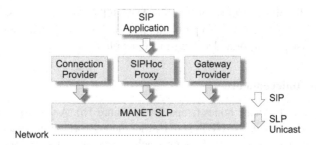

Fig. 2. Architecture Overview: *SIPHoc* Processes on a MANET node

not assume NAT, IPv6 or MobileIP. Moreover, any node in the network may act as a potential gateway: in SIPHoc gateways are established and discovered dynamically.

3   Architecture and System Components of SIPHoc

The SIPHoc architecture is shown in Figure 2. It is based on four components running as independent operating system processes within a node in the MANET. The components are divided into two groups, one for implementing SIP in the MANET, and one for connecting to the Internet.

- SIP in MANET components:
  - A *MANET SLP* layer providing a regular SLP (Service Location Protocol) interface but implementing efficient and decentralized service lookup functionality. It runs only on nodes where one of the other three components is present.
  - A *SIPHoc Proxy* with a standard SIP interface but implementing MANET specific functionality. It only runs on nodes with an end user applications. Each *SIPHoc Proxy* serves as an outbound SIP proxy for local SIP applications.
- Internet connectivity components:
  - A *Gateway Provider* that turns the node into a gateway if the node has Internet access.
  - A *Connection Provider* that manages connections of the node to the Internet when there is a gateway in the MANET.

The *SIPHoc Proxy* is accessed by the application through the standard SIP protocol. The *Distributed Service Locator* process is accessed using SLP. All processes shown in Figure 2 can be started and stopped independently of each other.

4   SIPHoc Components for Running SIP in MANETs

The two key problems to solve in this section are how to replace the centralized location service by a distributed solution, and how to find other proxies without relying on DNS.

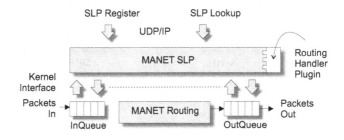

Fig. 3. MANET SLP architecture

4.1   MANET SLP

MANET SLP is a fully distributed service discovery platform for MANETs. MANET SLP provides a regular SLP interface over UDP for service registration and lookup (Figure 3). Services can be registered using the SLP *REGISTER* interface and looked up using the SLP *LOOKUP* interface. All services are *soft-state*, meaning that they expire after a specified period of time. The lifetime for locally stored services can be defined upon startup.

MANET SLP works by piggybacking sevice information onto routing messages (as also suggested in [24],[8]). This is done by capturing routing messages (using the *libipq* [1] library under linux) and extending them with service information. As pointed out above, this idea is not new. What is unique in MANET SLP is that the routing specific functionality is encapsulated within a *routing handler*. The routing handler is a software module that receives raw routing packets as input and generates altered packets that include the piggybacked service information. Whether the routing handler acts pro-actively and constantly disseminates information or only on demand (when a service is needed) depends on the underlying routing protocol. Which routing handler to use is decided at system startup. An additional advantage of this design is that, unlike in [13], routing protocols do not have to be modified to be used in SIPHoc.

4.2   SIPHoc Proxy

A standard SIP proxy/registrar accepts SIP registrations of a collection of users from certain domains. A SIPHoc proxy typically only accepts SIP registrations from users (applications) on that particular device. In addition to storing these registrations in its local location service table, each SIPHoc proxy uses MANET SLP to advertise itself as the contact address for these registered users (e.g., as the outbound proxy for those users). If a SIPHoc proxy receives an INVITE message and cannot find the target in its local location service table, it consults the MANET SLP layer and forwards the INVITE message to the proxy which was advertised as outbound proxy for this user (we call this procedure *dynamic outbound proxy selection*).

An alternative approach would have been to implement a distributed storage solution using MANET SLP where each proxy knows about all other SIP users in the MANET. This is very efficient but creates the same problems as the use of broadcast messages to register SIP applications across the MANET [16,12] (Figure 4). If each proxy can

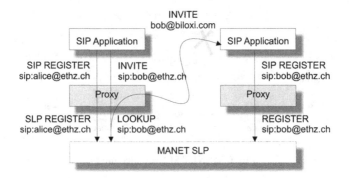

Fig. 4. Violation of the SIP message flow

find out the location of the final destination of the session by itself (through MANET SLP), SIP bindings are resolved directly at the caller's proxy and INVITE messages do not pass the callee's proxy. This violates the standard SIP message flow, where INVITE messages always pass through the proxy where the target is registered (Figure 1b). This violation creates problems with session mobility and session tear down.

In contrast to this, through dynamic outbound proxy selection, SIPHoc complies with the traditional SIP message flow. Moreover, the use of a proxy at each device creates an infrastructure that is by design fully decentralized.

4.3   SIPHoc Proxy Example

How the *SIPHoc Proxy* works can be best understood with an example (see Figure 5). The example maps the standard SIP message flow shown in Figure 1 to the SIPHoc proxy and MANET SLP components just described. We assume two users Alice and Bob. The IP addresses of the two machines of Alice and Bob are 192.168.220.1 and 192.168.220.2 respectively. Each user runs a *SIPHoc Proxy* on port 5060 and a SIP application on port 5062. Both machines are in the MANET, within an arbitrary hop-distance from each other. *ProxyA* is the proxy used by Alice and *ProxyB* that of Bob.

To register with SIPHoc, both users send their URI and contact address to their proxies (1 and 5, Figure 5)): *sip:alice@ethz.ch* and (192.168.220.1:5062 for Alice; *sip:bob@ethz.ch* and 192.168.220.2:5062 for Bob. The local SIPHoc proxy for each one of them will then store the corresponding entry in the local location service table (2,6). It will also contact the underlying MANET SLP and register the entry so that it is advertised by the MANET SLP module (3,4,7,8). Note that the entry in the local location service table differs from the entry sent to the MANET SLP in that the latter contains the contact address of the proxy (port 5060) rather than the one of the user (port 5062). To establish a SIPHoc session, assume Alice contacts Bob, Alice sends an INVITE message to *sip:bob@ethz.ch* (9). *ProxyA* checks whether the target SIP URI is in the local location service table (10). If that is not case, then it requests the entry from the MANET SLP layer (11-12). Once the contact address of the proxy of the user *sip:bob@ethz.ch* is found, the INVITE message is forwarded (13). There is no difference in whether a SIP proxy receives an INVITE message from the local user or from

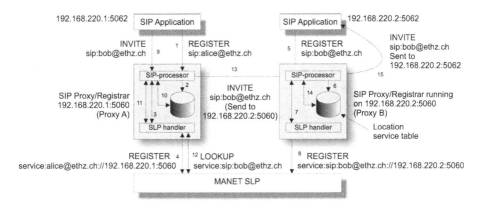

Fig. 5. SIPHoc Proxy/Registrar: dynamic outbound-proxy-selection

another proxy over the network. Hence, *ProxyB*, upon receiving the INVITE message, checks whether the requested SIP URI is available in its local location service table (14). In this case it will find the entry (registered by Bob as 192.168.220.2:5062), and can then forward the INVITE message to Bob (15).

4.4 SIPHoc over AODV and OLSR

When the SIPHoc proxy contacts the MANET SLP module, what happens depends on the underlying routing protocol. This is because, depending on how routing takes

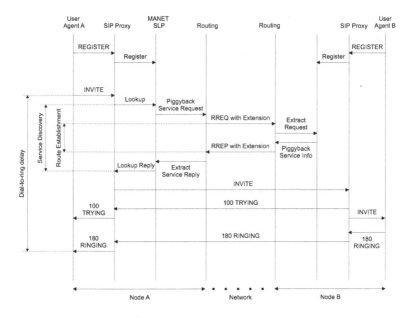

Fig. 6. SIP registration and call setup in a MANET using AODV

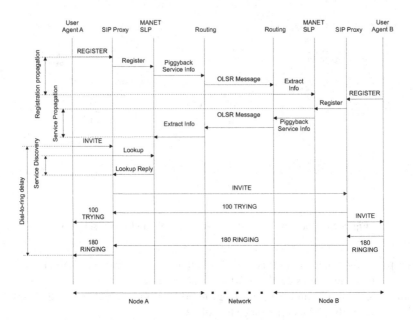

Fig. 7. SIP registrations and call setup in a MANET using OLSR

place, the MANET SLP will be either pro-active or act on demand. Currently we have implemented two different routing handlers. One for AODV [17] (on demand) and one for OLSR [4] (pro-active). As an example of the differences in terms of how services are found depending on the routing protocol, the message flow for session establishment in the case of AODV is shown in Figure 6 and for the case of OLSR in Figure 7. In an on demand routing handler (AODV), a lookup request from the SIPHoc proxy results in a *route request* from the routing protocol with the SIP information piggybacked to it [11]. In a pro-active routing handler (OLSR), the routing messages are exploited to constantly disseminate and maintain information across all MANET SLP modules. The advantage of the SIPHoc architecture (Figure 2) is that all these network properties are abstracted through the routing handler plug-in used in the MANET SLP layer and thus neither the SIPHoc proxy nor the SIP application are concerned with the routing protocol.

5   Internet-Connected MANETs

In this section we enhance the architecture described in the previous Section to support Internet connectivity.

5.1   Gateway Provider

A *Gateway Provider* is a process that can set up a node to become a *gateway* in case the node has Internet connection, and removes the *gateway* functionality in case the Internet connection is lost. *Gateway Provider* processes are started on nodes who want to

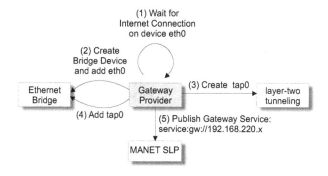

Fig. 8. Gateway Provider

act as gateways. A *gateway* is a node that is directly connected to the Internet and configured to provide Internet access to all the nodes within the MANET. Typically, these are nodes with multiple interfaces, since one interface is configured for communication with the MANET, and another interface is dynamically attached to the Internet. How a *Gateway Provider* works is shown in Figure 8. Once started, the *Gateway Provider* process keeps waiting for an Internet connection to become available (Figure 8, step 1). Detecting whether a node has Internet connection or not is done using a special *InternetDetectionAPI*. The idea is to exploit system support to efficiently detect a possible Internet connection. Our current implementation makes use of the operating system routing table. If an Internet connection has successfully been detected, say on interface *eth0*, the *Gateway Provider* process then creates a *bridge* device on that node and immediately adds interface *eth0* to the *bridge* (step 2). In a following step, a *layer-two tunnelling* device *tap0* is created (step 3) and also added to the *bridge* (step 4). The device *tap0* allows any node within the MANET to set up a *layer-two tunnel* connection to the gateway node. Since the tunnel device *tap0* is part of the *bridge*, traffic received on *tap0* is directly forwarded to the Internet via interface *eth0*. To provide MANET nodes with such gateway functionality, a *Gateway Provider* must however first register itself as a *gateway* service using the underlying *MANET SLP* service (step 5). Once a gateway service is registered, any node within the MANET may look up the gateway's location and connect to it. If the Internet connection is lost the service will be de-registered or will timeout, and both the tunnel endpoint *tap0* and the *bridge* will be removed.

5.2 Connection Provider

A *Connection Provider* is a process that sets up an *Internet connection* if a gateway can be found. *Connection Provider* processes are started on nodes who want an Internet connection. How a *Connection Provider* works is shown in Figure 9. Once started, the *Connection Provider* process periodically searches for a gateway service by performing an SLP lookup request (Figure 9, step 1). If a gateway service can be found[1], a *layer-two tunnel* connection to the gateway is established (step 2). To finally configure the node

---

[1] Currently, if multiple gateway services are found, the list of all gateways is passed to the tunnelling component.

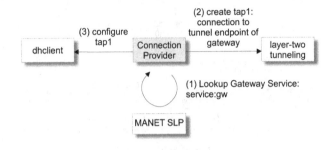

Fig. 9. Connection Provider

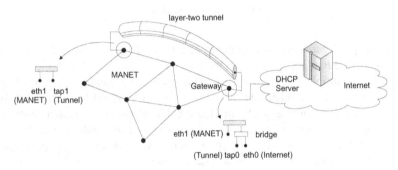

Fig. 10. Network state after the *Connection Provider* has successfully configured a node for Internet access

for Internet access, a DHCP request is triggered on that newly established *tap1* interface (step 3). Since the *tap0* interface at the gateway node is bridged towards the Internet, the DHCP request will eventually be answered by the DHCP server that is reachable from the gateway node. The mechanism of IP configuration is encapsulated in an *IPConfiguration* module with a well defined interface. This allows the *Connection Provider* to easily adapt to other ways of IP configuration such as, e.g., IPv6 auto-addressing or MobileIP. After the IP configuration on the *tap1* device is done, the corresponding node is not only able to communicate with any node in the Internet, but nodes from the Internet may also transparently connect to that node within the MANET. A more detailed perspective on how components such as *bridge* and *layer-two tunnel* interfaces interact with each other is given in Figure 10.

The proposed mechanism differs from previous work for MANET-Internet connectivity in that it combines both a dynamic approach (through the use of a Gateway-Provider and a Connection-Provider) with a routing independent approach (through layer-two tunneling) while still being message efficient (due to MANET SLP).

5.3 Enhancing the SIPHoc Proxy

The ultimate vision of a SIP infrastructure that works in both isolated and Internet connected MANETs is that clients can use their Internet registered SIP accounts[2]

---

[2] A SIP account associated with some official SIP provider in the Internet.

transparently in the MANETs. In other words, the only change should be the scope of the corresponding SIP URI which will vary depending on whether the MANET is currently connected to the Internet or not. For instance, assume again a user Bob in the MANET with SIP URI *sip:bob@ethz.ch*. Given that Bob's SIP account is officially associated with the SIP provider at *ethz.ch*, we would like calls to and from the Internet to become possible as soon as the MANET is connected. On the other hand, Bob should always be able to call any SIP user within the MANET – and vice versa – even if the MANET is currently disconnected from the Internet. To implement this vision of transparent and seamless SIP connectivity, two problems have to be solved: First, the proxy has to know whether the target node is in the MANET or outside. Second, the proxy has to make sure the contact address used during SIP session establishment is in fact reachable by the target user.

Let us first see how the proxy determines the SIP target. Suppose the MANET is currently connected to the Internet[3]. Besides registering users as described in section 4.2, the proxy now additionally forwards SIP REGISTER messages to the Internet if a responsible proxy for the specified domain is available. Upon receiving an INVITE message, the proxy immediately forwards the request to the Internet. If the INVITE process succeeds, the call is considered to be established. If the INVITE process fails – because either the target SIP URI is not registered with any proxy in the Internet, or the user is not online – the INVITE message will simply be forwarded to the responsible proxy in the MANET, if available. To minimize the call-to-ring delay, looking up the outbound-proxy is done concurrently with the forwarding of the INVITE message to the Internet. The workflow of a SIPHoc proxy as described is illustrated in Figure 11. The activities, highlighted grey and labeled "Continue as usual", refer to the procedures described in section 4.2

Let us now see how the proxy copes with SIP user contact addresses when having an Internet connection. Typically, nodes with Internet connection have multiple IP addresses assigned (see section 5.2). Let's call the IP address used in the MANET *internal* and the one used for communicating to the Internet *external*. The SIP applications we used implement static binding, meaning that they use the IP address determined at startup time to be included in the contact address field of any SIP message sent towards the proxy (REGISTER, INVITE). Since the *external* IP address is configured dynamically when Internet connectivity is available, SIP messages would carry contact addresses pointing to an *internal* IP address. In practice, for connections to and from the Internet, one would however like to include the *external* IP address in the contact header of the SIP message because these addresses are used later by the application to establish the actual session. For the application to know which address to include in the contact header, it would have to know about its connection state (Internet, MANET) and the one of the target. Since we want out-of-the-box SIP applications to run transparently in heterogeneous MANETs without the application having to be modified, we propose a concept called **SIP contact-address translation** to be implemented in the proxy. In Figure 11 this is illustrated by two additional activities before the final message forwarding. In the case of a SIP request (INVITE, REGISTER), the old contact address is first saved. Then, the

---

[3] The SIPHoc proxy detects an Internet connection using the InternetDetectionAPI described in section 5.1.

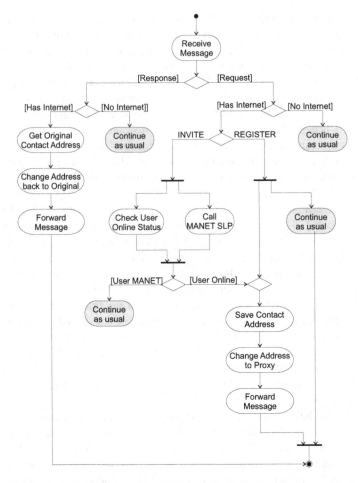

Fig. 11. Activity Diagram of the *SIPHoc Proxy* (SIP-Processor Component)

contact address is changed to the *external* IP address of the proxy. Once a response for a given request is received, the contact address is changed back to the original address that is used by the local SIP application (Figure 11). This keeps the application totally unaware of whether it communicates over the Internet or only within the MANET.

6   Case Study: VoIP in MANETs

6.1   VoIP

Since SIPHoc is strictly SIP compatible, it allows out-of-the-box SIP based VoIP applications to run transparently in MANETs. In this section we use Kphone as a VoIP application to evaluate our SIP infrastructure. However, we also have successfully tested SIPHoc with various other Softphones such as Linphone, Twinkle or Ekiga. From a user perspective, the metric of interest is the *dial-to-ring* delay, i.e., the time elapsed between

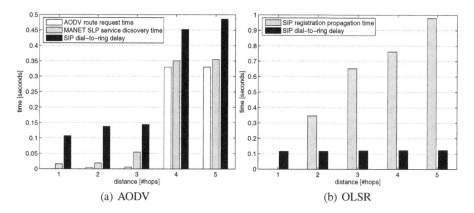

Fig. 12. Performance of SIPHoc in MANETs

the caller clicking the button on the calling terminal and the time the called party hears the ringing. This call setup includes a set of SIP messages (INVITE, TRYING, RING-ING) as well as the associated routing messages with their service extensions embedded. The duration of the call setup depends on the current locations of caller and callee (MANET, Internet) and on the routing protocol used (AODV, OLSR). The following two sections evaluate the session setup time for a) pure Ad Hoc environments and b) Internet-connected Ad Hoc networks.

6.2   Experimental Setup

The measurements were done using 6 notebook computers running Debian 3.1 (Sarge). Five of them had a 2.0Ghz Mobile Pentium 4 and were equipped with an integrated 11Mbit/s IEEE802.11b wireless network interface card and were running kernel 2.6.8. The sixth laptop had a Pentium M processor with 1.73GHz combined with a 54Mbit/s IEEE802.11g wireless network interface card (used at 11Mbit/s through configuration) and was running kernel 2.6.11. Because it would be difficult to find a spatial separation of the notebooks which would have required multihop communication between them, an artificial separation using packet filter rules was used: They were only allowed to communicate with their direct neighbors , all other traffic was dropped (by the default policy). All results are averages over a set of 10 tests. The routing performance was measured by restarting the AODV daemon and issuing an ICMP packet to the target host afterwards, so the time required for the route discovery could be calculated from entries in the log of the AODV daemon. The same goes for the service lookup times where the SLP daemons were restarted after every lookup.

6.3   Performance in a MANET

In Figure 12a we study the session setup time for the AODV case and relate the results to both the route establishment and the service discovery time. The x-axis in Figure 12a refers to the number of nodes on the path (hop distance) between the caller and the callee. A first observation from Figure 12a is that looking up a service using

MANET SLP only takes a few milliseconds longer than a simple route request for the same hop distance. Therefore, the price for piggybacking service information into routing messages is minimal. At the same time, MANET SLP reduces the time necessary to access a given service, since service lookup and route discovery take place simultaneously. As a direct conclusion from this, the SIP dial-to-ring delay is kept very low, only a few milliseconds more than the MANET SLP service discovery time. The overhead comes from the three additional messages involved in a SIP session setup (INVITE, Trying, RINGING). Please note that even if the SIPHoc proxy on the caller part would resolve the requested SIP URI by some magic oracle in zero time, the dial-to-ring delay would still be at least the sum of these 3 messages plus the route establishment time. Thus the measurements prove that SIPHoc reduces the dial-to-ring delay almost to the lowest value possible. The gap in time between three and four hops in Figure 12a is due to AODV's *expanded ring search* technique [17]. In an *expanding ring search*, the originating node initially uses a TTL equal 2 in the RREQ packet IP header and sets a timeout for receiving a RREP. If the RREQ times out without corresponding RREP, the originator broadcasts the RREQ again with the TTL incremented by 2 until a TTL threshold is reached[4]. In Figure 12a, nodes within a distance of three hops can be reached with a TTL value of 2 (one RREQ message), nodes within a distance of 4 and 5 hops, however, can only be reached with a TTL value of 4 (two RREQ messages) which leads to a gap in the route and discovery time.

While for the AODV case most of the overhead goes into dynamically looking up the outbound proxy during session establishment, the major overhead for the OLSR case is during the SIP registration phase. In Figure 12b we study the time needed for a SIP registration to be propagated across the network using OLSR. The x-axis of Figure 12b indicates the hop distance between the local proxy receiving the registration (source proxy) and the target. We see that even nodes being 5 hops apart from the source proxy receive the service information in less a second. Thus, already one second after a user has registered with its local proxy, all nodes within a hop distance of 5 nodes have the SIP binding of the given user accessible in their local MANET SLP process. Once the SIP binding of a user is available locally, the SIP dial-to-ring delay reduces to the time needed to send and receive the messages involved in a call setup (INVITE, Trying, RINGING), which is about 100ms (Figure 12b).

The conclusion from these results, both for AODV and OLSR, is that the *dial-to-ring* delay in an ad hoc network using *SIPHoc* is comparable to the route discovery time. In this sense, SIPHoc is close to optimal.

6.4   Internet-Connected Environment: Scenarios

The next experiment evaluates the dial-to-ring delay for Internet connections. The setup consists of 5 laptops[5] arranged to form a linear 4-hop network. On the MANET side, there is user Alice with no direct Internet access. User Bob is on the other extreme of the MANET and is on a node that – in some experiments – acts as gateway and has Internet access. A third user, Chris, is located in the Internet. We also assume a SIP proxy on *sip.ethz.ch* located in the Internet. We have evaluated the *dial-to-ring* delay

---

[4] Initial TTL value and increment can also be configured differently.

[5] DELL Latitude, 2Ghz Intel Pentium IV, 256 MB RAM.

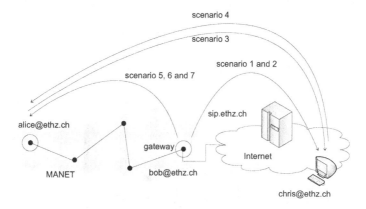

Fig. 13. Evaluation setup

in 7 scenarios as illustrated in Figure 13: (1) Bob calling Chris using an unmodified out-of-the-box SIP proxy[6] as a forwarding proxy for Bob; (2) Bob calling Chris using SIPHoc; (3) Alice calling Chris using Bob as a gateway; (4) Chris calling Alice using Bob as a gateway; (5) Bob calling Alice when Bob is disconnected from the Internet; (6) Bob calling Alice when Bob is connected to the Internet; and (7) Bob calling Alice when Bob is connected to the Internet and Alice is connected to the Internet using the gateway provided by Bob (therefore the INVITE message is routed through the Internet). We also include the cost of an AODV route request (8) for comparison.

6.5   Internet-Connected Environment: Experiments

Each set of bars in Figure 14 corresponds to the result of one scenario, with the x-axis representing the scenario identifier. For all scenarios except the first one, we consider both the case where AODV is used as a routing protocol and the case where OLSR is used. Scenarios 1 and 2 are SIP connections over the Internet. They allow to determine the cost of SIPHoc over a plain SIP infrastructure. The results show that the overhead of SIPHoc (scenario 2) is small compared with the cost of using a plain SIP proxy (scenario 1). The overhead comes from the *SIPHoc Proxy* that performs various checks (looking up whether the node has Internet connection or not, preparing MANET SLP lookup) before forwarding the actual INVITE message to *sip.ethz.ch*. Since the target user Chris in scenario 1 is located in the Internet, the SIPHoc proxy invite processing succeeds without the MANET SLP layer being involved (Figure 11). Thus, there is no difference between the dial-to-ring delay for AODV and OLSR in scenario 1. Scenarios 3 and 4 are in the range of scenario 2 indicating that the 4-hop latency in the MANET is rather negligible compared to the whole session setup time. Furthermore, scenarios 3 and 4 confirm that both directions, MANET-Internet and Internet-MANET, perform similarly. The reason why there is no significant difference between the AODV and the OLSR case is that the route between Alice and the gateway is established during the gateway discovery phase which takes place asynchronously in a separate process

---

[6] We have used the JAIN Proxy: http://snad.ncsl.nist.gov/proj/iptel

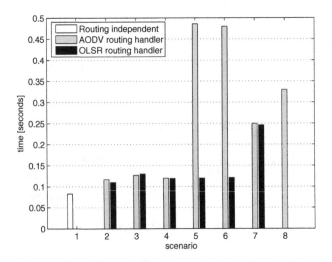

Fig. 14. *dial-to-ring* delay

(connection provider, Section 5.2) before the actual session establishment. In scenario 5, the target user cannot be found in the Internet, thus calls to the MANET SLP layer are necessary. If AODV and the corresponding MANET SLP routing handler is used, the dynamic discovery of the outbound-proxy (section 4.2) results in additional messages sent across the network, which increases the overall dial-to-ring time. The overhead is nevertheless in the range of a route request (scenario 8). This is because the outbound-proxy lookup and the route discovery take place simultaneously. If OLSR is used in combination with the corresponding MANET SLP routing handler, no overhead at all is observed when comparing scenarios 5 and 6 with scenarios 3 and 4. This is because the SIP registration information has been propagated across the network pro-actively, piggybacked on routing messages. In scenario 6, note that the MANET is considered to be connected to the Internet. However, since Alice uses an official SIP account, but is not connected to the Internet, the *SIPHoc Proxy* receives an offline response from *sip.ethz.ch* and then proceeds as in scenario 5, leading to a similar result. Scenario 7 has an impressive performance considering that the call goes through 4 hops in the MANET, the gateway and the Internet consecutively. The call is faster than the calls in scenarios 5 and 6 since no MANET SLP lookup is involved, but takes longer than scenarios 3 and 4 because both endpoints use a *SIPHoc Proxy*. The results for AODV and OLSR again match quite well since the SIPHoc proxy succeeds immediately to establish a session over the Internet and no MANET SLP call is necessary.

The results have shown that the overhead for calls to and from the Internet is within an acceptable range. This is mainly due to the strategy described in section 5, after which the SIPHoc proxy always first tries to establish a SIP session over the Internet and only uses dynamic outbound-proxy discovery if necessary. Since the overhead of calls to the Internet is negligible compared to the overhead within the MANET, the overhead in case a given user cannot be found in the Internet is almost zero.

6.6   Gateway Service

One important last question is how fast the gateway service can be discovered in the MANET. The answer depends on the routing protocol used. For the AODV case, the gateway service discovery time corresponds to the values for service discovery shown in Figure 12a. For the OLSR case, the gateway discovery time corresponds to the registration propagation time shown in Figure 12b.

To see whether tunnel maintenance affects the performance of the gateway, we have measured *dial-to-ring* delays for various setups with up to 1000 additional (idle) tunnel connections, without observing any recognizable slowdown.

We have also studied the packet overhead caused by the fact that the gateway is accessed through a layer 2 tunnel which wraps the packet and adds its own Ethernet and IP headers. The Ethernet header uses 14 bytes and the IP header 20 bytes. *openvpn*, used as tunneling application in our setting, sends its packets using UDP which adds another 8 bytes. This results in an overall overhead of 42 bytes per packet. Compared with the typical MTU of 1500 bytes per packet in Ethernet, an overhead of 42 bytes is almost irrelevant. For voice data, however, the audio data contained in a UDP packet is typically in the range of 160-172 bytes. A voice data packet on the wire without the tunneling overhead would therefore have a size of 214 bytes. With the tunnel header, the size of each packet increases to 256 bytes. This is an overhead of 20%. If only a few nodes in the network communicate through the gateway using tunneling this overhead will not have a large effect. If the network is big and most of the users communicate through the gateway, an overhead of 20% may decrease the available capacity.

6.7   Discussion

We have shown in sections 6.3 and 6.5 that SIPHoc provides a very efficient SIP middleware infrastructure for VoIP applications in both isolated and Internet connected MANETs. Our experiments illustrate that SIPHoc is able to establish sessions within a few hundred milliseconds, regardless whether the other party is located in the MANET or in the Internet. Due to the efficient architecture of SIPHoc, the overhead in the dial-to-ring delay stays in the order of a route discovery time, which is the lowest value possible since the cost of a route discovery has to be paid anyway.

7   Conclusion

In this paper we have presented *SIPHoc*, a middleware providing SIP-compatible session establishment in both isolated and Internet-connected MANETs. The advantages over existing work are that *SIPHoc* does not impose any network topology, does not involve any centralized components, does not require the modification of existing standards, is message efficient, and has an overhead comparable to MANET route requests. In the paper we have used VoIP to show how SIPHoc can be used by SIP-compatible applications to transparently establish sessions with other parties either located within the MANET or in the Internet. To the best of our knowledge, *SIPHoc* is the first complete implementation of a SIP infrastructure for MANETs and the only one that resolves all the limitations of existing work.

Acknowledgement

The work presented in this paper was supported (in part) by the National Competence Center in Research on Mobile Information and Communication Systems (NCCR-MICS), a center supported by the Swiss National Science Foundation under grant number 5005-67322.

References

1. The Netfilter/Iptables Project (June 2001), http://www.netfilter.org
2. amd Ki-Hyung Kim, H.-G.S., Jung, W.-D., Park, J.-S.: Performance of service location protocols in manet based on reactive routing protocols. In: Lorenz, P., Dini, P. (eds.) ICN 2005. LNCS, vol. 3421, Springer, Heidelberg (2005)
3. Chen, J.-J., Cheng, Y.-L., Tseng, Y.-C., Wu, Q.: A push-based voip service for an internet-enabled mobile ad hoc network. In: APWCS 2006. Proceedings of 3rd IEEE VTS Asia Pacific Wireless Comm. Symposium, IEEE Computer Society Press, Los Alamitos (2006)
4. Adjih, C., Laouiti, A., Minet, P., Muhlethaler, P., Qayyum, A., Viennot, L.: Optimized link state routing protocol (olsr). In: Clausen, T. (ed.) RFC 3626, Network Working Group (October 2003)
5. Dutta, A., Jain, R., Wong, K., Burns, J., Young, K., Schulzrinne, H.: Multilayered mobility management for survivable network. In: Proceedings of MILCOM (2001)
6. Egevang, K., Francis, P.: The IP Network Address Translator (NAT). RFC 1631 (Informational), Obsoleted by RFC 3022 (May 1994)
7. Engelstad, P., Zheng, Y.: Evaluation of service discovery architectures for mobile ad hoc network. In: WONS 2005: Proceedings of the Second Annual Conference on Wireless On-demand Network Systems and Services, IEEE Computer Society Press, Los Alamitos (2005)
8. Frank, C., Karl, H.: Consistency challenges of service discovery in mobile ad hoc networks. In: MSWiM 2004: Proceedings of the 7th ACM international symposium on Modeling, analysis and simulation of wireless and mobile systems, pp. 105–114. ACM Press, New York (2004)
9. Guttman, E., Perkins, C., Veizades, J., Day, M.: Service Location Protocol, Version 2. RFC 2608 (Proposed Standard), Updated by RFC 3224 (June 1999)
10. Jönsson, U., Alriksson, F., Larsson, T., Johansson, P., Gerald, J., Maguire, Q.: Mipmanet: mobile ip for mobile ad hoc networks. In: MobiHoc 2000: Proceedings of the 1st ACM international symposium on Mobile ad hoc networking & computing, pp. 75–85. IEEE Press, Piscataway (2000)
11. Kozat, U., Tassiulas, L.: Service discovery in mobile ad hoc networks: an overall perspective on architectural choices and network layer support issues. Ad Hoc Networks 2(1), 23–44 (2004)
12. Leggio, S., Manner, J., Hulkkonen, A., Raatikainen, K.: Session initiation protocol deployment in ad-hoc networks: a decentralized approach. In: IWWAN. 2nd International Workshop on Wireless Ad-hoc Networks (2005)
13. Li, L., Lamont, L.: A lightweight service discovery mechanism for mobile ad hoc pervasive environment using cross-layer design. In: Percom 2005: Proceeding of the 3rd International Conference on Pervasive Computing and Communications Workshops (2005)
14. Michalak, M., Braun, T.: Common gateway architecture for mobile ad-hoc networks. In: WON 2005: Second Annual Conference on Wireless On demand Network Systems and Services (2005)

15. Nilsson, A., Perkins, C.E., Tuominen, A.J., Wakikawa, R., Malinen, J.T.: Aodv and ipv6 internet access for ad hoc networks. SIGMOBILE Mob. Comput. Commun. Rev. 6(3), 102–103 (2002)
16. O'Doherty, M.: Pico sip. Internet Draft (February 2001)
17. Perkins, C., Belding-Royer, E., Das, S.: Ad hoc On-Demand Distance Vector (AODV) Routing. RFC 3561 (Experimental) (July (2003)
18. Perkins, C., Royer, E.: Ad hoc on-demand distance vector routing. In: Proceedings of the 2nd IEEE Workshop on Mobile Computing Systems and Applications, pp. 90–100 (February 1999)
19. Perkins, C.E.: Mobile-ip, ad-hoc networking, and nomadicity. In: COMPSAC 1996. Proceedings of International IEEE Computer Software and Applications Conference, vol. 00, p. 472. IEEE Computer Society Press, Los Alamitos (1996)
20. Rosenberg, J., Schulzrinne, H., Camarillo, G., Johnston, A., Peterson, J., Sparks, R., Handley, M., Schooler, E.: SIP: Session Initiation Protocol. RFC 3261 (Proposed Standard), Updated by RFCs 3265, 3853 (June 2002)
21. Rosenberg, J., Weinberger, J., Huitema, C., Mahy, R.: STUN - Simple Traversal of User Datagram Protocol (UDP) Through Network Address Translators (NATs). RFC 3489 (Proposed Standard) (Mar 2003)
22. Sailhan, F., Issarny, V.: Scalable service discovery for manet. In: PerCom 2005. Proceedings of the 3rd IEEE international Conference on Pervasive Computing and Communications, IEEE Computer Society Press, Los Alamitos (2005)
23. Sun, Y., Belding-Royer, E.M., Perkins, C.E.: Internet connectivity for ad hoc mobile networks. International Journal of Wireless Information Networks special issue on "Mobile Ad Hoc Networks (MANETs): Standards, Research, Applications" 9(2) (April 2002)
24. Ververidis, C., Polyzos, G.: Extended zrp: a routing layer based service discovery protocol for mobile ad hoc networks. In: Mobiquitous 2005: Proceedings of the Second Annual International Conference on Mobile and Ubiquitous Systems, IEEE Computer Society Press, Los Alamitos (2005)

Vector-Field Consistency for Ad-Hoc Gaming

Nuno Santos, Luís Veiga, and Paulo Ferreira

INESC-ID/Technical University of Lisbon
Distributed Systems Group
Rua Alves Redol N 9, 1000-029 Lisboa
{nuno.santos,luis.veiga,paulo.ferreira}@inesc-id.pt

Abstract. Developing distributed multiplayer games for ad-hoc networks is challenging. Consistency of the replicated shared state is hard to ensure at a low cost. Current consistency models and middleware systems lack the required adaptability and efficiency when applied to ad-hoc gaming. Hence, developing such robust applications is still a daunting task. We propose i) Vector-Field Consistency (VFC), a new consistency model, and ii) the Mobihoc middleware to ease the programming effort of these games, while ensuring the consistency of replicated objects. VFC unifies i) several forms of consistency enforcement and a multi-dimensional criteria (time, sequence and value) to limit replica divergence, with ii) techniques based on locality-awareness (w.r.t. players position). Mobihoc adopts VFC and provides game programmers the abstractions to manage game state easily and efficiently. A Mobihoc prototype and a demonstrating game were developed and evaluated. The results obtained are very encouraging.

Keywords: Consistency Management, Replicated Objects, Locality-Awareness, Multiplayer Games.

1 Introduction

The growing utilization of personal appliances such as PDAs and cell phones enables the proliferation of ad-hoc networks. Ad-hoc networks form spontaneously between two or more devices communicating via wireless interfaces. Due to their entertaining nature and motivated by this technological advance, distributed multiplayer games are particularly interesting to deploy in such environments. Once an ad-hoc network is formed, people may play these games irrespective of the place they are (e.g. public transports, restaurants) without the need for a structured network and without incurring into any connectivity expenses.

In distributed multiplayer games there is a need for data sharing between the network nodes (e.g. player positions, maps, scores). Enforcing data consistency requires additional communication for update propagation and synchronization operations. In ad-hoc networks, communication-intensive operations are critical and have a twofold negative impact. Firstly, the high latency, the reduced network bandwidth and the small processing capability of devices brings overheads that dramatically hinder game playability. Secondly, extensive access to the network

R. Cerqueira and R.H. Campbell (Eds.): Middleware 2007, LNCS 4834, pp. 80–100, 2007.

causes devices batteries to consume rapidly. In order to circumvent these negative impacts, game programmers tend to use programming tweaks, low level optimizations and error-prone message-passing approaches to keep the shared data consistent. As a side effect, software becomes harder to manage and less reliable.

Current approaches to optimistic consistency [1] relax the strict consistency model to reduce communication expenses. The common assumption is that applications may allow data inconsistencies up to a certain limit and enable application programmers to specify these limits according to the semantics of applications. The criteria for slacking consistency varies: by divergence between the values of replicas, on a time-basis [2], by applying application based predicates on replica values [3,4], sequential ordering [5], or combining several approaches [4,6]. However, these proposals are inadequate to cope with the dynamics of distributed games: consistency requirements change often and quickly throughout the game execution, namely w.r.t. the players' position in the *virtual world*. The above mentioned systems lack the required adaptability and are inefficient when applied to the ad-hoc scenario. On the other hand, current middleware for multiplayer games embodies the notion of *locality-awareness* (traceable to [7,8]) but offer a very limited consistency model [9], or use it just to drive load-balancing [10] and network traffic between servers [11].

In this paper, we propose a new consistency model for replicated objects called *Vector-Field Consistency* (VFC) and present *Mobihoc*, a middleware adopting VFC to support multiplayer distributed games in ad-hoc networks. A Mobihoc prototype was implemented on the J2ME platform. To demonstrate its feasibility, a distributed version of Pacman was implemented on top of Mobihoc. Both Mobihoc and Pacman were deployed and evaluated in real mobile phones (Nokia 6600) with good performance results.

VFC is an optimistic consistency model allowing bounded divergence of the object replicas. The VFC novelty is the following. VFC selectively and dynamically strengthens/weakens replica consistency based on the ongoing game state while elegantly managing i) how the consistency degree *changes* throughout game execution, and ii) how the consistency requirements are *specified*. The first issue is dealt by employing locality-awareness techniques. It considers that throughout the game execution, there are certain 'observation points' we call *pivots* (e.g. the player's position) around which the consistency is required to be strong and weakens as the distance from the pivot increases. Since pivots can change with time (e.g. if the player moves), objects consistency needs can also change with time. The second issue is handled by providing a 3-dimensional vector for specifying consistency degrees. Each dimension of the vector bounds the replica divergence in *time* (delay), *sequence* (number of operations) and *value* (magnitude of modifications) constraints. Game programmers parameterize VFC by specifying both the pivots and the consistency degrees according to game logic.

The advantages of VFC are manifold. First, it is flexible and easily perceived by game programmers: the consistency model based on pivots is intuitive and the parameterization settings allow the game programmer to specify the consistency requirements for a wide range of game scenarios. Second, from the players viewpoint, VFC allows user experience to proceed within acceptable parameters in the sense that, as far as the players are concerned, the rules of the game are being abided to, and users are provided with all the relevant information (e.g. immediate surroundings, opponents' scores) to make sensible game decisions. Also, by intelligently selecting the critical updates to send and postponing the less critical ones, VFC is efficient in the utilization of resources, it reduces network bandwidth usage and masquerades latency. Thus, for each particular game, programmers are able to specify the consistency requirements that enable a more efficient use of the network by tolerating bounded inconsistencies that do not jeopardize the overall game state and the players experience. This is mostly useful for those games where the number of updates to propagate is high and the interactivity with the user is demanding. Despite addressing multiplayer games, VFC and Mobihoc can also be used to develop any other cooperative applications based on replicated shared-data.

This paper is organized as follows. Section 2 briefly describes the VFC consistency model. Section 3 presents the Mobihoc architecture. Section 4 describes the implementation details of Mobihoc. Section 5 presents and discusses the obtained experimental results. Section 6 surveys the relevant related work and Section 7 draws some conclusions.

2   Consistency Model

In VFC, objects are positioned within a *virtual world*, an abstraction of an N-dimensional space. Without loss of generality, we consider the virtual world to be 2-dimensional. In many games these abstractions map immediately to the game semantics; for example, in the Pacman game, the virtual world is a 2-dimensional maze populated with objects such as avatars, ghosts and dots. Each node of the network has a local *view* consisting of a full local replica of the virtual world. Each view may have bounded inconsistencies. VFC characterizes how these inconsistencies are managed.

The remainder of this section describes the two main ideas underlying the VFC model: *consistency zones* describe how the consistency of object replicas varies in each view (see Section 2.1), and *consistency vectors* characterize the consistency degrees (see Section 2.2). Section 2.3, proposes two generalizations of the basic VFC model and systematizes the parameters for setting VFC from the game programmers' viewpoint.

2.1   Field-Generated Consistency Zones

Within a particular view, object consistency depends on their distance to a *pivot* (P). It is characterized by a position in the virtual world and it can move over time. A pivot can be an object (e.g. the Pacman player) or just a function (e.g. an editor cursor). Figure 1.a illustrates a virtual world populated with objects o_1, o_2, o_3, o_4 and o_5. The pivot (o_5) is signed with a star.

By analogy with the electric ($\vec{E}$) and the gravitational ($\vec{G}$) fields, a pivot generates a 'consistency field' determining the consistency of each object as a

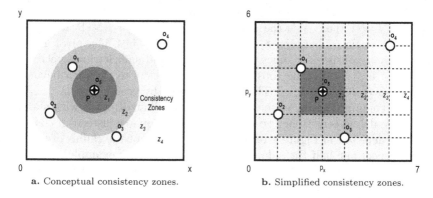

Fig. 1. Consistency zones centered on a pivot within a virtual world

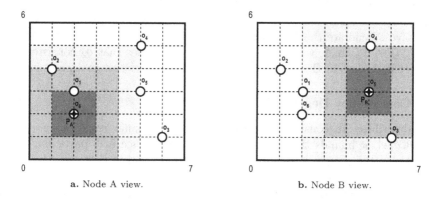

Fig. 2. Two views of the same virtual world

function of the distance between the object and the pivot. Thus, pivots generate *consistency zones*, iso-surfaces, ring shaped, concentric areas around them, such that the objects positioned within the same consistency zone are enforced the same consistency degree. For example, in Figure 1.a, pivot P is in the center of four consistency zones labeled z_i, where $0 \leq i \leq 4$. Objects o_2 and o_3 are enforced the same consistency degree since they are in z_3.

Each consistency zone maps to a *consistency degree* (c_i) of a *consistency scale*. A consistency scale $C = \langle c_1, \ldots, c_n \rangle$ is an ordered set of c_i, each specifying the consistency to be enforced within zone z_i. The property $c_i > c_{i+1}$ holds, meaning that c_i enforces stronger consistency than c_{i+1}. Thus, consistency zones are arranged monotonically; consistency degrees become weaker as the distance to P increases. In Figure 1.a, darker consistency zones impose stronger consistency requirements. For example, if P represents the player and the other objects are ghosts of the Pacman game, ghosts consistency weakens as they are farther from the player. Specification of consistency degrees is detailed in Section 2.2.

Consider λ_i the radius of the outer circumference of z_i. We define z_i as follows: i) if $i = 1$ then z_1 is the circle of radius λ_1, ii) if $i > 1$ then z_i refers to the area enclosed between z_i and z_{i-1} (a ring). Thus, if a pivot P is surrounded by n consistency zones, it is necessary and sufficient to specify λ_i to all i where $1 \le i < n$. The consistency zone z_n refers to the area beyond the circumference of radius λ_{n-1}. This is represented by vector $Z = [\lambda_1, ..., \lambda_{n-1}]$. Since it is computationally expensive to determine if an object is within a radial surface, we define consistency zones as concentric squares instead of concentric circles, as depicted in Figure 1.b. Also, λ represents not the radius of the outer circumference, but half the side of the outer square. For example, consistency zones of Figure 1.b are defined by $Z = [1, 2, 3]$ and objects are distributed by the following zones: $\{o_1, o_5\} \rightarrow z_1$, $\{o_2, o_3\} \rightarrow z_2$, $\{o_4\} \rightarrow z_3$.

Determining the consistency degree of an object depends on its relative position w.r.t. the pivots. Thus, the same object may have different consistency degrees in different views. Figure 2 illustrates this by depicting the views of two nodes, A (Figure 2.a) and B (Figure 2.b), respectively, with pivots P_A and P_B. Both pivots generate the consistency zone pattern $Z = [1, 2, 3]$. Hence, for example, $o_2 \rightarrow z_2$, in A, while $o_2 \rightarrow z_4$ in B. This implies that o_2 consistency is stronger in A than in B, which is expected since o_2 is closest to a pivot in A.

2.2   Consistency Degree Vectors

VFC describes the consistency degrees as 3-dimensional *consistency vectors* $\kappa = [\theta, \sigma, \nu]$. κ bounds the maximum objects divergence in a particular view, i.e. between the objects latest updates and their replicas in that view. In short, for each object o, κ bounds the staleness of o in a particular view. Each dimension is a numerical scalar defining the maximum divergence of the orthogonal constraints *time* (θ), *sequence* (σ), and *value* (ν)[1], respectively.

- *Time* – Specifies the maximum time a replica can be without being refreshed with its latest value, irrespective of the number of updates performed in-between. Consider that $\theta(o)$ provides the time passed from the last replica update. The *time* constraint κ_θ enforces that, at any time, $\theta(o) < \kappa_\theta$. This scalar quantity measures time in seconds.
- *Sequence* – Specifies the maximum number of lost replica updates, i.e. updates that were not applied to a replica. Similarly, consider that $\sigma(o)$ indicates the number of lost updates. The sequence constraint κ_σ enforces that, at any time, $\sigma(o) < \kappa_\sigma$. The unit is the number of lost updates.
- *Value* – Specifies the maximum relative difference between replica contents or against a constant (e.g. top-value). Consider that $\nu(o)$ provides this difference. The value constraint κ_ν enforces that, at any time, $\nu(o) < \kappa_\nu$. The unit of variation is a percentage. It captures the effects of updates on the object internal state and is implementation dependent (e.g. it may reflect a drift regarding the player score or the player life charge).

---

[1] Although in modern Greek, the *vee* sound is written using the letter β, we prefer to use the letter ν, for its resemblance with the latin v.

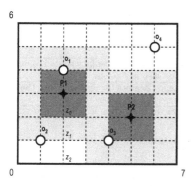

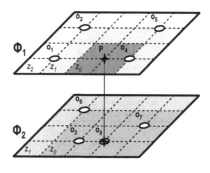

Fig. 3. Multi-pivot generalization   **Fig. 4.** Multi-zones generalization

The overall maximum divergence is obtained by the disjunction of all the κ vector dimensions. For example, consider the consistency vector $\kappa = [0.1, 6, 20]$. Hence, at maximum, replicas are outdated in $\kappa_\theta = 0.1$ seconds or $\kappa_\sigma = 6$ lost updates or with a $\kappa_\nu = 20\%$ variation in the replica internal state. To indicate the least possible requirements, i.e. no requirements on that dimension, we use '.' (mathematically, this symbol represents '∞'). For example, $\kappa = [0.1, 6, .]$ imposes no consistency constraints whatsoever regarding the replica internal state.

In VFC, consistency degrees are specified by κ vectors. In order to specify a consistency scale obeying $c_i > c_{i+1}$ with κ_i and κ_{i+1} vectors, the condition $\kappa_{i+1} > \kappa_i$ must hold, i.e. for every $\kappa_{i+1_u} \geq \kappa_{i_u}$ and there is at least one v such that $\kappa_{i+1_v} > \kappa_{i_v}$, $u, v \in \{\theta, \sigma, \nu\}$. For example, $C = \langle [0.2, 2, 10], [0.2, 5, 10] \rangle$ is a valid consistency scale: $[0.2, 2, 10]$ stands for a stronger consistency degree than $[0.2, 5, 10]$ because the number of admitted lost updates is higher in the latter (5) than in the former (2) and the other dimensions are equal. Also, we define $\kappa_M = [., ., .]$ as the highest consistency degree, and $\kappa_m = [0, 0, 0]$ as the lowest consistency degree, such that $\kappa_m \leq \kappa_i \leq \kappa_M$.

2.3   VFC Generalization

In this section we introduce two generalizations allowing a broader utilization of the VFC model: *multi-pivot* and *multi-zones* generalizations. The multi-pivot generalization admits more than one pivot per view. Figure 3 illustrates such a case, with two pivots P_1 and P_2 in the same view. Objects are assigned the consistency degree w.r.t. the closest pivot.

The multi-zones generalization allows different sets of objects to be characterized differently w.r.t. their consistency requirements. For example, in Pacman, objects standing for ghosts and for rooms may be characterized with different consistency requirements. Thus, n sets of objects may be assigned specifically: i) consistency zones, ii) consistency degrees, and iii) pivots. Specification of each set is designated by ϕ_i, where $1 \leq i \leq n$; ϕ refers to all ϕ_i. Figure 4 shows an example of two object set specific settings ϕ_1 and ϕ_2. The former characterizes

Parameter	Description
O_i	Subset of objects that the consistency specification refers to. O_i are exclusive meaning that for every two ϕ_i and ϕ_j of ϕ, if $o \in O_i \Rightarrow o \notin O_j$. Moreover, for every object o, there must be a ϕ_i such that $o \in O_i$.
Z	Consistency zone vector Z specifying how to draw the consistency zones around the pivots. It is $\#_Z$ sized and specifies $\#_Z + 1$ consistency zones.
C	Consistency scale characterizing the consistency degrees for applying into the consistency zones. It is $\#_C$ sized with $\#_C = \#_Z + 1$ consistency degrees.
V	Set identifying the pivot objects for each view of the virtual world.

Fig. 5. Table describing the ϕ parameters of VFC

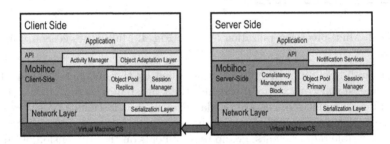

Fig. 6. Mobihoc architecture

objects $\{o_1, o_2, o_4, o_5\}$. The latter characterizes objects $\{o_3, o_6, o_7, o_8\}$. Both have the same pivot but different consistency zone specifications.

Summary. In order to specify the consistency requirements, game programmers need to provide the VFC ϕ settings by describing individual object sets ϕ_i. Each ϕ_i setting is described by $\phi_i = [O_i, Z, C, V]$, where $O_i \subseteq O$. Figure 5 presents a table summarizing these parameters. As an example, the ϕ settings relative to Figure 2 can be described by $\phi_1 = [O, Z, C, P]$, where $O = \{o_1, o_2, o_3, o_4, o_5, o_6\}$, $Z = [1, 2, 3]$, $C = \langle \kappa_m, [., 1, .], [., 2, .], \kappa_M \rangle$ and, finally, $V = \{A \rightarrow \{o_6\}, B \rightarrow \{o_5\}\}$. In this example, there is a single object set ϕ_1.

3 Architecture

Mobihoc is a middleware platform aimed at supporting the design of multiplayer distributed games for ad-hoc networks. Mobihoc enforces VFC by managing the game state between the network nodes and provides programmers with the adequate means to parameterize VFC according to game semantics.

Mobihoc follows a client-server architecture (see Figure 6).[2] Upon the establishment of the ad-hoc network, one of the nodes becomes the server. Naturally, the server device may also act as a client allowing all nodes to participate in the

---

[2] The rationale for this choice is mainly due to the limitations of the Bluetooth technology that imposes a single node of the network to relay all messages between any two nodes.

game. The server has a coordinating role regarding data management: write-lock management, update propagation and VFC enforcement. The client-server protocol is orchestrated by the Session Manager components of each peer. Communication is performed between clients and the server on a star like topology using the services of components Network Layer and Serialization Layer.

The remainder on this section presents, firstly, the mechanisms for reading/writing objects (Section 3.1) and, secondly, the mechanisms for VFC enforcement (Section 3.2), and exposes other relevant architecture components.

3.1 Read and Write Objects

The shared data is a collection of objects. Each node maintains local replicas of all objects in the Object Pool container. The server maintains a primary copy of the object pool while the clients keep replicas of such objects. From the architectural viewpoint, there is no restriction whatsoever w.r.t. the representation of data (e.g. object graphs, tuples, relations). Also, the Object Adaptation Layer maps the application data representation to the Mobihoc internal data representation.

Mobihoc allows clients to read and write objects through its API. Read operations are performed on the local replicas without locking requirements (clients may read stale data). Write operations need to acquire locks in order to prevent the loss of updates. The server manages locks centrally; clients exchange messages with the server to acquire and release them. Object updates are sent to the server when clients release locks. The server propagates the new object versions to the other nodes according to the VFC specification.

With the exception of lock messages (for obtaining and releasing locks), nodes operate periodically w.r.t. the interactions between them. The server, periodically, sends a message to all clients defining a *round*. This has a twofold implication. In each round, the server sends round messages to the clients; updates are piggybacked on the round messages and merged at client pools at reception time. On the other hand, it enables the execution of synchronized application handler functions (*activities*) at the client side. Whenever a round message is received the Activity Manager executes client activities. This feature may be used by many games based on turns. For example, activities may be used to update players locations, scores or other game state information. Since updates are received and merged before executing activities, the game programmers know that local replicas are stable when their activities execute.

3.2 Enforcement of the VFC Model

The Consistency Management Block (CMB) at the server side enforces the VFC model. The CMB coordinates the propagation of updates to clients according to the VFC consistency parameters specified by each client. There are two phases: the *setup phase* and the *active phase*. During the *setup phase*, clients register the objects to be shared and send their consistency parameters (VFC ϕ settings) to the server; the CMB aggregates all the clients ϕ settings. The *active*

CMB-Update-Received(o, u_o)
1   $D[o] \leftarrow 1$
2   Enqueue$(U, \langle o, u_o \rangle)$

CMB-Round-Triggered(t, M)
1   Merge(O, U)
2   $u \leftarrow$ New-Vector()
3   for $o \leftarrow 1$ to $\#_O$
4   do if $D[o] = 1$
5   then Add$(u, O[o])$
6            $D[o] \leftarrow 0$
7   for $c \leftarrow 1$ to $\#_C$
8   do Piggyback$(M[c], u)$

a. CMB update handler.   b. CMB round handler.

Fig. 7. Pseudo-code of CMB Version 1

phase is when clients may access the registered objects. In this phase, the server processes: 1) write requests (sent asynchronously by the clients piggybacked in lock release messages), and 2) round events (triggered periodically). The CMB is involved in handling both these events. It provides two functions that are called by the Session Manager (SM): CMB-Update-Received and CMB-Round-Triggered. As both functions are called, the CMB accumulates and computes the required information to build the clients' consistency views according to the previously specified ϕ settings. When called by the SM, the CMB-Round-Triggered function returns the updates to be sent to each client, which the SM piggybacks in the round messages.

In spite of implementing VFC, the CMB module offers a generic interface allowing Mobihoc to support different consistency models. The remainder of this section describes the internals of CMB that enforce VFC. The description of the CMB algorithm is performed gradually as three versions are progressively presented for a better understanding: 1) the CMB sends every client all updates performed since the last round event, 2) the CMB supports consistency degrees (κ vectors), 3) the CMB provides full VFC support, i.e. update sending obeys the ϕ settings specified by clients. For each step we describe the algorithms underlying CMB-Update-Received and CMB-Round-Triggered functions.

Version 1. In order to guarantee that all updates received since the last round event are sent to all clients in the next round, the CMB keeps track of which objects became dirty (i.e. were written) meanwhile in array D. Only the dirty objects are propagated to clients. Figure 7 presents the pseudo-code of the algorithms implementing this semantics. D has an entry per object of the object pool. Whenever the server receives an update, CMB-Update-Received is invoked setting the object as dirty in D and putting the update in the queue of pending updates U. At each round event, CMB-Round-Triggered is executed: it merges the pending updates in the object pool and sends all pending updates piggybacked in round messages to clients after testing the D dirty flags. D is then cleared meaning that the new versions were sent to all clients.

Version 2. This version considers that, instead of sending all updates to every client, there is a consistency vector κ, common to all clients. κ specifies when and which updates must be propagated to clients. Figure 8 presents the pseudo-code

```
CMB-Update-Received(o, u_o)                    CMB-Round-Triggered(t, M)
 1   S_σ[o] ← S_σ[o] + 1                         1   Merge(O, U)
 2   if S_σ[o] ≥ κ_σ or                          2   u ← New-Vector()
 3       |ν(u_o) − S_ν[o]| ≥ κ_ν                 3   for o ← 1 to #_O
 4     then D[o] ← 1                             4   do t_δ ← t − S_θ[o]
 5   Enqueue(U, ⟨o, u_o⟩)                        5       if D[o] = 1 or t_δ ≥ κ_θ
                                                  6         then Add(u, O[o])
                                                  7             D[o] ← 0
                                                  8             S_θ[o], S_σ[o], S_ν[o] ← t, 0, ν(O[o])
                                                  9   for c ← 1 to #_C
                                                 10   do Piggyback(M[c], u)
```

a. CMB update handler.   b. CMB round handler.

Fig. 8. Pseudo-code of CMB Version 2

of the algorithms that support consistency vectors. The $κ$ consistency vector expresses three orthogonal dimensions (time, sequence and value). Each dimension is evaluated independently and auxiliary data structures (S arrays) are kept for each dimension. Without loss of generality, we assume there is a single and fixed $κ$ vector for all clients, thus all clients receive the same updates obeying $κ$. Each dimension is evaluated as follows:

- *Time* – $S_θ$ keeps the time of the last sent update. Whenever this time exceeds the one specified by $κ_θ$, the update is sent (see Figure 8.b lines 4-5) and the CMB internal state (D and S arrays) is reset. The time is approximated to a multiple of the round period.
- *Sequence* – $S_σ$ is simply a counter of the number of updates that where received by the server since the last update was sent. There is a counter per object. When an update is received, this counter is incremented. When the counter exceeds the value $κ_σ$, the object is set to dirty in D in order to send the update in the next round (see Figure 8.a lines 1-4).
- *Value* – This qualitative dimension implies querying the object state to test when the difference to the last propagated version exceeds $κ_ν$. This query is evaluated by a function $ν$, provided by the game programmer and dependent of the game semantics. $S_ν$ keeps the query result of the last propagated version and do the test of Figure 8.a line 3 whenever an update is received.

Version 3. In order to fully support VFC, it is required to maintain per client consistency views. This imposes two extensions w.r.t. the CMB Version 2: 1) D and S become bidimensional matrices where the additional dimension regards individual client views, and 2) $κ$ vectors are computed per object, per view, according to clients $φ$ settings. To this extent, additional data structures are required: K, Z, C and P. K is a bidimensional matrix storing per object $κ$ vectors of each view, that are valid during a time slot. Z, C and P refer to the data structures related to the clients $φ$ settings (see Section 2.3).

Calculating $κ$ vectors is straightforward (see Figure 9, lines 11-18). Function $Φ(c, o) → ⟨Z, C, P⟩$ retrieves the $φ$ settings referring to o for each client view s: Z, C and P. The algorithm proceeds as follows: 1) determines in which consistency zone z_{closer} the object is, and 2) resolves and stores in K the object

CMB-UPDATE-RECEIVED(o, u_o)

```
1   for c ← 1 to #C
2   do if D[c, o] = 1
3       then continue
4       κ ← K[c, o]
5       S_σ[c, o] ← S_σ[c, o] + 1
6       if S_σ[c, o] ≥ κ_σ or
7          |ν(u_o) − S_ν[c, o]| ≥ κ_ν
8          then D[c, o] ← 1
9   ENQUEUE(U, ⟨o, u_o⟩)
```

CMB-ROUND-TRIGGERED(t, M)

```
1   MERGE(O, U)
2   for c ← 1 to #V
3   do u ← NEW-VECTOR()
4       for o ← 1 to #O
5       do κ ← K[c, o]
6           t_δ ← t − S_θ[c, o]
7           if D[c, o] = 1 or t_δ ≥ κ_θ
8              then ADD(u, O[o])
9                 D[c, o] ← 0
10                S_θ[c, o], S_σ[c, o], S_ν[c, o] ← t, 0, ν(O[o])
11             ⟨Z, C, P⟩ ← Φ(c, o)
12             z_closer ← −
13             for p ← 0 to #P
14             do ⟨p_x, p_y⟩ ← ⟨P[p].x, P[p].y⟩
15                ⟨o_x, o_y⟩ ← ⟨O[o].x, O[o].y⟩
16                z ← MAX(|p_x − o_x|, |p_y − o_y|)
17                z_closer ← MIN(z_closer, z)
18             K[c, o] ← C[Z[z_closer]]
19   PIGGYBACK(M[c], u)
```

a. CMB update handler.   b. CMB round handler.

Fig. 9. Pseudo-code of CMB Version 3

consistency degree κ. Regarding the first step, since the object may be positioned in more than one consistency zone, each one belonging to a pivot, it is necessary to know which of these consistency zones imposes strongest consistency requirements. This is found by detecting which pivot is closer to the object, hence the z variable to evaluate the distance to a pivot and z_{closer} to keep the shortest one. Finding the distance from object o to a pivot $P = \langle p_x, p_y \rangle$ implies discovering in which P centered square of side l the object $\langle o_x, o_y \rangle$ is positioned such that $z = l/2 = Max(|p_x − o_x|, |p_y − o_y|)$. Since consistency zones are delimited by squares centered in P, it is enough to compare z with half the length of the squares that bound a certain consistency zone (e.g. s_1 for the inner square and s_2 for the outer square). Thus, the object is ensured to be in a determined consistency zone if $s_1 < z \leq s_2$. The operation that provides the number of the consistency zone based on z_{closer} is $Z[z_{closer}]$ in line 18. After determining which is the consistency zone of the closest pivot, determining which is the corresponding consistency degree is simply done by consulting the C table.

4   Implementation

A prototype of Mobihoc was implemented on J2ME. Mobihoc can be deployed on J2ME MIDP 2.0 CLDC 1.0 compliant devices. The prototype design follows the architecture of Figure 6. In this section, we specify the most relevant implementation details of the internal components (Section 4.1) and provide a brief insight on how the game programmers specify the VFC ϕ settings (Section 4.2).

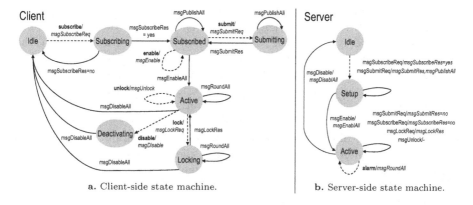

a. Client-side state machine.   **b.** Server-side state machine.

Fig. 10. Client and server Session Manager state machines

4.1   Implementation Internals

We adopted Bluetooth to support communication between the network nodes. The Network Layer (see Figure 6) uses JSR 82, the J2ME Bluetooth API, for discovery of nearby devices and services, management of active connections and sending/receiving data. Internally, the Network Layer is multithreaded in order to prevent blocking and increase parallelism. All messages exchanged between peers are implemented as Java objects.

Due to the lack of binary object serialization support in J2ME, a Serialization Layer was implemented in order to (un)marshal objects (see Figure 6). It requires objects to implement a specific interface allowing the middleware to read and write the object fields. The game programmer does not have to implement this code; a compiler was developed that transparently extends the application source code accordingly. Naturally, since it is not possible to access the already compiled class code, there are several limitations concerning the objects that can be serialized. The fields of the serializable objects are required to be: i) Java primitive types or, ii) serializable objects or, iii) arrays of primitive types/serializable objects or, iv) Vector and Hashtable objects of the Java API. Message objects exchanged via the Network Layer observe these restrictions.

Game programmers are invited to share data as Java object graphs. The current implementation of the Object Adaptation Layer maps directly the objects of the graph into objects individually managed and stored in the object pools. Further optimizations may assemble clusters of application level objects to be managed as single units. Notice that, since these objects require to be (de)serialized in order to be exchanged between clients and server, game programmers must follow the constraints imposed by the Serialization Layer.

The Mobihoc core consists of the CMB and the Session Manager components. The CMB internals implement the algorithms presented in Figure 9, regarding both the functionality and the data structures. The Session Managers of both the client and server sides execute the protocol that provides the Mobihoc services to the game programmers. Each implements its own state machine (see Figure 10).

Shaded circles represent the states; arrows between the states represent state transitions. State transitions are triggered by events. Each arrow description has two parts separated by a slash: the left side is the event name, the right side is the outgoing message sent to the remote peer. Straight arrows represent incoming messages, dashed ones represent API requests or internal events.

Due to space constraints it is not possible to fully explain the details of the Session Manager state machines. Briefly, Session Managers coordinate in order to enforce the two phases already presented in Section 3: the *setup* and the *active* phases. Broadly speaking, first, the server declares its intention to accept client connections and enters the SETUP state. Then, clients connect to the server and subscribe into its services. Clients may now submit to the server the objects to be shared, which the server forwards to every client. When the server receives an *enable* request, it switches to the ACTIVE state and the system enters the *active* phase. While in this state, the server sends periodic round messages and handles lock and release requests. Updates are received by the server piggybacked with the release messages. The system leaves this phase when clients send the server a *disable* request causing the server to switch to the IDLE state.

4.2   Integration with Programming Languages

For a consistency model to be widely used, it should be seamlessly integrated with popular programming languages, such as Java and C#. In this section, we describe how programmers can programmatically specify VFC ϕ settings.

Pivots are registered by name and objects are associated with them using the Mobihoc overloaded methods setPivot(String, Object) and setPivot(String, Object []). Sets of objects are selected by applying VFC declarative tags to object classes in source code, represented as Java *annotations* (@VFCPlane{}, @VFCZone{}) or .Net *attributes* ([VFCPlane()], [VFCZone()]) with parameters stating zone *ranges* and κ-tuple components (e.g. @VFCZone{int range, float time, int sequence, float valueDiff}).

Java support for annotations is limited. In J2SE, it disallows multiple applications of the same annotation (even with different parameters) to the same class. Therefore, we make use of composite annotations (e.g. @VFCPlane{} that encapsulates the parameters of multiple @VFCZone{} annotations). In J2ME, there is no support for annotations whatsoever. Therefore, they are parsed as source code comments and classes extended to bear annotation parameters as private static fields. In .Net (including .Net CF) there is support for multiple application of attributes to classes which eases programmers' lives (e.g. [VFCZone(range, time, sequence, valueDiff]) applied as [VFCZone(10,0.5,5,0.2)], [VFC Zone(20,1.5,15,0.6)] and [VFCZone(30,4.5,25,0.9)]).

To allow inspection of objects by Mobihoc, classes must implement the IVFCConsistency interface that describes three methods: getPosition for objects to provide their current coordinates in the virtual world, getValue to provide their internal data to be propagated, and valueDiff to provide an application-dependent measure (in percentage) of difference w.r.t. contents of another object.

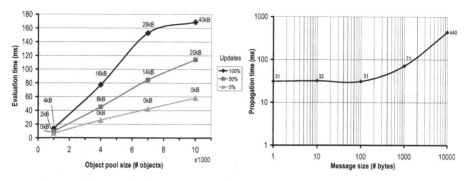

Fig. 11. Evaluation of CMB Version 3 round **Fig. 12.** Evaluation of message propaga-
handler   tion delays

5 Evaluation

The Mobihoc prototype was evaluated in a twofold perspective: quantitative
(Section 5.1) and qualitative (Section 5.2). The former consisted on a Mobihoc
performance study; several mini-benchmarks were implemented for this purpose. The latter evaluated the effectiveness of Mobihoc in developing distributed
games. We implemented a distributed Pacman game for this purpose. The code
was deployed and executed in Nokia 6600 phones.

5.1 Quantitative Evaluation

The main objective was to study the impact of VFC enforcement on the overall
Mobihoc performance. VFC is implemented in Mobihoc according to the CMB
Version 3 algorithm (see Figure 9). Due to space limitations, we focus our attention on the most costly operation – the CMB-ROUND-TRIGGERED function.
This function not only performs intensive computations but it is also executed
periodically, once per round. Observing the algorithm of Figure 9, it is straightforward to see that, disregarding the cost of the merging operation in line 1, the
overall cost is proportional to the number of clients. Thus, we implemented a
micro-benchmark in order to evaluate the algorithm cost for a single client.

Several experiments were conducted by running this micro-benchmark on
Nokia 6600 phones and measuring the execution time of the CMB-ROUND-
TRIGGERED function (at the server side) by varying two factors: i) the number
of objects in the pool (between 1000 and 10000 objects), and ii) the percentage of updates piggybacked in the round messages to the client (0%, 50% and
100% simulated update percentages).[3] Additionally, experiments were conducted
with the following fixed conditions: i) the simulated ϕ settings included 1 pivot
and small C and Z (arrays with 3 positions); ii) object payload was 4 bytes

---

[3] Updates are piggybacked in the round message if the test of line 7 is true. The micro-
benchmark simulated this setting according to the update percentage provided as
input.

Fig. 13. Two phones enroled in a distributed Pac-   **Fig. 14.** Game view in
man game   one phone

(e.g. 2 small integers for space coordinates). Figure 11 presents the performance measurements. Each result is annotated with the corresponding volume of data to be sent to the client.

In order to better perceive the real impact into the overall system performance, we also measured the cost of wireless communication. For this purpose, we implemented a second micro-benchmark, deployed it and executed it on two Nokia 6600 phones to measure network propagation time using Bluetooth. The size of the messages varied from 1 to 10000 bytes. Figure 12 presents the obtained propagation times which allows us to establish a comparison w.r.t. the VFC evaluation result.

Results show that as the number of updates (sent to clients) grows, the VFC overheads increases. Thus, we infer that performance is influenced by the VFC parameterization: weak consistency requirements cause less updates to be sent, increasing efficiency. Also, considering a reasonable number of objects, the computation time is less than the corresponding transmission time in the network. Hence, the VFC computation costs can be masqueraded if they are performed in parallel with the transmission of the updates to clients and there is still time to attend game logic and rendering on the clients. Further, since the propagation time is nearly stable for messages below 200 bytes, the CMB may be enhanced to adapt the number of updates in order to increase efficiency.

5.2 Qualitative Evaluation

To evaluate Mobihoc qualitatively, we implemented a distributed multiplayer version of the popular Pacman game. Our version of the game considers a maze divided into a matrix of 8×8 rooms; each room is assigned a 2-coordinate position. Players have access to the whole maze; yet, during the game, each player's device only shows the room where its avatar is in at that instant. If two players' avatars are in the same room, they can see each other. Figure 13 is a snapshot of two devices enroled in a Pacman game match. It captures a moment were both avatars are in the same room. Figure 14 displays a magnified screen of one of these devices showing the details of the game in that room, particularly the avatars and the room coordinates $(0,0)$ at the center of the screen.

The implementation of this game explores Mobihoc and VFC features for sharing the game state as follows. The maze is mapped to a bi-dimensional 8×8 virtual world. The game state referring to rooms, players and ghosts is implemented as objects with a position in the virtual world. Rooms are assigned a fixed coordinate regarding its overall location in the maze. Both players and ghosts, regardless of having fine grained positions within each room relevant for the game semantics, w.r.t. consistency, are also assigned a position referring to the room where they are at each moment. For each player, we consider that there is only one pivot assigned to its avatar. Also, we defined $Z = [0, 1]$ characterizing three consistency zones. The first zone affects the objects in the same room as the avatar; here, consistency is required to be strong. The second refers to the avatar adjacent rooms; it is a weaker consistency zone and it is relevant mainly when the avatar leaves the current room. The weakest consistency zone is beyond the adjacent rooms. We defined three consistency degrees based on the sequence dimension (σ).

This game, while being very simple and using few VFC features, demonstrates the usability of VFC and Mobihoc. Our experience, from the application programmer viewpoint, is that the model is intuitive, it is simple to describe consistency requirements and to programmatically use Mobihoc employing VFC as a consistency model. We believe it is straightforward to describe consistency requirements for more demanding game scenarios.

6   Related Work

In this section, we discuss relevant work related to ours. Since we are addressing consistency enforcement for multiplayer games in ad-hoc networks, we focus on: i) other work regarding optimistic consistency (see [1] for a thorough survey) in the presence of replicated data, ii) game development for ad-hoc and mobile networks using resource constrained devices such as PDAs and mobile phones, iii) other techniques leveraging *locality-awareness* (in games) to improve middleware performance and scalability, and iv) middleware support for game development and deployment.

Optimistic Concurrency and Divergence Bounding. Optimistic consistency techniques are mostly used in loosely-coupled scenarios (e.g. mobile computing). We find they are also suitable to multiplayer games in ad-hoc networks, as they may be employed to circumvent known issues associated with low bandwidth and high latency.

Real-time guarantees [2] allow an object replica to remain stale and still be used (i.e., without being refreshed) for a specified maximum time, before the replica must be made consistent. *Order bounding* [5] is used to limit the number of uncommitted updates that may be applied to a replica. This allows given transactions to proceed faster because they can ignore the effects of a bounded number of transactions preceding them.

Numeric bounding is introduced in TACT [4,6], a multi-dimensional consistency model that proposes its combination with order bounding. Numeric bounding is based on the notion of defining maximum quotas for allowable updates to each replica (e.g. $10 for a number of replicas of a $100 bank balance). Once the quota has been completely used by a replica (e.g. to withdraw money from the account), the replica can no longer be updated until it is made consistent w.r.t. operations performed on the other replicas. Although TACT proposes a multi-dimensional model for consistency enforcement and limiting replica divergence, it does not embody any notion of locality-awareness. There is no notion of spacial relation neither among individual data objects nor among users. The middleware is oblivious to them. State is simply represented as individual database records or shared/replicated variables in servers. Therefore, it cannot be used in game scenarios where the consistency degree required for an object varies with player position and corresponding *sensing* and *acting* ranges. Numeric bounding is also related with *escrow techniques* [3] on data updates which are employed by mobile databases during disconnection periods, such as *reservations* in Mobisnap [12].

In VFC, besides introducing support for locality-awareness in existing optimistic consistency techniques, we are also able to extend them. We leverage the fact that in the ad-hoc networks we address, there is a central node in charge of routing that is able to monitor all object updates. Therefore, we are able to further extend escrow and numeric bounding techniques, allowing application programmers to define limits on the *value divergence* resulting from updates performed by other nodes (instead of simply limiting their own updates in a conservative manner).

Game Development for Ad-hoc and Mobile Networks. The work in [13] compares the two dominant platforms for ad-hoc gaming (Java J2ME, and .Net Compact Framework) w.r.t. portability and performance of native code invocation, numerical and graphic code. It also studies the performance of several communication strategies (namely packet forwarding). Though providing insights on the environments we are addressing, it assumes a strict consistency model, with a centralized game server.

The work in [11] is focused on traffic selection according to its *urgency* (immediate forwarding) and *relevancy* (reliable delivery) to maintain scalability in wide-area scenarios in multiplayer games. Game developers must define statically, for each entity (e.g. class of objects), levels of urgency and relevance. The middleware generates code that assigns network resources dynamically during the game based on the provided requirements. Although offering control at some level over replica divergence, this work does not explore locality-awareness. Thus, the divergence of all objects of a given type (e.g. representing players) is bound by global parameters irrespective of their relative spatial position w.r.t. each player. This *one-size-fits-all* approach is inflexible and may waste bandwidth w.r.t. a more fine-grained and adaptive approach embodied in our proposal.

Locality Awareness in Large-Scale Multiplayer Middleware. The notions of locality-awareness can be traced back to *interest-management* [8], used to filter routing massive volumes of data in large-scale distributed simulations. Locality-awareness is employed in [10] to perform load balancing on massive multiplayer games. The authors propose a transparent mechanism to partition vast virtual worlds into a cluster of dedicated servers to ensure scalability. Based on their locations, players are redirected to servers in charge of the corresponding partition. As this approach is vulnerable to hot-spots in the game (e.g. crowding, player flocking), it employs heuristics when to reduce server load (by splitting highly populated partitions) and leverage idle resources (coalescing empty partitions in the same server).

The work described in [14] proposes the use of peer-to-peer (P2P) network topologies, such as Pastry [15], to handle massive multiplayer games, in a scalable and cost-effective way, due to the increased flexibility provided by self-organization, while obviating the need for dedicated servers. This also enables game creation and enrollment to be performed in a ad-hoc manner, instead of handled exclusively by central servers. These properties can be leveraged with locality-awareness in order to dynamically organize nodes in groups, reflecting common areas of interest within the virtual world. Therefore, updates to objects are only propagated to other nodes within the same group, which encloses an isle of consistency within the virtual world.

Communication between nodes is handled by multicast using Scribe [16]. Object state is kept consistent by employing a coordinator-based approach, analogous to the tokens employed in Mobihoc. The effects of varying population density, growth, message aggregation, and network dynamics are also studied. Programmers must explicitly pre-define the static partitioning of the virtual world, defining areas of interest. Consistency is therefore strictly enforced within each one and ignored outside altogether.

Matrix [9] proposes the use of locality-awareness by perceiving a multiplayer game as a *decomposable system* [7] where there is stronger interaction within each given *subsystem* (e.g. a room, a game level) than among different *subsystems* (e.g. across rooms). Based on this premise, a *radius* or *zone of visibility* can be identified for each event in the game, outside of which, the corresponding updates need not be propagated (e.g. a shot in another room). Thus, the system enforces *pockets* of *locally-consistent* state. Matrix requires programmers to explicitly tag individual packets carrying updates with their corresponding spatial coordinates where they took place in the game. With this information, the middleware checks the game visibility radius (a global parameter) and decides whether and where to forward the packet. While providing a very interesting approach based on localized consistency, Matrix also adheres to an overly limitative approach of *all-or-nothing* consistency, with no method of stating maximum replica divergence. Furthermore, it makes use of a global consistency radius instead of multiple and dynamic zones of consistency with different divergence bounds, as we propose.

The work in [17] also explores locality-awareness but w.r.t. actual physical location of players that must wear tags. It describes a number of experiments trying to determine how game accuracy and feed-back detail (e.g. graphics, sound) may be balanced against the communication latency observed.

Other Large-Scale Multiplayer Middleware. Regarding online games in wide-area networks, the work in [18] proposes to re-use server infrastructure to deploy several MMOG[4] side-by-side. It describes a service platform that can host a number of games on-demand, leveraging existing grid technology. The work described in [19] proposes a methodology to reduce human-resources costs in MMOG development. It makes use of message-oriented middleware, arguing that games typically operate in an event-driven manner. Protocol and message-handling code for clients and servers is automatically generated from message descriptors written in XML. Game and virtual-world logic is managed via *adapters*, which can be plugged-in asynchronously, on-the-fly within an entire running MMOG application. These works, while being relevant cases of employment of middleware to support online multiplayer games, are not targeted to the kinds of constrained devices and ad-hoc networks we are addressing.

7   Conclusions

In this paper we present a novel consistency model to manage replicated data (VFC) and a middleware platform (Mobihoc) adopting VFC to support multiplayer distributed games in ad-hoc networks. While some of previous works embody the notions of *consistency radius*, *locality of interest*, or isles of *localized consistency*, they adopt a rather *all-or-nothing approach*. Thus, objects inside an area of interest must be kept strongly consistent, while the values (or updates to it) of objects outside are simply discarded. VFC combines and extends more sophisticated consistency models (such as TACT), with the notions of *locality-awareness* in a unified model. VFC and Mobihoc provide intuitive, simple and flexible abstractions such that application programmers are able to easily express their consistency requirements according to application semantics. Moreover, VFC and Mobihoc are widely applicable, not being restricted to the development of distributed games for ad-hoc networks.

Regarding future work, we envisage to perform thorough empirical studies to compare the performance of VFC and Mobihoc with other game consistency protocols and frameworks. Also, we aim to employ our solution to different types of real games in order to i) analyze the benefit of our solution in terms of efficiency/playability, and ii) to explore the flexibility of VFC in parameterizing consistency requirements for different game scenarios. Although the partitioning of the game space into zones depends on the application semantics, we envisage to develop the mechanisms to help game programmers better deciding how to partition the game space into zones. Additionally, we intend to study how this approach scales across either number of objects or number of nodes, and possibly to redesign Mobihoc to environments other than ad-hoc networks.

---

[4] Massive Multiplayer Online Games.

Acknowledgments. The authors wish to acknowledge the students José Lopes and Tiago Bernardo for their implementation work in the Pacman game.

References

1. Saito, Y., Shapiro, M.: Optimistic replication. ACM Comput. Surv. 37(1), 42–81 (2005)
2. Alonso, R., Barbara, D., Garcia-Molina, H.: Data caching issues in an information retrieval system. ACM Transactions on Database Systems (TODS) 15(3), 359–384 (1990)
3. Krishnakumar, N., Jain, R.: Escrow techniques for mobile sales and inventory applications. Wireless Networks 3(3), 235–246 (1997)
4. Yu, H., Vahdat, A.: Design and evaluation of a conflit-based continuous consistency model for replicated services. ACM Transactions on Computer Systems (TOCS) 20(3), 239–282 (2002)
5. Krishnakumar, N., Bernstein, A.: Bounded ignorance: a technique for increasing concurrency in a replicated system. ACM Transactions on Database Systems (TODS) 19(4), 586–625 (1994)
6. Yu, H., Vahdat, A.: The costs and limits of availability for replicated services. ACM Transactions on Computer Systems (TOCS) 24(1), 70–113 (2006)
7. Simon, H.A.: The architecture of complexity. Proceedings of the American Philosophical Society 106, 467–482 (1962)
8. Morse, K., et al.: Interest Management in Large-scale Distributed Simulations. In: Information and Computer Science, University of California, Irvine (1996)
9. Balan, R., Ebling, M., Castro, P., Misra, A.: Matrix: Adaptive middleware for distributed multiplayer games. In: Alonso, G. (ed.) Middleware 2005. LNCS, vol. 3790, Springer, Heidelberg (2005)
10. Chen, J., Wu, B., Delap, M., Knutsson, B., Lu, H., Amza, C.: Locality aware dynamic load management for massively multiplayer games. In: Proceedings of the tenth ACM SIGPLAN symposium on Principles and practice of parallel programming, pp. 289–300. ACM Press, New York (2005)
11. Griwodz, C.: State replication for multiplayer games. In: Griwodz, C. (ed.) Proceedings of the 1st workshop on Network and system support for games, pp. 29–35 (2002)
12. Preguiça, N., Martins, J.L., Cunha, M., Domingos, H.: Reservations for conflict avoidance in a mobile database system. In: Proc. of the 1st Usenix Int'l Conference on Mobile Systems, Applications and Services (Mobisys) (2003)
13. Janecek, A., Hlavacs, H.: Programming interactive real-time games over WLAN for pocket PCs with J2ME and.NET CF. In: Proceedings of 4th ACM SIGCOMM workshop on Network and system support for games, pp. 1–8. ACM Press, New York (2005)
14. Knutsson, B., Lu, H., Xu, W., Hopkins, B.: Peer-to-peer support for massively multiplayer games. In: IEEE Infocom, IEEE Computer Society Press, Los Alamitos (2004)
15. Rowstron, A.I.T., Druschel, P.: Pastry: Scalable, decentralized object location, and routing for large-scale peer-to-peer systems. In: Guerraoui, R. (ed.) Middleware 2001. LNCS, vol. 2218, pp. 329–350. Springer, Heidelberg (2001)

16. Castro, M., Druschel, P., Kermarrec, A., Rowstron, A.: Scribe: a large-scale and decentralised application-level multicast infrastructure. IEEE Journal on Selected Areas Commun(JSAC) (Special Issue on Network for Support Multicast Commun.) 20(8), 100–110 (2002)
17. Mansley, K., Scott, D., Tse, A., Madhavapeddy, A.: Feedback, latency, accuracy: exploring tradeoffs in location-aware gaming. In: Proceedings of ACM SIGCOMM 2004 workshops on NetGames 2004: Network and system support for games, pp. 93–97. ACM Press, New York (2004)
18. Saha, D., Sahu, S., Shaikh, A.: A service platform for on-line games. In: Proceedings of the 2nd workshop on Network and system support for games, pp. 180–184 (2003)
19. Hsiao, T., Yuan, S.: Practical middleware for massively multiplayer online games. IEEE Internet Computing 9(5), 47–54 (2005)

Correlation-Based Content Adaptation
for Mobile Web Browsing

Iqbal Mohomed, Adin Scannell, Nilton Bila, Jin Zhang, and Eyal de Lara

Department of Computer Science
University of Toronto
{iq,amscanne,nilton,delara}@cs.toronto.edu,
jinyaozhang@utoronto.ca

Abstract. The resource impoverished environment on mobile devices results in a poor experience for users browsing the World Wide Web. Proxy-based middleware that transform content on the fly to better suit the resource conditions on a user's device provide a promising solution to this problem. A key challenge in such systems is deciding how to adapt content, especially when the same content has multiple uses that have varying adaptation requirements. In this paper, we show that it is possible to provide fine grain adaptation of multi-purpose content by detecting correlations in the adaptation requirements of past users across multiple objects on a web site, and using this history to make adaptation predictions for users encountered subsequently. To evaluate our technique, we built prototype page layout and image fidelity adaptation systems, and used these to gather traces from users browsing multi-purpose web content in a laboratory setting. Our experimental results show that using correlations to make adaptation predictions can significantly reduce bandwidth consumption, browsing time, energy usage and user effort required to adapt content.

Keywords: Content Adaptation, Mobile Devices, Customization, Web Browsing, Experimentation.

1   Introduction

The severe resource constraints on mobile devices make browsing the World Wide Web an unpleasant experience for users. At present, the majority of content on the Web is targeted towards use on desktop computers with ample displays and high-speed connections to the Internet. These assumptions do not hold in a mobile environment, where devices have small screens, low-bandwidth, limited battery capacity, processing capabilities, I/O facilities and storage. The problem of mobile web access is further complicated due to the considerable heterogeneity among different classes of devices (laptops, PDAs, cell phones, pagers, etc.). Also, as users move about naturally during the course of their activities, the mobile computers they carry with them experience significant variability in wireless connectivity – at one moment the user may be in range of an accessible well-connected, lightly loaded 802.11g access point, whereas at other times, she may only have access to a WWAN service (such as GPRS, CDMA 1X, etc.) that charges her based on the number of kilobytes that are transferred over the link.

R. Cerqueira and R.H. Campbell (Eds.): Middleware 2007, LNCS 4834, pp. 101–120, 2007.
© IFIP International Federation for Information Processing 2007

A promising solution to these problems is adaptation middleware, interposed in the network path between the client and web server, which automatically tailors content for individual mobile devices [1, 2, 3, 4, 5, 6, 7, 8, 9, 10]. For example, images on web pages can be served to the user at a reduced fidelity in order to conserve bandwidth and energy, and improve download times. Also, the layout and size of content objects (such as images) can be changed to better fit on a small display. However, a key challenge in such systems is *how* to identify appropriate adaptations. This is a difficult problem because optimal adaptation depends on the usage semantics of content (the user's purpose vis-à-vis the content) as well as the user's context (characteristics of the user's device as well as their surroundings).

In previous work [11, 12, 13], we introduced Usage-Aware Interactive Content Adaptation (URICA), an automatic adaptation technique that customizes content for mobile devices based on the content's usage semantics and the user's context. URICA learns how to adapt content from implicit feedback provided by users carrying out their tasks. This is achieved by having the system make an initial adaptation decision, and allowing users who are unsatisfied with the system's adaptation decision to take control of the adaptation process and make changes (e.g., increase the fidelity of a transcoded image or change the layout of a page). The successful adaptation is recorded and used in making future adaptation decisions for the same and other users. URICA works well when users utilize content in a similar manner. For example, Figure 1(a) shows histograms of image display sizes that satisfied users for two distinct images in a system that scales the dimensions of images to fit on a small screen. Here, making predictions using the history of individual objects works well; we see that presenting Image 1 at size 2 and Image 2 at size 9 will satisfy the majority of users. However, URICA is less effective for multi-purpose content, where objects on a web page are used for different tasks with varying adaptation requirements. Figure 1(b) illustrates the case when users can perform one of two tasks on a page. For the first task, they require a small version of Image 1 and a large version of Image 2, while these requirements are reversed in the second task. Here, if we only consider the history of the object that is being adapted, there is no single adaptation that will satisfy all users.

Fortunately, typical web tasks involve more than one object. This paper shows that for web tasks that involve multiple objects, it is possible to leverage the feedback provided by the user on a few initial objects to narrow the history used to make subsequent predictions to include only those users who have similar adaptation requirements. This is achieved by finding correlations in adaptation requirements *between different objects* on a web site using the history of previously encountered users. Once these correlations are uncovered, the interactive feedback provided by the user to adapt some objects can be used to adapt other related objects on the page or site. For example, for the content depicted in Figure 1(b), we can see from the adaptation history of the two images that the sizes of Image 1 and 2 are inversely correlated. Once this determination is made, if a user increases the size of Image 1, the system can automatically decrease the size of Image 2.

Correlation-based prediction works well for multi-purpose content because, while users can utilize the same content in different ways, it is quite likely that there are *at least some users who use the content in each of the different ways.*

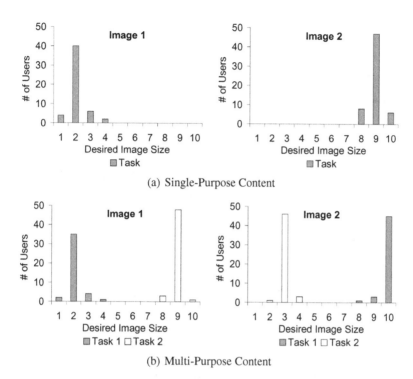

(a) Single-Purpose Content

(b) Multi-Purpose Content

Fig. 1. Histograms of image display sizes that satisfied past users. The vertical axis shows the number of users who desired each of the adaptations on the horizontal axis. When content is single-purpose (*a*), one adaptation decision works well for most users. For multi-purpose content (*b*), there may be correlations in the adaptation requirements of users across objects.

Correlation-based predictions can also be useful in the case of single-purpose content when users have different context. If the context in question affects adaptation requirements, the adaptation history of individual objects will be noisy just as in the case of multi-purpose content. That is, a single adaptation will not satisfy users with different context. In such situations, adaptation based on correlations will also be beneficial.

We experimented with two well-known machine learning techniques that enable correlations between objects to be uncovered automatically: Decision Stumps, which directly encodes relationships between the adaptation requirements of objects, and the Gaussian Mixture Model, which finds correlations implicitly by clustering users with similar adaptation requirements. Our experience showed that these techniques only perform well when users have an incentive to fix incorrect adaptation decisions made by the system. For instance, in a system that adapts the dimensions of images, users have a clear incentive to correct images that are larger or smaller than what they require. However, such incentives may not always exist. For instance, in a system that adapts image fidelity, if the initial set of images on a site is served to the user at a fidelity that is greater than that required, there is little incentive for the user to interact with these images to lower their fidelity given that the bandwidth to transfer the images would have already been spent. For these situations, we developed an algorithm called *all-in* that

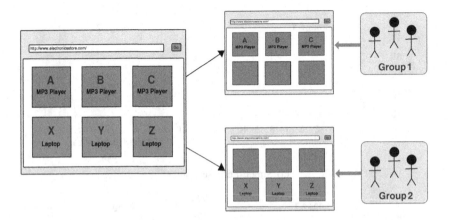

Fig. 2. A schematic of a web page with images of MP3 players and laptop computers. Users in group 1 are shopping for MP3 players, whereas those in group 2 are shopping for laptop computers. If the user improves the quality of one image of an MP3 player, it is likely that they will want the other MP3 player images at high quality as well (the same holds for laptop images).

clusters together the histories of past users with similar adaptation requirements, and as a user provides feedback, it rapidly narrows down a cluster of users with similar adaptation preferences.

We built two prototype adaptation systems for the purpose of evaluation. One scaled the dimensions of images on web pages and the other adapted their fidelity. We collected traces from users browsing multi-purpose content using our prototypes in a laboratory setting, and used these to evaluate the performance of alternative algorithms for making adaptation predictions. We found that making adaptation predictions using correlations results in significant performance improvements. For image scaling, we observed that using correlations to make predictions required 66% fewer user interactions. In the case of image fidelity adaptation, we observed that correlation-based predictions reduce bandwidth consumption by 63%, user interactions by 48%, energy consumption by 17% and time to completion by 20%.

The rest of this paper is organized as follows. Section 2 describes algorithms for multi-purpose content adaptation. Section 3 provides a description of our experiments. Section 4 presents the result of our evaluation. Finally, Section 5 discusses related work, and Section 6 concludes the paper and suggests avenues for future work.

2   Adapting Multi-purpose Content

When the same content can be used for multiple purposes, users may have varying adaptation requirements for the same object based on the particular task they are trying to perform on a web page or site. For example, Figure 2 shows the schematic of a web page that contains six images and represents the front page of an online retailer that sells MP3 players and laptop computers. The first three images on the page show MP3 players and the next three show laptop computers. A user who pays for downloads by the kilobyte will most likely not want to see all images at high quality - users shopping for MP3 players will want to see the top three images at a higher quality than the others (and vice versa). In this case, the varying adaptation requirements of different users leads to a noisy history for every object - no single adaptation will satisfy all users.

Fortunately, typical web tasks involve more than one object, and when there is correlation in the adaptation requirements of these objects, the feedback provided by users on a few objects can be used to adapt others. Continuing our previous example, the system can determine that users who want any one of the MP3 player images at high quality will likely want the other two at a high quality as well (the same holds for laptop images). The adaptation system would initially serve all images at low quality, and as soon as the user requests an improvement for one of the images (say, an image of an MP3 player), the system can improve the quality of not just that image, but also the quality of other images whose quality levels are highly correlated (the other images of MP3 Players).

It is important to note that objects do not have to be tagged with any meta-data by the content creator for this approach to work. Nor are users required to explicitly specify the task they are performing. The only information required is the history of how users have adapted objects on the page in the past, which is gathered automatically by the system at run-time.

In this section, we start by describing the two types of implicit feedback that can be provided by users in interactive adaptation systems: *two-sided feedback* and *one-sided feedback*. The type of feedback available plays a crucial role in the design and performance of algorithms that predict adaptation requirements. We then describe three algorithms for taking advantage of correlations in user preferences.

2.1 Type of Feedback

The type of adaptation being performed influences the nature of feedback provided by users. In some cases, the constrained resource cannot be recovered when an adaptation decision results in overconsumption. In such situations, users have no incentive to provide additional feedback to the adaptation system. That is, users only provide feedback until the adapted object is "good enough". We call this *one-sided feedback*. For example, in image fidelity adaptation, if the system serves an image at a fidelity that is lower than what is desired by the user, we can expect the user to interact with the system to obtain a higher fidelity representation. However, if the system provides a representation that is of a higher fidelity than that which is required, the user has no incentive to provide feedback. This is because the cost of downloading the higher quality representation has already been incurred. Thus, if the system provides an image at some initial fidelity level (say, level 5, where there are 10 fidelity levels in total) and the user does not improve the object, we cannot say for certain that the user required fidelity 5. We only know that the user may have desired a fidelity between 1 and 5.

In other cases, where overused resources can be reclaimed, users are motivated to keep interactively adapting an object until it has been appropriately customized. We call this *two-sided feedback*. For example, in image screen size adaptation, if the system overuses the screen real-estate resource, it can be reclaimed. Users have an incentive to shrink and enlarge images until they are suitable for their purpose.

2.2   Prediction Algorithms

We initially investigated two standard techniques from machine learning that enable correlation-based predictions: Decision Stumps, which directly encodes relationships between the adaptation requirements of objects, and the Gaussian Mixture Model, which finds correlations implicitly by clustering users with similar adaptation requirements. We observed these techniques to perform well when users provide two-sided feedback. However, when only one-sided feedback is available, these algorithms can perform badly if the system over-predicts on the initial set of objects on the page. For example, in a system that adapts image fidelity, if the initial set of images on a site is served to the user at a high fidelity, there is little incentive for the user to interact with these images to lower their fidelity, and the system cannot accurately gauge the user's adaptation requirements. This problem can be overcome by under-predicting on the initial set of objects as a way of *probing* for the user's true adaptation requirements. However, this can require the user to frequently interact with objects. To address this problem, we developed an algorithm called *all-in* that under-predicts without causing an excessive number of interactions.

Decision Stumps: In order to investigate the effectiveness of directly correlating the adaptation requirements of different images, a method using decisions stumps [14] for predicting adaptation requirements was implemented. A decision stump is a decision tree with only a single branch. In reference to the motivating example, it encodes a decision of the form: Was the required fidelity for image $X < 5$? If yes, then a fidelity of 5 is sufficient for image Y; otherwise 5 is not sufficient for Y. Several decision stumps (alternatively, they may be thought of as *rules*) are weighted and combined into a final model, which is used to make predictions. Each decision stump in this model represents some relationship between the object whose adaptation requirement is being predicted and some other object. The weighting of the decision stumps is calculated during training in order to minimize error; it may be thought of as specifying the relative predictive ability of each relationship. Due to the multiple decision stumps that compose a single model, more than one relationship can be captured and the multi-purpose nature of any given object preserved.

For each object (call this the target object) and every subset of the non-target objects, a distinct prediction model is generated. This model is generated by feeding the history of all user adaptation requirements for the given set of non-target objects along with the corresponding adaptation requirements for the target object into a training procedure. This training procedure uses boosting [15] which generates a set of decision stumps and weights that predict adaptation requirements with a low error rate. A model for each subset must be generated because, as we are encoding correlations directly, a prediction for an image X may be based on different images, depending on the set of objects for which the user has provided some feedback.

Predictions are made by selecting the appropriate model for the target image, and providing as input the already-specified set of required fidelities. For example, suppose we are generating predictions for the electronics retailer used in the motivating example of this section. Suppose the user has seen and possibly interacted with two images, X and A, and we must now predict a fidelity for the image Y. First, we retrieve our model that was trained with adaptation requirements for X and A and predicts Y. Based on the current user's requirements for X and A, we predict an appropriate requirement for Y. Since this model is a combination of decision stumps that involve rules regarding the required fidelities of X and A, we can simply evaluate them all and determine a final score. This final score corresponds to the predicted required fidelity. This process is repeated with all remaining images other than Y, as predicted images are loaded and the user provides feedback.

In the evaluation section, the use of this model with both one-sided and two-sided feedback is explored. This method may encode many complex relationships between objects, and requires no specification of parameters in advance (such as number of clusters). Unfortunately, the cost of training and generating the large number of models for this method may be high, although there could exist optimizations to alleviate this problem. Another disadvantage of this method is that it may also have a tendency to over-fit training data, especially for users with non-typical adaptation requirements. This may manifest itself as a single out-of-character requirement given by a user throwing off several predictions due to over-emphasis on a particular image.

For our implementation of this method, we used the MultiBoost [15] algorithm implemented by the Weka [14] toolkit. The MultiBoost algorithm combines AdaBoost [16] with wagging, and it was shown to be more effective in reducing error than either of its constituent techniques [15].

Gaussian Mixture Model: In a Gaussian mixture model, all sets of adaptation requirements are assumed to be sampled from a set of Guassian distributions spread throughout the space of all possible adaptation requirements. Given a set of training data, the parameters of the distributions are set by running an expectation-maximization (EM) algorithm in order to maximize the likelihood that the given data was sampled from the mixture of distributions. As input for this training procedure, all available history of user adaptation requirements is provided. The number of distributions must be selected a priori, however.

For prediction, based on a user's currently specified set of adaptation requirements and the training distributions, a candidate distribution for the user is selected by computing the likelihood of her belonging to each distribution, then selecting the most probable. The mean of this candidate distribution is used to provide any missing adaptation requirements. If this mean is insufficient for the user for some particular object, the most probable distribution with a higher adaptation requirement is selected for that object instead. Eventually, these adaptation requirements which are not well-represented may lead to the selection of a better candidate distribution.

Similar to the scenario given for decision stumps, suppose that we are serving images for users browsing the online electronics retailer. The user has seen and possibly interacted with the images X and A and we must now predict image Y. Based on their required fidelities for X and A, the probability of the user belonging to each Gaussian distribution d, $p(d)$, is computed. This is a calculation over only the images which the user has seen (X and A), in this case given by

$$p(d) = \alpha_d \prod_{i=\{X,A\}} \frac{1}{\sigma_d(i)\sqrt{2\pi}} exp(-\frac{(x_i - \mu_d(i))^2}{2\sigma_d(i)^2})$$

for each distribution d with means $\mu_d(i)$, standard deviations $\sigma_d(i)$ and prior α_d (all set by the EM training procedure). The distribution with the highest $p(d)$ is selected, call this d_{best}, and the means of d_{best} are used to provide a prediction for the adaptation requirements of other images. In this case, since we need to predict Y, we would use $\mu_{d_{best}}(Y)$, the mean of the distribution d_{best} for the image Y.

Logically, these distributions can be thought of as the center of clusters. During the training procedure, they will tend to each cover different groups of users' adaptation requirements. This model is representable in a compact way, and has the advantage that each distribution, or cluster, has an explicit variance for each object. This is useful for intentional overprediction and underprediction, based on user preference. For example, the user may favour underprediction in order to conserve bandwidth. Also, since the identification of a candidate cluster is based on all objects, a single odd requirement from a user is likely to have less of an impact on other predictions than in the case of decision stumps.

The *all-in* Algorithm: We designed the *all-in* algorithm[1] for use when only one-sided feedback is available, and investigate it in the context of image fidelity adaptation. The algorithm starts off by using the standard K-means clustering algorithm to partition users into multiple groups. The idea is that users within a group share similar adaptation requirements - not just for a single object but rather across all objects on a web page or web site. Once we have a set of clusters, the system transitions into prediction mode. The system then uses an online classification algorithm to make predictions.

The goal of the *all-in* algorithm is to rapidly classify the user into a single cluster. For each user, the adaptation decisions made by the system early on are aggressive in that they may be wasteful. However, once the system is able to correctly classify the user, it starts making moderate predictions, such as serving the mean of the image fidelities that was requested by other users within a cluster.

At the outset, the algorithm assumes that the user can belong to any cluster. Also, it computes an upper and lower threshold for each object in every cluster. These thresholds correspond to the range of values where an object's desired fidelity may lie, for users belonging to this cluster. We take the highest and lowest fidelity that was previously observed as the upper and lower threshold, respectively[2]. When serving an image initially, the algorithm makes an aggressive prediction: it serves the image at the lowest upper threshold across all clusters. If the user is not satisfied with this adaptation, she will request an improvement and the system will remove the cluster whose upper thresholds are violated. The process is repeated until the user no longer requests improvements to an object, and moves on to a different page or object. In this case, the system checks if there exist any clusters whose lower thresholds are violated, and removes them. Once the system has classified the user into a single cluster, the algorithm behaves less aggressively, and serves objects at the mean of the image fidelities that were requested by other users within the cluster.

---

[1] The phrase "all-in" is taken from poker where a player bets his entire stake on a hand. When there are only two players, this move forces the opponent to evaluate her hand and make a decision on whether to accept the bet ("call") or give up the hand ("fold").

[2] Other alternatives are possible, such as taking the endpoints of the 5-95 percentile range. This would help eliminate outliers in a production system.

It is possible for the system to reach a point where there is no cluster that the user can belong to. This can occur for two reasons: first, there may be no cluster that captures the current user's preferences or second, we may have removed the user from a cluster that she would otherwise have fit into because her adaptation preference on some prior object was radically different. With regards to making adaptation predictions for this particular user, we can do nothing about the first possibility. However, we can address the second by making all clusters valid again for the user. For the particular object under consideration, we give up, and serve it without any adaptation. In a production system, we can take the first possibility into account as well. Any time the system runs into a large number of users who cannot be classified, it can transition into training mode again, and regenerate the clusters.

2.3 Practical Considerations

Parameters, such as the number of clusters to use in the *all-in* algorithm, can be automatically determined in a production system. Once the system has encountered some number of users (say T, specified by the operator of the adaptation proxy), it can run profiling experiments that compare the performance that would have been experienced by the previously encountered users in different conditions. The experiments may compute a variety of performance metrics for different parameter settings, and the system can set parameters to be the values that result in the best performance. A single metric or a composition thereof can be used for this purpose, based on the goals of the proxy operator or the preferences of users. Indeed, if users specify different goals to the adaptation system, it can provide them with varying predictions tailored to their requirements based on the same history.

3 Experimental Methodology

To evaluate our prediction algorithms, we considered two types of adaptation: page layout and image fidelity. For each type of adaptation, we created a prototype that allows users to interactively adapt content. We used the prototypes to perform experiments in which participants adapted content in a laboratory setting. The traces of the user's adaptation decisions were then used to evaluate the prediction algorithms.

In this section, we first describe our trace gathering experiments. We then discuss the methodology used to evaluate the prediction algorithms on the collected traces.

3.1 Gathering User Traces

We conducted our experiments in a laboratory at the University of Toronto. For the experiments we recruited three groups of participants from the general student population. The first group adapted the layout of web pages, while the second and third groups adapted the fidelity of images on web pages. Table 1 summarizes the setup of the experiments. During the experiments, the prediction component of the adaptation system was disabled so that participants would have to interact with images in order to achieve an appropriate adaptation. That is, the system did not take advantage of past interactions of the current or previous users. This forces participants to reveal their true adaptation preferences as well as avoiding any effects arising from the ordering of participants in our study.

Page Layout Adaptation Experiment: The goal of our first experiment was to investigate a scenario in which users naturally provide two-sided feedback. We created a prototype page layout adaptation system that allowed users to increase and decrease the screen dimensions of images on a web page. While all of the participants in this study were given the same task to perform, we varied the device used to browse the web across individuals. Thus, the primary source of variation in the adaptation requirements of users is the difference in device context.

The experiment consisted of four web pages, each containing three images of postage stamps. For each page, participants were asked to modify the dimensions of the images in a manner such that it would be easy to identify differences between two images and find details on a third image. We obtained traces from 30 participants who were randomly divided into three sub-groups which used different simulated displays: a PocketPC SmartPhone, a PocketPC PDA and a Toyota GBook vehicular terminal. The setups for these traces are referred to in Table 1 as SmartPhone, PDA and GBook, respectively.

Image Fidelity Adaptation Experiments: The goal of our second and third experiment was to consider a case where users are only motivated to provide one-sided feedback. To this end, we created an image fidelity adaptation system in which the images on a web page are initially served at low fidelity (for faster download), and users can click on individual images to improve their fidelity. In these studies, different participants were given varying tasks. However, all of the participants performed their assigned tasks on the same device. As such, variations in the adaptation requirements of users stem from differences in their assigned task.

For these experiment, we designed two image-rich sites. The first, a movie posters site, had images of popular movie posters. The second, a map site, had a map of the University of Toronto's campus represented in a grid of 6 x 6 images. For each site, we designed three tasks, and each participant performed only one of those tasks. For the movie posters site, each task consisted of detailed questions pertaining to a different subset of the posters. For example, participants were asked to identify the director, title and release date of some of the movies. For the map site, participants were asked to provide directions from one given building to another within the university's campus. To accomplish these tasks, participants had to increase the fidelity of relevant images until sufficient details were visible. Participants were able to adjust image fidelities on a scale between 1 and 10. The tasks were designed so that participants would find some images in a web page relevant while others not as much.

For these experiments, participants used a laptop equipped with our adaptation system and an available network bandwidth of 56kbps, which is a reasonable approximation of a GPRS WWAN connection. We recruited 231 participants who were divided in six sub-groups of 37 to 40 individuals. Our setup is described in Table 1.

Table 1. Summary of experiments

Page Layout	# of Pages	Images per Page	Total Images	Setup	# of Users
Postage Stamps	4	3	12	SmartPhone Display	10
				PDA Display	10
				GBook Display	10
Image Fidelity					
Movie Posters	9	1	9	Task-1	37
				Task-2	37
				Task-3	37
Map	1	36	36	Path-1	40
				Path-2	40
				Path-3	40

3.2 Trace-Based Evaluation

In order to determine the effectiveness of each algorithm considered, we evaluated them using the traces collected from the participants in our experiments. For the page layout experiment, we collected for each participant, their required image dimensions for every image. From the fidelity experiment, we obtained for each participant their minimum required fidelity for every image.

To test each algorithm, we used leave-one-out cross-validation. That is, each algorithm was trained with the traces of all users except one. The algorithm was then used to predict the dimensions or fidelities of the images served to the user, depending on the experiment.

For this testing, we created a user simulator. At the start, the prediction algorithm provides an adapted version of each image on a page. The simulated user, based on the collected traces, goes through each of the images on the page in turn and provides an "interaction" for the first image it finds that is not properly adapted. When the simulated user provides an interaction, the prediction algorithm recalculates an appropriate adaptation for all of the images on the page and presents it to the simulated user once again. This process is repeated until all of the images are adapted according to the user's preferences.

For the page layout adaptation experiment, the primary metric used to evaluate the different algorithms is the number of user interactions. However, for the fidelity experiments, a number of metrics are used for evaluation: the number of user interactions required, fulfillment time, wasted bandwidth and energy consumed. Number of interactions is the number of times a user had to interact with the images in order to achieve her desired adaptation. Fulfillment time is the aggregate of interaction time (the time users spend interacting with images until their fidelity requirements are met) and download time. Wasted bandwidth is calculated as the amount of bandwidth used beyond what would be required by the user if all images were served at their exact required fidelity immediately. Energy consumed is the energy measure, in Joules, consumed by the device for viewing and downloading content.

In order to compute fulfillment time and energy consumption with our simulator, we measured the average interaction time from one of our user studies (2388 milliseconds).

We then ran several experiments on an HP iPAQ h6325 PDA in order to measure download speeds and energy characteristics of real hardware. With a GPRS connection, we observed effective download speeds of approximately 33kbps. When the device was idle, it consumed 0.67 Joules/second (with GPRS radio and backlight on) and when the device was downloading, it consumed 1.59 Joules/second.

For any particular algorithm, there is a clear trade-off between wasted bandwidth and the number of interactions: under-predicting the fidelity required for an image will lead to more user interactions and over-predicting the fidelity will lead to wasted bandwidth. However, good algorithms can perform well at both simultaneously. Indeed, a perfect prediction algorithm that knows the exact adaptation required by users (we call this *oracle*) would not waste any bandwidth, nor would it require any interactions by the user.

4   Experimental Results

In this section, we provide the results of our evaluation. We start by considering the case of two-sided feedback, which occurs naturally during the course of our page layout experiment. Next, we consider the performance of different algorithms when only one-sided feedback is available, as is the case in our fidelity adaptation experiments.

All of the results presented in this section are mean results, averaged across individual users over the entire web site for any given experiment. The algorithm that we use as our baseline for performance is the *single object history* (SOH) prediction algorithm from our previous work [12,13]. This algorithm makes adaptation predictions for each object by considering its adaptation history in isolation. For image fidelity adaptation, the SOH algorithm initially serves an image at the mean value of the fidelity that was desired by previously encountered users. If this is not satisfactory, the SOH algorithm provides a subsequent prediction by ignoring the desired fidelities below that which was just served, and recomputing the mean. For page layout adaptation, the initial prediction of the SOH algorithm is computed in the same way (taking the mean of the desired image sizes of previously encountered users). However, when a user decides to increase or decrease an image, the algorithm removes from the history all of the desired image sizes of previous users that are less than or greater than the size that was just provided, respectively. SOH makes the next prediction by computing the mean value from the remaining history.

4.1   Two-Sided Feedback

We tested both the decision stump algorithm and the Gaussian mixture model algorithm on the postage stamp experiment, where users were required to adapt images by re-sizing them. For this experiment, feedback was provided for predictions that were too high or too low. Because the images were already downloaded, there was no notion of bandwidth wasted for this experiment. Using the SOH algorithm, the mean number of interactions required of a user during the experiment was 15. By leveraging correlations between adaptation requirements however, the decision stumps algorithm achieved a mean of 5.1 interactions, while the Gaussian mixture model achieved 5.9 (with six distributions), both demonstrate a vast improvement over using only SOH.

Table 2. The performance of several variations of decision stumps on the movie poster dataset. We observe that significantly more bandwidth is wasted with one-sided feedback (*line 2*) than in the hypothetical case of perfect feedback (*line 1*). We also observe that under-prediction greatly reduces wasted bandwidth but comes at the cost of more interactions required of the user (*line 3*).

Variation	# of Interactions	Bandwidth Wasted (KB)
Perfect Feedback	2.50	200.74
One-Sided Feedback	0.32	830.19
Under-prediction on First Image with One-Sided Feedback	6.71	113.67

These results demonstrate that using correlation based prediction methods for cases where two-sided feedback is available is an excellent idea, and that standard machine learning techniques work well. After all, this a very straight-forward prediction problem.

4.2   One-Sided Feedback

One-sided feedback introduces a twist to the prediction problem. We compare the performance of our different algorithms and explore the effect of under-prediction on the movie posters experiment. We show that the *all-in* algorithm leverages this effect and provides strong performance across all studies where only one-sided feedback is available. Finally, we evaluate the algorithms on the movie posters experiment using two metrics of practical interest: fulfillment time and energy usage.

Without any adaptation, 2.70MB are transferred to download the 9 images in the movie posters experiment. However, if an oracle were to exist such that we were able to provide users with their desired fidelity, only 1.29MB would have been downloaded on average. That is, without adaptation, an average of 1.41 MB of bandwidth is consumed needlessly. Making predictions using single object history results in an average wastage of only 378KB of bandwidth; this occurs at an average cost of 5.4 interactions. When we consider how interactions are distributed across images, we observe that the users must interact with approximately two-thirds of the images on the web site.

In the case of image fidelity adaptation, only one-sided feedback is available. However, in order to establish the validity of the methods in general, we first consider the performance they achieve if users provided perfect feedback. For perfect feedback, we assume the algorithm knows by how much each image was over-predicted, without incurring any additional interactions (under-predictions still result in interactions). We then show results for the case where users provide one-sided feedback.

The first line of Table 2 shows the result of making predictions using decision stumps when perfect feedback is provided. We see that, beyond the single object history case, the amount of wasted bandwidth is reduced by 47%. In addition, the number of interactions is decreased from 5.4 to only 2.5. However, for image fidelity adaptation as the problem is made manifest (only one-sided feedback is available), the wastage increases significantly. The second line of Table 2 shows the result of making predictions under these conditions. Although the number of interactions required is minimal, the wasted bandwidth is significantly higher (830KB) than using the predictions generated by the single object history method (378KB).

Figure 3(a) shows the performance achieved when making predictions using a mixture of Gaussians when perfect feedback is available. The x-axis in the graph indicates the number of distributions that are created based on the observed training data. The y-axis on the left indicates the mean number of interactions required by each user and the y-axis on the right provides the mean wasted bandwidth per user. We observe that after about four distributions, the algorithm achieves consistent performance. With six distributions, users waste 212KB with 1.4 interactions. Like the decision stumps method, this represents a significant improvement over the predictions generated with only single object history which wastes 378KB with 5.4 interactions. When only one-sided feedback is given, the number of interactions remains consistently low, however, the wasted bandwidth climbs above 700KB. Figure 3(b) shows the performance of the Gaussian Mixture Model in this case.

We conclude that when only one-sided feedback is available, the two standard techniques that we considered suffer from poor performance.

Effect of Under-prediction: In situations where users only provide one-sided feedback, the performance of prediction algorithms that use correlations can be improved by purposely under-predicting on the initial set of images on a web page. We now show the performance of the decision stumps and Gaussian mixture model algorithms for the movie posters dataset when we under-predict on the first image.

The third line of Table 2 shows the result of making predictions using decision stumps, but with a purposeful under-prediction on the first image served. We see that the amount of wasted bandwidth is reduced by nearly 70% compared to the case where only single object history is used. However, this comes at the cost of more interactions, 6.7 versus 5.4 in the case of single object history.

Figure 4(a) shows the performance of the Gaussian mixture model with one-sided feedback for the case of six clusters. Due to the nature of the model, it is natural to under-predict on images by some standard deviation of the required fidelities of the object. The x-axis indicates the amount of under-prediction (in terms of the number of standard deviations). Similar to Figure 3, the y-axis on the left and right indicate the average number of interactions required per user and the average amount of

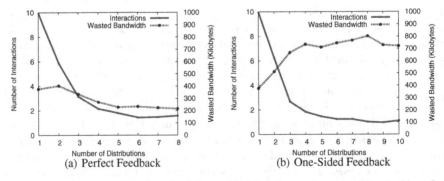

Fig. 3. The performance of the Gaussian Mixture Model on the movie posters dataset with perfect and one-sided feedback. We observe that significantly more bandwidth is wasted with one-sided feedback (*b*) than in the hypothetical case of perfect feedback(*a*).

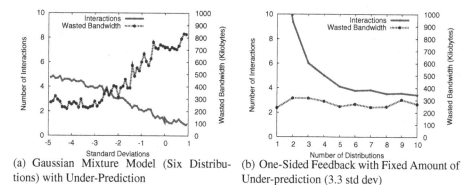

(a) Gaussian Mixture Model (Six Distribu-   (b) One-Sided Feedback with Fixed Amount of
tions) with Under-Prediction   Under-prediction (3.3 std dev)

Fig. 4. The effect of under-prediction on the Gaussian mixture model on the movie posters dataset.
We observe that wasted bandwidth decreases as we under-predict with more standard deviations
(*a*). For e.g., -4 on the x-axis refers to under-predicting the mean by four standard deviations.
Alternatively, for a fixed amount of under-prediction, we observe that GMM has far less wasted
bandwidth (*b*) compared to GMM with no under-prediction.

wasted bandwidth per user, respectively. If the algorithm under-predicts by 3.3 standard
deviations, compared to using single object history for predictions, users waste 45%
less bandwidth and require 1.4 fewer interactions. Figure 4(b) shows the performance
of the Gaussian Mixture Model when under-predicting by 3.3 standard deviations for
various numbers of distributions.

From these results, we conclude that under-prediction results in a significant
reduction in the amount of wasted bandwidth. However, doing so may result in more
interactions required of the user.

Performance of the *all-in* Algorithm: Figure 5(a) shows the performance achieved
when making predictions using the *all-in* algorithm for the movie posters data set.

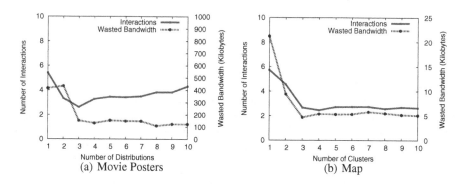

(a) Movie Posters   (b) Map

Fig. 5. The performance of the *all-in* algorithm on the studies where only one-sided feedback
is provided. We observe that *all-in* performs consistently well on all datasets for both wasted
bandwidth and number of interactions.

The x-axis indicates the number of clusters into which users may be classified. These clusters are created using the observed training data. Similar to the previous figure, the y-axes on the left and right indicate the mean number of interactions required by each user and the mean amount of wasted bandwidth per user, respectively. With respect to the number of interactions required, the algorithm performs optimally when there are three clusters. In this case, users waste only 138KB (a reduction of 63% compared to using single object history) at the cost of just 2.6 interactions (2.8 interactions less than single object history).

The *all-in* algorithm also performs well on the map experiment 5(b). When we compare the performance of the three methods, we find that the *all-in* algorithm has the best performance. One of the key features of the *all-in* algorithm is that until the user is isolated into a single cluster, the initial prediction made for each object is lower than the average fidelity required by users. When doing correlation-based adaptation with one-sided feedback, purposeful under-prediction for the first few objects provides significant benefit. This is because when the algorithm under-predicts, it forces the user to interact. This leads to an accurate history for a small set of objects, which can be leveraged to provide better quality predictions for the remainder of the objects on a web site.

Energy and Fulfillment Time: To characterize the exact benefits that the different methods may provide in practice, we evaluated all of them and several baseline and naive approaches with respect to fulfillment time and energy consumption. Figure 6 shows the fulfillment time and energy consumption for a number of adaptation policies: no adaptation (NA), single object histories (SOH), decision stumps (DS), decision stumps with under-prediction (DSU), Gaussian mixture model (GM), Gaussian mixture model with under-prediction (GMU), *all-in* (AI) and oracle (OR). Oracle, discussed earlier, is able to exactly predict the user's required fidelity, wasting no bandwidth nor requiring any interaction. It gives an upper bound on the performance of prediction algorithms.

For both fulfillment time and energy, we see that under-prediction results in significant improvement for both decision stumps and Gaussian mixture model. *all-in* performs the best for both fulfillment time and energy consumption, and performs close to oracle. In all cases, the correlation based approaches that use under-prediction offer both better fulfillment time and energy usage. Of all of them however, *all-in* also requires the fewest interactions.

4.3 Summary of Results

We first considered the performance of our prediction algorithms on an adaptation problem where two-sided feedback is available. We found that, in this case, all correlation-based techniques perform better than if we were to make predictions using only SOH. We then considered the algorithms' performance in the case where only one-sided feedback is available and found that for both the decision stumps and Gaussian mixture model algorithms, over-predictions on the initial set of objects lead to poor predictions for later objects. We modified these algorithms to perform under-prediction, which while reducing wasted bandwidth significantly, burdened the user by requiring more interactions. The *all-in* algorithm performed consistently well, even when only one-sided feedback was available, due to its aggressive under-prediction.

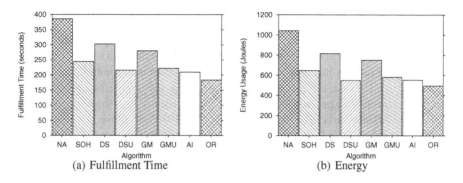

Fig. 6. The average fulfillment time and energy consumption per user for several adaptation techniques on the movie posters dataset

Finally, we considered the fulfillment time and energy consumed during the movie posters experiment by each of the algorithms. We found that the *all-in* algorithm outperformed all others, and provides effective fine-grain adaptation even in the case of multi-purpose content.

5   Related Work

There is significant research on content adaptation for mobile devices [1,2,3,4,5,6,8,9, 10,17,18,19,20], and even a few commercial adaptation systems have been deployed [1,21].

Content providers have traditionally adapted content manually, by offering device specific versions of their content. This approach places significant overhead on content providers as they need to maintain multiple versions of their content.

There has also been research on systems which automatically adapt content on-the-fly. Most automatic systems generate adaptation policies either based on rules [1,6,7, 20,22] or constraints [4,7,19,23]. In both approaches, adaptation policies are defined using high-level programming languages or mathematical formulas [22,23]. Rule-based systems rely on high-level rules to guide the adaptation process. When adapting an object, the system determines the subset of rules that apply and adapts accordingly (e.g., convert images larger than 50 KB to progressive JPEG images). Constraint-based adaptation extends rule-based adaptation to encode tradeoffs between possible adaptation strategies. A constraint captures, in a mathematical formula, the relationship between resource consumption and user satisfaction for a specific adaptation. An automatic solver adapts content by finding a solution that meets all constraints, minimizes resource consumption, and maximizes user satisfaction. Unfortunately, content providers cannot be expected to provide constraints or rules for every data object, as this imposes significant onus. As a result, small sets of rules apply to broad sets of content (e.g., all JPEG images are adapted the same way independent of their purpose or value to the user). Moreover, determining the relationship between user satisfaction and content metrics, such as resolution or frame rate, is hard and often depends on the semantics of the content being adapted and the user's task, which is rarely taken into consideration in these approaches.

In contrast, in our approach, end-users provide feedback for only a small subset of the content of web pages (by clicking on the objects), and the system is able to correctly adapt the larger set of content by considering the correlation in adaptation requirements of users. Also, because the end-user has control over the degree of adaptation, the system is guaranteed to provide adaptations that are satisfactory to the user.

End-user adaptation is also explored in [24, 25], however, those systems provide solutions specific to the layout of web pages on small screens, and as such do not explore correlations in user adaptation requirements.

Our work is related to previous efforts on recommendation-based systems. Most recommendation systems [26, 27, 28, 29] use collaborative filtering, in which people collaborate to help one another perform filtering by recording their reactions to documents they read. Balabanovic et al. [30] add the ability to evaluate and provide feedback in order to learn and improve on the recommendations. A collection of histories [31] can be created and then mined to recommend to the user a set of candidate functions and to detect users' erroneous behavior. Semantics can be used to build a model of the user [32] such as that used by online retailers like Amazon.com, which can then be used to recommend other items in the same class of products.

In our previous work, we introduced the URICA technique, which adapts single-purpose content based on the history of previously encountered users [12], and considers the context of those adaptations [13]. In this paper, we have shown how to provide fine-grain adaptation in the more challenging case of multi-purpose content. This is achieved by finding correlations in user adaptation requirements *between different objects* on a web site, and leveraging a user's feedback across multiple objects.

6   Conclusions and Future Work

In this paper, we showed that correlations in user adaptation requirements across different objects can be used to provide fine-grain adaptation for multi-purpose content. We considered two techniques from machine learning that enable correlation-based predictions: decision stumps, which directly encodes relationships between the adaptation requirements of objects, and the Gaussian mixture model, which finds correlations implicitly by clustering users with similar adaptation requirements. These techniques do not perform well when users have no incentive to correct over-predictions made by the system. We provide an algorithm called *all-in*, which groups together users with similar adaptation requirements and then makes predictions in a way that rapidly classifies users into a single cluster. We showed that for one-sided feedback, the *all-in* algorithm performs significantly better than other techniques when considering key metrics such as bandwidth usage, number of user interactions, fulfillment time, and energy consumption.

In the future, we intend to do a large scale, real-world deployment of an image fidelity adaptation system. The goal of this endeavor is to learn about the behavior of users performing interactive adaptation on web content outside a lab environment, and over an extended period of time. A version of this system for devices that can run the Firefox browser has already been made publicly available [33], and versions for the Minimo and Pocket Internet Explorer web browsers are currently being tested.

Acknowledgment

This research was supported Bell University Labs (BUL) under grant 480997, and by the Canadian Foundation for Innovation (CFI) and the Ontario Innovation Trust (OIT) under grant number 7739. Any opinions, findings, conclusions or recommendations expressed in this material are those of the authors and do not necessarily reflect the views of CFI, OIT, BUL or the University of Toronto.

References

1. Britton, K., Case, R., Citron, A., Floyd, R., Li, Y., Seekamp, C., Topol, B., Tracey, K.: Transcoding: Extending e-business to new environments. IBM Systems Journal 40(1), 153–178 (2001)
2. de Lara, E., Wallach, D.S., Zwaenepoel, W.: Puppeteer: Component-based adaptation for mobile computing. In: Proceedings of the 3rd USENIX Symposium on Internet Technologies and Systems, San Francisco, California (2001)
3. Fox, A., Gribble, S.D., Brewer, E.A., Amir, E.: Adapting to Network and Client Variability via On-Demand Dynamic Distillation. SIGPLAN Notices 31(9), 160–170 (1996)
4. Lum, W.Y., Lau, F.C.M.: A context-aware decision engine for content adaptation. IEEE Pervasive Computing 1(3), 41–49 (2002)
5. Noble, B.D., Satyanarayanan, M., Narayanan, D., Tilton, J.E., Flinn, J., Walker, K.R.: Agile application-aware adaptation for mobility. Operating Systems Review (ACM) 51(5), 276–287 (1997)
6. Smith, J.R., Mohan, R., Li, C.S.: Content-based transcoding of images in the Internet. In: Proceedings of the IEEE International Conference on Image Processing, Chicago, Illinois, IEEE Computer Society Press, Los Alamitos (1998)
7. Smith, J.R., Mohan, R., Li, C.S.: Transcoding internet content for heterogeneous client devices. In: Proceedings of the IEEE International Symposium on Circuits and Systems, Monterey, California, IEEE Computer Society Press, Los Alamitos (1998)
8. Sun, Z., Mahmud, J., Mukherjee, S., Ramakrishnan, I.V.: Model-directed web transactions under constrained modalities. In: WWW 2006. Proceedings of the 15th international conference on World Wide Web, ACM Press, New York, NY, USA (2006)
9. Borodin, Y., Mahmud, J., Ramakrishnan, I.: Context browsing with mobiles - when less is more. In: MobiSys 2007. Proceedings of the 5th international conference on Mobile systems, applications and services, pp. 3–15. ACM Press, New York, NY, USA (2007)
10. Zhuang, Z., Chang, T.Y., Sivakumar, R., Velayutham, A.: A3: application-aware acceleration for wireless data networks. In: MobiCom 2006. Proceedings of the 12th annual international conference on Mobile computing and networking, pp. 194–205. ACM Press, New York, NY, USA (2006)
11. Mohomed, I., Chin, A., Cai, J.C., de Lara, E.: Community-driven adaptation: Automatic content adaptation in pervasive environments. In: WMCSA 2004. Proceedings of the Workshop on Mobile Computing Systems and Applications, Lake District National Park, UK, pp. 124–133. IEEE Computer Society, Los Alamitos (2004)
12. Mohomed, I., Cai, J.C., de Lara, E.: Urica: Usage-aware interactive content adaptation for mobile devices. In: Proceedings of EuroSys 2006, Leuven, Belgium (2006)

13. Mohomed, I., Cai, J.C., Chavoshi, S., de Lara, E.: Context-aware interactive content adaptation. In: MobiSys 2006. Proceedings of the 4th international conference on Mobile systems, applications and services, pp. 42–55. ACM Press, New York, NY, USA (2006)

14. Witten, I., Frank, E.: Data mining: Practical machine learning tools and techniques (2005)

15. Webb, G.: Multiboosting: A technique for combining boosting and wagging. Machine Learning , 159–196 (2000)

16. Freund, Y., Schapire, R.: Experiments with a new boosting algorithm. In: Proc. of International Conference on Machine Learning, pp. 148–156 (1996)

17. Fox, A., Gribble, S.D., Chawathe, Y., Brewer, E.A.: Adapting to network and client variation using infrastructural proxies: Lessons and perspectives. IEEE Personal Communications 5(4), 10–19 (1998)

18. Katz, R.H.: Adaptation and mobility in wireless information systems. IEEE Personal Communications 1(1), 6–17 (1994)

19. Narayanan, D., Flinn, J., Satyanarayanan, M.: Using history to improve mobile application adaptation. In: Proceedings of the 3rd IEEE Workshop on Mobile Computing Systems and Applications, Monterey, California, IEEE Computer Society Press, Los Alamitos (2000)

20. Schilit, B.N., Trevor, J., Hilbert, D.M., Koh, T.K.: Web interaction using very small internet devices. IEEE Computer 35(10), 37–45 (2002)

21. iAnywhere Solutions: Avantgo, http://www.avantgo.com

22. Han, R., Bhagwat, P., LaMaire, R., Mummert, T., Perret, V., Rubas, J.: Dynamic adaptation in an image transcoding proxy for mobile web browsing. IEEE Personal Communications 5(6), 8–17 (1998)

23. Dotsenko, Y., de Lara, E., Wallach, D.S., Zwaenepoel, W.: Extensible Adaptation via Constraint Solving. In: Proceedings of the 4th IEEE Workshop on Mobile Computing Systems and Applications, Callicoon, New York, IEEE Computer Society Press, Los Alamitos (2002)

24. Bila, N., Ronda, T., Mohomed, I., Truong, K.N., de Lara, E.: Pagetailor: Reusable end-user customization for the mobile web. In: MobiSys 2007. Proceedings of the International Conference on Mobile Systems, Applications and Services, San Juan, PR, USA (June 2007)

25. Baudisch, P., Xie, X., Wang, C., Ma, W.Y.: Collapse-to-Zoom: Viewing Web pages on small screen devices by interactively removing irrelevant content. In: UIST 2004. Proceedings of the 17th Symposium on User Interface Software and Technology, Santa Fe, NM, USA (October 2004)

26. Goldberg, D., Nichols, D., Oki, B.M., Terry, D.: Using collaborative filtering to weave an information tapestry. Communications of the ACM 35(12), 61–70 (1992)

27. Terveen, L., Hill, W., Amento, B., McDonald, D., Creter, J.: Phoaks: a system for sharing recommendations. Commun. ACM 40(3), 59–62 (1997)

28. Balabanovic, M., Shoham, Y.: Fab: content-based, collaborative recommendation. Communications of the ACM 40(3), 66–72 (1997)

29. CiteSeer, http://citeseer.ist.psu.edu/

30. Balabanovic, M., Shoham, Y., Yun, Y.: An adaptive agent for automated web browsing. Journal of Visual Communication and Image Representation 6(4) (1995)

31. Ohsugi, N., Monden, A., Matsumoto, K.: A recommendation system for software function discovery. In: APSEC 2002. Proceedings of the 9th Asia-Pacific Software Engineering Conference, Gold Coast, Queensland, Australia (December 2002)

32. Ghani, R., Fano, A.: Building recommender systems using a knowledge base of product semantics. In: 2nd International Conference on Adaptive Hypermedia and Adaptive Web Based Systems, Malaga, Spain (May 2002)

33. Chameleon Homepage, http://adaptive.slup.cs.toronto.edu/

New Worker-Centric Scheduling Strategies for Data-Intensive Grid Applications*

Steven Y. Ko, Ramsés Morales, and Indranil Gupta

Department of Computer Science
University of Illinois, Urbana-Champaign
Urbana, IL 61801
{sko,rvmorale,indy}@cs.uiuc.edu

Abstract. Distributed computations, dealing with large amounts of data, are scheduled in Grid clusters today using either a *task-centric* mechanism, or a *worker-centric* mechanism. Because of the large data sets, the execution time is bounded by the cost of data transfer. In this paper, we introduce new worker-centric scheduling strategies that are novel in that they aim to implicitly exploit the locality of interest in order to reduce the cost of data transfer. Many Grid applications are characterized by such a locality of interest, *i.e.*, a file is often accessed by multiple tasks and, more importantly, a set of files that are accessed by one task are also likely to be accessed together by other tasks. Our new deterministic, as well as probabilistic, scheduling algorithms implicitly exploit this feature to improve running time. Our experiments are done with traces of a real Grid application (*Coadd*), and show that our algorithms are able to achieve utilization of over 90%, while reducing makespan significantly compared to task-centric approaches.

Keywords: worker-centric scheduling, task-centric scheduling, data-intensive applications, Grid environments.

1 Introduction

Data-intensive Grid applications are the applications that run on distributed Grid sites and are characterized by their access of large amounts of data sets. In attempting to minimize the execution time for such applications, schedulers of the Grid application are hampered by the sheer size of the data sets involved. While these data sets are mostly read-only and predefined, their size ranges from several terabytes to petabytes [1]. Examples of such data-intensive Grid applications can be found in many scientific domains such as Physics, Earth science, and Astronomy, *e.g.*, [2,3].

At run time, this large scale of the data sets makes it impractical to replicate all the data at every execution site, where the term "site" refers to a cluster of

---

* This work was supported in part by NSF CAREER grant CNS-0448246 and in part by NSF ITR grant CMS-0427089.

R. Cerqueira and R.H. Campbell (Eds.): Middleware 2007, LNCS 4834, pp. 121–142, 2007.

client machines ("workers"). Instead, the typical approach to structuring such a data-intensive Grid application (*i.e.*, the "job") is to partition the execution code into several small "tasks", and to divide up the data into several disjoint pieces, each of which we call a "file". Thus, each task requires a specific subset of the files that constitute the job data, and a site begins the execution of a given task by retrieving all those required files.

When running a data-intensive Grid application across a collection of several sites, one of the most challenging problems is the design of a (global) Grid scheduling algorithm. Specifically, since the cost of data transfer is a major bottleneck for the execution time [2,4,5,6], the main goal of the (global) scheduling algorithm becomes assigning tasks to sites in such a way as to reduce the frequency and amount of data transfer [4,5,6]. Fortunately, many data-intensive Grid applications exhibit *locality of interest, i.e.,* a file is often accessed by multiple tasks and also, a set of files that are accessed by one task are also likely to be accessed together by other tasks [7] (note: we will also use *data-sharing* whenever appropriate).

Our analysis of *Coadd* (Sloan Digital Sky Survey southern-hemisphere coaddition [2,3]) (explained in detail in Section 2.1) also shows the locality of interest in data-intensive Grid applications. There is a significant number of files accessed by multiple tasks (Figure 1(a)) and there is a large number of tasks that access the same set of files during their execution (Figure 1(b)). This locality of interest gives an opportunity to reduce the numbers of both redundant file transfers and file replicas, and is present in wide variety of applications including data mining, image processing, genomics [4], and spatial processing applications which consist of tasks that process overlapping regions [2].

Previously, locality of interest has been exploited for scheduling and workflow planning in Grid data-intensive applications. Casanova *et al.* [6], Ranganathan *et al.* [5] and Santos-Neto *et al.* [4] successfully demonstrated the benefits of their locality-aware schedulers over traditional schedulers. However, the scheduler design in all the mentioned papers is *task-centric, i.e.,* the global scheduler assigns a task to a worker, without considering whether or not the worker can start executing the task immediately after the task assignment.

We observe that such task-centric scheduling suffers from two major issues when dealing with data-intensive applications. First, there is a possibility of unbalanced task assignments, resulting in some sites being overloaded with tasks. Second, conditions at a site during scheduling time of a task may be different from the conditions at the site during execution of the task, because each task usually waits in the site's (or worker's) task queue for a while.

We argue that an alternative *worker-centric* scheduling [8,9], where a scheduling decision to a worker is made only when the worker can start executing the task immediately, is amenable to approaches that exploit locality in file accesses, and addresses both of these issues. In worker-centric scheduling, the times of task assignment to a worker are determined solely by the worker's preference based on its local criteria, *e.g.*, by using policies based on local CPU load, site queue length, time of the day, etc. The task execution begins as soon as the task arrives at the worker. The scheduling problem then becomes the one of designing a global scheduler that assigns the best possible as-yet-unscheduled task to the "best" worker, based on such characteristics as the files already present at the worker's site, and the data required by the unscheduled tasks.

There are two options for implementing worker-centric scheduling strategies - either (1) workers could *pull* tasks from a task repository associated with the global scheduler, when the worker's local policies allow it to do so; or (2) the global scheduler could *push* tasks out to workers, depending on the worker's preference. We consider only the pull variant ((1) above) since it is simpler and more practical. Henceforth in this paper, whenever we use the term "worker-centric", we will be referring to *only* the pull variant of the worker-centric algorithm.

In this paper, we present the first (to the best of our knowledge) worker-centric scheduling strategies that implicitly exploit the locality of interest in data-intensive Grid applications. We then demonstrate the advantages of worker-centric scheduling over task-centric scheduling for data-intensive Grid applications through experiments. In our worker-centric strategies, each worker requests a task from the global scheduler when convenient to the worker. Upon receiving this request, the global scheduler iterates over the list of as-yet-unscheduled tasks and finds the best task to assign to the worker. The "best" task could be selected according to a variety of metrics, which we discuss later in detail.

We propose three different metrics that consider the different aspects of locality of interest in data-intensive Grid applications, and aim to: (1) maximize the chance of reusing the data, and (2) to minimize the number of file transfers. Our simulation results with *Coadd* confirm that worker-centric scheduling gives better performance than task-centric scheduling in many scenarios. We select *Coadd* for all our experiments in this paper because (1) it is difficult to obtain Grid application traces, and (2) *Coadd* is a real Grid application used by several research organizations [2, 3] and it shows many typical characteristics of data-intensive Grid applications. Thus, we believe that our results will hold for many other data-centric Grid applications.

It is important to note that our Grid model is general, and *not* intended to specifically target production Grids such as Grid2003 [10]. Rather, we use the term "Grid" as a generic model, where a set of cooperating sites (a cluster of workers) can be used to execute a job (which consists of tasks sharing read-only data). Also, our scheduling strategies focus only on scheduling data-sharing tasks within a single large job (application), instead of multiple disconnected jobs injected into the system by different users. However, for realistic evaluation, we do simulate the presence of background jobs running concurrently with our main Grid job in our experiments in Section 4.

The rest of the paper is organized as follows. In Section 2, we present background information including the detailed problems of task-centric scheduling and advantages of worker-centric scheduling. Section 3 presents our basic algorithm and various metrics that we consider. Section 4 presents our simulation results and Section 5 discusses related work. Section 6 concludes our paper.

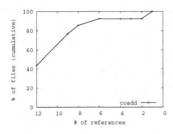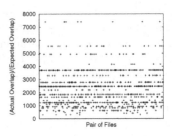

Fig. 1. (a) Coadd file access distribution. Note that the x-axis is in decreasing order, so each point in the CDF represents the minimum number of files accessed.(b) Locality of interest in Coadd.

2   Background and Basics

In this section, we motivate the scheduling problem by presenting the characteristics of data-intensive applications. We then elaborate on the two types of schedulers mentioned: task-centric and worker-centric. Lastly, we discuss scheduling issues for data-intensive applications.

2.1   Characteristics of Data-Intensive Applications

We discuss characteristics of data-intensive applications here to motivate the problem. As a real example, we use one particular application, *Coadd* (Sloan Digital Sky Survey southern-hemisphere coaddition [2,3]) in our discussion.

In general, tasks in a data-intensive application access a large set of files, thus data transfer time significantly affects the entire execution time (*i.e.* data-intensive applications are network-bound [11,4]). In addition, the tasks have a high degree of data-sharing among them, which gives an opportunity to reuse data in local storage [6,11,2,5,4].

For example, *Coadd* is a spatial processing application that has 44,000 tasks accessing 588,900 files in total. It is reported by Meyer *et al.* [2] that when it was run on Grid3 [10] with over 30 sites and 4,500 CPUs, it took roughly 70 days to complete. One of the reasons for the observed long completion time was the large number of files necessary for each task. Meyer *et al.* [2] state that these characteristics would also be expected in other spatial processing applications.

Our analysis of *Coadd* indeed confirms the characteristics of data-intensive applications. In *Coadd*, each task accesses a different number of files ranging from 36 to 181, and approximately 124 files on average. Moreover, roughly 90% of files are accessed by 6 or more tasks, as shown in Figure 1(a). If we assume that each file is fixed at 5MB as in [2], then the total size of all the files is roughly 2.8TB, and each of 44,000 tasks potentially requires 620MB of data transfer on average and up to 905MB in the worse case for each execution.

Considering the number of tasks and size of data transfers, it is desirable to reduce the redundant file transfers.

To show locality in *Coadd*, we first pick 1,000 sample pairs of files (say, A and B) accessed by *Coadd* tasks. We then plot the ratio between the actual number of tasks accessing both files, and the expected number of tasks accessing the same files. Figure 1(b) shows the result. The former (the actual number, say, C) is directly counted from our *Coadd* workload, and the later (the expected number) is derived from $\frac{a}{T} \times \frac{b}{T} \times T$, where T is the total number of tasks, and a, b are the numbers of tasks accessing A and B, accordingly. The Y-axis shows $C/(\frac{a}{T} \times \frac{b}{T} \times T)$. As we can see, the values are much larger than 1, which means that the number of tasks that access the same pair of files is much larger than statistically expected.

2.2   System Model

Before comparing task-centric to worker-centric solutions, we present our system model. We assume that:

1) A *job* is defined as an application composed of multiple parallel *tasks*. Each task does not need to communicate with other tasks in order to proceed (*i.e.*, a job is a Bag-of-Tasks [4]). However, tasks do share read-only files (data). These files are provided a priori along with the job specification.

2) There are multiple sites. Each site has at least one computation server or *worker* (and possibly multiple workers), and one data server to store data locally. We further assume that there is only one *data server* (or *local storage*) per site. If there are multiple data servers at a site, we consider all these data servers as combined storage. Storage size at a site is limited.

3) The data server of a site receives all file requests from the workers in the same site, and sends batch file requests for the missing files to the external file server. The data server processes requests one by one. This is more efficient than simultaneous requests, given the bandwidth limits.

4) Each task issues exactly one batch file request.

5) A worker starts executing a task by transferring all the files necessary for the task to the local data storage. After the transfer is over, the worker begins the actual computation of the task.

6) There is one external (global) scheduler that contains information about all tasks and gives tasks out on-demand to workers. Also, there is an external file server that has all the files necessary for all tasks, and hands them out to data servers on-demand.

7) Intra-site communication costs are negligible compared to inter-site communication costs.

8) In order to simplify our exposition, we will henceforth assume that all files are equally-sized. However, all our algorithms can be easily extended to variable sized files, by modifying the considered metrics to reflect the data size rather than the number of files.

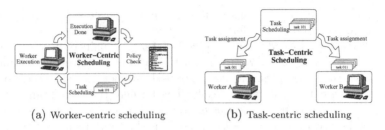

(a) Worker-centric scheduling   (b) Task-centric scheduling

Fig. 2. An illustration of worker-centric and task-centric scheduling

We use the following two terms throughout the paper:

1) *Makespan* [12] is the total execution time of the job in consideration. This is the main metric for performance measurement.

2) *Utilization* of worker A is defined as, *(total computation time of A) / (total execution time of A)*.

3) A task and a local storage (*i.e.* the data server at a site) are said to *overlap* with each other, when at least one file necessary for the task is already present in the local storage. We use the term, *overlap cardinality*, to indicate the number of overlapping files.

The main goals for a scheduling algorithm are then to: (1) reduce the make-span, (2) reduce the number of files transferred to sites, and (3) increase the utilization at workers.

2.3   Task-Centric and Worker-Centric Schedulers

We elaborate two types of schedulers, namely, task-centric schedulers and worker-centric schedulers. Figure 2 shows an illustration of worker-centric and task-centric scheduling. In essence, this categorization is based on whether or not a scheduling strategy considers immediate task execution of a worker after a task assignment.

Concretely, a scheduler is *worker-centric*, if the task assignment to a worker is done when the worker can start executing the task immediately. As mentioned before, we consider only the pull-based variant of worker-centric scheduling and the term "worker-centric" refers to this pull-based variant of worker-centric scheduler throughout the paper. This variant has each worker *pull* a task from a task repository associated with the global scheduler, when its *local policies* allow it. These local policies may be a function of CPU load, free RAM space, time of day, etc. For instance, a site could have a policy that Grid jobs are executed only over night or at a specific time of the day. Another policy might state that a site could execute Grid jobs only when the average CPU load has been below a specified threshold for a while. This architecture is similar to a server-client architecture - a worker requests a task to the scheduler, and the scheduler finds the "best" task for the worker according to a set of metrics and local policies of the worker. One example of this type of worker-centric strategies is the traditional *workqueue* algorithm, which dispatches a task in FIFO order to an idle worker [13].

On the contrary, a scheduler is *task-centric*, if a task assignment is done without considering whether or not the worker can execute the task immediately. For a given set of tasks and a set of workers, the global scheduler chooses the best match (based on its certain metrics other than immediate task execution) between workers and tasks, and assigns each task to the best worker. Each worker has a task queue and executes the tasks in the queue one by one; an empty queue means the corresponding worker is not executing tasks for that job. Typical metrics used by schedulers are CPU load, network bandwidth, data overlap, etc. For example, scheduling strategies in [5] and storage affinity-based schemes [11] are task-centric.

Since our focus in this paper is to show the effectiveness of worker-centric scheduling in exploiting locality compared to task-centric scheduling, we do not discuss various policies of worker-centric scheduling further. In Section 4, we first evaluate our task-centric and worker-centric strategies using a simple policy called *always available* - a worker requests a task from job X immediately after it finishes the previous task from the same job X. Later, to consider the effect of slowdown due to background CPU load, we experimentally study the effect of local jobs at individual workers (which might be submitted by local users or through other schedulers) - these background jobs run concurrently with tasks of the Grid job under consideration.

2.4   Scheduling Issues for Data-Intensive Applications

Several previous studies have identified that reusing data in local storage gives a dramatic performance improvement for data-intensive applications [6, 2, 5, 4]. Among others, studies by Ranganathan *et al.* [5] and Santos-Neto *et al.* [4] propose various task-centric scheduling strategies for data-intensive applications. Their studies suggest that making scheduling decisions based on data reuse indeed improve performance over other scheduling strategies that consider various different metrics altogether. Broadly, both types of strategies calculate and use the overlap cardinality (either the number of files or bytes) between all possible task-site pairs, in order to make the scheduling decisions.

The reason why schedulers considering overlap cardinality work better is intuitive. As we state in Section 2.1 and show in Figure 1(a), (a) data transfer time significantly affects the entire execution time of a data-intensive application, and (b) tasks have a high degree of data-sharing among themselves. This strategy also works well in the real world because data location is relatively static and easy to obtain compared to dynamic metrics such as network bandwidth and CPU loads [4].

2.5   Problems of Task-Centric Scheduling and Possible Solutions

We observe two problems from task-centric scheduling strategies. These problems are significant because data replication and task replication [5, 4] never address the second problem, although the first problem can be avoided by both mechanisms.

1) **Unbalanced Task Assignments:** As mentioned by Ranganathan *et al.* [5], task-centric scheduling with data reuse has the problem of overloading certain sites with popular files. Since the overlap cardinality is the primary metric when assigning a task, workers with popular files may be assigned more tasks than the workers with less popular files. Since this problem is inherent in task-centric scheduling, other mechanisms need to be used to avoid the problem, *e.g.*, data replication [5] and task replication [4].

With data replication, the system keeps track of the popularity of each file. If a file's popularity exceeds the pre-determined threshold, it is replicated to other sites. Thus, data replication helps to distribute the load of sites with popular files [5].

Task replication can also help to distribute the unbalanced load caused by popular files. With task replication, the scheduler first distributes its tasks according to the overlap cardinality. Once the initial assignment is done, the scheduler waits until at least one worker becomes idle. Then it picks a task already assigned to a worker and replicates it to the idle worker. If one of the workers finishes the task, the other worker cancels the task. The process is repeated whenever there is an idle worker. This strategy, called *storage affinity*, is proposed and evaluated by Santos-Neto *et al.* [4]. They show that a task-centric scheduler with data reuse and task replication performs better than other scheduling strategies with dynamic information such as CPU loads and available bandwidth.

2) **Long Latency between scheduling and execution:** Task-centric scheduling typically has long latency between scheduling and execution. The following two reasons cause this problem - (1) Since each worker accepts tasks passively from the scheduler and stores received tasks in its queue, there is latency between task assignment time and the actual execution time. (2) Since storage at a site is limited in size, some files required by a task may have been replaced by other required files between the scheduling and execution times of the task.

Therefore, it is possible that a worker was assigned a task because it had some files needed by the task, but at the time of execution, the worker might no longer have some of those files. This "premature scheduling decision" can cause performance degradation with small storage sizes as we show in Section 4.

2.6 Advantages of Worker-Centric Scheduling

In comparison to the above approach, worker-centric scheduling does not suffer from the unbalanced task assignment problem because a worker requests a new task to the scheduler only when its local policies allow it to execute a task. This means that it is not necessary to have other mechanisms to resolve the issue. Therefore, a worker-centric scheduler only needs to consider its scheduling metric, which leads to a simpler scheduler design.

In fact, both data replication and task replication are orthogonal mechanisms to improve performance in worker-centric schedulers. Thus, they might help the performance of worker-centric schedulers, but are not necessary. However, task-centric schedulers *require* other mechanisms because unbalanced task assignment caused by popular files actually *hurts* the performance of task-centric schedulers [5].

```
while(forever):
    req = GetNextRequest()
    if taskQueue is empty:
        wait for a task
    for each task t in taskQueue:
        CalculateWeight(t)
    t = ChooseTask(n)
    ReturnRequest(t)
```

Fig. 3. Pseudo-code of the basic algorithm. The global scheduler performs this algorithm whenever a worker requests a task.

In addition, worker-centric scheduling has short latency between scheduling and execution compared to task-centric scheduling. This arises because w.r.t. a worker, this is a *just-in-time* scheduling policy. Each worker executes a task as soon as the task has arrived at the worker. Thus, it does not suffer from the premature scheduling decisions.

In Section 3, we focus on worker-centric scheduling strategies and propose various metrics that consider data-reuse. We also show in Section 4 that worker-centric scheduling without additional mechanisms can achieve better performance in many scenarios than task-centric scheduling with additional mechanisms.

3   New Worker-Centric Scheduling Algorithms

In this section, we present our new worker-centric scheduling algorithms that attempt to exploit locality by considering data-reuse during scheduling.

3.1   Basic Algorithm

Our basic algorithm is shown in Figure 3. It is a worker-centric algorithm, with one global scheduler and multiple sites, each containing multiple workers. Upon receiving a request from a worker, the global scheduler calculates the weight of each as-yet-unscheduled task (*CalculateWeight()*) and chooses the best task to assign to the requesting worker (*ChooseTask()*). Notice that worker requests are processed sequentially. *CalculateWeight()* and *ChooseTask()* take into account the set of files already at the worker's site, and the set of files required by the worker, thus attempting to exploit locality. These are detailed next.

As mentioned in Section 2.2, for simplicity of exposition, we restrict our discussion to tasks that share equally-sized files. However, our algorithms can easily be extended to varied file sizes by merely considering a "file block" (instead of a file) as a unit of sharing among tasks.

3.2   *CalculateWeight()*

CalculateWeight() calculates a weight for each each task in order to exploit the locality of file access. This weight can be calculated via one of three possible metrics - *Overlap*, *Rest*, and *Combined*. Before further discussion, we need to define the following terms and conditions:

1) T: the set of all unscheduled tasks that the scheduler currently has in its queue.

2) F_t: the set of overlapping files between task t and the data storage at the site of the requesting worker.

3) $|t|$: the total number of files required by task t.

4) r_i: the number of past references of the file i at the local storage (*i.e.* data server) of the requesting worker, *i.e.*, the number of previously completed tasks at the site that accessed file i.

5) Task t is said to be *better* than task t', when

$Calculate Weight(t) > Calculate Weight(t')$

Now we consider three metrics that could be used by the scheduler.

1) *Overlap*: This metric is the overlap cardinality (discussed in Section 2.2). It counts the number of files that are needed by the given task and are already present in the local storage of the requesting worker. Thus, $|F_t|$ is the overlap cardinality. Intuitively, the goal of this metric is to maximize the chance of reusing the data already stored in the local storage of the requesting worker. As mentioned before, this metric is the primary metric of task-centric scheduling strategies in the previous studies.

2) *Rest*: This metric is the inverse of the number of files that need to be transferred in order to execute the given task, *i.e.*, $rest_t = \frac{1}{|t|-|F_t|}$. Intuitively, the goal of this metric is to minimize the number of files that need to be transferred. This is a complement of *overlap* metric conceptually.

3) *Combined*: For this metric, each data server keeps for each file the number of past references, *i.e.*, the number of previously completed tasks at the site that have accessed the file. It combines these past references and *rest* using an equation defined as follows. We define ref_t to be the total references of all the overlapping files of task t at the worker's site, *i.e.*, $ref_t = \sum_{i \in F_t} r_i$. Now, let $totalRef$ be the sum of all ref_t over all t in T (w.r.t. the requesting worker's site), *i.e.*, $totalRef = \sum_{t \in T} ref_t$. Also, let $totalRest$ be the sum of all $rest_t$ over all t in T, *i.e.*, $totalRest = \sum_{t \in T} rest_t$. Then, $combined_t = \frac{ref_t}{totalRef} + \frac{totalRest}{rest_t}$. Intuitively, this metric attempts to exploit locality of file access, and thus minimize both the number of files that need to be transferred as well as to prefer workers that accessed the same files in the past.

3.3   *Choose Task()*

Since the scheduler greedily assigns a task to a worker based on the value of *Calculate Weight()*, there is some possibility of sub-optimal assignments. One reason for this is the sequential nature of such worker-centric scheduling. For example, suppose worker h is a better candidate to execute task t than worker h', but worker h' requests a task right before worker h requests a task. In this

File ID / Site ID	file0	file1	file2
site0	N / A	12	6
site1	N / A	N / A	N / A
site2	10	1	5
site3	8	N / A	1
site4	N / A	N / A	1

Fig. 4. A reference table example. Each entry contains a reference counter. We use N/A to indicate that the entry is not present for the sake of demonstration.

case, the scheduler will assign task t to worker h' rather than h. This can happen quite often especially for data-intensive applications - since file transfer time is usually long after a task assignment, the global scheduler can receive a number of requests from different workers during the transfer. So it is possible that a better worker comes by while the previously-assigned worker has not even started processing, *i.e.*, it is still awaiting the file transfer to complete.

To take these types of scenarios into account, we use randomization when choosing a task through *ChooseTask(n)*. *ChooseTask(n)* then executes two steps. First, it chooses a set, T_n, of the best n tasks among all tasks (*i.e.*, tasks with n largest values calculated by *CalculateWeight()*), where n is a parameter. Second, it chooses one task among the best n tasks with a probability proportional to the *CalculateWeight()* values. Thus the probability of choosing task t is,

$$P_t = \frac{CalculateWeight(t)}{\sum_{k \in T_n} CalculateWeight(k)}.$$

If $n \geq 2$, this is a randomized approach. If $n = 1$, this is a deterministic approach that greedily chooses the best task. Notice that this procedure, in combination with *CalculateWeight()*), attempts to implicitly exploit the locality of file access.

3.4 Reducing Communication Cost

In order to make the scheduling decision for a requesting worker, we assumed above that global scheduler has all the necessary information about files currently stored at the requesting worker's site, namely, (1) names of files that the data server is currently storing, and (2) the reference count for each of these files. In other words, we assumed that the global scheduler implicitly maintains a *reference table*, as shown in Figure 4. In this table, there is one column per file in the job, and one row per site in the Grid. Each entry (i, j) specifies "reference count" for file j at site i. The reference count denotes the past references of file j at site i and also shows the presence of file j at site i.

There are two efficiency sub-problems that need to be addressed: how to maintain this table efficiently, and how to keep it updated with minimal network bandwidth overhead. The first sub-problem is addressed by having the global scheduler maintain a local hash table per site (row in the reference table), containing the names of files currently stored at that site along with their reference counts. File names are the keys for this data structure. Notice that lookup, insertion and deletion into this hash table are each $O(1)$ on expectation.

The bandwidth problem is addressed by piggybacking each task-requesting message, from a worker to the global scheduler, with the set of file names that have been replaced at the data server of the worker's site *since the last request from the same site*, *i.e.*, the list of names of files that were eliminated from the site's data server since its last request. The global scheduler deletes these file names from the hash table for that site. Then, once it makes the requested scheduling decision for the worker, the new files required by the assigned task are inserted into this hash table and the corresponding reference counts are initialized to 1. For all other files that are already present at the site and required by the assigned task, the global scheduler increments corresponding reference counts by 1. In this way, the communication between the worker to the global scheduler is reduced to only once per request no matter how many files are added and/or deleted from the site's data server.

This approach is very efficient for our considered cases. In spite of file-sharing across tasks, each task in our observed data-intensive applications typically accesses a relatively small number of files compared to the total number of files for a given application. For example, in the *Coadd* traces, no task accesses more than 181 files out of a total of 588,900, in spite of data-sharing. This also means that at most 181 files are replaced between two consecutive requests. Thus, assuming file names are 4 bytes each, the additional information piggybacked along with a worker request is at most 724 bytes in size, which is reasonably small.

3.5   Complexity

If $|T|$ is the number of currently waiting tasks, and $|I|$ is the maximal number of files required by any task, then the total communication complexity of our algorithm arises out of the per-request piggybacked information as described in the previous section - this is $O(|I|)$ per task assigned to a worker. Similarly, the computation complexity is $O(|I| + |T| \times |I|)$ per task assigned to a worker, with the first term accounting for the hash table operations, and the second one for the scheduler's operation itself. This is $O(|T| \times |I|)$, and more efficient than task-centric strategies used by Ranganathan *et al.* [5] and Santos-Neto *et al.* [4], which compare all pairs of tasks and sites. Their complexity is $O(|T| \times |I| \times |S|)$ (where $|S|$ is the total number of sites), even assuming the use of a hash table similar to that described in the previous section. Our approach is more efficient because we do not assume any knowledge (a priori or otherwise) about sites other than the requesting worker's.

4   Evaluation

In this section, we present our evaluation of worker-centric scheduling strategies and discuss the results.

4.1   Simulation Overview

To demonstrate the advantages of worker-centric scheduling over task-centric scheduling, we implement our basic algorithm with three metrics on the SimGrid simulator [14]. For comparison, we also implement *storage affinity* [4], a task-centric scheduling with data reuse and task replication.

We vary five main parameters in our experiments - (1) capacity of each data server, (2) number of workers per site, (3) computation time, (4) number of sites, and (5) file size. The default values for these parameters are summarized in Table 1, and used in our experiments unless otherwise noted. However, we vary each of these 5 parameters in our experiments to see the effects of different values. Throughout the experiments, the computation time of each task is linear to the number of files (*i.e., (number of files) * (unit computation cost)*).

Table 1. Default parameters for experiments

Unit computation cost	1,000 MFLOPS
capacity of each data server	6,000 files
number of workers per site	1
number of sites	10
file size	25 MB

Our main workload is *Coadd* (Sloan Digital Sky Survey southern-hemisphere coaddition [2,3]). As mentioned before, *Coadd* is a spatial processing application that has 44,000 tasks accessing 588,900 files in total. We use only the first 6,000 tasks of *Coadd* to finish our experiments in a reasonable amount of time. A total of 53,390 files are accessed by these 6,000 tasks. More workload characteristics are shown in Table 2. Although we only use the first 6,000 tasks, our workload characteristics remain similar to Figure 1(a).

4.2   Simulation Environment

Network Configuration: We use 5 different topologies, each with 90 sites, generated with Tiers topology generator [15]. Tiers is a structural topology generator that generates hierarchical cluster topologies. We use Tiers because it is well-supported by SimGrid, the simulator we use in our experiments. Only a subset of 90 sites are used in each experiment. For each topology, there are one global scheduler and one global file server which stores all the files. At each site, there are 30 workers and 1 data server. All 30 workers and the data server in a site share outgoing links to the global scheduler and the file server. Intra-site communication cost (cause by bandwidth and latency) is negligible. Inter-site communication cost is determined by underlying network links generated by Tiers. Each path between two sites consists of multiple network links, and the bandwidth and latency of each of these links determine the inter-site communication cost. Table 3 summarizes the average and standard deviation of bandwidth values between a site to the

Table 2. Characteristics of *Coadd* with 6,000 tasks

Total number of files	53,390
Max number of files needed by a task	101
Min number of files needed by a task	36
Average number of files needed by a task	78.4327

file server for each topology. Each worker's computation capacity (in MFLOPS) is chosen randomly from top500 list [16] and is uniformly divided by 100, since most of the 500 machines are too powerful. Each experiment is performed with 5 different topologies and the results are averaged over the 5 runs.

Table 3. Average bandwidth and standard deviation between a site and the file server

	Avg (MB/s)	Std dev
Topology 0	4.418	5.416
Topology 1	4.631	6.734
Topology 2	3.858	2.599
Topology 3	3.432	1.432
Topology 4	3.932	2.778

Background Jobs: We perform our experiments with background jobs as well as without background jobs. We use background jobs to evaluate the performance of different strategies in the presence of competing applications running on each site. Since a site is typically shared by different schedulers and local users, this gives us a more realistic setting.

We simulate background jobs through varying each worker's CPU load. A worker is always executing a task for the Grid job in question, but in addition it is also running background jobs. The background jobs thus slow down the execution of the task at the worker. The load due to these background jobs is simulated as follows: at each worker, once every 5 minutes, the background CPU load is picked as a floating-point number uniformly at random between 0 to 100. This becomes the worker's background load over the next 5 minutes. Considering that the total job execution time in our simulations is *O(tens to hundreds of days)*, we consider the granularity of 5 minutes to be fine-grained enough to capture dynamics of background jobs.

4.3   Algorithms

We compare the following 6 different algorithms. The first algorithm is task-centric; the rest are worker-centric.

1) *task-centric storage affinity* : The task-centric scheduling with data reuse and task replication [4]. This is a deterministic algorithm.
2) *overlap* : Our basic algorithm with the *overlap* metric. This is a deterministic algorithm.

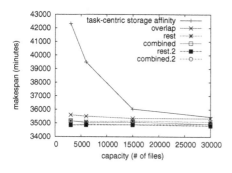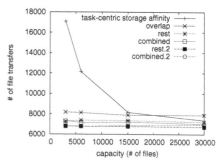

Fig. 5. (a) Makespan and (b) file transfers of each algorithm with different capacities of 3,000, 6,000, 15,000, and 30,000 files (with background jobs)

3) *rest* : Our basic algorithm with the *rest* metric. $n = 1$ for *ChooseTask(n)*. This is a deterministic algorithm.

4) *combined* : Our basic algorithm with the *combined* metric. $n = 1$ for *Choose-Task(n)*. This is a deterministic algorithm.

5) *rest.2* : Our basic algorithm with the *overlap* metric. $n = 2$ for *ChooseTask(n)*. This is a randomized algorithm.

6) *combined.2* : Our basic algorithm with the *overlap* metric. $n = 2$ for *Choose-Task(n)*. This is a randomized algorithm.

We have tried different values of n for *ChooseTask()*, but only 1 and 2 give good results. Thus, we only show the results of $n = 1$ and 2.

4.4   Capacity per Data Server

Figure 5(a) shows the makespan (*i.e.* total execution time) of each algorithm with different capacities of 3,000, 6,000, 15,000, and 30,000 files in the presence of background jobs. We do not present the results without background jobs since the performance characteristics are similar. Randomized algorithms, *rest.2* and *combined.2*, perform the best in all cases, which confirms that it avoids sub-optimal scheduling decisions described in Section 3.3. *Storage affinity* has a negative performance impact with smaller capacities because of premature scheduling decisions as discussed in Section 2.5. However, the performance becomes comparable to worker-centric scheduling as the storage size increases.

Figure 5(a) also shows the importance of considering the number of files that actually need to be transferred. Among the worker-centric strategies, *overlap* performs worse than other metrics because it does not explicitly consider the number of file transfers, while other metrics do. As we can see in Figure 5(b), *overlap* usually has higher number of file transfers than other metrics. Overall, the randomized algorithms appear to perform the best (*i.e.*, *rest.2* and *combined.2*).

The makespan of each metric in worker-centric scheduling shows steady behavior because the working set of a *Coadd* task is not big. As is shown in Table 2,

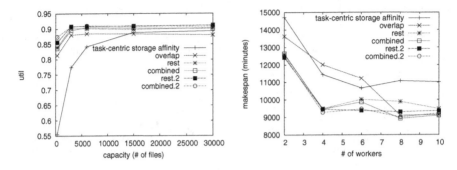

Fig. 6. (a) Average utilization at worker, with different capacities of 3,000, 6,000, 15,000, and 30,000 files (with background jobs) (b) Makespan with different numbers of workers at a site (without background jobs)

a task needs 101 files at most, and roughly 78 files on average. Thus, a storage with 3,000 files can actually give similar performance as a storage with, say, 10,000 files.

Figure 6(a) shows the average utilization of each worker (accounting for both the main Grid job and the background jobs). For *task-centric storage affinity*, the low utilization with the capacity of 3,000 files means that the greedy approach requests files more often than other strategies. This behavior shows (1) that randomized decisions can be better than taking what looks as the "best" decision at some particular time and, again, that (2) the *task-centric storage affinity* suffers from premature scheduling decisions.

Due to the lack of space, we do not present the utilization results without background jobs here. However, the utilization of each worker with background jobs is slightly higher than that of each worker without background jobs. There are two factors contributing to this result. The first factor is obviously background jobs running on each worker. The second factor is that it takes more time for a worker to finish a task with background jobs. Thus, the utilization goes higher with background jobs.

4.5   Number of Workers per Site

Figure 6(b) shows the makespan of each algorithm with different numbers of workers at a site. *combined.2* performs the best mostly, which shows that minimizing file transfers as well as considering past references helps to reduce the makespan. Overall, worker-centric scheduling metrics perform well with smaller numbers of workers, but *storage affinity* performs well with larger numbers of workers. Also, randomized algorithms that consider the number of file transfers perform better than others.

The makespan of each algorithm flattens as the number of workers increases. In some cases, the performance is worse with more workers (in Figure 6(b))! We can understand the reason behind this behavior with two factors that contribute to the makespan. First, as the number of workers increases at a site, the contention at the

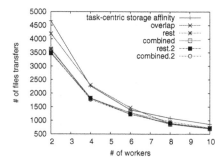 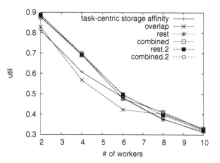

Fig. 7. (a) Average number of file transfers per worker with different numbers of workers at a site (b) Average worker utilization, with different numbers of workers at a site. We only show the results without background jobs, since the presence of background jobs does not show any different behavior.

data server of the site increases. Since the data server processes each request one by one so as to minimize the redundant file transfers (as mentioned in Section 2.2), this contention is unavoidable. This factor has a negative impact on the makespan (*i.e.* increases it). On the contrary, as the number of workers increases, the number of files that can be shared by the workers also increases. This factor has a positive impact on the makespan. The interaction of these two factors results in different behaviors of different algorithms.

Table 4. Result of the *rest* metric at a site with 2 workers, 4 workers, 6 workers, and 8 workers. All numbers are averages per worker. Note that *rest* shows the worst makespan with 6 workers at a site.

	waiting time (hrs)	transfer time (hrs)	# of file transfers
2 workers	3.59	30.35	3998.5
4 workers	40.32	45.45	2086.5
6 workers	98.35	33.85	1335.17
8 workers	75.93	18.81	906.38

To validate the reason, Figure 7(a) shows the number of file transfers per worker and Figure 7(b) shows the corresponding utilization. It shows that the average number of file transfers per worker decreases as the number of workers increases. Thus, it shows that good file-sharing is achieved intra-site as the number of workers increases. In addition, Table 4 shows the result of the *rest* metric at one particular site with 2, 4, 6, and 8 workers. It shows (1) average waiting time that a file request spends at the data server's waiting queue, (2) transfer time that it takes to transfer all the files from the external file server to the data server, and (3) associated number of file transfers.

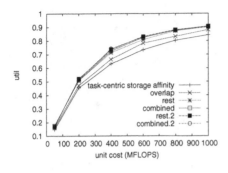 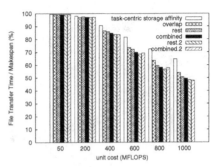

Fig. 8. (a) Average utilization per worker, and (b) total file transfer time compared to makespan, for different unit computation costs of 50, 200, 400, 600, 800, and 1,000 MFLOPS

In the case of 2 workers in Table 4, the contention at each data server and the file server is very low compared to other settings, simply because there are fewer workers. Thus, the waiting time and the transfer time are rather small even though the number of file transfers is high.

We can reason why the performance is sometimes worse with more workers with the data of 4 workers, 6 workers, and 8 workers. If we look at the data in this range, both the average number of file transfers and the average transfer time decrease as the number of workers increases, but the average waiting time peaks at 6 workers. This means that the reduced transfer time is not enough to compensate the increased competition at the data server for *rest* with 6 workers at a site. For the same reason, other algorithms sometimes exhibit a worse makespan with more workers.

4.6   Effect of Computation Time

With our default parameter values in Table 1, the average utilization per worker is usually more than 90%, which means that each worker spends most of its time on computation. Thus, we perform an experiment with smaller values of unit computation time in order to understand how different computation-to-communication ratios affect the behavior of each strategy. As mentioned before, the computation time of each task is linear to the number of files that it needs to process, *i.e., (computation time) = (number of files) * (unit computation cost)*. We vary the unit computation cost in this experiment.

Figure 8(a) and Figure 8(b) show that our experiment covers a wide range of communication-to-computation ratio. As shown in Figure 8(a), the utilization of each worker (*i.e., (total computation time of the worker) / (total execution time of the worker)*) varies from roughly 0.2 to 0.9. Also, Figure 8(b) shows that the file transfer time (*i.e.,* communication time) takes from roughly 50% to almost 100% of the entire makespan. Thus, our experiment covers a wide range of communication-to-computation ratio, and still captures the characteristic of long communication time in data-intensive applications. Although Figure 8 shows the

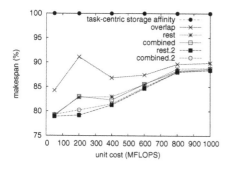 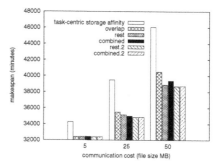

Fig. 9. (a) Makespan (percentile) of each algorithm with different unit computation costs of 50, 200, 400, 600, 800, and 1,000 MFLOPS (b) Makespan with different file sizes (both with background jobs)

results without the presence of background jobs, the overall behavior remains similar even with background jobs. Note that file transfer time does not directly contribute to worker utilization as in Figure 8. The reason is because computation is parallelized, and hence, most workers are busy with doing computation even when the file server transfers files. This explains a seemingly inconsistent behavior of Figure 8, in which the file transfer time takes roughly 50% with the unit computation cost of 1,000 MFLOPS in Figure 8(b), even when the average utilization of each worker is roughly 90% in Figure 8(a).

Figure 9(a) shows the makespan (with background jobs) of each algorithm in percentile scale using task-centric storage affinity as a baseline comparison. We do not present the results without background jobs since they exhibit similar behaviors. Overall, we observe that the performance trend remains similar across different strategies even with various computation-to-communication ratios. Worker-centric strategies perform better than the task-centric storage affinity in terms of makespan. In the best case, worker-centric *rest* takes roughly 28% less makespan time than *task-centric storage affinity*. Also, the gap between task-centric storage affinity and other strategies generally becomes wider as the unit computation cost decreases. This is an expected behavior since file transfer time becomes more dominating in total execution time as the unit computation cost decreases.

4.7   Number of Sites

Figure 10(a) shows the makespan of each algorithm with different numbers of sites and Figure 10(b) shows the number of file transfers accordingly. Generally, the makespan of each algorithm reduces as the number of sites increases, as expected. *combined.2* performs the best, which again confirms that minimizing file transfers as well as considering past references helps to reduce the makespan. In the best case, *combined.2* takes roughly 17% less makespan time than *task-centric storage affinity*. Randomized algorithms perform better than deterministic algorithms, which again shows that it avoids sub-optimal scheduling decisions described in Section 3.3.

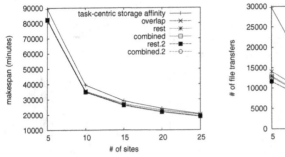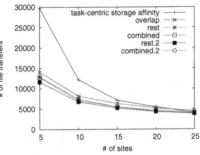

Fig. 10. (a) Makespan with different numbers of sites (b) Number of file transfers with different numbers of sites (both with background jobs)

4.8 File Size

Figure 9(b) shows the makespan of each algorithm with different file sizes. We choose small (5MB), middle (25MB), and large (50MB) file sizes. The makespan grows almost linearly as the file size grows. Since all algorithms consider files as the primary metric, various file sizes do not result in dramatically different behaviors. *combined.2* shows the best performance just like many other scenarios shown before. The general behavior remains the same even in the presence of background jobs.

5 Related Work

Spatial Clustering [2] creates a task workflow based on the spatial relationship of files in the input data set. It improves data reuse and diminishes file transfers by clustering together tasks with high input-set overlap. Two drawbacks to this approach are that (1) it cannot handle new jobs arriving asynchronously, and (2) it is application specific.

Storage Affinity [4] also addresses file reuse for data-intensive applications. The algorithm computes a data affinity value for each task, for each site, according to the input set of each task and the data currently stored at a site's networked storage. To address inefficient CPU assignments, they propose replicating tasks, also based on the storage affinity. The algorithm shows improved makespan and good data reuse, specially when compared to the XSufferage [17] scheduling heuristic.

Decoupling data scheduling from task scheduling was proposed by Ranganathan *et al.* [5]. The work evaluates four simple task scheduling mechanisms and three simple data scheduling mechanisms. Best results are obtained when a task is scheduled to a site that has a good part of its input data already in place, combined with proactive replication of a popular input data-set to a random/least-loaded site.

A pull-based scheduler is proposed by Viswanathan *et al.* [8]. It employs an Incremental Based Strategy, where a scheduler determines how to fraction a job among available workers, based on worker's computing speed and estimated buffer. This work completely ignores data transfer time, and requires knowledge of CPU speed and memory size in all workers.

Rosenberg *et al.* [9] study global scheduling strategies in the Grid-like environments theoretically. Their scheduling strategies focus mainly on *DAGs of tasks*, where tasks are inter-dependent and pre-ordered, and the dependency structure follows DAG (Directed Acyclic Graph). Although they discuss *pull* and *push* strategies, their studies do not assume (1) data-intensive applications (transfer time, storage capacity, data correlation, etc), (2) data-sharing, and (3) task-independence. Thus, the issues are not related to our work.

6   Conclusion and Future Work

We argued that worker-centric scheduling is more desirable than task-centric scheduling to exploit locality of interest present in data-intensive applications. We base our argument on two problems of task-centric scheduling, namely, unbalanced task assignments and premature scheduling decisions. We proposed various metrics, both deterministic and randomized, that can be used with worker-centric scheduling and found that metrics considering the number of file transfers generally give better performance over metrics considering the overlap between a task and a storage. We also found that worker-centric scheduling algorithms achieve better or comparable performance to task-centric scheduling, with the randomized approaches performing best. Our future work includes quantifying how much data-sharing is required for our algorithms to be effective, and using multiple applications to evaluate the performance of our algorithms.

References

1. Allcock, W.E., Bester, J., Bresnahan, J., Chervenak, A.L., Foster, I.T., Kesselman, C., Meder, S., Nefedova, V., Quesnel, D., Tuecke, S.: Secure, efficient data transport and replica management for high-performance data-intensive computing. CoRR cs.DC/0103022 (2001)
2. Meyer, L., Annis, J., Mattoso, M., Wilde, M., Foster, I.: Planning Spatial Workflows to Optimize Grid Performance. Technical Report, GriPhyN 2005-10 (2005)
3. Sekhri, V.: Lessons Learned on Summer 04 Grid SDSS Coadd, https://www.darkenergysurvey.org/the-project/simulations/sdss-grid-coadd/sum mer-04-grid-coadd
4. Santos-Neto, E., Cirne, W., Brasileiro, F.V., Lima, A.: Exploiting Replication and Data Reuse to Efficiently Schedule Data-Intensive Applications on Grids. In: Feitelson, D.G., Rudolph, L., Schwiegelshohn, U. (eds.) JSSPP 2004. LNCS, vol. 3277, Springer, Heidelberg (2005)
5. Ranganathan, K., Foster, I.T.: Decoupling Computation and Data Scheduling in Distributed Data-Intensive Applications. In: Proc. of HPDC-11 (2002)
6. Casanova, H., Obertelli, G., Berman, F., Wolski, R.: The AppLeS Parameter Sweep Template: User-Level Middleware for the Grid. In: Proc. of SC (2000)
7. Iamnitchi, A., Doraimani, S., Garzoglio, G.: Filecules in High-Energy Physics: Characteristics and Impact on Resource Management. In: Proc. of HPDC-15 (2006)

8. Viswanathan, S., Veeravalli, B., Yu, D., Robertazzi, T.G.: Design and Analysis of a Dynamic Scheduling Strategy with Resource Estimation for Large-Scale Grid Systems. In: Proc. of GRID (2004)
9. Rosenberg, A.L., Yurkewych, M.: Guidelines for scheduling some common computation-dags for internet-based computing. IEEE Transactions on Computers 54(4) (April 2005)
10. Foster, I.T., et al.: The Grid2003 Production Grid: Principles and Practice. In: Proc. of HPDC-13 (2004)
11. de Silva, D.P., Cirne, W., Brasileiro, F.V.: Trading Cycles for Information: Using Replication to Schedule Bag-of-Tasks Applications on Computational Grids. In: Proc. of Euro-Par 2003 (2003)
12. Pinedo, M.: Scheduling: Theory, Algorithms and Systems, 2nd edn. Prentice Hall, New Jersey, USA (2001)
13. Cirne, W., Brasileiro, F., Sauv, J., Andrade, N., Paranhos, D., Santos-Neto, E., Medeiros, R.: Grid Computing for Bag of Tasks Applications. In: Proc. Third IFIP I3E (September 2003)
14. Legrand, A., Marchal, L., Casanova, H.: Scheduling Distributed Applications: the SimGrid Simulation Framework. In: Proc. of CCGrid (2003)
15. Doar, M.B.: A Better Model for Generating Test Networks. In: Proc. of Globecom. (1996)
16. Top 500 list, http://www.top500.org
17. Casanova, H., Zagorodnov, D., Berman, F., Legrand, A.: Heuristics for Scheduling Parameter Sweep Applications in Grid Environments. In: 9th Heterogeneous Computing Workshop (2000)

Interactive Resource-Intensive Applications Made Easy

H. Andrés Lagar-Cavilla[1], Niraj Tolia[2], Eyal de Lara[1], M. Satyanarayanan[2],
and David O'Hallaron[2]

[1] University of Toronto
[2] Carnegie Mellon University

Abstract. Snowbird is a middleware system based on virtual machine (VM)
technology that simplifies the development and deployment of *bimodal* applications. Such applications alternate between phases with heavy computational-
resource needs and phases rich in user interaction. Examples include digital
animation, as well as scientific, medical, and engineering diagnostic and design
tools. Traditionally, these applications have been manually partitioned into distributed components to take advantage of remote computational resources, while
still providing low-latency user interaction. Instead, Snowbird lets developers
design their applications as monolithic units within a VM, and automatically
migrates the application to the optimal execution site to achieve short completion
time and crisp interactive performance. Snowbird does not require that applications be written in a specific language, or use specific libraries, and it can be
used with existing applications, including closed-source ones, without requiring
recompilation or relinking. Snowbird achieves these goals by augmenting VM
migration with an interaction-aware migration manager, support for graphics
hardware acceleration, and a wide-area peer-to-peer storage system. Experiments
conducted with a number of real-world applications, including commercial
closed-source tools, show that applications running under Snowbird come within
4% of optimal compute time, and provide crisp interactive performance that is
comparable to native local execution.

Keywords: Bimodal Applications, Migration, Virtual Machines, Thin Clients,
Interactive Response, Variable Thickness.

1 Introduction

A growing number of applications in many domains combine sophisticated algorithms
and raw computational power with the deep knowledge, experience and intuition
of a human expert. Examples of such applications can be found in simulation and
visualization of phenomena in scientific computing, digital animation, computer-aided
design in engineering, protein modeling for drug discovery in the pharmaceutical
industry, and computer-aided diagnosis in medicine. These *bimodal* applications
alternate between resource-intensive *crunch phases* that involve little interaction,
and *cognitive phases* that are intensely interactive. During the crunch phase, short
completion time is the primary performance goal, and computing resources are the
critical constraints. During the cognitive phase, crisp interactive response is the primary
performance goal, and user attention is the critical constraint.

R. Cerqueira and R.H. Campbell (Eds.): Middleware 2007, LNCS 4834, pp. 143–163, 2007.

Optimizing both phases is important for a good user experience, but achieving this end is complicated by the large disparity in the performance goals and bottlenecks of the two phases. Today, developers manually split a bimodal application into a distributed set of components [1,2,3,4]. Crunch phase components are executed on compute servers or server farms. Distant data servers are sometimes used because datasets are too large to cache or mirror locally, or are constrained by organizational or regulatory policies that forbid caching or mirroring. In contrast, cognitive phase components are executed locally where they can take advantage of local graphics acceleration hardware. Unfortunately, this approach requires developers to manage communication and coordination between application components, and to be aware at all times of whether a particular component will be executed locally or remotely. This adds software complexity above and beyond the intrinsic complexity of the application being developed, and hence slows the emergence of new bimodal applications.

This paper introduces Snowbird, middleware based on virtual machine (VM) technology that simplifies the development and deployment of bimodal applications. Snowbird masks the complexity of creating a bimodal application by wrapping the application, including all its executables, scripts, configuration files, dynamically linkable libraries, and operating system, into a migratable VM. During execution, Snowbird automatically detects phase transitions in the application and migrates the VM containing its complex web of dependence to the optimal execution site. Snowbird does not require applications to be written in a specific language, nor to be built using specific libraries. Existing closed-source applications can use Snowbird without recoding, recompilation, or relinking.

Snowbird extends existing VM technology with three mechanisms: an interaction-aware migration manager that triggers automatic migration; support for graphics hardware acceleration; and a peer-to-peer storage subsystem for efficient sharing of persistent VM state at Internet scale. Experiments conducted with a number of real-world applications, including commercial closed-source tools such as the Maya 3D graphics animation package, show that applications running under Snowbird come within 4% of optimal crunch completion times, while exhibiting crisp interactive performance that is comparable to native local execution.

From a more abstract perspective, Snowbird can be viewed as a tool that provides seamless transitions between thick and thin client modes of execution. It has long been known that the strengths of thick and thin clients complement each other. Thin clients are attractive in CPU-intensive and data-intensive situations because application execution can occur on remote compute servers close to large datasets. Unfortunately, high network latency and jitter between the application execution site and the user site can lead to poor interactive performance. Thick clients offer a much better user experience in that situation. By transparently morphing an application between thick and thin client modes of execution, Snowbird gives a user the best of both worlds.

2   Design and Implementation

The dominant influence on the design of Snowbird was our desire to simplify the creation and deployment of bimodal applications without imposing onerous constraints

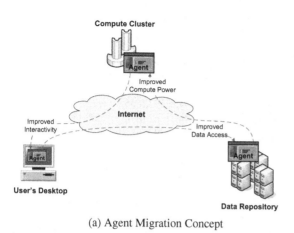

Life Cycle Commands
createagent *agentname*
launch *agentname*
kill *agentname*
purge *agentname hostname*

Migration Commands
suspend *agentname*
resume *agentname hostname*
suspend-resume *agentname*
                        hostname

Admin Commands
addhost *agentname hostname*
sync *agentname hostname*
movehome *agentname*
                    newhome
listhosts *agentname*

(a) Agent Migration Concept   (b) Snowbird Commands

Fig. 1. Snowbird Overview

on developers. The use of VM technology is the key to achieving this goal. It allows a developer to focus on the creation of a single monolithic entity rather than the more difficult programming task of creating a distributed system. This monolithic entity, called an *agent,* is the migratable embodiment of an application that transparently and seamlessly relocates itself to achieve optimal performance. At run time, Snowbird automatically detects phase transitions and migrates the agent to the optimal execution site. The example illustrated in Figure 1(a) shows an agent that starts at the user's desktop to provide good interactive response during a cognitive phase. It then migrates to several remote sites, where it leverages the superior compute power of a shared-memory multiprocessor and improved I/O performance from proximity to a large dataset. The agent then returns to the desktop for the next cognitive phase.

The logical encapsulation provided by an agent eases the complexity of developing and deploying a bimodal application. Simplicity is reinforced by the fact that all the paraphernalia associated with a large application (such as other processes, dynamically linked libraries, and specific OS features upon which an application relies) is atomically moved with the same containing agent. Hence no application-specific code has to be pre-installed in order to run on a site. An agent only requires SSH access credentials to execute on a Snowbird-enabled site. The SSH credentials are also used to encrypt all communications. Note that an agent can be a tool chain composed of several processes executing simultaneously or sequentially in a pipeline fashion.

Snowbird's use of VM technology offers three significant advantages over existing approaches to code mobility. First, applications do not have to be written in a specific language, to be built using specific libraries, or to run on a particular OS. Second, legacy applications do not have to be modified, recompiled, or relinked to use Snowbird. This greatly simplifies real-world deployments that use proprietary rather than open-source applications. Third, migration is transparent and seamless to the user, beyond the obviously desirable effects of improved interactive or computational performance.

A second factor influencing Snowbird's design is our desire to support applications at an Internet scale, particularly those using remote datasets over WAN links. It is

Table 1. Internet2 Round Trip Times

End Points	RTTs (ms)			
	Min	Mean	Max	c
Berkeley – Canberra	174.0	174.7	176.0	79.9
Berkeley – New York	85.0	85.0	85.0	27.4
Berkeley – Trondheim	197.0	197.0	197.0	55.6
Pittsburgh – Ottawa	44.0	44.1	62.0	4.3
Pittsburgh – Hong-Kong	217.0	223.1	393.0	85.9
Pittsburgh – Dublin	115.0	115.7	116.0	42.0
Pittsburgh – Seattle	83.0	83.9	84.0	22.9

end-to-end latency, not bandwidth, that is the greater challenge in this context. Table 1 shows recent round-trip time (RTT) values for a representative sample of Internet2 sites [5]. The theoretical minimum RTT values imposed by speed-of-light propagation, shown in the last column c, are already problematic. Unfortunately, technologies such as firewalls and overlay networks further exacerbate the problem, causing the minimum observed RTT values to far exceed the substantial propagation delays. Although bandwidths will continue to improve over time, RTT is unlikely to improve dramatically. These performance trends align well with the design of Snowbird; the critical resource in VM migration is network bandwidth, while the critical resource for crisp interaction is RTT.

A third factor influencing Snowbird's design is the peer-to-peer (P2P) relationship between migration sites that is implicit in Figure 1(a). Since Snowbird can migrate to any Internet site for which it possesses SSH credentials, there is no notion of clients or servers. Solely for purposes of system administration, Snowbird associates a *home* host with each agent. This is typically a user's desktop machine or so some other nearby computer where the user spends most of her time interacting with the agent. The home host acts as the authoritative machine on which the commands shown in Figure 1(b) are issued. The command line interface for Snowbird includes commands for managing an agent's life cycle, for controlling agent migration, and for system administration. Migration control commands are typically used by the migration manager described in Section 2.2. However, they are available for explicit user control, if desired.

Sections 2.1 to 2.4 present more details on four specific aspects of Snowbird. Section 2.1 expands upon our use of VM technology. Section 2.2 describes the interaction-aware migration manager. Section 2.3 describes the use of hardware-accelerated graphics by VM applications. Section 2.4 presents Snowbird's wide-area peer-to-peer storage subsystem for sharing persistent VM state.

2.1   Choice of VM Technology

The current version of Snowbird is based on the Xen 3.0.1 VMM. We chose Xen because its open-source nature makes it attractive for experimentation. However, our design is sufficiently modular that using a different VMM such as VMware Workstation will only require modest changes.

Snowbird uses VM migration [6,7] to dynamically relocate the agent from a source to a target host. To migrate an agent, its VM is first suspended on the source. The suspended VM image, typically a few hundred MBs of metadata and serialized memory contents, is then transferred to the target, where VM execution is resumed. Snowbird uses *live-migration* [8] to allow a user to continue interacting with the application during agent relocation. This mechanism makes migration appear seamless, by iteratively prefetching the VM's memory to the target while the VM continues to execute on the source host. When the amount of prefetched VM memory reaches a critical threshold, a brief pause is sufficient to transfer control.

Modern VMMs allow the creation of VMs with multiple virtual CPUs regardless of the underlying number of available physical cores. Thus, when migrating from uniprocessor to multiprocessor hosts, Snowbird agents are able to transparently leverage the increased computing power by configuring their containing VMs as SMPs.

2.2   Interaction-Aware Migration Manager

While users can explicitly control migration decisions using the commands in Figure 1(b), Snowbird provides system-controlled agent relocation as one of its key features. In other words, the decision to migrate, the choice of migration site, and the collection of information upon which to base these decisions can all happen under the covers in a manner that is transparent to the user and to the agent.

A key feature of Snowbird is that it accounts for the quality of the application's interactive response when making its migration decisions. This is in stark contrast to the large body of related work on automated process migration policies [9], which concentrates on computationally-intensive applications devoid of interactions. Snowbird uses an *interaction-aware migration manager* module that bases its decisions on three sources: *interactivity sensors* that extract relevant data from the Snowbird user interface; *performance sensors* that extract their data from the VMM; and *migration profiles* that express the migration policy as transitions of a finite state machine triggered by sensor readings. Snowbird's clean separation between policy and mechanism simplifies the use of different profiles and sensors.

Interactivity sensors. The interaction sensor is built into Snowbird's agent graphical user interface, described in the next section. As shown in Figure 2, the interaction sensor collects a stream of time-stamped events corresponding to keyboard/mouse inputs and screen updates. The intensity of the user's interactive demand and the quality of the agent's response can both be inferred from this stream.

Our measure of *interaction intensity* is the number of input events per unit of time. Our measure of *interactive response quality* is the number of frames per second triggered by an input event. This metric can be derived by assuming that all screen updates are causally related to the most recent input event. The frames per second (FPS) triggered by that input event is thus the number of related screen updates divided by the time from the event to the last of those updates. The FPS metric reflects both the smoothness and the swiftness of an interactive response. Remote interaction usually relies on non-work-conserving thin-client algorithms such as VNC [10] that under adverse network conditions skip frames to "catch up" with the output. Skipping frames in this manner results in jerky on-screen tracking of mouse and keyboard inputs that

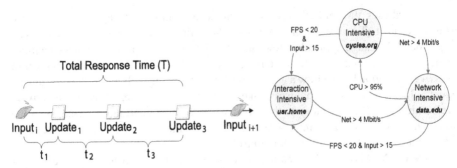

Fig. 2. Interaction Intensity and Smoothness   **Fig. 3.** Example Partial FSM

can be annoying and distracting. For work-conserving thin-client algorithms like X, a low FPS rating means that the same amount of screen updates happened in more time, resulting instead in a sluggish response. We thus quantify the quality of the interactive response of an event window as the average FPS yielded by all the inputs in that window. High interaction intensity combined with a low-quality response is the cue used by the migration manager to trigger a remote-to-local transition.

Performance Sensors. Snowbird provides performance sensors for *CPU utilization*, and *network utilization*. These sensors periodically poll the VMM for an agent's share of CPU time, and the number of bytes transmitted on its network interfaces, respectively. The poll interval is configurable with a default value of one second.

Migration Profiles. A migration profile defines a finite state machine (FSM) that is used to model the agent's behavior. As shown in Figure 3, each state in this machine characterizes a particular level of resource demand and/or interaction. Profile rules define when and how sensor readings should trigger state transitions. The profile also specifies the amount of past sensor information that should be averaged to evaluate the rules, which defaults to ten seconds. Each state defines an optimal execution site. The mapping of application profile-defined FSM states to hosts is dependent on the infrastructure available to each particular user. While the figure exemplifies the typical FSM derived from the three sensors we implemented, profile writers are free to generate more complex FSMs using more sensors and states.

Profile creation involves a characterization of an agent's resource usage and may be done by application developers or by third-parties such as user groups, administrators, or technically adept users. In the absence of an application-specific profile, the migration manager uses a generic profile that identifies typical crunch and cognitive phases. The default profile is shown in Figure 3; most of its values are fairly intuitive and conservative. We use the long-established 20 FPS threshold [11] to trigger interactive response-based migrations. The input threshold of 15 inputs per window of ten seconds is derived from observations of the average input event generation rate in our experiments. We were able to use this generic application profile for all the experiments described in Section 3.5.

We plan to augment the Snowbird migration manager with many of the features developed by the process migration community in the scope of automated migration,

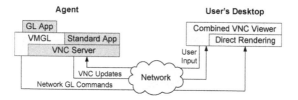

Fig. 4. 3D Support in Snowbird

such as selecting destination sites based on their current load [9]. One relevant concern in our environment is the handling of applications with overlapping crunch and cognitive phases, that could compromise the agent's stability by "thrashing" between the two states. The straightforward solution we have implemented is to specify a priority favoring interactive performance when conflicting migration rules are simultaneously triggered. Another solution would be to invoke hysteresis mechanisms [12] to prevent the migration manager from adopting this erratic behavior.

2.3   Hardware-Accelerated Graphical Interface

The graphical user interface for an agent has to comply with two requirements. First, a user should be able to interact seamlessly with an agent, regardless of its current location. Second, many of the applications targeted by Snowbird (such as scientific visualization and digital animation), require the use of 3D graphics acceleration hardware, a feature absent from most virtualized execution environments.

Snowbird uses VMGL [13] to meet these requirements. VMGL includes an enhanced thin client interface based on VNC [10], and provides agents with access to 3D graphics hardware acceleration. When the agent is running on a remote host, the thin client protocol is used to communicate screen updates and user inputs (i.e., keystrokes and mouse) over the network. When the agent runs on the user's desktop, the network becomes a loopback connection. Interaction is never interrupted during agent relocation because network connections persist through live-migrations: for relocations within the same L2 subnet, a gratuitous ARP-reply binds the agent's IP address to the new physical host. Relocations across subnets are supported with VPN tunnels or L2 proxys like VNETs [14].

VMGL provides applications running in a VM access to 3D graphics hardware acceleration by virtualizing the OpenGL API. This cross-platform API for 3D applications is supported by all major graphics hardware vendors. We use library preloading to masquerade as the system's native GL driver and intercept all GL calls made by an application. GL primitives are then forwarded over the network, using the WireGL protocol [15], to a remote rendering module where they are rendered directly by 3D graphics acceleration hardware. Although this setup allows complete flexibility, we expect the rendering module to execute in the user desktop's administrative VM, physically co-located with the agent VM during cognitive phases.

Figure 4 shows how we adapted VMGL for use in Snowbird. GL primitives bypass the VNC server and are rendered using 3D hardware on the user's desktop. Updates from non-3D APIs (e.g. Xlib) used by standard applications are rendered by the VNC server on its virtual framebuffer and shipped to the viewer. A modified VNC viewer

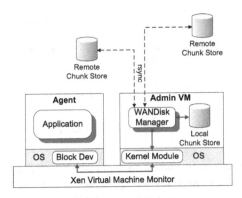

Fig. 5. WANDisk Storage System Architecture

composes both streams and offers a combined image to the user. Input events are handled entirely by the thin client protocol. Similar mechanisms can be used to support the Direct3D rendering API for Windows VMs [16].

2.4 The WANDisk Storage System

VM migration mechanisms only transfer memory and processor state; they do not transfer VM disk state, which is typically one to three orders of magnitude larger (many GBs). Therefore, each VM disk operation after migration usually involves network access to the source host. While this is standard practice on the LAN environments that are typical of VM deployments in data centers (SANs, Parallax [17], distributed file systems like Lustre), it is unacceptable for the high-latency WAN environments in which we envision Snowbird being used. A distributed storage mechanism is thus needed to take advantage of read and update locality in disk references. Furthermore, while several WAN-optimized distributed storage choices were available to us, none of them satisfied two key characteristics of the Snowbird deployment model. First, there are multiple symmetric hosts on which an agent might run, thus precluding storage systems that are limited to a single replica support (DRBD), and systems that centralize data transfers on a server (NFS, AFS, Coda [18], VM disk mechanisms used by the Collective [7] and Internet Suspend/Resume [6], etc). Second, in this P2P-like model there is no need to maintain complex multiple-writer synchronization protocols [19], as the agent executes – and modifies its underlying disk state – in a single host at a time.

We have therefore implemented a distributed storage system called WANDisk, that provides efficient WAN access to multiple replicas of an agent's virtual disk. To provide flexibility in the choice of migration site, WANDisk follows a P2P approach where any Internet host can maintain a persistent replica of the agent's state. To reduce data transfers, WANDisk relies on the persistence of the replicas, which are created on demand as new migration sites are identified. WANDisk's replica control mechanism uses two techniques for optimizing the efficiency of agent migration. First, lazy synchronization is used to avoid unnecessary data transfers to inactive migration sites or for unused parts of a virtual disk. Second, differential transfers are used between replicas to reduce synchronization overhead.

Figure 5 shows the two-tiered WANDisk architecture, which consists of a *kernel module* and a user-space *disk manager*, both operating within Xen's administrative VM. The kernel module presents a pseudo block device that is mapped to an agent's virtual block device. All agent-originated block requests are handled by the pseudo block device and redirected into the user-space disk manager.

The disk manager partitions the agent's virtual disk into *chunks* and uses a *chunk table* to keep track of versioning and ownership information. Chunk size is configurable at agent creation time; we use a chunk size of 128 KB in our experiments, which we have found to work well in practice. As the agent modifies blocks in its virtual block device, the mapped chunk's version number is incremented, and its ownership transferred to the host where the agent is executing. Each host thus "owns" the chunks which the agent modified while executing there. Before the agent accesses any of those chunks at a different host, the chunk table will point WANDisk to the location of the freshest copy. The chunk table is thus the only piece of metadata necessary for the correct execution of WANDisk, and becomes a crucial addition to an agent's migratable state. To account for this, we have modified live migration in Xen to include the chunk table; however, actual chunk transfers are not involved in the critical path of agent migration. WANDisk fetches chunks exclusively on-demand, using the rsync algorithm [20] to perform efficient differential data transfer.

The heavyweight sync command shown in Figure 1(b) is available for bringing any replica up to date under explicit user control. This command may be used for performance or reliability reasons. The command blocks until the replica at the specified migration site is both complete and up to date. At this point, agent execution can continue at that site even if it is disconnected from other replicas.

3   Usage Experience and Experimental Evaluation

We have gained hands-on usage experience with Snowbird by applying it to four bimodal applications from distinct application domains. None of these applications was written by us, and none had to be modified for use with Snowbird. Two of the applications (*Maya* and *ADF*) are commercial closed-source products whose success in the marketplace confirms their importance. The other two applications (*QuakeViz* and *Kmenc15*) have open source user communities. Section 3.1 describes these applications in more detail.

We found that using these applications with Snowbird was straightforward. Installing each as an agent was no more complex or time-consuming than installing it on a native machine. The only extra step was the creation of an application profile for the migration manager. Our generic application profile proved to be adequate for these four applications, but we recognize that some customization effort may be needed in the case of other applications.

This positive qualitative experience leads to a number of quantitative questions. What performance overheads does Snowbird incur? How much does it improve task completion time in the crunch phase, and crispness of interaction in the cognitive phase? How close is Snowbird's performance to that achievable through optimal partitioning (which is necessarily application-specific)?

The rest of this section describes our answers to these and related questions. Section 3.1 begins by describing the four applications and the benchmarks based on them. Section 3.2 then describes our approach to balancing realism and good experimental control in the cognitive phase, even in the face of unpredictable user behavior. Sections 3.3 and 3.4 describe our experimental setup. Finally, Section 3.5 presents our results.

3.1 Application Benchmarks

To demonstrate Snowbird's broad applicability, we experimented with applications that are representative of the domains of professional 3D animation, amateur video production, and scientific computing, and include both open source as well as commercial closed source products. For each application, we designed a representative benchmark that consists of a crunch and a cognitive phase.

Maya *(Digital Animation, closed source)*
This is a commercial closed source high-end 3D graphics animation package used for character modeling, animation, digital effects, and production-quality rendering [21] . It is an industry standard employed in several major motion pictures, such as *"Lord of the Rings,"* and *"War of the Worlds."* Our benchmark encompasses the typical work involved in completing an animation project. During the 29-minute cognitive phase, a digital character is loaded, a number of intermediate positions are generated by tweaking the character's skeleton and joints, and the animation pattern is scripted. The user periodically visualizes a low-fidelity preview of the animation, which Maya generates using graphics hardware acceleration. The crunch phase consists of rendering a photo-realistic version of each frame in the animation. This is a highly parallelizable CPU-intensive process that does not use graphics hardware. Maya allows the crunch phase to be initiated on a remote compute server, thus providing a case of application-specific partitioning against which to compare Snowbird.

QuakeViz *(Earth Sciences, open source)*
This is an interactive earthquake simulation visualizer, and the only benchmark that accesses a remote dataset. Our benchmark consists of the visualization of a 1.9 GB volumetric dataset depicting 12 seconds of ground motion around a seismic source in the Los Angeles Basin [22]. In our experiments, this dataset is stored on the remote compute server and accessed via NFS. During the crunch phase, QuakeViz mines the dataset to extract ground motion isosurfaces, surfaces inside the volume for which all points are moving in the same direction and at the same speed. The result is a set of triangular meshes depicting isosurfaces at successive time steps. Transformations such as smoothing and normals calculation are applied to the meshes to generate a more visually appealing result. In the cognitive phase, the isosurface meshes are rendered on the screen, and the user studies the seismic reaction by moving forwards or backwards in time and zooming, rotating, or panning the isosurfaces. Our benchmark explores 30 different time-steps during its 23-minute long cognitive phase.

ADF *(Quantum Chemistry, closed source)*
This is a commercial closed-source tool, used by scientists and engineers to model and explore properties of molecular structures [23]. In the ADF benchmark, the crunch

phase consists of performing a geometry optimization of the threonine amino-acid molecule, using the Self-Consistent Field (SCF) calculation method. ADF distributes this intensive calculation to multiple CPUs using the PVM library, providing a second case of application-specific partitioning against which to compare Snowbird. The SCF calculation generates results that are visualized in a subsequent cognitive phase, such as isosurfaces for the Coulomb potential, occupied electron orbitals, and cut-planes of kinetic energy density and other properties. Analysis of these properties through rotation, zooming, or panning, are examples of the actions performed during the 26 minute-long cognitive phase.

Kmenc15 *(Video Editing, open source)*
This is an open-source digital editor for amateur video post production [24]. Users can cut and paste portions of video and audio, and apply artistic effects such as blurring or fadeouts. Kmenc15 can process and produce videos in a variety of standard formats. This benchmark does not exploit graphics hardware acceleration. In the 15-minute cognitive phase of our benchmark, we load a 210 MB video of a group picnic and split it into four episodes. We then edit each episode by cropping and re-arranging portions of the recording and adding filters and effects. The crunch phase converts the four edited episodes to the MPEG-4 format. Kmenc15 converts the four episodes in parallel, exploiting available multiprocessing power.

3.2 Interactive Session Replay

One of the challenges in evaluating interactive performance is the reliable replay of user sessions. To address this problem, we developed *VNC-Redux*, a tool based on the VNC protocol that records and replays interactive user sessions. During the session record phase, VNC-Redux generates a timestamped trace of all user keyboard and mouse input. In addition, before every mouse button click or release, VNC-Redux also records a snapshot of the screen area around the mouse pointer. During replay, the events in the trace are replayed at the appropriate times. To ensure consistent replay, before replaying mouse button events the screen state is compared against the previously captured screen snapshot: if sufficient discrepancies are detected, the session must be reinitialized and replay restarted. Screen synchronization succeeds because VNC, like most other thin client protocols, is non work-conserving and can skip intermediate frame updates on slow connections. This results in the client always reaching a stable and similar (albeit not always identical) state for a given input. Therefore, given an identical initial application state, the entire recorded interactive session can be reliably replayed.

Unfortunately, the simple screen synchronization algorithms used by other replay tools [25] do not work well in high-latency environments. These algorithms typically perform a strict per-pixel comparison with a threshold that specifies the maximum number of pixel mismatches allowed. Something as simple as a mouse button release being delayed by a few milliseconds due to network jitter can cause a 3D object's position to be offset by a small amount. This offset causes the algorithm to detect a large number of pixel mismatches, stalling replay.

To address this problem, we developed an algorithm based on Manhattan distances to estimate image "closeness". For two pixels in the RGB color space, the Manhattan distance is the sum of the absolute differences of the corresponding R, G, and B values. If a pixel's Manhattan distance from the original pixel captured during record is greater than a given distance threshold, it is classified as a pixel mismatch. If the total number of pixel mismatches are greater than a pixel difference threshold, the screenshots being compared are declared to be different. Our experiments confirm that this improved matching algorithm works well over high latency networks.

3.3   Experimental Configurations

We investigate four configurations for executing bimodal applications:

- *Local Execution:* The application executes exclusively in an unvirtualized environment on a typical desktop-class machine. During interactive phases, 3D graphics are rendered using locally available hardware acceleration. This represents the best scenario for cognitive phases, but the worst case for crunch phases.
- *Remote Execution:* The application executes exclusively in an unvirtualized environment on an SMP compute server located behind a WAN link and close to external datasets. This represents the best scenario for crunch phases. As the user interacts with the application over a WAN link using a standard VNC thin client, 3D rendering on the remote server is software based, representing the worst case for the cognitive phases.
- *Partitioned:* The application executes in an unvirtualized environment on the desktop-class machine, but is able to ship intensive computation to the remote compute server in an application-specific manner. This execution mode combines the best of remote and local execution, but is fully dependent on application support and requires multiple installations of the application. Not all of our benchmarks provide this mode of execution.
- *Snowbird:* Snowbird is used to dynamically switch between local and remote execution modes, independently of application support or lack of it. Both the user's desktop and remote compute server run the Snowbird infrastructure: Xen VMM, WANDisk, the hardware-accelerated agent GUI, and the migration manager. All benchmarks are initiated in an agent running at the user's desktop, with the WANDisk state at all hosts initially synchronized. The single generic application profile is used for all of our experiments.

By running the complete benchmark in each of the Remote and Local modes, we obtain two sets of results. First, a measure of what is clearly undesirable: running the crunch phase on an underpowered configuration (Local), and interacting with an application executing behind a WAN link (Remote). By comparing against these results we quantify the benefits of Snowbird in terms of reduced completion time for the crunch phase and improved interactive performance for the cognitive phase.

Conversely, the execution of the crunch and cognitive phases on the Remote and Local configurations, respectively, represents the ideal application partitioning. This provides an upper bound on the performance of any manual partitioning, as each phase is executed in the most advantageous location and no cost for communication overhead or added computational complexity is included. We compare Snowbird's performance against these set of results to quantify its overhead.

Finally, we can compare Snowbird to manual application partitioning for those applications that provide that option. While we expect manual application partitioning to be very close to optimal performance for both application phases, we also expect Snowbird to provide similar crunch and interactive performance.

3.4   Experimental WAN Testbed

Our experimental testbed consists of a user desktop, which is a 3.6 GHz Intel Pentium IV equipped with an ATI Radeon X600 Graphics Processor Unit (GPU), and a compute server, which is a four-way SMP (two dual-threaded cores) 3.6 GHz Intel Xeon. The desktop and server communicate through a NetEm-emulated WAN link with a bandwidth of 100 Mbit/s and RTTs of 33, 66, and 100 ms. These RTTs are conservative underestimates of the values observed between US and Europe, as shown in Table 1. We use a paravirtualized 2.6.12 Linux kernel for the Snowbird experiments and Fedora's 2.6.12 Linux kernel for the non-Snowbird experiments. Both kernels are configured with 512 MB of RAM. Agent VMs are configured as 512 MB SMP hosts, allowing them to fully utilize the computing power of the compute server's multiple cores. Snowbird uses the WAN-optimized HPN-SSH [26] protocol for data transfers.

3.5   Results

This section present the results of our experiments with the four benchmarks introduced in Section 3.1. All benchmarks include a cognitive and a crunch phase. In Maya and Kmenc15, the cognitive phase precedes the crunch phase, whereas in QuakeViz and ADF, the cognitive phase follows the crunch phase. Maya and ADF are the only applications we used that provide a partitioned execution mode. Unfortunately, the partitioned execution mode of ADF badly underperformed in our WAN testbed: with a 33 ms RTT, crunch phase completion time expands to roughly six times as much as in thin client mode. The vendor-supplied partitioning is designed for tightly-connected cluster computing and hence uses a very "chatty" synchronization protocol. This is an example of Snowbird overcoming the negative effects of an application-specific partitioning scheme that was not designed for WANs.

Crunch Phase. Figure 6 shows the total completion time of the crunch phase for the benchmarks and configurations investigated. Each result is the mean of five trials; error bars show the observed standard deviations. For reasons explained earlier, partitioned execution results are not presented for ADF. As Figure 6 shows, Snowbird outperforms local execution by a significant margin. Since the impact of RTT on crunch phase performance is very small, we only show it for Snowbird. The crunch phases of all the benchmarks are CPU intensive and benefit from the increased computational power of the multiprocessor server. QuakeViz also takes advantage of the lower latency and increased bandwidth to its dataset, located on the compute server. More specifically, at 33 ms RTT, Snowbird approximately halves the length of the crunch phase for all applications, and comes within 4 to 28% of the ideal performance of the remote configuration. For Maya, it comes within 4 to 9% of the performance obtained through vendor-supplied partitioning.

Table 2 shows how long it takes the migration manager to detect the transition into the crunch phase, and how long it takes to migrate the agent to the remote compute

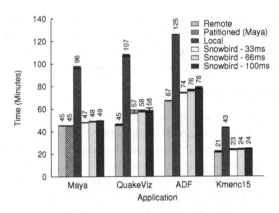

Fig. 6. Crunch Phase Completion Time

Table 2. Crunch Phase Migration Time

	Time (seconds)								
	Latency = 33 ms			Latency = 66 ms			Latency = 100 ms		
Application	Detect	Migrate	Suspend	Detect	Migrate	Suspend	Detect	Migrate	Suspend
Maya	10.8	51.9	3.5	10.8	53.5	4.7	11.5	58.2	5.6
QuakeViz	8.1	49.9	3.5	8.1	49.9	5.0	8.1	55.6	6.3
ADF	12.5	62.0	4.9	11.5	62.0	6.2	13.1	64.9	6.7
Kmenc15	8.1	51.8	4.7	9.1	54.0	5.7	8.4	59.5	6.7

server. Each result in this table is the mean of five trials, and the largest standard deviations observed for Detect, Migrate, and Suspend are 22%, 4%, and 7% of the corresponding means. As Table 2 shows, the maximum time taken by the migration manager is 14 seconds. Even with the worst-case latency of 100 ms, agent migration never takes more than 70 seconds to complete. In all cases, the agent spends less than 1.5 minutes on the user's desktop after it enters a crunch phase, which amounts to less than 5% of the total benchmark time. The table also shows that the maximum time for which an agent would appear to be unresponsive to user input during migration is six seconds or less. This is an order of magnitude smaller than the best value attainable without live migration (512 MB of VM RAM at 100 Mbit/s $\simeq$ 41 s).

Cognitive Phase. Figure 7 shows the Cumulative Distribution Functions (CDFs) of the number of FPS per interaction for each of our four benchmarks under three configurations: local, remote, and Snowbird. Plots to the right indicate better performance than plots to the left. We show results for different network RTTs for the remote and Snowbird configurations. The cognitive phases for QuakeViz and ADF start on the remote compute server soon after the crunch phase terminates. The migration manager detects this transition and migrates back to the user's desktop. On the other hand, the cognitive phase of Maya and Kmenc15 start with the agent already running on the user's desktop. We do not include results for Maya and ADF's partitioned mode, as they are practically identical to local interaction.

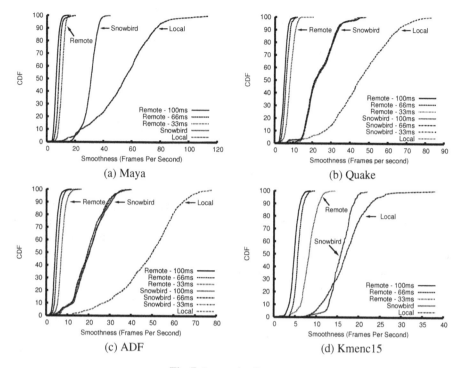

Fig. 7. Interactive Response

Our results show that Snowbird delivers a much better cognitive performance than remote interaction. More importantly, the median number of FPS delivered by Snowbird is above the long-established 20 FPS threshold needed for crisp interactivity [11]. In general, Snowbird's quantitative interactive performance is between 2.7 to 4.8 times better than that delivered by a thin client, with the interactive response in thin client mode rarely exceeding 10 FPS. Even though the agent has to migrate from the compute server to the user's desktop, Snowbird's cognitive performance tends to be independent of the WAN latency. Further, the network latency has a negligible impact on both the time taken before the decision to migrate is made and the time required to migrate the agent; we omit the migration time results for cognitive phases as they are very similar to those in Table 2.

The results also show that the FPS delivered by Snowbird is not as high as in unvirtualized local interaction. Local execution experiments delivered anywhere between 1.1 to 2.6 times more FPS in the median case. Nevertheless, once the agent migrates to the local host, in our subjective experience, the user experience delivered by Snowbird is indistinguishable from that of the native configuration for all of the benchmarks.

Summary. Our results confirm that Snowbird offers significant benefits for bimodal applications. Without any application modifications, relinking, or binary rewriting, such applications are able to improve crunch performance through remote infrastructure. This improvement is achieved without compromising cognitive performance. Even when an application vendor supplies a partitioned mode of operation for cluster computing, Snowbird is able to offer comparable performance (within 4%), and in some cases greatly exceed its benefit over WANs.

4   Implementation Limitations and Future Extensions

The Snowbird prototype has certain limitations in functionality and performance. Some of these limitations arise from our goal of rapidly creating an experimental prototype rather than a robust, complete and efficient product. Other limitations have deeper roots in the design of Snowbird, and will therefore require more effort to overcome.

One limitation is that parallel Snowbird applications execute in a single SMP virtual machine. While the current trend of aggressively scaling processors to a hundred or more cores favors our design, some applications might be inherently designed to use multiple machines in a large cluster. Extending Snowbird to those applications would require new mechanisms such as "gang VM migration" that treat a group of VMs as a unit. We anticipate that these mechanisms will be conceptually simple, but their implementation may involve nontrivial complexity.

A second limitation arises from our use of hardware virtualization. At startup, an application might configure itself to take advantage of vendor-specific extensions to the x86 instructions set architecture, such as Intel's SSE or AMD's 3DNow!. Upon migration to different hardware, the application will crash when it attempts to execute an unsupported instruction. One possible solution is to use dynamic binary rewriting. Another approach is to extend Snowbird so that it never attempts migration to an incompatible destination.

A third limitation is that Snowbird assumes a distinct separation of crunch and cognitive phases. Applications that consistently overlap these phases will not benefit from Snowbird. More generally, Snowbird is beneficial only when its agility of adaptation exceeds the rate of change of application behavior, and when remote execution provides sufficient improvement to overcome the cost of migration. Figure 8 illustrates this tradeoff for crunch phases. The horizontal axis shows migration time in minutes, which depends on the quality of the Snowbird implementation. This measure of system agility includes both the swiftness with which migration can be triggered, and the efficiency with which it can be completed. The vertical axis shows the crunch speedup when executing remotely, which depends on the application and the available remote resources. Each curve plots the relation $speedup = C/(C - migration\_time)$ for three hypothetical applications, where C is the crunch phase completion time when executing locally. Above each curve, Snowbird is beneficial; the expected performance gain exceeds the migration cost. Below each curve, Snowbird becomes harmful, as its migration cost eclipses any potential performance gains.

The simple model shown Figure 8 illustrates how improving migration time broadens the set of applications for which Snowbird is applicable. For a given speedup, workloads with smaller crunch time benefit as migration time decreases. And for a given crunch time, swifter migration reduces the constraints on the quality of the remote resources needed. Conversely, high migration times limit the applicability of Snowbird to applications with long crunch phases, or to remote platforms capable of yielding very

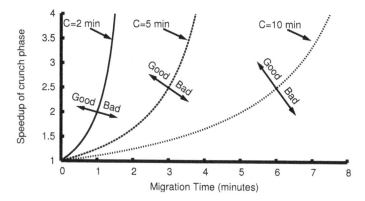

Fig. 8. When Is Snowbird Useful?

high speedups. In the current prototype, detection and change of modality occur in roughly 10 seconds, while the migration that follows typically takes about 60 seconds plus lazy WANDisk chunk fetches. Mapping these values to Figure 8 indicates that crunch phases below ten minutes and speedups below a factor 2 will probably not show benefits with the current prototype.

It should be noted that a complementary attribute of agility is *stability*, which characterizes the ability of the implementation to avoid frivolous migrations that may lead to thrashing. It is well known from control theory that agility and stability are two sides of the same coin, and have to be considered together in the design of an adaptive system. Improvements to Snowbird's agility may necessitate more sophisticated mechanisms for stability.

5   Related Work

To the best of our knowledge, Snowbird is the first system that exploits VM technology for the purpose of simplifying the development and deployment of bimodal applications. Closest in spirit to Snowbird is the large body of process migration research [9,12,27,28]. Although extensively investigated for over two decades, no operating system in widespread use today supports process migration as a standard facility. We conjecture that this is because process migration is a brittle abstraction: a typical implementation involves so many external interfaces that it is easily rendered incompatible by a modest change. Snowbird implements a more resilient abstraction because the code and state implementing these interfaces is part of the OS that is transported with the application.

Language-based code mobility is another well-explored approach to moving computation. Relevant examples of work in this genre are Emerald [29] and one.world [30]. Java's remote method invocation framework has made this approach feasible and relevant to a range of computing environments. Snowbird's language-independent approach has the advantage of preserving substantial investments in legacy libraries, tool chains, and applications. It is also flexible with respect to code structure: an application can be a single monolithic process, or it can be a tool chain with scripts that glue the chain together. The crunch phase can have a finer structure, such as the use of multiple large datasets each of which is located at a different Internet site.

Snowbird can function as an adjunct to Grid computing middleware toolkits such as Globus [31] and Condor [32], that are widely used by the scientific computing community today. Snowbird complements the functionality provided by these toolkits by transforming a single monolithic application into an entity that can be easily migrated under toolkit control. More recently, the use of VMs has also been advocated for the Grid [14,33], as enablers of simpler security and manageability abstractions.

Researchers have also developed toolkits for distributed visualization of large remote datasets. Examples include Dv [34], Visapult [2], SciRun [4], and Cactus [3]. Unlike Snowbird, these tools require applications to be written to a particular interface and are therefore useful only when application source code is available.

From a broader perspective, Snowbird was inspired by the substantial body of recent work on applying VM technology to a wide range of systems problems, including security [35], mobile computing [6,36], and software maintenance [7]. Since the first technical report to describe our work [37], others have examined related techniques. Sandpiper [38] is a migration manager for cluster area networks that does not consider interaction-triggered relocations. Similar to VMGL, Blink [39] virtualizes GL-based 3D-rendering, but is specific to Xen-paravirtualized Linux. Bradford et al. [40] provide a virtual disk relocation scheme for the wide area with a full-prefetch policy that adds several minutes of downtime during migration.

6   Conclusion

A growing number of bimodal applications alternate between resource-intensive crunch phases and intensely interactive cognitive phases. The crunch phase may be CPU-intensive, memory-intensive, data-intensive, or some combination of all three. The cognitive phase must avoid sluggish or jerky responses in order to ensure low user distraction. This demands low end-to-end latency and may also require the use of local graphics acceleration hardware.

Snowbird simplifies the creation of bimodal applications by masking the distributed systems complexity of resource management, synchronization, and data consistency. It presents the simple programming abstraction of a VM to the developer, and assumes full responsibility for seamlessly migrating this VM to the best execution site. In experiments that include closed-source commercial applications, Snowbird offers crisp interactive performance that is superior to the best achievable through remote execution. At the same time, it is able to bring remote resources to bear on crunch phase performance. Without user or developer intervention, Snowbird is able to promptly detect application transitions between crunch and cognitive phases, and to automatically migrate the application to the most appropriate execution site.

An alternative viewpoint is to regard Snowbird as a tool that enables seamless transitions between the thin and thick client modes of execution. Thin clients are favored due to their ability to harness remote resources, while thick clients provide an unparalleled user experience during highly interactive tasks. By transparently morphing an application between the thick and thin client modes of execution, Snowbird gives a user the best of both worlds.

In closing, Snowbird's extensive use of multiple machines to meet the needs of a single user reflects an evolutionary trend that began with timesharing (fraction of a machine per user) and continued through personal computing (single machine per user) and client-server computing (local machine plus remote machines in fixed roles). Snowbird proposes a new step in this evolution by seamlessly and transparently using local and remote machines in flexible roles.

Acknowledgments

We thank Rajesh Balan for his involvement with earlier versions of this work. We also extend our gratitude to Nilton Bila, Angela Demke Brown, Debabrata Dash, Jan Harkes, Lionel Litty, Jing Su, Adin Scanell, and Alex Varshavsky for their feedback on early versions of this paper. We thank Beatriz Irigoyen for her help with ADF, Julio Lopez for his help with QuakeViz, Brian Paul for his help with Chromium, and Karan Singh for his help with Maya. Finally, we acknowledge the many and useful suggestions from the anonymous reviewers of this paper.

This research was supported by the National Science Foundation (NSF) under grant number CNS-0509004, the National Science and Engineering Research Council (NSERC) of Canada under grant number 261545-3 and a Canada Graduate Scholarship, by the Canadian Foundation for Innovation (CFI), and the Ontario Innovation Trust (OIT) under grant number 7739. Any opinions, findings, conclusions or recommendations expressed in this material are those of the authors and do not necessarily reflect the views of the NSF, NSERC, CFI, OIT, Carnegie Mellon University, or the University of Toronto. All unidentified trademarks mentioned in the paper are properties of their respective owners.

References

1. Afework, A., Beynon, M.D., Bustamante, F., Demarzo, A., Ferreira, R., Miller, R., Silberman, M., Saltz, J., Sussman, A., Tsang, H.: Digital Dynamic Telepathology - The Virtual Microscope. In: Proc. American Medical Informatics Association (AMIA) Annual Fall Symposium, Lake Buena Vista, FL (November 1998)
2. Bethel, W.: Visapult: A Prototype Remote and Distributed Visualization Application and Framework. In: Proc. SIGGRAPH Annual Conference, New Orleans, LA (July 2000)
3. Goodale, T., Allen, G., Lanfermann, G., Masso, J., Radke, T., Seidel, E., Shalf, J.: The Cactus Framework and Toolkit: Design and Applications. In: Palma, J.M.L.M., Sousa, A.A., Dongarra, J.J., Hernández, V. (eds.) VECPAR 2002. LNCS, vol. 2565, Springer, Heidelberg (2003)
4. Parker, S., Johnson, C.: SCIRun: A Scientific Programming Environment for Computational Steering. In: Proc. ACM/IEEE Supercomputing, San Diego, CA, Dec 1995, IEEE Computer Society Press, Los Alamitos (1995)
5. National Laboratory for Applied Network Research (NLANR): RTT And Loss Measurements, http://watt.nlanr.net/active/maps/ampmap_active.php
6. Satyanarayanan, M., Kozuch, M.A., Helfrich, C.J., O'Hallaron, D.R.: Towards Seamless Mobility on Pervasive Hardware. Pervasive and Mobile Computing 1(2), 157–189 (2005)

7. Sapuntzakis, C.P., Chandra, R., Pfaff, B., Chow, J., Lam, M.S., Rosenblum, M.: Optimizing the Migration of Virtual Computers. In: OSDI 2002. Proc. 5th USENIX Symposium on Operating Systems Design and Implementation, Boston, MA (December 2002)
8. Clark, C., Fraser, K., Hand, S., Hansen, J.G., Jul, E., Limpach, C., Pratt, I., Warfield, A.: Live Migration of Virtual Machines. In: NSDI 2005. Proc. 2nd Symposium on Networked Systems Design and Implementation, Boston, MA (May 2005)
9. Barak, A., Guday, S., Wheeler, R.G.: The MOSIX Distributed Operating System. LNCS, vol. 672. Springer, Heidelberg (1993)
10. Richardson, T., Stafford-Fraser, Q., Wood, K.R., Hopper, A.: Virtual Network Computing. IEEE Internet Computing 2(1) (January/February 1998)
11. Airey, J.M., Rohlf, J.H., Brooks, F.P.J.: Towards Image Realism with Interactive Update Rates in Complex Virtual Building Environments. ACM SIGGRAPH Computer Graphics 24(2), 41–50 (1990)
12. Powell, M.L., Miller, B.P.: Process Migration in DEMOS/MP. In: SOSP 1983. Proc. 9th ACM Symposium on Operating Systems Principles, Bretton Woods, NH (October 1983)
13. Lagar-Cavilla, H.A., Tolia, N., Satyanarayanan, M., de Lara, E.: VMM-Independent Graphics Acceleration. In: VEE. Proc. 3rd Conference on Virtual Execution Environments, San Diego, CA (June 2007)
14. Sundararaj, A.I., Dinda, P.A.: Towards Virtual Networks for Virtual Machine Grid Computing. In: Proc. 3rd Virtual Machine Research and Technology Symposium, San Jose, CA, pp. 177–190 (May 2004)
15. Buck, I., Humphreys, G., Hanrahan, P.: Tracking Graphics State for Networked Rendering. In: Proc. ACM SIGGRAPH/EUROGRAPHICS Workshop on Graphics Hardware, Interlaken, Switzerland, pp. 87–95. ACM Press, New York (2000)
16. VMware, http://www.vmware.com/pdf/ws6_manual.pdf
17. Warfield, A., Ross, R., Fraser, K., Limpach, C., Hand, S.: Parallax: Managing Storage for a Million Machines. In: HotOS. Proc. 10th Workshop on Hot Topics in Operating Systems, Santa Fe, NM (June 2005)
18. Satyanarayanan, M.: The Evolution of Coda. ACM Transactions on Computer Systems 20(2) (May 2002)
19. Muthitacharoen, A., Morris, R., Gil, T., Chen, B.: Ivy: A Read/Write Peer-to-peer File System. In: OSDI 2002. Proc. 5th USENIX Symposium on Operating Systems Design and Implementation, Boston, MA (December 2002)
20. Tridgell, A., Mackerras, P.: The rsync Algorithm. Technical Report TR-CS-96-05, Computer Science, Australian National University, Canberra, Australia (1996)
21. Maya, http://www.autodesk.com/maya
22. Akcelik, V., Bielak, J., Biros, G., Epanomeritakis, I., Fernandez, A., Ghattas, O., Kim, E.J., Lopez, J., O'Hallaron, D., Tu, T., Urbanic, J.: High Resolution Forward and Inverse Earthquake Modeling on Terasacale Computers. In: Proc. ACM/IEEE Supercomputing, Phoenix, AZ, IEEE Computer Society Press, Los Alamitos (2003)
23. te Velde, G., Bickelhaupt, F.M., Baerends, E.J., Guerra, C.F., van Gisbergen, S.J.A., Snijders, J.G., Ziegler, T.: Chemistry with ADF. Computational Chemistry 22(9), 931–967 (2001)
24. Kmenc15, http://kmenc15.sourceforge.net/
25. Zeldovich, N., Chandra, R.: Interactive Performance Measurement with VNCPlay. In: Proc. USENIX Annual Technical Conference, FREENIX Track, Anaheim, CA (April 2005)
26. Rapier, C., Stevens, M.: High Performance SSH/SCP - HPN-SSH, http://www.psc.edu/networking/projects/hpn-ssh/
27. Douglis, F., Ousterhout, J.: Transparent Process Migration: Design Alternatives and the Sprite Implementation. Software Practice and Experience 21(8) (August 1991)
28. Milojičić, D.S., Douglis, F., Paindaveine, Y., Wheeler, R., Zhou, S.: Process Migration. ACM Computing Surveys 32(3) (September 2000)

29. Jul, E., Levy, H., Hutchinson, N., Black, A.: Fine-grained Mobility in the Emerald System. ACM Transactions on Computer Systems 6(1) (February 1988)
30. Grimm, R., Davis, J., Lemar, E., Macbeth, A., Swanson, S., Anderson, T., Bershad, B., Borriello, G., Gribble, S., Wetherall, D.: System Support for Pervasive Applications. ACM Transactions on Computer Systems 22(4) (November 2004)
31. Foster, I., Kesselman, C.: Globus: A Metacomputing Infrastructure Toolkit. Journal of Supercomputer Applications and High Performance Computing 11(2) (June 1997)
32. Thain, D., Tannenbaum, T., Livny, M.: Distributed Computing in Practice: The Condor Experience. Concurrency and Computation: Practice and Experience 17 (February-April 2005)
33. Figueiredo, R.J., Dinda, P.A., Fortes, J.A.B.: A Case For Grid Computing On Virtual Machines. In: ICDCS. Proc. 23rd International Conference on Distributed Computing Systems, Providence, RI (May 2003)
34. López, J., O'Hallaron, D.: Evaluation of a Resource Selection Mechanism for Complex Network Services. In: HPDC. Proc. IEEE International Symposium on High-Performance Distributed Computing, San Francisco, CA (August 2001)
35. Dunlap, G.W., King, S.T., Cinar, S., Basrai, M.A., Chen, P.M.: ReVirt: Enabling Intrusion Analysis Through Virtual-machine Logging and Replay. In: OSDI 2002. Proc. 5th USENIX Symposium on Operating Systems Design and Implementation, Boston, MA (December 2002)
36. Kozuch, M., Satyanarayanan, M.: Internet Suspend/Resume. In: Proc. 4th IEEE Workshop on Mobile Computing Systems and Applications, Callicoon, NY, IEEE Computer Society Press, Los Alamitos (2002)
37. Lagar-Cavilla, H.A., Tolia, N., Balan, R., de Lara, E., Satyanarayanan, M., O'Hallaron, D.: Dimorphic Computing. Technical Report CMU-CS-06-123, Carnegie Mellon University (April 2006)
38. Wood, T., Shenoy, P., Venkataramani, A., Yousif, M.: Black-box and Gray-box Strategies for Virtual Machine Migration. In: NSDI 2007. Proc. 4th Symposium on Networked Systems Design and Implementation, Cambridge, MA (April 2007)
39. Hansen, J.G.: Blink: Advanced Display Multiplexing for Virtualized Applications. In: NOSSDAV. Proc. 17th International Workshop on Network and Operating Systems Support for Digital Audio and Video, Urbana-Champaign, IL (June 2007)
40. Bradford, R., Kotsovinos, E., Feldmann, A., Schiöberg, H.: Live Wide-Area Migration of Virtual Machines including Local Persistent State. In: VEE. Proc. 3rd Conference on Virtual Execution Environments, San Diego, CA (June 2007)

Garbage Collecting the Grid:
A Complete DGC for Activities

Denis Caromel, Guillaume Chazarain, and Ludovic Henrio

INRIA Sophia Antipolis, CNRS - I3S - Univ. Nice Sophia Antipolis
BP 93, 06902 Sophia Antipolis Cedex - France
First.Last@inria.fr

Abstract. Grids are becoming more and more dynamic, running parallel applications on large scale and heterogeneous resources. Explicitly
stopping a whole distributed application is becoming increasingly difficult. In that context, there is a strong need to free resources a soon as
they become useless, leading to automatic termination, using distributed
garbage collecting techniques. We propose in this paper a new distributed
garbage collector for active objects taking into account cycles but with
a complexity similar to the distributed garbage collector of Java/RMI.
The algorithm is based on a different approach to collect acyclic and
cyclic garbage. On one hand, acyclic garbage is collected by knowing the
immediate referencers of an active object and detecting the lack of these
referencers. This behavior with respect to acyclic garbage is common
to the distributed garbage collector of RMI. On the other hand, cyclic
garbage is detected by considering the recursive closure of all the referencers of an active object and finding cycles of active objects waiting
for requests. These cycles are found by letting idle active objects make a
consensus on a common final activity. The algorithm is fully distributed
and has been implemented with no modifications to the local garbage
collector. Benchmarks have shown the scalability of the algorithm in a
grid context.

Keywords: distributed garbage collection, cycle detection, grid computing.

1 Introduction

Computer grids can be used to deploy complex and long running applications
made of distributed activities. To optimize the resource usage of the global application, it is important to free resources held by idle activities as soon as possible.

When these grid applications are written in a high level language such as Java,
the underlying platform exposes a local garbage collector to simplify the memory
management. The automatic garbage collection mechanism has been adapted to
objects accessible over a network in the form of distributed garbage collectors,
abbreviated DGC. Currently, the most used DGC implementation seems to be
the one of RMI [1,2]. However, this DGC is unable to collect distributed cycles
of garbage since it is based on a reference listing [3] approach. Recent cyclic

R. Cerqueira and R.H. Campbell (Eds.): Middleware 2007, LNCS 4834, pp. 164–183, 2007.
© IFIP International Federation for Information Processing 2007

distributed garbage collector [4] typically suffers from a large space complexity, because each process has a view of the whole distributed system.

This paper presents a DGC geared towards the collection of distributed activities which is able to collect both acyclic and cyclic garbage, typically referred to as a complete DGC. Activities are represented by the active object [5] model which provides asynchronous method calls to the object model, thus is well suited to grid applications. More precisely, active objects are remotely accessible objects with their own thread of activity and requests queue.

As they attempt to find cycles of active objects, complete DGC algorithms need a view of the reference graph in order to find cycles in it.

The contributions of this paper consist of:

- a method to build the reference graph between activities without modifying the local garbage collector,
- the identification of cycles of idle activities as cyclic garbage instead of the more common unreachable strongly connected component,
- a DGC algorithm using this characterization of cyclic garbage and
- experimental results of an implementation of this DGC algorithm.

The rest of the paper is organized as follows: section 2 describes the construction of the reference graph which provides the necessary input for the DGC algorithm. How the algorithm identifies garbage (both acyclic and cyclic) based on this reference graph is described in section 3 while section 4 discusses some implementation issues as well as the complexity of the algorithm. Experiments are described in section 5. Finally, section 6 discusses the related work, and some future work ends the paper.

2   The Reference Graph

A crucial aspect of the garbage collection of activities is determining which other activities still hold references to the activity currently being examined and may activate it later on. The references between different activities are in fact transitive references, since there can be a chain of local pointers between the active object and the remote reference. This is identical to the graph summarization technique in [4].

This work is built upon the active object model which permits some assumptions, but these assumptions are not fundamental to the DGC algorithm. One of these assumptions is the *no-sharing property* described below, and we will describe in the discussion in Section 4.1 an approach to relax this requirement.

2.1   The No-Sharing Property

As the distribution of activities on the grid is often unknown beforehand, activities should typically not share (by aliasing) references to the same passive object (standard object). Since references to other activities are represented by passive objects called stubs, such stubs of remote objects are not shared either.

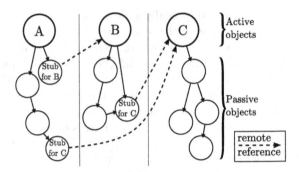

Fig. 1. The no-sharing property: no passive objects are referenced by more than one active object

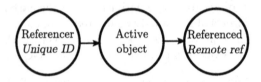

Fig. 2. Remote references are needed for referenced active objects, but only a unique ID is needed to track referencers

This rule[1], illustrated in Figure 1, is called the *no-sharing property*. With this property, once we know that a given active object references a given stub, we can assume that this stub will always be exclusively referenced by this same active object. This property allows, as we will see in the next section, to build the reference graph without modifying the local garbage collector.

2.2   Building the Reference Graph

An active object maintains two kinds of relationship with other active objects. There are referencers and referenced active objects. The connectivity require-ments for these two kinds of active objects are different. On one hand, the DGC algorithm will try to contact referenced active objects, so an access to the remote references used by the application is needed. On the other hand, referencers only need to be identified by a unique ID, as the DGC algorithm will never try to directly contact them. Concretely, as seen in Figure 2, the DGC algorithm will only try to contact referenced active objects and will just store the ID of the active objects contacting it. This is an important property of the algorithm in that it does not require more connectivity than the deployed application. This

---

[1] Practically speaking, the only way to defeat this rule is to put a remote reference in some static variable since communications between local or remote active objects always go through a serialization and deserialization step, so no sharing is possible with only these communications.

aspect is particularly useful in grid contexts where the deployment has to deal with connectivity limitations like firewalls and NATs.

The proposed reference graph can be built transparently on top of a local garbage collector. The graph is constructed by hooking into the deserialization of stubs, and by remembering which local active object A (i.e. the recipient of the message) triggered the deserialization, then A can add the stub target B to its list of referenced active objects. When A subsequently sends a DGC message to B, B will add A to the list of its referencers.

Iterating this process of adding edges between active objects builds the reference graph. The reference graph is represented for each active object instance by the list of its remote references. However, a local active object instance may reference several stubs representing the same remote active object. As a consequence, it is crucial to keep track of all of these stubs, as only the disappearing of all of them indicates that an edge should be removed in the reference graph. Instead of independently tracking these stubs, a more efficient way is to add a common tag (a reference to a dummy object) in every stub instance for the same remote object owned by the same local active object, and then the DGC just has to keep a weak reference to this tag in order to detect the local garbage collection of all of these stubs.

3 The Distributed Garbage Collector Algorithm

The distributed garbage collector algorithm relies on the following *Garbage* property to discriminate garbage activities:

$$\forall x, Garbage(x) \Leftrightarrow (\forall y, y \rightarrow^* x \Rightarrow Idle(y)) \tag{1}$$

An active object (x) is said to be garbage if and only if the reflexive transitive closure of its referencers (y) is idle, the active object x is included in the reflexive transitive closure of its referencers. The concept of local idleness $(Idle(x))$ for an active object must be provided by the middleware.

The *Garbage* property is verified using two different approaches for acyclic and cyclic garbage. On one hand, acyclic garbage is found by ensuring that the set of the direct referencers of an active object is empty, this satisfies the *Garbage* property. On the other hand, cyclic garbage is found by letting an active object make a consensus on a "final activity clock" by the reflexive transitive closure of its referencers.

3.1 Detecting Acyclic Garbage Using a Heartbeat

To detect acyclic garbage we request that referencers of an activity periodically send a *DGC message* to the referenced activity in a heartbeat fashion. Its frequency, thereafter referred to as *TTB* for TimeToBeat, is a constant known by all participating active objects in the distributed system. Therefore, increasing TTB lowers the overhead of the DGC but makes it slower to reclaim garbage.

If an active object receives no DGC messages for a certain amount of time, it considers itself as garbage, and is thus destroyed. This amount of time is called *TTA* for TimeToAlone. This parameter designates the delay after which an active object considers it must have received a DGC message from all of its referencers.

When a local active object deserializes a reference to a remote active object, it makes sure that at least one DGC message is sent to this remote active object at the next broadcast. In other words, even if the reference is quickly garbage collected, the algorithm remembers that one DGC message must be sent anyway. This ensures that a reference to a remote active object that would be quickly exchanged between two other active objects receives DGC messages to keep it alive.

The TTA value should satisfy the formula $TTA > 2 * TTB + MaxComm$ with $MaxComm$ being an upper bound on the communication time between active objects. This formula ensures that referencers always get a chance to send a DGC message before declaring that no messages were received. The worst case is an active object A giving just before its broadcast a reference B to another active object C that has just broadcasted. If the B stub on A is collected just after giving it to C, then C will have to wait $2 * TTB + Comm$ without receiving DGC messages from A or C, $Comm$ being the time to send the reference.

3.2   Detecting Cyclic Garbage by Making a Consensus

The very high level view of our algorithm to find distributed cyclic garbage is to traverse the recursive closure of an active object's referencers in order to find cycles of idle activities. This traversal checks at each step that the currently visited active object is idle. An active object may not be able to directly contact its referencers (firewall, NAT), hence the traversal is done in the opposite direction, using the periodic DGC messages described in the previous section. The outcome of the traversal is not affected by this restriction on the direction as a traversal in the correct direction is simulated over the traversal in the opposite direction.

This traversal builds a reverse spanning tree over the reference graph. This means that every active object except the originator (maker of the consensus)

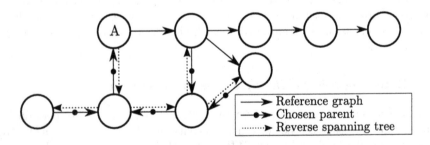

Fig. 3. A reference graph and an associated reverse spanning tree: the reverse spanning tree is used by the originator to make a consensus on its "final activity clock"

promotes a single of its referenced active objects as its parent. The reverse spanning tree is represented by active objects knowing their parent instead of their children because of the connectivity restrictions. Figure 3 shows a reference graph and a possible reverse spanning tree rooted at A over this graph. This tree permits to explore the recursive closure of A's referencers even if it contains cycles.

Activity Clock. The traversal ensures that all visited active objects are idle. As this is obviously a source of races, for each active object the local check is more thorough.

The cyclic garbage collector algorithm requires every active object to maintain a *named* Lamport logical clock [6], which is used to determine which activity was the last active. The clock is *named* in the sense that the ID of the active object incrementing the clock is embedded in the clock. This active object is called the owner of the activity clock. This additional information provides a total ordering of the named clocks by letting the comparison function of two activity clocks first compare the clock values and then the active object IDs if the clock values are identical.

The essence of using a Lamport logical clock is that if an active object receives a DGC message with a clock which is more recent than its own view of the clock, it updates its clock accordingly. When an active object A increments the activity clock $ID : Value$, it turns it into $A : Value + 1$. A garbage cycle is detected by an active object A when the following conditions are met:

– the recursive closure of A's referencers have a common activity clock called *final activity clock* and
– A is the owner of this final activity clock and is idle.

In order to check that every recursive referencer of an active object has the same activity clock, we construct a reverse spanning tree among the active objects having the same activity clock. If all the recursive referencers agree on the activity clock, then the spanning tree will span all the referencers; which will finally agree on the garbage collection: the consensus will be transmitted over a tree. If some referencers have a different activity clock, then at least one of these referencers references an active object of the spanning tree, and this referenced active object will not agree on the consensus for the final activity clock: no active object is garbage collected.

The activity clock is used to regulate the concurrent execution of the distributed garbage collection and the application which may modify the reference graph through the passing of objects as parameters or return values. The relevant occasions when the activity clock is incremented will be detailed after.

DGC Messages and Responses. For active objects to agree on a final activity clock, all active objects first need to be notified of the new activity clock. To this end, an active object sends DGC messages containing the activity clock to all the active objects it references. The agreement on a consensus is detected by interpreting the DGC responses active objects send upon reception of a DGC message. The precise traversal is discussed in more detail below.

DGC messages flow from the referencers to the referenced active objects in order to advertise their view of the final activity clock while DGC responses flow in the opposite direction (on the same connection) to propagate the activity clock candidate for a consensus. DGC messages also contain the acceptance (or not) of the consensus candidate received in the previous DGC response. Between two active objects DGC messages and responses cannot race with application messages as they are sent over the same FIFO connection.

The reference graph traversal is not a traditional traversal where messages are forwarded as soon as they are received. On the contrary, DGC messages are sent every TTB; DGC responses are sent only in response to DGC messages. The effect is that there are no DGC phases, it is a continuous process.

The content of a DGC message is:

- **sender ID:** used to detect new referencers and to know which DGC response's final activity clock the consensus boolean refers to,
- **final activity clock:** to propagate the final activity clock throughout the reference graph,
- **consensus:** a boolean indicating the acceptance of the final activity clock received in the previous response; this is actually in response to the previous DGC response.

The consensus boolean in a DGC message is set according to these rules:

- **if the destination is the parent:** the conjunction of the consensus values of the sender's direct referencers and the local agreement of the sender,
- **if the sender has a parent which is not the destination:** whether the sender locally agrees with the final activity clock (only the local agreement).

The content of a DGC response is:

- **final activity clock consensus candidate:** the consensus attempt by the traversal,
- **has parent:** boolean indicating if the referenced active object can be a parent, this ensures that the reverse spanning tree is rooted at the originator.

The reverse spanning tree is constructed by having every active object promote one of its referenced active objects as its parent. The reverse spanning tree will conduct the consensus from the active objects to the originator. The *hasparent* boolean in the DGC response checks if the sending active object has chosen a parent or is itself the consensus originator. This ensures that the chosen parent leads to the originator.

An active object updates its view of the final activity clock in the graph using its own activity clock and the DGC messages. It also stores the last DGC message of its referencers in order to compute the consensus boolean value.

The activity clock contained in the DGC response is never used to update an active object's clock, only to try to build a consensus. For example, in Figure 4, if the cycle C1 is busy it will propagate activity clocks in the cycle C2, but the latter will never propagate activity clocks in the cycle C1. As references are oriented, C2 must not prevent C1 from being garbage collected.

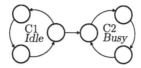

Fig. 4. Activity clocks are not propagated in DGC responses, otherwise C2 would prevent C1 from being garbage collected until C2 is garbage too

Making a Consensus. An idle active object decides that a consensus has been made when all of its referencers sent it a DGC message with the consensus boolean set for its own final activity clock. This is also the current final activity clock of the originator, and the one it sent in the previous DGC responses. The active object detecting the garbage cycle is the root of the reverse spanning tree. Let us see what this means for an active object to be in this state:

- it has propagated its final activity clock in a part (or the whole) of the recursive closure of its referenced active objects,
- the recursive closure of its referencers have all accepted this final activity clock.

An active object needs to propagate its final activity clock only in the part of its referenced active objects that belongs to the same cycle as itself, hence not necessarily all of its referenced active objects.

When is the activity clock incremented. The activity clock is incremented on these three occasions:

Active object becoming idle. This is the primary reason for the existence of the clock. During a traversal, active objects could alternate between being idle and busy (i.e. an active object receives and starts serving requests before the traversal completes) so the outcome of the traversal would be inconsistent. In this case, with the clock, active objects can be idle but still disagree on the proposed final activity clock.

Loss of a referencer. According to the rules for detecting garbage cycles, the active object that breaks the cycle is the owner of the final activity clock, provided that it is idle. As a consequence, we have to enforce that the owner of the final activity clock be in the recursive closure of referencers.

Consequently when an active object detects that one of its referencers has disappeared (i.e. it has not received DGC messages from this referencer in a TTA period), it must increment its activity clock. This is also the reason why active objects track the list of their referencers IDs.

Therefore, when an active object disappears, its referenced active objects increment their activity clocks, so that cycles without external referencers cannot agree upon an unowned activity clock. The latter could result in a cycle where all active objects have a common final activity clock, but as the owner of this final activity clock is not in the cycle, it cannot break the cycle.

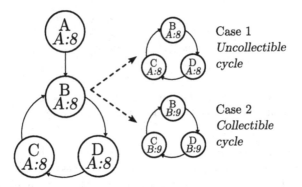

Fig. 5. The loss of a referencer must be detected to avoid uncollectible cycles

In Figure 5, the active object A references a cycle and propagated its final activity clock in this cycle. When A terminates the cycle should not keep its final activity clock that belongs to nobody in the cycle (Case 1). Instead B should notice that it lost a referencer (A) and then should increment its activity clock to obtain B:9 (Case 2).

Loss of a referenced. The reverse spanning tree built over the active object references is built by, for each activity, choosing a single referenced active object and considering it as its parent. An active object tells to its referenced active objects if its activity clock is the same as the referenced's one, but will tell to its parent if its referencers and itself agree on the final activity clock. This simulates a graph traversal with the references other than the parent being the nodes already visited, in order to avoid cyclic dependencies. To justify this traversal, let

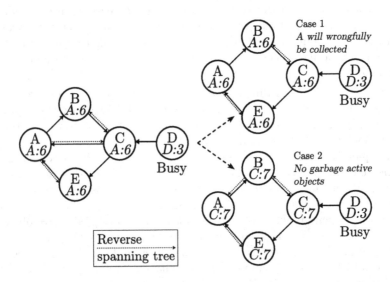

Fig. 6. The loss of a referenced must be detected to avoid collecting live cycles

us suppose instead that an active object would propagate an agreement on a final activity clock only if it received such an agreement from all of its referencers, in this case a consensus would never be reached in cycles.

Therefore, when an active object loses a reference, it may actually lose its parent. And without its parent, an active object will have nobody to tell if its referencers disagree about the final activity clock. In Figure 6, only D is busy, so it prevents the cycle from being garbage collected. C's parent in the reverse spanning tree is A, so C will tell to A that the consensus is rejected, but will not tell it to E as it is not its parent. If the reference edge from C to A disappears, nobody will say to A that the consensus is rejected, and the cycle will wrongfully be garbage collected. The solution is to increment the activity clock when a reference disappears.

The active object A will nevertheless detect the loss of a referencer (C), but detecting the loss of a referenced ensures that C does not have a final activity clock from someone else and no parent, a condition that would break the reverse spanning tree.

3.3   Algorithms

Here we show a pseudo-code version of the four DGC algorithms for: the recursive agreement of the referencers, the broadcasting every TTB, the reception of a DGC message and the reception of a DGC response. For clarity, they have been simplified by omitting the following details: the management of referencers and referenced active objects, the activity clock incrementation in the three cases seen in Section 3.2, and the error handling.

Algorithm 1. $referencers.agree(clock)$: Recursive agreement on $clock$?

---

for all $referencer$ **in** $referencers$ **do**
    if $referencer.clock \neq clock$ **or** $referencer.consensus = $ **false then**
        return false
return true

Algorithm 2. Every TTB on every active object AO

---

if $AO.isIdle()$ **then**
    if $now() - AO.lastMessageTimestamp > TTA$ **then**
        $AO.terminate()$ // acyclic garbage
    if $AO.clock.owner = AO$ **and** $AO.referencers.agree(AO.clock)$ **then**
        $AO.terminate()$ // cyclic garbage
for all $dest$ **in** $AO.referenced$ **do**
    $consensus \leftarrow AO.isIdle()$ **and** $dest.lastResponse.clock = AO.clock$ **and**
        $(AO.clock.owner = AO$ **or** $AO.parent \neq$ **nil) and**
        $(AO.parent \neq dest$ **or** $AO.referencers.agree(AO.clock))$
    $dest.sendMessage(AO.id, consensus, AO.clock)$

Algorithm 3. Reception of a DGC *message* by active object AO

---

if *message.clock* > *AO.clock* then
    $AO.clock \leftarrow message.clock$
    $AO.parent \leftarrow$ **nil**
$AO.referencers[message.sender].clock \leftarrow message.clock$
$AO.referencers[message.sender].consensus \leftarrow message.consensus$
$AO.lastMessageTimestamp \leftarrow now()$
$hasParent \leftarrow AO.parent \neq$ **nil** or $AO.clock.owner = AO$
return $response(AO.clock, hasParent)$ // DGC response

Algorithm 4. Reception of a DGC *response* from *ref* by active object AO

$ref.lastResponse \leftarrow response$
if $response.clock = AO.clock$ and $response.hasParent$ and
                     $AO.parent =$ **nil** and $AO.clock.owner \neq AO$ then
    $AO.parent \leftarrow ref$

---

4   Discussion

4.1   Middleware Integration

The DGC algorithm has been implemented on top of the Java platform which provides a local garbage collector albeit one with a very restricted public interface. In spite of these restrictions we have decided against modifying the Java Virtual Machine or the compiler, because doing so makes applications harder to debug and hinders portability. In the rest of this section, we provide guidelines for the integration of the DGC algorithm in a middleware, taking the ProActive [7] middleware as reference.

The ProActive middleware is a Java implementation of active objects. Method calls on active objects are transparently asynchronous as they return a *future*. A future is an object that serves as a placeholder for the actual result. After an asynchronous call, execution continues on the caller side and the caller will transparently wait for the return value of the call when first using the future.

Idle Active Objects. The DGC algorithm requires the ability to decide if an active object is busy or idle. An active object is typically implemented as a server listening for requests and serving them. Hence, in the case of single threaded active objects, it is easy to decide whether an activity is currently busy serving a request or not: an active object waiting for requests is said to be idle.

Some kinds of active objects are never idle, they would be the roots in a local garbage collector. In this DGC, the roots are:

- registered active objects as anyone can look them up at any time, this is identical to marking the registry as a root when the implementation permits (registry implemented as an active object),

- dummy active objects used as referencers when non active code references an active object.

The second item needs more explanation. It was stated that the referencers of an active object are active objects too. This is not always the case for example when some `main()` method acquires a reference to a remote active object, it is not part of an active object. To this end, the middleware creates a dummy active object that has no activity but provides the non functional properties needed by the middleware and the DGC. This allows the assumption that all referencers are active objects.

Reference Orientation. Reference edges are oriented, therefore a busy referenced active object will not prevent an idle referencer from being garbage collected, as seen in Figure 4. This implies that a referenced active object may not be able to update a future with its value for its referencer (caller) if the latter was garbage collected. This property is not necessary for garbage collection but fits with the middleware as the receipt of an updated future cannot wake up an idle activity by itself. An active object waiting for a future is busy as waiting for a future can only be done during the service of a request. Hence, this property is accepted as it is more aggressive towards garbage. Nevertheless, we could get rid of this property by dropping the orientation of references edges in a middleware where the reception of a future can wake up an idle activity, with a callback mechanism for example.

The Process Graph. If the no-sharing property is not desired or available we cannot reliably build a local reference graph without stopping all the threads or modifying the local garbage collector. Therefore, only a coarser graph would be available in this case: the graph of address spaces (processes). The bounds of address spaces are clearly identifiable as a serialization and a deserialization step are always needed to cross them. The graph of processes contains the same vertices as the reference graph, to wit, all objects in the distributed system. The edges (x, y) of this graph (P) can be determined from the reference graph (R) with the following formula:

$$\forall (x, y) \in R, \forall x' \in Proc(x), \forall y' \in Proc(y), (x', y') \in P \qquad (2)$$

x, x', y, y' are active objects and $Proc(x)$ is the process hosting the active object x. Using the process graph instead of the reference graph makes the DGC algorithm implementable on a broader range of middlewares, but limits its ability to find cyclic garbage to whole processes. For instance, a garbage cycle spanning some processes where some active objects are still live will not be collected if only the process graph is available.

The DGC of RMI uses another graph: each remote object maintains the list of stubs targeting this remote object, as dictated by the reference listing approach. Edges in this graph thus connect vertices of different types: stubs to remote objects, hence this graph is not suitable for cycle detection as it does not contain edges from remote objects to stubs.

4.2 Asynchrony - Real-Time Needs

This DGC algorithm is not fully asynchronous because, as seen in Section 3.1, it requires an upper bound on the communication time. Fully asynchronous distributed garbage collectors, while resistant to transient failures, have the limitation that undetected failures can prevent garbage collection as these are indistinguishable from transient failures. Consequently, and like the DGC of RMI, our algorithm is hard real-time as a missed deadline can cause a malfunction in the application if an active object is wrongfully garbage collected. However, the synchronization between active objects is very loose as it is represented by $TTA - 2 * TTB$. As this difference can be made as large as needed, deadlines can therefore be pushed arbitrarily far away, obviously slowing down the DGC.

For deadlines in the range of minutes (the common case) care must be taken to avoid letting TCP timeouts be the cause of missed deadlines. To this end, a basic TCP streaming socket should be avoided for the broadcasting because of its synchronous nature as blocking on a socket will delay for no reason the remaining of the broadcast. The alternative is to broadcast in parallel using either non-blocking I/O, asynchronous I/O or threads.

Another cause of missed deadlines can be the pauses caused by the local garbage collector. This was significant enough to justify the increase of the default lease time of the RMI DGC from one minute to one hour [8] in Sun Java 1.6. In our experiments, we have not yet found the need for these long deadlines.

4.3 Complexity Analysis

The presented distributed garbage collector works by building the reference graph and then a reverse spanning tree. Nevertheless, at no point in time is the whole graph known by a single active object. Active objects keep information only about their immediate neighbors (referencers and referenced active objects).

To sum up, for each active object, the added size in data structures is proportional to the numbers of referencers and referenced active objects.

DGC messages and responses between active objects are of fixed size and are exchanged every TTB between every couple of referencer/referenced active objects.

Figure 7 shows an abridged example with the main steps both in the presence of garbage, and when a single object prevents the formation of garbage. The time complexity of finding garbage can be determined by reviewing the steps (as shown in Figure 7) needed to detect a garbage cycle:

1. propagating the final activity clock through the reference graph (DGC messages),
2. propagating the consensus candidate through a reverse spanning tree (DGC responses),
3. propagating the consensus decision through the reference graph (DGC messages).

These steps proceed in an unsynchronized parallel fashion as the construction of the reference graph in the different active objects may be at different steps.

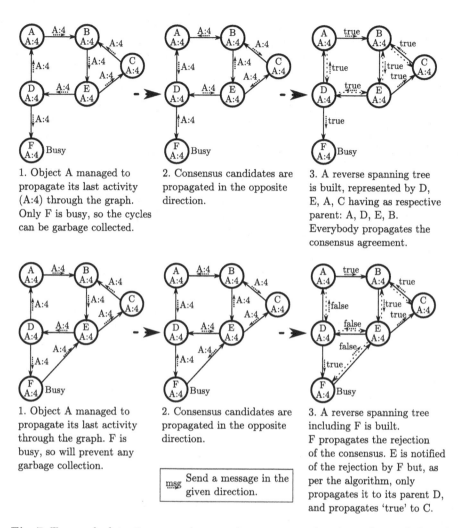

1. Object A managed to propagate its last activity (A:4) through the graph. Only F is busy, so the cycles can be garbage collected.

2. Consensus candidates are propagated in the opposite direction.

3. A reverse spanning tree is built, represented by D, E, A, C having as respective parent: A, D, E, B. Everybody propagates the consensus agreement.

1. Object A managed to propagate its last activity through the graph. F is busy, so will prevent any garbage collection.

2. Consensus candidates are propagated in the opposite direction.

| msg | Send a message in the given direction. |

3. A reverse spanning tree including F is built. F propagates the rejection of the consensus. E is notified of the rejection by F but, as per the algorithm, only propagates it to its parent D, and propagates 'true' to C.

Fig. 7. Two cycle detection examples: a garbage compound cycle, and a single live object preventing the compound cycle from being collected. The three steps are separated but their execution is actually unsynchronized.

To evaluate the time complexity, we introduce h as the maximum height of all spanning trees and reverse spanning trees for the distributed system to consider, which can be bigger than the diameter of the reference graph. The maximum height spanning tree represents the time needed to propagate DGC messages while the maximum height reverse spanning tree represents the time needed to propagate the DGC responses; they may not be equal as the reference graph may not be exclusively made of cycles. Then the order of the time to detect a garbage cycle is in $O(h * TTB)$.

After detecting a garbage cycle, to evaluate the time needed to fully collect it we need to take into account an optimization in the algorithm. For simplicity reason, this optimization has not been introduced in Section 3.2 as it is not required by the algorithm. When a consensus is made, the active object finding itself in a dead cycle waits during TTA before terminating. During this time it stops sending DGC messages as it does not need anymore to keep its referenced active objects alive, and it gives DGC responses indicating that a consensus has been reached in order to propagate the information through the referencers. This behavior is not required by the algorithm as it could simply terminate a single active object and expect the acyclic or cyclic garbage collector to go on with the remaining active objects. Nevertheless, cyclic data structures can contain sub-cycles so that the acyclic garbage collector cannot take care immediately of the remaining active objects. For this reason, and as will be shown by the benchmarks, we argue that propagating the result of the consensus is an important optimization, otherwise the acquired knowledge is partially dropped and the consensus process must start again for the sub-cycles. Therefore, a fourth step is added to go from the detection of a garbage cycle to its full collection:

4. propagating the consensus acceptation through a reverse spanning tree (DGC responses).

With this optimization in mind, a precise order of the time to garbage collect a cycle is in $O(h * TTB) + TTA$. The added TTA recalls that all active objects in cyclic garbage wait during TTA before terminating, so the last one will wait needlessly during TTA.

5   Experiments

For the experiments, the DGC algorithm has been implemented in the ProActive middleware.

In all of the following benchmarks, we measured the total network traffic by using an instrumented local SOCKS server [9] on every machine. All JVMs are instructed to forward all of their connections to the local SOCKS server which then simply forwards the connection and prints its transferred size at the end. Thus, our communication numbers only include the TCP payload but are not impacted by unrelated network traffic. Accounting only TCP is enough as all communications are over RMI, and the DNS usage is extremely low. Also, DGC messages and responses transmitted inside a single JVM are not accounted as they are directly passed by reference.

5.1   Hardware, Network and Software Environment

The following experiments have been realized on clusters in three sites of the French Grid'5000 [10] platform: Bordeaux, Sophia and Rennes. We used 49 nodes from Bordeaux, 39 from Sophia and 40 from Rennes, totalizing 128 nodes. Hardware and software details follow:

– **Bordeaux**: AMD Opteron 248 or Intel Xeon EM64T 3GHz, Dual CPU, 2G RAM, Gigabit Ethernet, RTT latency: 0.2ms. Debian 4.0 x86_64, Linux-2.6.18, Sun Java 1.5.0_10.

- **Sophia**: AMD Opteron 2218, Dual CPU, 4G RAM, Gigabit Ethernet, RTT latency: 0.1ms. Rocks 3.3.0 x86_64, Linux-2.4.21, Sun Java 1.5.0_10.
- **Rennes**: Intel Xeon 5148 LV, Dual CPU Dual Core, 2G RAM, Gigabit Ethernet, RTT latency: 0.1ms. Ubuntu 6.10 x86_64, Linux-2.6.19.1, Sun Java 1.5.0_10.

The RTT network latencies between sites are as follows: 8ms between Rennes and Bordeaux, 10ms between Bordeaux and Sophia, 20ms between Rennes and Sophia.

5.2   NAS Benchmarks

We used a ProActive/Java implementation of some of the NAS Parallel Benchmarks [11], this implementation uses explicit termination of active objects, therefore we know the earliest time at which objects could be garbage collected. Hence, we could measure both the overhead in computation time and the time required by the DGC to collect all the active objects at the end.

This NAS Benchmarks implementation is the worst case in terms of communication overhead for the DGC algorithm as every active object has a reference to every other active object because of global barriers. By this account, every TTB there is a communication between every couple of active objects. Nevertheless, the DGC algorithm itself is not exercised much as the reference graph is static: references are created at initialization time and are not changed thereafter.

This benchmark shows the impact of the DGC on a real workload. The DGC parameters are set in a slightly aggressive manner as the TTB is set to 30 seconds and the TTA to 61 seconds as per the formula in Section 3.1.

The tested kernels are:

- **CG:** A conjugate gradient method used to compute an approximation to the smallest eigenvalue of a large, sparse, symmetric positive definite matrix.
- **EP:** An embarrassingly parallel kernel.
- **FT:** A 3-D partial differential equation solution using FFTs.

The benchmarks are class C on 256 active objects with a round-robin distribution. We show the average and standard deviation of the total bandwidth consumed over 3 runs. The overhead is evaluated as $\frac{T_{dgc}-T_{nodgc}}{T_{nodgc}}$. The DGC algorithm is independent of the communication pattern, so a heavily communicating kernel like CG or FT will experience a lower overhead than a lightly communicating kernel like EP.

As expected, the bandwidth overhead of a lightly communicating benchmark like EP is very high as most of the communication is caused by the DGC algorithm. The DGC time is the time between when the benchmark has its result and when the DGC collects all the active objects. As the TTB was set to 30 seconds, the benchmark shows that the 256 active objects are collected in 15 or 17 DGC messages/responses broadcasting iterations. This speed is caused by two factors. The first one is the optimization that consists in propagating a notification that a garbage cycle has been found to all the members of the cycle. Without this

Kernel	No DGC		DGC		Overhead
	Average	Std. dev.	Average	Std. dev.	
CG	194351.81 MB	3965.60 MB	223639.83 MB	1532.94 MB	15.07 %
EP	69.75 MB	0.56 MB	717.92 MB	47.00 MB	929.28 %
FT	41999.48 MB	3383.64 MB	48187.78 MB	873.03 MB	14.73 %

Fig. 8. Bandwidth overhead

Kernel	No DGC		DGC		Overhead	DGC time	
	Average	Std. dev.	Average	Std. dev.		Average	Std. dev.
CG	3529.45 s	27.11 s	3190.00 s	5.41 s	-9.62 %	534.31 s	26.77 s
EP	8.36 s	0.54 s	8.37 s	0.44 s	0.12 %	530.41 s	42.40 s
FT	424.40 s	7.31 s	427.66 s	2.46 s	0.77 %	457.41 s	3.61 s

Fig. 9. Time overhead

optimization, after each consensus, a single active object is collected and the consensus must start again. The other reason for the speed is the fact that the reference graph in this benchmark is a complete graph, so consensus attempts are quickly propagated throughout the graph.

The negative time overhead for CG can be explained by the differences in the network usage caused by the DGC algorithm. The ProActive middleware is built on top of RMI and the DGC algorithm does its broadcast in a separate thread. By default, RMI closes the sockets it opens after 15 seconds [12] of inactivity. Consequently, the DGC broadcasting implicitly opens the sockets in its own thread and the benchmark code will not be slowed down by the latency of opening a TCP connection. Experimenting with a very high `connectionTimeout` value, hence preventing the closing of RMI sockets, gives a positive overhead. The running time rises from 2488.2 seconds without the DGC to 2499.23 seconds with the DGC, giving an overhead of 0.44%. However, the drawback of this kind of tuning is the increase in resource usage as sockets are accumulated and never closed.

These NAS benchmarks have shown that the time overhead of the DGC algorithm is insignificant, the bandwidth overhead in slightly communicating applications is important but does not result in a slowdown of the application.

5.3   DGC Torture Test

A special purpose test to stress the DGC algorithm was made. This is a simple master/slave application where slaves continuously exchange references between themselves and the master during at least ten minutes, then become idle. Thus a very complex reference graph is created and the DGC has to destroy it after the ten minutes of intense activity.

The only data exchanged by active objects consists in the remote references, so the communication overhead of the DGC is predominant. We measured the impact of changing the TTB and TTA values on the total communication size and total time.

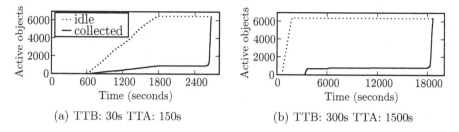

(a) TTB: 30s TTA: 150s   (b) TTB: 300s TTA: 1500s

Fig. 10. Evolution of the number of idle and garbage collected active objects

Experiments have been realized in the same hardware and software environment as the NAS with 128 machines, each of them hosting 50 slave active objects. The total number of active objects is therefore 6401, including the master active object.

In Figure 10 we can see that active objects start to become idle after their last running iteration 600 seconds after being started. During this phase, some acyclic garbage is quickly reclaimed, then the consensus is being made. Finally, thanks to the optimization that consists in notifying the referencers when a garbage cycle is found the whole graph is rapidly collected. The total bandwidth consumed for the TTB values 30s and 300s are respectively 1699MB and 2063MB. For reference, without the DGC algorithm, the total bandwidth consumed is 228MB and the last active object finishes after 1718 seconds.

This benchmark has shown that the DGC algorithm scales to a large number of active objects with a very dynamic reference graph.

6   Related Work

One can find lots of distributed garbage collector algorithms in the literature, we will concentrate here on a representative sample. We exclude special purposes algorithms having requirements like a central server or migration support.

In the DGC algorithm [4] by Veiga and Ferreira, cycle detection messages traverse the reference graph and grow information about it. Referencers are called dependencies and represent the still unknown part of the graph. At each step of the traversal, the cycle detection message may add some unresolved dependencies or may resolve some of them depending on the traversed object. A garbage cycle is identified as such when it has no more unresolved dependencies; one of its elements is then terminated. A drawback of this approach is that the growth of the message is limited only by the total size of the distributed system, so the communication overhead can become large.

The DGC algorithm presented by Le Fessant [13] is based on the propagation of marks from referencers to their referenced objects. Marks have a color: black for activities, white for idleness, and gray if both colors were encountered. These marks are generated by local roots and remote objects, a cycle is detected when a remote object receives only its own mark with the white color. This algorithm requires a tight cooperation with the local garbage collector. Unfortunately, no information is provided about the time complexity for the collection of cycles.

Lang, et al. [14] describe a DGC algorithm based on the construction of hierarchical groups over the reference graph. Each group performs a mark and sweep to destroy cycles it fully contains. The determination of groups leaves room for optimization by the application. But, as cycles are collected depending on the formed groups, no indication is given of the time needed to detect a cycle.

7   Future Work

7.1   Dynamic Parameters

The presented algorithm is configured by only two parameters: TTB and TTA. They are supposedly constant and known to every active object in the distributed systems. Two improvements are considered:

- allowing each active object to specify its own TTB and TTA value,
- dynamically adjusting the TTB and TTA in respect to the presence of suspected garbage and according to the communication rate.

The first envisioned improvement addresses the cases of applications with disparate garbage collection needs. A distributed application can be composed of a static part and a more dynamic one. The more dynamic part would benefit from smaller TTB and TTA, resulting in faster garbage collection, while the static part would lower its DGC overhead by increasing TTB and TTA.

Then, dynamically adjusting them becomes attractive in order to augment the broadcasting frequency when some garbage is suspected, i.e. when an active object gets a parent and some of its referencers agree with the consensus, or lower it when the distributed system is highly loaded.

7.2   Breadth First Spanning Tree

The DGC algorithm makes a consensus by traversing a reverse spanning tree, therefore the height of the reverse spanning tree influences the speed of finding garbage cycles. Shallow reverse spanning tree are thus preferred as their traversal is faster. Currently, the reverse spanning tree is constructed by choosing the first referenced active object with the right response as the parent. This produces shallow trees by relying on the time to reply, that is, one edge should be traversed faster than two unless the broadcasts are fortuitously synchronized. Nevertheless, a proper algorithm to ensure that the height is minimal is being considered.

8   Conclusion

We have shown a practical algorithm and its implementation for complete distributed garbage collection including cycles of garbage. Though this algorithm can be adapted to any distributed environment, it is particularly precise in a middleware featuring the no-sharing property, as in the active objects model. Cycle detection is based on a consensus reached by exploring a reverse spanning tree, but the algorithm does not require more connectivity than the original application. To summarize, the algorithm only relies on the knowledge of idle processes, and of their remote references. Also, benchmarks have shown the scalability of the algorithm in grid contexts. All these properties make our algorithm particularly adapted to any middleware having only a limited control over the local garbage collector, and in particular for grid computing.

Acknowledgements. Experiments presented in this paper were carried out using the Grid'5000 experimental testbed, an initiative from the French Ministry of Research through the ACI GRID incentive action, INRIA, CNRS and RENATER and other contributing partners.

The authors would like to thank Christian Delbé and Stijn Mostinckx for their extensive reviews and helpful comments.

References

1. Wollrath, A., Riggs, R., Waldo, J.: A Distributed Object Model for the Java System. Computing Systems 9(4), 265–290 (1996)
2. Birrell, A., et al.: Distributed Garbage Collection for Network Objects. Digital, Systems Research Center (1993)
3. Plainfosse, D., Shapiro, M.: A survey of distributed garbage collection techniques. In: Proceedings of the International Workshop on Memory Management (1995)
4. Veiga, L., Ferreira, P.: Asynchronous Complete Distributed Garbage Collection. In: IPDPS 2005. Proceedings of the 19th IEEE International Parallel and Distributed Processing Symposium, vol. 01, IEEE Computer Society Press, Los Alamitos (2005)
5. Caromel, D., Henrio, L.: A Theory of Distributed Object. Springer, Heidelberg (2005)
6. Lamport, L.: Time, clocks, and the ordering of events in a distributed system. Communications of the ACM 21(7), 558–565 (1978)
7. Baduel, L., Baude, F., Caromel, D., Contes, A., Huet, F., Morel, M., Quilici, R.: Programming, Deploying, Composing, for the Grid. In: Grid Computing: Software Environments and Tools, Springer, Heidelberg (2006)
8. RMI gcInterval is too short by default. Sun Bug Database (2004), http://bugs.sun.com/bugdatabase/view_bug.do?bug_id=6200091
9. Nylon. SOCKS 4 and 5 server, http://monkey.org/~marius/pages/?page=nylon
10. Cappello, F., Caron, E., Dayde, M., Desprez, F., Jeannot, E., Jegou, Y., Lanteri, S., Leduc, J., Melab, N., Mornet, G., Namyst, R., Primet, P., Richard, O.: Grid'5000: a large scale, reconfigurable, controlable and monitorable Grid platform. In: Grid'2005 Workshop, Seattle, USA, November 13-14,2005, IEEE/ACM (2005)
11. Bailey, D., Harris, T., Saphir, W., van der Wijngaart, R., Woo, A., Yarrow, M.: The NAS Parallel Benchmarks 2.0. The International Journal of Supercomputer Applications (1995)
12. ConnectionTimeout property, http://java.sun.com/javase/6/docs/technotes/guides/rmi/sunrmiproperties.html#connectionTimeout
13. Le Fessant, F.: Detecting distributed cycles of garbage in large-scale systems. Principles of Distributed Computing (PODC), Rhodes Island (August 2001)
14. Lang, B., Queinnec, C., Piquer, J.: Garbage collecting the world. In: Proceedings of the 19th ACM SIGPLAN-SIGACT symposium on Principles of programming languages, pp. 39–50 (1992)

XenSocket: A High-Throughput Interdomain Transport for Virtual Machines

Xiaolan Zhang[1], Suzanne McIntosh[1],
Pankaj Rohatgi[1], and John Linwood Griffin[2]

[1] IBM T.J. Watson Research Center, 19 Skyline Drive, Hawthorne, NY 10532, USA
{cxzhang,skranjac,rohatgi}@us.ibm.com
[2] Arlington, Virginia, USA

Abstract. This paper presents the design and implementation of XenSocket, a UNIX-domain-socket-like construct for high-throughput interdomain (VM-to-VM) communication on the same system. The design of XenSocket replaces the Xen page-flipping mechanism with a static circular memory buffer shared between two domains, wherein information is written by one domain and read asynchronously by the other domain. XenSocket draws on best-practice work in this field and avoids incurring the overhead of multiple hypercalls and memory page table updates by aggregating what were previously multiple operations on multiple network packets into one or more large operations on the shared buffer. While the reference implementation (and name) of XenSocket is written against the Xen virtual machine monitor, the principle behind XenSocket applies broadly across the field of virtual machines.

Keywords: shared-memory IPC, interdomain communication, virtual machine, stream processing, security architectures, Xen.

1 Introduction

Virtual machine technologies offer a number of benefits in the design of middleware. These include the ability to make more efficient use of hardware resources and to minimize network overhead by colocating multiple parties acting on the same data on the same physical machine. In addition, virtualization can provide increased robustness and security by isolating different applications and critical system components into separate protection domains within the same physical system. Finally, virtual machine technologies facilitate efficient monitoring and resource control of these different protection domains or partitions to ensure that adequate resources are available to critical domains. Figure 1 illustrates, at a conceptual level, how security can be improved by employing virtualization.

Unfortunately, the disappointing I/O performance of virtual machines has limited their adoption in application domains that require data-intensive, high-throughput network computing. Even with the recent advances in virtualization technology, virtual network and interdomain communication performance remain a problem. Taking the Xen [3] version 3.0.2 virtual machine monitor as an

R. Cerqueira and R.H. Campbell (Eds.): Middleware 2007, LNCS 4834, pp. 184–203, 2007.
© IFIP International Federation for Information Processing 2007

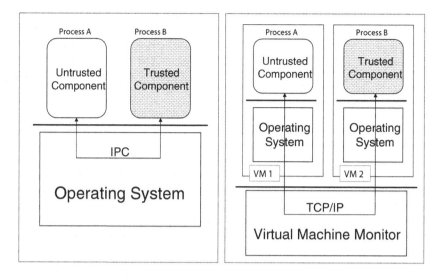

(a) Monolithic Approach   (b) Virtualization Approach

Fig. 1. Improved Security via Virtualization. In (a), the untrusted component might compromise the Operating System on which it is running which in turn leads to compromise of the trusted component running on the same OS. By isolating the trusted and untrusted components into separate Virtual Machines in (b), it is significantly more difficult for the untrusted component to affect the integrity of the trusted component. We are assuming that, because the Virtual Machine Monitor (VMM) is much smaller compared to a modern monolithic kernel, it is therefore much harder to break.

example, Figure 2 shows the transport throughput of two guest domains on the same machine communicating through a TCP connection. For comparison, the figure also shows the throughput of two Unix processes communicating through a UNIX domain socket stream on a native Linux system. As shown in the figure, the disparity is enormous, 13952 Mb/s for a UNIX domain socket vs. a mere 130 Mb/s for a TCP socket.

Analyses of the literature, combined with our own empirical observations, led us to speculate that a large source of overhead in Xen's interdomain networking was caused by the overhead of the TCP/IP stack as well as the repeated issuance of hypercalls to invoke Xen's page flipping mechanism. As described by Barham et al. [3], the Xen virtual machine monitor supports an atomic operation that updates the page tables in two virtual machines to swap the mapping of a pair of pages between the domains. This operation is used to implement a zero-copy network transmission from one domain to another: data in a network packet is page-aligned in one domain, the operation is invoked, and the data is now resident in the other domain. While this is a useful general solution for low-bandwidth messaging between domains, we speculated that it led to low throughput and high processor overhead for inter-domain communication bound applications.

To address these problems we designed and built XenSocket—a specialized interdomain transport based on memory buffers that are shared statically between a pair of domains. Applications inside a domain access this shared memory segment using the standard POSIX socket API, from which we derived the name XenSocket. A XenSocket is conceptually similar to a UNIX domain socket as would be provided by an operating system for interprocess communication; we note that we cannot simply use UNIX domain sockets for same-system component-to-component communication due to the need for virtualization-based isolation as described above.

The idea of using shared memory buffers for interprocess communication is obviously not new. However, one critical design issue for the virtualized environment is that information leakage is a sincere concern in a scheme that involves the direct sharing of memory resources between two dissimilar virtual machines (such as Domain-0 and an unprivileged domain). Special care must be taken to ensure that the integrity of the interdomain protections are maintained after the shared memory channel is torn down or after a workload is complete.

Another contribution of this paper is our exposition of one of several potentially useful techniques for high-throughput interdomain messaging in a virtual machine environment. Our sockets-based interface to the shared-memory-based transport provides a straightforward integration mechanism for large applications that require a mix of intra-machine and inter-machine communications.

We have realized an implementation of XenSocket against the Xen 3.0.2 release. Beyond Xen, the technique of using shared memory buffers for high-throughput communications applies generally across the field of virtual machines as well as other low-level resource protection schemes such as microkernels.

We summarize the key contributions of our paper below:

1. We designed and implemented an interdomain transport on Xen using shared memory. Our approach requires no modification to Xen or the Operating System.
2. Our design takes special care to maintain the interdomain protection provided by the original security architecture.
3. We measured the performance of our implementation and compared with previous approaches.
4. We demonstrated that security can be achieved with marginal performance loss—we were able to achieve throughput close to that of a native Unix Domain Sockets with much better security and robustness guarantees than we otherwise could with a monolithic kernel approach.

The remainder of this paper is organized as follows. Section 2 presents an example of a complex middleware application and details the existing performance problems we encountered with Xen. Section 3 describes our high-level design objectives with XenSocket. Section 4 discusses details of our Xen-based implementation. Section 5 presents the performance of our reference implementation. Section 6 describes related work. Section 7 discusses current status, open issues and future work surrounding XenSocket. Section 8 presents our concluding remarks.

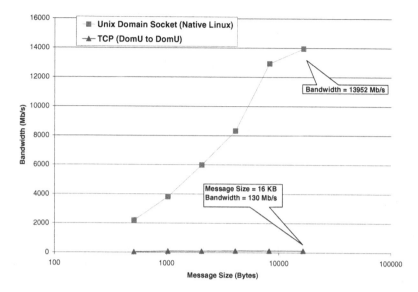

Fig. 2. Performance Comparison of TCP vs. Unix Domain Sockets as a Function of Message Size

2 Background and Motivation

2.1 A Motivating Example: System S

Outside the context of this paper, we are involved in building the security architecture for the large-scale distributed stream processing system known as System S being developed at IBM Research. The goal of System S is to extract important information by analyzing voluminous amounts of unstructured and mostly irrelevant data. Example applications for System S include analyzing audio, video and data feeds carrying information about financial, business and current events in order to support trading activities in financial institutions, and supporting responses to disasters such as Hurricane Katrina, based on analysis of vehicular movements, traffic and other sensors, news reports etc. System S has been designed to simultaneously address a number of challenges including

- **Rapid Reconfiguration:** The system must be quick to adjust to external events and the changing requirements and priorities of its users to the rapidly evolving data forms and types.
- **Perpetual Overload:** The system is required to "process" orders of magnitude higher data rates than existing systems, so a design goal has been to ensure that it functions well at high load. In fact, the system is designed to operate under a perpetual state of overload and must adjust its resource allocations to support the highest priority activities. This means that there will not be enough processing resources to completely analyze all the data being ingested, nor the bandwidth to transmit all the intermediate results,

nor the storage to store all the data, so applications have to be designed to be resilient to variations in processing resources and to operate despite missing data.

- **System Security and Information Confidentiality:** The system must be resilient against compromise from data-driven attacks originating from the ingested data and must adequately protect the confidential information being processed within it from unauthorized disclosure.
- **Heterogeneity:** System S has to be designed to be a distributed system running on a heterogeneous collection of platforms, each specialized for particular types of processing.

The Stream Processing Core (SPC) is the middleware component of System S that hosts the distributed stream processing applications over heterogeneous hardware platforms and manages the stream connections, resources and dataflow autonomically. From a logical perspective, applications running on System S consist of multiple software-based processing and analysis components known as Processing Elements (PEs) which can communicate with each other via a unidirectional data stream abstraction. Each application can therefore be viewed as a directed graph with the PEs as nodes and the streams as edges, and at any point in time multiple applications could be running concurrently within System S. The SPC is responsible for providing both the execution environment for the PEs running in the system as well as the underlying data transport mechanism that implements the streams abstraction. The actual PE's are processes that are scheduled throughout a large physical installation and communicate with the rest of the system via the abstractions provided by a Streams Library (SL) that is linked into the PE executable. This library is also responsible for providing the streams API to the PEs, with the actual data transport across PEs managed by a separate data routing and transport component known as the Data Fabric. Each PE takes in chunks of data (known as stream data objects or SDOs) from one or more incoming streams, operates atomically and collectively on the input SDOs, and passes out results in the form of SDOs into one or more outgoing streams. These output SDOs are then transferred by the PE's streams library to the Data Fabric, which is then responsible for transporting them to the Streams Library of the subsequent PEs that need to consume them.[1]

2.2 Security Requirement of System S and Virtualization

Virtualization technology is an important component of the System S architecture. Although virtualization is not yet pervasively used throughout the system, it is critically needed in select places for the purposes of aggregation, colocation and most importantly for security and robustness. Given the large attack surface of applications analyzing large quantities of unstructured data of all types, it is

---

[1] The interested reader will find more information on the scale and scope of the System S components in the treatment by Amini et al. [1] and on the Web; only those details that motivate the design of our high-throughput messaging system are included in this paper.

highly likely that application PEs and even the operating systems hosting them could be compromised by exploits within the ingested data. The security architecture for System S (see Section 6 in [4]) therefore requires that application PEs that are not robust enough to handle low-integrity external data be confined and restricted in the way they can interact with other PEs as well as the rest of the system. This could be done by exploiting the protections provided by a virtualization layer; for example PEs operating on streams with different security or privacy labels could be isolated from each other and the virtualization protection could also be used to ensure the integrity of System S itself, in that trusted portions of the system (such as the Data Fabric modules that route SDOs between PEs) exist either on standalone physical machines or in isolated virtual machines, so as to be protected from damage from poorly designed or compromised PEs. In particular, the security architecture calls for the PEs and the Data Fabric to be resident in separate partitions or nodes, whereas in the current implementation these reside on the same node and the Streams Library transports the SDOs back and forth from the Data Fabric using Unix Domain Sockets.

2.3   Performance Requirement of System S

The fundamental performance bottleneck of System S is designed to be the saturation of the network links between each processing component [7]. In other words, throughput—the number of chunks per second passing through the system (or between components)—is a key metric of goodness for our purposes.[2]In contrast, the latency incurred by chunks moving from component to component does not have an important impact on the overall performance of the Stream Processing Core, and the fraction of processing time consumed for each chunk is expected to be negligible in comparison with the fraction of the network capacity consumed by each SDO.

2.4   Problem Statement

Unfortunately, our empirical experience with Xen as a virtualization platform for System S showed that interdomain communication using the Xen virtual network fell well short of the throughput metrics identified for the project. In addition, the processor overhead consumed by the virtual network infrastructure was substantial enough to take away resources needed by each SDO. Specifically, domain-to-domain throughput capped out at around 130 Mb/s to 142 Mb/s (13-14% of the available raw physical network capacity), while maxing out the CPU utilization of the guest domains and requiring 18-20% of the processor in Domain-0.

The inefficiency of virtual machines as regards same-system networking performance is a well-known problem. In the literature, Menon et al. use profiling to explain some inefficiencies in the Xen virtual network [13], and in follow-up work

---

[2] Actually, the metric of goodness in System S is the utility of the work done within the system [2], but networking throughput remains a key bottleneck.

Menon, Cox, and Zwaenepoel discuss performance optimizations to the network stack that leverage the fact that two domains on the same system are not constrained by physical network effects such as small packet sizes and the need to calculate and verify checksums [12]. Through these optimizations the authors achieve a maximum receive throughput of 970 Mb/s and transmit throughput of 3310 Mb/s. While these improvements are noteworthy, the performance of the resulting system still falls short compared to that of Unix Domain Sockets (over 10,000 Mb/s, see Figure 2).

In order to support the use of virtualization in our distributed stream processing application, our objective is to achieve throughput performance on both the send and receive paths at speeds approaching those of a UNIX domain socket for mid-sized messages (tens or hundreds of kilobytes).

3   Design

XenSocket provides a sockets-based interface to one or more large shared memory buffers for domain-to-domain communication. We make the design assumption that a XenSocket provides a one-way tunnel between a sender domain and a receiver domain. As discussed in Section 7, this assumption is not a requirement of a shared-memory-based transport; rather, the choice was made to conserve memory in the event that only one-way communications are needed.

Our shared-memory-based system is especially appropriate for asymmetric broadcast communications, where one domain sends a lot of information to multiple other domains on the same system (perhaps including an I/O domain for retransmission to other physical machines) without expecting to receive anything in return other than an acknowledgment of receipt.

3.1   Shared Memory and Circular Buffers

XenSocket was designed to test our hypothesis that per-packet page flipping is a large source of inefficiency in the Xen virtual network design. This was inspired in large part by the work of Menon, Cox, and Zwaenepoel [12] who demonstrated substantial performance gains in the Xen virtual network by transmitting more information per hypercall and, notably, replacing some instances of page flipping between domains with a memory copy between the domains.

XenSocket uses shared memory for message passing. There are two types of memory pages shared by each endpoint of a XenSocket: a descriptor page and buffer pages. The descriptor page is used to store control information. The buffer pages together form the circular buffer. When a socket connection is established between two domains, a shared memory region is reserved by one domain and mapped by the other domain. This shared memory is treated as a circular buffer: the sender writes data into this buffer, and the receiver reads directly from the buffer in FIFO order. This design differs from the well-utilized method of using Xen communication rings and page flipping, where data are first placed onto a memory page by the sender and then that page is remapped into the receiver's address space.

3.2 Sharing and Security

When sharing pages between domains of different trust levels (say, between an unprivileged domain and Domain-0), it is important that pages are only shared from the less-trusted domain and only mapped by the more-trusted domain. This design is to prevent the less trusted domain from launching a Denial of Service (DoS) attack on the more trusted domain by repeatedly establishing XenSocket connections to the more trusted domain without tearing them down, eventually exhausting the resources of the more trusted domain. We refer to the less-trusted domain as the *server* domain, since it provides the pages used for the circular buffer. The more-trusted domain is then the *client* domain, since it maps these pages into its own memory space. Note that the label of server and client is independent of which domain acts as the sender of data and which as the receiver.

It is currently necessary for the designer of a shared-memory-based transport to consider this, as Xen does not support the forced revocation by the hypervisor of a mapped page by a domain. This security design must be enforced by the existing security architecture of the application using an explicit policy, as Xen by default does not assign trust labels to domains (other than the hardwired fact that Domain-0 is more trusted than any other domain). One way of implementing this is through sHype, the secure hypervisor architecture for Xen [16].

Each XenSocket uses one descriptor page per one-way connection. The descriptor page is mapped read-write by both domains and is used for transmission of control information passing between the domains. An alternate design is possible where each domain provides its own descriptor page that is readable by both domains but only writable by itself. However, such a split design is both undesirable (from the standpoint of only wanting less-trusted domains to expose pages) and unnecessary, as long as none of the domains use the information in an unsafe, unchecked manner. In other words, if there is operationally-sensitive information that domain S shares with domain R, then S should keep the authoritative copy of the information in memory that is not shared or visible to R. In this way, if R overwrites the copy of this information on the shared page, it will not affect the correct operation of S—R's overwrites will only impact R itself.

3.3 A Sockets Interface to Shared Memory

In XenSocket, a sender application in one domain can create a socket (just as it would create a socket for TCP/IP-based communication or Unix Domain Sockets) and use send() (or write()) to push data into the socket. A receiver application in another domain can also create a socket and use recv() (or read()) to pull data from the socket. The choice of a sockets-based interface was initially made because existing System S components such as the Stream Processing Core (SPC) already make use of a sockets interface in their communications, but we believe that a sockets-based interface is a generally useful one to support the migration of distributed applications into a virtual machine environment.

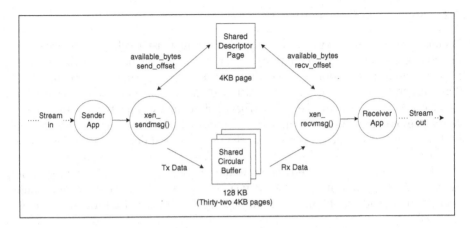

Fig. 3. XenSocket Architecture

In our design, a domain does not specify whether it will be a sender or a receiver on a XenSocket; this choice is indicated the first time the domain issues a `write()` or `read()` operation on the socket—after issuing a command of one type (e.g., `write`), any commands of the opposite type (`read`) will immediately return with a failure code.

4   Implementation

XenSocket is a socket-based solution for increasing interdomain throughput in Xen. Its APIs follow from standard socket APIs. Underneath this socket API, XenSocket uses shared memory for implementing high-throughput, interdomain data transfer. Our implementation is based on Xen version 3.0.2. XenSocket compiles into a kernel module and currently requires no changes to Xen or Linux. Work is in progress to port the implementation to newer versions of Xen.

XenSocket allocates two shared memory regions accessible by both the sender and receiver. One region consists of just one 4KB page for storage of state and control variables shared by the sender and receiver, which is called the descriptor page. The second region is comprised of multiple 4KB buffer pages that form one shared circular buffer. In our present implementation, thirty-two pages are allocated to realize a 128 kilobyte circular buffer. Figure 3 shows the architecture of the XenSocket implementation.

4.1   User Perspective

From a user perspective, XenSocket has a simple sockets-based interface, so chosen because of its simplicity and because existing components in our application already communicated over a socket interface. In this section we show how an application would use the XenSocket API, highlighting the differences between XenSocket API and standard socket API.

Server (Receiver)	Client (Sender)

s = socket();
 	
. . .
 	
gref = bind(s, xaddr);
 	
. . .
 	
recv(s);
 	
. . .
 	
. . .
 	
shutdown(s);
	s = socket();
	
	. . .
	
	. . .
	
	connect(s, xaddr);
	
	send(s);
	
	. . .
	
	shutdown(s);

Fig. 4. XenSocket Usage Example

Figure 4 illustrates the time sequence whereby XenSockets are established and used by a client (sender) and server (receiver) in a typical scenario[3]. The receiver in one domain first creates a socket by calling the socket() API. It then calls the bind() API to bind the socket to an address (xaddr). Additionally, it allocates physical memory to establish both a descriptor page and a shared circular buffer. Unlike the normal bind() call, which returns an error code indicating success or failure, the XenSocket bind() call returns the grant table reference to the descriptor page (gref) on success so that the sender can later use it to establish the sharing of that page. The bind() API also allocates an event channel to be used for communication with the sender whose identity, its domain number, is passed in as part of the socket address (xaddr) parameter. The receiver then calls read() or recv() for receiving data. The receiver blocks until it detects data in the circular buffer. The receiver calls shutdown() upon detecting that the sender has ended the connection.

The sender similarly calls socket() to create a socket just as the receiver does. The sender then calls connect(), supplying the receiver's domain ID and the grant table reference of the shared descriptor page[4], both are part of the xaddr parameter. The connect() call gets the addresses of the physical pages of the shared circular buffer, which were placed in shared memory when the receiver called bind(), and maps them into the virtual address space of the sender. Additionally, it establishes the other end of the event channel facilitating communication of events between the client and server. With all this in place, the sender can now transmit data by calling send() or write() to deposit data into the circular buffer. The sender shuts down when all data has been sent.

4.2 Data Transfer

One core piece of the implementation is an efficient data transfer algorithm using atomic operations provided by the Linux kernel. A sketch of the send

---

[3] Note that although in this example, the server acts as a receiver and the client as a sender, the mapping between the server and the receiver (similarly the client and the sender) is not fixed, as discussed in Section 3.2.

[4] In our current implementation, the grant table reference value is passed to the connect() call manually, however in the future we intend to automate this.

```
Procedure: xen_sendmsg
Input      : target_bytes
Output     : written_bytes
begin
    num_bytes ← 0;
    written_bytes ← 0;
    while written_bytes < target_bytes do
        num_bytes ← atomic_read(available_bytes);
        num_bytes ← min(num_bytes, target_bytes);
        if num_bytes = 0 then
            wait with timeout;
            continue;
        end
        write num_bytes into circular buffer;
        send_offset ← (send_offset + num_bytes) mod BUFFER_SIZE ;
        atomic_sub(available_bytes, num_bytes);
        signal receiver of newly available data;
        written_bytes ← written_bytes + num_bytes ;
    end
    return written_bytes;
end
```

Algorithm 1. Send Algorithm. The use of atomic operations eliminates the need for conventional locks and thus improves performance.

```
Procedure: xen_recvmsg
Input      : target_bytes
Output     : read_bytes
begin
    num_bytes ← 0;
    read_bytes ← 0;
    while read_bytes < target_bytes do
        num_bytes ← atomic_read(available_bytes);
        num_bytes ← min(num_bytes, target_bytes);
        if num_bytes = 0 then
            wait with timeout;
            continue;
        end
        read num_bytes from circular buffer;
        recv_offset ← (recv_offset + num_bytes) mod BUFFER_SIZE ;
        atomic_add(available_bytes, num_bytes);
        signal sender of newly available space;
        read_bytes ← read_bytes + num_bytes ;
    end
    return read_bytes;
end
```

Algorithm 2. Receive Algorithm

and receive algorithms is shown in Algorithm 1 and Algorithm 2 respectively. Pseudo procedures starting with `atomic` indicate atomic operations. The send and receive algorithms use one shared control variable, `available_bytes`, which indicates the number of bytes available for write in the circular buffer. Both the sender and the receiver maintain local read/write offsets into the circular buffer, which are not shared.

Currently, our implementation supports only blocking reads and writes. When there is no room in the circular buffer for writing, `send()` will block. The sender will remain in a wait loop, awaking periodically, until space becomes available in the circular buffer. Similarly, `recv()` blocks when the buffer is empty. It remains in the blocking state until data is available for read. The sender signals the receiver of available data via the event channel when more data is written to the buffer. Similarly, the receiver signals the sender of available space when more data is consumed from the buffer.

4.3   Connection Teardown

Unlike Unix Domain Sockets, where either endpoint of the connection can shut down independent of the other, care must be taken to tear down a connection in XenSocket to ensure a smooth unmapping process because of the shared resources between the two endpoints. Since the server is the one that allocates the shared resources, our current implementation of XenSocket ensures that the client shut down first. If we had allowed the server to shut down first, the descriptor page, event channel, and circular buffer would all have been torn down, making communication between the client and server for the purpose of synchronization impossible. On the other hand, the shutdown API provides the user applications with the capability of initiating a shutdown at either endpoint. To support this, our shutdown implementation uses two shared control variables to serialize the shutdown. `shutdown()` first detects whether the client or the server is the caller. In the former case, the shutdown proceeds as usual, and one shared variable is set to indicate that the client has shutdown. The server application is notified of this condition after all data sent by the client has been emptied from the circular buffer. The server application can then issue a `shutdown` call, which properly deallocates all shared resources. If the server application issues a `shutdown()` call first, a second shared control variable is set to indicate that the server has initiated a shutdown and waits for the client to shut down first. When the client detects such a situation, it immediately stops sending data and returns an error code to the application, which in turn will eventually issue a `shutdown()` call. The shutdown process then proceeds as if the client had initiated the shutdown first.

Our XenSocket implementation is resistant against misbehaving server domains. We assume that the high integrity client domain is trustworthy and therefore can be relied upon to behave correctly. In our implementation, the client domain is non-blocking – it merely notifies the server domain that it has initiated a shutdown. Therefore, if the server misbehaves, it will only hurt itself.

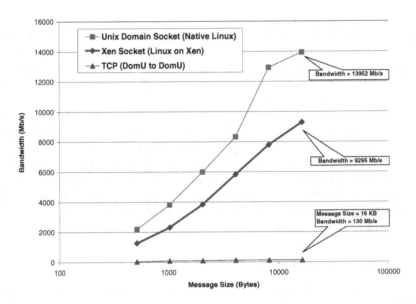

Fig. 5. Throughput Comparison of XenSocket vs. Unix Domain Sockets and TCP for Message Sizes Between 512 Bytes and 16 KB. XenSocket achieves up to 72 times the throughput of standard TCP stream at message size of 16 KB.

5   Performance Evaluation

We evaluated our XenSocket implementation on an IBM HS20 blade with dual 2.8GHz Pentium Xeon processors and 4GB RAM. We use netperf version 2.4.2 as our primary benchmark. All data reported was run on Xen version 3.0.2 and Linux version 2.6.16.18. Each test was run 3 times, with the average reported. All experiments were run in single CPU mode with hyper-threading disabled to minimize performance variation.

5.1   Performance for Common Message Sizes

Figure 5 shows the reported throughput as a function of message size for XenSocket between two guest domains, as compared to that for Unix Domain Sockets of two processes on native Linux, and that for unmodified TCP between two DomUs. As demonstrated in the figure, XenSocket achieves up to 72 times the throughput of standard TCP stream in the peak case (message size = 16 KB). However, XenSocket still lags Unix Domain Sockets by 33% in this case. We are very encouraged by this initial performance result and are continuing to optimize XenSocket further.

The gradual increase of the throughput as the message size increases indicates that at small message sizes, the performance is dominated by the per-message call overhead (one system call plus one Xen Hypercall each side). When the message size increases, the performance becomes dominated by the overhead of

Table 1. CPU Utilization vs. Achieved Throughput in XenSocket. As discussed in Section 2, the existing Xen virtual network requires 18-20% CPU usage in Domain-0 to transfer only 130-142 Mb/s between two guest domains.

Throughput	CPU Utilization		
	Sender	Receiver	Domain-0
3320 Mb/s	6%	11%	1%
972 Mb/s	3%	4%	0%
136 Mb/s	0%	2%	0%

actually transferring the data. At the message size of 16 KB, XenSocket reaches a peak throughput of 9295 Mb/s. At this rate, the CPU utilizations of both guest domains reach 100%, whereas Domain-0 remains at near zero CPU utilization.

A direct comparison with the results of Menon et al. [12] is not illustrative, as described below, but it is useful to point out the design choices that cause our results to differ. Their results are asymmetric, with a maximum receive performance of 970 Mb/s and a maximum transmit performance of 3310 Mb/s. In addition, there is a big difference between running the benchmark in the driver domain and in the guest domain. In our case, since we run both the receiver and the sender on the same machine, we only look at the maximum bandwidth that can be achieved between the two. Additionally, since XenSocket does not require Domain-0 to be involved in the data exchange, it does not make much difference whether the sender (or receiver) resides in the driver domain or the guest domain.

To make the comparison more complete, we also look at the CPU utilization of XenSocket at performance close to 3310 Mb/s, 970 Mb/s and 130 Mb/s, the maximum transmit and receive throughputs achieved in Menon et al., and in unmodified TCP on Xen (see Section 2). We modify netperf to sleep at a certain rate so as to bring down the performance to the specific target level. Since the throughput varies at each run, it is difficult to fix the throughput at exactly a static value. Thus, we chose the throughput level that is closest to the target level. The CPU utilization at the sender and receiver is taken from the statistics reported by netperf. For Domain-0, we use the percentage of total processor time spent idle reported by the `vmstat` tool. Table 1 lists the CPU utilization of the sender and receiver guest domains, and domain-0. At 3320 Mb/s, the CPU utilization is around 6% for the sender and 11% for the receiver. At 972 Mb/s, the CPU utilization is around 3-4% for the sender and the receiver. At 136 Mb/s, the CPU utilization is close to 0% for the sender and about 2% for the receiver. In all cases, Domain-0 is mostly idle.

Note that this is not an exact apples to apples comparison for two reasons: First, we run the sender and the receiver on the same machine, whereas in the case of Menon et al., the sender and the receiver are evaluated separately. Secondly, we have different assumptions on the intended usages of XenSocket than that of Menon et al. Our intended applications are high-throughput distributed stream systems, thus we relax the latency requirement, and can do batching at the receiver side. In contrast, Menon et al. have to support interactive

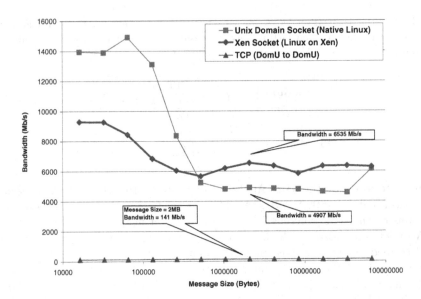

Fig. 6. Throughput Comparison of XenSocket vs. Unix Domain Sockets and TCP for Large Message Sizes. Both XenSocket and Unix Domain Sockets see a large dropoff when the message size reaches 512 KB and then stabilize around 5-6 Mb/s. The performance curves invert at message size of 512 KB where XenSocket outperforms Unix Domain Sockets.

networking, and therefore have to dispatch any network packet received from the network immediately to the receiver.

Despite these differences, we believe that the comparison is still meaningful in that it highlights the unique features of our approach and shows how the differences in the two approaches affect performance.

5.2   Performance for Larger Message Sizes

Figure 6 shows the throughput of XenSocket, Unix Domain Sockets and TCP for large message sizes (ranging from 16 KB to 64 MB). It's interesting to note that for both XenSocket and Unix Domain Sockets, the throughput starts to drop off after a certain message size (16 KB for XenSocket and 64 KB for Unix Domain Sockets), then stabilizes when the message size is larger than 512 KB. Interestingly, XenSocket performs about 33% better than Unix Domain Socket (6534 Mb/s vs. 4907 Mb/s for message size of 2 MB). For TCP, the throughput is virtually unchanged at about 141 Mb/s.

We investigated the cause of the performance drop off for large message sizes using the OProfile tool [10] and its extension to Xen [13]. Our initial results indicate that there is a strong correlation between the throughput performance and the L2 cache hit ratio. We thus believe that the drop off is caused by some caching effects of the L2 cache. Another indication that this is due to cache effects comes from the fact that performance of the Unix Domain Socket varies across identically configured hardware platforms. A precise characterization of the performance variation and pinpointing the causes will require further research. It suffices to say that the variation is comparable to the performance difference between XenSocket and Unix Domain Socket, confirming that XenSocket indeed achieves throughput close to that of Unix Domain Socket.

6 Related Work

Our approach is inspired by previous research on using shared memory buffers for interprocess communication. As an earlier example, we note the use of cached fast buffers by Druschel, Peterson, and Davie [5] in their optimization of the OSIRIS network adaptor. More recently, Götz implemented a shared-memory-based transport for high-throughput data transfer in the L4 microkernel [6]. There are also examples other than our work on System S that motivate high-throughput communication in a VM environment, such as the virtualization of a transaction processing system that contains multiple front-end web servers, interconnected database servers, and back-end storage system nodes.

The Xway project [8] also uses a sockets interface over a shared-memory transport to improve Xen interdomain communications throughput. The Xway and XenSocket projects were developed independently but share similar designs. The core difference is the type of socket interface presented to the user or application. With Xway, applications create sockets using the existing AF_INET protocol family. Modified INET socket code creates a shared-memory transport whenever both endpoints are on the same physical host. The Xway design allows deployment of the shared-memory transport without requiring changes to existing applications. With XenSocket, sockets are created using a new AF_XEN protocol family. The XenSocket design enables communication between domains that do not have virtual network devices or that do not share a common Internet Protocol-based network interface. This level of isolation is important for System S security and in such architectures as that described by Payne [15].

The PROSE System prototype developed by Van Hensbergen and Gross [17] uses shared buffers for low-latency IPC in a hybrid microkernel-and-virtual-machine environment. Their work focuses on latency and no performance details are available for bandwidth benchmarks. In addition, their approach uses polling at the receiving side, which leads to more CPU usage than a non-polling algorithm.

Liu et al [11] looked at improving device I/O of Virtual Machines by leveraging the virtualization capabilities of the device itself and bypassing the VMM all together for performance critical operations. The idea was inspired by early work on OS-bypassing I/O where user-level applications can directly access physical devices in order to improve performance. While their approach shares similar principle with ours in that both try to improve performance by minimizing the involvement of the VMM, there are two fundamental differences between the two approaches. In our approach, the VMM is always involved in the communication (e.g., it's never bypassed). In addition, our approach does not involve physical devices. Rather, it only concerns the communication of two VMs on the same physical platform.

An orthogonal area of memory sharing research on virtual machines focuses on improving the *spatial* efficiency of memory usage. For example, Kloster et al [9] employs hashing to locate identical pages that belong to different VMs and transparently share the page among VMs, thereby reducing the total number of required physical pages. Because the pages are identical, and sharing is performed transparently from the VM's perspective, there is no security implication of this optimization, except for the possibility of opening up potential side channels.

7   Discussion

As described above, our design of a XenSocket is a one-way communications pipe between two domains. While the traditional view of a socket is a two-way mechanism, we chose the one-way design as a balance between our desire to minimize overall system impact and our interest in ensuring a large circular buffer to avoid stalling by the sender or receiver. A more complete design would include variable-size circular buffers whose logic is capable of adapting the buffer reservation size to the actual usage of the buffer. In this way a two-way socket could be the norm, where the initial circular buffer size is small but grows to most efficiently match the demand. A variant on this idea would be to dynamically move pages between the two circular buffers in order to adapt the buffer size to the workload while maintaining a constant amount of memory reservation per XenSocket.

An unexplored aspect of our design for XenSocket is its use in a local multicast environment; i.e., in the case where one domain sends identical messages to a constant set of multiple other domains on the same system. When one or more of these other domains act as an external network bridge, this could represent a multicast to applications running both in local domains and on remote systems. The descriptor page in our design could be extended to include acknowledgments from each of the receiving domains. This would reduce the memory and computational pressure on the sending domain—both in comparison with the design presented in this paper and with the original Xen virtual network—as the sending domain would only have to copy each message once into a shared memory buffer instead of performing work for each receiving domain. However, it remains to be explored the degree to which such an approach is open to denial-of-service attacks when one domain chooses not to acknowledge on a timely basis the data it receives, filling up the circular buffer and therefore halting the information flow.

There are other aspects of performance optimization that we have not yet explored. For example, we can offload control of memory transfers into and out of the shared memory space to the DMA controller or the I/O memory management units. Resource contention may become an issue for multiple instances of XenSocket running in parallel due to the extra memory copies needed into and out of the circular buffer. However, we note that even in the original Xen page-flipping scheme for virtual networks, it is still necessary to copy data into and out of the pages that are flipped. Another optimization is to implement the shared pages in the hypervisor memory, which is mapped to all VMs. An advantage of this approach is reducing the number of cache and TLB flushes due to context switches. A disadvantage is that it does not scale to large number of concurrent connections. A third optimization is using cooperative scheduling mechanisms such as gang scheduling [14], where the sender and the receiver are scheduled together to minimize waiting time.

A hardware trend that is relevant to our work on XenSocket is the emergence of multi-core processors. In a virtualized multi-core environment—where a currently-open question is "what are we going to do with all those cores?"— one class of applications that will map well to the environment contains those distributed applications that compute sequential analyses over large local data sets. Examples of these are image recognition or feature extraction applications. While such applications could be written as large multi-threaded programs with a common shared memory pool, we postulate that the preservation of isolation boundaries combined with a distributed message-passing paradigm will provide the most useful transition path for minimally-modified distributed software architectures into a multi-core environment.

8 Conclusion

As virtualization becomes more widely deployed, we foresee a growing number of applications that require high-performance interdomain communication. This is in part driven by security and reliability concerns—by separating components of a complex software system into different domains, one achieves better isolation among the components, thus improving security and reliability. For example, in our target application, a large-scale distributed stream processing system consisting of components with different trust levels, our security design mandates that components of different trust levels must be placed either on separate machines or on separate virtual machines, in both cases with a proper security-label-based gating of communication between the machines. Achieving this with only marginal degradation of communication performance in a virtual machine environment is particularly crucial for our target application whose success depends on the ability to transfer large amounts of data rapidly between the distributed application components.

In this paper we present XenSocket, a shared-memory-based construct that provides a POSIX sockets-based mechanism for high-throughput interdomain communications. XenSocket draws on best-practice work in this field and avoids incurring the overhead of multiple hypercalls and memory page table updates by aggregating what were previously multiple operations on multiple network packets into one or more large operations on the shared buffer. Our performance evaluation indicates that with XenSocket we have successfully achieved our goal of same-system interdomain transport throughput that approaches that of interprocess communication using UNIX domain sockets.

We have released the source code for our XenSocket reference implementation under the name **XVMSocket**. XVMSocket is freely available at the SourceForge open source software development web site [18] for use under the terms of the GNU General Public License.

Acknowledgments

We would like to thank our colleagues from IBM Research, Ronald Perez, Douglas Lee Schales, and Volkmar Uhlig, and our colleagues in the IBM Linux Technology Center, Anthony Liguori, Ryan Harper, Muli Ben-Yehuda, and Eric Van Hensbergen, and Jose Santos from Hewlett Packard for insightful discussions and comments. Reiner Sailer, Stefan Berger and Wesley Most helped in the initial Xen setup. And finally, we thank our anonymous reviewers for their careful review and helpful comments on improving this paper.

References

1. Amini, L., Andrade, H., Bhagwan, R., Eskesen, F., King, R., Selo, P., Park, Y., Venkatramani, C.: SPC: A distributed, scalable platform for data mining. In: DMSSP 2006: Proceedings of ACM SIGKDD Workshop on Data Mining Standards, Services and Platforms, Philadelphia, PA, USA (2006)
2. Amini, L., Jain, N., Sehgal, A., Silber, J., Verscheure, O.: Adaptive control of extreme-scale stream processing systems. In: ICDCS 2006 (2006)
3. Barham, P., Dragovic, B., Fraser, K., Hand, S., Harris, T., Ho, A., Neugebauer, R., Pratt, I., Warfield, A.: Xen and the art of virtualization. In: SOSP 2003: Proceedings of the nineteenth ACM Symposium on Operating Systems Principles, pp. 164–177. ACM Press, New York (2003)
4. Cheng, P., Rohatgi, P., Keser, C., Karger, P.A., Wagner, G.M., Reninger, A.S.: Fuzzy multi-level security: An experiment on quantified risk-adaptive access control. Technical Report RC24190, IBM Research, Yorktown Heights, NY, USA (Feburary 2007)
5. Druschel, P., Peterson, L.L., Davie, B.S.: Experiences with a high-speed network adaptor: A software perspective. In: SIGCOMM 1994: Proceedings of the Conference on Communications Architectures, Protocols and Applications, pp. 2–13. ACM Press, New York (1994)
6. Götz, S.: Asynchronous communication using synchronous IPC primitives. Diploma thesis, System Architecture Group, University of Karlsruhe, Germany (May 2003)
7. Jain, N., Amini, L., Andrade, H., King, R., Park, Y., Selo, P., Venkatramani, C.: Design, implementation, and evaluation of the linear road benchmark on the stream processing core. In: SIGMOD 2006. Proceedings of the 2006 ACM SIGMOD International Conference on Management of Data, pp. 431–442. ACM Press, New York (2006)
8. Kim, K.-H.: Personal communication (May 1, 2007), http://lists.xensource.com/archives/html/xen-devel/2007-05/msg00122.html
9. Kloster, J.F., Kristensen, J., Mejlholm, A.: Efficient memory sharing in the xen virtual machine monitor. Technical report, Aalborg University (January 2006), https://services.cs.aau.dk/public/tools/library/files/rapbibfiles1/1136884892.pdf

10. Levon, J., Elie, P.: http://oprofile.sourceforge.net/about/
11. Liu, J., Huang, W., Abali, B., Panda, D.K.: High Performance VMM-Bypass I/O in Virtual Machines. In: 2006 USENIX Annual Technical Conference, Boston, Massachusetts, USA, pp. 29–42 (June 2006)
12. Menon, A., Cox, A.L., Zwaenepoel, W.: Optimizing network virtualization in Xen. In: 2006 USENIX Annual Technical Conference, Boston, Massachusetts, USA, pp. 15–28 (June 2006)
13. Menon, A., Santos, J.R., Turner, Y., Janakiraman, G.J., Zwaenepoel, W.: Diagnosing performance overheads in the Xen virtual machine environment. In: VEE 2005: First International Conference on Virtual Execution Environments, Chicago, Illinois, USA, pp. 13–23 (June 2005)
14. Ousterhout, J.K.: Scheduling techniques for concurrent systems. In: ICDCS 1982: 3rd International Conference on Distributed Computing Systems, pp. 22–30 (1982)
15. Payne, B.D., Sailer, R., Cáceres, R., Perez, R., Lee, W.: A layered approach to simplified access control in virtualized systems. Operating Systems Review 41(3), 12–19 (2007)
16. Sailer, R., Jaeger, T., Valdez, E., Perez, R., Berger, S., Griffin, J.L., van Doorn, L.: Building a MAC-based security architecture for the Xen opensource hypervisor. Technical Report RC23629, IBM Research, Yorktown Heights, NY, USA (June 2005)
17. Van Hensbergen, E., Goss, K.: PROSE I/O. In: IWP9 2006: First International Conference on Plan 9, Madrid, Spain (December 2006)
18. XVMSocket, http://sourceforge.net/projects/xvmsocket/

Creating Private Network Overlays for High Performance Scientific Computing

Edward Walker

Texas Advanced Computing Center, The University of Texas at Austin, Austin,
Texas 78758, USA
ewalker@tacc.utexas.edu

Abstract. In this paper we describe an approach in creating private network overlays in user-space to support the dynamic creation of personal clusters on-demand. These personal clusters are created by submitting job proxies to High Performance Computing (HPC) clusters. Job proxies contribute CPU resources back to the personal cluster when they eventually run, allowing application jobs to execute on them in a system call virtualized run-time environment. The virtualized run-time environment enables additional personal cluster-wide services to be interposed, including a private network overlay instantiated for each personal cluster created. The interposed private network overlay allows the personal clusters to tunnel IP traffic thorough gateway nodes at each contributing HPC cluster site in order to provision resources across private networks, survive transient network outages, support critical services like distributed filesystems, and in some cases, improve network transfer throughput across the wide-area network. This paper describes our design and implementation strategy, and concludes with some general guiding principles to aid other projects of a similar nature.

Keywords: High performance computing, resource management, cluster computing, overlay networks.

1 Introduction

We describe our experience in implementing a user-space private network overlay across High Performance Computing (HPC) clusters to support a TeraGrid production software system called MyCluster [1][2].

TeraGrid is a multi-year, multi-million dollar, NSF funded project to build the world's largest HPC cyberinfrastructure for open scientific research [3]. The project currently links nine resource provider sites across the continental United States, providing in aggregate over 200 teraflops of compute resource and four petabytes of online disk storage. Resources on the TeraGrid include HPC clusters, visualization clusters, and online data collections, accessible through a 30 Gbps wide-area network (WAN) backbone.

MyCluster is a system for provisioning resources from distributed HPC sites into personal clusters created on-demand. These personal clusters can be created on a

R. Cerqueira and R.H. Campbell (Eds.): Middleware 2007, LNCS 4834, pp. 204–222, 2007.

per-user, per-experiment, basis, allowing them to be used as job containers for experiments conducted within a personalized computing laboratory. In 2006, the system was used to acquire over 800,000 CPUs for researchers on the TeraGrid to support computational experiments across a broad range of scientific disciplines [5][6].

The MyCluster system provisions resources for building personal clusters by deploying semi-autonomous agents at each HPC site. These semi-autonomous agents, reacting to local and global load conditions, submit and manage job proxies through the local scheduler at each HPC site. Job proxies then contribute CPUs back to the personal clusters when they are run by the local scheduler. Job proxies also allow application jobs, submitted into the personal cluster, to execute in a system call virtualized run-time environment where additional cluster-wide services are interposed in user-space.

MyCluster enables users to select a commodity job management system to aggregate the provisioned CPU resources into their personal clusters. Job management systems that are supported, in various stages of prototype to production form, include Condor [7][8], Sun Grid Engine (SGE) [10] and OpenPBS [9]. Users therefore benefit from using a single, well-known interface to interact with their jobs across the heterogeneous clusters on the TeraGrid. Users also benefit from the ability to reuse the plethora of tools that have been developed for these systems over the years.

Finally, MyCluster is a completely user-space system, with no requirement for administrator privilege for deployment. This choice allows the system deployment model to easily scale, allowing it to aggregate any HPC cluster accessible across the internet. A user can simply invoke a self-installer at a site, boot-strap a personal version of the system, and enable the provisioning of resources from that site for computational experiments.

Within the context of the MyCluster project, we have been developing a system for building private network overlays across HPC clusters to enable the seamless creation of personal clusters. Like MyCluster, the system is deployable in user-space, without administrator privilege. It allows the creation of a class B network, enabling compute nodes in internal networks to acquire a virtual IP address, advertise it, and exchange messages between each other using the standard BSD network socket interface. Programs do not have to be recompiled to use the network overlay. Our system transparently tunnels IP (TCP and UDP) traffic through a series of packet relays in the overlay to deliver message packets between addresses in the private network.

The network overlay instills some critical properties to the MyCluster system. First, the network overlay enables MyCluster to provision resources from HPC clusters with compute nodes in internal networks, allowing its deployment on most HPC cluster configurations. Second, the network overlay allows MyCluster to survive transient WAN outages, providing increased quality of service guarantees for long running experiments executing in the personal clusters. Third, the network overlay allows the WAN distributed filesystem XUFS [4] to be deployed within the personal cluster. This allows jobs running in the personal cluster to transparently access files from the submission directory across remote sites, emulating the shared filesystem in a real cluster. Fourth, in some cases, the network overlay improves transfer throughput across the WAN, enabling more efficient bulk data transfers across remote sites.

The rest of this paper will be as follows. Section 2 compares our work against other similar projects described in the literature. Section 3 describes the design and implementation of our network overlay in detail. In particular, it describes the mechanisms used to transparently interpose our overlay behavior into unmodified applications, the algorithm used to provide fault-tolerance to applications using our overlay, an *optional* kernel patch to improve the potential performance of one version of our system, and a brief overview of how a distributed filesystem is enabled by our overlay. Section 4 describes the experimental evaluation of our network overlay on the local area network (LAN) and on the TeraGrid WAN. It also describes some apparent anomalies in our experimental results, and determines their cause. The section also examines how much overhead is introduced to HPC applications running in our virtualized run-time environment. Finally, section 5 derives some important guiding principles from our experience, and concludes this paper.

2 Related Work

MyCluster creates personal clusters using resources across the WAN. It is therefore related to the projects like Cluster-On-Demand (COD) [12][13], VioClusters [14], In-VIRGO [15], WOW [16] and Virtual Workspaces [17]. In particular, VioClusters, InVirgo and WOW also create network overlays using the technologies VIOLIN [26], Virtuoso [24][25], and IPOP [27] respectively.

At the risk of over simplifying, these systems adopt the same basic approach of instantiating a system virtual machine with its network device bridged to a TAP device, configured in promiscuous mode, on the host computer. Marshalling processes on the host computer then forward Ethernet frames from the TAP device, originating from the system virtual machine, to the external network as UDP packets or, more interestingly, as packets to a P2P overlay like Brunet [29]. Conversely, un-marshalling processes on the host computer forward Ethernet frames it receives from the external network back to the TAP device into the system virtual machine.

The use of system virtual machines provides many useful properties to these projects. In particular, system virtual machines ensure resource, fault and security isolation between applications running on the same server. These isolation properties are important in IT hosting environments and infrastructures like PlanetLab [28] where multiple applications may be consolidated on the same server hardware. System virtual machines also offer the opportunity for users to ensure a correct operating system environment for their running jobs. This guarantees some level of quality of service, in terms of expected operating system environment, when jobs run. Our system however does not use system virtual machines for a number of reasons.

The first reason why we do not use system virtual machines is because the isolation properties offered by them are not as compelling a reason for their use in HPC clusters. This is because running jobs are already naturally resource isolated by the job schedulers on HPC clusters. These job schedulers fairly allocate time and space on the cluster nodes to jobs requesting them. Thus, for the period of time when the job runs, no other users are consuming resources on the same nodes. Also, HPC jobs are user-level processes that do not require kernel modifications, i.e. the installation of kernel modules. Unlike IT hosting environments where applications with special kernel module requirements may cause crashes and affect other running applications on the same server, HPC jobs run on dedicated compute nodes in isolation from other jobs in the cluster. Thus, a fault in a HPC job does not affect other running jobs in a cluster. Finally, the compute nodes in many HPC clusters are within private networks, completely isolated from the corporate and external network. Also, these nodes are re-imaged on a weekly or bi-weekly basis. Thus compute nodes already offer good security isolation.

The second reason why we do not use system virtual machines is because of the finely tuned execution environments in HPC clusters. HPC clusters have many software packages that are compiled and configured by HPC specialist to run well at the site. Also, these HPC clusters have operating system environments that are configured to reduce phenomena like operating system jitter [11], and to function well with internal components like the high-speed interconnect and parallel filesystem. For example, the IBM GPFS [30] and Lustre [31] filesystems on many HPC clusters work with only a small subset of Linux kernel versions which need to be further patched with vendor-specific modifications. These site-specific requirements severely restrict the choice of operating systems that can be instantiated by the user anyway.

The third reason why we do not use system virtual machines is because they often require the pre-installation of administrator-level components like virtual machine monitors, and/or hypervisors. Even with type II virtual machine monitors [18] (e.g. VMWare Workstation and User-Mode-Linux) setting up external networking for these virtual machines require bridge devices like TUN/TAP to be set up and configured in promiscuous mode. These actions require administrator permission, limiting the broad applicability of the approach only to sites that have agreed to deploy the appropriate configuration.

The fourth reason why we do not use system virtual machines is because each virtual machine instance requires a root filesystem image to boot. Root filesystem images are typically at least 500 megabytes in size, and this needs to be distributed across the WAN and replicated for every virtual machine instance created. For large HPC computational runs, there could be many thousands of virtual machines in use, requiring the replication and management of multiple gigabytes of image files.

Our network overlay project is also related to other tools that support IP traffic tunneling between private networks and the WAN. These tools include SOCKS [19], GCB [22], OpenSSH, OpenVPN [20] and PPTP [21]. All these tools have at least one deficiency which prevented their use in our system. SOCKS does not allow connections from an external network to a node in a private address space, while GCB assumes that the node in the private address space has at least outbound external network connectivity in order to operate correctly. In many cluster configurations, compute nodes have no external network connectivity in any direction. Also, OpenSSH, OpenVPN and PPTP represent point-to-point solutions, i.e. from a client to a gateway node. They do not easily cater for the scenario our network overlay supports, i.e. multiple nodes behind multiple gateways joining a private network infrastructure, without requiring extensive scripting and additional coding effort. Also, all the above technologies do not assign virtual IP addresses to the compute nodes in the private network. This is needed to prevent addressing conflicts for nodes from multiple internal networks.

Realm-Specific IP (RSIP) [23] is an experimental IETF proposal that is very similar to our network overlay solution. RSIP allows nodes in a private address space to register and temporarily lease a public IP address from a RSIP gateway. These nodes can then advertise their addresses and have external connections to them relayed through the RSIP gateway. There are however a number of problems with RSIP. First RSIP it is not widely implemented. It is intended as a replacement for NAT, but this has not occurred. Second, RSIP leases public IP addresses to the nodes in the private address space. This approach limits the number of available addresses that can be used.

3 Design and Implementation

3.1 MyCluster Overview

MyCluster builds Condor, SGE or OpenPBS clusters when a user creates a *virtual login session*. Within this virtual login session, users can submit, monitor and manage jobs through a single job management interface, emulating the experience of a traditional cluster login session. Fig 1 shows an example of a SGE virtual login session.

```
ewalker@blanco ~]$ vo-login -S
Enter GRID pass phrase:
Spawning on tg-login.tacc.teragrid.org
Spawning on tg-login3.ncsa.teragrid.org
Setting up VO participants ......Done

Welcome to your MyCluster/Sun Grid Engine environment
To shutdown environment, type "exit"
To detach from environment, type "detach"

blanco(grid)% agent_jobs
GATEWAY: lonestar.tacc.utexas.edu
    753018 (RUNNING)
GATEWAY: tg-login3.ncsa.teragrid.org
    526521.tg-master.ncsa.teragrid.org (RUNNING)
blanco(grid)% qhost
HOSTNAME        ARCH       NPROC  LOAD  MEMTOT  MEMUSE  SWAPTO  SWAPUS
-------------------------------------------------------------------------
global          -            -      -     -       -       -       -
mc1-14          glinux       2    0.03   2.0G   79.1M    2.0G    0.0
mc1-9           glinux       2    0.00   2.0G   92.6M    2.0G    0.0
tg-c491         ia64linux    2    0.65   3.9G  383.3M    5.9G   23.5M
tg-c861         ia64linux    2    0.00   3.9G  404.7M    6.0G   16.5M

blanco(grid)% qsub -t 1000 sub.cmd
your job-array 1.1000-1000:1 ("sub.cmd") has been submitted
blanco(grid)% qdel 1
ewalker has registered the job-array task 1.1000 for deletion
```

Fig. 1. Formatted snapshot of a SGE virtual login session

A high level overview of the MyCluster processes relevant to the discussion in our paper is shown in Fig 2. When a user first starts a virtual login session, the system remotely spawns a *proxy manager* at the head node of each of the clusters contributing resources to the session. These proxy managers submit and manager *job proxies* to the local scheduler at the site. When the local scheduler runs the job proxy, it starts the job starter daemon for the job management system selected for the session, i.e. Condor, SGE or OpenPBS. The job starter daemon then registers back to the master processes at the job submission host across the WAN. Jobs submitted to

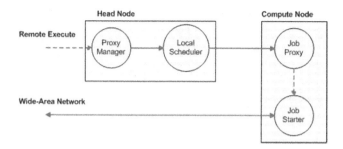

Fig. 2. MyCluster process architecture overview

the personal cluster can then be dispatched to the newly registered job starter, with the user seeing an expanding and shrinking cluster as these job starter daemons register and terminate over time.

3.2 Private Network Overlay Architecture

The MyCluster system requires the provisioned compute nodes in a virtual login session to have full bi-directional access to the external network. This is to allow the job starter to register and accept jobs from the job management master processes in the personal cluster. Many of the TeraGrid clusters have compute nodes with full network connectivity to the TeraGrid WAN, and thus MyCluster is easily supported on these systems.

However, to enable MyCluster to be deployed on HPC clusters with the more traditional configuration where compute node are within a private network, a network overlay has been implemented to enable external network connectivity for these job starters.

The network overlay we have implemented allows a private class B network to be deployed, instantiated, and destroyed by user–level processes, requiring no administrator privilege, pre-installed virtual machine or outbound WAN connectivity for the compute nodes. Using interposition methods, our solution overrides the socket system calls in the application process to allow connections between privately assigned class B IP addresses to be tunneled through a series of subnet routers. These subnet routers run as user-level processes and are strategically located at the head (or some gateway) node of the clusters with access to the external network.

Subnet routers initialize their internal route tables by reading a route table file `.uvpn_route_<id>` created for each virtual network instance. This file specifies, for a particular session, the subnet to which the host cluster belongs and the contact addresses for routers of other subnets in the network overlay.

Fig 3 shows the augmented MyCluster process architecture with the network overlay support for routing IP traffic between compute nodes provisioned by a virtual login session. When a user starts a virtual login session, each host cluster is allocated a subnet in a virtual class B network and a subnet router is spawned at the head node. Each node provisioned by a job proxy is then assigned a virtual IP address in the subnet, with the home router (at the cluster head node) keeping a database of real to virtual IP address mapping.

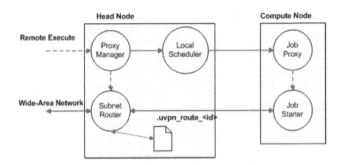

Fig. 3. MyCluster process architecture with a network overlay

When the application process in a job proxy, i.e. the job starter, invokes the `connect()` system call to an address within the private network, a series of connections are made to establish an IP packet relay path between the source and destination addresses. First, the interposed `connect()` makes a connection to the home router and sends a connection header containing the source and destination address end-points associated with the desired virtual connection. The format of the connection header is shown in Fig 4.

0	7	15	31
OPCODE	FLAG	NOP	
Source virtual IP address			
Source port			
Destination virtual IP address			
Destination port			

Fig. 4. Network overlay connection header

The home router then searches its route table for the location of the peer router responsible for the subnet associated with the virtual destination address. A connection is then made to the peer router and the connection header forwarded. The peer router, on receiving the connection header, looks up the real IP address associated with the virtual destination address, and makes a connection to this real address. The connection header is then forwarded to the destination process, which then stores the information contained in the connection header for future reference.

When the relay path is finally created from the home router, through the peer router, to the real IP address, the `connect()` call returns the socket descriptor for this relay. Equivalently, the `accept()` call, which is also interposed at the destination, returns the socket descriptor for the other end of this relay. This relay connection simulates a dedicated leased-line, allowing the processes at both ends to issue `send` (or `write`) and `recv` (or `read`) calls to exchange bytes between them. If a process decides to query information associated with the socket connection, we interpose the `getsockname()` and `getpeername()` calls to return the information associated with the virtual connection, instead of information associated with the real connection to the home routers.

3.3 Interposition Mechanisms

The system supports two mechanisms for interposing our network overlay functionality into the BSD socket call interface. The first uses the UNIX shared object preloading mechanism available in most UNIX variants. For example, on Linux this involves defining the location of a shared object in the LD_PRELOAD environment variable. This shared object will then be used by the linker to override the system shared library implementation of the socket interface, allowing our overlay behavior to be interposed.

Table 1. Interposed socket system calls

PRELOAD	PTRACE
Connection-less based protocols	
`sendto, recvfrom`	`sendto, recvfrom`
Connection based protocols	
`connect, accept`	`connect, accept`
Shadow socket management	
	`socket, listen, bind,` `setsockopt`
Connection information	
`getsockname,` `getpeername`	`getsockname,` `getpeername`
Connection termination	
`close`	`close`
Shadow socket duplicate tracing	
	`dup, dup2, fctnl, fork`

The shared library preloading mechanism however only works on dynamic linked executables. Furthermore, some UNIX variants, in particular AIX, do not support the preloading mechanism. To remedy this, we provide an alternative mechanism to interpose our overlay functionality. This alternative mechanism uses the UNIX ptrace debugging interface. The ptrace interface allows a parent process to monitor the execution of its children processes, allowing system calls in the children processes to be traced and modified by manipulating the CPU architecture registers prior to and after their invocation.

The socket calls interposed by the two mechanisms are shown in Table 1. The preloading mechanism interposes the connect() and accept() calls to support the creation of the virtual connection relay for connection based protocols. For connection-less protocols, the sendto() and recvfrom() calls are also interposed. The getsockname() and getpeername() calls are interposed to return the correct information about the virtual connection as explained before.

Finally, the close() system call is interposed to allow the managed termination of virtual connections.

The preloading mechanism allows our system to directly query and manipulate socket descriptors in the interposed application. Interposing the overlay functionality using the ptrace mechanism however requires additional effort. The ptrace monitoring process runs in a separate process image, making querying and manipulating socket descriptors in the monitored application process difficult.

To overcome this difficulty, our strategy for the ptrace mechanism is to implement the overlay functionality in the parent monitoring process itself. Overlay connections are established between shadow sockets in the ptrace monitoring processes that exactly mirror the sockets created in the application processes. Fig 5 illustrates the basic idea.

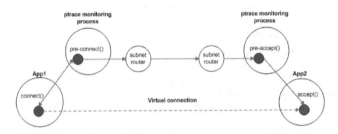

Fig. 5. Shadow sockets negotiate relay connection between ptrace parent processes

For every successful socket() invocation in the interposed application process, the ptrace monitoring process also creates an equivalent shadow socket. Subsequent calls to bind(), listen(), and setsockopt() on a socket in the application process causes the same action to be performed on its associated shadow socket in the ptrace monitoring process.

To avoid clashes in the local network port namespace, the application requested port number for the bind() call on the original socket is replaced with a free port in the range [51000, 52000]. Only the shadow socket is allowed to bind to the application requested port number instead. Note in particular that the shadow socket at the receiving peer is now set to listen to the application requested port instead of the original socket. To avoid confusing the user application, the getsockname() call is interposed to return the application requested port for the original socket when it is invoked.

When a TCP connection is initiated in a network overlay using the ptrace mechanism, the connecting application process is redirected to connect to a dynamically created relay thread in the monitoring parent. The shadow socket that is associated with the original socket then creates the virtual connection relay to the monitoring parent at the receiving peer as described before. The monitoring parent at the receiver peer then connects to the socket in the application process which is listening on the alternative port we had previously assigned it to.

Messages to/from the virtual connection are then routed through the additional relay thread in the monitoring parent to/from the subnet routers. The information contained in the connection header for the virtual connection is maintained in the monitoring parent at either end-point, and the getpeername() and getsockname() calls in the application are interposed to return this information as necessary.

3.3.1 Tracing Duplicate Socket Descriptors

In order to properly terminate virtual connections, the ptrace mechanism also needs to closely trace socket descriptors that are duplicated within and across processes. To do this, our network overlay system also traces the dup(), dup2(), fcntl() and fork() system call. For the fork() call in particular, our system will check if any shadow sockets has the FD_CLOEXEC flag set. If it is not set, the socket descriptor is expected to be duplicated in the new process.

When a socket descriptor is duplicated, we increment a reference count to a structure record we maintain for each shadow socket. Subsequent close() calls on the duplicated socket descriptor decrements this shared reference count. When the reference count reaches 0, the shadow socket is then closed, and any associated virtual connection terminated.

3.4 Tolerating WAN Outages

An important benefit of creating our network overlay is the WAN fault tolerant properties it instills to the end-points in the virtual connection. The IP packet relay created by our network overlay effectively isolates the connected application processes at either end-points from the less reliable WAN. When a network outage causes the connection between peer subnet routers to be temporarily disconnected, this disconnection is not propagated to the end-points.

To prevent the lose of in-flight messages during a WAN outage, Fig 6 details the WAN recovery algorithm used in our network overlay. Messages that are sent from the application to the subnet router are immediately forwarded to the destination socket connected to a peer subnet router in the connection relay. If the forwarding is successful, a count s_bytes is incremented with the number of bytes sent, while at the destination peer subnet router, the count r_bytes is incremented with the number of bytes received. The message itself is also appended to a circular buffer of sent messages. The size of this circular buffer is equal to the size of the socket's internal send buffer size, i.e. SO_SNDBUF.

If the subnet router fails to forward an application message, the message is appended to an unsent message file and the subnet router periodically (every 5 minutes) attempts to reconnect with the peer subnet router in the connection relay.

When the connection with the peer subnet router is re-established, a hand-shake is performed to ensure recovery of any lost in-flight data. First, the peer router sends its r_bytes count to the reconnecting router. Second, the reconnecting router compares this against its s_bytes count. Third, if the s_bytes value is larger then the received r_bytes value, the reconnecting router sends s_bytes-r_bytes bytes from the circular buffer of sent messages. Fourth, the reconnecting router then forwards the content of the unsent message file to the peer router, after which the connection relay resets back to its original fault-free state.

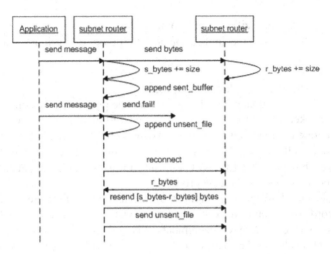

Fig. 6. WAN outage recovery algorithm

3.5 Personal Global File Namespaces

The network overlay allows compute nodes provisioned in the virtual login session to communicate with the submission workstation from which the personal cluster is created. An important collateral benefit is that this provides the ability for compute nodes, provisioned from an internal private network, to mount the XUFS distributed filesystem enabling jobs running on them to access files from the submission directory. XUFS allows the submission directory to be mounted in user-space and, like our network overlay, can be deployed, instantiated and destroyed without administrator privilege. Also, similar to our network overlay solution, XUFS uses interposition mechanism to allow this transparent remote access to files and directories. More details about XUFS can be found in our prior publications [3].

3.6 "ptrace is slow"

In adopting the ptrace debugging mechanism as one method of imposing our network overlay functional into the socket interface, we have often encountered the comment "ptrace is slow". This is usually accompanied by anecdotal stories supporting the claim. Later in section 4.4, we examine the overhead of running a collection of HPC benchmarks representing different workload types in our ptrace interposed environment. We will see later that for many HPC workloads this assertion is not necessarily true.

In this section we look at the degenerate case where a program's execution time is dominated by many repeated system calls. An example of such a degenerate case is a program whose only task is reading and writing a very large file using very small read/write message buffers. Later we show in section 4.1 an example of such a degenerate case in one of our scenarios in the experimental evaluation of the TCP throughput of our network overlay solution

In these degenerate cases, the `ptrace` mechanism is expected to introduce large overheads. This is because the ptrace mechanism causes the operating system to stop the application process every time a system call is invoked. This allows the monitoring parent process to examine and modify the execution of the application as necessary. Furthermore, this stop-start behavior occurs twice for every system calls invoked in the application process; once prior to a system call invocation and once after it has been completed by the operating system.

We have implemented an optimization to the ptrace mechanism in Linux to allow the monitoring process to selectively decide what system calls are of interest to it. For example, our network overlay mechanism is only interested in a subset of the socket system calls. Often repeated system calls like `send()`, `write()`, `recv()`, and `read()` do not need to be interposed by our system. This design choice is deliberate to ensure we introduce as little overhead to the original application as possible.

The optimization we have implemented in Linux introduces a new PTRACE_SYSCALL_MASK option to the ptrace system call. We allow the monitoring process to use a bit-mask data structure to selectively set the bits associated with system calls of interest to it. The monitoring process then uses this bit-mask as the input parameter to the `ptrace()` system call when the PTRACE_SYSCALL_MASK option is used. The ptrace mechanism then only stops the application processes when a system call defined in this bit-mask is invoked. A code fragment illustrating how this option is used by a monitoring process who is only interested in the `open()` system call is shown below:

```
scall_set syscall_mask;

SC_ZERO(&syscall_mask);
SC_SET(__NR_open, &syscall_mask);
ptrace(PTRACE_SYSCALL_MASK,pid,&syscall_mask,__NR_open+1);
```

We have implemented this ptrace enhancement in the Linux kernel version 2.6.16 [32]. We show in our experimental evaluation section later that this improves the performance in all our scenarios when comparing the TCP connection throughput performance in our network overlay against the native socket connection throughput. We are encouraged by this, and also by the fact that this option is already under discussion by the mainline Linux development community, albeit in a different implementation version [33].

4 Experimental Evaluation

4.1 Local Area Network TCP Throughput Evaluation

In this section, we describe results from experiments comparing the TCP transfer throughput of a native connection versus a connection through the proposed network overlay on a local area network (LAN). The experiments were conducted between two Linux 2.6.16 X86_64 hosts connected through a 100 Mbs switch. Each host was designated a subnet, with a subnet router running on each. For all experiments, the TCP throughput was measured using NETPERF [34]. Fig 7 illustrates the LAN experiment setup for the network overlay.

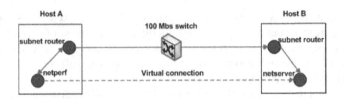

Fig. 7. LAN experiment setup for the network overlay

Table 2 shows the TCP throughput on the LAN using a native TCP socket connection versus a connection made through the network overlay using the preloading mechanism. The network overlay connection shows no degradation in throughput performance compared to the native connection.

Table 2. TCP throughput (Mbs) of native connection versus connection through the overlay using the preload mechanism

Send size (bytes)	100	200	300	400	500	600	700	800	900	1000
Native	93.95	94.03	94.03	94.03	94.03	94.03	93.99	94.02	94.03	94.02
preload	94.2	94.25	94.3	94.27	94.31	94.28	94.28	94.3	94.29	94.3

Fig 8 shows the TCP throughput on the LAN using a native TCP socket connection versus a connection made through the network overlay using the ptrace mechanism. The experiment show the throughput performance degrading considerably for small send sizes. This experiment demonstrates the degenerate case expounded on in section 3.6. For small send sizes, many more send() system calls are invoked, causing the application process to be stopped much more frequently then when large send sizes are used.

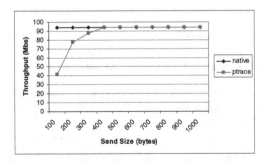

Fig. 8. TCP throughput (Mbs) of native connection versus network overlay connection using the ptrace mechanism

Table 3 shows the TCP throughput on the LAN using a native socket connection versus a connection made through the network overlay using the ptrace mechanism with the PTRACE_SYSCALL_MASK enhancement enabled. We see that the network overlay connection shows no degradation in throughput.

Table 3. TCP throughput (Mbs) of native connection versus connection through the overlay using the ptrace mechanism (PTRACE_SYSCALL_MASK enhancement enabled)

Send size (bytes)	100	200	300	400	500	600	700	800	900	1000
Native	93.95	94.03	94.03	94.03	94.03	94.03	03.99	94.02	94.03	94.02
Ptrace+enh	94.29	94.28	94.3	94.28	94.28	94.31	94.3	94.3	94.29	94.3

4.2 Wide Area Network TCP Throughput Evaluation

In this section, we describe results from experiments comparing the TeraGrid WAN TCP transfer throughput of a native connection versus that of a connection through our network overlay. The experiments were conducted between an SDSC cluster compute-node and the NCSA cluster head node, with the network overlay subnet routers deployed at the cluster head nodes. All IP traffic was tunneled through the firewall at each site using one of the free ports in the range [50000,51000] open for traffic between the two sites. For all experiments, the TCP throughput was measured using NETPERF. Fig 9 illustrates the experimental setup. The PTRACE_SYSCALL_MASK ptrace option was not tested in the experiments in this section because we did not have to the opportunity to patch the running kernels at these sites.

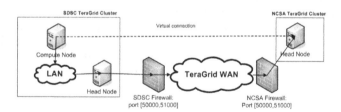

Fig. 9. TeraGrid WAN experimental setup for the network overlay

Fig 10 shows the TCP throughput on the TeraGrid WAN using a native connection versus connections through the network overlay using the different interposition mechanisms. The TCP throughput through the network overlay show no perceptible overhead, except for the degenerate case for small send sizes when the ptrace interposition mechanism is used. The throughput in the network overlay using the ptrace mechanism shows a 21% degradation in performance for the 100 byte send size scenario. However, we note that because of the lower bandwidth of the WAN, this degradation is not as pronounced as that observed in the LAN experiments.

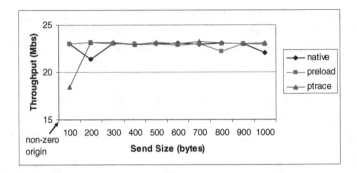

Fig. 10. TCP throughput of native connection versus network overlay connections between NCSA and SDSC

4.3 TCP Throughput Anomaly

An experiment was conducted on the TeraGrid WAN between TACC and NCSA with the setup similar to Fig 9, except with the SDSC cluster replaced with the TACC cluster. Fig 11 shows the TCP throughput of a native connection and a network overlay connection between a TACC cluster compute-node and the NCSA cluster head node. The network overlay configuration tunnels the TCP connection through a relay between subnet routers located at the TACC and NCSA cluster head nodes. Surprisingly, the results show a 500% improvement in the TCP throughput using the network overlay compared to the native TCP socket connection.

After some investigation, this apparent anomaly was explained by the different network device configurations at the compute and head nodes on the TACC cluster. The TACC cluster compute nodes had their network device MTU (Maximum Transmission Unit) set to the default 1500. This MTU value is optimized for the LAN rather than the WAN, because the network device was also used for mounting the internal NFS (network file system) home directories on the compute node. However, the TACC cluster head node had its network device MTU set to 9000, optimized for sending jumbo packets across the WAN. Therefore, rerouting IP traffic through the head node improved the TCP throughput performance across the WAN significantly.

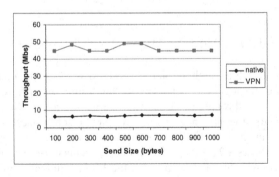

Fig. 11. TCP throughput of native connection versus network overlay connection between TACC and NCSA

4.4 Execution Overhead

In this section, we investigate the overhead introduced when HPC applications are executed in the system call virtualized environment where the network overlay and distributed filesystem (XUFS) services are interposed.

Fig 12 (a) and (b) show the run-time of the applications in the NAS [35] and BioBench [36] benchmarks respectively. We ran the benchmarks in our virtualized environment and compared the run-times when executed natively. All benchmarks were run on a Linux 2.6.16 kernel X86_64 host with one gigabyte of memory.

Most of the benchmark applications show no perceptible overhead when executed in our system call virtualized run-time environment. Only the FASTA application in the BioBench benchmark exhibited a 19% degradation in performance when executed in the ptrace interposed environment.

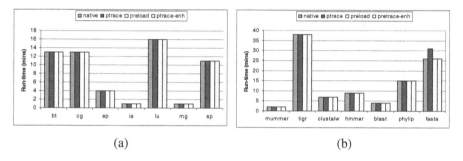

(a)   (b)

Fig. 12. Run-times of NAS (a) and BioBench (b) benchmarks in the system call virtualized run time environments

All the benchmark applications, except FASTA, have system call profiles similar to the BLASTP system call invocation histogram shown in Fig 13 (a). The BLASTP profile illustrates the read, compute, and write phases common to most HPC applications. The profile also shows that the majority of the run time is dominated by the compute cycle.

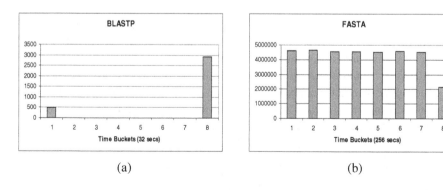

(a)   (b)

Fig. 13. Histogram of system call frequency for BLASTP (a) and FASTA (b)

In contrast, for FASTA we see a more evenly spread system call invocation profile across the entire run-time of the application, as shown in Fig 13 (b). But because of the compute bound nature of FASTA, this mitigates the overhead introduced by the ptrace mechanism to only 19% in our case.

5 Conclusions

We have described our mechanism for providing a network overlay to support the creation of personal clusters in the MyCluster system. The system is unique in providing a completely user-space solution, requiring no pre-installation of virtual machine monitors or hypervisors. Furthermore, our solution provides additional fault-tolerance to application processes communicating over the WAN and throughput benefits in certain deployment scenarios.

Some general principles can be derived from our experience to help guide other projects building similar widely distributed system call virtualized run-time environments.

First, user-space interposition mechanisms do not provide the properties of resource, fault, and security isolation, but they are highly appropriate for augmenting the properties of the native system to enable more productivity for the user. Consider if the required level of isolation guarantees is already satisfied by the system, and if needed, consider the range of alternative mechanisms for providing this, such as QoS schedulers [38], kernel-level interposition techniques [39][40] or full system virtual machines. For example, MyCluster currently provides isolation properties through personal cluster containers with HPC cluster QoS schedulers assigning dedicated resources for each instance.

Second, shared object preloading is a very efficient user-space interposition mechanism and should be used where possible to implement overlay behavior. Where appropriate this can be used in conjunction with other techniques for providing isolation properties to the system.

Third, the ptrace debugging interface is an acceptable mechanism to interpose overlay behavior for compute-bound applications. For non compute-bound applications which frequently invoke system calls, high execution overheads can be expected. However, new ptrace system call options like PTRACE_SYSCALL_MASK can be implemented to mitigate this.

Fourth, WAN fault-tolerant properties can be transparently added into network applications by isolating the connection end-points from the WAN in an overlay. This can be used to ensure legacy applications, originally developed for the LAN, are able to survive transient network outages in the less reliable WAN.

Finally, network bulk transfer throughput across a WAN can be improved by routing network connections through WAN optimized intermediaries in an overlay. The cost of implementing additional connection hops can sometimes be more then compensated by the gain in transfer throughput.

References

[1] Walker, E., Gardner, J.P., Litvin, V., Turner, E.L.: Personal Adaptive Clusters as Containers for Scientific Jobs, Cluster Computing, vol. 10(3) (September 2007)

[2] Walker, E., Gardner, J.P., Litvin, V., Turner, E.L.: Creating Adaptive Clusters in User-Space for Managing Scientific Jobs in a Widely Distributed Environment. In: CLADE 2006. Proc. of IEEE Workshop on Challenges of Large Applications in Distributed Environments, Paris (July 2006)

[3] NSF TeraGrid, http://www.teragrid.org

[4] Walker, E.: A Distributed File System for a Wide-Area High Performance Computing Infrastructure. In: WORLDS 2006. Proc. of the 3rd USENIX Workshop on Real, Large Distributed Systems, Seattle (November 2006)

[5] Walker, E., Guiang, C.: Challenges in Executing Large Parameter Sweep Studies Across Widely Distributed Computing Environments. In: CLADE 2007. Proc. of IEEE Workshop on Challenges of Large Applications in Distributed Environments, Monterrey (June 2007)

[6] Walker, E.: How to Run A Million Jobs in Six Months on the NSF TeraGrid. Proc. of TeraGrid 2007 (June 2007)

[7] Condor, High Throughput Computing Environment, http://www.cs.wisc.edu/Condor/

[8] Litzkow, M., Livny, M., Matka, M.: Condor – A Hunter of Idle Workstations. In: Proc. of the International Conference of Distributed Computing Systems, pp. 104–111 (June 1988)

[9] Portable Batch System, http://www.openpbs.org

[10] Sun Grid Engine, http://gridengine.sunsource.net/

[11] Kerbyson, D.J., Pakin, S., Petrini, F.: The Case of the Missing Supercomputer Performance: Achieving Optimal Performance on the 8,192 Processors of ASCI Q. In: Proc. of ACM/IEEE Conference on High Performance Networking and Computing (SC03), Phoenix, Arizona, pp. 15–21 (November 2003)

[12] Chase, J., Grit, L., Irwin, D., Moore, J., Sprenkle, S.: Dynamic Virtual Clusters in a Grid Site Manager. In: Proc. of the 12th Intl Symp on High Performance Distributed Computing (HPDC-12) (2003)

[13] Ramakrishnan, L., Grit, L., Iamnitchi, A., Irwin, D., Yumerefendi, A., Chase, J.: Toward a Doctrine of Containment: Grid Hosting with Adaptive Resource Control. In: SC 2006. Proc. Of the ACM/IEEE Conference on High Performance Networking and Computing, Tampa, FL (November 2006)

[14] Ruth, P., McGachey, P., Jiang, X., Xu, D.: VioCluster: Virtualization for Dynamic Computational Domains. In: Cluster 2005. Proc. of the IEEE International Conference on Cluster Computing, Boston, MA (September 2005)

[15] Adabala, S., Chadha, V., Chawla, P., Figueiredo, R., Fortes, J., Krsul, I., Matsunaga, A., Tsugawa, M., Zhang, J., Zhao, M., Zhu, L., Zhu, X.: From Virtualized Resources to Virtual Computing Grids: The In-VIGO System, Future Generation Computer Systems (2004)

[16] Ganguly, A., Agrawal, A., Boykin, P.O., Figueiredo, R.: WOW: Self-Organizing Wide Area Overlay Networks of Virtual Workstations. In: Proc. of the 15th IEEE Intl. Symp. On High Performance Distributed Computing (HPDC-15), Paris (2006)

[17] Keahey, K., Doering, K., Foster, I.: From Sandbox to Playground: Dynamic Virtual Environments in the Grid. In: Proc. of the 5th International Workshop in Grid Computing (2004)

[18] Goldberg, R.: Architectural Principles for Virtual Computer Systems. PhD thesis, Harvard University (February 1973)

[19] Leech, M., Ganis, M., Lee, Y., Kuris, R., Koblas, D., Jones, L.: SOCKS: Protocol Version 5, IETF RFC 1928 (March 1996)

[20] OpenVPN, http://www.openvpn.net

[21] Hamzeh, K., Pall, G., Verthein, W., Taarud, J., Little, W., Zorn, G.: Point-to-point Tunneling Protocol (PPTP), IETF RFC 2637 (July 1999)

[22] Son, S., Livny, M.: Recovering Internet Symmetry in Distributed Computing. In: Proc. of the 3rd Intl. Symp. On Cluster Computing and the Grid (CCGrid), Tokyo, Japan (May 2003)

[23] Borella, M., Lo, J., Grabelsky, D., Montenegro, G.: Realm Specific IP: Framework, IETF RFC 2102 (July 2000)

[24] Dinda, P., Sundaraj, A., Gupta, A.: Dynamic Topology Adaption of Virtual Networks of Virtual Machines. In: Proc. of the 7th Workshop on Languages, Compilers and Run-time Support for Scalable Systems (October 2004)

[25] Sundararaj, A., Dinda, P.: Towards Virtual Networks for Virtual Machine Grid Computing. In: Proc. of the 3rd USENIX Virtual Machine Research and Technology Symposium, San Jose, CA (May 2004)

[26] Jiang, X., Xu, D.: Violin: Virtual Internetworking on Overlay Infrastructure. In: Proc. of the 2nd International Symposium Of Parallel and Distributed Processing and Applications (December 2004)

[27] Ganguly, A., Agrawal, A., Boykin, P.O., Figueiredo, R.: IP Over P2P: Enabling Self-Configuring Virtual IP Networks for Grid Computing. In: IPDPS 2006. Proc. of the 20th IEEE Intl. Parallel and Distributed Processing Symposium, Rhodes Island, Greece (2006)

[28] PlanetLab, http://www.planet-lab.org/

[29] Boykin, P.O., Bridgewater, J., Kong, J., Lozev, K., Rezaei, B., Roychowdhury, V.P.: Brunet software library, http://brunet.ee.ucla.edu/brunet/

[30] Schmuck, F., Haskin, R.: GPFS: A Shared-Disk File System for Large Computing Clusters. In: Proc. of the 1st USENIX Conference on File and Storage Technologies (FAST), Monterey, CA (2002)

[31] Schwan, P.: Lustre: Building a File System for 1,000-node Clusters. In: Proc. of Ottawa Linux Symposium (2003)

[32] PTRACE_SYSCALL_MASK Linux 2.6.16 patch, http://www.tacc.utexas.edu/~ewalker/syscall_mask.patch

[33] "Virtual Time" posting, LWN.net 29/ (1798), http://lwn.net/Articles/

[34] NETPERF, http://www.netperf.org/netperf/

[35] Bailey, D., Barszcz, E., Barton, J., Browning, D., Carter, R., Dagum, L., Fatoohi, R., Fineberg, S., Frederickson, P., Lasinski, T., Schreiber, R., Simon, H., Venkatakrishnan, V., Weeratunga, S.: The NAS Parallel Benchmarks, RNR Technical Report, RNR-94-007 (March 1994)

[36] Albayraktaroglu, K., Jaleel, A., Wu, X., Franklin, M., Jacob, B., Tseng, C.W., Yeung, D.: BioBench: A Benchmark Suite of Bioinformatics Applications. In: ISPASS 2005. Proc. of the 2005 IEEE Intl. Symp. on Performance Analysis of Systems and Software, Austin TX (March 2005)

[37] Globus Security Infrastructure, http://www.globus.org/toolkit/docs/4.0/security/

[38] Aurrecoechea, C., Campbell, A.T., Hauw, L.: A Survey of QoS Architectures. Multimedia Systems 6(3) (May 1998)

[39] Davoli, R., Goldweber, M., Gardenghi, L.: UMView: View-OS implemented as a System Call Virtual Machine. In: OSDI 2006. Poster at USENIX Operating System Design and Implementation (2006), http://www.usenix.org/events/osdi06/posters/davoli.pdf

[40] Soltesz, S., Poltzl, H., Fiuczynski, M.E., Bavier, A., Peterson, L.: Container-based Operating System Virtualization: A Scalable, High-performance Alternative to Hypervisors. In: Proc. of 2nd ACM EuroSys Conference, Lisbon, Portugal (March 2007)

A Cost-Effective Distributed File Service with QoS Guarantees

Kien Le, Ricardo Bianchini, and Thu D. Nguyen

Department of Computer Science, Rutgers University
{lekien, ricardob, tdnguyen}@cs.rutgers.edu

Abstract. Large-scale, value-added Internet services composed of independent cooperating or competing services will soon become common place. Several groups have addressed the performance, communication, discovery, and description aspects of these services. However, little work has been done on effectively composing paid services and the quality-of-service (QoS) guarantees that they provide. We address these issues in the context of distributed file storage in this paper. In particular, we propose, implement, and evaluate a cost-effective, QoS-aware distributed file service comprising a front-end file service and back-end (third-party) storage services. Our front-end service uses mathematical modeling and optimization to provide performance and availability guarantees at low cost by carefully orchestrating the accesses to the back-end services. Experimental results from our prototype implementation validate our modeling and optimization. We conclude that our approach for providing QoS at low cost should be useful to future composite Internet services.

Keywords: Distributed storage, quality of service, cost optimization.

1 Introduction

Large-scale, value-added Internet services composed of independent cooperating or competing services will soon become common place. We refer to these services as *composite services*. Two technology trends suggest this new class of services: the progress toward ubiquitous Internet connectivity even from devices with limited resources, and the increasing adoption of service communication, discovery, and description standards, such as the Simple Object Access Protocol (SOAP), the Universal Description, Discovery and Integration Service (UDDI), and the Web Service Definition Language (WSDL). Together, these trends are forcing functionality and data into the network infrastructure in the form of remotely accessible services.

Composite services promise anytime, anywhere access to powerful services and vast data sets. A composite service may use constituent services that provide complementary functionality or data. For example, a composite stock service might use a service that provides stock quotes in some currency and a service that translates an amount of money (e.g., a stock quote) in one currency into another. In contrast, a composite service may use services that provide the same functionality or data. For example, a composite job-scheduler service might use multiple job-execution services. Regardless of type, we expect that composite services and their constituent services will provide service-level agreements (SLAs) for a monetary charge.

R. Cerqueira and R.H. Campbell (Eds.): Middleware 2007, LNCS 4834, pp. 223–243, 2007.
© IFIP International Federation for Information Processing 2007

In terms of structure, composite services are organized into a front-end service and multiple independent back-end services. The front-end service monitors and aggregates the back-end services, whereas the back-end services communicate with the front-end service but not with each other. In the above examples, the stock and job-scheduler services are called front-end services, whereas the stock-quote, currency-exchange, and job-execution services are called the back-end services.

For several years, researchers have been studying composite services in one form or another in the CORBA, Grid, and Web Service communities. These works have mostly focused on the performance, communication protocols, discovery mechanisms, and description of these composite services. Little work has been done on effectively composing paid services and the quality-of-service (QoS) guarantees that they provide.

In this paper, we address these issues in the context of distributed file storage. In particular, we propose, implement, and evaluate a cost-effective, QoS-aware composite file service comprising a front-end file service and back-end (third-party) storage services. The composite file service is intended to support soft real-time applications that involve large data files, such as the visualization of large-scale scientific data (e.g., [1]). For these applications, it is important to guarantee that data files will be available a large fraction of the time, and that a large percentage of file accesses will be served within a certain amount of time.

The composite service provides "soft" availability and performance guarantees, i.e. in extreme scenarios, such as a network partition separating front-end and back-end services, the guarantees may be violated. When these violations occur, the service compensates users for the violations.

Our front-end service allows users to choose the performance and availability guarantees that they desire on a per-file basis. Based on the chosen availability guarantee, the front-end service replicates the file across the back-end services. Based on both chosen guarantees, the back-end services' behaviors, and their SLAs, the front-end service intelligently distributes the requests across the back-end services to provide the chosen guarantees at low cost.

The front-end service uses mathematical modeling and optimization to carefully orchestrate the accesses to the back-end services. More specifically, the front-end service combines two algorithms: Base and OptWait. Base is reminiscent of traditional job scheduling. It sends each request to one of the back-end services that replicate the corresponding file, according to a ratio determined by the mathematical machinery to meet the file's performance guarantees while minimizing access cost. In contrast, OptWait is more sophisticated. It may actually send each request to multiple back-end services in turn (starting with the cheaper ones) until the request is satisfied. The amount of time it waits for each service to respond is determined mathematically and depends on the probability that the service will return a reply during that time and on the file's performance guarantee. Because we can mathematically decide on the best algorithm, our composite service picks the best algorithm for each file.

Because our initial focus (and the focus of this paper) is on the request-distribution aspect of our work, we have implemented a prototype of our composite service with a single front-end file server. The server implements the NFS protocol and executes our mathematical machinery. It communicates with client machines using a standard NFS protocol over UDP, whereas it communicates with back-end services using XML over HTTP. Several Internet storage services, e.g. Amazon.com's S3 [2], could implement the back-end services. However, for greater control of our experiments, we implemented our own back-end services, which provide data blocks named by absolute number.

Experimental results from our prototype implementation validate our modeling and optimization approach. Our analysis of the algorithms studies several different parameters, including the performance and availability guarantees, and the characteristics and behavior of the back-end services. Our most important results show that our composite service is successful at providing the guarantees that it promises. The results also show that, independently, Base and OptWait provide the lowest cost in different parts of the parameter space, whereas our combined system always produces the lowest cost.

2   Related Work

Our work builds upon previous research on service composition, QoS-aware resource management, and distributed file and storage systems.

Service composition. This has been an important research topic in the Web Services community, e.g. [3,4]. These works typically consider the QoS-aware composition of services from constituent services that provide complementary computational functionality. For this reason, they do not consider request-distribution policies across the services. Our work differs from these efforts as we study request-distribution policies that are both QoS- and cost-aware, across functionally-equivalent constituent services.

QoS-aware resource management. A large body of work has been done on this topic, especially in the context of networks, server clusters, and grid environments, e.g. [5,6,7]. These works consider resource allocation, provisioning, reservation, and negotiation, as well as admission-control policies in guaranteeing QoS (and sometimes optimizing costs) for the systems' users.

The extent of the performance guarantees provided by our composite service is limited to the front-end and back-end services' behaviors, as well as the communication between front-end and back-end services; the composite service cannot provide performance guarantees about the communication between clients and the front-end service. All other works on server-side QoS guarantees have this same limitation. We envision combining our QoS guarantees with those of future networks to completely eliminate this limitation. Nevertheless, an easy approach to tackle this problem with current network technology is to place front-end servers on the same local-area network as clients. In this approach, the front-end server could be an appliance, like today's load balancing or storage appliances.

Although we can benefit from previous QoS works in managing the resources of our front-end service and by leveraging network QoS, this paper focuses on request distribution across the black-box back-end services, which allow us no control over their resource allocation. In fact, the back-end services can themselves be distributed. The only information about them that we rely upon is their SLAs.

Distributed file and storage systems. Most of the research in distributed file and storage systems has been focused on cluster or local-area network environments, in which resources are dedicated to the system and owned by the same administrative entity, e.g. [8,9,10]. Due to their low communication latencies, these systems are amenable to small data and meta-data transfers. In contrast, peer-to-peer file and storage systems have also become prominent in recent years, e.g. [11,12,13]. These works have typically concentrated on achieving extreme performance scalability and availability in the presence of high churn in the online membership of constituent nodes.

Although our composite file service can be seen as a peer-to-peer system in the strictest sense, it lacks a few defining characteristics of previous systems, such as peers that often become unavailable. Further, we are interested in pushing the boundaries of traditional distributed file systems, such as NFS, by using them across the wide area. Two papers have addressed the effect of high latencies on file system traffic [14,15], but neither of them considered QoS or costs. We expect Internet block-storage services to become widespread in the future, as protocols such as iSCSI become more popular.

Summary of contributions. As far as we know, this paper is unique in a few respects. First, our work seems to be the first to focus on cost- and QoS-aware request distribution across third-party services. Second, our OptWait request-distribution algorithm departs from traditional scheduling policies by potentially assigning a request to multiple back-end services in turn. Finally, our approach of considering the entire set of recent response times from each back-end service, rather than using a single metric such as the recent average response time or the maximum recent response time, in mathematically determining request distributions is also novel.

3   Our Composite File Service

In this section, we discuss the basic principles behind our composite file service, our request-distribution algorithms, and our current implementation.

3.1   Basic Principles

Overview. As already mentioned, our composite file service comprises a front-end file service and a number of back-end block-storage services. The front-end service translates the file system API, e.g. create, read, write, unlink, into block accesses that are forwarded to one or more back-end services. The front-end service composes the user-requested guarantees from the back-end services at low cost. In fact, even if a single storage service could provide the required guarantees directly to the user (who could use a local file system and iSCSI, for example, bypassing the front-end service), the composite file service could still provide them for a lower cost, e.g. by forwarding some of the requests to a back-end service with lower cost per access whenever possible.

In our design, the front-end service is implemented by a number of distributed servers for both performance and availability. Each user mounts the file system through one of the front-end servers, which is chosen using a separate Web interface listing all available front-end servers and their geographical locations. The same file system can be mounted concurrently at different front-end servers. However, the front-end service provides no consistency guarantees when read-write and write-write file sharing is not done on the same front-end server. When the same front-end server is used, strong consistency is

Table 1. Notation and definitions

Notation	Definition
A_{front}	Availability of the front-end service
A_i	Availability guarantee provided by back-end service i
(P_i, L_i)	Performance guarantee provided by back-end service i:
	When service is available, $P_i\%$ of requests should be served in L_i time
(c_i^r, c_i^w, c_i^s)	Read, write, and storage costs of back-end service i
A_f	Availability requested by the creator of file f
(P_f, L_f)	Performance requested by the creator of file f:
	When service is available, $P_f\%$ of requests should be served in L_f time
H_f	Set of back-end services that store file f
S_f	Size of file f
r_f, w_f	Expected percentage of reads and writes to file f
R_f, W_f	Actual percentage of reads and writes to file f
P_f^r, P_f^w	Percentage of reads and writes to file f that complete in L_f time
$CDF_i(L)$	Percentage of requests served by back-end service i in L time
p_i	Probability of sending a request to back-end service i (optimized by Base)
(l_i, p_i)	Length of wait at back-end service i and expected percentage of
	requests served by i during the wait (optimized by OptWait)
$Cost(f)$	Expected monetary cost of serving file f
$AccessCost_t(f)$	Actual monetary cost of serving file f during interval t
$TotalCost(f)$	Actual monetary cost of serving file f over all intervals

guaranteed. To guarantee high availability and fault tolerance, all data and meta-data are replicated across several back-end services. Furthermore, the front-end servers only store soft state, such as a disk cache of meta-data, and keep write-ahead logs of updates in the back-end. All files are accessible from an inode-map stored at a few specific back-end services (and cached on the disks of the front-end servers). Thus, if a front-end server fails, the user can mount the file system through another front-end server, which can take over for the failed server using its write-ahead log.

The back-end block-storage services may be provided by different service providers. Although our front-end service treats the back-end services as "black boxes", we do assume that each back-end service is bounded by an SLA with the front-end file service. In particular, each back-end service i promises to meet an availability guarantee of A_i and a performance guarantee of (P_i, L_i) at a cost of (c_i^r, c_i^w, c_i^s). The two guarantees specify that service i will be servicing access requests $A_i\%$ of the time and, when it is available, $P_i\%$ of the accesses will complete within time L_i. The SLAs are defined over a long period of time, say one month, so that short-lived performance anomalies do not cause SLA violations. The cost tuple (c_i^r, c_i^w, c_i^s) specifies that each read access costs c_i^r, each write access costs c_i^w, and each unit of storage per unit of time costs c_i^s. Table 1 summarizes the notation used in our modeling.

In computing request distributions, the front-end service uses the availability and cost information from the SLAs with the back-end services. Instead of relying on the performance guarantees provided by the back-end services in computing distributions, we use the latency of requests as observed at the front-end service to encompass the latency of the wide-area network. Specifically, the front-end service monitors the latency of block accesses to each back-end service over two periods of 12 hours per day. The request distributions computed during a period of 12 hours are based on the cumulative distribution function (CDF) of the latencies observed during the same period of the day before. For example, the request distributions computed during the afternoon on Wednesday are based on the latencies observed during the afternoon on Tuesday. This approach is motivated by the cyclical workloads of many Internet services [5]. We plan to investigate more sophisticated approaches for considering block access latencies as future work.

File creation and access. When a file f is first created, the user can specify a desired availability guarantee of A_f and a performance guarantee of (P_f, L_f). (Files for which the user requests no guarantees are stored at a single back-end service and served on a best-effort basis.) These desired characteristics, if accepted by the front-end service, determine that it must be able to serve access requests to f $A_f\%$ of the time and that $P_f\%$ of the requests must complete within time L_f, when the service is available. If a file access request involves $n > 1$ blocks, the target latency for the request becomes nL_f. Again, these guarantees are defined over a long period of time, e.g. one month.

Obviously, we can only meet the requested availability if the front-end service itself is more available than A_f. If that is the case, it will choose a set of back-end services H_f to host f that meets (or exceeds) A_f. The front-end service randomly selects back-end services from three classes – inexpensive, medium, and expensive – one at a time in round-robin fashion. These classes are likely to correspond to services with generally high, medium, and low response times, respectively, although that is not a requirement. Assuming that failures are independent, the front-end service will select a set of back-end services that satisfies the following inequality:

$$A_{front} \times \left(1 - \prod_{i \in H_f} (1 - A_i)\right) \geq A_f \qquad (1)$$

where A_{front} is the availability of the front-end service. This formulation assumes that the back-end services are always reachable from the front-end service across the network. However, it can be easily replaced by more sophisticated formulations without affecting the rest of the system.

The front-end will choose a minimal set H_f in the sense that, if any back-end service is removed from H_f, the remaining set would no longer be able to meet A_f. Once H_f has been chosen, the front-end service will solve a cost-optimization problem for the two algorithms and choose the one that produces the lowest cost for f.

At this point, file f can be accessed by clients. On a read to f, the front-end service will forward a request to a subset of H_f for each needed block according to the chosen algorithm. On a write, the front-end will forward the request to all back-end services in H_f to maintain the target data availability, while concurrently writing to the write-ahead log if necessary. The front-end service only waits for the possible write ahead and one back-end service to process the write before responding to the client. In the background, the front-end service will ensure that the write is processed by the other back-end services in H_f as well. When write sharing is done through the same front-end server, this approach to processing writes favors lower latency without compromising strong consistency; the pending writes can be checked before a subsequent read is forwarded to the back-end.

Optimizing costs. Our request-distribution algorithms, Base and OptWait, are run by the front-end service to minimize the cost of accessing the back-end services in H_f. As mentioned above, their respective optimization problems are solved at first during file creation, but they may need to be solved again multiple times over the file's lifetime. In particular, whenever the file is opened, a new distribution is computed but only if the current distribution is stale, i.e. it was not computed based on the same period of the day before. After the back-end services are selected and the request distribution is computed, the front-end service can inform the client about the cost of each byte of storage and the (initial) average cost of each block access, given the requested guarantees. Note that the cost of accessing the write-ahead logs is not included in the cost computations; this cost is covered by our service fees (discussed below).

Because we select the H_f back-end services randomly from three classes of services, our cost optimization produces a "locally" optimal cost; it is possible that this cost will not be the lowest possible cost (i.e., the "globally" optimal cost) for a system with a large number of back-end services. Attempting to produce the lowest possible cost would involve searching an exponentially large space of back-end service groupings, which could take hours/days of compute time to explore meaningfully, even if a heuristic algorithm were to be used. We plan to explore this issue in our future work.

The front-end accumulates the access costs accrued during the periods of stable request distribution, i.e. in between consecutive changes to the request distribution. The overall cost of the composite service is then the sum of the costs for each stable period. Periodically, say every month, the front-end service charges each of its users based on how many accesses and how much storage the front-end service required of its back-end services on behalf of the user. Formally, the total cost to be charged is:

$$TotalCost(f) = \sum_{\forall t} AccessCost_t(f) + S_f \sum_{i \in H_f} c_i^s \qquad (2)$$

where $AccessCost_t(f)$ is the access cost of each period t of stable request distributions since the last calculation of $TotalCost(f)$ and S_f is the maximum size of the file since the last calculation of $TotalCost(f)$. We define $AccessCost_t(f)$ exactly below.

Service fees and compensation. Finally, note that the costs incurred by the front-end service are actually higher than the sum of $TotalCost(f)$ for all files. As mentioned above, the cost of accessing the write-ahead logs is not included in $TotalCost(f)$. In addition, when the client load is low, the front-end service may need to send additional accesses to the back-end services to properly assess their current performance (and availability). These extra accesses increase costs for the front-end service; the extra cost can be amortized across the set of users as a "service fee".

Further, there may be situations in which the guarantees provided by the front-end service are violated. For example, the network between the front-end service and some of the back-end services may become unusually slow or back-end services may start violating their SLAs. As mentioned above, the front-end service responds to these situations by recomputing its request distributions accordingly, but the recomputations may not occur early enough. Nevertheless, in case of back-end SLA violations, the front-end service will be compensated for them and the compensations can be passed on to its users. In case of network problems, the front-end service can use its service fees to compensate users.

3.2 Base

In Base, a read request to a file f is forwarded to a single back-end service $i \in H_f$ with probability p_i. (Writes are sent to all back-end services in H_f.) Base computes these probabilities so as to minimize the cost of servicing accesses to f while respecting the performance guarantees requested for the file. Formally, Base needs to minimize:

$$Cost(f) = r_f \sum_{i \in H_f} p_i c_i^r + w_f \sum_{i \in H_f} c_i^w \tag{3}$$

subject to the following two constraints:

$$1. \, \forall i \in H_f, p_i \geq 0 \text{ and } \sum p_i = 1 \qquad 2. \, r_f P_f^r + w_f P_f^w \geq P_f$$

where r_f is the fraction of read block accesses to f, w_f is the fraction of write block accesses to f, P_f^r is the percentage of read accesses that complete within L_f, and P_f^w is the percentage of write accesses that complete within L_f.

Equation 3 computes the average cost of reads and writes, reflecting the read-to-write ratio ($r_f : w_f$), and the fact that each read incurs the cost of only 1 back-end access according to the probabilities p_i (hence $p_i c_i^r$), while each write incurs the cost of accessing all back-end services. Constraint 1 states that the probabilities of accessing each back-end service in H_f have to be non-negative and add up to 1. Constraint 2 requires that the percentage of reads and writes that complete within L_f time must be at least P_f to meet the guarantees requested by the user.

We then define P_f^r and P_f^w as:

$$P_f^r = \sum_{i \in H_f} p_i CDF_i(L_f) \qquad P_f^w = \max_{i \in H_f}(CDF_i(L_f)) \tag{4}$$

where the $CDF_i(L)$ operator produces the percentage of requests satisfied within L time by back-end service i, as observed at the front-end service. P_f^w is determined by the best performing back-end service because the front-end forwards each write in parallel to all back-end services and replies to the client when the first one completes.

Equations 3 and 4 together with the two constraints completely define Base's optimization problem, except for how to determine r_f and w_f. The user can optionally estimate r_f and w_f and pass them as parameters at file creation time. If the user does not provide this information, we split constraint 2 above into two parts, $P_f^r \geq P_f$ and $P_f^w \geq P_f$, and instantiate Equation 3 with the assumption that $r_f = 1$ and $w_f = 0$. This approach correctly but conservatively ensures that the solution to the optimization problem provides the required guarantees for f. For details on this point, please refer to the longer, technical report version of this paper [16].

After each period t of stable request distributions computed by Base, we compute the cost of accessing the H_f back-end services during the period as:

$$AccessCost_t(f) = R_f \sum_{i \in H_f} p_i c_i^r + W_f \sum_{i \in H_f} c_i^w \qquad (5)$$

where R_f is the number of read requests and W_f is the number of write requests serviced during period t.

Finally, note that a malicious client is not able to lower its access costs by providing fake values for r_f and w_f, since these costs are computed based on the actual requests made by the client during each period of time.

3.3 OptWait

In OptWait, the front-end service takes the different approach of possibly forwarding a read request to more than one back-end service. In particular, the front-end service forwards each read request to the back-end services in sequence, from least to most expensive, waiting for a bounded amount of time for each service to respond before trying the next service.

The basic idea behind Opt-Wait is illustrated in Figure 1, which shows three performance CDFs for three back-end services. Let us assume that the left-most curve represents the most expensive service, whereas the right-most curve represents the least expensive service. OptWait would first forward a request to the least expensive service, waiting for an amount of time l_1. This would allow OptWait to take advantage of the percentage of requests (p_1) that complete fairly quickly. If the

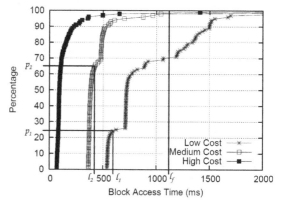

Fig. 1. Performance CDFs for three services. An OptWait distribution might specify that a request should be forwarded to multiple back-end services in turn.

request did not complete within l_1 time, OptWait would then forward the request to the medium-cost service and wait for some wait time l_2. Again, the goal would be to leverage the steep part of the medium-cost service's CDF. If, after $l_1 + l_2$ time, the request still had not completed at either back-end service, OptWait would then forward the request to the most expensive service and wait for the request to complete at any of the three back-end services.

The key to OptWait is setting appropriate l_i times. Like in Base, we do so by optimizing the access cost under the performance constraints imposed by the guarantees requested by the user. Assuming H_f with 3 back-end services, our problem is to minimize the following equation:

$$
\begin{aligned}
Cost(f) = r_f[p_1 C_1 \\
+((1 - CDF_1(l_1 + l_2))p_2 + CDF_1(l_1 + l_2) - p_1)(C_1 + C_2) \\
+(1 - (1 - CDF_1(l_1 + l_2))p_2 - CDF_1(l_1 + l_2))(C_1 + C_2 + C_3)] \\
+w_f \sum_{i \in H_f} c_i^w
\end{aligned}
$$

(6)

where $p_i = CDF_i(l_i)$, $CDF_i(l) = 0$ when service i is not being used for reads (i.e., $l_i = 0$), $C_i = 0$ when service i is not being used for reads and $C_i = c_i^r$ when it is, and $l_i = \infty$ when i is the last service being used for reads. (We only present the equation for the restricted case of 3 back-end services for clarity and because of space constraints. We refer the interested reader to [16] for the general formulation.)

Equation 6 computes the cost of writes in the same manner as the Base cost function (Equation 3), as the two algorithms treat writes in the same way. More interestingly, it computes the cost of reads by summing up the multiplication of the probability that each back-end service will need to be accessed by the cost of doing so. For example, if services 1 and 2 are used for reads, the first two lines of the equation compute the cost, whereas the third line becomes 0. The first line multiplies the probability that service 1 replies within l_1 time (p_1) by the cost of accessing service 1. For the requests that are not serviced by service 1 within l_1, service 2 would be activated. Thus, the second line of the equation sums up the probability that service 1 does not reply within $l_1 + l_2$ time but service 2 does reply within l_2 time ($(1 - CDF_1(l_1 + l_2))p_2$), and the probability that service 1 replies after l_1 but before $l_1 + l_2$ time ($CDF_1(l_1 + l_2) - p_1$). The second part of the cost is obtained by multiplying this probability by the cost of making one access to service 1 and one access to service 2.

Equation 6 should be minimized subject to the following constraints:

$$1. \; \forall i \in H_f, l_i \geq 0 \qquad 2. \; r_f P_f^r + w_f P_f^w \geq P_f$$

where constraint 1 simply states that times have to be non-negative and constraint 2 is the same as that for Base. (Just as for Base, the front-end service can break constraint 2 into two parts and compute costs for $r_f = 1$ and $w_f = 0$, if the user does not provide information about r_f and w_f as a parameter.) We define P_f^w just the same as for Base, since the two algorithms handle writes in the same way. In contrast, P_f^r is defined as:

$$
\begin{aligned}
P_f^r = CDF_1(L_f) \\
+(1 - CDF_1(L_f))CDF_2(L_f - l_1) \\
+(1 - CDF_1(L_f))(1 - CDF_2(L_f - l_1))CDF_3(L_f - l_1 - l_2)
\end{aligned}
$$

(7)

where again $CDF_i(l) = 0$ when service i is not being used for reads.

In plain English, the first additive component of Equation 7 represents the probability that the least-expensive service will reply in a timely manner (within L_f time) if it is used, the second component is the probability that service 2, if used, will reply in a timely manner (given that a request is only forwarded to it after l_1 time) but not service 1, and so on. (Again, because the general formulation and its closed form [16] are hard to read, we only present the equation for a system with exactly 3 back-end services.)

After each period t of stable request distributions computed by OptWait, we compute the cost of accessing the H_f back-end services during the period by replacing r_f and w_f in Equation 6 by R_f and W_f, respectively.

3.4   Implementation

We have implemented a prototype front-end file service called Figurehead to explore our request-distribution algorithms in real systems with real workloads. Although Figurehead should be supported by multiple geographically distributed servers in practice, it is currently based on a single node as a proof-of-concept implementation.

Figurehead consists of four components: an NFS version 2 facade that allows the file service to be accessed through standard NFS clients, a file system that supports the NFS facade and uses remote back-end block services for storage, an optimization module that computes the best request distribution strategy, and a module that constantly monitors the performance of the back-end services. All components were written in Java and run in user space. Relevant details about these four components are as follows.

NFS facade. The multi-threaded NFS facade accepts NFS remote procedure calls via UDP. It implements the NFS version 2 protocol almost completely; the only calls that have not been implemented are those dealing with symbolic links.

The one complication that the NFS protocol poses for Figurehead is that opens and closes are not sent through to the server. Thus, whenever the NFS facade receives a create or the first access to an unopened file, it opens the file and caches the opened-file object returned by the file system. A cached opened-file object is closed and discarded after it has not been accessed for 5 minutes.

File system. The file system behind our NFS facade uses the same meta-data scheme to represent a file as the Linux ext2 file system. The inode was changed to include information about the availability and performance guarantees requested by the creator of a file. An inode-map maps each inode to the set of back-end services that is hosting the file. All data and meta-data except for the inode-map are stored at the back-end services in 8-KByte blocks. The file system communicates with the back-end services over a Web Service interface, namely the RPC implementation from Apache Axis [17].

When a file is first created, the file system chooses a set of back-end services to host the file as described in Section 3.1. It then allocates an inode, saves the availability and performance guarantees for the file in the inode (along with other traditional file-system information, such as owner and time of creation), enters the mapping of $inode\text{-}number \rightarrow H_f$ into its inode-map, and writes the inode to the appropriate back-end services. The file system also opens the file.

When a file is opened, the file system extracts the set of back-end services that is hosting the file (H_f) from the inode-map, obtains their access time CDFs from the monitoring module, reads the inode to obtain the performance guarantees, and asks the request distribution module to compute the best request distribution strategy for the file. This last step is not necessary when the file is being re-opened and the current request distribution was computed based on the same period of the day before. To determine whether to recompute a request distribution, Figurehead maintains information about when each distribution is computed. When a previous request distribution exists but a new computation is required, the computation is performed in the background and adopted when completed. When client requests arrive, the file system uses the file meta-data to identify the corresponding blocks and forwards the appropriate block operations to the back-end services. Reads are handled according to the current request distribution, whereas writes are forwarded to all back-end services in H_f.

The file system maintains a write buffer to ensure that each write to a file f eventually reaches all of the nodes in H_f. When a write request arrives, the file system assigns a thread per back-end service in H_f the task of ensuring that the write eventually reaches a particular back-end. Each write is then discarded from the write buffer once it has propagated to all back-ends in H_f. We assume that the back-end services can handle small "overwrites;" that is, a write that only partially overwrites a previously written block can be sent directly to the back-end services without having to read the old data and compose a new complete-block write. This avoids making small overwrites more expensive than a complete-block write because of the need to read the block.

The file system implements two levels of meta-data caching. First, all meta-data is currently cached on a local disk (and is never evicted) using a Berkeley database [18]. This cache reduces the number of accesses to the back-end services by eliminating repeated remote meta-data accesses. In fact, the cache makes the meta-data accesses to the back-end services relatively infrequent for the large-file applications we target (dominated by reads and/or overwrites), so these accesses are not currently reflected in our mathematical machinery. Second, file-specific meta-data, i.e. inodes and indirect blocks, are cached in memory for open files as the meta-data is accessed. This avoids repeatedly accessing the cache on disk for a stream of accesses to the same file. Meta-data of an open file that is cached in memory is evicted when the file is closed. Our policy of holding a file opened in the NFS facade for 5 minutes beyond its last access implies that meta-data for an open file is also cached in memory by the file system for the same amount of time.

Finally, since the NFS clients cache data themselves, our file system (in fact, the entire front-end service) does not cache data at all.

Request-distribution module. This module solves the optimization problems posed by Base and OptWait, and chooses the algorithm that produces the lowest cost. The Base optimization problem is solved using the linear programming solver lp_solve [19] and produces the p_i probabilities with a precision of a few decimal places. Unfortunately, minimizing cost in OptWait is not a linear programming problem. To solve it, we consider all feasible combinations of the probabilities p_i's (in steps of 1% in our current implementation) for the back-end services in H_f to compute the best l_i's wait times. Even though this is essentially a brute force approach, it does not take long to compute as the size of H_f is small (typically two or three), even for high P_f requirements. We report running times for this module in Section 4.

Monitoring module. This module is responsible for monitoring each back-end service in terms of its performance as seen at the front-end service. Specifically, this module probes each back-end service periodically with regular block accesses (every 5 seconds in our current implementation). With the access times measured from these accesses, this module constructs the performance CDF for the service.

Figurehead limitations. Currently, Figurehead has three limitations. First, as we mentioned above, it is implemented by a single server, rather than a collection of geographically distributed servers. Second, we have not yet implemented the write-ahead log for crash recovery. Third, the monitoring module currently does not use information from regular accesses to the back-end services, always issuing additional block accesses to assess their performance (and availability). These extra accesses increase costs and would not be required when the regular load on the back-end services is high enough. We are currently addressing these limitations.

4 Evaluation

In this section, we first explore and compare the two request distribution algorithms over the space of different costs and back-end service behaviors. We then study the impact of using past access time data to predict current behaviors of the back-end servers. Finally, we evaluate our prototype Figurehead implementation, and validate that it provides the performance guarantees computed by the mathematical machinery.

Ideally, we would like to study our system using actual back-end services on the Internet. However, at this point, there are not enough of them to provide a large range of data. Thus, we have collected access times over a period of close to one month from 50 PlanetLab machines to support our evaluation. These data were collected by running a simple block-storage service on each machine, populating each service with 5120 blocks, and randomly accessing a block according to a Poisson process with mean inter-access time of 1 second from a client machine located at our site.

4.1 Base vs. OptWait

We first compare Base and OptWait mathematically assuming fixed access time CDFs for the back-end services. In particular, we chose data from three PlanetLab nodes, `planetlab2.cs.umass.edu`, `planetlab1.cs.unibo.it`, and `planet-lab.iki.rssi.ru`, whose CDFs are shown in Figure 1. We study a set of three nodes because they provide a sufficiently rich space to understand the behaviors of the two algorithms, yet is not overly complicated to explain.

Overall results. Figure 2 plots the average cost $(Cost(f))$ achieved by Base and OptWait for a read-only workload as a function of the per-file guaranteed latency (L_f), with a per-file percentage guarantee (P_f) of 95%. (The results are similar for other P_f values.) Each of the curves represents a different combination of algorithm and per-access cost for each back-end service. For example, the curve labeled OptWait [5,10,15] represents the cost computed by OptWait

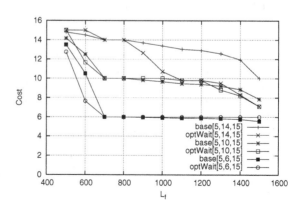

Fig. 2. Costs achieved by Base and OptWait vs. L_f, assuming a read-only workload and $P_f = 95\%$

Table 2. Costs and distributions with back-end service costs = [5,10,15] and $P_f = 95\%$. The Base distributions are listed as $[p_1, p_2, p_3]$, whereas the OptWait distributions are listed as $[(l_1, p_1), (l_2, p_2), (l_3, p_3)]$. l_1, l_2, l_3 are given in ms.

L_f (ms)	Base Cost	Base Dist	OptWait Cost	OptWait Dist
500	14.17	[0,17,83]	15.00	[(0,0),(0,0),(∞,100)]
600	12.50	[0,50,50]	11.65	[(0,0),(511,89),(∞,100)]
700	10.00	[0,100,0]	10.00	[(0,0),(∞,100),(0,0)]
800	10.00	[0,100,0]	10.00	[(0,0),(∞,100),(0,0)]
900	9.83	[3,97,0]	10.00	[(0,0),(∞,100),(0,0)]
1000	9.66	[7,93,0]	10.00	[(0,0),(∞,100),(0,0)]
1100	9.46	[11,89,0]	9.80	[(923,68),(0,0),(∞,100)]
1200	9.40	[12,88,0]	9.80	[(923,68),(0,0),(∞,100)]
1300	9.21	[16,84,0]	8.80	[(794,62),(∞,100),(0,0)]
1400	8.85	[23,77,0]	8.20	[(923,68),(∞,100),(0,0)]
1500	7.86	[43,57,0]	7.10	[(1404,86),(0,0),(∞,100)]
1600	5.00	[100,0,0]	5.00	[(∞,100),(0,0),(0,0)]

when $c_1^r = 5$, $c_2^r = 10$, and $c_3^r = 15$ fractions of dollar per access (what fraction exactly is irrelevant to our study). Table 2 lists the optimized costs and request distributions for Base and OptWait for costs [5,10,15].

From these figures, we can see that neither Base nor OptWait is always better than the other. At the extremes, i.e. at very low or very high latency guarantees, the two algorithms behave the same because there is no room for optimization. For very low latency guarantees, the only choice is to use the most expensive service all the time (if it is possible to meet the guarantee at all). For very high latency guarantees, the obvious best choice is to use the cheapest service all the time.

In between these extremes, the relative behavior of Base and OptWait depends on the shapes of the access time CDFs of the back-end services, as well as their costs. For example, consider the costs achieved by Base and OptWait for cost [5, 10, 15] at latency guarantees of 500ms and 600ms. At 500ms, Base achieves lower cost than OptWait because it is able to use the medium-cost service 17% of the time, whereas OptWait cannot yet use the medium-cost service (see Table 2). In this case, for p_2 in OptWait to be greater than 0, l_2 would have to be at least 365ms, leaving insufficient time for accessing the high-cost service should the request fail to complete at the medium-cost service within l_2. At 600ms, OptWait does better than Base because its greater use of the medium-cost service, 89% vs 50%, more than offsets the 11% of the time that it has to use both the medium-cost and high-cost service.

In general, we observe that Base can typically start using a lower-cost back-end service before OptWait as the guaranteed response time increases. This is because Base never resends requests. However, eventually, OptWait can use the lower-cost service more aggressively because it can avoid the tail of the CDF by re-sending requests to the more expensive services as needed.

Table 3. Costs and distributions with $P_f = 95\%$, as a function of L_f and back-end service costs. The Base distributions are listed as $[p_1, p_2, p_3]$, whereas the OptWait distributions are listed as $[(l_1, p_1), (l_2, p_2), (l_3, p_3)]$. l_1, l_2, l_3 are given in ms.

L_f (ms)	Back-End Costs	Base Cost	Base Dist	OptWait Cost	OptWait Distribution
1200	[5,10,15]	9.40	[12,88,0]	9.80	[(923,68),(0,0),(∞,100)]
1200	[5,6,15]	5.88	[12,88,0]	6.00	[(0,0),(∞,100),(0,0)]
1200	[5,14,15]	12.92	[12,88,0]	9.80	[(923,68),(0,0),(∞,100)]
1300	[5,10,15]	9.21	[15.79,84.21,0]	8.80	[(794,62),(∞,100),(0,0)]
1300	[5,6,15]	5.84	[15.79,84.21,0]	6.00	[(0,0),(∞,100),(0,0)]
1300	[5,14,15]	12.58	[15.79,84.21,0]	9.50	[(1064,70),(0,0),(∞,100)]
1400	[5,10,15]	8.85	[23.08,76.92,0]	8.20	[(923,68),(∞,100),(0,0)]
1400	[5,6,15]	5.77	[23.08,76.92,0]	6.00	[(0,0),(∞,100),(0,0)]
1400	[5,14,15]	11.92	[23.08,76.92,0]	8.30	[(1285,78),(0,0),(∞,100)]

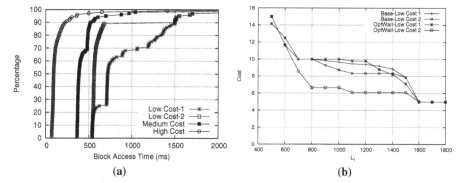

Fig. 3. (a) CDFs for 4 back-end services. (b) Access cost achieved by Base and OptWait when using two different sets of three back-end services {low-cost-1, medium-cost, high-cost} and {low-cost-2, medium-cost, high-cost}. Both with cost [5,10,15] and $P_f = 95\%$.

Impact of the back-end service costs. Observe that Base's distribution of requests is independent of the ratio between the costs of the three back-end services. That is, as long as $c_3^r > c_2^r > c_1^r$, Base will choose the same set of distribution probabilities (p_1, p_2, p_3) regardless of the ratios $c_1:c_2:c_3$. OptWait, on the other hand, may alter its distribution strategy based on the cost ratios. For example, consider in Table 3 the distributions computed for L_f within the interval [1200ms, 1400ms] for costs [5, 6, 15] vs. [5, 10, 15]. For [5, 10, 15], OptWait chooses to use either the low- and medium-cost or low- and high-cost services. For [5, 6, 15], OptWait only chooses to use the medium-cost service. This is because the medium-cost service is only slightly more expensive than the low-cost service; immediately choosing it is less costly than potentially having to forward the request to two services.

Impact of the shape of the CDFs. Base and OptWait also behave differently with respect to the shapes of the CDFs. In general, Base's behavior depends on the three key points $CDF_1(L_f)$, $CDF_2(L_f)$, and $CDF_3(L_f)$, whereas OptWait's behavior depends on the shape of all CDFs between 0% and $CDF_i(L_f)$. These dependencies can be seen clearly in Figures 3(a) and (b). Figure 3(a) shows the CDFs for 4 back-end services from which we derived two sets of three services {low-cost-1, medium-cost, high-cost} and {low-cost-2, medium-cost, high-cost}.

Figure 3(b) shows that OptWait behaves significantly better when using low-cost-2 in the interval [600ms, 1600ms] because low-cost-2 is substantially "steeper" than low-cost-1. Base is also able to leverage low-cost-2's better behavior to improve its cost, but less so than OptWait. The reason is that Base only leverages the fact that low-cost-2 gives a better $CDF_1(L_f)$ than low-cost-1, rather than the fact that low-cost-2 gives an additional 30% of requests completing under 700ms over low-cost-1 in this interval.

4.2 Validating the Mathematical Machinery

We now validate our mathematical approach when servicing actual file system workloads. We also validate that the prediction of back-end service behaviors using past access time data do not significantly degrade our QoS guarantees. First, we use simulation to analyze the mathematical approach independent of the details of an actual implementation. Next, we evaluate our prototype implementation.

Workloads. We use two realistic workloads. The first models an interactive visualization application, where the user is navigating through a large amount of data–for example, a large rendering model or large scientific data set. This application is exactly the type of soft real-time application that Figurehead is designed to support.

This workload is constructed based on publications on visualization systems [20,21,22], and has the following attributes: a random Poisson read access stream with a mean interarrival time of 50ms on a large data file. It currently does not make a difference to Figurehead whether a read stream is random or sequential, since Figurehead does not currently do any prefetching or caching. We assume a random read access stream because these accesses are dependent on the user's interactive navigation.

The second workload models a scientific application running on a grid environment. Although this is not a classical soft real-time application, it still constitutes an interesting workload because predictability of data access can significantly reduce the burden of resource management and coordination of the stages of a multi-stage application such as the one described in [23].

This workload is constructed based on data extracted from [1,23,24,25], and has the following attributes: a sequential read access stream from a single large file followed by a sequential write access stream to the same file. This read/write access stream represents a multi-phase application with an initial read phase to load input data and a final write phase that saves the computed results. We assume that intermediate results generated between the initial and final phases are stored on local storage rather than a file system such as Figurehead. We further assume that the initial input data and the final results have the same size; thus, the read-to-write ratio is 1:1. Finally, both the read and write access streams are Poisson processes with mean interarrival times of 50ms.

Because the WAN latencies we consider are larger than 50ms, we assume that the access streams of both applications are generated by a number of concurrent threads.

Table 4. Simulation results with $(P_f, L_f) = (95\%, 600ms)$ and costs [5,10,15]. **V** denotes the visualization workload, **S** the scientific workload, **B** the Base algorithm, and **O** the OptWait algorithm. **Expected** is the percentage of requests expected to complete before L_f as computed by the algorithm. **Simulated** is the actual percentage of requests that completed before L_f in a simulation run. **Min, Max, Avg** are the minimum, maximum, and average values across 18 runs using 18 half-day traces from the PlanetLab machines.

	V-B		S-B		V-O		S-O	
	Expected	Simulated	Expected	Simulated	Expected	Simulated	Expected	Simulated
Min	95	95.06	95	95.28	95.2	95.61	95	95.56
Max	95	95.89	95	97.28	97.36	97.89	97.33	98.56
Avg	95	95.48	95	96.07	96.22	96.57	95.7	96.78

Simulation using *a priori* knowledge of back-end service behaviors. Our first experiment is as follows. Take a trace of the three machines whose overall behaviors are shown in Figure 1 over a period of 9 days. Construct a CDF for each back-end service for each 12-hour period of the 9 days. For each 12-hour period, use the corresponding CDF to compute the distribution using Base and OptWait for $P_f = 95\%$, $L_f = 600ms$, costs [5,10,15], and $c^r = c^w$ for all back-end services. Then, simulate Figurehead's response time for 18000 accesses for each workload using the 12-hour traces that were used to construct the CDFs. This corresponds to statistical oracular knowledge of the behaviors of the back-end services.

Table 4 shows the results for 18 runs of each application/distribution algorithm pair, where each run was performed using a distinct half-day period of the 9-day trace. For both workloads under Base and OptWait, the simulation always leads to exceeding the QoS guarantee. This is because we construct and use the CDFs in a conservative manner. In particular, each CDF is represented by a set of 100 discrete points, representing the latency corresponding to each percentage point on the CDF. Now suppose that the mathematical engine needs a percentage value corresponding to the latency 1000ms. If our CDF has the points (999ms, 95%) and (1001ms, 96%), then we would return 95%, rather than an interpolated value between 95% and 96%. We choose this conservative approach because an interpolated value would be optimistic sometimes but pessimistic other times, making the mathematical machinery less predictable.

An additional interesting observation to make is that mathematically, Base always achieves a distribution that should theoretically give the exact P_f required (in this case, 95%). OptWait, on the other hand, because of our discrete approach for computing the best distribution, typically overachieves compared to the required P_f. (Note that, for $L_f = 600ms$, OptWait achieves lower cost than Base despite this overachievement.) As shall be seen, this overachievement makes OptWait more robust when the CDF is computed based on past data.

Impact of using past access times to predict current back-end service behaviors. We now consider the impact of not having *a priori* information on the expected behaviors of the back-end services. In particular, as mentioned in Section 3.1, we run the same experiments as above but use a CDF constructed from the response times observed in the same 12-hour period 1 day ago to predict each back-end service's behavior in the

Table 5. Simulated results for $(P_f, L_f) = (95\%, 600ms)$ and costs [5,10,15] when using data access times from 12 hours ago to predict the current behaviors of back-end services. The notation is the same as in Table 4. **Failures** is the number of 12-hour simulation runs that did not meet the QoS guarantee.

	V-B		S-B		V-O		S-O	
	Expected	Simulated	Expected	Simulated	Expected	Simulated	Expected	Simulated
Min	95	92.72	95	94.28	95.2	93.83	95	95.67
Max	95	97.72	95	98.33	97.36	98.83	97.33	98.61
Avg	95	95.35	95	96.11	96.24	96.42	95.76	96.8
Failures	0	5	0	6	0	5	0	0

current 12-hour period (e.g., 8am-8pm from Tuesday to predict behavior for 8am-8pm Wednesday). Table 5 shows the results for 16 12-hour runs (we could not use the first two half-day periods because they did not have any past history for prediction).

As expected, past data is not a perfect predictor of current behavior. This leads to a number of 12-hour simulation runs where Figurehead would not be able to achieve the QoS guarantee. In fact, approximately 35% of the runs missed the QoS guarantee under Base. OptWait has a comparable failure rate for the Visualization workload but was perfect for the Scientific workload. As already mentioned, OptWait is somewhat more resilient to the imperfect predictor because it typically overachieves compared to the required P_f. On the other hand, the imperfect predictor can also lead the 12-hour runs to achieve more than the QoS requirement, i.e. more than P_f of the requests complete within L_f time. In fact, the **Max** values for both Base and OptWait are larger in Table 5 than in Table 4.

However, the most important observation here is that *both request-distribution algorithms provide the performance guarantees that they promise* when the entire 8 day period is considered (see the simulated **Avg** entries). (Recall that QoS guarantees are defined over long periods of time, such as one month.) The reason for this result is that the QoS requirement is exceeded during the majority of the 12-hour periods, which more than compensates for the many fewer periods when the requirement is not met.

4.3   Prototype Behavior

We now validate that our prototype, Figurehead, actually provides the performance guarantees computed by the mathematical machinery. All results reported below were obtained by running on 5 PCs connected by a Gb/s Ethernet switch. Each PC is configured with 1 hyper-threading Intel Xeon 2.8 GHz processor, 2 GBytes of main memory, and 25 GBytes of disk space. Three of the machines were used as back-end block servers and one as the client. The other machine ran Figurehead. We always assume that the three back-end services are needed to meet the client's specified availability requirement. Again, all the experiments assume $P_f = 95\%$, $L_f = 600ms$, costs [5,10,15], and $c^r = c^w$ for all back-end services. To mimic a wide-area network, we inserted delays to the completion times of accesses to the back-end services. We use the same 9-day trace as in the last subsection; the delays were randomly chosen from the appropriate half-day period. (We used the traces instead of running the back-end services themselves on PlanetLab nodes for repeatability.)

Microbenchmarks. We first present results from microbenchmarks to illustrate the performance of Figurehead. For these microbenchmarks, we did not inject any network delays so that performance reflects what is achievable over a LAN. We also assume that r_f and w_f are known ahead of time; i.e., r_f is 1 when measuring read performance and 0 when measuring write performance. We measured write performance for appends (rather than overwrites) to a file.

Using these microbenchmarks, we find that the times required to read and write 1 byte of data are approximately 30ms and 66ms, respectively. Appends are more expensive than reads because they require writing meta-data. Overall, Figurehead reads and writes are about one order of magnitude slower than on a local disk. The higher access latency of Figurehead arises mainly from using a Berkeley database as disk cache and the Web Services interface to access the back-end block servers. These inefficiencies can be easily eliminated in a production-grade implementation. However, the fairer comparison is between accessing a back-end service through Figurehead and accessing it directly, both on a WAN. Because network trips dominate in this scenario, Figurehead would impose a much lower overhead. For example, the lowest average latency we measured for the PlanetLab nodes is 165ms. Given this latency, Figurehead would impose roughly a 30% degradation when all accesses are appends.

Another important issue is the overhead of computing request distributions. The time to solve a Base and OptWait optimization problem is approximately 710us and 14ms, respectively. We found that, while the time to solve OptWait does increase with L_f, it does so quite modestly. The reason for the slight time increase is that a higher L_f tends to generate a larger search space in OptWait. Finally, these optimization times do not change significantly with changing P_f and so we do not show those results here.

Macrobenchmarks. Finally, we ran the two workloads described in the last section concurrently against a running instance of our Figurehead prototype. We ran each workload/distribution algorithm pair 4 times, each time for a distinct half-day period from the 9-day trace (the first 4 half-day periods). Overheads from the system (e.g, computing time inside the Figurehead front-end) led to a degradation in meeting the QoS requirement P_f by almost nothing to at most 1%. Detailed measurements show that the main sources of overheads were synchronization delays, inaccuracies in the sleep function used to emulate WAN latencies, and accessing the Berkeley DB. Despite these overheads, *the prototype consistently provides the proper guarantees when all the periods are considered.*

5   Conclusions

In this paper, we addressed the issue of composing functionally-equivalent, third-party services into higher level, value-added services by developing a distributed file service. In this context, we proposed two request-distribution algorithms that optimize costs at the same time as providing performance and availability guarantees. To achieve this goal, both algorithms rely on information about the behavior of the third-party services to mathematically determine the request distributions. While one algorithm is reminiscent of traditional scheduling policies, the other departs significantly from these policies, as it may schedule the same request at multiple third-party services in turn.

We found that both algorithms provide the guarantees that they promise. Comparing the algorithms, we found that neither is consistently the best. Nevertheless, using our mathematical modeling, the system can actually select the best algorithm for each file a priori. Experimental results from our prototype implementation characterized its performance and the optimized access costs under the two algorithms.

Composite services such as the one we studied are in the horizon. Based on our experience and results, we believe that these services can benefit from our modeling and optimization approach for guaranteeing quality-of-service at low cost.

References

1. Shasharina, S.G., Wang, N., Cary, J.R.: Grid Service for Visualization and Analysis of Remote Fusion Data. In: Proceedings of the International Workshop on Challenges of Large Applications in Distributed Environments (June 2004)
2. Amazon: Amazon Simple Storage Service, http://aws.amazon.com/s3
3. Gu, X., Nahrstedt, K.: Distributed Multimedia Service Composition with Statistical QoS Assurances. IEEE Transactions on Multimedia 8(1) (February 2005)
4. Zeng, L., Benatallah, B., Ngu, A., Dumas, M., Kalagnanam, J., Chang, H.: QoS-Aware Middleware for Web Services Composition. IEEE Transactions on Software Engineering 30(5) (May 2004)
5. Chase, J., Anderson, D., Thackar, P., Vahdat, A., Boyle, R.: Managing Energy and Server Resources in Hosting Centers. In: Proceedings of the Symposium on Operating Systems Principles (October 2001)
6. Krauter, K., Buyya, R., Maheswaran, M.: A Taxonomy and Survey of Grid Resource Management Systems for Distributed Computing. Software–Practice and Experience 32(2) (February 2002)
7. Subramanian, L., Stoica, I., Balakrishnan, H., Katz, R.: OverQoS: An Overlay Based Architecture for Enhancing Internet QoS. In: Proceedings of the Symposium on Networked Systems Design and Implementation (March 2004)
8. Gibson, G.A., Nagle, D.F., Amiri, K., Butler, J., Chang, F.W., Gobioff, H., Hardin, C., Riedel, E., Rochberg, D., Zelenka, J.: A Cost-Effective, High-Bandwidth Storage Architecture. In: Proceedings of the International Conference on Architectural Support for Programming Languages and Operating Systems (October 1998)
9. Radkov, P., Yin, L., Goyal, P., Sarkar, P., Shenoy, P.: A Performance Comparison of NFS and iSCSI for IP-Networked Storage. In: Proceedings of the USENIX Conference on File and Storage Technologies (March 2004)
10. Thekkath, C.A., Mann, T.P., Lee, E.K.: Frangipani: A Scalable Distributed File System. In: Proceedings of the Symposium on Operating Systems Principles (October 1997)
11. Bhagwan, R., Tati, K., Cheng, Y.C., Savage, S., Voelker, G.M.: Total Recall: System Support for Automated Availability Management. In: Proceedings of the Symposium on Networked Systems Design and Implementation (March 2004)
12. Dabek, F., Kaashoek, M.F., Karger, D., Morris, R., Stoica, I.: Wide-Area Cooperative Storage with CFS. In: Proceedings of the Symposium on Operating Systems Principles (October 2001)

13. Rowstron, A., Druschel, P.: Storage Management and Caching in PAST, a Large-Scale, Persistent Peer-to-Peer Storage Utility. In: Proceedings of the Symposium on Operating Systems Principles (October 2001)
14. Martin, R., Culler, D.: NFS Sensitivity to High Performance Networks. In: Proceedings of the International Conference on the Measurement and Modeling of Computer Systems (May 1999)
15. Ng, W.T., Hillyer, B., Shriver, E., Gabber, E., Ozden, B.: Obtaining High Performance for Storage Outsourcing. In: Proceedings of the USENIX Conference on File and Storage Technologies (January 2002)
16. Le, K., Bianchini, R., Nguyen, T.D.: A Cost-Effective Distributed File Service with QoS Guarantees. Technical Report DCS-TR-615, Department of Computer Science, Rutgers University (August 2007)
17. Apache: Apache Axis, http://ws.apache.org/axis/
18. Olson, M.A., Bostic, K., Seltzer, M.I.: Berkeley DB. In: Proceedings of the USENIX Annual Technical Conference, FREENIX Track (June 1999)
19. Berkelaar, M.: LP_Solve, ftp://ftp.es.ele.tue.nl/pub/lp_solve/
20. Almeida, J.M., Krueger, J., Eager, D.L., Vernon, M.K.: Analysis of Educational Media Server Workloads. In: Proceedings of the International Workshop on Network and Operating Systems Support for Digital Audio and Video (June 2001)
21. Crandall, P.E., Aydt, R.A., Chien, A.A., Reed, D.A.: Input/Output Characteristics of Scalable Parallel Applications. In: Proceedings of the ACM/IEEE conference on Supercomputing, IEEE Computer Society Press, Los Alamitos (1995)
22. Wong, W.M.R., Muntz, R.R.: Providing Guaranteed Quality of Service for Interactive Visualization Applications (poster). In: International Conference on Measurement and Modeling of Computer Systems (June 2000)
23. Thain, D., Bent, J., Arpaci-Dusseau, A.C., Arpaci-Dusseau, R.H., Livny, M.: Pipeline and Batch Sharing in Grid Workloads. In: Proceedings of the IEEE Symposium on High Performance Distributed Computing, IEEE Computer Society Press, Los Alamitos (2003)
24. Nieuwejaar, N., Kotz, D.: The Galley Parallel File System. In: Proceedings of the ACM International Conference on Supercomputing, ACM Press, New York (1996)
25. Wang, F., Xin, Q., Hong, B., Brandt, S., Miller, E., Long, D., McLarty, T.: File System Workload Analysis for Large-Scale Scientific Computing Applications. In: Proceedings of the IEEE/NASA Goddard Conference (April 2004)

R-Capriccio: A Capacity Planning and Anomaly Detection Tool for Enterprise Services with Live Workloads

Qi Zhang[1], Ludmila Cherkasova[2], Guy Mathews[2], Wayne Greene[2], and Evgenia Smirni[1]

[1] College of William and Mary, Williamsburg, VA 23187, USA*
{qizhang,esmirni}@cs.wm.edu
[2] Hewlett-Packard Laboratories, Palo Alto, CA 94304, USA
{lucy.cherkasova,guy.mathews,wayne.greene}@hp.com

Abstract. As the complexity of IT systems increases, performance management and capacity planning become the largest and most difficult expenses to control. New methodologies and modeling techniques that explain large-system behavior and help predict their future performance are now needed to effectively tackle the emerging performance issues. With the multi-tier architecture paradigm becoming an industry standard for developing scalable client-server applications, it is important to design effective and accurate performance prediction models of multi-tier applications under an enterprise production environment and a real workload mix. To accurately answer performance questions for an existing production system with a real workload mix, we design and implement a new capacity planning and anomaly detection tool, called *R-Capriccio*, that is based on the following three components: *i)* a *Workload Profiler* that exploits locality in existing enterprise web workloads and extracts a small set of most popular, core client transactions responsible for the majority of client requests in the system; *ii)* a *Regression-based Solver* that is used for deriving the CPU demand of each core transaction on a given hardware; and *iii)* an *Analytical Model* that is based on a network of queues that models a multi-tier system. To validate *R-Capriccio*, we conduct a detailed case study using the access logs from two heterogeneous production servers that represent customized client accesses to a popular and actively used HP Open View Service Desk application.

1 Introduction

As IT and application infrastructures become more complex, predicting and controlling the issues surrounding system performance and capacity planning become a difficult and overwhelming task. For larger IT projects, it is not uncommon for the cost factors

* This work was largely completed in the summer of 2006 when Qi Zhang did an internship at HPLabs. E. Smirni are supported in part by the National Science Foundation (ITR-0428330). Currently, Qi Zhang is employed by MicroSoft and can be reached at the following address: qizha@microsoft.com. E. Smirni has been partially supported in part by the National Science Foundation under grants ITR-0428330 and CNS-0720699, and by a gift from Hewlett-Packard.

R. Cerqueira and R.H. Campbell (Eds.): Middleware 2007, LNCS 4834, pp. 244–265, 2007.

related to performance tuning, performance management, and capacity planning to result in the largest and least controlled expense. Application performance issues have an immediate impact on customer satisfaction. A sudden slowdown can affect a large population of customers, can lead to delayed projects, and ultimately can result in company financial loss. It is not unusual for a piece of new hardware to be added into the infrastructure to alleviate performance issues without fully understanding where the problem really is.

With complexity of systems increasing and customer requirements for QoS growing, the research challenge is to design an integrated framework of measurement and system modeling techniques to support performance analysis of complex enterprise systems in order to explain large-system behavior. Predicting and planing future performance is of paramount importance for the commercial success of enterprise systems.

Large-scale enterprise development projects are relying more and more on the *Service-Oriented Architecture* (SOA) design. This approach provides a collection of mechanisms and interfaces for a dynamic enterprise IT environment to connect applications where classic, data-processing legacy systems can be integrated with agile, web-based front-end applications. Application servers provide a standardized platform for developing and deploying scalable enterprise systems. As a result of this, application servers are a core component of an enterprise system and an integral part of a new trend towards building service-oriented architectures. Today, the *three-tier architecture* paradigm has become an industry standard for building scalable client-server applications.

In multi-tier systems, frequent calls to application servers and databases place a heavy load on resources and may cause throughput bottlenecks and high server-side processing latency. Typically, preliminary system capacity estimates are done by using synthetic workloads or benchmarks which are created to reflect a "typical application behavior" for "typical client requests". While capacity planning based on synthetic workloads or benchmarks can be useful at the initial stages of design and development of a future system, it may not be adequate for answering more specific questions about an existing production system. Often, a service provider does need to answer the following questions:

- How many additional clients can be supported by the existing system *i)* while still providing the same performance guarantees, e.g., response time under 8 sec., and *ii)* assuming that new clients perform similar activities as already existing clients in the system, i.e., the system processes the same type of workload?
- If the client activities and behaviors change over time in a specified way, how is the performance of the system affected?

In this work, we propose a new capacity planning framework, called *R-Capriccio*, for practical capacity evaluation of existing production systems under "live" workloads that can provide answers to all of the above questions. *R-Capriccio* can assist in providing answers for advanced "what-if" scenarios in system capacity analysis where the evaluated system operates under a diverse workload mix. *R-Capriccio* is comprised of the following key components:

- *Workload profiler*: The profiler extracts a set of most popular client transactions, called *core* transactions, to characterize the overall site workload and the most popular client sessions at the site.
- *Regression-based solver*: Using statistical regression, the solver approximates the resource cost (CPU demand) of each core transaction on a given hardware. Thus a real workload mix can be directly mapped into the corresponding CPU demand requirements.
- *Analytical model*: For capacity planning of multi-tier applications with session-based workloads, an analytic model based on a network of queues is developed, where each queue represents a tier of the application.

Another important problem that needs to be addressed is a preliminary analysis of performance issues that often occur during the application updates and new software releases: this is also known as *anomaly detection*. Typically, when a new software release is introduced and unexpected performance problems are observed, it is important to separate performance issues that are caused by a high load of incoming workload from the performance issues caused by possible errors or inefficiencies in the upgraded software. R-Capriccio can be used to distinguish the performance issues that are not caused by the existing system workload and essentially be used as an alarm to identify anomalies in the system operation.

For most production multi-tier services the I/O traffic (both network and disk) is not a system bottleneck. The memory requirements increase linearly with the number of concurrent users in the system [2] and can be computed in a straightforward way. In this work, we concentrate on systems with CPU bottlenecks and evaluate the capacity requirements for support of a given workload with a specified constraint on the latency of user response times. This additional latency constraint makes this modeling problem non-trivial and challenging.

A prerequisite for applying our framework is that a service provider collects the following information:

- the application server access log that reflects all processed client requests and client activities at the site, and
- CPU utilization at all tiers of the evaluated system.

Thus the *problem* is to approximate the *CPU costs* of different client transactions at different tiers, and then use these cost functions to evaluate the resource requirement of scaled or modified transaction workload mix in order to accurately size the future system. In this work, we continue developing the approach that is based on linear regression for approximating the CPU transaction cost in a system running the TPC-W benchmark [24]. However, it is much more challenging to apply and validate this modeling approach with real, live workloads that exhibit much more complex and diverse behavior than the synthetic TPC-W benchmark.

To validate our approach, we use a 1-month long access logs and CPU utilization data from two heterogeneous application servers that provide customized client access to a popular and actively used HP service: Open View Service Desk (OVSD). We demonstrate that the proposed regression method provides a simple, but powerful solution to accurately approximate CPU transaction costs for both heterogeneous application servers under study. We use the results of the regression method to parameterize an analytic model of queues. We then use the analytic model to complete the last step of the capacity planning process and derive the maximum number of clients that the studied application servers can support for a given workload mix under different constraints on transaction response times.

The rest of the paper is organized as follows. Section 2 provides a detailed workload analysis and a workload profiler. Section 3 introduces our regression-based method for deriving the CPU cost of the site transactions. Section 4 presents the analytic model for predicting multi-tier application performance. Section 5 presents related work. Finally, a summary and conclusions are given in Section 6.

2 Workload Characterization

In this section, we analyze a 1-month trace collected from the heterogeneous application servers at the OVSD business portal during July 2006. This trace has a detailed information about each processed request, including its arrival and departure time, request URL, and client session ID.

2.1 Units of Client/Server Activities

Since often service providers are interested in capacity planning rules for their production systems under live, real workloads, we need to understand properties of these workloads, and identify a set of workload characteristics that are essential for a capacity planning framework.

We first define *client activity* as follows. Typically, a client communicates with a web service (deployed as a multi-tier application) via a web interface, where the unit of activity at the client-side corresponds to a download of a web page. In general, a web page is composed of an HTML file and embedded objects such as images. Typically, the HTML page is dynamically generated by the application server, and depending on the application and its business logic, the page generation may involve issuing multiple (or none) database calls. A browser retrieves a web page by issuing a series of HTTP requests for all objects: first it retrieves the main HTML file and after parsing it, the browser retrieves all the embedded images. Thus, at the server side, a web page retrieval corresponds to processing of multiple smaller objects that can be retrieved either in sequence or via multiple concurrent connections. It is common that a web server and application server reside on the same hardware, and shared resources are used by the application and web servers to generate main HTML files as well as to retrieve page embedded objects[1]. In the access logs that we obtained from the OVSD application server, there are both types of entries: web page requests and subsequent entries for embedded images. The HTTP protocol does not provide any means to delimit the beginning or the end of a web page: this is why it is very difficult to accurately measure the aggregate resources consumed due to web page processing at the server side. In this work, we define a *transaction* as a *web page* accessed by the client (also called *web page views*).

---

[1] It is common for applications in many production systems implemented using the PHP web-scripting/application development language [15].

Client access to a web service occurs in the form of a *session* consisting of multiple individual transactions (web pages). For example, in an e-commerce site, placing an order through the web site involves further requests relating to selecting a product, providing shipping information, arranging payment agreement, and finally receiving a confirmation. Thus, for a customer trying to place an order, or a retailer trying to make a sale, the real measure of such a web service performance is its ability to process the entire sequence of individual transactions needed to complete a higher-level logical transaction. The number of such concurrent client sessions that a multi-tier system can support without violating transaction response time is a measure of system capacity.

In this section, we present the analysis of OVSD workload performed by our *Workload Profiler*:

- first, it characterizes a set of client transactions and extracts the distribution of transactions over time;
- second, it characterizes a set of user activities by analyzing and extracting the session characteristics over time.

2.2 Transactions

In our analysis, we consider a reduced trace that contains only transactions (web page views) as discussed above. We omit all embedded images, style sheets, and other format-related primitives. Moreover, we further distinguish a set of unique *transaction types* and a set of client accesses to them. For static web pages, the URL uniquely defines a file accessed by clients. For dynamic pages the requests from different users to the same web page URL may appear as requests to different URLs due to the client-specific extension or a corresponding parameter list. We carefully filter out these client-specific extensions in the reduced trace.

There are 984,505 transactions in the reduced trace. Fig. 1 illustrates the number of transactions in each hour. It reflects a typical enterprise diurnal access pattern, i.e., high loads during work hours, and low loads during nights and weekends. In addition, the studied workload exhibits a regular and predictable load pattern.

Overall, in the reduced trace, there are 756 different unique transactions (or transaction types). Fig. 2 shows the cumulative distribution function (CDF) of client accesses to different transaction types ranked by the transaction popularity. The transaction with *rank 1* represents the most popular transaction type. Fig. 2 reflects that the studied workload exhibits a very high degree of reference locality: i.e., a small subset of site transactions is responsible for a very high percentage of client accesses, e.g.,

- the top 10 transaction types accumulate 79.1% of all the client accesses;
- the top 20 transaction types are responsible for 93.6% of the site accesses;
- the top 100 transaction types account for 99.8% of all site accesses.

This characterization is consistent with earlier works [5,6,7] that have demonstrated that web server and e-commerce workloads exhibit a high degree of reference locality. Complementary to the characterization of the most frequently accessed files, we also see that the percentage of the files that are requested only a few times over an entire month is very high for this site. These rarely accessed files may play a less important role in the capacity planning framework, as we demonstrate later.

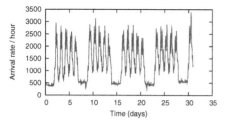

Fig. 1. Arrival rate of transactions for each hour in July, 2006

Fig. 2. CDF of the transaction types

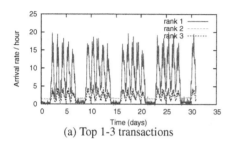

(a) Top 1-3 transactions

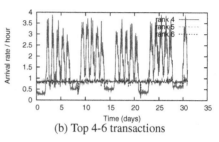

(b) Top 4-6 transactions

Fig. 3. Arrival rate of the first 6 most popular transactions across time

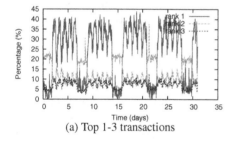

(a) Top 1-3 transactions

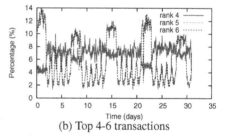

(b) Top 4-6 transactions

Fig. 4. Portions of the transactions belonging to the top 6 popular transactions across time

Fig. 3 shows the arrival rates of the transactions for the 6 most popular types over time, and Fig. 4 shows the percentages of these transaction types in the workload mix over time. Each point in these figures corresponds to one-hour statistics. The figure shows that the transaction mix is not stationary over time. For example, the most popular, rank 1 transaction can cotribute to 15% to 40% in the workload depending on the hour of the day. Similar observations apply to other transactions as well.

Traditional capacity planning methodologies usually examine peak loads and system utilization to conclude on the number of clients that can be handled by the system. These methods aim to accommodate variations in load while assuming that the set of workload transactions is stationary, i.e., that the distribution of different transaction types is fixed. Many of industry standard benchmarks are built using this principle [3,4]. But real workloads rarely exhibit this feature as shown by the analysis above. Therefore, instead

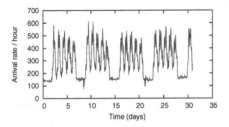
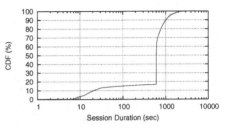

Fig. 5. Arrival rate of sessions for each hour in July, 2006

Fig. 6. CDF of the session durations

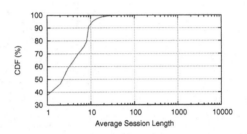

Fig. 7. CDF of the session length

of focusing on loads solely, a robust capacity planning methodology must also consider the changing workload mix since the system capacity directly depends on the types of user activities.

2.3 Sessions

Understanding user activities at the session level is essential for capacity planning, as *the number of concurrent sessions* in the trace is actually a representation of *the number of concurrent clients* handled by the system. Fig. 5 displays the arrival rate of new sessions over time, which follows the same trends as the transaction arrivals. Additionally, it indicates that the high load of transactions during peak time is mainly due to the increased number of customers.

Fig. 6 shows the CDF of client session durations. A session duration is defined as the time between the beginning of the first transaction and the end of the last transaction with the same session ID. The most typical session duration is around 600 seconds. It is related to the *timeout* parameter in the application server: if a session is inactive for 600 seconds it is timed out by the server.

Fig. 7 gives the CDF of the session length, i.e., the number of transactions within each session. Most sessions have a small number of transactions, i.e., 93.1% of the sessions have less than 10 transactions, and 37.6% of the sessions have only one transaction.

Since the traces are collected independently at two application servers supported by heterogeneous machines with different CPU speeds, we turn to the workload in each server to further understand the session-based behavior of users.

2.4 Workloads of Different Servers

In this sub-section, we present the workload and utilization analysis of each of the two application servers, which then is used by our capacity planning framework to show that the framework can effectively support heterogeneous resources.

The two application servers handle client requests after a load balancing point. Fig. 8 shows that the load balancing in this system works well. A similar number of transactions are dispatched to each of the two servers, and both exhibit the characteristics of the entire workload as described above. [2] Server 2 has a faster CPU. As a result, its CPU utilization is lower compared to server 1 (see Fig. 9). Most of the time, CPU utilization in both servers is under 10%. Note that for each weekend, there is a spike of CPU utilization which is related to administrator back-up tasks.

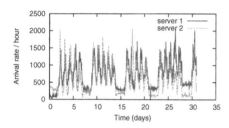
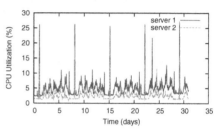

Fig. 8. Arrival rate of transactions of each application server

Fig. 9. Average CPU utilization of each application server

Fig. 10 shows the average number of concurrent sessions over time processed separately by server 1 and by server 2. During peak time, there are about 60 concurrent sessions for each server, but during the weekends, the number of concurrent sessions decreases to 10.

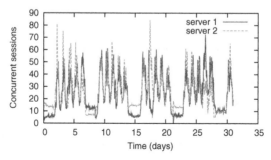

Fig. 10. Average number of concurrent sessions of each application server

---

[2] The workload mixes and the transaction popularity ranking at each server are similar to the entire system. We do not report the figures here due to space limitation.

When server 2 receives a slightly higher number of requests than server 1 (since server 2 has a faster CPU, and its typical CPU utilization is lower), this leads to a slightly higher number of concurrent sessions hosted by the server 2 as shown in Fig. 10.

2.5 Summary of Workload Analysis

To summarize, the following observations have to be taken into account for an accurate capacity planning and performance evaluation of production systems with live workloads:

– The transaction mix varies over time and hence can not be treated as a fixed, stationary distribution.
– The workloads exhibit a strong locality property, i.e., a small number of transaction types are responsible for a large fraction of client requests.
– Most of users have a high think time.

The *Workload Profiler* collects a set of the following metrics over time: *i)* the average CPU utilization, *ii)* the number of different transactions, *iii)* the number of concurrent sessions, and *iv)* the client think times. These metrics are collected for each time window of 1 hour (this is a tunable tool parameter) and for each application server. These metrics can then be used to parameterize the analytic model in Section 4.

3   CPU Cost of Transactions

In this section, we use a statistical regression-based approach for an efficient approximation of CPU demands of different transaction types. We have introduced this approach in our earlier paper [24], where we evaluated it by using a testbed of a multi-tier e-commerce site that simulates the operation of an on-line bookstore, according to the classic TPC-W benchmark [4]. The challenge is to apply and validate this technique with real, live workloads that exhibit much more complex and diverse behavior than synthetic ones. With the knowledge of CPU demands of transactions one can easily compose the resource requirement of scaled or modified transaction mixes. Thus, this methodology can be directly applied to production systems and can be used to explain large-scale system behavior and predict future system performance. In this section, we analyze challenges of applying this method to production systems operating under live, real workloads, and introduce an optimization technique that enables an efficient use of the proposed approach.

3.1 Regression Methodology

To capture the changes in server workload we observe a number of different transactions over fixed length time intervals, denoted as *monitoring windows*. The transaction mix and system utilization are recorded at the end of each monitoring window.

Assuming that there are totally M transaction types processed by the server, we use the following notations:

- T is the length of the monitoring window;
- N_i is the number of transactions of the i-th type, where $1 \leq i \leq M$;
- $U_{CPU,n}$ is the average CPU utilization at the n-tier during this monitoring window;
- $D_{i,n}$ is the average service time of transactions of the i-th type, at the n-tier of the systems, where $1 \leq i \leq M$.
- $D_{0,n}$ is the average CPU overhead related to activities that "keep the system up". There are operating system processes or background jobs that consume CPU time even when there is no transaction in the system.

From the utilization law, one can easily obtain Eq. (1) for each monitoring window [8]:

$$D_{0,n} + \sum_i N_i \cdot D_{i,n} = U_{CPU,n} \cdot T. \tag{1}$$

Because it is practically infeasible to get accurate service times $D_{i,n}$ (since it is an over-constrained problem), we let $C_{i,n}$ denote the approximated CPU cost of $D_{i,n}$ for $0 \leq i \leq M$. Then an approximated utilization $U'_{CPU,n}$ can be calculated as

$$U'_{CPU,n} = \frac{C_{0,n} + \sum_i N_i \cdot C_{i,n}}{T}. \tag{2}$$

To solve for $C_{i,n}$, one can choose a regression method from a variety of known methods in the literature. Finding the best fitting method is outside of the scope of this paper. In all experiments, we use the Non-negative Least Squares Regression (Non-negative LSQ) provided by MATLAB to get $C_{i,n}$. This non-negative LSQ regression minimizes the error

$$\epsilon = \sqrt{\sum_j (U'_{CPU,n} - U_{CPU,n})_j^2} \quad ,$$

such that $C_{i,n} \geq 0$, where j is the index of the monitoring window over time.

3.2 Applying Regression to a Production System with Live Workload

We use the one-month trace analyzed in Section 2 to evaluate the accuracy of the regression-based method described above. We had to limit our validation exercise to the application server tier because we could not get relevant CPU utilization measurements at the database tier.

For each 1-hour time window[3] the *Workload Profiler* provides the average CPU utilization as well as the number of transactions N_i for the i-th transaction type, where $1 \leq i \leq M$. The OVSD trace profile has the format shown in Table 1.

When we first introduced and applied the regression-based technique for evaluating the transaction cost in [24], there were only 14 different transaction types in TPC-W. The analysis of OVSD workload revealed that the real workloads often have a much higher number of transaction types, e.g., OVSD workload operates over 756 different transaction types. In order to apply the regression technique to OVSD workload we

---

[3] In [24], we showed that a larger monitoring window improves the accuracy of regression results. For the production system under study a monitoring window of 1 hour produced the best results.

Table 1. An example of transaction profile in server 1

Time (hour)	N_1	N_2	N_3	N_4	$\cdots$	N_{756}	$U_{CPU}(\%)$
1	21	15	21	16	$\cdots$	0	13.3201
2	24	6	8	5	$\cdots$	0	8.4306
3	18	2	5	4	$\cdots$	0	7.4107
4	22	2	4	7	$\cdots$	0	6.4274
5	38	5	6	7	$\cdots$	0	7.5458
$\cdots$							

would need to collect more than 756 samples of 1-hour measurements. Such a collection would require to observe this workload for more than 1-month before we would collect enough "equations" for evaluating the OVSD transaction cost.

The workload analysis presented in Section 2.2 shows that the studied workload exhibits a very high degree of reference locality, i.e., a small subset of site transactions is responsible for a very high percentage of client accesses, e.g., the 100 most popular transactions already cover 99.8% of all client accesses. From the other side, there is a high percentage of transactions that are rarely accessed, i.e., so called, "one-timers". We divided the original 1-month trace in two halves. The additional workload analysis revealed that there are 203 transactions that are accessed only once in the first half of the trace, and which are not accessed in the second half of the trace. Similarly, there are 189 transactions that are accessed only once in the second half of the trace, and which are not accessed in the first half of the trace. The non-negative LSQ regression used in this paper returns "0" as a typical value for "rare" variables, since there is not enough information in the original set of equations to produce a more accurate solution.

So, the question is whether accurate performance results can be obtained by approximating the CPU cost of a much smaller set of popular (*core*) transactions. In other words, if we use regression to find the CPU cost of a small number of *core* transactions, can this small set be useful for an accurate evaluation of the future CPU demands in the system?

Following this idea, we only use the columns N_1 to N_K and U_{CPU} in Table 1 to approximate C_i for $1 \leq i \leq K$. The approximated U'_{CPU} of every hour is then computed by these N_1 to N_K and C_1 to C_K values.

We also consider the results produced by the non-negative LSQ regression method when K is equal to 10, 20, 60 and 100 transactions respectively. We use the relative error of the approximated utilization as the metric to validate the regression accuracy. For every hour, the relative error of the approximated utilization is defined as

$$Error_R = \frac{|U'_{CPU} - U_{CPU}|}{U_{CPU}}. \tag{3}$$

We divide the OVSD trace into two parts. The first half is used as a training set to solve for the CPU cost C_i using the non-negative LSQ regression method. The second half is treated as a validation set. Because the administration jobs during weekends might introduce a significant noise to the CPU utilization, the training set for the regression consists of data from workdays only.

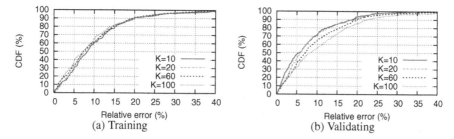

Fig. 11. Server 1. CDF of relative errors under a different number of of core transactions chosen for a regression method: (a) training set, (b) validating set.

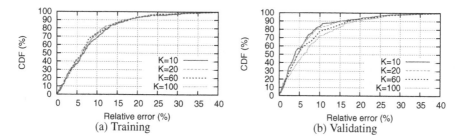

Fig. 12. Server 2. CDF of relative errors under a different number of core transactions chosen for a regression method: (a) training set, (b) validating set.

The regression method produces similar results for the two heterogeneous application servers in the system. Figs. 11-12 show the CDF of the relative errors for training and validating sets for servers 1 and 2, respectively.

The regression results can be summarized as follows:

- Overall, the non-negative LSQ regression achieves good results for all examined values of K, i.e., when the regression method is applied to approximate the CPU cost of the top 10, 20, 60, or 100 most popular transactions. For the training set, at least 60% of the points have relative errors less than 10%, and at least 90% of the points have relative errors less than 20% (see Figs. 11(a) and 12(a)). The method's accuracy for the validating set is only slightly worse (see Fig.11(b), 12(b)).
- Larger K achieves a higher accuracy for the training set. However, this improvement is not significant: for $K = 100$ there is only a 4% improvement compared to the results with the top 10 transactions.
- The larger values of K, e.g., $K = 100$, show a worse prediction accuracy for the validating set compared to K equal to 10 or 20 core transactions as shown in Fig. 11 - 12. These results again can be explained by the workload properties. While we consider 100 most popular transactions, the last 80 of them only responsible for 6% of the client requests. These transactions have an irregular access pattern. Some of those transactions appear only in the first or second half of the trace

(while not being a "one-timer"). As a result, computing the individual cost of these transactions does not help to evaluate the future CPU demands, and introduces a higher error compared to the regression based on a smaller transaction set.

Regression produces the best results when a representative set of core transactions is used and rarely accessed transactions are omitted. Since some of the rarely accessed transactions might only appear in the first half of the trace, while some different rarely accessed transactions may only appear in the second half of the trace, it is beneficial to use only core transactions in linear regression as well as in the overall capacity planning. The additional CPU overhead that is due to the rarely accessed transactions is "absorbed" by the CPU cost of the core transactions. Consequently, a small additional CPU usage by the distinct and rarely accessed transactions is accounted via the CPU cost of the most frequently and consistently accessed core transactions.

We conclude that considering the top 20 *core* transactions (i.e., $K = 20$) leads to the most accurate results. Note that the top 20 transactions are responsible for 93.6% of the total transactions in the analyzed trace. Therefore, selecting the top K transactions that account for 90% - 95% of all client accesses for the regression method results in a good representative subset of the entire workload. The regression solver produces a solution for 200 equations with 20 variables only in 8 millisecond. In general, the common least squares algorithms have polynomial time complexity as $O(u^3 v)$ when solving v equations with u variables, and hence, can be efficiently used as a part of on-line resource evaluation method [1]. Combining the knowledge of workload properties with statistical regression provides a powerful solution for performance evaluation of complex production systems with real workloads.

3.3 Anomaly Detection

Shortened product development cycle, frequent software updates, and more complex integration dramatically increase the risk of introducing poorly performing applications. Consequently, another problem that needs to be addressed is a preliminary analysis of performance issues that often occur during the application updates and new software releases: this is also known as *anomaly detection*. Typically, when a new software release is introduced and unexpected performance issues are observed, it is important to make sure that these performance issues are not caused by the current workload, i.e., system overload due to a higher rate of client requests. When the system performance can not be explained by the existing workload mix in the system, it suggests that the observed performance issues might be caused by the latest software modification. Thus, it is important to evaluate the resource usage caused by the existing transaction mix in the system, and to generate the alarm events when system utilization significantly deviates from the predicted utilization value computed from the existing workload.

Using the observed workload mix we compute the expected CPU utilization of the system U'_{CPU} by Eq. 2 and compare it against the measured CPU utilization U_{CPU} for the same time period. The service provider can set a threshold Th that defines the acceptable deviation of expected system utilization U'_{CPU} from the observed utilization U_{CPU}. If

$$\frac{U_{CPU} - U'_{CPU}}{U'_{CPU}} \geq Th \qquad (4)$$

then our tool generates an alarm event. We only consider the situations when the measured CPU utilization is significantly higher than the expected one, since in this case, something else besides the observed workload causes performance problems.

Fig. 13 demonstrates the anomaly detection feature of the tool for the OVSD trace with $Th = 2$. Our method accurately predicts CPU utilization caused by this mix. Over weekends our method has generated the alarm warnings (marked with circles in Fig. 13) indicating that something else, besides the transaction processing, happens in the system. During these time intervals the predicted and observed utilizations are drastically different. Our method correctly identifies a non-typical CPU utilization caused by a set of additional administrative tasks, extensively performed over weekends (see remarks about this in Section 2.4), and which had nothing to do with the processed transaction mix.

While in this paper, we defined an anomaly situation as one where observed CPU utilization significantly exceeds predicted CPU utilization, one can consider a symmetrical situation where observed CPU utilization is significantly lower than predicted CPU utilization as a result of transaction mix, and verify the reasons behind it: for example, it might be related to unavailable embedded objects in the serviced web pages due to some storage subsystem problems. Currently, we are working on optimizing the regression technique that provides a better support for performance anomaly detection as well as on designing a technique for tuning the threshold parameters that minimize false positive alarms.

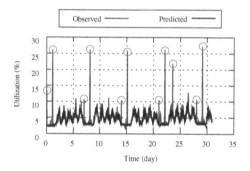

Fig. 13. Anomaly detection with R-Capriccio

4   Capacity Planning

Modern Internet servers typically employ a multi-tier structure consisting of web servers, application servers and databases as given in Fig. 14. Each tier gets the requests from its preceding tier, and may generate certain requests to its successor. For scalability, a tier may consist of several replicated servers. These servers may be heterogeneous, and a dispatcher may employ a special load balancing strategy for distributing the incoming requests across the replicated servers.

Due to the session-based client behavior, a multi-tier system is usually modeled as a closed system with a network of queues (see Fig. 15). The number of clients in the system is fixed. When a client receives the response from the server, it issues another

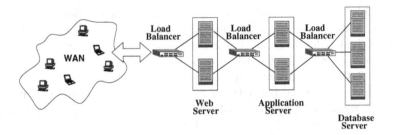

Fig. 14. A multi-tier structure of a server

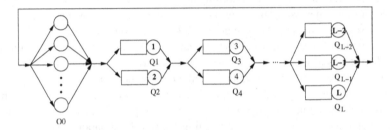

Fig. 15. Queuing network modeling of a multi-tier closed system

request after certain think time. This think time is modeled as an infinite server Q_0 in Fig. 15. Once the service time in each queue is obtained, this closed system can be solved efficiently using Mean-Value Analysis (MVA) [8].

Workload characterization of real traces in Section 2 shows that the workload mix changes over time, and hence the service time could not be modeled as a fixed distribution for the entire lifetime of the system but one can treat the workload as fixed during shorter time intervals (e.g., 1 hour). R-Capriccio performs the capacity planning procedure for each monitoring time window of 1 hour and then combines the results across these time points to get the overall solution [4].

4.1 MVA

MVA is based on the key assumption that when a new request enters a queue, this request sees the same average system statistics in the system as without this new request. Fig. 16 presents a description of the detailed MVA algorithm [22].

The visit ratio V_i (definition in Fig. 16) is controlled by the load balancing policy. For example, if the load balancing policy used is equally partitioning the transactions across all servers, then the number of visits V_s to server s in tier l is equal to $1/m_l$, where m_l is the number of servers in tier l.

---

[4] For the TPC-W benchmark and most production multi-tier services CPU is a typical system bottleneck. However, in practice, when one needs to make a projection of the maximum achievable system throughput, additional "back of the envelope" computations for estimating memory and network requirements under the maximum number of concurrent clients are required to justify this maximum throughput projection.

Inputs:
N = number of clients
Z = think time
L = number of servers
S_i = service time per visit to the i-th queue
V_i = number of visits to the i-th queue

Outputs:
X = system throughput
Q_i = average number of jobs at the i-th queue
R_i = average response time of the i-th queue
R = system response time (excluding think time)
U_i = utilization of the i-th queue

1. Initialization: for $i = 1$ to L do $Q_i \leftarrow 0$
2. Iterations:
   for $n = 1$ to N do
   a. for $i = 1$ to L do
      $$R_i = S_i(1 + Q_i)$$
   b. $R = \sum_{i=1}^{L} R_i V_i$
   c. $X = \dfrac{n}{Z + R}$
   d. for $i = 1$ to L do $Q_i = XV_iR_i$
3. for $n = 1$ to L do
   a. $X_i = XV_i$
   b. $U_i = XS_iV_i$

Fig. 16. The MVA algorithm [8]

Note that the original MVA (as in Fig. 16) takes the number of clients N as input, and computes the average performance metrics for a system with N clients. In capacity planning, the number of clients is unknown. In the contrary, the model needs to be solved for exactly this unknown variable. Here, we assume that the Service Level Agreement (SLA) specifies a threshold Γ_R (i.e., upper bound) of the average transaction response time. Then the condition in step **2** of MVA is changed to the following condition: "while $R \leq \Gamma_R$ do".

4.2 Case Study

In this section, we demonstrate how *R-Capriccio* helps to answer the following capacity planning question:

– How many clients can be supported by the existing system:
  • providing the desirable performance guarantees, e.g., response time under Γ_R, and
  • assuming that the system processes a given (varying, non-stationary) type of workload?

The detailed sequence of steps performed by *R-Capriccio* is summarized in Fig. 17.

---

1. **Workload profiler:**
   For each monitoring window w, and each server s:
   a. collect the number of transactions $N_{i,s,w}$ of each type i;
   b. collect the average utilization $U_{s,w}$.
   For each monitoring window w:
   a. select the top K most popular transaction types;
   b. collect the transaction mix in the system,
      i.e., the percentage p_i of the transactions for type i
      for all $1 \leq i \leq K$;
   c. collect the average think time Z_w.

2. **Regression-based solver:**
   For each server s:
   Compute the cost function $C_{i,s}$ for each transaction
   type i as described in Section 3, where $1 \leq i \leq K$.

3. **Analytical model:**
   For each monitoring window w:
   a. approximate the service time S_s for each server s as
      $S_s = \sum_{i=1}^{K} p_i \cdot C_{i,s}$;
   b. compute the maximum number of clients MAX_w can
      be handled with average response time less than Γ_R
      using MVA algorithm.
   Build the profile with entry as (w, MAX_w).
   Find the minimal MAX_w value X.
   X is the number of concurrent customers the system can support
   with the average transaction response time less than Γ_R

Fig. 17. The R-Capriccio Framework

The first two steps of R-Capriccio that use the *Workload Profiler* and the *Regression-based Solver* have been presented in the previous two sections. We use the same workload as input to the third step of the analytic model. In the case study, we had to limit our capacity planning exercise to the application server tier (which is a bottleneck tier in the OVSD service) because we could not get relevant CPU utilization measurements at the database tier (this particular database was shared across a few different services, and we had only access to the OVSD part of the application servers).

Since the traces are collected from the two servers independently, we treat each heterogeneous server as an independent system. Later, we show how to combine the capacity planning results from those heterogeneous servers together.

All the experiments are conducted for the top 20 most popular transaction types, i.e., K is set to 20. Following step **3.a.** in Fig. 17, we approximate the average service time for each 1-hour time interval for both servers as shown in Fig. 18. Because server 2 has a faster CPU, it is expected that it has a smaller service time than server 1. For each time interval there is a vector of parameters representing the average think time, the average

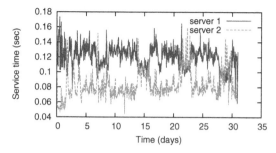

Fig. 18. Approximated service time using the CPU cost of the top 20 transaction types

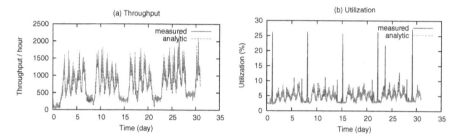

Fig. 19. Server 1. Measurements versus analytic model: a) Throughput of transactions; b) CPU utilization.

service time, and the number of concurrent clients. We apply the MVA model at each time interval for each server.

Fig. 19(a) shows the validation results by comparing the throughput of the analytic model and the measured transaction throughput of server 1. The analytic model captures the real system behavior well, i.e., 90% of the relative errors are below 18.7%. Comparisons of the throughput of the analytic model and the measured session throughput of server 2 are of similar accuracy.

Fig. 19(b) compares the average measured utilization over time with the utilization results provided by the analytic model. We observe a nearly perfect match between the measured and analytic results. Except for the utilization spikes observed in the real system measurements over weekends that are due to special administration-related tasks as discussed in Sections 2.4 and 3.3. Our method predicts a much lower CPU utilization using the observed transaction mix for these time periods. This presents an additional functionality of R-Capriccio that can help in generating "alarm" conditions when predicted utilization for processing the existing workload significantly deviates from the system measurements. The analytic results for server 2 show a similar performance trends and are not presented here for brevity.

Fig. 20 and Fig. 21 illustrate the CDF of the maximum number of clients that can be supported by server 1 and server 2 under the changing OVSD transaction mix over time, where the transaction response time is limited by Γ_R equal to 1, 3, 6 and 10 seconds respectively. These results are computed using the same think time and service time as in the above experiments.

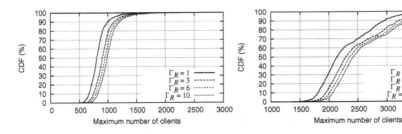

Fig. 20. Server 1: CDF of the maximum number of clients under different threshold Γ_R of the average response time

Fig. 21. Server 2: CDF of the maximum number of clients under different threshold Γ_R of the average response time

The summary of results are shown in Table 2. As expected, server 2 has a much higher capacity than server 1. Higher values in threshold Γ_R allow for a larger number of clients to be supported by the system.

Table 2. Maximum number of clients under different Γ_R

Γ_R(sec)	Server 1	Server 2	Total
1	472	1349	1821
3	528	1478	2006
6	565	1534	2099
10	608	1580	2188

The capacity of the entire application server composed of these two heterogeneous servers is determined by the load balancing policy as well. For example, if the SLA defines that the average transaction response time is not higher than 1 second, the studied application server can handle 1821 concurrent clients but only if the load balancer is aware of the heterogeneous capacity of these two servers and can split the load proportionally to server capacity. If the load balancer partitions transactions equally, capacity reduces to 944, just half of the previous one. Such a big difference indicates the significant impact of a load balancing policy on system capacity as heterogeneous CPU speeds must be taken into account.

5   Related Work

Performance evaluation and capacity planning of software and hardware systems is a critical part of the system design process [8]. There is a number of capacity planning techniques proposed for different popular applications.

Among these techniques, queuing theory is a widely used methodology for modeling a system behavior and answering capacity questions [16,17,18]. Modeling of a single-tier system, such as a simple HTTP server, has been studied extensively. Even for a multi-tier structure which is employed ubiquitously for most servers, the system is usually abstracted as the most bottle-necked tier only: in [16], only the application tier for the e-commerce systems are modeled by a M/GI/1/PS queue; similarly in [19] the application tier with N node cluster is modeled by a G/G/N queue. Recently B. Urgaonkar et al. proposed analytic models for both open and closed multi-tier systems [17,18]. These models are validated by synthetic workloads running in real systems. However the expense of accurately estimating model parameters, i.e., service times and visit ratios, from each server log makes this model difficult to apply in production environments. Direct measurements in [18] do not characterize transactions as we do in this paper. Moreover, existing capacity planning methods are based on evaluating the system capacity for a fixed set of typical user behaviors. Once the service time is estimated, it is consistent throughout the planning procedure. This approach does not consider the fact that a changing workload for the same system has different service times and may result in different system capacity. Our experiments show that such techniques as those in [18] may fail to model a real system because of its dynamic nature.

In this paper, we use a similar closed multi-tier model as in [18], but in contrast to [18] or other examples in the existing literature of capacity planning, we propose a methodology that does not need a controlled environment for analytic model parameterization. Instead of characterizing the overall service time of every server, we use a statistical regression method to approximate the service cost of individual transactions. This CPU cost function together with the transaction mix help to approximate the system service time that varies with the changing transaction mix.

The use of statistical methods in capacity planning has been proposed in the early 80's [9,8], but the focus was on a single machine/cluster that is much simpler than current large-scaled multi-tiered systems. Recently statistical methods are getting more attention in computer performance analysis and system performance prediction. In [20] the authors use multiple linear regression techniques for estimating the mean service times of applications in a single-threaded software server. These service times are correlated with the Application Response Measurement package (ARM) data to predict system future performance. In [21],[23] the authors focus on transaction mix performance models. Based on the assumption that transaction response times mostly consist of service times rather than queueing times they use the transaction response time to approximate the transaction service demand. The authors use linear regression to identify performance anomalies in past workloads and to scrutinize their causes. We do not use measured transaction response times to derive CPU transaction demands (this approach is not applicable to the transactions that themselves might represent a collection of smaller objects). One of their basic assumptions is that the transaction mix consists of a small number of transaction types.

We have introduced a statistical regression-based approach for the CPU demand approximation of different transaction in our earlier paper [24], where we evaluated this approach by using a testbed of a multi-tier e-commerce site that simulates the operation of an on-line bookstore, according to the classic TPC-W benchmark [4]. Using the TPC-W benchmark, we demonstrated that the use of linear regression provides promising results. However, TPC-W operates using only 14 transaction types. In this work, we continue applying the linear regression technique for approximating the CPU transaction cost as was introduced in [24] but in a much more challenging environment. Here, we applied and validated this technique with real, live workloads that exhibit much more complex and diverse behavior than the synthetic TPC-W benchmark. Among the contribution of the current paper is a novel approach that illustrates how the regression-based technique can be applied to the production sites with large set of transaction types. By applying the regression to a set of popular, so-called "core" transactions (that are responsible for 90% - 96% of the site traffic) we are able to obtain the accurate estimates of transaction CPU cost that can be used for a variety of performance anomaly detection cases and capacity planning tasks in the production sites with real, live workloads.

6 Conclusion

In this paper, we present *R-Capriccio*, a new capacity planning framework which provides a practical, flexible and accurate toolbox for answering capacity planning and anomaly detection questions for multi-tier production systems with real workloads. More importantly, it can be used for explaining large-scale system behavior and predicting future system performance.

We used the access logs from the OVSD application servers to demonstrate and validate the three key components of R-Capriccio: the workload profiler, the regression-based solver, and the analytic model. In our capacity planning framework, we identify the set of most popular *core* transactions and sessions for building a site profile, compute transaction cost, and size the future system under the real workload. In order to derive the resource cost of each core transaction (i.e., CPU time required for corresponding transaction processing), we observe a number of different core transactions over fixed length time intervals and correlate these observations with measured server utilization for the same time interval. Using a *non-negative least-squares regression* method we approximate the resource cost of each core transaction. The statistical regression works very well for estimating the CPU demands of transactions that themselves might represent a collection of smaller objects and where the direct measurement methods are not feasible.

While this paper concentrates on evaluating the CPU capacity required for support of a given workload, we believe that regression methods can be efficiently applied for evaluating other shared system resources. We plan to exploit this avenue in our future work.

References

1. Ari, B., Giivenir, H.A.: Clustered Linear Regression. Knowledge-Based Systems 15(3) (2002)
2. Capacity Planning for WebLogic Portal, http://edocs.bea.com/wlp/docs81/capacityplanning/capacityplanning.html
3. The Workload for the SPECweb96 Benchmark, http://www.specbench.org/osg/web96/workload.html
4. TPC-W Benchmark, http://www.tpc.org
5. Arlitt, M., Williamson, C.: Web Server Workload Characterization: The Search for Invariants. In: Proc. of the ACM SIGMETRICS 1996 Conference, Philadelphia, PA (May 1996)
6. Almeida, V., Bestavros, A., Crovella, M., de Oliveira, A.: Characterizing Reference Locality in the WWW. Technical Report, Boston University, TR-96-11 (1996)

7. Arlitt, M., Krishnamurthy, D., Rolia, J.: Characterizing the Scalability of a Large Web-based Shopping System. J. ACM Transactions on Internet Technology 1(1) (August 2001)

8. Menasce, D., Almeida, V., Dowdy, L.: Capacity Planning and Performance Modeling: from mainframes to client-server systems. Prentice Hall, Englewood Cliffs (1994)

9. Kachigan, T.M.: A Multi-Dimensional Approach to Capacity Planning. In: Proc. of CMG Conference 1980, Boston, MA (1980)

10. Cherkasova, L., Tang, W.: Sizing the Streaming Media Cluster Solution for a Given Workload. In: CCGrid 2004. Proc. of the 4th IEEE/ACM, Chicago, USA (2004)

11. Rolia, J., Cherkasova, L., Arlitt, M., Andrzejak, A.: A Capacity Management Service for Resource Pools. In: Proc. of the Fifth Int. Workshop on Software and Performance (2005)

12. Chase, J.S., Anderson, D., Thakar, P., Vahdat, A., Doyle, R.: Managing Energy and Server Resources in Hosting Centers. In: SOSP. Proc. of the 18th ACM Symposium on Operating System Principles (2001)

13. Sarris, D., Hofer, J.: Capacity Planning for e-Commerce Systems With Benchmark Factory, www.dlt.com/quest/

14. Klerk, L., Bender, J.: Capacity Planning. Microsoft TechNet (2000), http://www.microsoft.com/technet/archive/itsolutions/ecommerce

15. PHP HyperText preprocessor, www.php.net

16. Villela, D., Pradhan, P., Rubenstein, D.: Provisioning Servers in the Application Tier for E-Commerce Systems. In: Proc. of IWQoS 2004, Montreal, Canada (2004)

17. Urgaonkar, B., Shenoy, P., Chandra, A., Goyal, P.: Dynamic Provisioning of Multi-tier Internet Applications. In: ICAC 2005. In Proc. of the 2nd IEEE International Conference on Autonomic Computing, Seattle (June 2005)

18. Urgaonkar, B., Pacifici, G., Shenoy, P., Spreitzer, M., Tantawi, A.: An Analytical Model for Multi-tier Internet Services and its Applications. In: Proc. of the ACM SIGMETRICS'2005, Banff, Canada (June 2005)

19. Ranjan, S., Rolia, J., Fu, H., Knightly, E.: QoS-Driven Server Migration for Internet Data Centers. In: Proc. of IWQoS 2002, Miami, FL (May 2002)

20. Rolia, J., Vetland, V.: Correlating Resource Demand Information with ARM Data for Application Services. In: Proc. of the ACM Workshop on Software and Performance (1998)

21. Kelly, T.: Detecting Performance Anomalies in Global Applications. In: WORLDS 2005. Second Workshop on Real, Large Distributed Systems (2005)

22. Jain, R.: The Art of Computer Systems Performance Analysis: Techniques for experimental Design, Measurement, Simulation, and Modeling. Wiley-Interscience, NY (1991)

23. Stewart, C., Kelly, T., Zhang, A.: Exploiting Nonstationarity for Performance Prediction. In: Proc. of EuroSys 2007, Lisbon, Portugal (March 2007)

24. Zhang, Q., Cherkasova, L., Smirni, E.: A Regression-Based Analytic Model for Dynamic Resource Provisioning of Multi-Tier Applications. In: ICAC 2007. Proc. of the Fourth International Conference on Autonomic Computing, Jacksonville, FL, p. 27 (2007)

AVMEM - Availability-Aware Overlays for Management Operations in Non-cooperative Distributed Systems[*]

Ramsés Morales, Brian Cho, and Indranil Gupta

Dept. of Computer Science
University of Illinois at Urbana-Champaign
Urbana IL 61801
{rvmorale, bcho2, indy}@cs.uiuc.edu

Abstract. Monitoring and management operations that query nodes based on their availability can be extremely useful in a variety of large-scale distributed systems containing hundreds to thousands of hosts, e.g., p2p systems, Grids, and PlanetLab. This paper presents decentralized and scalable solutions to a subset of such availability-based management tasks. Specifically, we propose AVMEM, which is the first *availability-aware overlay* to date. AVMEM is intended for generic non-cooperative scenarios where nodes may be selfish and may wish to route messages to a large set of other nodes, especially if the selfish node has low availability. Under this setting, our concrete contributions are the following: (1) AVMEM allows arbitrary classes of *application-specified predicates* to create the membership relationships in the overlay. In order to avoid selfish nodes from exploiting the system, we focus on predicates that are random and consistent. In other words, whether a given node y is a neighbor of a given node x is decided based on a consistent and probabilistic predicate, dependent solely on the identifiers and availabilities of these two nodes, but without using any external inputs. (2) AVMEM protocols discover and maintain the overlay spanned by the application-specified AVMEM predicate in a scalable and fast manner. (3) We use AVMEM to execute important availability-based management operations, focus-ing on range-anycast, range-multicast, threshold-anycast, and threshold-multicast. AVMEM works well in the presence of selfish nodes, scales to thousands of nodes, and executes each of the targeted operations quickly and reliably. Our evaluation is driven by real-life churn traces from the Overnet p2p system, and shows that AVMEM works well in practical settings.

Keywords: Membership protocols, availability variation, predicates, management, distributed algorithms, P2P systems.

[*] This material is based upon work supported by the National Science Foundation (NSF) under CAREER award CNS-0448246 and ITR award CMS-0427089.

R. Cerqueira and R.H. Campbell (Eds.): Middleware 2007, LNCS 4834, pp. 266–286, 2007.

1   Introduction

Today's large-scale distributed settings contain hundreds to thousands of hosts, and include Grids [5,10,29], peer-to-peer (p2p) systems, and geographically-distributed clusters such as PlanetLab [20]. Modern and emerging distributed applications running in such settings will have to address two challenges: heterogeneous availability variation of underlying hosts, and the requirement for system-wide monitoring operations. Further, these challenges have to work even under non-cooperative situations, where hosts may behave selfishly.

The availability of hosts (i.e., their fraction uptime) in any of these systems varies widely across both time and across hosts. For instance, in the Overnet p2p system 50% of hosts have a 10-day availability lower than 30% [3]. This heterogeneity across space and time is visible even in Grid applications. For instance, Grid5000 designers report that each machine reboots several tens of times *per day*, depending on the applications that are scheduled to run on it [5].

Orthogonally, in addition to this heterogeneity, several researchers and industrial companies have pointed out the dire need for monitoring and management of end-user distributed applications. Jim Gray opined that management was the most difficult problem for any distributed system [19]. The 2005 NSF report on "Grand Challenges in Distributed Computer Systems" lists among its primary concerns real-time management, automated monitoring, and dealing with heterogeneity in distributed systems [7]. Finally, end-user applications routinely form 24% to 33% of the TCO (Total Cost of Ownership) of today's clusters [26].

Finally, it is well-known that p2p and Grid systems (e.g., @Home-style applications, or spread over multiple institutions) consist of many nodes that are selfish and would like to obtain maximum benefit from the overlay, in spite of their low availability. For instance, Adar and Huberman point out in [1] that as many as 70% of nodes in Gnutella are freeloaders. Authors have looked at avoiding the effect of selfish nodes for multicast, e.g., [12], however, we believe we are the first to look at availability-based management tasks under a non-cooperative node model.

The conjunction of the above three concerns motivates the problem of designing middleware that executes *availability-based* monitoring and management tasks for such distributed settings. To stay concrete, we consider four specific types of such availability-based tasks (which we sometimes also refer to as *queries*), each with significant and varied uses:

I. Threshold-multicast and Threshold-anycast: Multicast (or anycast) to all nodes with availability $> b$ (where $b \in [0, 1)$), starting from any arbitrary initiator node. This would be useful for both control and data operations. Control operations include selecting a supernode in a p2p system with a minimal threshold availability, e.g., akin to [13,14,16]. Data operations include a publish-subscribe or multicast application where packets are sent out to only nodes above a certain availability, e.g., [21]. Such a multicast application would *incentivize* hosts to have higher availability, in order to obtain good reliability.

II. Range-multicast and Range-anycast: Multicast (or anycast) to a node with availability in range $[b, b + \delta] \subseteq [0, 1]$, starting from any arbitrary initiator node. This operation can be used to *fingerprint* characteristics of the nodes within an availability range, e.g., one could find out the average bandwidth of nodes below a certain availability, in order to understand the correlations. In addition, threshold anycast would be useful for selection of replica locations for a file [4,6], and of deployment instances for a distributed Grid application [5].

There are many other availability-based management operations not listed above that may be desired by applications. However, we find that all of the existing overlays in literature are *availability-agnostic* while selecting neighbors, thus making it inefficient to run the above classes of tasks. This observation motivates the need for an *availability-aware overlay*, that would support availability-based management operations like the ones listed above.

1.1 Design Goals, Challenges, and Principles

A decentralized solution to the availability-based management problems just described consists of two components: (I) an overlay among the nodes that helps each node maintain a set of neighbors (or a *membership list*), based on the availabilities of these nodes; and (II) operations to execute the desired management operations by leveraging this overlay. Furthermore, these components require an *availability monitoring* service, which can be queried to learn the availability of any node in the system.

In building the overlay (component (I) above), we face two challenges. The first arises because we consider a system model where nodes may be *selfish*. Under this setting, nodes (especially those with low availabilities) would like to have as many other nodes (possibly of high availability) in their own membership list, and to communicate with them. Further, these selfish nodes may wish to flood the network with copies of a genuine anycast or multicast request they received[1]. To address this challenge, we select neighbors of a given node x, based on the availabilities of the nodes, in a manner that is *consistent* in spite of changes in the system.

Concretely, given a node x and y, let $M(x, y)$ be a binary variable that denotes whether y is a valid entry in x's membership list or not. Consistency requires that the value of $M(x, y)$ depend only on the addresses (IP and port) of x, y, and their availabilities $av(x), av(y)$ as reported by the availability monitoring service. $M(x, y)$ should not be influenced by any external factors such as other nodes in the system, the system size, or churn in the system (i.e., nodes joining and leaving the system), etc. Notice that consistency allows both the recipient node y of any message and a third node to verify the value of $M(x, y)$, regardless of other factors in the system. This implies that any node x (selfish or otherwise) will be able to send messages only to other nodes y that are legitimately its neighbors under the consistent predicate, i.e., for which $M(x, y) = 1$.

---

[1] Corruption of messages is not considered here, as it is an orthogonal problem, and how to tolerate it has been previously addressed [17].

The second challenge arises from the fact that we would like to maintain connectivity in the overlay as well as support efficient anycast and multicast operations, yet maintain only a small number of neighbors. A small number of neighbors translates to a lower bandwidth, memory, and computation overhead. In order to ensure connectivity, scalability, and efficiency, we require the neighbor selection criteria to be *flexible*, besides being consistent. Our approach addresses this challenge by coupling consistency with *randomization*.

Finally, for component (II) above, we would like to execute anycast and multicast operations in a manner that is *fast* (i.e., has low latency), *scalable* (i.e., uses a small number of messages), and *reliable* (i.e., manages to complete successfully). We address this challenge by using a variety of techniques, ranging from flooding and greedy approaches, to gossip and simulated annealing.

1.2   Other Related Work and Eliminated Solutions

Using a centralized solution to execute the management tasks mentioned is prohibitive because this would limit the number of simultaneous tasks that can be addressed, especially if these tasks are for the multicast variants above. It is well-known that such central-database solutions are rather ineffective at providing real-time answers to instantaneous queries.

In the realm of decentralized solutions, one potential alternative is to leverage p2p ring-based distributed hash tables (DHTs) such as Pastry [22] or Chord [24]. Such an approach would decide DHT nodeIDs for nodes based on the node's availability, rather than a hash of its IP address. Although this allows management tasks to be resolved via the DHT routing algorithm itself, this approach causes an unacceptable amount of churn in the DHTs. This churn arises since a nodeID changes with the node's availability, besides the fact that nodes are continuously going offline and coming online. In addition, when using ring-based DHT routing the latency for answering a range-multicast task is linear in the number of nodes involved, thus making it inefficient.

Another alternative could be p2p solutions that are specially built to support range searches (or range queries) such as skip trees, graphs and others [2,9,23,30], or content-based publish-subscribe architectures like Sub-2-Sub [28]. In this approach, nodes would be organized and placed in the overlay based on their current availability, so that anycast and multicast tasks could be executed by doing a range search on the appropriate availability range. Once again however, there is a high degree of churn in the system; as nodes' availabilities change over time, their positions in the overlay will move around as well. Further, p2p range query structures are known to be difficult to manipulate under concurrent operations. Note that no system targets range or threshold operations under a selfish node model.

Finally, we would like to eliminate broadcast-based solutions that flood out the multicast or anycast to all nodes, since this is inefficient, unscalable, and causes spam to nodes outside the target range.

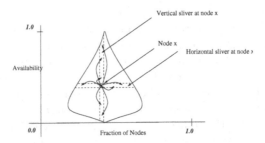

Fig. 1. AVMEM membership lists at a node x: Horizontal Sliver and Vertical Sliver

1.3   Contributions of This Paper

In order to meet the above goals, this paper presents AVMEM which, to the best of our knowledge, is the first proposed availability-aware membership protocol. AVMEM explicitly leverages availability information of nodes in the system while selecting neighbors. AVMEM avoids the effects of selfish nodes, and allows efficient execution of our targeted availability-based management operations. Concretely, each node in AVMEM maintains two small membership lists: a *horizontal sliver* (HS) and a *vertical sliver* (VS). The horizontal sliver at node x contains a small (random) subset of nodes with availability "close" to $av(x)$, the availability of x. In contrast the vertical sliver contains a small (random) subset of nodes from among those with availability that is not in the vicinity of $av(x)$. This is illustrated in Figure 1.

Most importantly, AVMEM supports an arbitrary class of *membership predicates* that are random and consistent. This gives an application developer the choice from a family of AVMEM predicates in order to build the appropriate overlay for their application. The horizontal and vertical slivers at each node are selected in a *randomized and consistent fashion* by using the application-specified predicate. This maintains connectivity, reduces the effect of selfish nodes, and provides efficiency, scale and reliability for the management operations.

We discuss and analyze the family of predicates supported by AVMEM in Section 2. Then, in Section 3, we present decentralized AVMEM protocols that achieve scalable and fast discovery as well as updating of neighbors at each node. Finally, we solve: (1) anycast by using greedy and simulated-annealing approaches, and (2) multicast by using either a flooding or a gossip-based approach. We have implemented AVMEM, and we present trace-based simulations in Section 4. Specifically, we use churn traces from the Overnet p2p system [3] to evaluate and compare the effectiveness the management operations, as well as to microbenchmark the behavior of the AVMEM overlay itself. Due to the novelty of AVMEM, we prefer to do a thorough and comprehensive evaluation, rather than creating a strawman system to make comparisons. We conclude in Section 5.

2   AVMEM Membership Graph Predicates

This section presents a range of predicates for creating random and consistent membership graphs (or overlays) that are availability-aware. Section 3 will describe the discovery of membership graphs for any such given predicate.

Basics and Notation: The availability of a node x, as reported by the availability monitoring service, is denoted as $av(x)$. Further, the identifier (hash-based or IP-port) of node x is denoted as $id(x)$. Given two nodes x and y and a membership predicate, $M(x, y)$ is a binary variable that indicates whether node x (with availability $av(x)$) should contain node y (with availability $av(y)$) in its membership list or not.

Due to our principles of randomization and consistency, we use the following framework for the AVMEM predicate in the rest of the paper:

$$M(x, y) \equiv \{H(id(x), id(y)) \leq f(av(x), av(y))\} \qquad (1)$$

Here, $H(.)$ is a (consistent) normalized cryptographic hash function with range $[0, 1]$, used for its randomization – a normalized version of SHA-1 or MD-5 could be used for this purpose. Further, f is a function that takes as input a pair of variables in the range $[0, 1]$, and outputs a value that lies in $[0, 1]$.

The above predicate means that for given nodes x, y, node x will include y in its membership list only if the value of $H(id(x), id(y))$ is less than the value of $f(av(x), av(y))$. This provides consistency, since the value of $M(x, y)$, as specified by equation 1, depends only on the identifiers and availabilities of nodes x and y, but not on anything else in the system. Further, regardless of who evaluates the condition 1 above, it will produce the same result for nodes x, y.

Since we assume that H is a fixed and well-known function, the actual AVMEM predicate is thus determined by the nature of f. For instance, if $f(., .) = p, (p \in [0, 1])$, then we derive a random overlay (like SCAMP[8] or CYCLON[27]), but with the additional property of consistency. In other words, for this example, given two nodes x and y, then $M(x, y) = 1$ consistently with probability p.

Section 2.1 next discusses a family of interesting AVMEM predicates specified under the framework of equation (1). Section 2.2 analyzes these predicates.

2.1   A Family of Availability-Aware AVMEM Predicates

We consider a family of interesting predicates that leverage the known probability distribution function (PDF) of the availability variation in a given system. The availability variation PDF in several deployed p2p systems has been observed to remain fairly stable from one day to another [25]. Notice that such information can be collected and analyzed offline by either a crawler or a central server. This information can then be communicated to all nodes at pre-run-time and used consistently. Suppose the PDF of the availability distribution of the system is specified as $p : [0, 1] \rightarrow [0, 1]$, i.e., $p(a) \cdot da$ is the *fraction* of nodes with availability between a and $(a - da)$, when $da \rightarrow 0$. Then, our canonical AVMEM predicate is specified as:

$$f(av(x), av(y)) = \begin{cases} hs(av(x), av(y), p(.)) & \text{if } |av(x) - av(y)| < \epsilon. \text{ [Hor. Sliver]} \\ vs(av(x), av(y), p(.)) & \text{otherwise. [Vertical Sliver]} \end{cases}$$

Recall that a horizontal sliver at node x is defined as a partial list of nodes (called horizontal sliver neighbors of x in the overlay) with "similar" availability as node x. According to the above framework, we use an availability range of $(\pm\epsilon)$ around $av(x)$ as candidate nodes for the horizontal sliver at node x. The value of ϵ is fixed globally, and *does not depend on the target ranges of multicast or anycast operations (or vice-versa)*. Our experiments find that using $\epsilon = 0.1$ suffices to give good scalability and reliability for management tasks.

To understand the horizontal sliver concept intuitively, the reader may realize that the horizontal sliver is somewhat like similar notions in DHTs, i.e., like the "leaf table entries" in Pastry [22], and the "successors/predecessors" in Chord [24]. However, our setting is different since those systems deal with hashed nodeIDs, while we are dealing with availability space instead. The horizontal sliver helps to maintain a connected overlay among nodes with availability around $av(x)$. Notice that if there are L such nodes, the number of neighbors has to be $O(log(L))$, selected uniformly at random, for connectivity to hold with high probability (w.h.p.) [8].

On the other hand, a vertical sliver at node x is defined as a random sample of nodes with availabilities ranging all the way from 0 to 1. The goal of a vertical sliver is to maintain connectivity throughout the system via a sufficient number of "long-distance" links (in availability space) among nodes. This is most akin to the routing table entries in Pastry or Chord DHTs [22,24]. However, once again, we are dealing with the availability space rather than hashed nodeIDs, thus our problem setting is quite different.

Below we describe and analyze several AVMEM predicates. Some of these predicates will assume knowledge of the expected system size (i.e., number of online nodes) as a parameter N^*. In p2p systems [3,?], overlays like PlanetLab, and Grid systems, the actual number of online nodes varies within a small constant factor of N^*. Thus, N^* need not be accurate – our algorithms and analysis hold even when the actual system size is off by a constant factor from the value of N^*, although they might cease to hold with an order of magnitude variation. Just like the availability PDF, the value of N^* can be calculated offline by crawlers, and communicated to all nodes consistently. N^* would not be changed even if the actual number of online nodes changes.

While $vs()$ and $hs()$ can be arbitrary, below we first discuss several useful options for selecting the vertical sliver (i.e., different vertical sub-predicates) and then for selecting the horizontal sliver (i.e., different horizontal sub-predicates).

I. Vertical Sub-Predicate Possibilities: There are several ways of specifying the vertical sliver sub-predicate, i.e., $vs()$. We discuss three options below, in increasing order of complexity. We are most interested in the second option (I.B) and analyze it in detail in Section 2.2. The first option we discuss is availability-independent:

$$vs(av(x), av(y), p(.)) = d_1, d_1 = O(\tfrac{log(N^*)}{N^*}) \text{ [I.A: Constant Vertical Sliver]}$$

This predicate works best in a system where the availability PDF distribution is a uniform one. However, distributed systems rarely have homogeneous availability PDFs. This motivates us to consider other predicates that are more expressive. We derive a very generic vertical sliver sub-predicate:

$$vs(av(x), av(y), p(.)) = min(\tfrac{c_1 \cdot log(N^*)}{N^* \cdot p(av(y))}, 1.0) \text{ [I.B: Logarithmic Vertical Sliver]}$$

Here, c_1 is a constant. Section 2.2 proves that this predicate ensures a *uniformity of coverage of the availability space* (Theorem 1). In other words, for any availability range $[b, b + \epsilon]$ (non-overlapping with $[av(x) - \epsilon, av(x) + \epsilon]$), a node x will have the same expected number of vertical sliver neighbors in this range, *regardless of the value of b*.

Finally, one may desire that the density of vertical sliver neighbors in an infinitesimal interval around a value b becomes smaller and smaller as the absolute value of $|b - av(x)|$ becomes larger and larger. This would provide an overlay somewhat akin to Pastry routing table entries and Chord finger table entries, where neighbors are chosen with exponentially increasing distance as one moves away (there, in the hashed nodeID space). This is realized by the following predicate, as proved in Corollary 1.1 of Section 2.2:

$$vs(av(x), av(y), p(.)) = min(\tfrac{c_1 \cdot log(N^*)}{N^* \cdot p(av(y)) \cdot |av(y) - av(x)|}, 1.0)$$
$$\text{[I.C: Logarithmic-Decreasing Vertical Sliver]}$$

II. Horizontal Sub-Predicate Possibilities: Just like for vertical slivers, there are several possible horizontal sliver sub-predicates. We enumerate two of them below. The second of these predicates (I.B) is more interesting, and is analyzed in Section 2.2.

The first option is to select a constant fraction of the nodes that lie in the availability range $[av(x) - \epsilon, av(x) + \epsilon]$. The predicate is:

$$hs(av(x), av(y), p(.)) = d_2, d_2 = O(\tfrac{log(N^*)}{N^*}) \text{ [II.A: Constant Horizontal Sliver]}$$

Although this ensures connectivity w.h.p. among the nodes in this availability range, it involves too many nodes. Specifically, it is possible that the range $[av(x) - \epsilon, av(x) + \epsilon]$ contains much fewer nodes than N^*. This raises the possibility that the size of the horizontal sliver at a node x can be reduced. This leads us to the following predicate:

$$hs(av(x), av(y), p(.)) = min(\tfrac{c_2 \cdot log(N^*_{av(x)})}{N^{*min}_{av(x)}}, 1.0)$$
$$\text{[II.B: Logarithmic-Constant Horizontal Sliver]}$$

Here, c_2 is a constant. This formulation involves two new parameters - $N^*_{av(x)}$ and $N^{*min}_{av(x)}$. First, $N^*_{av(x)}$ is the expected number of online nodes in the availability range $[av(x) - \epsilon, av(x) + \epsilon]$. Mathematically, this can be derived from the PDF of the availability distribution. That is, $N^*_{av(x)} = N^* \times \int_{av(x)-\epsilon}^{av(x)+\epsilon} p(a)da$, where $N^* =$ the stable system size. Second, $N^{*min}_{av(x)}$ is the *minimum* number of expected online nodes present in any availability interval of width ϵ that lies wholly within $[av(x) - \epsilon, av(x) + \epsilon]$. This can also be calculated from the PDF of the availability distribution as follows: $N^{*min}_{av(x)} = N^* \times (min\{\int_v^{v+\epsilon} p(a)da, [v, v+\epsilon] \subseteq [av(x) - \epsilon, av(x) + \epsilon]\})$.

Note that these values can be easily calculated from a discretized PDF distribution of the system created from a small sample set of nodes. $\int_v^{v+\epsilon} p(a)da$ is merely the number of nodes that have availability lying in this interval, divided by the total number of entries in the discretized PDF.

Section 2.2 shows, via Theorems 2 and 3, that the logarithmic constant vertical sliver sub-predicate maintains connectivity w.h.p. among all nodes lying in the range $[av(x) - \epsilon, av(x) + \epsilon]$.

2.2   Analysis of AVMEM Predicates

In this section, we show that the logarithmic vertical sliver ensures uniformity of coverage in the availability space (Theorem 1), the logarithmic-constant horizontal sliver ensures connectivity among online nodes whose availabilities lie close to each other (Theorem 2), and that the above two sliver rules together ensure a small, scalable set of online neighbors for each node in the system (Theorem 3).

Theorem 1. The logarithmic vertical sliver sub-predicate (equation I.B) ensures that, given a node x, for any $a \in [av(x) - \epsilon, av(x) + \epsilon]$, the expected *number* of online nodes with availability in an (infinitesimally small) interval around a, that are vertical sliver neighbors of node x, does not depend on the value of a.

Proof. The expected number of online nodes, in the vertical sliver of node x, that have their availabilities lying in an interval of size da around a, is given as $=p(av(y))da \cdot N^* \times \frac{c_1 \cdot log(N^*)}{N^* \cdot p(av(y))} = c_1 \cdot log(N^*)da$. This is independent of a. □

Corollary 1.1. The logarithmic-decreasing vertical sub-predicate (equation I.C) selects online neighbors that are at exponentially increasing distances from node x, where distances are measured in the availability space $av(.)$. (The proof follows along similar lines as Theorem 1.)

Theorem 2. The logarithmic-constant horizontal sliver (equation II.B) sub-predicate ensures that for a given node x, the sub-overlay consisting of all online nodes with availabilities in the interval $[av(x) - \epsilon, av(x) + \epsilon]$ is connected w.h.p.

Proof. For the given node x, define X^+ as the set of all online nodes (other than x itself) that have availability $\in [av(x), av(x)+\epsilon]$. Similarly, define X^- as the set of all online nodes (other than x) that have availability $\in [av(x) - \epsilon, av(x))$. We will show the proof in three parts: (i) the sub-overlay graph of nodes in X^+ is connected w.h.p., (ii) the sub-overlay graph of nodes in X^- is connected w.h.p., and (iii) x knows at least one node in X^+ and at least one node in X^- w.h.p.

For any node u, define $N^{*+}_{av(u)}$ and $N^{*-}_{av(u)}$ as the expected number of online nodes lying respectively in the upper half and lower half of the interval $[av(u) - \epsilon, av(u) + \epsilon]$. That is, $N^{*+}_{av(u)} = N^* \times \int_{av(u)}^{av(u)+\epsilon} p(a)da$, and $N^{*-}_{av(u)} = N^* \times \int_{av(x)-\epsilon}^{av(u)} p(a)da$.

We first prove (i), and the proof of (ii) follows analogously. For any node $y \in X^+$, notice first that the interval $[av(y) - \epsilon, av(y) + \epsilon]$ wholly contains the interval $[av(x), av(x) + \epsilon]$. We use a well-know result from [8] that in a graph of M nodes, if each node has $\Omega(log(M))$ neighbors that are selected at random, then the graph is connected w.h.p.

Firstly, from the definition of the logarithmic-constant horizontal sliver rule, notice for each node u that belongs to X^+, the probability of y picking u as neighbor is independent of where $av(u)$ lies. Thus, neighbors are picked uniformly at random. Secondly, we need to show that if there are $M = N^{*+}_{av(x)}$ nodes in the interval X^+, each node in that interval has an expected $\Omega(log(M))$ online neighbors lying in X^+. From the horizontal sliver rule at node y, the expected number of online nodes from the interval X^+ that y has as neighbors is:

$$= \int_{av(x)}^{av(x)+\epsilon} (c_2 \cdot \frac{log(N^*_{av(y)})}{N^{*min}_{av(y)}} \times (N^* \cdot p(a)))da$$

$$= \frac{c_2 \cdot log(N^*_{av(y)})}{N^{*min}_{av(y)}} \cdot N^{*+}_{av(x)}$$

$$\geq c_2 \cdot log(N^*_{av(y)}), \text{ (since } N^{*+}_{av(x)} \geq N^{*min}_{av(y)})$$

$$\geq c_2 \cdot log(N^{*+}_{av(x)}), \text{ (since } N^*_{av(y)} \geq N^{*+}_{av(x)})$$

This completes the proof of (i), and thus (ii). Finally, to prove (iii), notice that we can derive, based on the same reasoning as above, the probability of x knowing at least one node in the set X^+, and at least one node in X^-, as:

$$\geq (1 - (1 - \frac{c_2 \cdot log(N^*)}{N^{*+}_{av(x)}})^{N^{*+}_{av(x)}}) \times (1 - (1 - \frac{c_2 \cdot log(N^*)}{N^{*-}_{av(x)}})^{N^{*-}_{av(x)}})$$

$$\geq (1 - e^{-c_2 \cdot log(N^*)}) \cdot (1 - e^{-c_2 \cdot log(N^*)})$$

$$\geq (1 - \frac{2}{(N^*)^{c_2}})$$

$\square$

Theorem 3. The logarithmic-constant horizontal sub-predicate (equation II.B) and the logarithmic vertical sub-predicate (equation I.B) , together, ensure that the total expected number of online neighbors (vertical sliver + horizontal sliver) at a given node x: (i) is at most $(N^*_{av(x)} - 1 + c_1 \cdot log(N^*))$; and (ii) $O(log(N^*))$ if $N^{*min}_{av(x)} = \theta(N^*)$.

Proof. Consider a node x. From the discussion of Theorem 1's proof, the expected number of online vertical sliver neighbors at x is:

$$= \int_0^{av(x)-\epsilon} c_1 \cdot log(N^*)da + \int_{av(x)+\epsilon}^1 c_1 \cdot log(N^*)da \leq c_1 \cdot log(N^*)$$

Since the horizontal sliver at node x can contain at most $(N^*_{av(x)} - 1)$ nodes, this proves the part (i) of the theorem.

To show (ii), we use a similar derivation as in the discussion of Theorem 2's proof. We can show that the expected number of online horizontal sliver neighbors of node x is:

$$\leq \int_{av(x)-\epsilon}^{av(x)+\epsilon} (c_2 \cdot \frac{log(N^*_{av(x)})}{N^{*min}_{av(y)} \cdot \epsilon} \times (N^* \cdot p(a)))da = c_2 \cdot \frac{log(N^*_{av(x)})}{N^{*min}_{av(y)}} \times N^*$$

Since $N^{*min}_{av(x)} = \theta(N^*)$ and $N^*_{av(x)} \leq N^*$, this is $O(log(N^*))$.   □

3   AVMEM Maintenance and Management Operations

We first discuss in Section 3.1 how nodes discover their AVMEM neighbors according to any application-specified predicate. Then, Section 3.2 describes how the anycast and multicast operations are executed atop the AVMEM overlay.

3.1   AVMEM Membership Maintenance

In this subsection, we first describe the techniques used by AVMEM to *discover and maintain* neighbors, i.e., horizontal sliver (HS) and vertical sliver (VS) neighbors, in conformity with the application-specified AVMEM predicate. We then analyze the optimality of this protocol, and check whether the memory, bandwidth, and discovery time scale to medium-scale systems.

For discovery and maintenance, we leverage two types of existing services in a black-box manner. These services are:

1. an *availability monitoring service*, e.g., centralized, or distributed such as AVMON [18]; and
2. a *decentralized shuffling partial membership service*, e.g., SCAMP [8], CY-CLON [27], T-MAN [11], LOCKSS [15].

An availability monitoring service is defined as one that can be queried for the long-term availability (e.g., raw, or aged) of any given node. It returns an answer that is reasonably accurate, and that is reasonably consistent over time. The level of accuracy and consistency of course depends on the actual availability monitoring protocol itself. The more accurate and consistent it is, the better our AVMEM discovery will perform. For our practical implementation, we leverage our own availability monitoring service called AVMON [18]; our experiments show that this gives good results. Furthermore, AVMON's overhead is low; for instance, in a system with 2000 nodes, the average node bandwidth is 6.81Bps, average node memory is 52 Bytes, and average node CPU time is 0.57ms per minute.

A decentralized shuffling membership service allows a node to maintain a random list of some of the nodes in the system (irrespective of any predicate). This is a *weakly consistent list* that is incomplete, and may even contain stale entries. Further, this list is shuffled, i.e., its contents are continuously changed by the underlying shuffling protocol, so that given a node y and node x that stay long enough in the system, the entry for node y will *eventually* appear in the shuffled list at node x. For our practical implementation, we could have chosen any one of existing systems such as SCAMP [8], CYCLON [27], T-MAN [11], LOCKSS [15], etc. However, we chose to use our AVMON implementation's underlying *coarse view* mechanism [18], which fulfills the requirements of shuffling membership. This simplifies the overall design of our system, and Section 4 shows this approach performs well in practice.

Given the above two services, the core AVMEM maintenance protocol consists of two sub-protocols: (I) a Discovery sub-protocol, and (II) a Refresh sub-protocol. The discovery protocol enables nodes to discover new AVMEM relationships and thus HS and VS neighbors. On the other hand, the refresh protocol continuously checks whether existing HS and VS neighbors still satisfy the predicate, and eliminates them if they do not. Each sub-protocol is elaborated below.

I. Discovery Sub-Protocol: At any given node x, the discovery protocol runs periodically, i.e., once every *discovery protocol period* time units (typically 1 minute). It iterates through the entries in the coarse view (i.e., the shuffled membership list). For each entry node y that is not already in $HS(x) \cup VS(x)$, it queries the availability monitoring service for the availability of y, and checks the AVMEM predicate to see if y is a valid HS or VS neighbor of x. If one of these sub-predicates evaluates to true, then y is included in $HS(x)$ or $VS(x)$, as appropriate. We will soon analyze the discovery time of this protocol.

II. Refresh Sub-protocol: The refresh sub-protocol periodically iterates through the entries of the $HS(x)$ and $VS(x)$ lists. For each node y in these lists, the sub-protocol queries the availability monitoring service for y's current availability, and evaluates the appropriate AVMEM predicate to see if $M(x,y) = 1$ or not. If $M(x,y)$ has become 0, then y's entry is deleted from the appropriate list. It is easy to see that once $M(x,y)$ becomes false, node x will delete y from its AVMEM membership list within a worst case time of 1 *refresh protocol period*. In our implementation, we found that using a refresh period of 20 minutes suffices for reasonable maintenance of AVMEM predicates.

Discovery Protocol - Optimality and Reality Check: The underlying shuffling membership protocols we are considering (SCAMP[8], CYCLON[27], T-MAN[11], LOCKSS[15], AVMON's coarse view [18]) all maintain a view of size v at each node, where the entries in this view are randomly selected as well as continuously shuffled[2]. For AVMEM, we are concerned about the memory, computation, and bandwidth spent by a node on the one hand, and the discovery time for neighbors on the other hand. The former three scale linearly with v - memory is of course v, computation comes from evaluating the predicate periodically for each entry in the view (thus v), and bandwidth from fetching the availability information for these entries ($O(v)$).

---

[2] Since we are using AVMON [18], this v would be the same as cvs in [18], i.e., AVMON's "coarse view size".

Discovery time is defined as follows: given a pair of nodes x and y for which $M(x, y) = 1$, this is the time until x actually includes y in its $HS(x)$ or $VS(x)$, as appropriate. The discovery time depends on the operation of the underlying shuffling protocol, but fortunately, the fact that there is constant shuffling tells us that the expected time for a given node y to appear in x's view is $O(\frac{N}{v})$.

In order to optimize the above concerns, we thus wish to minimize $f(v) = v + \frac{N}{v}$. Differentiating this with v, gives $\frac{df(v)}{dv} = 1 - \frac{N}{v^2} = 0$, or $v = O(\sqrt{N})$, which is a minimum. This is a reasonably small number for medium-scale systems. Even for $N = 100,000$, $v = \sqrt{N} \simeq 320$. With 20 B per entry and a 1 minute protocol period, the per-node memory is 6.3 KB, and the bandwidth is 105 Bps. Finally, if the average discovery time is $\frac{N}{v}$ protocol periods, this turns out to be around 5 hours. This is reasonable given that large-scale Grid computations run for several days, users survive in p2p systems for months, and PlanetLab nodes are up for years.

3.2   Management Operations over AVMEM

In this section, we describe algorithms for executing the four operations laid out in Section 1, namely: threshold-multicast, threshold-anycast, range-multicast, and range-anycast. For ease of exposition, we first discuss the two anycast operations, and then the multicast operations.

I. {Threshold, Range} Anycast: We discuss how to route an anycast message intended for range R – a threshold anycast follows a similar approach, where the range R stretches from the threshold to 1.0. A node x receiving an anycast message checks to see if it itself lies within range R - if yes, then the anycast is successful and we are done. Each anycast has a TTL (time-to-live) that is decremented by 1 at each virtual hop. If this TTL value is 0 the message is not forwarded. In any other case the message is forwarded to another node. We discuss three approaches for forwarding of an anycast below.

• Greedy Forwarding: Node x forwards the anycast to an AVMEM neighbor that lies inside R. If there is no such neighbor, x selects as the next hop the neighbor whose availability is closest to r.

• Retried Greedy Forwarding: To increase the reliability for anycasts, we allow nodes to retry a prospective next-hop if the previous candidate was not responsive (i.e., was found to be offline). To implement this, we introduce an integer parameter $retry$, initialized to k at the initiator. Each forwarded message carries the value of $retry = k$. This parameter determines the number of nodes tried using the greedy metric, before dropping the message. Specifically, each next-hop node is required to acknowledge receipt of the anycast message - failing this, the previous hop node will decrement the value of $retry$ by 1, and retry its next-best neighbor, according to the greedy metric (i.e., distance to range target R). The retrying stops when either $retry$ reaches 0, or there are no more next-best nodes left in the AVMEM neighbor list of node x.

• Simulated Annealing: An alternative approach is to follow simulated annealing, where the probability of choosing a random next-hop is high initially (in the first few hops) but decreases as the anycast proceeds. Specifically, we choose $p = e^{-\Delta/ttl}$, where ttl = remaining time to live, and Δ = the Euclidean distance between the edge of R and the availability of the current next-hop under consideration. At each hop, a random next-hop can be selected (from among the AVMEM neighbors) with probability p, as the list of neighbors is traversed, otherwise the greedy approach is used (with probability $(1 - p)$).

A few notes are due about the above approaches. Each of the above three variants naturally has three flavors, depending on whether only the horizontal sliver neighbors of x are used (HS-only), only the vertical sliver is used (VS-only), or whether both are used (HS+VS). To be generic, we referred to the considered set of sliver neighbors as merely "AVMEM neighbors" above. Thus, we have a total of nine algorithms. Section 4 presents data on the most promising variants.

Further, when node x is considering potential next-hops for an anycast, it uses *cached* values of availabilities for its neighbors. Typically, these cached values were fetched the last time the refresh operation was done at node x - this eschews querying the availability service for each forwarded message. Section 4 evaluates how much using cached values allows flooding attacks by selfish nodes.

II. {Threshold, Range} Multicast: For these operations, we once again consider only the range R; the threshold-based variant follows similarly. The multicast operation follows a two-stage process: an anycast into the range R, followed by a multicast within the range. The anycast follows the techniques listed above. Hence, we now discuss multicast only when the initiator is within the range R. Once a node x has received a multicast message M for a range R (where $av(x) \in R$), it can use one of two approaches for forwarding it:

• Flooding: Node x forwards the multicast to *all* its AVMEM neighbors that lie in range R. Any duplicate copies of the multicast are ignored, and the forwarding is done only once. This is a highly reliable approach, but is wasteful since each node will receive multiple copies of the multicast - in the worst case, it may receive one copy from each of its in-neighbors.

• Gossip: To avoid the above overhead, we use a gossip-based approach. Here, node x (after receiving the multicast) *gossips* the multicast M. It does so periodically - once every *protocol period* seconds, it selects up to *fanout* of its AVMEM neighbors: (1) whose availabilities lie within the range R, and (2) to whom x has not already forwarded M. These neighbors could be selected randomly, but for our implementation we use a deterministic iteration through the list in order to select gossip targets. The node repeats the above process for N_g protocol periods after it first receives the multicast. Any duplicate copies of the multicast it receives are eliminated. We select N_g and fanout so that $(N_g \times fanout) = log(N^*)$, thus ensuring dissemination w.h.p. via gossip [8].

Just as for anycast, there are three variants for each of the above two approaches - HS-only, VS-only, and HS+VS, depending on which set of AVMEM neighbors are used for the operations. This gives us a total of six algorithms. We implemented all these options, and Section 4 presents data from the best ones.

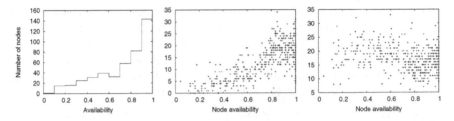

Fig. 2. System Snapshot of Online Nodes showing: (a) the distribution of online nodes (b) the size of horizontal slivers and (c) the size of vertical slivers with respect to availability (each dot in the plot stands for a node). There are 442 online nodes.

4   Experiments

We implemented AVMEM in C, and present evaluation results from a discrete event simulation. In order to be realistic, we inject churn (availability variation) traces from the Overnet p2p system [3] into our system. These traces were originally collected over a 7 day period, at 20 minute intervals, for a fixed population of 1442 hosts, and are injected as such. By default, we build and use AVMEM overlays using the two sub-predicates of Logarithmic Vertical Sliver (equation I.B) and Logarithmic-Constant Horizontal Sliver (equation II.B), from Section 2. We evaluate both the AVMEM overlay (Section 4.1) as well as the management operations atop it (Section 4.2).

4.1   Microbenchmarks: AVMEM Overlay Properties

Overlay Properties: We evaluate whether the number of horizontal and vertical sliver neighbors in our implementation follow theoretical predictions. The system was allowed to warm up for 24 hours, and a snapshot was taken of online nodes. Figure 2(a) shows that the availability distribution of online nodes in this snapshot is highly skewed, making this trace set a good test for our algorithms.

Figures 2(b,c) respectively show the distributions of horizontal sliver size and vertical sliver size at all these online nodes. From Figure 2(c), it is clear that the median values of the vertical sliver sizes are uncorrelated to the availability, as expected. Figure 2(b) shows an increasing median value of the horizontal sliver size with node availability. Yet, Figure 3 demonstrates that this increase is only sublinear - the horizontal sliver size grows sublinearly with the total number of nodes present within $\pm\epsilon$ availability. Finally, Figure 4 counts the total number of *incoming* vertical sliver links to nodes in different availability ranges. We observe that this number is largely uncorrelated to the distribution of nodes (seen in Figure 2(a)). Thus, we conclude that the AVMEM slice sizes follow theoretical analysis, even under a realistic churn model.

Attack Analysis: We first evaluate the effect of a *flooding attack*, where a selfish (or malicious) node wishes to send out a message to all nodes that are not part of its AVMEM neighbor list(s). Although each node checks each incoming

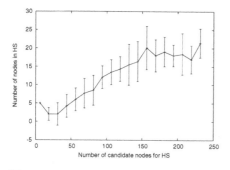

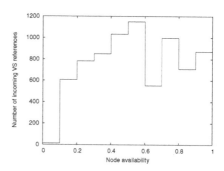

Fig. 3. Horizontal Sliver Scaling: Size of horizontal sliver at a node grows sub-linearly with total number of nodes within ϵ availability of the node. Standard deviation plotted symmetrically but no data was negative.

Fig. 4. Vertical Sliver Link Distribution: Number of incoming vertical sliver links to an availability range is uniform ($[0,0.1]$ skewed as it has one node)

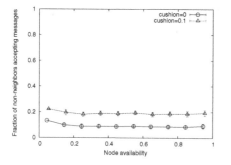

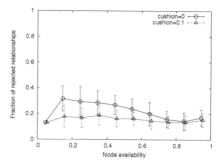

Fig. 5. Flooding Attack: Fraction of peers that are not currently neighbors that would accept communications. Measurement averaged across 0.1-wide availability ranges.

Fig. 6. Legitimate Rejection Rate: Fraction of nodes that will reject communications from an AVMEM in-neighbor. Measurement averaged across 0.1-wide availability ranges.

message to verify if its sender is a valid in-neighbor (according to the AVMEM predicate), and reject it if not, this is open to attacks due to several reasons: (1) nodes may use cached and stale availability information to do this check, and (2) availability information reported by our underlying AVMON service could give inconsistent or inaccurate answers. Figure 5 (line for cushion=0) depicts that regardless of the availability of the selfish node, fewer than 10% of nodes outside of its AVMEM neighbor list accept its flooding message. This is reasonable - it means that to receive an audience from one additional peer, a selfish node must obtain information about 10 additional peers.

Second, we evaluate how the above inaccuracies and cached information affect the rejection of valid messages sent to AVMEM neighbors. Figure 6 shows that this number is below 30% regardless of the sending node's availability. To reduce

this effect further, we add a constant *cushion* to the right hand side of equation
(1) in Section 2, i.e., to function f. This reduces the rejection rate to below 20%
while slightly increasing the effect of flooding attacks (see also Figure 5). This is
reasonable - it means that a node attempting to forward a message will have to try
only an expected $\frac{1}{0.8} = 1.25$ neighbors before succeeding. From these two attacks,
we conclude that AVMEM provides uniform attack resilience and acceptance rate
for legitimate messages, *independent of the sending node's availability*.

4.2 Management Operations over AVMEM

In order to explore anycasts and multicasts systematically, we select the initiator
node in one of three ways, and the target range in one of three ways, thus
effectively giving us nine combinations for each management operation. Although
we evaluated all the nine combinations, for brevity, we show data for only the
most interesting ones below. Specifically, the initiator is chosen as either (1)
LOW $\in [0, 0.3333)$, or (2) MID $\in [0.3333, 0.6666)$, or (3) HIGH $\in [0.6666, 1.0)$. For
threshold operations (anycasts or multicasts), the target availability range was
either 0.25, or 0.49 or 0.90. For range operations, the target availability range
was either one of $[0.2, 0.3]$, or $[0.44, 0.54]$, $[0.85, 0.95]$. Each point on any plot is
the average of 5 different protocol runs, each with 50 messages.

Basic Anycast Operations: We first evaluate anycast based on greedy forwarding using VS-only, HS-only, and HS+VS, as well as simulated annealing
with HS+VS (see Section 3.2). The retried-greedy variation will be discussed
soon. All anycasts are sent with $TTL = 6$. Among the nine options discussed
above, the following four settings were the most interesting. First, Figure 7 shows
the results for a range-anycast experiment with initiator in the MID and target
$[0.85, 0.95]$. All variants gave a 100% success rate for messages, with all except
HS-only finishing w.h.p. within 1 hop. This makes intuitive sense as messages
will not travel far in availability space by using HS-only.

Second, Figure 8 shows the number of delivered range anycasts out of 50
sent, from nodes in availability range HIGH to three different target availability
ranges: $[0.85, 0.95]$, $[0.44, 0.54]$, and $[0.2, 0.3]$. The third of these is the harshest
scenario, since it is very likely that either (1) there are no nodes online in the
low availability ranges, or (2) the anycast takes a longer path via low-availability
nodes, and thus has a high probability of being dropped inside the overlay, as
its TTL expires. Of the multiple options, HS+VS comes out the best.

Retried-Greedy Anycast: Figure 9 shows the reliability and latency of
retried-greedy forwarding, for different values of *retry*, under the harshest possible scenario of the initiator in HIGH and target range $[0.2, 0.3]$. The latency
on each virtual hop here was selected uniformly at random from the interval
$[20ms, 80ms]$. Notice that even under such harsh scenarios, $retry = 8$ gives as
good a performance as the 60% delivery plateau, with a low average latency of
739ms.

Benefit of AVMEM Predicate: In order to compare the usefulness of the
horizontal (logarithmic-constant) and vertical (logarithmic) sub-predicates used

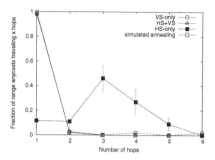

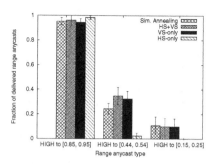

Fig. 7. Range Anycast: Hops required to delivery when sending from MID to range [0.85, 0.95]

Fig. 8. Range Anycast under increasingly harsh scenarios: Lower target availability ranges have lower success rate

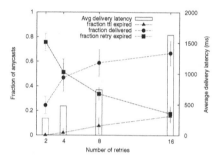

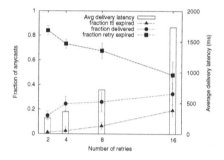

Fig. 9. Retried Greedy Anycast in harsh environment: Anycasts sent to target availability range [0.15, 0.25] from nodes in HIGH

Fig. 10. Retried Greedy Anycast (Random Overlay, instead of AVMEM): Anycasts sent to target availability range [0.15, 0.25] from nodes in HIGH

in the above AVMEM overlay, we ran exactly the same range-anycast operation from Figure 9, but *over a random overlay graph* similar to those created by alternative membership protocols like SCAMP [8], CYCLON [27], T-MAN [27], etc. For fairness, the outdegree of each node in the random graph is $O(log(N^*))$. Figure 10 shows the data for this, and should be compared against Figure 9. A look at these figures tells us that for management operations: (1) overlays based on AVMEM predicates give a higher success rate than random graphs, while (2) both achieve similar latencies.

Multicast Operations: Figure 11 shows the latency performance of range- and threshold-multicast, using both flooding (default) and lower-cost gossip ($fanout = 5$, $N_g = 2$, gossip period=1 s). The latency for each multicast is the worst case, i.e., it is the time of the *last receiving* node obtaining the multicast. The CDF shows that this stays below 300ms for flooding, and 5.5s for gossiping. Figure 12 shows that the spam factor for multicasts is low, i.e., the

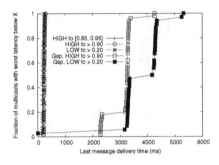

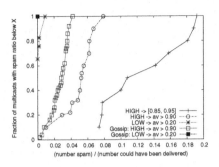

Fig. 11. Multicast Latency CDF: Latency of last message delivered for each multicast

Fig. 12. Multicast Spam Ratio CDF: Ratio of number of multicasts received by a node outside target range, to number of valid nodes in range

fraction of multicasts overflowing the target range, and reaching a node outside is below 8% for most cases, except the topmost case where data is skewed by the small number of nodes in the target range. Finally, Figure 13 shows that flooding gets a reliability above 90%, while gossip reaches 70%. Bandwidth savings due to gossip may thus be worthwhile to applications less concerned about reliability.

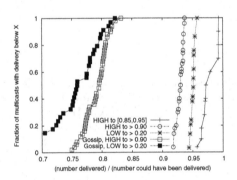

Fig. 13. Multicast Reliability CDF: Fraction of nodes inside target range, that received a multicast

5 Conclusions

We have presented the design and evaluation of AVMEM, an availability-aware overlay. We showed that AVMEM overlay construction is scalable and that a set of availability-based management operations can be run efficiently and reliably on this overlay.

Our experimental evaluation using realistic overlay traces shows that the theoretical properties hold in our implementation. Selfish nodes are implicitly kept under control and good overlay connectivity is achieved by the proposed

AVMEM predicates. This allows in reliable and scalable anycast and multicast operations to availability ranges.

References

1. Adar, E., Huberman, B.A.: Free riding on Gnutella. First Monday 5(10) (2000)
2. Aspnes, J., Shah, G.: Skip graphs. In: Proc. ACM-SIAM SODA, pp. 384–393 (2003)
3. Bhagwan, R., Savage, S., Voelker, G.: Understanding availability. In: Kaashoek, M.F., Stoica, I. (eds.) IPTPS 2003. LNCS, vol. 2735, pp. 135–140. Springer, Heidelberg (2003)
4. Bhagwan, R., Tati, K., Cheng, Y.-C., Savage, S., Voelker, G.M.: Total Recall: System support for automated availability management. In: Proc. Usenix NSDI (2004)
5. Cappello, F., et al.: Grid 5000: A large scale, reconfigurable, controlable and monitorable Grid platform. In: Proc. GRID (2005)
6. Chun, B.-G., et al.: Efficient replica maintenance for distributed storage systems. In: Proc. Usenix NSDI, pp. 45–58 (2006)
7. Kaashoek, F., et al.: Report of the NSF Workshop on Research Challenges in Distributed Computer Systems, http://www.nsf.gov/cise/cns/geni/workshop_report.pdf
8. Ganesh, A., Kermarrec, A.-M., Massoulie, L.: Peer-to-peer membership management for gossip-based protocols. IEEE Transactions on Computers 52(2), 139–149 (2003)
9. Harvey, N., Jones, M.B., Saroiu, S., Theimer, M., Wolman, A.: Skipnet: A scalable overlay network with practical locality properties. In: Proc. USITS (2003)
10. IBM. The Oceano Project, http://www.research.ibm.com/oceanoproject/
11. Jelasity, M., Babaoglu, O.: T-Man: Gossip-based overlay toplogy management. In: Brueckner, S.A., Serugendo, G.D.M., Hales, D., Zambonelli, F. (eds.) ESOA 2005. LNCS (LNAI), vol. 3910, pp. 1–15. Springer, Heidelberg (2006)
12. Li, H., Clement, A., Wong, E., Napper, J., Roy, I., Alvisi, L., Dahlin, M.: BAR gossip. In: Proc. Usenix OSDI (2006)
13. Liang, J., Kumar, R., Ross, K.W.: The fasttrack overlay: A measurement study. Computer Networks 50(6), 842–858 (2006)
14. Lo, V., Zhou, D., Liu, Y., Gauthier-Dickey, C., Li, J.: Scalable supernode selection in peer-to-peer overlay networks. In: Proc. IEEE Hot-P2P, pp. 18–27. IEEE Computer Society Press, Los Alamitos (2005)
15. Maniatis, P., Roussopoulos, M., Giuli, T.J., Rosenthal, D.S.H., Baker, M., Muliadi, Y.: Preserving peer replicas by rate-limited sampled voting. In: Proc. SOSP, pp. 44–59 (2003)
16. Min, S.-H., Holliday, J., Cho, D.-S.: Optimal super-peer selection for large-scale p2p system. In: Proc. ICHIT, pp. 588–593 (2006)
17. Minsky, Y.M., Schneider, F.B.: Tolerating Malicious Gossip. Distributed Computing 16(1), 49–68 (2003)
18. Morales, R., Gupta, I.: AVMON: Optimal and scalable discovery of consistent availability monitoring overlays for distributed systems. In: Proc. ICDCS (to appear, 2007)
19. Patterson, D.: A conversation with Jim Gray. ACM Queue 1(4) (June 2003)
20. Peterson, L., Anderson, T., Culler, D., Roscoe, T.: A blueprint for introducing disruptive technology into the internet. In: Proc. HotNets (October 2002)

21. Pongthawornkamol, T., Gupta, I.: AVCast: New approaches for implementing availability-dependent reliability for multicast receivers. In: Proc. IEEE SRDS, IEEE Computer Society Press, Los Alamitos (2006)
22. Rowstron, A., Druschel, P.: Pastry: scalable, distributed object location and routing for large-scale peer-to-peer systems. In: Proc. IFIP/ACM Middleware, ACM Press, New York (2001)
23. Shu, Y., Ooi, B., Tan, K.-L., Zhou, A.: Supporting multi-dimensional range queries in peer-to-peer systems. In: Proc. P2P, pp. 173–180 (2005)
24. Stoica, I., Morris, R., Karger, D., Kaashoek, F., Balakrishnan, H.: Chord: A scalable peer-to-peer lookup service for Internet applications. In: Proc. ACM SIGCOMM, pp. 149–160. ACM Press, New York (2001)
25. Stutzbach, D., Rejaie, R.: Understanding Churn in Peer-to-Peer Networks. In: Proc. 6th ACM SIGCOMM IMC, pp. 189–202. ACM Press, New York (2006)
26. TechWise Research Inc.: Are some RISC-based clusters easier to manage than others (2004), http://h71000.www7.hp.com/openvms/whitepapers/sm_whitepaper.pdf
27. Voulgaris, S., Gavidia, D., van Steen, M.: CYCLON: Inexpensive membership management for unstructured P2P overlays. Journal of Network and Systems Management 13(2), 197–217 (2005)
28. Voulgaris, S., Riviere, E., Kermarrec, A.-M., van Steen, M.: Sub2Sub: self-organizing conten-based publish-subscribe for dynamic large scale collaborative networks. In: Kaashoek, M.F., Stoica, I. (eds.) IPTPS 2003. LNCS, vol. 2735, Springer, Heidelberg (2003)
29. Weiss, T.: Grid computing gets push from Sun, IBM and Compaq. Computer World (November 2001)
30. Zheng, C., Shen, G., Li, S., Shenker, S.: Distributed Segment Tree: Support of range query and cover query over DHT. In: Proc. IPTPS (2006)

iManage: Policy-Driven Self-management for Enterprise-Scale Systems

Vibhore Kumar, Brian F. Cooper, Greg Eisenhauer, and Karsten Schwan

College of Computing
Georgia Institute of Technology
Atlanta, GA 30332
{vibhore,eisen,schwan}@cc.gatech.edu
Yahoo! Research
2821 Mission College Blvd.
Santa Clara, CA 95054
cooperb@yahoo-inc.com

Abstract. It is obvious that big, complex enterprise systems are hard to manage. What is not obvious is how to make them more manageable. Although there is a growing body of research into system self-management, many techniques are either too narrow, focusing on a single component rather than the entire system, or not robust enough, failing to scale or respond to the full range of an administrator's needs. In our *iManage* system we have developed a policy-driven system modeling framework that aims to bridge the gap between manageable components and manageable systems. In particular, iManage provides: (1) *system state-space partitioning*, which divides a large system state-space into partitions that are more amenable to constructing system models and developing policies, (2) *online model and policy adaptation* to allow the self-management infrastructure to deal gracefully with changes in operating environment, system configuration, and workload, and (3) *tractability and trust*, where tractability allows an administrator to understand why the system chose a particular policy and also influence that decision, and trust allows an administrator to understand the system's confidence in a proposed, automated action. Simulations driven by scenarios given to us by our industrial collaborators demonstrate that iManage is effective both at constructing useful system models and in using those models to drive automated system management.

Keywords: Policies, Self-Management, Bayesian Networks, Enterprise-Systems.

1 Introduction

Consider large systems that are integral parts of an enterprise's IT infrastructure. Examples of such systems include those supporting enterprise websites, or inventory management subsystems, or even the distributed information systems supporting a company's daily operations. Administrators managing these systems are not only expected to keep them running, but in addition, many such systems must meet certain processing constraints, be highly available, offer differentiated levels of Quality of Service (QoS), meet certain Service Level Agreements (SLAs), and may be subject to unforeseen demands.

R. Cerqueira and R.H. Campbell (Eds.): Middleware 2007, LNCS 4834, pp. 287–307, 2007.
© IFIP International Federation for Information Processing 2007

Unfortunately, even the occurrence of seemingly routine events like load changes, node and link failures, software patches, or modifications of certain environmental parameters can cause such systems to behave in unexpected ways, often resulting in their failure to meet current objectives. Given these facts and acknowledging enterprises' growing reliance on their computing infrastructures, solutions must be found for system self-management. These solutions must be driven by high level business goals, be open and receptive to administrators, cope with dynamic changes in requirements and conditions, and scale from small, tightly managed individual subsystems to large company-wide support infrastructures.

The existing tools and techniques for enabling self-management of enterprise-scale systems are insufficient because they are either too general or are too specific. For instance, the state-of-the-art system management tools deployed at large enterprises include software suites like IBM's Tivoli, which is a systems management platform and HP's OpenView (now combined with Mercury), which can be used for managing large-scale systems and networks[1] These tools are equipped with methods for system monitoring and for graphically displaying system status to administrators. However, their functionality for automated symptom determination, reasoning about symptom causes, and taking appropriate corrective actions remains rudimentary, in part due to the lack of standards and more importantly, due to the general nature of these tools. In contrast, researchers have successfully embedded self-managing capabilities into specific well-defined subsystems like database backends [28], request schedulers for multi-tier web services [8] and others. To complement the self-management work being done for specific subsystems, several researchers have been focusing on issues like policy-specification language [11], model building techniques [4] and efficient monitoring schemes [1]. Similarly, there has been some excellent research in the domain of automating specific tasks that are required for enabling self-management. A particular effort of note is the work on automated problem diagnosis, presented in [9,32]. The work focuses on using the monitoring data gathered from a system to detect service level objective violations and correlating the violation to earlier violations for gaining useful insights. While automating subsystems and problem diagnosis is important, these specific techniques must be combined into a comprehensive framework in order to be effective for complex systems.

The goal of our research is to develop abstractions and methods that help bridge the gap between (i) the excellent progress made in the general domain of self-management, like automation of well-defined subsystems or specialized techniques for self-management tasks vs. (ii) the more general challenges posed by managing more complex and/or larger IT infrastructures and applications. Toward this end, we build on such prior work for online system management, we adopt the use of online monitoring and behavior detection tools and techniques [10], and we endorse the use of ECA policies to describe and build our self-management framework. To also address the broader management challenges posed by complex and dynamic IT applications and infrastructures, however, we propose a novel representation of the system state-space that is geared towards policy-based self-management, and we develop new techniques for dealing with the problems of *scale, dynamism, tractability* and *trust*. Tractability here refers to an

---

[1] IBM, Tivoli, HP, OpenView and Mercury are registered trademarks of their respective owners.

administrator's ability to understand current management actions undertaken by the system and to the system's ability to expose its reasoning for those actions. To achieve the goal of system manageability, our system, iManage, offers the following tools:

- *A system modeling framework* - iManage collects system parameters and metrics (collectively called *system variables*) into a single representation of the system state-space, and identifies which actions are available to change the system state.
- *A scheme for reducing the complexity of the system model* - Since a typical system model is too complex to be used or even properly constructed, our tools provide mechanisms to partition the state-space into smaller units that are easier to deal with. These *micro-models* allow us to more precisely model critical aspects of the system, and to more effectively develop policies.
- *Techniques for evolving system models* - Policies that are appropriate under one set of conditions may become invalid as operating conditions and the environment changes. iManage provides techniques for evolving system models and policies, including methods to learn new policies and incorporate human knowledge and experience to refine the policies.
- *Techniques for quantifying our confidence in a system model* - In order for our system models to be useful, the system administrator must be able to trust them. iManage associates a confidence value with each self-management policy, and allows the administrator to both understand and use this confidence value when deciding whether to let the system manage itself.

In the following section we motivate the iManage approach by describing certain subsystems and properties of the operational information system deployed by Delta Air Lines, one of our industry partners. Our interactions with the administrators and developers at that site have motivated much of this work.

1.1 Motivating Example

The Passenger Information Delivery System – PIDS (shown in Figure 1) – is a middleware developed at Delta Technology, Inc. to serve two important needs of the airline. First, it is responsible for managing the passenger data sourced from the airline's TPF mainframe. Second, it provides access to passenger information via events and service interfaces. The PIDS middleware, which according to estimates by Delta Technology processes around 9.5 billion events annually, ensures near real-time delivery of processed events to 'consumers' – programs that need to receive the events – and to a database of current booking and flight information used in activities like those in support of Delta's web site. PIDS collects data from all over the airline. While much of its information comes out of the airline's TPF-based Deltamatic Reservation and Operational Support System (OSS), additional inputs like gate information, information about weather, etc. arrive from airports throughout Delta's worldwide system. Further passenger information is provided by the reservation system. Finally, most planes generate and transmit their own landing time, which is provided to PIDS via FPES (the flight progress event system).

There are hundreds of variables associated with the PIDS system that capture the current state of the PIDS servers, the current load conditions, client specific metrics and

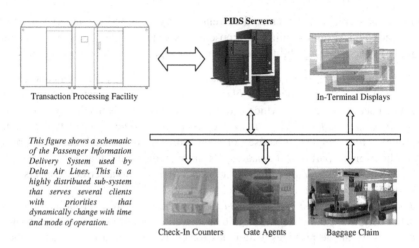

This figure shows a schematic of the Passenger Information Delivery System used by Delta Air Lines. This is a highly distributed sub-system that serves several clients with priorities that dynamically change with time and mode of operation.

Fig. 1. Some Interactions in the PIDS Middleware System

several others. Some of these variables are enumerated in Table 1. A system administrator manages the system by virtue of having the ability to modify some of these variables, examples including the number of client service threads or the number of workflow service threads. More specifically, such modifications of state variables constitute the set of actions allowed for managing the system. The actions of a system administrator to respond to an event (like increased workflow processing delay) are based on his wisdom (mental model of the system behavior) and the prevailing conditions (values of different variables representing the current state). However, partial (and sometimes complete) failures of PIDS middleware are not uncommon, often resulting in delayed and/or canceled flights, and eventually leading to loss of revenue. Such failures can be attributed to the scale of the PIDS middleware and to the dynamic load conditions posed by the application domain.

The above example justifies our focus on the issue of scalability when designing our self-management framework. Moreover, in order to deal with the dynamic load conditions experienced by the PIDS middleware one must make use of self-management techniques that can continuously evolve. Finally, our interaction with the system administrators running the PIDS middleware motivated the need to keep the humans in the self-management loop and in control of the adaptation actions which translated to the requirements for tractability and trust.

1.2   Road Map

The rest of this paper is organized as follows. In Section 2 we present an overview of the overall approach, introduce the system state-space model used by the iManage framework and describe the requirements for policy enablement. Section 3 focuses on the specifics of our approach by describing the algorithms and techniques used by our framework, these include - the partitioning algorithm, the model building technique and the specifics of policy learning, adaptation and the confidence attribute. In Section 4

Table 1. Some variables associated with the PIDS middleware

Variable	Description
	Global Variables
E2EL	The end-to-end latency introduced by the processing workflow.
ELPP	The average queuing delay at individual PIDS processing nodes.
CLIE	Number of cache access clients being served at any time.
ETTR	Expected time to recover from a failure.
EDRR	Events dropped in last 100,00,000 events.
CSTH	Client service threads at individual PIDS processing nodes.
WSTH	Workflow service threads at individual PIDS processing nodes.
NGAG	Number of active boarding gates
NBCA	Number of active baggage claim
NCIC	Number of active check-in counters
NOVR	Number of active overhead displays
	Gate Agent Variables
TTFD	Time to flight departure
DEST	Identifies whether a flight is domestic or international
NPAS	Number of passengers scheduled to board the flight

we present the evaluation of our techniques. Section 5 discusses the related work and finally, we conclude in Section 6 with some open problems for further research in this area.

2   Overview and State-Space Model

In this section we present an overview of our solution approach, which is followed by a formal description of iManage's system state-space model and thereafter we present the requirements for policy-enablement of an enterprise-system. The formal model is used in the following sections to formally describe the various algorithms and techniques used by the iManage framework.

2.1   Solution Overview

The iManage framework for policy-driven self-management of enterprise-scale systems provides an abstraction of a system state-space, where each axis represents an identifiable system variable (e.g., end-to-end delay, throughput, etc.). The state-space model specifically identifies two sets of variables - one set contains the variables that determine the operational status of the system and the other set contains the variables that can be modified to affect the state of the system. The first set is used for specifying the goals or SLAs and the second set is used to determine 'actions' that later become part of ECA policies for the system. In order to manage the system one needs to establish a model that connects the set of action variables to the set of goal variables. However, given the scale of the state-space for enterprise-scale systems and the fact that the system can exhibit different behaviors in different state sub-spaces, modeling the state-space is not straight-forward. The iManage framework utilizes a novel state-space partitioning scheme to deal with the problems of scale and heterogeneous system behavior. iManage then makes use of tree augmented naive Bayesian networks or TANs to build 'micro-models' for each partitioned sub-space that results from the state-space partitioning algorithm. As a result, the system model becomes a collection of the 'micro-models' constructed for each sub-space. In case some goal violation is detected, the system model is consulted to arrive at new values for the set of action variables. In terms of policy the goal violation becomes the *event*, the value of system variables at the time of violation become the *condition* and the assignment of new values to the set of action variables becomes the *action*. Since, probabilistic models are used to arrive at a solution in case of goal violation, even the suggested policy actions are associated with a certain probability of bringing the system to a state of non-violation, this probability acts as the confidence attribute for the policy. A policy is enforced only when the confidence attribute exceeds the threshold set by a system administrator.

2.2 System State-Space Model

The following convention is used to describe the system state-space model. We use boldface capital letters such as, $\mathbf{V}, \mathbf{V}_\phi$ to denote sets, and assignment of values to variables in these sets are denoted by regular capital letters such as V_1, V_2. Similarly, we use boldface lower case letters such as, $\mathbf{v}_i, \mathbf{v}_j$ to represent variables that occur in the sets, and regular lower case letters such as, v_1, v_2 denote specific values taken by those variables.

We consider a system whose state can be represented by a set $\mathbf{V}$ of n variables $\{\mathbf{v}_1, ..., \mathbf{v}_n\}$, which are not necessarily independent. Out of these n variables the system's operational status (like failed, stable, unstable, etc.) can be determined by using only a subset $\mathbf{V}_\phi$ (an example of such variable would be the delay experienced by the users of an enterprise's website) of the state variables in $\mathbf{V}$. Therefore, $\mathbf{V}_\phi$ is the set of variables of interest as far as the system's operational status is concerned.

Furthermore, we associate the system with a set $\mathbf{A}$ of m action interfaces $\{\mathbf{a}_1, ..., \mathbf{a}_m\}$, such that an instance $\mathbf{a}_1$ of action interface variable $\mathbf{a}_i$ represents an action that can be invoked on the system. The invocation of an action $\mathbf{a}_1$ on a system state V_1 is denoted by $\Omega(\mathbf{a}_1, V_1)$, which possibly translates the system to a new state. The effect of invocation of action $\mathbf{a}_1$ on an instance of a system state-space variable v_1 is similarly represented using $\omega(\mathbf{a}_1, v_1)$. The above discussion is used to arrive at the following definition of a deterministic action-variable pair.

Definition 1. *A tuple $(\mathbf{a}_i, \mathbf{v}_i)$ is said to be a deterministic action-variable pair if $\omega(\mathbf{a}_j, v_k)$ is known for all instances $(\mathbf{a}_j, v_k)$ of $\mathbf{a}_i$ and $\mathbf{v}_i$.*

The set of all deterministic action-variable pairs of a system constitutes the set $\mathbf{D}$, and the set of all state-space variables that occur in any tuple in the set $\mathbf{D}$ constitute the set $\mathbf{V}_\alpha$, also called the set of actionable variables. The following lemma holds for all members of the set $\mathbf{V}_\alpha$.

Lemma 1. *If v_1 and v_2 are two possible values of the state-space variable $\mathbf{v}_\alpha^i \in \mathbf{V}_\alpha$ then there exists an instance $\mathbf{a}$ of $\mathbf{a}_i$ such that $(\mathbf{a}_i, \mathbf{v}_\alpha^i) \in \mathbf{D}$ and $\omega(\mathbf{a}, v_1) = v_2$.*

In order to manage a system, and affect its status, one needs to be able to deterministically modify the value of variables contained in $\mathbf{V}_\phi$. However, we only know of ways to deterministically modify the value of variables contained in $\mathbf{V}_\alpha$. Therefore, if one could discover a function χ that maps the space of variables of interest, $\mathbf{V}_\phi$ to the space of actionable variables, $\mathbf{V}_\alpha$ then one would be able to manage the system as described next. Let, $V^{current}$ represent the current state of a system and $V_\phi^{current}$ and $V_\alpha^{current}$ represent values of the corresponding sets of variables $\mathbf{V}_\phi$ and $\mathbf{V}_\alpha$. Now, if the system needs to be translated to a new feasible state such that the variables of interest take the value V_ϕ^{goal}, then one should be able to determine V_α^{goal} using the function χ and then use the set $\mathbf{D}$ to determine the actions required to change the value of variables in $\mathbf{V}_\phi$ from $V_\alpha^{current}$ to V_α^{goal}.

Note that the set of variables in $\mathbf{V} - (\mathbf{V}_\phi \cup \mathbf{V}_\alpha)$ are not redundant and as we shall see in Section 3.1 they play an important role in determining the function χ. An example of such variable would be a measurement of number of disk-operations - such a variable is usually not a member of $\mathbf{V}_\phi$, which is used to determine acceptable system operational status; and this metric, in general, cannot be deterministically affected by allowed system actions (e.g. allocating another disk-array). However, such variables may give hints about the actions to be taken to remedy a certain problem.

To put the above discussion in context, such a system model can be readily applied to the example discussed in Section 1.1. For example, the list of variables, enumerated in Table 1, constitute the set $\mathbf{V}$ of state variables for the PIDS system. The set of variables $\{E2EL, CLIE\}$ are the variables of interest as far as the operational status of the PIDS middleware is concerned and therefore constitute the set $\mathbf{V}_\phi$ (this corresponds to two of the several requirements imposed on the PIDS middleware -*the processing workflow should not introduce a delay of more than 1 second* and *the system should be able to handle 3000 concurrent requests from the clients*). The set $\mathbf{V}_\alpha = \{CSTH, WSTH\}$ constitutes the set of variables that have action associations.

Limitations. In the above discussion we assumed that all the variables that constitute the system state-space are known. This is not true for several systems where due to considerations like monitoring overhead and complexity some of these variables might not be monitored. However, the probabilistic modeling techniques used by our framework are able to perform sufficiently well even when some of the variables are not listed as members of the system state-space, or are not monitored by the system. One must note that failure to include some important state-space constituents may lead to a system model which might not be manageable.

The second limitation arises from the fact that the function χ might return multiple possible instances of the set $\mathbf{V}_\alpha$ corresponding to the goal state represented by V_ϕ^{goal}. For example, if V_ϕ^{goal} corresponds to reduction in end-to-end delay for a three tier web-server then there may exist multiple actions like increasing the number of front-end servers or upgrading the backend database server that may lead to reduction in end-to-end delay. Our probabilistic techniques will suggest the solution which has the highest probability of resolving the problem without any guarantees about the efficiency or optimality of the solution. This opens up the possibility of a difference between 'manageable' and 'efficiently' or 'optimally' manageable system. However, in this paper we will limit ourselves to the concept of manageability.

2.3   Enabling Policies

There are certain requirements that should be met by any system to become eligible for policy-driven self-management. Firstly, the system should be able to measure and export the current value of variables that constitute the state-space for the system. One can think of this as 'dials' on a control dashboard used for managing a very large system. Secondly, the ability to modify some of the variables is also central to the idea of policy enablement. One can similarly think of this capability as the 'knobs', which can deterministically change the value displayed on some 'dials'. In terms of our system state-space model, the variables represented by 'dials' are the variables in the set $\mathbf{V}$. The variables which have an associated 'knob' constitute the set $\mathbf{V}_\alpha$. The 'knobs' can in turn be used to take actions specified using $\omega(\mathbf{a}_i, v_\alpha^j)$.

In order the enable policies in a policy-ready system we need to have a way for representing the policies, mechanisms that discover and learn policies at runtime, ways to enforce policies and techniques for keeping the policies updated for the current system environment. The following sub-sections briefly describe our approach to handling these issues. Some of these issues will later be dealt in detail in Section 3.

Policy Specification - We use a modified form of the well accepted event-condition-action (ECA) format for specifying the policies. The ECA specification is very useful when it comes to enforcing policies for any system. We however, extend the specification to include a confidence-attribute that is related to the probability of the policy having a desired effect when the action specified as part of the policy is taken under appropriate conditions. The *event* in our policy description is a change in the value of some variable(s) in $\mathbf{V}_\phi$. The *condition* that triggers the action associated with the policy is specified over the set of variables in $\mathbf{V}$. The *action* is similarly specified as the modification in the value of some variables contained in $\mathbf{V}_\alpha$.

Policy Discovery - We believe that all policies cannot be specified and that the system may need to discover some policies on the fly. We use a novel state-space partitioning scheme, described in Section 3.1 to first reduce the system state-space under consideration at any instant. Then for each partition we make use of greedy algorithm to discover the most important variables from the set $\mathbf{V}_\alpha$ (i.e. the right knobs). We finally make use of Bayesian networks to build 'micro-models' of the the state-space corresponding to each partition, thereby enabling us to find the values to which the 'knobs' should be adjusted to. We elaborate on these techniques in the following sections.

Policy Enforcement - The interfaces that export the current value of system variables are continuously monitored for any changes. These changes in the value of some variables may cause some policy to evaluate its condition and if the condition evaluates to true the action specified as part of the policy is taken. In simple words, when a problem occurs (i.e. the value on some dials signals something bad) the self-management subsystem tries to (1) find the 'right-knobs' and then (2) adjusts them to some appropriate new values. The enforcement of any policy is also contingent on the confidence-attribute, which should be more than a system-wide threshold set by the system administrator. This gives the administrator a control over the degree of self-management.

Policy Refinement - Policies that are either specified or are learnt by the system may need to be changed because the conditions under which such policies are valid may change with time. An instance of this would be the addition of more nodes to the network underlying the operational information system. Such instances may lead to changes in threshold values that trigger an action specified as part of the policy. Our techniques are able to keep track of such changes in the environment and in response, they suitably modify the policies.

3 Solution Approach

The system state-space model proposed in Section 2.2 showed that $\mathbf{V}$, $\mathbf{V}_\phi$, $\mathbf{V}_\alpha$, $\mathbf{A}$, $\mathbf{D}$ and χ are the parameters that should be known for arriving at a self-management solution for a system. One can safely assume that for most of the systems the sets $\mathbf{V}$, $\mathbf{V}_\phi$, $\mathbf{V}_\alpha$, $\mathbf{A}$ and $\mathbf{D}$ are known apriori. This implies that the system variables, the variables of interest and the deterministically modifiable variables along with the ways to modify them are known. This is true for enterprise-scale systems where the system variables like number of network nodes, link capacities, etc. are known, similarly the variables of interest like end-to-end delay are also known apriori and lastly one knows of variables like allocated buffer-length at network nodes which can be deterministically modified by changing some system parameters. The problem is to find the function χ, and this means that we need to find a way to model the system. Remember that the function χ relates the variables in $\mathbf{V}_\phi$ to the variables in $\mathbf{V}_\alpha$ and the function χ can change for different values of variables in $\mathbf{V} - (\mathbf{V}_\phi \cup \mathbf{V}_\alpha)$. Once the function χ has been determined for the system state-space, one can easily find and/or adapt the actions that form part of the policy specification.

However, building a model (i.e. determining χ) for understanding the behavior of an enterprise-scale system is a tough task. This can be attributed to the fact that in such systems there are a large number of variables (e.g., bandwidth, workload, queue length at servers, etc.), each one of which can potentially affect the state of the system and more often than not these variables also interact amongst themselves. For example, in a certain sub-space of the system's state-space the bandwidth between participating nodes may be the bottleneck and any modification to the priority of processes may have little or no effect on the observed performance. The situation may similarly be reverse for some other system state sub-space where server capacity may be the bottleneck and any modification to the inter-node bandwidths may have no effect on the observed performance. The two insights that follow from the above discussion are that -

1. Finding a single function to model the entire state-space of an enterprise-scale system might lead to very crude and incorrect system models.
2. There exists system state sub-spaces where the effect of certain variables can essentially be ignored from the system model.

The above discussion motivates the need to partition the system state-space. The following sub-section elaborates on the specific requirements for the partitioning scheme and then describes the partitioning algorithm in detail.

3.1   System State-Space Partitioning

The aim of our partitioning scheme is to create system state-space partitions such that -

- the involved system variables exhibit some homogeneity in their behavior inside the partition, which is beneficial for building the system model.
- the number of 'knobs' required to manage the system within the partition is minimized, which is beneficial for the purpose of learning and adapting the actions specified as part of policy.

To incorporate the concept of partition homogeneity we create partitions such that operational states contained in the partition are close to each other. Note that partition homogeneity corresponds to macro-level states of the system, for instance in one partition the underlying network may be the bottleneck (making server capacity redundant) while in some other partition the server capacity may be the bottleneck (similarly making the network capacity redundant). In order to minimize the 'knobs' we want to ensure the partitions are created such that the 'knobs' needed in one partition are possibly not needed in the other. This corresponds to making partitions which are orthogonal to each other. The partitioning algorithm employed by our framework is described next.

The Partitioning Algorithm. A system state can be defined as the binding of appropriate values to the variables contained in the set $\mathbf{V}$. The partitioning algorithm aims to partition many such observed system states to achieve the objective mentioned in the previous section. We define a partition to be a collection of observed system states. A partition inherits the sets $\mathbf{V}$ and $\mathbf{V}_\phi$ from the system state-space but the sets $\mathbf{V}_\alpha$, $\mathbf{A}$ and $\mathbf{D}$ can vary between the partitions.

Let, S be the observed operational states contained in the initial system state-space partition for which $\mathbf{D}$ defines the association of action interfaces in $\mathbf{A}$ with the variables in $\mathbf{V}_\alpha$. For simplicity the discussion here assumes that it is possible to define a measure of normalized distance between any two operational states. Techniques for doing such operations exist and interested readers may refer to well-known techniques like Mahalanobis distance [24]. We define an operator $\delta_\mathbf{R}$ over a pair of operational states from a partition, which finds the normalized distance between the two operational states considering only the dimensions contained in the set $\mathbf{R}$, where $\mathbf{R} \subseteq \mathbf{V}$. We also define the operation θ over a pair of operational states from a partition. The operation θ finds the number of places in which the two states differ, considering only the dimensions corresponding to the set $\mathbf{V}_\alpha$ for the partition under investigation. Finally, we define

$$v(s_1, s_2) = \eta \times \delta_\mathbf{V}(s_1, s_2) + \mu \times \theta(s_1, s_2) \tag{1}$$

where, η and μ can take values from the range [0,1] and these are used to configure v for weighted distance and orthogonality. To evaluate if we need to partition a given system state-space P, we try find a subset $\mathbf{V}'_\alpha$ of $\mathbf{V}_\alpha$ such that

$$\sum_{\forall s_i, s_j \in S} \delta_{\mathbf{V}_\alpha - \mathbf{V}'_\alpha}(s_i, s_j) \leq \Delta_{max} \tag{2}$$

$$|\mathbf{V}'_\alpha| \leq f \tag{3}$$

where Δ_{max} is a user defined parameter that represents the maximum allowed representation error for the actionable variables and f represents the maximum number of actions that can be used to manage the system in the given partition. We employ a greedy approach for finding $\mathbf{V}'_\alpha$, i.e. we add the member of $\mathbf{V}_\alpha$ to $\mathbf{V}'_\alpha$ which causes the greatest reduction in the L.H.S. of the equation 2. We repeat the above process until the L.H.S. becomes lesser than Δ_{max}, at this point we look at the cardinality of the set $\mathbf{V}'_\alpha$ - if the cardinality is less than f we do not partition the system state-space, otherwise we proceed to partition the system state-space. The $\mathbf{V}'_\alpha$ so determined becomes the $\mathbf{V}_\alpha$ for the partition. We start by finding a pair of states s_1 and s_2 from the set of all such pairs contained in the set S such that $\upsilon(s_1, s_2)$ is maximized. The pair s_1 and s_2 acts as the seed for the two new system state sub-spaces S_1 and S_2 that will be created. We then iterate through the remaining operational states in the set S, adding the operational state s_i to S_1 if $\delta_{\mathbf{V}}(s_i, s_1) \leq \delta_{\mathbf{V}}(s_i, s_2)$. One can alternatively use the centroid of existing operational states in the evolving partitions to determine the membership. Once the two new partitions S_1 and S_2 have been created, we find the set $\mathbf{V}_\alpha$ for them using the greedy approach described above. If the criteria defined by Δ_{max} and f is not met by any partition then we repeat the above scheme for that partition. We now enumerate the advantages of the partitioning scheme for the purpose of enabling policy-driven self-management.

- *Simplifies Policy Learning.* Our approach intelligently reduces the space of possible actions that could be taken in response to an event. This greatly simplifies the process of correlating the events to actions for the purpose of determining ECA policies.
- *Assists in Problem Diagnosis.* The system might migrate through a series of system state 'partitions' before ending in an unacceptable state (e.g. SLA violation). The path followed by a system before a failure may contain information about the events that may have led to a failure, and can therefore assist in problem diagnosis and constructing complex policies.
- *Simplifies Problem Resolution.* If a system enters an unacceptable state during its operation then the model corresponding to the partition to which this unacceptable state belongs can possibly be used to arrive at a resolution to the problem.
- *Reducing Monitoring Overhead.* The partitions that are created by our algorithm allow us to ignore a subset of variables when the system is operating in that partition. This can potentially allow us to monitor such variables at reduced frequencies. However, we have not fully explored this possibility.

Once the system state-space has been partitioned we build a system *micro-model* corresponding to each partitioned sub-space. A system model in our framework consists of several micro-models each one of which models a sub-space of possible system states. The micro-model to be applied is determined based on the current state of the system. Since, we attempt to model only a small partition of the entire system state-space at a time we are able to build models even for systems with a very high number of variables. This makes our approach highly scalable. A similar approach was presented in [32], which made use of an ensemble of probabilistic models to detect SLO violations, and was shown to perform significantly better than the approach which used a single monolithic model to detect violations. The approach works by adding new models when the existing models do not accurately capture the current system behavior.

3.2 Building System Micro-models

We want to create *micro-models* such that they can predict the the values for the variables in $\mathbf{V}_\alpha$ given the values for the variables in $\mathbf{V} - \mathbf{V}_\alpha$. Here we take advantage of the fact that our system state sub-spaces have a reduced dimension in terms of actionable variables. For all the variables in $\mathbf{V}_\alpha$ we exhaustively enumerate all the possible values and create a new variable $\mathbf{c}$ which can take values corresponding to such an exhaustive enumeration. For example, if $|\mathbf{V}_\alpha| = 2$ and each variable in $\mathbf{V}_\alpha$ can take 3 discrete values then $\mathbf{c}$ can take 9 distinct enumerated values. We assume that the actionable variables take discrete values and if the variable is continuous, one can use existing techniques to discretize continuous data (actually the Bayesian modeling techniques, which are referred to in this paper make use of such techniques). The system state space $\mathbf{V}$ can now be represented as $\{\mathbf{c}\} \cup (\mathbf{V} - \mathbf{V}_\alpha)$.

To find the best value from the variable $\mathbf{c}$ which helps translate the system to a desired state we resort to making using of probabilistic modeling techniques. We use a variant of Bayesian network [16] called the Tree Augmented Naive Bayes [15] or TANs to probabilistically model the system state-space. A Bayesian network is represented as an acyclic graph whose vertices encode random variables and the edges represent statistical dependence relations among the variables and local probability distributions for each variable given values of its parents. The main advantage of using a Bayesian network (or one of its variants) is that their representation provides and easy way to inspect the relationships between the involved variables. This allows an expert to embed his knowledge or the common wisdom into the self-management framework by proposing an initial model, which can be further refined using learning techniques. Furthermore, by simple inspection an expert can single out any faults in the learnt system model. Our choice for making use of TANs was driven by the fact that unrestricted forms of Bayesian network are computationally very costly to build as they need to evaluate all the dependencies amongst the set of random variables. A TAN, on the other hand allows only a tree structured dependence amongst the set of random variables (other than the class variable) and is therefore cheaper to build and has been shown to perform almost as well as the unrestricted version. A TAN model when used as a classifier is able to determine the following probability

$$p = Pr(\mathbf{x}|\mathbf{a}_1, \mathbf{a}_2, ..., \mathbf{a}_n) \tag{4}$$

for the set $\{\mathbf{a}_1, \mathbf{a}_2, ..., \mathbf{a}_n, \mathbf{x}\}$, from a given training set. The variable $\mathbf{x}$ assumes a special status in this equation and is called the class variable and the other variables are called the attributes.

To create the micro-model we designate the newly formed variable $\mathbf{c}$ as the class variable and the remaining variables, i.e. the set of variables in $\mathbf{V} - \mathbf{V}_\alpha$ are designated as attributes. The resulting micro-model is able to determine the following probability.

$$p = Pr(\mathbf{c}|\mathbf{V} - \mathbf{V}_\alpha) \tag{5}$$

The above equation determines the probability of the variable c taking a certain value given the values of the variables in the set $V - V_\alpha$. This procedure for achieving a desirable and feasible system state is as follows. Let, $V^{current}$ represent the current system state and V^{goal}_ϕ represent the new desired values for the set V_ϕ. To find the values of variables in V_α that can possibly lead to the goal state, we create the set $V' = V - V_\alpha$. We create an instance V^{goal} of the set V' by assigning the corresponding values from the set $V^{current}$ and thereafter resetting the values corresponding to the set V_ϕ using the values from V^{goal}_ϕ. We then use the instance V^{goal} to find the instance c^{goal} of variable c that maximizes Equation 5. The values of V_α corresponding to c^{goal} so determined are used as the new values for actionable variables.

Discussion. Note that the state depicted by V^{goal} may not exist in a real system. This is because the variables that are contained in $V - V_\phi \cup V_\alpha$ inherit their values from the state instance $V^{current}$, and it may so happen that when the system translates to the new goal state, the values for variables other than the variables of interest and actionable variables may also change. However, experimental results presented in Section 4 show that the predicted values of V_α are mostly able to achieve the goal state. This can be attributed to the fact that attribute discretization adds some degree of tolerance causing some smaller changes not to be reflected until they occur at the points where discretization partitions the continuous data space. Another important consideration for future work may be the consideration of the magnitude of change in the values of the variables in V_α, a solution that requires smaller change in magnitude may sometimes be preferred over the most probable solution.

3.3   Policy Learning, Adaptation and Confidence Attribute

The system state space model and the micro-model play a central role in supporting the task of policy learning. The high-level directives or goal statements are described over the set of variables contained in the set V_ϕ. For example, a high-level directive like delay $< 20msec$ can be used to learn the corresponding policy using the procedure described next. The framework instantiates a trigger for capturing delay $\geq 20msec$ which acts as the *event* in terms of policy. If at any time the *event* occurs the current system state $V^{current}$ is used in conjunction with system sub-space micro-model to arrive at a corrective *action*. The event, the current system state (condition) and the corrective action is recorded as a policy. Due to space limitations we cannot give the full details of policy construction here. Interested readers may refer to an extended version [20] of this paper.

In a dynamic system the micro-models may evolve with time. This may cause some learned policies to become invalid with time because the corrective actions that were determined using an earlier version of the model may not be applicable any more. Policy adaptation requires periodic evaluation of the actions specified as part of the learned policies.

The confidence-attribute associated with each policy helps us to deal with the issue of administrator's *trust* in our self-management framework. The confidence-attribute for a policy is equal to the probability p determined using the Equation 5. The system administrator can declare a threshold value to have control over the policies that will be enforced. Only the policies with a confidence-attribute greater than the threshold value are autonomically enforced by the self-management framework.

3.4 Implementation

We have implemented the system state-space partitioning algorithm in C++, which takes as input a set of data which contains actual observed values from a running (or simulated) system and the index of variables which can be modified deterministically. The user also needs to provide values for the partitioning parameters η, μ, Δ_{max} and f as defined in Section 3.1. The output from the partitioning algorithm is the set of partitions and the corresponding index of variables which can be modified deterministically. The output is generated in the well-known C4.5 format to facilitate further processing. We then make use of jBNC [17], a java based implementation for the Bayesian networks to build a TAN micro-model corresponding to each partition. The TAN is then used for finding corrective actions, policy adaptation, etc.

4 Experiments

Our goal was to study the suitability of our techniques in managing large enterprise-scale systems where a large number of variables can potentially affect the state of the system. In this section, we present our findings based on simulation experiments under a variety of workloads and operating conditions. Our techniques, for instance, were able to detect bottleneck nodes in our simulation of a PIDS-like middleware and were able to avoid several SLA violations that would have otherwise occurred. We start with a description and validation of the simulator testbed, which is followed by a brief description of the workload and evaluation metrics. We present our experimental results starting from Section 4.3.

4.1 Simulator Testbed

We wanted to evaluate our techniques for self-management using applications that are representative of the ones used by large enterprises. We evaluated the possibility of using well-known benchmarks and real-enterprise applications for putting our techniques to test. However, we soon realized that the applications available to us in our lab environment (like RUBiS [26] and an implementation of industrial middleware from Delta Technology [12]) were not instrumented well enough to sense and actuate a sufficiently large set of variables, and often changing any environment parameter (like maximum number of worker threads, number of MySQL connections, memory allocations and MySQL cache size) required restarting the application for the changes to take effect. Of course, in order to use our techniques, these systems could be enhanced to provide more monitoring and dynamically tunable parameters. Furthermore, it was not possible for us to make use of such applications for a large-scale (say 500 underlying nodes) evaluation of our techniques.

In order to overcome the problems mentioned above we decided to design a well instrumented simulator for simulating a large system implementing service oriented architecture (SOA). An implementation of SOA contains a set of services running on a

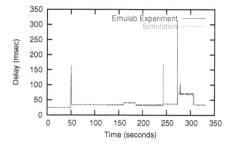 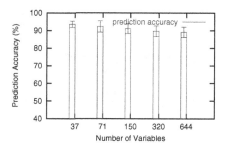

Fig. 2. Validation of the SOA simulator against an emulation at Emulab

Fig. 3. iManage's scalability with number of observed system variables

distributed network of nodes that can be invoked by sending a message to the service, messages may or may not be generated as a result and if the messages are generated they may be forwarded to the source, to a sink or to some other service(s). The PIDS middleware described in Section 1.1 can be implemented as a SOA. Our SOA simulator consists of four main components - server, service, network-link and client. A server represents a processing facility with a limited number of cycles per second, a limited memory, connections to other servers and ability to throttle server frequency at the expense of more power. A service represents a software which accepts certain types of messages, possibly generates some messages in response and determines the server cycles that will be used to process a certain message type given the available memory. There may be more than one service running on a server and they may have different priorities. A network-link has an associated bandwidth, delay, and cost per unit of data transmitted. Finally, a client represents a source or a sink for the messages. An event source has a rate of generating events that can vary with time. A sink measures the incoming event-rate, the average delay for update propagation and the current delay measured over a recent window.

A simulation can be started by providing a network topology which instantiates the basic distributed network of servers and network-links, this is followed by addition of some services for processing messages and some clients. The simulation is run for a pre-specified amount of time and it dumps the state at configurable regular intervals. We make use of these state dumps to evaluate to build system models and then use these system models to arrive at policies for managing the simulated system. The network topologies for the simulations were generated using the GT-ITM [30] generator.

4.2 Simulator Validation

To validate our simulator we compared the measurement we got from our simulator with the ones we got from using the same experimental setup on Emulab [14] testbed. Our experimental setup consisted of a 13 node topology and an event processing graph that consisted of 3 sources, 2 services and 2 sinks. On the Emulab testbed we created the specified 13 node topology and then made use of the IFLOW middleware [22] to setup the event processing graph. We instantiated the same setup using our simulator. The services were configured to take a specified amount of time for processing the

Table 2. Effect of partitioning parameters on $|\mathbf{V}_\alpha|$ & number of partitions

		Original		Partition	
f	Δ_{max}	$|\mathbf{V}|$	$|\mathbf{V}_\alpha|$	avg $|\mathbf{V}_\alpha|$	partition count
3	0.1	71	11	2.8	5
4	0.2			4.0	3
3	0.1	227	31	2.7	7
4	0.2			3.8	5

Table 3. Comparison between the accuracies (in %age) of single and micro-models

Data Set		Model Type
$|\mathbf{V}_\alpha|$	Single Model	Micro-Model
71	89.4 ± 2.8	92.3 ± 3.2
277	86.3 ± 1.9	90.7 ± 2.3

incoming events depending upon the incoming event type, and server load. We measured the event propagation delay between a source and a sink under a variety of variations which included events that take different processing times, variation in event rate from sources and change in event-size. The same event workload was used for both the Emulab testbed and the simulator. The measurement of event propagation delay for both the Emulab testbed and the simulator is shown in Figure 2. Our simulator was able to closely follow the behavior of real emulation testbed for the same experimental setup paving the way for simulations at a larger scale.

4.3   Microbenchmarks

We ran two simulations with 8 and 32 servers, each for 4 simulated hours. The two simulations dumped 71 and 227 state variables, respectively every 30 seconds. During the course of simulation we kept modifying the system conditions like the event rates from the sources, modifying the server frequencies, using alternate high or low-cost links to the destination and changing the priorities for various services running at a server. We also ran the simulation for another 20 minutes, dumping data at every 30 seconds to evaluate the accuracy of generated models. We collected 3 such sets of observations.

The first experiment focused on determining the effect of partitioning parameters Δ_{max} and f on the number of partitions that are created for a given system state-space and the average number of actionable variables that appear across the partitions. The results obtained by using one set of observation from the simulation described above are shown in Table 2. The table enumerates results from two set of simulations described above which generated 480 observed system states each. The results show that our techniques were able to significantly reduce the average number of actionable variables. For example our partitioning scheme was able to able to achieve a 90% reduction in number of actionable variables per partition for a system state-space with 31 variables. As far as the number of partitions are concerned, they are an important contributors towards the scalability of our techniques. However, a very high number of partitions may lead to partitions that may have a very sparse population leading to bad system models. The number of actionable variables are required to be low for our techniques to be effective as long as the manageability of the system partition is maintained, which can be controlled by setting a low value for Δ_{max}.

The next experiment was conducted to examine the effect of partitioning on the accuracy of the system models. To construct a single system state-space model for the set of observations collected earlier we proceeded as follows. We eliminated any $\mathbf{V}_\alpha$ from

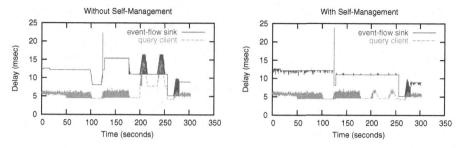

Fig. 4. Delays from the SOA simulator with and without self-management

the set if it did not change its value during the simulation run. This reduced $|\mathbf{V}_\alpha|$ to ≈ 5 and ≈ 11 for the simulations with 71 and 227 variables, respectively. Notice that even with a discretization factor of 2 for each variable, the simulation with 227 variable had $2^{11} = 2048$ possible values for the variable **c**. In the real world this translates to the confusion of which 'knobs' to turn to fix the system. Using the technique described in 3.2 we then constructed the single system models. For building micro-models corresponding to the partitioned sub-spaces we did not have to perform the pruning of the set $\mathbf{V}_\alpha$ as the partitioning algorithm takes care of removing the redundant members from the set $\mathbf{V}_\alpha$. The micro-models were then constructed for each of the partitioned sub-space. We used the generated models to predict the value of actionable variables given the value of other system variables from the test data set. Results reported in Table 3 show that the specialized micro-models work better than a single model at correctly predicting the values of variables in $\mathbf{V}_\alpha$.

To examine the effect of the number of observed system variables (i.e. $|\mathbf{V}|$) on the accuracy of predicting the right values for the variables in $\mathbf{V}_\alpha$ we conducted the following experiment. We used our SOA simulator to simulate systems that had 37, 71, 150, 320 and 644 variables that could be observed. Each system was simulated under varying workload conditions with appropriate corrective actions being taken at several points in the simulation. The time a system was simulated for was proportional to the number of variables being observed for that system. The smallest system with 37 variables was simulated for 1 hour simulation time. We used our techniques to build models for each of the systems and then used 10 minutes of generated test data to calculate the prediction accuracy corresponding to each model. We repeated the experiment 3 times. Results shown in Figure 3 show a slight decrease in prediction accuracy with the increase in number of observed system variables. However, the prediction accuracy only shows a linear trend in decrease as the number of variables are increase exponentially. We acknowledge that the results obtained may be highly dependent on the training set and the test data set that were generated during the simulation.

4.4 Evaluation of the Self-management Framework

The next set of experiments was conducted to evaluate the end-to-end efficiency of our framework in managing large-scale systems. We study the impact of suggested policy actions and the confidence attribute on the end system metrics at runtime. The simulations were conducted for a system with 227 variables and consisted of 32 simulated server nodes.

The simulation setup consisted of an event-flow that contained 3 sources, 2 services and 1 sink, and 2 query response services which received a stream of queries from a co-located client. Each event-flow service was located on a separate server but shared the server with another query response service. The variables that could be modified included the priority of the event-flow service thread, the priority of the query service thread and the frequency of the server. The dynamic workload conditions were simulated by varying the event rates from the sources and the query clients. The metrics of interest included $delay_{flow}$ and $delay_{query}$. The goals for the simulation run were specified as $delay_{flow} < 12.5msec$ and $delay_{query} < 7.5msec$, and both the threads were assigned the same priority. Figure 4 shows the delay observed at the event-flow sink and at one of the query client with and without self-management. Our techniques were mostly able to avoid any violations of the specified goals. The confidence threshold for this experiment was set to 85.0%.

We next conducted an experiment using the above setup to examine any unwanted behavior that may happen due to low confidence-threshold. When the confidence threshold was reduced to 75.0%, we actually observed delays at the event-flow sink that were more than the delays observed without the self-management in place. Confidence thresholds even lower than 75.0% made the system behave erratically when self-management was turned on. This was corroborated by re-examination of some of our earlier data used for prediction accuracy experiments. 90.0% of the predictions that lead to false predictions had a confidence-attribute lesser than 65.0%. These findings can be attributed to the use of probabilistic models by our framework. A low-confidence threshold means that there is possibility that a certain other assignment of values to variables in V_α also has a high probability of occurrence. This may lead to two assignments having almost the same probability of occurrence leading to a higher chance of erroneous choice of assignment by the system.

5   Related Work

Policy Research
There has been a lot work in the domain of using policies for simplifying the management tasks associated with system administration. Over the last decade, researchers, both in academia and industry, have focused on issues like policy specification languages [11], frameworks [5,27] and toolkits [23]. The research presented in this paper builds on the work done in the above mentioned areas and is a logical next-step, as the focus is on applying the policy-research to the management intensive domain of enterprise-scale systems. The policy research in the domain of automated network management that deals with issues like security, access control and other associated management tasks [29,25] justifies our stand on studying the impact and application of policy research to another rich domain. More recently, researchers have started evaluating the pros and cons of applying policy research for managing IT systems at large business enterprises [7]. This research, which is in its nascent stages, promises to provide systems that will manage themselves in accordance to high-level business goals [2]. The issues concerning human expertise and policy representation have also been explored in a recent paper [18].

Autonomic Computing & Self-Managing Systems
The task of implementing self-managing systems is a multi-step process in which policies can play an important role. Policies are a way to dictate the behavior of a self-managing system. This is in line with the vision of autonomic computing - 'to design computing system that can manage themselves given high-level objectives from administrators' - as described in [19]. There has been a lot of work in the domain of enabling self-management for a wide variety of systems. The SLA-based approach to manage systems has been explored by number of researchers [31]. In our prior work, we had focused on enabling self-management capabilities for distributed data stream systems [21,22]. Some researchers have also explored the use of rule-based self-management approach for managing applications [4]. The use of utility-functions for self-management has also been explored in specific reference to event-based systems [6] and an interesting take on aggregate utility-functions is presented in [3]. It turns out that defining utility-functions for enterprise-scale applications is a tough task because it may not be possible to mathematically model all the factors that can potentially affect the state of the enterprise system.

Bayesian Networks & Problem Diagnosis
Bayesian networks or the Belief networks have found applicability in a number of AI domains and they represent one of the best classification tools available to researchers. A tutorial on Bayesian networks is presented in [16]. Several specializations of the Bayesian networks have been proposed in literature the most important ones being the Naive Bayes [13] and the Tree Augmented Naive Bayes or the TANs [15]. In reference to applying Bayesian networks for modeling computer systems, a very innovative approach for correlating instrumentation data to system states is presented in [9]. This was later extended in [10] to develop signatures that could be used to more efficiently correlate the SLA violations that may occur in a system. More recent work in this domain makes use of an ensemble [32] of system models for the purpose of problem diagnosis. The work presented in this paper not only detects possible violations of higher level goals by the system but also suggests appropriate corrective actions to arrive at a solution for the problem.

6   Conclusions and Future Work

In this paper we described a system modeling framework that collects the system parameters and metrics into a unified abstraction, we call the system state-space, and identifies the actions that can be used to manage the system. To deal with complex system state-spaces, typical of enterprise-scale systems, we presented techniques that can be used to reduce the complexity and to more precisely model critical aspects of the system, and to more effectively develop policies. Additionally, iManage has capabilities for dealing with dynamic environment and for letting the administrator incorporate human knowledge and experience to refine the policies. Finally, the confidence-attribute associated with the policies learnt by iManage framework allows the administrator to fine-tune the enforcement of such policies. As part of the future work we are trying to address the issues related to monitoring overhead and making use of dynamic Bayesian networks to incorporate the consideration of time into the system model.

References

1. Agarwala, S., Schwan, K.: Sysprof: Online distributed behavior diagnosis through fine-grain system monitoring. In: ICDCS (2006)
2. Aiber, S., Gilat, D., Landau, A., Razinkov, N., Sela, A., Wasserkrug, S.: Autonomic self-optimization according to business objectives. In: ICAC (2004)
3. AuYoung, A., Grit, L., Wiener, J., Wilkes, J.: Service contracts and aggregate utility functions. In: HPDC (2006)
4. Bhat, V., Parashar, M., Liu, H., Khandekar, M., Kandasamy, N., Abdelwahed, S.: Enabling self-managing applications using model-based online control strategies. In: ICAC (2006)
5. Bhide, M., Gupta, A., Joshi, M., Mohania, M., Raman, S.: Policy framework for autonomic data management. In: ICAC (2004)
6. Bhola, S., Astley, M., Saccone, R., Ward, M.: Utility-aware resource allocation in an event processing system. In: ICAC (2006)
7. Cai, Z., Kumar, V., Cooper, B.F., Eisenhauer, G., Schwan, K., Strom, R.E.: Utility-driven management of availability in enterprise-scale information flows. In: van Steen, M., Henning, M. (eds.) Middleware 2006. LNCS, vol. 4290, Springer, Heidelberg (2006)
8. Chand, A., Elmeleegy, K., Cox, A.L., Zwaenepoel, W.: Causeway: System Support for Controlling and Analyzing the Execution of Multi-tier Applications. In: Alonso, G. (ed.) Middleware 2005. LNCS, vol. 3790, Springer, Heidelberg (2005)
9. Cohen, I., Chase, J.S., Goldszmidt, M., Kelly, T., Symons, J.: Correlating instrumentation data to system states: A building block for automated diagnosis and control. In: OSDI (2004)
10. Cohen, I., Zhang, S., Goldszmidt, M., Symons, J., Kelly, T., Fox, A.: Capturing, indexing, clustering, and retrieving system history. In: SOSP 2005 (2005)
11. Damianou, N., Dulay, N., Lupu, E., Sloman, M.: The ponder policy specification language. In: Sloman, M., Lobo, J., Lupu, E.C. (eds.) POLICY 2001. LNCS, vol. 1995, Springer, Heidelberg (2001)
12. Delta technology home. As viewed on (04/22/2007), http://www.deltadt.com/
13. Domingos, P., Pazzani, M.J.: On the optimality of the simple bayesian classifier under zero-one loss. Machine Learning 29(2-3), 103–130 (1997)
14. Emulab: network emulation testbed home. As viewed on (04/22/2007), http://www.emulab.net/
15. Friedman, N., Geiger, D., Goldszmidt, M.: Bayesian network classifiers. Machine Learning 29(2-3), 131–163 (1997)
16. Heckerman, D.: A tutorial on learning with bayesian networks. Technical report, Microsoft Research, Redmond, Washington (1995)
17. jBNC: Bayesian network classifier toolbox. As viewed on (04/22/2007), http://jbnc.sourceforge.net/
18. Kandogan, E., Campbell, C., Khooshabeh, P., Bailey, J., Maglio, P.: Policy-based management of an e-commerce business simulation: An experimental study. In: ICAC (2006)
19. Kephart, J.O., Chess, D.M.: The vision of autonomic computing. Computer 36(1), 41–50 (2003)
20. Kumar, V., Cooper, B.F., Eisenhauer, G., Schwan, K.: iManage: Policy-driven self-management for enterprise-scale systems. Extended Version, http://www.cc.gatech.edu/~vibhore/inTransit/policy-ext.pdf
21. Kumar, V., Cooper, B.F., Schwan, K.: Distributed stream management using utility-driven self-adaptive middleware. In: ICAC (2005)
22. Kumar, V., et al.: Implementing diverse messaging models with self-managing properties using iflow. In: ICAC (2006)

23. Lymberopoulos, L., Lupu, E.C., Sloman, M.S.: Ponder policy implementation and validation in a cim and differentiated services framework. In: NOMS (2004)
24. Mahalanobis, P.: On the generalised distance in statistics. In: Proc. of the National Institute of Science of India 12 (1936)
25. Minsky, N.: A scalable mechanism for communal access control. In: NCAC (2005)
26. RUBiS: home page. As viewed on (04/22/2007), http://rubis.objectweb.org/
27. Web services policy framework. As viewed on (04/22/2007),
    http://www-128.ibm.com/developerworks/library/specification/
    ws-polfram/
28. Weikum, G., Mnkeberg, A., Hasse, C., Zabback, P.: Self-tuning Database Technology and Information Services: from Wishful Thinking to Viable Engineering. In: Bressan, S., Chaudhri, A.B., Lee, M.L., Yu, J.X., Lacroix, Z. (eds.) CAiSE 2002 and VLDB 2002. LNCS, vol. 2590, Springer, Heidelberg (2002)
29. Wright, M.J.: Using policies for effective network management. International Journal of Network Management 9(2), 118–125 (1999)
30. Zegura, E.W., Calvert, K., Bhattacharjee, S.: How to model an internetwork. In: IEEE Infocom., IEEE Computer Society Press, Los Alamitos (1996)
31. Zhang, L., Ardagna, D.: Sla based profit optimization in autonomic computing systems. In: ICSOC 2004 (2004)
32. Zhang, S., Cohen, I., Symons, J., Fox, A.: Ensembles of models for automated diagnosis of system performance problems. In: DSN (2005)

Middleware Support for Adaptive Dependability

Lorenz Froihofer, Karl M. Goeschka, and Johannes Osrael

Vienna University of Technology
Institute of Information Systems
Argentinierstrasse 8/184-1
1040 Vienna, Austria
{lorenz.froihofer,karl.goeschka,johannes.osrael}@tuwien.ac.at

Abstract. Generic middleware can often not provide satisfactory solutions, but neither is it acceptable to let the application developer reinvent the wheel each time. Therefore, middleware shall support reuse of infrastructural services while leaving the application in control. In particular, we contribute with a middleware approach to support adaptive dependability by balancing integrity and availability in distributed systems. To achieve this goal, we add a new middleware service for explicit runtime management of data integrity constraints. In order to provide the desired balancing with respect to an application's requirements and environment conditions, our approach supports the application developer with explicit interaction between middleware, application, and metadata. Based on our prototype implementation, we show how adaptive balancing of integrity and availability improves the overall dependability. The performance impairments of our approach are typically worth their costs in systems where the read-to-write ratio is high or write performance is not a limiting factor.

Keywords: Middleware, dependability, adaptivity, constraint consistency, inconsistency, replication.

1   Introduction

Today's software systems often face availability requirements of 24 hours per day, 7 days a week. While availability close to 100% is already hard to achieve in a healthy system, e.g., due to system maintenance operations, the situation becomes even worse if parts of a system suffer from failures and the system therefore operates in a degraded mode. However, availability (the readiness for correct service) is only one attribute of dependability [1]. Integrity, the absence of improper system alterations, is another. Within our work, we focus on consistency of data with respect to data integrity constraints, i.e., *constraint consistency* [2]. The constraints stem from an application's requirements and have typically to be satisfied in the course of business transactions. Consistency of the constraints themselves, e.g., whether they represent conflicting requirements, is not within the focus of our work.

Failures are threats to dependability and hence to availability and integrity. While failures affecting availability might lead to a non-responsive system, integrity violations may lead to inconsistent data. We focus on node and link

R. Cerqueira and R.H. Campbell (Eds.): Middleware 2007, LNCS 4834, pp. 308–327, 2007.
© IFIP International Federation for Information Processing 2007

failures, assuming the *crash failure model [3] for nodes*—pause-crash for server nodes—and *links may fail by losing some messages but do not duplicate or corrupt messages*. Link failures may subsequently lead to network partitions, effectively splitting a system into parts that are not able to communicate. However, as node and link failures cannot be differentiated at the time when they occur [4], we initially treat node failures as partitions with a single node. Whether a node or link failed can be detected after the node is reachable again.

Replication [5], the process of maintaining several copies (replicas) of the same entity (data item, object), is well-known to provide fault tolerance for improved availability in case of node and link failures. The replication of entities, however, introduces a new integrity criterion: *replica consistency*. Replica consistency requires that replicas of an entity are consistent according to the used replica consistency model, e.g., 1-copy-serializability [6] or looser consistency models like ε-serializability [7] and eventual consistency. As replica consistency may impair constraint consistency, it is in the focus of our work as well.

It is well known that **C**onsistency, **A**vailability, and **P**artition-tolerance (CAP) cannot be optimized independently of each other. This interdependency is stated more precisely in the (strong) *CAP principle* [8,9] providing that *only two of the three requirements can be achieved*, e.g., a system can be available and consistent but not be partition-tolerant. However, the weak CAP principle specifies that *the stronger guarantees are provided for two of these properties, the weaker guarantees can be provided for the third*. Obviously, these three properties have to be balanced according to an application's requirements. Moreover, it would be beneficial if the system could adapt to changing requirements during runtime, e.g., due to node or link failures.

While in the past adaptation mechanisms were incorporated into software on a per system basis, where they are hard to change, reuse, or analyze, the proliferation of such systems suggests to include adaptation support into the middleware. Thus, the adaptation mechanisms can be reused in numerous systems, analyzed separately from the system being adapted, and easily changed to incorporate new adaptations. Moreover, they provide a natural home for encoding the expertise of system designers and implementers about adaptation strategies and policies.

It is important to note that we are *not* aiming at *transparent* adaptivity: While the initial motivation to introduce middleware stems from the goal to re-use infrastructure code and encapsulate it behind coherent service interfaces for the application programmer, soon transparency was introduced to conceal the distribution of components from the user and the application programmer, so that the system is perceived as a single coherent system rather than as a collection of independent components. Different kinds of transparency have been standardized by ISO (International Standardization Organization, ISO 10746-1:1998, http://www.iso.org/) and ANSA (Advanced Network Systems Architecture) [10] and have been in the focus of middleware research.

Unfortunately, generic transparency (if not impossible at all) often comes at the cost of impaired performance and other quality properties. Additionally, users or application developers sometimes require knowledge about certain distribution aspects (e.g., in the presence of certain failure scenarios). Consequently, transparency in itself is not the ultimate design goal of a distributed system, but neither is it advisable to unconditionally follow the so-called "end-to-end argument" that some properties can only reasonably be provided under consideration of the application semantics and therefore have to be actually implemented by the application itself. Rather should middleware support the integration of applications with configurable re-used infrastructure services.

If application requirements are available during run-time in a processable form, they can explicitly be manipulated, configured, and processed by the application as well as the middleware, which allows such a system to balance or trade certain requirements against each other during run-time. By applying these principles, the application can be left in control to avoid costly generic solutions. In particular, we contribute with a middleware approach to support adaptive dependability by balancing integrity and availability. In order to provide the desired balancing with respect to an application's requirements and environment conditions, our approach supports the application developer with explicit management of data integrity constraints.

Paper Overview. First, Sect. 2 introduces our concept of balancing availability and integrity before Sect. 3 describes a prototype implementation with explicit runtime constraint consistency management. Section 4 then provides evaluation results and corresponding conclusions. We give an insight into related work in Sect. 5 and conclude this paper in Sect. 6.

2   Balancing Concept

For investigating the trade-off between integrity and availability, we concentrate on *data-centric* systems [11], which have their focus on the (business) data, typically stored in database management systems and represented by the business objects (entities) of an application and the relations between them. The Enterprise JavaBeans (EJB) platform, for example, represents such business objects by entity beans. Furthermore, our focus is on distributed object systems where communicating objects reside on different nodes. The main reason for having objects distributed among nodes and not being centralized is strong ownership of these nodes, e.g., the objects might be bound to some hardware facilities or different administrative domains. Application data are encapsulated by objects and their relationships and are modified by (possibly nested) invocations of methods of these objects.

One example for such an application scenario is a distributed telecommunication management system (DTMS) [12]. The DTMS is a software application that manages voice communication systems (VCS), installed at different sites. Each site has its own instance of a DTMS, but configuration of the VCS requires DTMS instances of different sites to cooperate. The hardware facilities of the VCS are represented by objects within the DTMS that are bound to the site of the VCS for decentralized management reasons—a failure of a DTMS site should not have effects beyond the specific site. The objects of the DTMS are subject to integrity constraints that possibly span objects of multiple sites, e.g., the configuration parameters for a voice communication channel have to be consistent to enable communication between different sites.

Fig. 1. Simplified ATS model with constraint

Another application scenario, where a prototype has been implemented by an industry partner based upon our middleware, is a distributed alarm tracking system (ATS) [13]. A simplified model of this system is given in Fig. 1 for our studies within this paper. The simplified ATS has two objects Alarm and Repair-Report. Alarms are managed by administrative operators while the repair reports are filled out by technical operators. The alarmKind determines which kinds of components might have to be repaired (affectedComponent). Hence, the system applies certain integrity constraints between an Alarm and a RepairReport. The example provided in Fig. 1 specifies that an alarm with alarmKind= "Signal" can only be removed by repairing a component that is either a "Signal Controller" or a "Signal Cable". Administrative operators and technical operators are working at different locations, potentially accessing different servers. If a network split occurs between these servers, the system should still be available to all of them and allow to make progress.

2.1   Constraints and Consistency Threats

Generally, data integrity constraints are predicates on data, evaluating to true, if a constraint is satisfied, or false, if it is violated. In our case, constraints are defined upon a class model, e.g., by using the Object Constraint Language (OCL) for Unified Modeling Language (UML) class diagrams. We follow the well-established approach to differentiate between preconditions (bound to and checked before a specific method invocation), postconditions (bound to and checked after a method invocation), and invariant constraints (bound to a certain class—the *context class*) [14]. For invariant constraints, we further differentiate between hard (checked at the end of an operation during a transaction) and soft constraints (checked at the end of a transaction) [15]. Invariant constraints are defined solely on the state of objects (static constraints) and hence can be validated at any time. Dynamic constraints defined on state transitions, sequences or temporal predicates are not in the primary focus of our work.

While pre- and postconditions are explicitly bound to methods and hence have to be triggered before or after method invocations, invariants are bound to a certain class and the triggering methods for validation of invariants have to be specified. Triggering constraint validation of invariant constraints upon each call to a method of the context class or only upon each call to a public method of the context class are two possible options. However, invariant constraints have at least to be checked whenever a method that potentially might lead to a constraint violation—an *affected method* of the constraint—was called.

Although an invariant constraint is defined for a certain context class, affected methods might belong to other classes as well. For our example in Fig. 1, the constraint ComponentKindReferenceConsistency has to be checked whenever the alarmKind of an Alarm or the componentKind of a RepairReport is changed. Consequently, Alarm.setAlarmKind(...) and RepairReport.setComponentKind(...) are affected methods of the constraint ComponentKindReferenceConsistency while the constraint itself is an *affected constraint* of these methods with two *affected objects*, an Alarm object and a RepairReport object. Obviously, the affected methods of a constraint cannot generically be determined without further knowledge of the constraint. Moreover, checking the ComponentKindReference-Consistency constraint if only the description of an alarm is changed (caused by following the "trigger constraint at all public method invocations" paradigm) unnecessarily impairs performance. Due to these reasons, we only trigger constraint checking for affected methods specified by the application developer.

In a distributed system, where objects are located at different nodes, constraint validation is affected by node and link failures as some affected objects might not be available. If the objects are replicated, we might be able to validate the constraints (partially based on backup copies). However, if updates on replicas are allowed in different partitions, we cannot be sure whether the validation is reliable, because backup replicas of affected objects might be stale due to an update in another partition. For example, if the technical operator of an ATS application sets componentKind in a RepairReport while the system operates in degraded mode. The administrative operator might have changed the corresponding Alarm in the meantime in another partition. Consequently, the constraint validation performed because of the changed RepairReport is not fully reliable. Hence, we call such a situation a *consistency threat* [2].

2.2   Availability Improvements and Reconciliation

Systems with a strict consistency model require to block or abort operations if a consistency threat occurs. However, some constraints might not be critical for "sufficiently" correct system operation and can temporarily be relaxed (traded). The application developer decides which constraints are tradeable and specifies the according metadata about the constraint. During runtime, the middleware is responsible to appropriately trigger constraint validation.

Whenever a consistency threat is detected and the corresponding constraints are tradeable, the middleware triggers the negotiation process to decide whether to accept or not accept the current consistency threat. Negotiation can either be performed descriptively, e.g., accept the threat if no affected objects are older than n seconds, or algorithmically via an application callback. In an algorithmic negotiation process, the application may associate application-specific information with accepted threats. Whether a threat is accepted can be decided by the callback handle provided by the application developer on its own, or it might even contact the end user for a threat-specific decision. However, if the threat is not accepted, the current transaction is aborted. If the consistency threat is accepted, the middleware stores this threat (including the application data) to be re-evaluated at a later time when node or link failures are repaired.

After two partitions are reunified (node or link failure repaired), our system starts the reconciliation phase. First of all, the replication protocol starts to propagate updates performed in one partition to the replicas in the other partition(s). If replica (write-write) conflicts are detected, conflict resolution can either be performed generically, e.g., by performing a rollback to previous states, or application-specific, e.g., through an application callback by the replication protocol. However, replica conflicts are also provided to the constraint consistency component in order to support re-establishment of constraint consistency.

After replica consistency is re-established, constraint consistency has to be restored (constraints are defined upon objects and not between replicas of a single object). For this purpose, the stored consistency threats are re-evaluated. If re-evaluation is successful, i.e., the corresponding constraint is satisfied, no inconsistency was actually introduced by the consistency threat—if not, appropriate actions have to be taken. Such actions, again, can be generic (e.g., roll-back) or application-specific (e.g., call-back) including compensation. One further generic option is to validate constraints based on different selections of replicas for objects with replica conflicts detected during replica reconciliation. If any of these combinations satisfies the constraint, the solution can automatically be established or be presented to the application for confirmation.

2.3   Relationship to the Concept of Transactions

Traditional systems apply ACID (Atomicity, Consistency, Isolation, Durability) transactions [16], requiring that all four properties are met. Replication ("R") can synchronously be bound to transactions. However, in case of node or link failures, synchronous update propagation would block. Consequently, update propagation can be relaxed to asynchronous behavior, e.g., synchronous per network partition, to avoid blocking. Moreover, if constraints cannot be checked (unreachable objects) or cannot reliably be checked (stale backup copies involved), constraint consistency (the "C") needs to be relaxed, too. Interestingly, Coulouris et al. [17] do not include consistency in their list of transaction properties and rather specify that the "C" is under the responsibility of the application developer.

Fig. 2. Trading transactional properties for adaptive dependability

Atomicity ("A") is not relaxed in principle in our approach, although one business transaction (completed as a single transaction in a healthy system) may result in two or more transactions (one in degraded mode and one or more transactions to resolve conflicts during reconciliation). These considerations rather correspond to the concepts of atomic transactions [18] vs. business activities [19] in the area of Web services (WS). However, in our approach we did not follow these ideas and consequently bound atomicity, isolation, and durability strictly to transactions. Consequently, replication and constraint consistency management operate then on top of such "AID" transactions, see Fig. 2.

3   Middleware Support

These concepts for adaptive dependability have been integrated into a platform independent system architecture [20], which has been implemented in different prototypes using several technologies (EJB, CORBA, .NET). Within this section, we first provide how our general concepts and the general architecture were mapped to and integrated into the EJB middleware platform as provided by the JBoss application server (AS). Second, we contribute with a detailed description of constraint consistency management as a new middleware service.

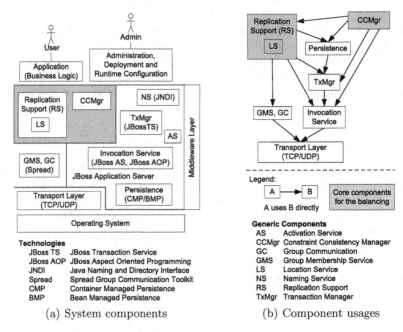

(a) System components   (b) Component usages

Fig. 3. EJB/JBoss AS specific system architecture

3.1   System Architecture

Two components of our architecture are primarily responsible for the balancing of availability and integrity, the *replication support* (RS) and the *constraint consistency manager* (CCMgr) provided within the grey areas of Fig. 3. Other important components are the *invocation service*, used for interception of point-to-point invocations, the *transaction manager*, managing distributed transactions, *persistence* to store application data, information about consistency threats, and historical replica versions to allow for rollback during reconciliation, the *group membership service* to detect node and link failures, and the *group communication* component that is used for update propagation (from primaries to backups) by the replication support. The *naming service*, allowing for name to object bindings, and the *activation service*, responsible for appropriate activation of objects, are not of immediate interest within our platform.

Although quite common and concise, the layered representation in Fig. 3(a) is not sufficient to illustrate how the components cooperate by using each other: First, strict layering is often not possible and second, layering does not imply actual usage. Therefore, Fig. 3(b) further provides an overview of usage-relations between the major components. This part of the figure shows that transaction management and invocation service are the two central services where almost all of the other services depend upon.

3.2   Constraint Consistency Management

Explicit runtime constraint consistency management is a new middleware service we introduced for balancing integrity and availability. In our approach, constraints are explicitly available during run-time and validated upon request of the middleware. The specification/implementation of constraints is up to the application developer as they result from the application requirements. On the other hand, triggering the validation of constraints as well as detection and management of consistency threats is performed by the middleware.

Explicit (Runtime) Constraint Representation. Obviously, constraints are processed by the middleware (management, triggering validation, etc.) as well as the application (performing the actual validation). Hence, this concept needs a contract between the two parties. For this purpose, we encapsulate the integrity constraints within explicit constraint classes similar to Verheecke et al. [21]. The primary contract between middleware and application is the Constraint.validate(ctx : ConstraintValidationContext) method (Fig. 4) that has to be implemented by the application developer and provides true or false as return value or throws an exception to indicate that constraint checking is impossible, e.g., due to unreachable objects. The middleware's responsibility is to ensure that validate(...) is called appropriately. Moreover, the beforeMethodInvocation(...) call to a constraint supports postconditions that check whether state transitions caused by a method call are correct. Within this call, a postcondition might store some values (state before the method invocation) and check during the call to validate(...) whether the method invocation actually produced a correct result with respect to the state before the method invocation.

The content of the ConstraintValidationContext provided to validate(...) depends on the type of a constraint and the circumstances under which the constraint is validated. It generally contains:

- The *context object* for invariant constraints, i.e., their "starting point" for constraint validation. Starting from this object, the constraint is able to reach all objects that are needed for validation of the constraint. For example, the context object for the OCL expression context Person inv: getAge() >= 18 would be an instance of the context class Person.
- The called object, called method, and method arguments for preconditions.
- The called object, method, method arguments, and result for postconditions.

To allow the middleware to trigger constraint validation appropriately, the affected methods have to be specified in addition to the constraints. Moreover,

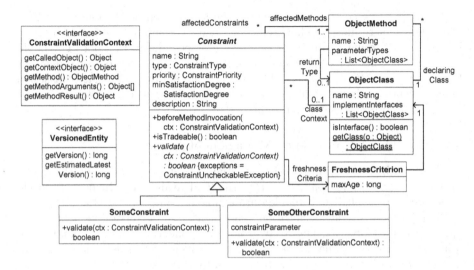

Fig. 4. Constraint runtime model

the context class can be specified for invariant constraints. Some invariant constraints, however, may not need a context object as they, for example, use a query operation to get their affected objects.

Finally, constraints may have associated freshness criteria (maximum age), one per affected class of objects (ObjectClass). These classes have to implement the VersionedEntity interface that allows to retrieve the version of the object getVersion() and the estimated latest version getEstimatedLatestVersion(). The estimated latest version is the one that the object would expect to have. For example, if an object is usually updated every n seconds and the last update producing version v happened $3n$ seconds ago, getVersion() would return v while getEstimatedLatestVersion() would return $v + 3$, indicating that the object most probably missed 3 updates. This mechanism can be used by the application developer to specify conditions for the negotiation of consistency threats.

Constraint Configuration and Registration. To allow appropriate validation, we need to know which constraints are affected by which method invocations. As motivated in Sect. 2.1, we require the application developer to declare constraints and affected methods as well as other details about a constraint, e.g., the constraint type or freshness criteria, in a configuration file. Similar to the EJB deployment descriptor, the constraint configuration file is read after deployment of an EJB application. The information contained in this file is then used to register the constraints within a constraint repository. This constraint repository allows to look up constraints, e.g., by class, method, or constraint type. Listing 1.1 provides an example of a constraint specification within the configuration file.

The constraint ComponentKindReferenceConsistency implements the integrity constraint of the ATS application provided in Fig. 1. It is a hard constraint, specifies that the constraint implementation requires a context object, it can be relaxed

Listing 1.1. Constraint configuration example

```
name="ComponentKindReferenceConsistency"
  type="HARD" priority="RELAXABLE" contextObject="Y"
  minSatisfactionDegree="UNCHECKABLE">
  <class>ComponentKindReferenceConstraint</class>
  <context-class>RepairReport</context-class>
  <affected-methods><affected-method>
    <context-preparation>
      <preparation-class>CalledObjectIsContextObject</preparation-class>
    </context-preparation>
    <objectMethod name="setAffectedComponent">
      <objectClass>RepairReport</objectClass>
        <arguments><argument>java.lang.String</argument></arguments>
    </objectMethod>
  </affected-method><affected-method>
    <context-preparation>
      <preparation-class>ReferenceIsContextObject</preparation-class>
      <params><param name="getter" value="getRepairReport"/></params>
    </context-preparation>
    <objectMethod name="setAlarmKind">
      <objectClass>Alarm</objectClass>
        <arguments><argument>java.lang.String</argument></arguments>
    </objectMethod>
  </affected-method></affected-methods>
</constraint>
```

during degraded mode, and the negotiation process will accept any consistency threats (minSatisfactionDegree= "uncheckable")—if no negotiation callback handle is registered by the application to be dynamically contacted for a threat-specific decision. A consistency threat occurs whenever the satisfaction degree of a constraint is possibly_satisfied or possibly_violated (constraint validation based on possibly stale objects) or uncheckable (e.g., due to unreachable objects). Considering constraint violations the least acceptable situation and satisfied constraints the desired case, we apply the following ordering of satisfaction degrees: violated < uncheckable < possibly_violated < possibly_satisfied < satisfied.

The <class> element specifies the Java implementation class of the constraint that will be instantiated while the configuration file is read during the deployment of an EJB application. The <context-class> is the class of the context object (RepairReport) required for constraint validation. Within the <affected-methods> element, affected methods of the constraint are provided. Each affected method is specified by stating the declaring class, the method name, and the method parameters. As the constraint is implemented for a specific context class, the ConstraintValidationContext (see Fig. 4) must be initialized appropriately. Values such as called object, called method, and method parameters are already set by the middleware. However, the <preparation-class> is responsible to extract the context object based on these values. The context object for the method RepairReport.setAffectedComponent(...) is the called object itself while the context object for the method Alarm.setAlarmKind(...) is obtained by calling getRepairReport() upon the called object (an instance of Alarm).

Constraint Consistency Manager. The CCMgr is notified by the invocation service before and after method invocations. Upon such notifications, the CCMgr looks up preconditions, postconditions, hard and soft invariant constraints and triggers validation according to their constraint type. To allow such behavior of the CCMgr it is also registered with the transaction manager (TxMgr) as a transactional resource to take part in the two-phase commit. If any constraints are violated, the CCMgr sets the state of the current transaction to "rollback-only". Hence, any constraint violation (or unacceptable consistency threat) prevents an ongoing transaction from successful commit.

In degraded system mode, the CCMgr provides additional functionality to support the integrity/availability balancing by interacting with the replication support in order to detect consistency threats caused by possibly stale objects. Typically, in order to provide replication transparency, respectively application independence from a particular replication protocol, a proxy object serves as interface between the application and the replication protocol. For the application, this proxy object provides a local view onto the logical object based on the reachable replicas. In our case, this object view becomes possibly stale if updates on the same logical object can occur in another network partition. Whether or not an object[1] is possibly stale depends on the presence of node or link failures and the underlying replication protocol. For example, in the primary partition protocol [22], each object accessed in a non-primary partition is possibly stale. In the case of the primary-per-partition protocol [23], objects are possibly stale in every network partition. However, before the CCMgr triggers the validation of a constraint, it starts to gather accessed objects, see Fig. 5. After the constraint validation returns, the CCMgr asks the replication manager whether any of these objects are possibly stale. If this is the case, the validation result (satisfaction degree) of the constraint is changed from satisfied to possibly_satisfied, or from violated to possibly_violated, as the constraint validation is not fully reliable. If there were any unreachable objects, the validation result of the constraint is uncheckable. These situations indicate a consistency threat and trigger negotiation of the threat.

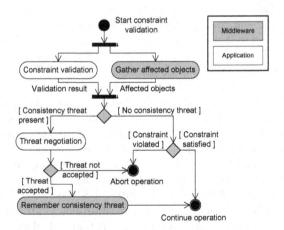

Fig. 5. Detection and negotiation of consistency threats

---

[1] For simplification, we use the term "object" as synonym for the local object view onto the logical object.

To perform algorithmic negotiation, the application must register a negotiation callback handler with the CCMgr. Such a negotiation handler is bound to the current transaction and responsible to decide whether to accept or not accept arising consistency threats. If no negotiation handler is registered at the CCMgr, declarative negotiation is performed based on the current satisfaction degree, the configured minimum satisfaction degree, and—if applicable—given freshness criteria. For this process, the current satisfaction degree of the constraint is compared with the minimum satisfaction degree. Moreover, the difference getEstimatedLatestVersion() - getVersion() is compared with the maximum age defined by available freshness criteria. Both, minimum satisfaction degree and optional freshness criteria are specified in the constraint configuration file.

Not accepting a consistency threat results in rollback of the current transaction. If a consistency threat is accepted, the consistency threat as well as application-specific information associated with the threat is persisted and used later during the constraint reconciliation phase. Reconciliation of constraint consistency is performed after reconciliation of replica consistency. Consequently, the CCMgr only starts its work after having received a notification from the replication manager that it has finished its reconciliation work.

To reconcile constraint consistency, the constraint consistency manager looks up accepted consistency threats and re-evaluates the corresponding constraints. If a constraint is satisfied, no inconsistency was introduced during degraded mode and the data about the consistency threat are removed. If a constraint is still threatened (node or link failures affecting the constraint are still present), re-evaluation of the corresponding threat is postponed until further repair. If a constraint is violated, an inconsistency was introduced during degraded mode and appropriate actions have to be taken to satisfy the constraint.

Invocation Interception. A key requirement for middleware integration of constraint consistency management is the possibility to intercept invocations. In EJB, each component and hence entity bean must provide a home and a business interface. These interfaces are implemented by the EJB container (a JBoss proxy in our case). After a call to the interface implementation, the EJB container can perform several middleware tasks, e.g., association of a security context or transaction with the call, before it finally forwards the call to the bean implementation.

In the case of JBoss, the JBoss proxy builds up an object representing the invocation and passes this object through an interceptor chain where each interceptor invokes the next interceptor until the final interceptor invokes the bean instance. The result of the invocation is passed back in the reverse order. The interceptors are responsible to provide middleware services for the invocation—enhanced by constraint consistency management and replication in our case. Fortunately, the invocation interceptors of the chain can be specified in a configuration file of the JBoss AS and therefore enhancing JBoss with additional functionality is rather easy to achieve. Consequently, it was only necessary to implement a new interceptor and put it into the interceptor chain. This interceptor is then responsible for appropriately including the CCMgr within the process of an invocation. The implementation of the replication protocol is based on the ADAPT replication framework [24], which also hooks into JBoss through custom interceptors.

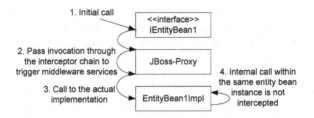

Fig. 6. JBoss invocation interception

Unfortunately, the interceptor chain is only traversed if the invocation comes from a call to the interface which is passed through the interceptor chain by the JBoss proxy (EJB container). If the bean instance calls another method on itself, this (internal) invocation is not intercepted, e.g., call number four in Fig. 6. This behavior would prevent any affected constraints of internal invocations from being checked. This issue can be solved by using the JBoss aspect-oriented programming (AOP) framework with which plain Java method invocations can be intercepted. Similarly to the approach above, the AOP framework transforms invocations into explicit invocation objects and calls interceptors registered with the AOP framework. Hence, we are able to use the same approach as above for triggering constraint validations for internal invocations as well.

3.3 Replication Support

To maximize availability for systems capable of applying our concept of adaptive dependability, the middleware should provide replication support. Within our prototype, we implemented the primary-per-partition protocol (P4) [23] to replicate the state of entity beans. The P4 behaves like a traditional primary-backup replication protocol in a healthy system with the specific setup that each object might have its primary on a different node instead of using only a single designated primary server node. However, during degraded mode, a temporary primary is chosen per partition. This further increases availability because operations can be performed on objects in different partitions as long as only non-critical constraints are affected. During repair, detected conflicts are solved either by rollback to previous states or by an application-specific compensation callback—potentially even involving a system operator.

However, the reconciliation process of the replication protocol has an influence on the handling of constraints and consistency threats. Consequently, constraints are further divided in intra- and inter-object constraints to address this fact. Intra-object constraints are constraints that can be evaluated on a single object and require access to the (primitive/value) attributes of the object only. Inter-object constraints need access to more than a single object.

If the replica reconciliation process resolves replica conflicts (replicas of a single logical object were written in different partitions) through selection of one copy (and not by creating a new state for the object by merging values of disjoint sets of attributes of the different replicas), a differentiation of integrity constraints into intra- vs. inter-object constraints is useful. In this case, intra-object constraints will not be violated retrospectively by the replica reconciliation process. Therefore, constraint validations based upon possibly stale objects can still return satisfied or violated instead of possibly_satisfied or possibly_violated for intra-object constraints. This reduces the number of consistency threats and hence the amount of associated information gathered during degraded mode and required to be processed in the constraint reconciliation phase. Inter-object constraints could be further classified into intra-class (all objects of the same class, e.g., uniqueness of an attribute for all objects of a class) and inter-class (objects of different classes, e.g., Fig. 1) constraints. Although this differentiation is useful for constraint implementation, it is not significant with respect to our balancing of dependability.

4   Evaluation

For our performance measurements, we used a mixture of different computers, each between 2–3 GHz and 1 GB of RAM, connected via 100 MBit Ethernet network links. The configuration denoted as "No DeDiSys" is a standard JBoss AS 4.0.4 with JBoss TS 4.2.1b1 as transaction service for distributed transactions and MySQL 5.0.21 for persistent storage. The "DeDiSys" configuration additionally applies the principles provided within this paper as well as the P4 replication protocol and is measured in healthy mode as well as degraded mode. In order to ensure repeatability of the tests, we used the script-based DedisysTest application described in [13].

The test case performed for measurement started with the creation of 1000 entity beans. Afterwards, a setter for String attributes of these entity beans was called 1000 times followed by 1000 calls getter methods of String attributes and 1000 calls to an empty method without associated constraints. The next steps only applicable to the DeDiSys configurations were 1000 calls to an empty method with a satisfied constraint and 1000 calls to an empty method with violated constraints. Constraint satisfaction or violation was achieved by simply returning true or false within the Constraint.validate(...) method in order to eliminate the validation overhead for reasonable overhead comparison. Details on this issue are available in [25]. To measure the behaviour in degraded mode when consistency threats occur, we called an empty method with an associated constraint 1000 times. The occurring consistency threats were negotiated with a dynamic negotiation handler and persisted afterwards. Finally, the 1000 entity beans created in the first step were deleted. Obviously, the create and delete case operate on 1000 different objects. The "accepted threat" case is the primary issue to investigate for the degraded mode and therefore split into a good case and bad case scenario. The values for the other operations were obtained by taking the average of 1000 operations on the same object and 1000 operations on different objects, i.e., one operation per object.

Figure 7 provides an overview of the performance of three different system configurations. "No DeDiSys" is performed on a single node (the fastest one), "No DeDiSys (average of 3 nodes)" is the average of the single-node performance of the three nodes taking part in the replicated setting, and the two DeDiSys configurations (healthy and degraded mode) use a setting with three replicated nodes. One drawback of the DeDiSys configurations is that creation, change,

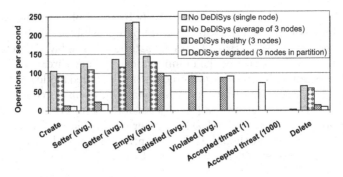

Fig. 7. No DeDiSys vs. DeDiSys in healthy and degraded mode

and deletion of entity beans is slower than the "No DeDiSys" setting. There are two main reasons for this performance loss. First, the replicated setting has to store data about the replicas of entity beans, e.g., JNDI name and primary key to identify the corresponding entity bean and the (serialized) request used to create the entity bean (required to create backup replicas). Second, propagating the update messages from the primary copies to the backup copies requires network access in contrast to the single-node "No DeDiSys" setting. Although an efficient implementation of the P4 protocol was not in our primary focus, the provided figures give a rough estimation of the expected performance loss due to fault- and partition-tolerant replication.

Moreover, we observe that operation in degraded mode is slightly slower for write operations than operation in healthy mode. This is primarily caused by keeping a history of states per replica (requires database access). However, this comparison serves only to show the overhead of degraded mode compared to healthy mode if the number of nodes is equal. In practice, such a situation can not occur as at least a single node will not be reachable and therefore the number of nodes in degraded mode is at least one less than in healthy mode. Consequently, the degraded mode might be even faster than the healthy mode for operations triggering the replication protocol. Whether this is true for a certain application further depends on the configuration of constraints and hence the number of consistency threats produced during degraded mode as the data about consistency threats have to be replicated, too. On the other hand, read performance decreases with a reduced number of nodes in a partition.

The case where methods without associated constraints were called shows the interception overhead introduced by our middleware enhancement as well as the ADAPT replication framework [24]. This is on the one hand the time required by the constraint consistency manager, e.g., accessing the constraint repository to search for affected constraints, and on the other hand running through the replication component that does not replicate if the called method is not a setter changing the state of an entity bean. In this case, the performance drops to about 73% of the "No DeDiSys" configuration, which we consider quite a good achievement as 22% of the 27% loss are caused by the ADAPT replication framework [24]. Consequently, the *overhead introduced by our middleware enhancement for empty operations is about 5%.*

Handling of satisfied and violated constraints only occurs in the DeDiSys configurations as this is a new middleware service added by our prototype. Although there are some minor differences between satisfied and violated constraints in certain scenarios, they show the same performance in average for the healthy as well as the degraded mode.

The "accepted threats" case for operation in degraded mode primarily shows the overhead introduced by consistency threat negotiation as well as persistence and replication of consistency threats in addition to the time required to handle satisfied constraints. In order to investigate a good case and a bad case scenario, we performed 1000 operations on a single object producing 1000 identical consistency threats[2] on the one hand and 1000 operations producing 1000 different consistency threats on the other hand. Of course, depending on the system configuration, even more than 1000 threats would be possible. The good case scenario shows the advantage of storing identical threats only once. Consequently, only a single threat has to be stored in this case and we could serve 74 business operations per second. On the other hand, the bad case scenario requires replication and persistence of 1000 different consistency threats, which is a rather costly operation. In this case, we could only serve three business operations per second. Obviously, this case heavily depends on the specific application. However, the operation in *degraded mode shows the greatest benefit of our approach* compared to traditional systems that either block, i.e., are unavailable, or operate in an uncontrolled inconsistent way—thereby impairing dependability in one or the other way.

Although the contribution of this paper is not focused on an efficient implementation of the P4 replication protocol, the effects of introducing replication are of course an interesting aspect to investigate. Our implementation of the P4 protocol uses synchronous update propagation from the primary to all currently reachable nodes. While this slows down updates (create, setter, delete), the performance of read operations is enhanced as reads can be performed on any node.

Figure 8 shows that the performance of one node using DeDiSys (and hence the P4 replication protocol) drops to 71% for entity bean deletion, 43% for entity bean creation, and 57% for local writes. This primarily shows the overhead of the ADAPT replication framework and the replication protocol through database accesses to persist details about entity bean replicas. Adding a second DeDiSys-node further reduces update performance to 28% (delete), 15% (create), and 22% (writes) compared to the "No DeDiSys" case. This shows a little bit less than 50% performance of the single DeDiSys node case, caused by the fact that the primary first executes the update and afterwards propagates the updates synchronously to the backups. Even though the backup nodes process the update messages from the primary in parallel, adding additional nodes decreases update performance slightly further.

On the other hand, read performance is increased by roughly 50% of the single node per additional node, starting from 78% of the "No DeDiSys" case

---

[2] Two consistency threats are identical if they refer to the same constraint and—if applicable—to the same context object.

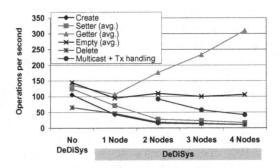

Fig. 8. Replication effects on different operations

for the single node scenario and reaching 227% in the four node replicated setting. Empty methods operate at a rather constant ratio independent of the number of nodes in the system. The reason for this is that they do not trigger update propagation on the one hand. On the other hand, as these methods do not adhere to any naming convention, we consider them as write operations—to be on the safe side—and therefore execute them only on the primary node. This behaviour is the same as for the test cases with satisfied and violated constraints. However, the backup nodes show no CPU load for non-update operations and hence can serve further client requests.

In order to investigate the theoretical maximum of (update) operations possible per second due to restrictions of group communication and transaction handling, we started a transaction, sent 1000 ping messages from the primary to the backups, associated the transaction context at the backups, responded with a **pong** message to the primary and finally committed the transaction. This is the "Multicast + Tx handling" case in Fig. 8. Obviously, the round-trip time of multicasts and transaction handling become more and more influential with an increased number of nodes, limiting the possibilities for performance improvements.

We conclude that only under extremely demanding performance requirements the performance impairment due to explicit constraint management may turn out to be a problem, see also [2,25] for further details. On the other hand, synchronous replication significantly reduces system performance for update operations while the performance of read operations is improved. Therefore, synchronous replication should be applied if the read to write ratio is high and/or write performance is not the limiting factor. In other cases, asynchronous replication protocols or only partial replication (updates are only propagated to some but not all nodes within the system) should be applied.

5   Related Work

The balancing of integrity and availability has already been investigated with respect to isolation [26,27] and replica consistency [28,7,29] and different strategies to optimistic replication are already well-known [30]. The focus of our work to trade constraint consistency for availability did not yet receive too much attention. Balzer [31] uses pollution markers to temporarily allow and denote constraint violations in a healthy system to allow certain business cases. The application using this approach tolerates inconsistency in the way that reports are marked appropriately if they contain data affected by pollution markers. Although our stored consistency threats roughly correspond to pollution markers, Balzer accepts constraint violations in a healthy system and does not consider node or link failures while we aim at fully consistent data in the healthy system and accept consistency threats during degraded mode. However, integration of both approaches would most likely provide further benefits to an application developer.

Representing data integrity constraints as explicit constraint classes was inspired by Verheecke et al. [21] who perform a transformation from UML class diagrams enhanced with OCL constraints into Java objects and Java constraint checking classes. Their approach generates skeletons for the classes with hardwired triggers for constraint validation while we require that constraints are explicitly manageable at runtime for adaptivity with respect to node and link failures. However, the specification of affected methods of a constraint, is a rather tedious task. To relieve the application developer from this work as well as from the implementation of the constraints themselves, the model driven approach used by Verheecke et al. could be integrated with our constraint checking framework. Consequently, entity beans, constraints and metadata could be generated based on UML models annotated with OCL constraints.

ADAPT [24] provides a replication framework to allow rapid prototyping of replication protocols in J2EE (Java 2 Enterprise Edition) environments. This framework is based upon the JBoss AS. The primary mechanism used is invocation interception at the client side as well as at the server side. The replication protocol building upon this framework is notified about different events, such as creation of, calls to, and deletion of enterprise beans. Consequently, this framework proved quite useful for our prototype implementation of the P4 replication protocol.

6   Summary and Conclusion

This paper presents a middleware approach to support adaptive dependability by balancing integrity and availability. We show how explicit runtime management of constraints as a middleware service can support the application to provide the envisaged balancing with respect to an application's requirements and environment conditions. This concept allows detection and negotiation of consistency threats as a means to bound the potentially introduced inconsistency during degraded mode. According to our prototype implementation and additional evaluation studies [2,25], performance impairment due to explicit constraint consistency management is not an issue while the performance loss through synchronous replication is acceptable if (i) the read-to-write ratio is high, (ii) the number of replicated nodes within the system is small, and/or (iii) write performance is not a limiting factor. However, our approach increases availability at the expense of increased aggregate complexity during system reconciliation. Therefore, this system mode is subject to improvements and future research questions.

Acknowledgments

We thank Hubert Künig for many in-depth discussions, Markus Horehled and Klaus Fuchshofer who contributed major parts of the proof-of-concept EJB prototype implementation integrated into the JBoss application server, and Dominik Ertl who was strongly involved in the performance tests. We further thank the anonymous reviewers for their useful comments. This work has been partially funded by the European Community under the FP6 IST project DeDiSys (Dependable Distributed Systems, contract 004152, http://www.dedisys.org/).

References

1. Avižienis, A., Laprie, J.C., Randell, B., Landwehr, C.E.: Basic concepts and taxonomy of dependable and secure computing. IEEE Trans. Dependable Sec. Comput. 1(1), 11–33 (2004)
2. Froihofer, L., Osrael, J., Goeschka, K.M.: Decoupling constraint validation from business activities to improve dependability in distributed object systems. In: Proc. 2nd Int. Conf. on Availability, Reliability and Security, pp. 443–450. IEEE Computer Society, Los Alamitos, CA (2007)
3. Cristian, F.: Understanding fault-tolerant distributed systems. Communications of the ACM 34(2), 56–78 (1991)
4. Fischer, M.J., Lynch, N.A., Paterson, M.S.: Impossibility of distributed consensus with one faulty process. J. ACM 32(2), 374–382 (1985)
5. Helal, A.A., Heddaya, A.A., Bhargava, B.B.: Replication Techniques in Distributed Systems. Kluwer Academic Publishers, Dordrecht (1996)
6. Bernstein, P.A., Hadzilacos, V., Goodman, N.: Concurrency Control and Recovery in Database Systems. Addison-Wesley, Reading (1987)
7. Pu, C., Leff, A.: Replica control in distributed systems: an asynchronous approach. In: SIGMOD 1991: Proceedings of the 1991 ACM SIGMOD international conference on Management of data, pp. 377–386. ACM Press, New York (1991)
8. Fox, A., Brewer, E.A.: Harvest, yield and scalable tolerant systems. In: Workshop on Hot Topics in Operating Systems, pp. 174–178 (1999)
9. Gilbert, S., Lynch, N.: Brewer's conjecture and the feasibility of consistent, available, partition-tolerant web services. SIGACT News 33(2), 51–59 (2002)
10. Architecture Projects Management: The advanced network systems architecture (ANSA) reference manual (1989), http://www.ansa.co.uk/ANSATech/89/ANSAREF/
11. Osrael, J., Froihofer, L., Kuenig, H., Goeschka, K.M.: Scenarios for increasing availability by relaxing data integrity. In: Cunningham, P., Cunningham, M. (eds.) Innovation and the Knowledge Economy - Issues, Applications, Case Studies, vol. 2, pp. 1396–1403. IOS Press, Amsterdam (2005)
12. Smeikal, R., Goeschka, K.M.: Fault-tolerance in a distributed management system: a case study. In: ICSE 2003: Proceedings of the 25th International Conference on Software Engineering, pp. 478–483. IEEE Computer Society, Washington, DC (2003)
13. Künig, H. (ed.): FTNS/EJB system design & first prototype & test report. Technical Report D3.2.2, DeDiSys Consortium (2007), http://www.dedisys.org/
14. Meyer, B.: Applying design by contract. Computer 25(10), 40–51 (1992)
15. Jagadish, H.V., Qian, X.: Integrity maintenance in object-oriented databases. In: Proceedings of the 18th International Conference on Very Large Data Bases, pp. 469–480. Morgan Kaufmann Publishers Inc., San Francisco (1992)

16. Haerder, T., Reuter, A.: Principles of transaction-oriented database recovery. ACM Comput. Surv. 15(4), 287–317 (1983)
17. Coulouris, G., Dollimore, J., Kindberg, T.: Distributed Systems - Concepts and Design, 4th edn. Addison-Wesley, Reading (2005)
18. Arjuna, BEA, Hitachi, IBM, IONA, Microsoft: Web services atomic transaction (2005),
    http://www-128.ibm.com/developerworks/library/specification/ws-tx/
19. Arjuna, BEA, Hitachi, IBM, IONA, Microsoft: Web services business activity framework (2005), http://specs.xmlsoap.org/ws/2004/10/wsba/
20. Osrael, J., Froihofer, L., Goeschka, K.M., Beyer, S., Galdámez, P., Muñoz Escoi, F.D.: A system architecture for enhanced availability of tightly coupled distributed systems. In: Proceedings of the 1st International Conference on Availability, Reliability and Security, IEEE Computer Society, Los Alamitos (2006)
21. Verheecke, B., Straeten, R.V.D.: Specifying and implementing the operational use of constraints in object-oriented applications. In: Proceedings of the Fortieth International Conference on Tools Pacific, Australian Computer Society, Inc,. pp. 23–32 (2002)
22. Ricciardi, A., Schiper, A., Birman, K.: Understanding partitions and the non partition assumption. In: IEEE Proc. of Fourth Workshop on Future Trends of Distributed Systems, IEEE Computer Society Press, Los Alamitos (1993)
23. Beyer, S., Bañuls, M.C., Galdámez, P., Osrael, J., Muñoz Escoi, F.: Increasing availability in a replicated partitionable distributed object system. In: Guo, M., Yang, L.T., Di Martino, B., Zima, H.P., Dongarra, J., Tang, F. (eds.) ISPA 2006. LNCS, vol. 4330, Springer, Heidelberg (2006)
24. Babaoglu, Ö., Bartoli, A., Maverick, V., Patarin, S., Vuckovic, J., Wu, H.: A framework for prototyping J2EE replication algorithms. In: Meersman, R., Tari, Z. (eds.) On the Move to Meaningful Internet Systems 2004: CoopIS, DOA, and ODBASE. LNCS, vol. 3291, pp. 1413–1426. Springer, Heidelberg (2004)
25. Froihofer, L., Glos, G., Osrael, J., Goeschka, K.M.: Overview and evaluation of constraint validation approaches in Java. In: ICSE 2007: Proceedings of the 29th International Conference on Software Engineering, pp. 313–322 (2007)
26. Berenson, H., Bernstein, P., Gray, J., Melton, J., O'Neil, E., O'Neil, P.: A critique of ANSI SQL isolation levels. SIGMOD Rec. 24(2), 1–10 (1995)
27. Herlihy, M., Wing, J.: Linearizability: a correctness condition for concurrent objects. ACM Trans. Program. Lang. Syst. 12(3), 463–492 (1990)
28. Davidson, S.B., Garcia-Molina, H., Skeen, D.: Consistency in a partitioned network: a survey. ACM Comput. Surv. 17(3), 341–370 (1985)
29. Yu, H., Vahdat, A.: Design and evaluation of a conit-based continuous consistency model for replicated services. ACM Trans. Comput. Syst. 20(3), 239–282 (2002)
30. Saito, Y., Shapiro, M.: Optimistic replication. ACM Comput. Surv. 37(1), 42–81 (2005)
31. Balzer, R.: Tolerating inconsistency. In: Proceedings of the 13th international conference on Software engineering, pp. 158–165. IEEE Computer Society Press, Los Alamitos (1991)

Consistent and Scalable Cache Replication for Multi-tier J2EE Applications[*],[**]

Francisco Perez-Sorrosal[1], Marta Patiño-Martinez[1], Ricardo Jimenez-Peris[1], and Bettina Kemme[2]

[1] Facultad de Informática, Universidad Politécnica de Madrid (UPM), Spain
{fpsorrosal,mpatino,rjimenez}@fi.upm.es
[2] McGill University, Quebec, Canada
kemme@cs.mcgill.ca

Abstract. Data centers are the most critical infrastructure of companies demanding higher and higher levels of quality of service (QoS) in terms of availability and scalability. At the core of data centers are multi-tier architectures providing service to applications. Replication is heavily used in this infrastructure for either availability or scalability but typically not for both combined. Additionally, most approaches replicate a single tier, making the non-replicated tiers potential bottlenecks and single points of failure. In this paper, we present a novel approach that provides both availability and scalability for multi-tier applications. The approach uses a replicated cache that takes into account both the application server tier (middle-tier) and the database (back-end). The underlying replicated cache protocol fully embeds the replication logic in the application server. The protocol exhibits good scalability as shown by our evaluation based on the new industrial benchmark for J2EE multi-tier systems, SPECjAppServer.

Keywords: scalability of middleware, replication, caching, reliability, fault-tolerance.

1 Introduction

The new vision of Enterprise Grids [1] is demanding for the creation of highly scalable and autonomic computing systems for the management of companies' data centers. Data centers are the most critical infrastructure of companies demanding higher and higher levels of quality of service (QoS) in terms of availability and scalability. At the core of data centers lies a multi-tier middleware architecture providing services to applications. A multi-tier architecture provides separation of concerns in regard to presentation (front end), business logic (middle-tier), and data storage (back-end). Clients interact with the front end, which acts as a client of the middle-tier or application server. Most computation is done at this level and data is stored in the back-tier.

[*] Patent pending.
[**] This work has been partially funded by the Spanish Research Council (MEC) under TIN2004-07474-C02-01, TIN2007-67353-C02-01, by the Madrid Research Foundation, S-0505/TIC/285 (cofunded by FEDER & FSE), by EUREKA/ITEA S4ALL (04025) funded by MITyC (FIT-3400005-2007-20) and by Automan (ARC funded by INRIA).

R. Cerqueira and R.H. Campbell (Eds.): Middleware 2007, LNCS 4834, pp. 328–347, 2007.

Replication can provide both scalability (load can be distributed across the replicas), and fault-tolerance (load submitted to a failed replica can be redirected to available replicas). Recent work on multi-tier replication, however, only replicates the application server tier while using a single database [2,3,4,5,6,7]. We call these shared database approaches *horizontal replication* (they replicate a single tier). The main shortcoming is that the shared database becomes a bottleneck and a single point of failure. An alternative is to replicate both tiers independently. However, attaining a consistent integration in a scalable way is still an open problem [8]. Furthermore, some of the approaches, e.g., FT-CORBA [9,10] or [6] for J2EE focus on availability and use either primary-backup or active replication. Thus, they do not address scalability since neither technique allows the sharing of load among replicas.

J2EE application servers cache an object oriented view of the database items used by the application. In order to keep this view consistent with the database, application servers implement a concurrency control policy for the cache. They typically provide serializability as correctness criteria, implemented via locking or optimistic schemes, since databases have relied on serializability for a long time. However, today many databases provide snapshot isolation as the highest isolation level (e.g., Oracle, PostgreSQL, FireBird, etc.) and others implement it (MS SQL Server). Therefore, current application server implementations are incorrect when used with databases providing snapshot isolation. Snapshot isolation provides a similar level of isolation as serializability (it passes the tests for serializability of standard benchmarks such as the ones from TPC). Snapshot isolation is usually implemented via a multi-version mechanism in which transactions see a snapshot of the database as of transaction start [11]. Therefore, readers and writers do not interfere. In contrast, when implementing serializability, read-write conflicts lead to blocking or aborts, reducing the potential concurrency and the performance of the system. That is avoided by snapshot isolation.

In this paper we propose a replicated multi-version cache that improves performance by avoiding frequent access to the database. It also provides availability, consistency, and scalability. In our architecture each application server is connected to a local copy of the database. The pair of application and database server is the unit of replication (*vertical replication*). This avoids that the database becomes a single point of failure and a bottleneck. Our replication solution is fully implemented within the application server tier on top of an off-the-shelf database. This fact is important for pragmatic reasons since it enables the use of the replication platform with any existing database and without requiring access to the database code. The replicated cache is based on snapshot isolation. That is, using a single server, the cache provides caching transparency, i.e., its semantics is the same as a system that does not use caching. In a replicated system, it provides one-copy correctness and fault-tolerance, that is, the replicated system behaves as a non-replicated system (consistency) that never fails.

To the best of our knowledge this paper is the first to provide a scalable and integrated solution for the replication of both the application server and database tier. It is also the first paper to implement snapshot isolation for the cache of the application server tier so that it works properly with a database based on snapshot isolation. We have implemented the replicated multi-version cache and integrated it into a commercial open source J2EE application server, JOnAS [3]. The performance of the implementation has

been evaluated with the new industrial benchmark, SPECjAppServer [12]. The prototype outperforms the non-replicated application server and shows good scalability in
terms of throughput and response time.

In the remainder of the paper, Section 2 introduces background on J2EE and snapshot isolation. Sections 3 and 4 present the replication model and the cache protocol,
respectively. Failure handling is described in Section 5. The performance evaluation is
shown in Section 6. Section 7 presents related work, and Section 8 conclusions.

2   Background and Motivation

2.1   J2EE

J2EE [13] is a framework that provides a distributed component model along with other
useful services such as persistence and transactions. J2EE components are called *Enterprise Java Beans* (EJBs). In this paper, we consider the EJB 2.0 specification. There
are three kinds of EJBs: *session beans* (SBs), *entity beans* (EBs) and *message driven
beans*. We will not consider message driven beans in this paper. SBs represent the business logic and are volatile. SBs are further classified as stateless (SLSBs) and stateful
(SFSBs). SLSBs do not keep any state across method invocations. In contrast, SFSBs
are associated with a client and keep session related information across invocations.

EBs model business data and are stored in some persistent storage, usually a
database. EBs are shared by all the clients. An EB typically represents a tuple of the
database. Thus, the set of EBs can be viewed as a cache of the database. Therefore,
EBs are accessed within the context of transactions. EBs are typically managed by the
application server (*container managed persistence*). The J2EE application server (AS)
takes care of reading from and writing to the database by generating the adequate SQL
statements (object oriented to relational model translation). Furthermore, it implements
some concurrency control mechanism on the cache to satisfy the isolation level provided by the database, typically serializability.

In J2EE, transactions are coordinated by the *Java Transaction Service* (JTS). Transactions access this service using the *Java Transaction API* (JTA). In J2EE transactions
can be handled either explicitly (*bean managed transactions*) or implicitly (*container
managed transactions*, CMT). With CMTs, the container intercepts bean invocations
and demarcates transactions automatically. We will focus on CMTs.

2.2   Snapshot Isolation

Snapshot Isolation (SI) [11] is a multi-version concurrency control mechanism used
in databases (e.g., Oracle, PostgreSQL, MS SQL server). One of the most important
properties of SI is that readers and writers do not interfere. This is a big gain compared
to serializability, the traditional correctness criteria for databases, where a locking implementation prevents concurrent reads and writes on the same object while optimistic
concurrency control aborts the reader.

SI can be implemented as follows. The system maintains a counter C of committed
transactions. At commit time, C is incremented and the new value is assigned to the
committing transaction T as *commit timestamp* $CT(T)$. At start, a transaction T receives

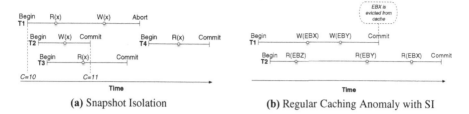

(a) Snapshot Isolation   **(b)** Regular Caching Anomaly with SI

Fig. 1. Snapshot Isolation

as *start timestamp ST(T)* the current value of C. When a transaction writes a data item x, it creates a new (private) version of x. When reading a data item x a transaction T either reads its own version (if it has already performed a write on x) or it reads the last committed version as of the start of T. That is, it reads the version created by a transaction T' so that $CT(T')$ is the maximum CT of all transactions that wrote x and $CT(T') \leq ST(T)$. By reading from a snapshot, reads and writes do not interfere. However, if two concurrent transactions want to write the same data item, SI requires one to abort. Such conflicts can be detected at commit time. When a transaction T wants to commit, a validation phase checks whether there was any concurrent transaction T' (i.e. $CT(T') > ST(T)$) that already committed and wrote a common data item. If such a transaction exists T aborts, otherwise it commits. If T commits, its changes (writeset) are made visible to other transactions that start after T_i commits.

Fig.1(a) shows an example with four transactions. We assume $C = 10$ and the transaction T with $CT(T) = 10$ updated x (not shown in the figure). Now $T1, T2$ and $T3$ start concurrently and all receive as start timestamp the value 10. $T2$ writes x. Its validation succeeds and $CT(T2)$ is set to 11. $T3$ reads the version of x created by T. Since it is read-only, no validation is necessary and it does not receive a commit timestamp. $T1$ reads the version of x created by T, and then writes x creating its own version. When $T1$ wants to commit, however, validation fails since there is a committed transaction $T2$, $CT(T2) > ST(T1)$, and $T2$ also wrote x. Therefore, $T1$ has to abort. Finally, $T4$ starts after $T2$ commits and receives $ST(T4) = 11$. It reads the version of x created by $T2$.

2.3   Application Server Caching and Replication

J2EE implementations provide caching for entity beans as follows. An entity bean (EB) represents a cached tuple of the database. We denote the entity bean representing tuple x as EBX. When accessing an EB, if it is not in memory the corresponding tuple is read from the database. If the EB is updated, the associated tuple will be updated at the database when the corresponding transaction commits. The EB is then cached in memory so that it can be directly accessed by further transactions. Access to EBs is typically controlled via locking in order to provide serializability. However, this can lead to executions that neither provide serializability nor snapshot isolation when the database system uses snapshot isolation.

Let's look at an example. Assume two transactions $T1$ and $T2$ start concurrently at the application server (Fig.1(b)). $T1$ wants to write x and y. For that, the application

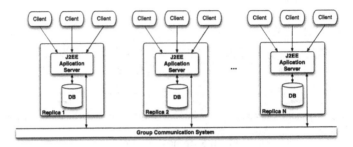

Fig. 2. Replication model

server reads the values of x and y into EBX and EBY, respectively, $T1$ gets locks and updates both beans. Concurrent transaction $T2$ reads z into EBZ, and then wants to read y but is blocked because $T1$ has a lock on EBY. Now $T1$ commits. The new values for x and y are written to the database and the locks are released. Both EBX and EBY remain cached. $T2$ receives the lock on EBY and reads the current value of EBY, namely the value written by $T1$. Now assume the cache replacement policy evicts EBX from the cache. Later, $T2$ wants to read x. x is reread into a new incarnation of EBX. However, since the database uses snapshot isolation and $T2$ is concurrent to $T1$ in the database, the old value of x is read. Therefore, $T2$ reads for y the value written by $T1$ but for x a previous value. This does neither conform to snapshot isolation nor to serializability.

In order to avoid the anomalies of J2EE caching when used with a snapshot isolation database, we propose a multi-version cache for EBs that enforces snapshot isolation. For each EB, instead of keeping a single copy in the cache, a list of potentially more than one version is cached. Each bean version EBX_i of data item x is tagged with the commit timestamp i of the transaction that created (and committed) this version. Additionally, the multi-version cache is replicated at several application servers in order to provide scalability, and availability. The semantics of the replicated multi-version cache is as if there was a single multi-version cache providing snapshot isolation (consistency).

3   Replication Model

We consider a vertical replication model in which a J2EE application server (AS) and a database (DB) are collocated in the same site [8]. This is the unit of replication, also called replica. Each AS communicates with its DB and with the remaining ASs. That is, DBs are not shared among ASs. The set of all replicas is called a *cluster* (Fig.2).

In here, we are interested in container managed transactions, where each client request is automatically bracketed as a transaction by the application server. This means, there is a one-to-one relationship between requests and transactions. Clients call methods of a session bean, and the session bean may access other session or entity beans. A client can be connected to any of the replicas. That replica will execute the transactions of the client. The changes of update transactions have to be executed at all replicas.

Our protocol uses a group communication system [14] for communication among the replicas. The next section discusses the replication protocol when no failures occur. Section 5 discusses failure handling.

4   Replication Protocol

In this section, we describe the multi-version cache replication protocol (Fig.3). We first present the main ideas and then discuss the protocol in detail.

Overview
When a request is submitted to a replica, a transaction is started at the application server (AS) and at the database (DB). The transaction might read data that is already cached at the AS or that has to be read from the DB. The cache protocol makes sure that the correct version is read according to snapshot isolation. If the transaction is read-only, it simply commits locally and the result is returned to the client. If the transaction updates a data item x, a new private version of the corresponding entity bean EBX is created. At commit time, the replication protocol multicasts all EB versions created by the transaction (i.e. its *writeset*) using a total order multicast provided by the group communication system. That is, although different replicas might multicast at the same time, all replicas receive all writesets in the same order. At each replica, the replication protocol now validates incoming writesets in the same order. If validation determines that a concurrent transaction that already validated had an overlapping writeset, validation fails and the transaction is aborted. If validation succeeds, the replica assigns a commit timestamp, tags the EB versions of the transaction with the commit timestamp and adds them to the cache. Then the transaction commits at AS and DB. When the transaction commits at the local replica, the result is returned to the client. Each replica validates the same set of update transactions in the same order, and decides on the same outcome for each individual transaction. Thus, each committed transaction has the same commit timestamp at each replica.

Protocol Details
We now discuss in detail how transactions are executed. When a transaction is submitted to a replica R, the replica starts a local transaction T at the local AS and a transaction t at the local DB. The correlation between AS transactions and DB transactions is stored in a table (Fig.3 line 6). Each transaction T at the AS will be associated with a *start timestamp* $ST(T)$ when it starts (line 3), and a *commit timestamp* $CT(T)$ at commit time (line 54) which is assigned from a counter that is increased every time a transaction commits. The start timestamp $ST(T)$ of a transaction T is the highest commit timestamp $CT(T')$, and indicates that T should read the committed state that existed just after the commit of T'. We assume that the initial start timestamp is 0 at all replicas. Each bean version $EBX_{CT(T)}$ of a data item x is tagged with the commit timestamp $CT(T)$ of the transaction T that updated (and committed) this version. When a transaction T reads a data item x it has written before, it reads its own version (lines 10-11). Otherwise, it first looks for EBX in the cache. It reads the version EBX_i such that $i \leq ST(T) \wedge \nexists EBX_j : i < j \leq ST(T)$, i.e. it reads the last committed version as of the time it starts (lines 12-13). If no appropriate bean is cached in memory, the

transaction reads x from the DB and the corresponding EBX version is created (lines 15-18). Since a transaction is started at the DB when a transaction starts at the AS, and the DB provides snapshot isolation, the DB will return the correct version for x. This process guarantees that each transaction observes a snapshot as of the start of the transaction and therefore it does not violate snapshot isolation. Since the DB does not show the versions associated to tuples, when a version of data item x is read from the DB the corresponding tag of the EBX version is unknown. Thus, the bean is tagged with -1.

In order to guarantee that transactions always read the appropriate bean version, the cache guarantees that for each data item x the following holds: (i) If both T and T' updated x, and $CT(T') > CT(T)$ and the version $EBX_{CT(T)}$ is cached, then $EBX_{CT(T')}$ is also cached. That is, if the cache contains a certain version of a bean, then it also contains all later versions of this bean; (ii) If there exists a version $EBX_{CT(T)}$ and there exists an active local transaction T' that is concurrent to T, i.e., $ST(T') > CT(T)$, then $EBX_{CT(T)}$ is cached. That is, a version is cached at least as long as there exists a concurrent local transaction that has not yet terminated. Having all these versions cached is important for reads.

Note that our approach requires the DB to provide snapshot isolation. This is needed because the cache cannot keep the entire database, i.e., all versions of all tuples. To show that snapshot isolation is needed at the DB level, assume the DB uses the isolation level read committed (or serializability via locking). Assume further that a transaction T_i reads and modifies x while a concurrent transaction T_j updates y and commits. Assume now further that T_i wants to read y and, due to lack of memory, the version of EBY that T_i needs to read, was evicted from the cache. Hence, it has to read it from the DB. Assuming transactions run at the DB with read committed (or serializability) isolation level, T_i reads the value of y committed by T_j. That is, it will not read the value of EBY at the time T_i started. Thus, the AS cannot provide by itself the snapshot isolation level.

In snapshot isolation, when two concurrent transactions update the same data item, only one may commit, the other has to abort. In order to detect such conflicts early, we use locking and version checking. When a transaction T_i wants to update a data item x, it has to first acquire a write lock on EBX (line 25). Write locks guarantee that at most one transaction updates data item x at any time. If another transaction holds a lock on EBX, T has to wait until the lock is released which is done at transaction abort (line 45) or commit (line 73). Lock requests are inserted into a FIFO wait-queue, i.e., when a transaction releases a lock the first in the wait queue receives it. Once a transaction T has a lock, a version check on the version EBX_j with the highest version number in the cache is performed. If $j > ST(T)$, then this version was created by a concurrent, already committed transaction, and T must abort (lines 26-27). If no such version exists, T can perform the update, i.e., create its own version and add it to its writeset (line 29-31). For now, this version is only seen by T itself. This guarantees that a transaction observes its own updates (lines 10-11) and prevents other transactions from observing uncommitted changes.

When a transaction wants to commit, if the transaction was read-only it is simply committed at the DB (lines 36-37). Otherwise, the writeset is multicast to all replicas using a total order multicast (line 39). All replicas in the multicast group (including senders) receive all messages in the same order. When a replica processes such a

Data:
timestamp = 0;
cache = ∅ ;
committedTx = ∅;
transactionTable = ∅;
mutex;;
oldestActiveTx = array[1..NumberReplicas] of Int = 0;

1 begin(T)
2 | set mutex ;
3 | ST(T) = timestamp;
4 | WS(T) = ∅;
5 | t = begin transaction in the DB;
6 | store(transactionTable, T, t);
7 | release mutex ;
8 end
9 read(T, EBX)
10 | if $EBX_{Tprivate} \in WS(T)$ then
11 | | return $EBX_{Tprivate}$;
12 | else if
      $\exists EBX_i \in cache : i = max(j) \mid EBX_j \in cache \wedge j < ST(T)$
   then
13 | | return EBX_i ;
14 | else
15 | | t = getTx(transactionTable, T);
16 | | EBX_{-1} = read(t,EBX) from the DB;
17 | | cache = cache $\cup\{EBX_{-1}\}$;
18 | | return EBX_{-1};
19 | end
20 end
21 write(T, EBX, value)
22 | if $\exists EBX_{Tprivate} \in WS(T)$ then
23 | | write($EBX_{Tprivate}$, value);
24 | else
25 | | acquire lock on EBX for T;
26 | | if $\exists EBX_i \in cache \mid i > ST(T)$ then
27 | | | abort(T);
28 | | else
29 | | | create($EBX_{Tprivate}$);
30 | | | WS(T) = WS(T) $\cup\{EBX_{Tprivate}\}$;
31 | | | write($EBX_{Tprivate}$, value);
32 | | end
33 | end
34 end
35 commit(T)
36 | if WS(T) == ∅ then
37 | | Commit (getTx(transactionTable, T)) in DB;
38 | else
39 | | multicast(WS(T), T, minLocalTx(transactionTable));
40 | end
41 end

42 abort(T)
43 | $\forall EBX_{Tprivate} \in$ WS(T) do
44 | | delete($EBX_{Tprivate}$);
45 | | release lock on EBX;
46 | end
47 | abort getTx(T) in DB;
48 | delete(transactionTable, T);
49 end
50 upon delivery of (WS(T), T, oldestLocalActiveTx)
51 | set mutex;
52 | oldestActiveTx[Sender(T)] = oldestLocalActiveTx;
53 | if $\nexists T_K \in committedTx : ST(T) > CT(T_k) \wedge$
      $WS(T) \cap WS(T_K) \neq \emptyset$ then
54 | | CT(T) = ++ $timestamp$;
55 | | if $local(T)$ then
56 | | | $\forall EBX_{Tprivate} \in$ WS(T) do
57 | | | | replace tag $Tprivate$ with tag $CT(T)$;
58 | | | | cache = cache $\cup\{EBX_{CT(T)}\}$;
59 | | | end
60 | | else
61 | | | t = begin transaction in the DB;
62 | | | store(transactionTable, T, t);
63 | | | $\forall EBX_{Tprivate} \in$ WS(T) do
64 | | | | if $\exists$ local transaction LT that has lock on EBX then
65 | | | | | abort(LT)
66 | | | | end
67 | | | | acquire lock on EBX for T (put lock request at begin of
               wait queue);
68 | | | | replace tag $Tprivate$ with tag $CT(T)$;
69 | | | | cache = cache $\cup\{EBX_{CT(T)}\}$;
70 | | | end
71 | | end
72 | | commit (getTx(transactionTable, T)) in the DB;
73 | | $\forall EBX \in WS(T)$ release lock on EBX;
74 | | committedTx = committedTx $\cup\{T\}$;
75 | | delete(transactionTable, T));
76 | release mutex;
77 end
78 garbageCollection()
79 | oldestTx = min(oldestActiveTx);
80 | $\forall T \in$ committedTx do
81 | | if $CT(T) < ST(oldestTx)$ then
82 | | | committedTx = committedTx - {T} ;
83 | | end
84 | end
85 | oldestLocalTx = oldestActiveTx[R];
86 | $\forall EBX \in$ cache do
87 | | if $\exists EBX_i \in cache \wedge i \neq -1 \wedge i < ST(oldestLocalTx)$ then
88 | | | cache = cache - EBX_i;
89 | | | if $EBX_{-1} \in cache$ then cache = cache-EBX_{-1};
90 | | end
91 | end
92 end

Fig. 3. Replicated Cache Protocol for Replica R

message (line 50), the corresponding transaction performs a final validation (line 53). This will help to find conflicts among transactions that executed at different replicas. Since all transactions perform deterministic validation in the same order, all replicas decide on the same outcome. A transaction passes validation, if there is no transaction in the system that is concurrent, already committed and has overlapping changes.

When a transaction T passes validation, it receives a commit timestamp (line 54). At the local replica, the private versions are tagged with the commit timestamp and added to the cache (lines 55-59). T and the corresponding DB transaction t commit and the locks are released (lines 72-73). Note that committing the DB transaction automatically propagates the changes to the DB. The protocol keeps track of all committed transactions (line 74) for validation purposes. At a remote replica, a DB transaction is started for T (lines 61-62). T first gets the locks on the data items. If a local transaction T' has a lock on one of the data items it has to abort because it is concurrent to T, has updated the same data item and is not yet validated and committed (lines 64-65). T has to be the first to get the lock (line 67). Then, the versions sent in the message are tagged with the commit timestamp and added to the cache (lines 68-69). From there, the transaction commits as in the local replica (lines 72-75).

If a transaction T does not pass validation, nothing has to be done. At remote replicas, the message can simply be discarded since nothing has yet been done on behalf of T. At the local replica, T can only fail validation if a conflicting remote transaction T' was received between sending and receiving T. In this case, however, as described above T' found the lock held by T and T was already forced to abort.

Note that messages are processed serially, that is, one after the other, in order to guarantee that validation and commit order are the same at all replicas. Furthermore, starting transactions have to be coordinated with committing transactions in order to guarantee that transactions see, in fact, the correct snapshot. Therefore, an appropriate mutex is set (lines 2,7, 51 and 76).

Examples
We illustrate the execution along two examples. Fig.4 shows an example of the evolution of the cache on a single replica (ignoring the replication part). We assume the cache is empty and the commit counter is at value 10. Transactions $T1$ and $T2$ obtain the same start timestamp (10) and each creates a corresponding DB transaction. Then, $T2$ reads x. Since no bean version exists in the cache, the data item is read from the DB and a version EBX_{-1} is created. The value of x is a. Now $T1$ reads x and y. Since EBX_{-1} is cached and $-1 \leq 10$, $T2$ reads EBX_{-1}. Furthermore y is read from the DB and stored in EBY_{-1}. Its current value is b. Now $T1$ updates EBX to the value c and EBY to the value d. For that, it creates private versions of EBX and EBY. Finally, it requests the commit. It receives commit timestamp $CT(T1) = 11$, the versions are tagged with this timestamp and added to the cache. The corresponding DB transaction commits meaning that the changes are transferred to the DB. Since the DB implements SI, new versions for both x and y are created also in the DB. When $T2$ now reads y, it does not read EBY_{11}, since $11 > ST(T2)$. Instead, it reads EBY_{-1} that is, the old value b of y. Since $T2$ is read-only, it simply commits in the DB and no commit timestamp is assigned.

In our second example (Fig. 5) we assume two replicas $R1$ and $R2$. We assume the commit counter at each replica is 10 when transaction $T1$ starts at $R1$ and $T2$ at $R2$. Both receive start timestamp 10. Now assume both read data item x, reading it from the local DB and loading it into EBX_{-1}. The current value is a. Now both transactions update EBX. Since they run in different replicas, both acquire the lock, and create their own private EBX versions. $T1$ sets the new value b, $T2$ sets the new value c. When $T1$ and $T2$ finish at their local replicas, their changes are multicast. Let us assume the total order is $T1, T2$ and there is no other concurrent conflicting transaction. Let's first have a look at $R1$. When $T1$ is delivered at $R1$, its validation succeeds. $T1$ is local at $R1$. It receives the $CT(T1) = 11$ and its version is tagged ($EBX_{11} = b$) and added to the cache. $T1$ commits at the DB. When now $T2$ is delivered at $R1$ validation fails since $T1$ is concurrent ($CT(T1) > ST(T2)$), conflicts, and has already committed. Therefore, nothing is done with $T2$ at $R1$. At replica $R2$ transactions are validated in

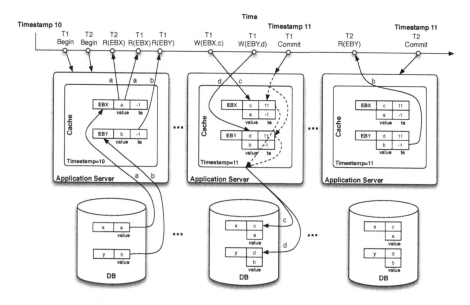

Fig. 4. Evolution of the cache in a single replica

the same order. $T1$'s validation succeeds. $T1$ is a remote transaction at $R2$ and has to acquire the locks. However, $T2$ has a lock on EBX. $T2$ is local and has not yet validated. Therefore, it is aborted, its private version discarded and its lock released. $EBX_{11} = b$ is created and added to the cache. The value is propagated to the DB and the transaction committed. When later $T2$ is delivered at $R2$, validation fails. The transaction has already aborted, and nothing has to be done. Therefore, the two replicas commit the same transactions and keep the same values (with the same version tag) in both the cache and the DB.

Dealing with Creation and Deletions of EBs. Creation and deletion of EBs is also handled by the protocol (not shown in Fig. 3). When a new EB is created (no corresponding data item exists in the DB), a private version is created for the transaction and there is no other version available. A lock is also set on the EB to prevent concurrent creations of the same EB (with the same primary key). When the transaction commits, the version becomes available for transactions that started after the creating transaction committed and the corresponding tuple is inserted in the DB.

Deletions create a tombstone version of the EB. The tombstone is also a private version of the transaction until commitment. If the transaction tries to access the EB, it will not find it, since the protocol will find the tombstone and recognize the EB as deleted. When the transaction commits, the tombstone version will become public. Even after transaction commit previous versions of the EB cannot be removed, since there might be active transactions associated to older snapshots (all transactions that started before the one that deleted the EB committed), that may read the older EB version.

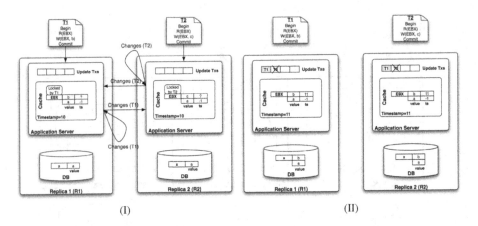

Fig. 5. Two concurrent conflicting transactions

Garbage Collection. Since EB versions are kept in memory (in the cache), they should be removed to free space in the cache when they are not needed. For this purpose, there is a garbage collection mechanism that discards unneeded EB versions (Fig.3 garbageCollection). Each replica removes versions that are older than the oldest start timestamp among local active transactions (lines 85-88). If a version of an EB, EB_i, is not needed (there is no local active transaction with start timestamp smaller than i), then version EB_{-1} is also not needed, since EB_{-1} is older (line 89). Moreover, if EB_{-1} is not evicted from the cache and a new transaction T ($ST(T) > i$) reads EB, it would read EB_{-1}, which is incorrect, since it should read a later committed version (EB_i or even a later version, since $ST(T) > i$).

Uncommitted updated EBs are pinned in the cache. If the cache gets full with pinned EBs, the J2EE application server writes locked EBs from the cache to a local disk repository (not the database) by means of a standard hibernation mechanism. Thanks to this, our versioning is not affected by the eviction policy of the cache. When a hibernated EB is going to be accessed the AS brings the hibernated EB to memory including all EB versions and their tags. Note that updated EBs whose changes have been committed will be evicted from the cache according to the cache policy.

Writesets ($committedTx$) are also garbage collected. Since they are used for validation, a writeset can only be garbage collected when there are no more active concurrent transactions in the system (lines 79-82).

Session Replication. Stateful session beans (SFSBs) keep conversational state from a client and their replication is not required to provide consistency and availability of EBs. However, if they are not replicated, a failure of a replica will cause the loss of the conversational state kept in the SFSB corresponding to all previously run transactions by the client at that replica. The conversation could not be resumed after the failover, what results in loss of session availability. For this reason, the replication protocol also replicates the state of SFSBs after each method invocation. Papers [15,7] focus on this topic.

5   Failure Handling

Clients connect to the application server through stubs that are obtained from the application server through JNDI (Java Naming and Directory Interface). Since stubs are generated by the application server, the necessary replication logic can be incorporated in a way fully transparent to clients. We have extended the stubs to be able to perform replica discovery and load-balancing, relying on IP-multicast. When a client wants to connect, the stub IP-multicasts a message to an IP-multicast address associated to the application server cluster. Clients are identified by a unique client identifier. When the replicas in the cluster receive a connection request, one of them (depending on the client identifier) returns to the stub a list of available replicas (their IPs) as well as an indication of their current load. Replicas multicast information about their load periodically (e.g., piggybacked on the writeset message). The stub then selects a replica randomly with a selection probability inversely proportional to the load of the replicas to attain load balancing. The stub connects to the selected replica and sends all client requests to this replica (sticky client). Each request receives a unique number (a counter kept at the stub that is incremented after each successful request).

The AS replicas build a group using the group communication service. The group communication system provides the notion of view (currently connected cluster members). Whenever a member fails, the available members are informed via a view change message. The group communication system provides strong virtual synchrony that guarantees that the relative order of delivering view changes and multicast messages is the same at all replicas. The total order multicast used for the writeset messages in the replication protocol also provides reliable delivery guaranteeing that all available replicas receive the same set of messages [14]. Furthermore, the writeset also contains the client identifier, request identifier plus the response that is going to be returned to the client. The remote replicas store for each client the latest request identifier, the outcome of the transaction (commit/abort), and in case of commit, the response.

Let us now consider the failover logic at the application server side. Each replica consists of a pair of AS and DB. If any of them fails or the site in which they are collocated fails, the replica is considered as failed. If only the AS or the DB fails, the other component automatically shuts down. We assume only crash failures.

At the client side the failure will be detected when the stub times out waiting for the response to an outstanding request. The stub will reconnect to a new replica and resubmit that request. Notice that we are considering container managed transactions, where each client request will be automatically bracketed as a transaction. Thus, there is a one-to-one relationship between requests and transactions. A failure can now occur at two logical timepoints. (1) The replica failed before multicasting the writeset related to the request to the other replicas. (2) The replica failed after multicasting the writeset.

If there have been previous interactions with that client, the new replica to which the stub connects to will have the last state of the stateful session bean (SFSB) associated to the client and processes the resubmitted client request in the following way. In case (1), the new replica does not yet have any information about this request and thus, will process it as a new request. In case (2) it has already stored the request identifier and the outcome of the corresponding transaction. It recognizes the resubmitted request as a duplicate for which it has already the outcome stored. If the outcome was commit, it returns the response to the client. Otherwise, it returns an exception to the client notifying that the transaction was aborted since snapshot isolation could not be guaranteed (the failed replica would have done the same if it had not failed).

6   Evaluation

6.1   Evaluation Setup

The evaluation has been performed in a cluster of 10 machines connected through a 100 Mbps switch. Sites have 2 AMD Athlon 2GHz CPUs, 1 GB of RAM, two 320 GB hard disks and run Fedora Linux. Each replica consists of one JOnAS v4.7.1 application server (AS) and a PostgreSQL v.8.2 database. JGroups [16] is used as group communication system.

We use the dealer application of SPECjAppServer in our evaluation. SPEC-jAppServer is a benchmark developed by SPEC (System Performance Evaluation Cooperative) to measure the performance of J2EE application server implementations [12]. In this application there is a workload generator (driver) that emulates automobile dealers interacting with the system through HTTP. The driver injects three different transaction types: purchase vehicles (25%), manage customer inventory (25%), browse vehicle catalog (50%). Browse transactions are read-only, purchase transactions have a significant amount of writes, and management transactions exhibit the highest fraction of updates. The main parameter in the tests is the injection rate (Ir), which models the injected load. The number of clients is Ir $\times$ 10. The SPECjAppServer specifies a maximum response time for all requests (2 seconds). Furthermore, the response time corresponding to the 90% percentile may be at most 10% higher than the average response time. The throughput is measured as the business transactions completed per second (Tx/sec).

We compare the results of our replicated multi-version cache with the traditional caching of JOnAS (no replication) and a replicated application server (JOnAS) with 2 replicas sharing a single database (horizontal replication) where only stateful session beans are replicated.

6.2   SPECjAppServer Benchmark Results

Fig. 6(a) shows the overall throughput with increasing loads. The figure shows graphs for traditional caching without replication, horizontal replication with 2 replicas (HR Shared DB) and our approach for 1-10 replicas. The first noticeable fact is that traditional caching and horizontal replication can only handle a load up to 3 Ir. In contrast, our replicated multi-version cache outperforms these two implementations by a factor of 2, even if there is only one replica. The reason is that the multi-version cache is able to avoid many database reads compared to regular caching. Horizontal replication did not help because the shared database was already saturated with two application server replicas. With 3 replicas (not shown), the system deteriorated and did not even achieve an Ir of 1. The replicated multi-version cache is able to handle a load up to 14 Ir achieving a throughput of 14 Tx/sec with 10 replicas compared to a load of 6 Ir and throughput

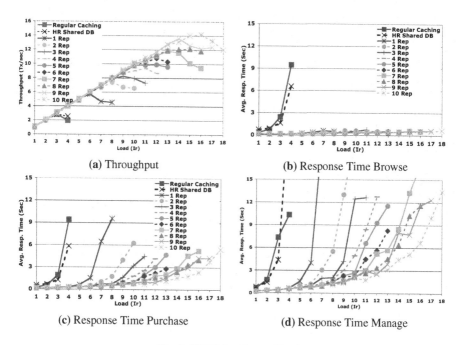

(a) Throughput

(b) Response Time Browse

(c) Response Time Purchase

(d) Response Time Manage

Fig. 6. SPECjAppServer Results

of 6 Tx/sec with a single replica (and 3 Ir resp. 3 Tx/sec with traditional caching). That is, by adding new replicas a higher number of clients can be served.

At the beginning, adding a new replica will increase the throughput by 2 Tx/sec, after a certain number of replicas the increase is 1 Tx/sec. From nine to ten replicas the gain is around 0.5 Tx/sec. The reason is that changes performed by update transactions have to be applied at all replicas. By increasing the load each replica spends more time applying changes and has less capacity to execute new transactions. Nevertheless, the scale-up achieved with our approach by far outperforms horizontal replication.

Even when the replicated cache configurations saturate (the throughput is lower than the injected load), configurations with a higher number of replicas exhibit a more graceful degradation. For instance, for Ir =13, both the 5-replica an 8-replica configuration are saturated. However, the achieved throughput with 8 replicas is higher than with 5 replicas, providing clients a better service. This is very important, since it will help the system to cope with short-lived high peak loads without collapsing.

Fig. 6(b-d) show the response time for browse, purchase and management transactions with increasing load. Interestingly, browse transactions (i.e., read-only transactions) are not affected by the saturation of update transactions. As can be seen in Fig. 6(b) the response time graphs are almost flat independently of the number of replicas even at high loads when the system reaches saturation. The reason is that for read-only queries our application server caching is very effective avoiding expensive database access in many cases. Also, read-only transactions do not require communication. We can observe that both regular caching and horizontal replication saturate with Ir = 3, since the response times increase exponentially for browse transactions.

Purchase transactions (Fig. 6(c)) are quite different since they are update transactions. The response time for all configurations reaches saturation (it grows exponentially) at some time point. The response times for traditional caching and horizontal replication are worse than for the multi-version approach even for low loads showing that our caching strategy saves expensive access to the database. Furthermore, the replicated architecture provides low response times until saturation is reached. Finally, the more replicas the system has, the more graceful is the degradation of the response time at the saturation point. This is important since acceptable response times can be provided in case of short-lived peaks.

The different behavior of the purchase transactions compared to browse transactions has to do with the fact that update transactions propagate their changes to all the replicas in the system, and also have to write changes to the database. Thus, a higher overhead is created leading to worse response time. This behavior is even more noticeable in the case of manage transactions, which have the highest percentage of updates (Fig. 6(d)). Again, however, degradation of response times is more graceful with larger number of replicas.

6.3   CPU Analysis

In this section we look at the CPU usage of the database and the application server during 16 minutes of executing the benchmark. Each of the following figures shows two graphs. One graph is the CPU usage of the database and the other is the overall CPU usage. The gap between the two graphs is mostly the application server (and replication protocol) CPU usage.

The results for regular caching and our multi-version cache with a single replica for Ir = 4 are shown in Fig. 7. At this load, the system is saturated with a 100% usage of the CPU with 1 replica and regular caching (Fig. 7(a)). The database consumes most of the CPU. There are depressions in the utilization graph of the database. They have to do with the way PostgreSQL handles updates. Periodically, when buffers are full, it stops transaction processing and forces data to disk. This results in underusing the CPU. The single replica multi-version cache configuration shows a significantly smaller CPU usage (Fig. 7(b)). The CPU usage of the database is much smaller due to the multi-version cache. This saves database access and reduces the CPU resources required by the database instance. Thus, the system is not saturated for Ir = 4.

Examining the 2-replica configuration of our replicated cache for Ir = 4 (Fig. 8(a)), the results are quite different. Although there are some high peaks in the CPU usage, the area covered is much smaller than for the 1-replica configuration. The overall CPU usage has been significantly reduced. This means that for the same load the overhead at each replica is smaller, resulting in an effective sharing of the load. In the 6-replica configuration and Ir = 4 (Fig. 9(a)), CPU usage is even further reduced with a very low amount of CPU devoted to the database. This explains the scalability of our approach. The more replicas in the system, the better the load is distributed.

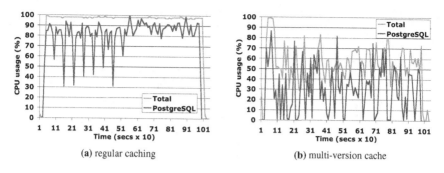

Fig. 7. CPU usage: One replica, Ir = 4

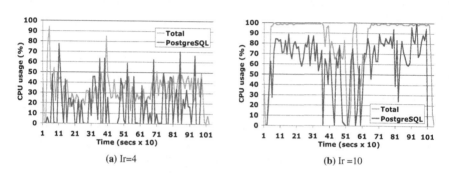

Fig. 8. Multi-version cache. CPU usage: Two replicas

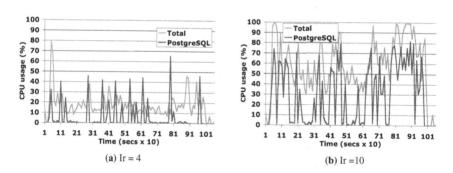

Fig. 9. Multi-version cache. CPU Usage: Six replicas.

Fig. 8(b) shows the 2-replica configuration when it is saturated at Ir = 10. At this load, the database usage of the CPU amounts to 80% which means that the database is the bottleneck. The 6-replica configuration is not saturated in this setting (Fig. 9(b)) since the CPU usage of the database is lower. This confirms the effective distribution of the entire load (application server and database load) among replicas, which results in the scalability of the approach.

Another important conclusion is the efficacy of collocating application and database server on the same site which distinguishes our vertical replication approach from

Table 1. JProfiler Results

	No Replication	Replication	When
JGroups		130,00	update tx
Replication Classes		143,00	update tx
Entity Serialization		3,20	update tx
SFSB Serialization		4,91	SFSBs update
Entity bean caching	152,00	110,00	always
DB Access	227,00	110,00	always

previous solutions. It enables adapting the CPU resources needed by each kind of server without replica configurations. The operating system takes care of distributing CPU to the servers according to their needs.

6.4　Profiling Tool Results

We also used a profiling tool, JProfiler, to analyze the differences in response time between the application server with and without the multi-version cache. It measures both the replication overhead and the savings obtained by the multi-version cache. Since the profiling tool introduces a very high overhead, the profiling could only be done with a single replica and the lowest Ir of 1. The results show the overall number of seconds spent during the whole experiment on methods with different functionalities (Table 1). The group communication system (JGroups) and the replication classes introduce a non-negligible overhead as expected. However, it must be noticed that read only transactions (50% of the load) are not affected by this overhead. The multi-version cache compensates the replication overhead by improving the caching efficiency and reducing the database access (rows at the bottom) in a 27.6% and 51.5%, respectively.

6.5　Scalability Analysis

In this section we measure the scalability of the replicated cache, i.e., how much we can increase the load when increasing the number of replicas. To measure the scalability we take the response time (RT) threshold of the SPECjAppServer benchmark, 2 seconds, and observe for each configuration (i.e. number of replicas) the maximum load (Ir) for which the response time remained below the 2-second threshold. Additionally, in order to observe the behavior under peak loads, we have also measured the maximum load for a 5-second threshold.

Fig. 10 shows the scalability results. For browse transactions we do not show any graphs since for all tested replica configurations and injected Ir the response time was well below 2 seconds. For purchase transactions, we can see that for small configurations the sustainable load increases sharply when increasing the number of replicas, while it only increases slightly when there are already many replicas in the system. This means, 5 replicas are able to manage a total of 110 clients (Ir = 11), that is, an average

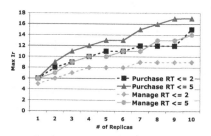

Fig. 10. Scalability Analisys

of 110/5=22 clients per replica. 10 replicas manage 150 clients (Ir = 15), that is, an average of 15 clients per replica. Still, scalability is considerably good considering the substantial fraction of updates involved in purchase transactions.

For manage transactions the system does not scale as well as for purchase transactions. This is expected since manage transactions have a higher percentage of updates resulting in a higher replication overhead. For this kind of transactions the system does not scale beyond 6 replicas for the 2-second threshold. However, if we look at the tolerance to peak loads (threshold RT $<= 5$ secs) having additional replicas is beneficial. Manage transactions with a threshold RT$<=5$ scale almost as well as purchase transactions. That is having 10 replicas, the system can still provide reasonable response time (below 5 seconds) at high loads, while this is not the case for 6 replicas.

7   Related Work

Early work in application server replication looked mainly at CORBA and focused on fault-tolerance [9]. This work resulted in the FT-CORBA specification [17], where the application server is replicated and the database is shared (horizontal replication). This results in solutions providing availability for the application server tier. Replication of CORBA with transactional consistency has been addressed in [10].

[15] presents a primary-backup approach for the replication of J2EE servers. It provides session availability, as we do in this paper. However, being primary-backup does not provide any scalability. [7] is also a primary-backup approach for the replication of J2EE servers supporting multiple transactional patterns (e.g. several client requests may be encapsulated within one server transaction or a single client request can initiate several server transactions). [2] introduces a caching algorithm for J2EE application servers. Application servers are replicated and share the database (horizontal replication). Consistency is guaranteed through a certification protocol. At commit time, every read entity bean is re-read to check whether it was modified. This approach has the shortcoming of all horizontal approaches since the shared database becomes the bottleneck. The certification is heavier than the validation of our replication protocol since it has to re-read every read entity bean.

On the theoretical side, papers [5,4] defined formally exactly-once correctness in multi-tier systems. They study the replication of stateful and stateless application servers with a shared database. In these proposals, each client request is executed as a single transaction. For each transaction a "marker" is inserted in a shared database. The new primary will look for this marker during failover in order to ensure exactly once execution of each client request. In this case, the database is a single point of failure. [6] applies this technique in a J2EE environment.

In contrast to aforementioned approaches, our proposed replicated cache provides both scalability and availability and avoids that the shared database becomes a single point of failure and a bottleneck.

[18] also explores middle-tier caching. The authors propose a freshness approach for data consistency in which inconsistency is bounded to miss a maximum number of update transactions (termed freshness). This consistency is very relaxed and contrasts sharply with the strong consistency provided by our approach. The simulation performed in the paper is evaluated with an ad-hoc benchmark. Our approach provides a high level of consistency via snapshot isolation and it is a real implementation evaluated with an industrial benchmark.

[19] studies different approaches for providing consistent caching in dynamic web applications. This approach shares the same strong consistency goal as our multi-version cache. The main difference lies in that our approach also provides scalability.

Clustering (replication) is a facility provided by many commercial J2EE application servers. However, current approaches focus on the replication of SFSBs and rely on a shared database. This is the case of JBoss open source J2EE application server [20], Oracle9iAS [21], WebLogic clustering [22] and WebSphere 6.0 [23]. The state of SFSBs is multicast to the rest of the replicas after each method invocation. JBoss Cache is a replicated transactional cache for entity beans with a shared database [24]. It provides two ways to maintain data consistency: replication and invalidation. With replication, every entity bean in the cache is replicated to the rest of the replicas at the end of a transaction. That includes all data read by the transaction, which may be a huge amount of data. If the invalidation policy is used, only the primary keys of the entity beans are sent. Then, these entity beans are invalidated in the cache of the rest of the replicas, which must read the entity beans from the database. Moreover, there is a two-phase-commit protocol (2PC) in order to commit a transaction resulting in a very heavy-weight protocol. This approach only provides availability of the application server tier, and does not provide scalability, unlike our replicated cache.

8   Conclusions

We have presented a replicated multi-version cache that achieves integral replication of multi-tier systems. The replication protocol takes into account both the application server and the database encapsulating the replication logic within the application server. This enables the use of off-the-shelf databases. The replicated multi-version cache scales even for update workloads, and takes advantage of modern snapshot-isolation databases such as Oracle and PostgreSQL. The implementation is based on a commercial J2EE application server, JOnAS. A thorough evaluation has been performed using an industrial benchmark, SPECjAppServer, and the results have demonstrated the good scalability of the approach.

References

1. Enterprise Grid Alliance: EGA Reference Model (2005)
2. Leff, A., Rayfield, J.T.: Improving application throughput with enterprise javabeans caching. In: ICDCS 2003. International Conference on Distributed Systems (2003)
3. Bull: JOnAS Clustering, https://wiki.objectweb.org/jonas/Wiki.jsp?page=JOnASClustering
4. Frølund, S., Guerraoui, R.: Implementing e-transactions with asynchronous replication. IEEE Trans. Parallel Distributed Systems 12(2), 133–146 (2001)
5. Frølund, S., Guerraoui, R.: e-transactions: End-to-end reliability for three-tier architectures. IEEE Trans. Software Engineering 28(4), 378–395 (2002)
6. Wu, H., Kemme, B., Maverick, V.: Eager Replication for Stateful J2EE Servers. In: DOA 2004. Proc. of Int. Symp. on Distributed Objects and Applications, pp. 1376–1394 (2004)
7. Wu, H., Kemme, B.: Fault-tolerance for stateful application servers in the presence of advanced transactions patterns. In: SRDS 2005. Proc. of the Int. Symp. on Reliable Distributed Systems, pp. 95–108 (2005)
8. Kemme, B., Jimenez, R., Patiño, M., Salas, J.: Exactly once interaction in a multi-tier architecture. In: VLDB DIDDR Workshop (2005)
9. Narasimhan, P., Moser, L.E., Melliar-Smith, P.M.: Eternal - a component-based framework for transparent fault-tolerant CORBA. Software: Practice and Experience 32(8) (2002)
10. Zhao, W., Moser, L.E., Melliar-Smith, P.M.: Unification of Transactions and Replication in Three-Tier Architectures Based on CORBA. IEEE Transactions on Dependable and Secure Computing 2(1), 20–33 (2005)
11. Berenson, H., Bernstein, P., Gray, J., Melton, J., O'Neil, E., O'Neil, P.: A critique of ANSI SQL isolation levels. In: ACM SIGMOD Conference, pp. 1–10. ACM Press, New York (1995)
12. SPEC: SPECjAppServer 2004 Benchmark (2004), http://www.spec.org/jAppServer/
13. Sun Microsystems: Java 2 Platform Enterprise Edition v1.4 (2003)
14. Chockler, G.V., Keidar, I., Vitenberg, R.: Group communication specifications: A comprehensive study. ACM Computer Surveys 33(4) (2001)
15. Perez-Sorrosal, F., Patiño-Martínez, M., Jiménez-Peris, R., Vuckovic, J.: Highly Available Long Running Transactions and Activities for J2EE Applications. In: ICDCS. Proc. of the IEEE Int. Conf. on Distributed Computing Systems (2006)
16. JGroups: A Toolkit for Reliable Multicast Communication, http://www.jgroups.org
17. OMG: Fault Tolerant CORBA. Object Management Group (2000)
18. Bernstein, P.A., Fekete, A., Guo, H., Ramakrishnan, R., Tamma, P.: Relaxed-currency serializability for middle-tier caching and replication. In: SIGMOD Conference, pp. 599–610. ACM Press, New York (2006)
19. Attar, M., Ozsu, M.T.: Alternative architectures and protocols for providing strong consistency in dynamic web applications. WWW Journal 9(3), 215–251 (2006)
20. The JBoss Group: JBoss Application Server, http://www.jboss.org
21. Oracle: Oracle9iAS Containers for J2EE. EJBs Developer's Guide, Rel. 2 (9.0.4) (2003)
22. BEA Systems: WebLogic Server 7.0. Programming WebLogic Enterprise JavaBeans (2005)
23. IBM: WebSphere 6 Application Server Network Deployment (2005)
24. The JBoss Group: JBoss Cache, http://labs.jboss.com/jbosscache/

CLASP: *Collaborating, Autonomous Stream Processing Systems*

Michael Branson[1], Fred Douglis[2], Brad Fawcett[1], Zhen Liu[2], Anton Riabov[2], and Fan Ye[2]

[1] IBM Systems and Technology Group, Rochester, MN USA
[2] IBM T.J. Watson Research Center, Hawthorne, NY USA

Abstract. There are currently a number of streaming data analysis systems in research or commercial operation. These systems are generally large-scale distributed systems, but each system operates in isolation, under the control of one administrative authority. We are developing middleware that permits autonomous or semi-autonomous streaming analysis systems (called "sites") to interoperate, providing them opportunities for data access, performance improvements, and reliability far exceeding that available in a single system. Unique characteristics of our system include an architecture for the management of multiple cooperation paradigms depending on the degree of trust and dependencies among the participating sites; a multisite planner that converts user-specified declarative queries into specifications of distributed jobs; and a mechanism for automatic recovery of site failures by redispatching failed pieces of a distributed job. We evaluate our architecture via experiments on a running prototype, and the results demonstrate the advantages of multisite cooperation: collaborative jobs that share resources, even across only a few sites, can produce results 50% faster than independent execution, and jobs on failed sites can be recovered within a few seconds.

Keywords: System S, streaming data analysis, Grid computing, Virtual Organizations, planning.

1 Introduction

Data stream processing systems take continuous streams of input data, process that data in certain ways, and produce ongoing results. There are currently a number of data stream processing systems in research [1,2,3,4] or commercial [5] operation. These systems are generally large-scale distributed systems, but each system operates in isolation, under the control of one administrative authority. Generally speaking, data that are brought into one such system are available to any application running on the system, and similarly any data created by one application are immediately available to other applications. This sharing is conducive to improving performance and scalability through the synergy of overlapping queries within one system [4,6]. However, the scale and functionality of an individual system can still be limited when facing extreme data rates (e.g.,

R. Cerqueira and R.H. Campbell (Eds.): Middleware 2007, LNCS 4834, pp. 348–367, 2007.

telemetry from radio telescopes [7]) or complex environments (e.g., supporting real-time disaster response). Additionally, resources (such as input data streams) that are available to one system are inaccessible to other systems.

In this paper we describe a middleware for Collaborating, Autonomous Stream Processing systems (**CLASP**). It sits above separate data stream processing systems and enables these systems to cooperate. We assume that each system, which we call a *site* in the larger cooperative environment, is at least partly autonomous. Thus the extent to which different sites cooperate is a matter of policy, determined by the administrators of each of the sites involved.

CLASP allows sites to benefit in several respects. They can share data sources that were owned and available individually. Thus a site can access a much wider spectrum of data input, greatly increasing the breadth of its analysis. They can share *derived* streams, which are processed results of existing applications, thus avoiding duplicating processing done by other sites and improving efficiency. They can help each other absorb any sudden increase in workload or decrease in resources by rebalancing processing across sites. They can also improve the reliability of job execution by recovering jobs from failed sites.

The middleware has been designed and prototyped in the context of System S [8], a project within IBM Research to enable sophisticated stream processing using arbitrary application logic (rather than relational algebra operations such as used in several other streaming analysis systems [1,2,3]). Although some details like application interfaces are specific to System S, the architecture itself is generic enough for the interoperation of streaming systems of other kinds.

We make several contributions in this paper. We analyze what functions are needed for stream processing sites to collaborate and propose an architecture that provides them. We extend the traditional Virtual Organization [9] (VO) concept to allow sites to form different VO structures based on the degree of mutual trust and coordination. We implement the architecture on a representative streaming system (System S) to demonstrate its feasibility and evaluate the benefits sites can gain through real testbeds and applications.

The rest of the paper is organized as follows. The next section describes System S in greater detail. Policies governing site interaction follow in Section 3. The architecture of **CLASP** is described in Section 4. Section 5 reports experimental results using a real testbed and application. The paper finishes with related work and conclusions.

2   System S

The goal of System S is to extract important information from voluminous amounts of unstructured and *mostly* irrelevant data. Example applications of such a system include analyzing financial markets (predicting stock value by processing streams of real-world events) [5], detecting patterns of fraudulent insurance claims, supporting responses to disasters such as Hurricane Katrina (based on vehicle movement, available supplies and recovery operations), or processing sensor data such as telemetry from radio telescopes [7] or volcanic activity [10].

We summarize the architecture of System S as a representative of streaming systems and describe some of its key components:

User Interface (UI) Users pose *inquiries* to the system through a front end to answer certain high-level queries. For example, "Show me where all bottled water is in the hurricane area." After the raw data have been processed by application logic (e.g., filtered, joined, and analyzed), results are passed back to the UI via data streams, where they can be presented to the user for further exploitation.

Inquiry Service (INQ) accepts specifications of the desired final results in a format called Inquiry Specification Language (ISL), which depicts the semantic meaning of the final results and specifies user preferences such as which data sources to include or exclude [11]. Given an inquiry, a *Planner* subcomponent [12] automatically composes data sources and processing in the form of jobs to produce desired results. It then submits such jobs to the Job Management component for execution.

Job Management (JMN) A job in System S is a set of interconnected *Processing Elements* (PEs), which process incoming stream objects to produce outgoing stream objects that are routed to the appropriate PE or storage. The PEs can perform stateless transformation or much more complicated stateful processing. System S reuses PEs among different applications when possible to avoid redundant processing.

Stream Processing Core (SPC) manages the execution of PEs [13,8]. It supports the transport of streams consisting of Stream Data Objects between PEs and into persistent storage. It also provides adaptive connectivity and fine-grained scheduling of communicating applications.

With the exception of INQ, these components map reasonably closely to other data stream analysis systems and are used here as a representative example. INQ is, by comparison, unique to System S: other systems do not have such automatic application composition capability and jobs are usually hand-crafted.

Each System S site runs an instance of each of these system components, possibly as a distributed and fault-tolerant service [14]. Each site may belong to and be managed by a distinct organization; administrators who manage one site generally have no control over another site. Collaboration among multiple sites is thus similar to Grid Computing [9]: sites share resources but retain substantial local autonomy.

As with the Grid, sites that want to collaborate for common goals and benefits can negotiate and form *Virtual Organizations* (VOs) [9]. However, there exist unique requirements in the streaming context, including the need for higher degrees of scalability and various administrative relationships among sites. Section 3 describes how we address these issues.

3   Virtual Organizations and Common Interest Policies

Sites that want to collaborate can form VOs. The members of a VO formalize their permissible interoperations as a *Common Interest Policy* (CIP), which specifies how they may share various types of resources and processing. VOs can be either *Federated* or *Cooperative.*

A Federated VO has an appointed leader site that assumes a coordination role and is able to exert a level of control over the other sites. This VO is appropriate when the sites share a common set of goal(s) that they want to achieve, or are all subject to a common authority. It allows the VO Lead to optimize resource and processing usage for the common good of the VO.

In a Cooperative VO, there is no central point of authority. VO members interact as peers of each other; they are independent and may have separate agendas. They may interoperate out of altruism, giving access to some resources freely, or they may charge a cost for access (cost could be monetary or credits in some sort of virtual economy).

VOs may have different relationships with each other. A whole VO can be included hierarchically as a member of another larger VO [15,16]. This allows sites to scale up for wide scope of collaboration. Two or more VOs may have common members which belong to these VOs simultaneously. The kinds of resources the common members share within each of these overlapping VOs, however, can be completely different. The exact resource sharing within the VO is specified by its CIP terms.

3.1   CIP Terms and Agreements

A CIP contains terms that dictate resource sharing, such as:

- Which set of data streams and locally stored data can be shared by which other remote sites. The set can be defined based on attributes such as the data type or data rate.
- Which set of processing resources can be used to run jobs from which other sites; which kinds of PEs coming from which other sites will the local site execute.
- In times of failure, which sites will perform what function (e.g., monitor, backup data, recover jobs) of the failure recovery process.

The CIP is known by all the members in a VO. By specifying these terms, VO members advertise resources that others may request to use. However, it does not guarantee access, since multiple members may request a resource that can only be used exclusively. Therefore, a VO member must reserve a resource in advance by establishing an *agreement* with the providing member to secure access to the resource for some duration.

Besides defining the kinds of resource sharing that are possible in a VO, the CIP also specifies what parameters are associated with an agreement (such as quality of service levels, costs, and limitations on the resource usage). Once established, this agreement must then be referenced when accessing this resource. The agreement's terms and conditions, along with costs and penalties, will be continuously monitored by some auditing functions at both System S sites providing and consuming the resource.

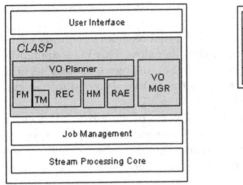

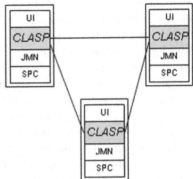

(a) CLASP architecture   (b) Multiple collaborating sites

Fig. 1. CLASP architecture includes several components. They provide the functions needed for sites to collaborate.

This notion of agreement shares similarities with the WS-Agreement specification from the Grid community [17]. For System S, a portion of a CIP term serves as the analogy to the WS-Agreement Agreement Factory and provides the creation template that is needed for creating an agreement between the provider and consumer of the resource. More details are presented in Section 4.2.

4   Architecture

4.1   Overview

Figure 1(a) shows the detailed CLASP architecture on one site. UI, JMN and SPC are single-site components and CLASP is between the UI and JMN. Multiple sites can work together through the interaction of their CLASP middleware (illustrated in Figure 1(b)). CLASP has a number of components providing various functions to support collaboration.

VO Manager deals with the construction of VOs and decisions on permissible cross-site resource usage; Section 4.2 provides details.

VO Planner produces plans utilizing resources from within the VO and partitions a global plan into a distributed job containing multiple subjobs. It is described further in Section 4.3.

Resource Awareness Engine (RAE) provides information about available resources to the VO Planner; see Section 4.4.

Remote Execution Coordinator (REC) extends JMN to the multi-site case by deploying distributed jobs submitted by the VO Planner. Each subjob in a distributed job may run on a different site (elaborated upon in Section 4.5).

Tunneling Manager (TM) manages tunnels that transmit streams from PEs on one site to PEs on another site (details in Section 4.5).

VO Failover Management (FM) handles site monitoring, arrangement of backup sites, and recovery of jobs after site failures. Failover is discussed elsewhere [18] and summarized in Section 4.6.

VO Heterogeneity Management (HM) is intended to manage the mapping or translation of data types, database schemas, security and privacy labels, and similar features between sites; see Section 4.7 for a brief discussion.

4.2   VO Management

The CLASP prototype supports the formation and management of VOs by using text-based CIP definition files. Each VO has a corresponding CIP file, containing three types of terms: VO type, membership, and sharing. Every CIP file must indicate whether the VO is federated or cooperative. For every member of the VO, there must be a membership term, specifying either a site member or a VO member. The CIP file may contain numerous sharing terms. Each sharing term defines what resources can be shared between which two sites, with attributes and their values, agreement creation parameters (separated by semicolons). Below is an example sharing term:

2;2;siteA;siteB;MONITOR_SITE_FOR_FAILURE;SHOULD;
COST:10:INITIATION_COST:100;
SITE_TO_MONITOR:MANDATORY:MIN_MONITORING_FREQ:OPTIONAL:
ACTION_UPON_FAILURE:MANDATORY

This term has a type (2, resource sharing), an index (2) of this term among those of the same type, identifiers of the sites involved (provider is siteA and consumer is siteB), what resource is being shared (site monitoring capability), access advice (SHOULD), attributes such as cost and initiation cost (10, 100), and what parameters are available when the term is used as an template to create an agreement, including which parameters are mandatory (e.g. action upon failure) or optional (e.g minimum monitoring frequency). We are currently moving to XML, which will provide a more structured framework for this specification.

We expect human administrators to negotiate and install CIP terms on their sites. To create a VO, one site's VO management component parses the CIP file and contacts other sites' VO management components about the creation of the new VO. When there are hierarchical VO members, all descendants of VO members are notified recursively about the new VO. Once a VO is in place, components can establish agreements according to the CIP terms. A component (such as the Failover Manager) does this by first querying its local VO Management for the set of candidate CIP terms that are applicable to its requirements.

For example, if it needs to find possible providers in a VO to monitor a particular site, it submits a query specifying this capability. VO Management will then search and return the matching CIP terms within the specified VO. The FM component will then analyze the terms and conditions of the returned candidate CIP terms and select the "best" one, e.g. a site that can monitor at a small cost. After filling in the creation parameters such as monitoring frequency, it calls local VO Management, which will in turn contact the VO Management on the provider site to establish the agreement. That VO Management component must contact the providing component and gain its commitment to support the agreement. Once established, the agreement will be referenced when making the inter-site request. The agreement is terminated after its lifetime, or explicitly by the requester.

4.3   VO Planner

The VO Planner is unique to System S. It automatically produces plans that utilize data sources and PEs from all sites in the VO. It accepts inquiries that describe the semantics of desired final results in Inquiry Specification Language (ISL) [11]. The Planner reads in the semantic description of data sources and the required input and output streams of PEs, and uses a branch and bound search algorithm [12] to find plans that can produce the final results.

Given one inquiry, the Planner produces multiple distributed plans in the form of flow graphs, consisting of interconnected PEs and data sources. These plans have different performance/cost tradeoffs and can be presented to the user, who can decide which one to deploy. The planner then partitions the selected plan into multiple sub-plans, each of which is a subjob assigned to one member site for execution. The planner also inserts tunneling PEs into subjobs; each pair of sink and source tunneling PEs transport one stream across sites. Finally, a distributed job that contains multiple subjobs, each of which contains a normal job (for data processing) and multiple tunneling PE jobs (for data transportation), is produced and submitted for execution.

Plan composition within the VO Planner is implemented using a plan solver module that operates on an abstract formulation expressed in Stream Processing Planning Language (SPPL) [12]. SPPL is designed to enable efficient planning in stream processing by introducing language primitives that natively model streams. The semantics of data sources and PEs are represented using OWL ontology [19] files. Since the semantic descriptions are relatively static, these files do not change frequently. When a site joins a VO, it can copy these files over to the VO Planner's site.

4.4   Resource Awareness Engine

Resource awareness refers to the propagation of information about data sources, PEs, and other kinds of resources among multiple collaborating sites. Sites need such remote resource information for operations such as planning, failure recovery. Such information may be stored in relational or semantic data stores, shared memory, or text files. The component that facilitates information propagation among sites is the *Resource Awareness Engine* (RAE).

We intend to use ROADS [20], a resource discovery service, as the basis for this component. ROADS allows multiple sites to query and search for resource information from others. The RAE components on these sites will form a tree hierarchy, whose exact topology depends on the trust and administrative relationships among sites. Each site's RAE will publish its resource information in a highly condensed summary format. The summaries from child sites will be aggregated by a site's RAE and propagated further up the tree. Thus each RAE will have the aggregated summary about the resource information of all its descendants, and the root RAE obtains the summary of all resource information.

When a site needs to query resource information, it sends a query to the root RAE. The root will evaluate the query against the summaries of its child branches, and find out which branches have the required resource information. It will forward the query down these branches. Each RAE in the hierarchy will follow the same process. Finally the RAEs possessing matching resource information will return it to the requesting site. The details about how summaries are produced and queries are evaluated against them can be found in [20].

For the prototype described in this paper, the RAE is integrated directly with the VO Planner. That is, the Planner is given a configuration file with the description of data sources in each site in its VO. Then as it generates new distributed jobs, the Planner augments its view of available derived streams to include the newly created streams on each site, which it can reuse when needed.

4.5 Distributed Execution

The Remote Execution Coordinator (REC) is responsible for the execution of distributed jobs. The VO planner submits a distributed job to the REC of the *owner* site, which is the one from which the inquiry was received. This REC will coordinate the execution of the subjobs, including their recovery upon failures. The REC dispatches the subjobs to the RECs on the corresponding execution sites, as specified by the planner. An example is illustrated in Figure 2. Site 3 is the owner site and its REC executes the third subjob and dispatches two other subjobs to Sites 1 and 2 for execution. The REC at the owner site maintains a subjob table about which subjobs are running at which other site. The table is used for recovery of subjobs on failed sites.

The REC executing a subjob first parses its Job Description Language (JDL) to identify one normal job, and multiple tunneling PE jobs. One thread is launched to handle each of them. The thread customizes the JDL, such as assigning a host for each PE. Then it deploys the job through its local Job Management. For a source PE job, the REC needs to contact the local Tunneling Manager responsible for assigning the network address and port on which the source PE will be listening for incoming connections. It deploys the source PE job and reports the assigned network location to the REC at the owner site. For a sink PE job, the REC needs to query the REC of the owner site for the network location of the corresponding source PE. Then it configures and deploys the sink PE job.

4.6 Failure Recovery

Failover in **CLASP** has been described elsewhere [18], with emphasis on the problem of identifying which sites are most appropriate for failure recovery in a large-scale VO with many available alternatives. Here we describe the implementation for detecting and handling failures.

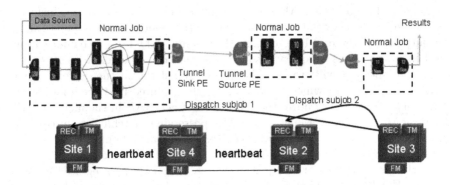

Fig. 2. Execution of a distributed job consisting 3 subjobs. Owner Site 3 executes one subjob, and dispatches two subjobs to Site 1 and 2 for execution. Site 4 monitors Sites 1 and 2.

The FM at the owner site arranges the failover monitoring for sites executing subjobs. By querying CIP terms, it finds which sites can monitor the liveness of execution sites, using periodic heartbeat messages. When an execution site fails, the FM at a monitoring site detects the failure and notifies the owner site. The REC at the owner site examines the subjob table and finds out which subjobs were running on the failed site. It then dispatches these subjobs to a new execution site, selected from candidate sites returned from VO Management. Algorithms by Rong, et al. [18] can be used for the selection. The new execution site will deploy the subjob.

Although executing normal jobs is straightforward, re-establishing broken tunnels needs special attention. To recover tunnel sink jobs, the REC at the new execution site queries the network location for corresponding tunnel source jobs, then configures and executes the tunnel sink job. The recovery of tunnel source jobs is a bit complex, as the old tunnel sink job might still be sending data to the failed site. The REC deploys such jobs and notifies the owner site about the new network location. The FM at the owner site will inform other execution sites to terminate tunnel sink jobs that send streams to the failed site. These tunnel sink jobs will be restarted using the new network locations of recovered tunnel source jobs. During the above process, new agreements might be created for additional monitoring and execution.

We also envision recovering critical applications from failed sites, even when they run entirely within the site that fails. This will require advance registration of the jobs to resubmit, with an agreement with another site to monitor the site making the request and to restart the critical applications if needed.

4.7   Heterogeneity

Our current prototype assumes a homogeneous environment. In the more general case, each site may have differences in its operating environment. This heterogeneity can arise in the runtime environment, type system, security and privacy policies, user namespace, and other aspects.

The general approach to heterogeneity is through *mapping functions* and common base agreements. The CIPs that govern how sites interoperate must specify operations to perform to ensure consistency. Differences in data types will be handled through explicit conversion functions: for example, converting a nine-digit US ZIP code into a five-digit one would involve truncating the additional level of detail. For security, System S assumes lattice-based [21] secrecy and integrity policy models [22]. Each site will understand the format and implied relationships of security labels used by all sites; the access rights and restrictions encoded within a security label are uniformly applicable throughout all the sites. We will address operation in heterogeneous environments in the future.

5   Experimentation

5.1   Test Environment

We have implemented the **CLASP** architecture in Java (with the exception of the tunneling PEs, written in C++). The prototype currently has about 40,000 lines of code. We use a testbed that consists of Linux SUSE 9 machines. Each machine has 2 Xeon 3.06 GHz CPUs, 800MHz, 512KB L2 cache, 4G memory and 80G Hard drive. They are connected through a 1Gbps LAN. Multiple machines can be grouped together as a System S site, which **CLASP** runs above. For most experiments, we use a Federated VO that contains four sites, one of which is a backup site, while the others are execution sites.

The goal of experiments is two-fold. 1) Quantify the benefits collaborating sites can gain compared to operating individually. We use the total number of produced results as the main metric. 2) Benchmark the time overhead of basic operations of CLASP, such as planning, job submission, and failure recovery. This gives us a basic understanding of the efficiency of the system.

To evaluate our system, we use an application we entitle "Enterprise Global Service" (EGS). EGS is intended for enterprises to monitor the quality of service of their customer service personnel. Customers talk with service representatives through a corporate VoIP network. A business analyst can issue various inquiries to examine the status of employee services. These inquiries include: find the location and "courtesy level" of a particular employee, find the satisfaction level of a particular customer, etc. We use a VoIP traffic generator [23] to produce the VoIP streams between employees and customers. Each inquiry's job contains about 15 PEs and a job produces results continuously during its lifetime.

Figure 3 shows an example of two distributed jobs deployed in the VO. Each of the two jobs (location of SHIMEI, location of EMILY) has three subjobs, running on Sites 1, 2 and 3. Roughly speaking, these jobs work as follows: A source PE pulls in all streams from the traffic generator. An annotator PE extracts Real Time Protocol fields and turns them into SDO attributes, then a value-based filter PE removes background noise. A speaker detection PE detects the identities of persons; location/courtesy/satisfaction analyzing PEs produce

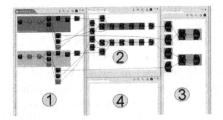

Fig. 3. Two distributed jobs are deployed within a VO of 4 sites. Each job has 3 subjobs that run on Sites 1, 2 and 3. Tunnel PEs connect subjobs across sites.

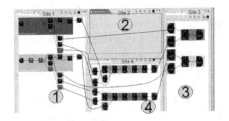

Fig. 4. After Site 2 fails, the two subjobs running on Site 2 are recovered on Site 4. Tunnel PEs are reconnected so that the two distributed jobs continue producing results.

the location, courtesy or satisfaction of persons. Their results are joined and then filtered based on which person the inquiry is looking for. The final results are reported and shown in a GUI.

Among all the PEs, location/courtesy/satisfaction analyzing PEs are the most computing-intensive. Beyond the mimimum processing required to perform the required tasks, the amount of extra processing they perform on each incoming SDO, defined as the *load level*, can be tuned. In the experiments we vary the load level for them to evaluate the system behavior under different computation intensities; zero load level corresponds to normal processing.

Figure 4 shows what happens after Site 2 fails. Site 4 detects the failure and notifies the owning site, Site 3, which recovers the failed subjobs on Site 4. The tunnel PEs are reconfigured such that cross-site data streams reconnect to the same subjobs recovered at the new site.

5.2   Result Production

We measure the performance of our prototype in several respects. We first compare the number of results obtained by collaborating sites in a VO, or using sites individually, under the same inquiry load. We produce three sets of inquiry load. Within each set, there are 6 inquiries submitted to each of the three execution sites in a VO. An individual site uses its own data sources and resources to produce plans and run the jobs. The sharing of streams is confined within each site. When the same 18 inquiries are submitted to the VO, the VO planner produces jobs that can reuse remote derived streams across sites.

Due to the sharing of more common processing, jobs running in a VO will generally produce results more efficiently. The more common processing across sites, the higher the savings by sharing existing processing. The three sets of inquiries correspond to different degrees of sharing (shown in Table 1). In the first set, the 6 inquiries (2 location, 2 courtesy, 2 satisfaction) submitted to each site are the same. When a new instance of the same inquiry is submitted, only additional tunneling and result reporting PEs are needed. They correspond to the maximum degree of cross-site sharing.

Table 1. The 3 sets of inquiries used in the experiments **loc** refers to getting the location of an employee; **cor** obtains their courtesy; and **sat** computes customer satisfaction

Set	Site 1	Site 2	Site 3
Set 1	loc SHIMEI	loc SHIMEI	loc SHIMEI
maximum	loc FAYE	loc FAYE	loc FAYE
reuse	cor SHIMEI	cor SHIMEI	cor SHIMEI
	cor FAYE	cor FAYE	cor FAYE
	sat SHIMEI	sat SHIMEI	sat SHIMEI
	sat FAYE	sat FAYE	sat FAYE
Set 2	loc SHIMEI	cor LEONARD	sat SHIMEI
minimum	loc FAYE	cor NORMAN	sat LEONARD
reuse	loc ENRIQUE	cor MARK	sat MARK
	loc NAOMI	cor FAYE	sat EMILY
	loc LEONARD	cor ENRIQUE	sat NAOMI
	loc EMILY	cor SHIMEI	sat FAYE
Set 3	loc ENRIQUE	cor FAYE	sat FAYE
average	sat EMILY	sat NORMAN	cor MARK
reuse	cor NAOMI	sat FAYE	sat LEONARD
	sat NORMAN	cor EMILY	sat NORMAN
	loc MARCIA	cor NORMAN	loc SHIMEI
	sat SHIMEI	loc MARCIA	cor LEONARD

In the second case, each site has a distinct set: Site 1 has only location inquiries, Site 2 only courtesy inquiries, and Site 3 only satisfaction inquiries. This corresponds the minimum degree of sharing. Inquiries of different sites can share only a few PEs such as the source PE and background noise reduction PE. They have to do the most computing-intensive processing (finding location/courtesy/satisfaction) by themselves. The third set is a middle ground between the two. Each site has a random mixture of inquiries, including different types and person names. The degree of sharing is less than the first but greater than the second set. This is likely what would happen in reality. For each set, we vary the computation intensity of jobs by changing the load level. We let jobs run for 2 minutes, and average the results over five runs.

Figure 5 compares the total number of results of all the 18 jobs in set 1 when running in the VO or individually. They produce about the same amount when the load level is zero. As the load level increases, running in the VO can produce as much as 50% more results, because jobs can tap into the processed results across sites and avoid duplicating common processing. For those running at an individual site, however, they can only tap into processing within the same site. We also examined the number of results produced by each individual job, when running in a VO or one site. The phenomena is similar and we do not elaborate due to space limitations.

Figure 6 compares the number of results for set 2. Jobs running in a VO produce slightly fewer results than in set 1. The reason is that the cost paid for sharing

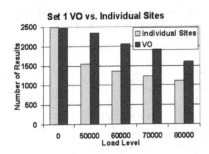

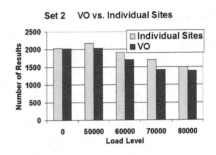

Fig. 5. The total number of results produced by the 18 jobs in set 1, running at individual sites or within the VO

Fig. 6. The total number of results of all the 18 jobs for Set 2, running at individual sites or within the VO

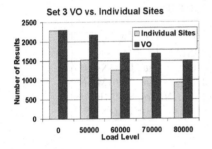

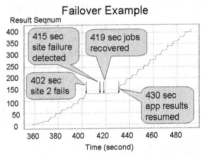

Fig. 7. The total number of results for all the 18 jobs for Set 3, running in VO or individual sites

Fig. 8. The job sequence number as a function of time. Once detected, failed jobs are recovered in about 3.5s.

offsets the benefits. In set 2, each site has only one type of job (location, courtesy or satisfaction). Jobs at different sites do not share computation-intensive processing. Thus running in a VO does not reduce the amount of processing much.

On the other hand, there is a cost to pay for a VO. Extra tunneling PEs are one factor. Another is a synchronization effect. A PE consuming SDOs slowly may cause its producing PE to wait since reliable transport is used to send SDOs between PEs. Other consuming PEs receiving SDOs from the same producing PE will have to wait as well. Thus one job that runs more slowly affects other jobs when they share input streams. Set 2 is the worst case where little processing can be shared across sites, thus the savings are not enough to cover the cost.

Figure 7 shows the comparison for set 3. The result is quite similar to that of set 1: running in a VO produces more results. This similarity is because each site has a random sequence of jobs that contains all different types and person names. The common processing across different sites is significant. The VO allows jobs to reuse the processing across site, thus producing results more efficiently.

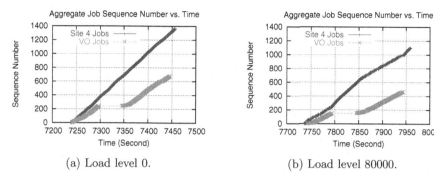

(a) Load level 0.   (b) Load level 80000.

Fig. 9. The aggregate result sequence number for jobs running in a VO and on Site 4 with varying load levels

5.3   Failover

Sites in a VO can backup and recover jobs for each other when some of them fail. Figure 8 shows the details about one VO job's result sequence number change for failover. Around time 402.5s a site fails, then after another 13s the failure is detected. (The detection time depends on the heartbeat interval, which can be set to achieve the desired detection speed.) In about 3.5s the failed jobs are recovered. Since the job needs some time to rebuild the lost state, it resumes producing results 10s later.

We use the number of results produced to demonstrate the advantage of failover. We run three types of jobs on Sites 1-3 in a VO. Site 4 is monitoring Sites 1-3. Upon the failure of any of them, Site 4 will recover subjobs running on the failed site. Site 4 also runs three types of jobs on itself. We let all jobs run for one minute, then we kill Site 1. After jobs are recovered on Site 4, we let them run for another two minutes.

Figure 9(a) shows the *aggregate sequence number* as a function of time, for all VO jobs and all Site 4 jobs, when the load level is zero. At any time, the aggregate sequence number for a collection of jobs is defined as the total number of results produced by these jobs up to that time. Starting around time 7240s, all jobs are producing results. At around 7300s, Site 1 fails. The aggregate sequence number for VO jobs stays flat, while for Site 4 jobs it is still increasing. After Site 4 detects Site 1's failure and recovers its subjobs (around 7350s), the VO jobs start to produce results. Since the load level is low, there is sufficient processing capacity on Site 4 to accommodate the failed subjobs without affecting those of its own. The speed of sequence number increase for Site 4 after failover remains about the same as before.

Figure 9(b) shows the same comparison under load level 80000. The sequence numbers increase more slowly. Eventually Site 4's and VO jobs produce about 1100/450 results, less than the 1400/650 results when the load level is 0. Although jobs for both Site 4 and VO produce less results, it is still much better than without failover (the VO jobs would not produce any more results).

Another interesting observation is that Site 4's jobs produce results more quickly between 7800-7850s. This is due to the lack of any synchronization effect during recovery. Since all jobs receive input streams from the same data source, more jobs will slow down the producing rate of the data source. When VO jobs have failed but not recovered, only Site 4's jobs are consuming data.

5.4 Planner

Plan Solver Performance. We measure the time it takes the VO planner to find plans that produce the desired final results. The Stream Processing Planning Language (SPPL) solver we use to implement the VO planner has been evaluated within one single site. It is scalable with large numbers of PEs, source and plan sizes [12]. The VO planner adds tunneling PEs to plans and optimizes plans for distributed metrics such as minimizing cross-site bandwidth consumption, calculated using bandwidth consumption for PEs and sources that produce cross-site streams.

We run the VO planner on a 3GHz Intel Pentium 4 PC with 4 GB memory. We use a setting that includes 5 sites. Data sources are uniformly randomly assigned to a site and each data source is available at that site only. PEs are available on all sites. This is reasonable because PE code can be easily transfered and installed at other sites (assuming they are secure and trusted). PEs and sources are given randomly constructed descriptions of their inputs and outputs, and random output bandwidth.

Since there could be many PEs that are not relevant to an inquiry, the processing graphs are likely to be of relatively small sizes. However, the planner still takes time to search through plans including irrelevant PEs. To model this scenario, we vary the number of PEs per site from about 72 to 1500, most of which are not relevant to the specified goal. To ensure plans that produce a given final result do exist, we generate random global processing graphs first and use their final results as input to the planner. There exist only 2 candidate plans of 6 nodes each (excluding tunneling PEs) for the goal. We average the results over 10 runs.

The planning time as a function of the number of PEs per site is presented in Table 2. We can see that it takes the planner less than one second to find the optimal plan for sites having up to about 160 PEs. Even in the case of 1500 PEs, it is only a little bit over 8s. Since many streaming jobs are expected to run for a long time, spending a few seconds to find an optimized one is reasonable.

We further evaluate the time to the first plan as a function of the plan size, i.e., the number of PEs in the plan (see Table 3). In all cases the planner can find a reasonably good plan within about a second. In general, the larger the plan size, the greater the time it takes. However, this time is not completely monotonic with the size of the plan, because the search time depends on the structure of individual plans as well.

Since proving optimality is a more difficult problem, it takes long time to decide whether a discovered plan is optimal. However, empirical results show that plans found initially are close to optimal ones. In 10 randomly generated planning

Table 2. Planning times for optimal 6-PE plans, as a function of the number of PEs per site

Number of PEs per site	Time to Optimal Plan (s)
72	0.37
102	0.36
162	0.51
312	1.46
612	2.20
1512	8.39

Table 3. Planning times for the first plan, as a function of the total number of PEs in the plan

Number of PEs	Time to first plan (s)
5	0.17
10	0.592034
20	0.753005
40	0.680179
50	1.01968
100	0.966948

problems that require 6 PEs and sources in the plan, the solver considered on average 104 candidate plans. The first plan is found between the first 7.3% and 25% of the plan search time. This plan is within 1.2% of the optimal one, using a quality measure that combines an additive PE and source quality metric and inter-site bandwidth consumption.

Hence, when the search takes longer than several seconds, we terminate the search early and present the current plan for deployment assuming that it is close to the optimal. We leave further improvement on the scalability of the SPPL solver to future work.

Agreements-Driven Replanning. A prerequisite to successfully deploy a distributed job is that all agreements are established. To avoid incurring possible costs before job deployment, the planner does not establish agreements at planning time. Instead, agreements are established when the job is being deployed. If not all of the required agreements can be established, one must replan.

We have measured the time that replanning takes in the EGS application by distributing the job to 3 sites and configuring the sites to reject initial agreements. The planner then replans the jobs with higher priority (and possibly higher site-dependent execution budget). Replanning was performed 3 times before deployment, resulting in higher job priorities and different plan partitioning. The whole cycle requires less than 7s. Although in this case replanning happens completely automatically, the VO planner provides APIs for developing more sophisticated GUIs to allow human feedback when replanning is needed.

5.5   Job Deployment Time

To understand the responsiveness of the system, we also measure the time it takes to deploy a distributed job. This is from the submission of the JDL of a distributed job, to the dispatching of its subjobs to other sites, until finally all subjobs are up and ready to process data. We use the same JDLs as before and they each contain about 20 PEs (including tunneling PEs).

Figure 10 shows the detailed time breakdown for a distributed job, with three subjobs, each of which has two tunnel jobs and one normal job. For each subjob,

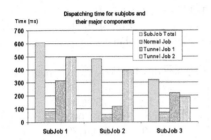

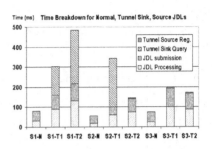

Fig. 10. The dispatching time details of a distributed job, from submission to finally it is deployed and ready to run

Fig. 11. The detailed breakdown of each subjob. Subjob 1 has two tunnel sink jobs, subjob 2 has one sink and one source, subjob 3 two sources.

a separate thread is launched to dispatch it to the corresponding site. Thus the overall time is dominated by the longest subjob. After a site receives a subjob, it processes the JDL first, then it launches one thread for each of the jobs: the normal job and the two tunnel jobs. The time for a subjob is in turn dominated by the job taking the longest time. From Figure 10, subjob 1 takes the most time, about 600ms. The other two subjobs take about 500ms and 400ms, respectively. Within each subjob, one tunnel job takes the longest time. The whole distributed job takes about 700ms.

Figure 11 shows the finer breakdown for each normal job and tunnel job. We find that the tunnel sink query takes the longest time. The reason is that, although a tunnel sink job can be deployed almost simultaneously as its tunnel source end, it has to query and wait for the tunnel source to register the listening IP address and port. Thus a tunnel sink is always deployed later than its source end. We plan to explore a "gateway" approach where multiple cross site streams can be multiplexed between a pair of gateway PEs to further improve the performance.

6   Related Work

CLASP has a strong relationship, yet significant differences, with two general areas of computing: Grid computing [9] and streaming data analysis [3,2,1]. With respect to Grid computing, a recent article [24] highlights the similarities between cooperative stream processing and Grid computing. They describe similar environments: "distributed, multidisciplinary, collaborative teams" that attack problems in a distributed fashion due to the nature of their various "intellectual, computational, data, and other resources." Indeed, our system adopts some Grid constructs, such as VOs. In addition, there has been substantial work in matchmaking between different organizations based on required capabilities (e.g., Liu, et al. [25] and the recent work on WS-Agreements [26,17]).

At the same time, there are a number of important differences. Our architecture supports multiple cooperation paradigms, including Federated and

Cooperative (peer-to-peer) VOs. It allows sites to collaborate more closely, with hierarchical layers of VOs to provide arbitrary scalability. This is suitable for complex stream processing that cannot be easily broken into smaller and similar pieces and requires complementary contributions from all sites. The distributed planning component of System S is significantly more sophisticated and flexible than the Grid models.

Borealis [3] is a distributed stream processing analysis system with a number of similarities to System S. It has explicit support for fault tolerance [27] as well as contracts to "sell" load between sites in a federated system [28]. **CLASP**, using System S, differs fundamentally from Borealis and other stream processing systems such as STREAM [1] and TelegraphCQ [2] in a number of aspects. First, although each such system itself can be distributed, there is no support for streaming systems belonging to different administrative authorities to work together. They cannot benefit from the sharing of data streams and processing to improve efficiency, reliability, or the breadth, depth and scale of analysis.

Second, System S supports generic application-specific processing rather than database operations— a more difficult problem due to higher complexity, development costs and times to completion [29]. System S has an Inquiry Specification Language that allows users to specify application declaratively at semantic level. This is very important to allow users focus on application level tasks, rather than deal with the complexity of finding the optimum set and interconnection of data sources and PEs.

7 Conclusions and Future Work

In this paper we have demonstrated that **CLASP**, our middleware for cooperating data stream processing sites, enables such sites to increase the scale, breadth, depth, and reliability of analysis beyond that available within a single site. Experiments with our prototype have demonstrated the performance benefits gained from reusing processing from other sites, as well as quantifying some of the overhead incurred in the system. There also exist other more qualitative benefits, such as access to remote data sources to broaden the breadth of analysis.

One of the important aspects we will investigate in the future is what mechanisms are needed to support security and trust. The current system works in a benign environment. When sites do not have full trust for each other, or some of them are selfish or even malicious, security checks should be enforced. In addition, as the system evolves, we will incorporate features such as fully dynamic resource awareness and support for heterogeneity.

We also plan to investigate the scalability of the system. Our testbed was a small number of sites, which is probably consistent with typical interoperating agreements one might expect from a system of this sort: in a real system, each site would itself be a very large-scale distributed system. Beyond that, we are currently experimenting with issues regarding large, multilateral agreements, particularly in competitive economic environments in which sites do not provide resources simply out of altruism.

Acknowledgments

We thank the anonymous referees, Lisa Amini, Nagui Halim, Anand Ranganathan, Bill Waller, and the rest of the System S team for helpful feedback on the design of **CLASP** and/or earlier drafts of this paper.

References

1. The STREAM Group: STREAM: The Stanford stream data manager. IEEE Data Engineering Bulletin 26(1) (2003)
2. Chandrasekaran, S., et al.: TelegraphCQ: Continuous dataflow processing for an uncertain world. In: Conference on Innovative Data Systems Research (2003)
3. Abadi, D.J., et al.: The design of the Borealis stream processing engine. In: CIDR 2005 - Second Biennial Conference on Innovative Data Systems Research (2005)
4. Pietzuch, P., et al.: Network-aware operator placement for stream-processing systems. In: ICDE 2006. Proc. the 22nd International Conference on Data Engineering (2006)
5. Streambase Systems, Inc.: Streambase (2007), http://www.streambase.com/
6. Repantis, T., Gu., X., Kalogeraki, V.: Synergy: Sharing-aware component composition for distributed stream processing systems. In: ACM/IFIP/USENIX 7th International Middleware Conference, pp. 322–341 (2006)
7. Risch, T., Koparanova, M., Thide, B.: High-performance GRID Database Manager for Scientific Data. In: WDAS-2002. Proceedings of 4th Workshop on Distributed Data & Structures (2002)
8. Jain, N., et al.: Design, implementation, and evaluation of the linear road benchmark on the stream processing core. In: SIGMOD 2006. 25th ACM SIGMOD International Conference on Management of Data, ACM Press, New York (2006)
9. Foster, I., Kesselman, C., Tuecke, S.: The anatomy of the Grid: Enabling scalable virtual organizations. In: Sakellariou, R., Keane, J.A., Gurd, J.R., Freeman, L. (eds.) Euro-Par 2001. LNCS, vol. 2150, Springer, Heidelberg (2001)
10. Werner-Allen, G., et al.: Deploying a Wireless Sensor Network on an Active Volcano. IEEE Internet Computing 10(2), 18–25 (2006)
11. Bouillet, E., et al.: A semantics-based middleware for utilizing heterogeneous sensor networks. In: Proceedings of the 3rd IEEE International Conference on Distributed Computing in Sensor Systems, pp. 174–188. IEEE Computer Society Press, Los Alamitos (2007)
12. Riabov, A., Liu, Z.: Scalable planning for distributed stream processing systems. In: Proceedings of ICAPS 2006 (2006)
13. Amini, L., et al.: Adaptive control of extreme-scale stream processing systems. In: Proceedings of ICDCS 2006 (2006)
14. Jacques-Silva, G., et al.: Towards autonomic fault recovery in system-s. In: Proceedings of the 4th IEEE International Conference on Autonomic Computing, IEEE Computer Society Press, Los Alamitos (2007)
15. Kim, K.H., Buyya, R.: Policy-based Resource Allocation in Hierarchical Virtual Organizations for Global Grids. In: SBAC-PAD 2006. Proceedings of the 18th International Symposium on Computer Architecture and High Performance Computing, pp. 36–46 (2006)
16. Branson, M., et al.: Autonomic operations in cooperative stream processing systems. In: Proceedings of the Second Workshop on Hot Topics in Autonomic Computing (2007)

17. Andrieux, A., et al.: Web Services Agreement Specification (WS-Agreement), Version 2006/07. GWD-R (Proposed Recommendation), Grid Resource Allocation Agreement Protocol (GRAAP) WGGRAAP-WG (2006)
18. Rong, B., et al.: Failure recovery in cooperative data stream analysis. In: ARES 2007. Proceedings of the Second International Conference on Availability, Reliability and Security, Vienna (2007)
19. W3C Recommendation: Web ontology language (OWL) (2004)
20. Yang, H., et al.: Resource discovery in federated systems with voluntary sharing (2007) (in submission)
21. Sandhu, R.: Lattice-based access control models. IEEE Computer (1993)
22. IBM: Security in System S (2006), http://domino.research.ibm.com/comm research_pro-jects.nsf/pages/system_s_security.index.html
23. Anderson, K.S., et al.: SWORD: Scalable and flexible workload generator for distributed data processing systems. In: The 37th Winter Simulation Conference, pp. 2109–2116 (2006)
24. Foster, I.T., Kesselman, C.: Scaling system-level science: Scientific exploration and IT implications. IEEE Computer 39(11), 31–39 (2006)
25. Liu, C., et al.: Design and evaluation of a resource selection framework for grid applications. In: Proceedings of the 11th IEEE Symposium on High-Performance Distributed Computing, IEEE Computer Society Press, Los Alamitos (2002)
26. Ludwig, H., Dan, A., Kearney, B.: Cremona: An Architecture and Library for Creation and Monitoring of WS-Agreements. In: ICSOC 2004. ACM International Conference on Service Oriented Computing, ACM Press, New York (2004)
27. Balazinska, M., Balakrishnan, H., Madden, S., Stonebraker, M.: Fault-Tolerance in the Borealis Distributed Stream Processing System. In: ACM SIGMOD Conf., Baltimore, MD, ACM Press, New York (2005)
28. Balazinska, M., Balakrishnan, H., Stonebraker, M.: Contract-based load management in federated distributed systems. In: Symposium on Network System Design and Implementation (2004)
29. Stonebraker, M., Çetintemel, U., Zdonik, S.B.: The 8 requirements of real-time stream processing. SIGMOD Record 34(4), 42–47 (2005)

A Policy Management Framework for Content-Based Publish/Subscribe Middleware

Alex Wun and Hans-Arno Jacobsen

University of Toronto
Toronto, Canada
{wun,jacobsen}@eecg.utoronto.ca

Abstract. Content-based Publish/Subscribe (CPS) is a powerful paradigm providing loosely-coupled, event-driven messaging services. Although the general CPS model is well-known, many features remain implementation specific because of different application requirements. Many of these requirements can be captured in policies that separate service semantics from system mechanisms, but no such policy framework currently exists in the CPS context. In this paper, we propose a novel policy model and framework for CPS systems that benefits from the scalability and expressiveness of existing CPS matching algorithms. In particular, we provide a reference implementation and several evaluation scenarios that demonstrate how our approach easily and dynamically enables features such as notification semantics, meta-events, security zoning, and CPS firewalls.

Keywords: Publish/Subscribe, Policy, Security, Configurability.

1 Introduction

To date, many publish/subscribe (pub/sub) systems have been developed to provide loosely-coupled, event-driven messaging services [1,2,3,4,5,6]. In particular, the Content-based Publish/Subscribe (CPS) paradigm is designed to support flexible and dynamic enterprise applications by routing on message content rather than destination identities or explicit network routes. Although the general CPS model is well understood, many CPS feature details still remain non-standardized for the good reason that different application scenarios have different requirements. While some CPS features can be addressed with system reconfigurability [7,8], others are more suitably expressed in policies that separate application requirements from infrastructure mechanisms [9,10]. For example, advanced features such as notification semantics, meta-events, security zoning, and CPS firewalls are appropriate for being realized as policies. These kinds of novel CPS features depend on being able to dynamically change system behaviour and are achievable through the flexibility of policies. However, no such policy framework currently exists in the CPS context. To address this problem, we present a content-based policy framework that is scalable, expressive, and extensible. Our policy framework supports a novel approach that applies policies based on the results of content-based matching. We find that this approach

R. Cerqueira and R.H. Campbell (Eds.): Middleware 2007, LNCS 4834, pp. 368–388, 2007.

enables many unique CPS capabilities that would otherwise be difficult or costly to achieve. In particular, we present a novel *post-matching* policy model capable of achieving scalable and expressive CPS policies. We also present a reference implementation of our policy framework using the PADRES [1] CPS middleware platform and a number of evaluation scenarios to highlight several unique and novel CPS features that become possible with our approach.

We first overview related work in Sec. 2 before presenting the concepts for our policy framework in Sec. 3. Our implementation is presented in Sec. 4 and several scenarios used to evaluate our approach are presented in Sec. 5. Finally, we conclude and discuss future work in Sec. 6.

2 Related Work

While there has been little research to date on policies in the CPS context, we are aware of the following related work. Opyrchal et al. [11] address issues of publication privacy in the context of pervasive environments using a centralized policy engine. Our work is different from theirs in many respects since they focus specifically on providing access control on publications. In addition to being distributed, our policy framework does not specifically target access control policies but also general feature and service policies such as notification semantics. Belokosztolszki et al. [12] incorporate Role-Based Access Control (RBAC) into the Hermes pub/sub system [3]. They address issues of policy management, broker trust, and access control optimization. Our work represents a different approach to pub/sub policies that targets issues orthogonal to RBAC in unstructured rather than structured overlays. Sturman et al. [13] propose a pub/sub architecture capable of message transformations. Our focus is not on the transformations themselves, but a framework that can support specifying policies on when and how to perform transformations among other features. In general, we are introducing a policy model that has significant expressiveness benefits complementing existing work.

Reconfigurable pub/sub systems allow the customization of middleware to suit the needs of different applications. Cugola and Picco [7] address issues of overlay and routing configurability by implementing a modular system architecture customizable at deployment time. Sivaharan et al. [8] present a component-based framework that allows pub/sub systems to easily cope with the diversity of mobile and heterogeneous network environments. Both are flexible systems that can be reconfigured with different pub/sub semantics as necessary. Our work is complementary because it addresses a different problem of separating system policies from mechanism, allowing applications to specify how a configured and running system should provide its services based on message content. Indeed, a benefit of our approach is that the main framework can be implemented in well-componentized, interceptor-based, or aspect-oriented system architectures without too much difficulty.

---

[1] http://padres.msrg.utoronto.ca (extended version of paper also available)

In the domain of traditional network environments, there is already a significant amount of work on policies addressing various issues from Quality of Service (QoS) to network management and security [14,15,16]. Stone *et al.* [17] present a survey of existing network policy languages and also propose their own Path-based Policy Language. Their approach explicitly declares the nodes in a network path to which policies are applicable. This approach is clearly not suitable in the CPS domain since it fundamentally conflicts with the paradigm of decoupling clients from message routing details. Agrawal *et al.* [18] present a policy-based system for autonomic management of computing resources. However, their work is again applicable in a different domain. The WS-Policy framework [19] focuses on providing an extensible syntax to express policies between Web service endpoints. However, not only is our focus on developing an actual policy mechanism rather than a syntax for expressing policies, the distributed CPS domain also has many concerns not addressed by end-point interactions such as routing. Existing policy frameworks for traditional network environments generally do not migrate easily into the CPS domain.

3   Content-Based Policy Framework

In this section, we introduce the main concepts of our content-based policy framework and discuss the implications of our approach with respect to policy composition and application in a distributed CPS system.

3.1   The Post-matching Policy Model

Since content-based matching algorithms are an integral part of CPS systems, the natural intuition is to protect these systems by enforcing policies before messages reach the matching algorithm. Although our policy framework supports enforcing policies before matching, such an approach does not easily achieve content-based expressiveness without duplicating the functionality of matching algorithms and incurring additional overhead. CPS systems generally provide highly scalable and expressive message filtering capabilities already [1,2,20]. By leveraging the high-performance matching algorithms that already exist, it is possible to build a policy framework that achieves the same scalability and expressiveness as the host CPS system itself. The basic concept behind our policy framework is summarized in Alg. 1 using an event-condition-action policy model [21].

In this model, a *content-based match event* serves as the trigger for policy *application*, which involves evaluating policy conditions and executing policy actions. Hence, we refer to this semantic as the *post-matching policy model*. While the model itself is deceptively simple, it enables a powerful policy framework since any application context that surfaces as message content is also reflected in the policy framework. Note that since we only depend on the notion of a content-based match event, this model is applicable to any CPS system that performs

when content-based match occurs
    if *additional policy condition(s) satisfied* **then**
        perform
            $Action_1$;
            $\ldots$;
            $Action_n$;

Algorithm 1. Post-matching policy model

matching at the message granularity[2]. The remainder of this paper focuses on the post-matching policy model even though we also support enforcing policies before matching in our framework.

3.2 Policy Framework Approach

More formally, our approach associates each filter F (advertisement or subscription) with an optional *policy statement* T[3], which contains one or more *policy rules*. Policy rules specify the conditions to evaluate and actions to execute when the policy is applied. When a message M is processed by a CPS broker, the matching algorithm computes a set $\Phi = \{(F_1, T_1), (F_2, T_2) \ldots (F_n, T_n)\}$ of matching filters F_i and their associated policy statements T_i containing policy rules applicable to M. Applying the policies $T_1 \ldots T_n$ against M involve evaluating the conditions and executing the actions specified in the policy rules of each policy statement. The result of applying the policies could include the rejection of M for routing, transformations on the format or content of M, or the triggering of other actions such as broker state maintenance and debugging. Essentially, our policy framework extends the CPS paradigm by giving applications the ability to specify policies intercepting content-based match events. In Sec. 5, we present example scenarios to highlight the benefits of the post-matching model and this approach.

It is important to note that the computation of Φ does not require any additional processing beyond what is already performed by the existing matching algorithm. If M is a publication, then Φ contains matching advertisements and subscriptions as computed by the matching algorithm. If M is a subscription, then Φ contains matching advertisements. For example, suppose a client issues two advertisements $A_1 = [(x < 100), (y < 50)]$ and $A_2 = [(x > 75), (y < 100)]$ to its local broker. Policies T_{a1} and T_{a2} are associated with advertisements A_1 and A_2, respectively. When the broker receives a subscription $S_1 = [(x > 25), (y < 75)]$ that intersects with both A_1 and A_2, the application of both policies T_{a1} and T_{a2} against S_1 is triggered. In contrast, a subscription $S_2 = [(x < 100), (y > 75)]$ would only trigger application of policy T_{a2} because the subscription only intersects with advertisement A_2. Suppose there is a further policy T_{s1} associated with S_1. Then a publication $P_1 = [(x, 90), (y, 30)]$ would trigger application

---

[2] This excludes matching algorithms that compress message sets into bit vectors, for instance, but includes topic-based approaches.

[3] From here on, we will use the terms "policy statement" and "policy" synonymously.

of all three policies T_{a1}, T_{a2}, and T_{s1} against P_1. In contrast, a publication $P_2 = [(x, 30), (y, 30)]$ only triggers application of policies T_{a1} and T_{s1}. In this way, the content-based expressiveness of the hosting CPS system is reflected in the policy framework.

Although we have discussed our approach in the context of advertisement-based semantics, these concepts are equally applicable in the context of subscription-based semantics.

3.3   Implications for Policy Composition

Deploying an application in a CPS system involves the decomposition of application contexts into messages. In this process, the application developer thinks in terms of event schemas[4] and event spaces[5]. Consequently, it is natural for an application developer to compose an overall policy by designing policies around the event schemas and event spaces that make up the application. By associating policies with filters, we implicitly achieve policy composition [22] with content-based expressiveness. For example, consider a supply-chain scenario where inventory report publications $P_i = [(class, report), (d_1, x_{i1}) \ldots, (d_n, x_{in})]$ with many data attributes are issued regularly. A management application subscribing to reports may consider d_1 to be a critical attribute. As such, if the value x_{i1} of that attribute is above a certain threshold, then the client would like to know the identity of the previous overlay hop of the message for tracking purposes. On the other hand, if x_{i1} is below a certain value, then the remaining attributes are uninteresting so the client would like the broker to remove them before delivering the notification. To achieve this, the management application can issue two subscriptions $S_1 = [(class=report), (d_1 > X_{high})]$ and $S_2 = [(class=report), (d_1 < X_{low})]$ with policies T_1 and T_2 associated with each, respectively. Policy $T_1 = AppendPrevHop()$ specifies a single action that appends the attribute ($PrevHop\ ID$) to the notification while policy $T_2 = RemoveAttributes(d_2, \ldots, d_n)$ specifies a single action that removes the given list of attributes from the notification. With these policies in place, notifications delivered to the management application may now have an extra $PrevHop$ attribute, missing $d_2 \ldots d_n$ attributes, or both depending on the value of the d_1 attribute. Furthermore, the management application is able to specify this notification policy without affecting other clients subscribing to the same events since the policies are only associated with subscriptions belonging to the management application clients. In this example, policies T_1 and T_2 have been composed together to specify a notification semantic for inventory reports by leveraging the content-based filtering capabilities of subscriptions, which already exist as a fundamental concept in CPS systems. No additional policy-specific composition language or content-based processing is needed in our approach. In contrast, a generic policy framework layered on top of the CPS system would need to explicitly process the contents of publications to achieve the same result.

---

[4] Advertisements or message type definitions.
[5] The set of all possible messages matching a filter.

3.4   Interception Points in CPS Overlays

The CPS policy concepts we have presented so far are equally applicable in both centralized and distributed CPS systems [1,2,4,20]. In particular, we have addressed *when* policy application occurs – either before or immediately after a content-based match event. For distributed CPS systems however, it is equally important to address *where* in the overlay policy application occurs. For instance, are policies only applied at edge brokers? Or are they applied at every overlay hop? Since there are valid scenarios for either case, our approach lets applications specify where policy application occurs based on *interception points*.

The three important interception points are ingress, egress, and routing, which correspond to the brokers at which a message enters, leaves, and routes through an overlay. Fig. 1 illustrates the concept of interception points. Note that for a single isolated overlay, ingress and egress points correspond to the brokers at which injection and notification occurs between brokers and clients. However, in a federated CPS system, ingress and egress points correspond to the brokers at the edges of sub-overlays.

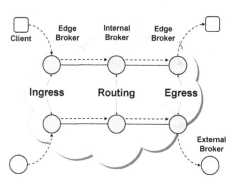

Fig. 1. Policy interception points

4   Policy Framework Implementation

In this section, we present the implementation of our policy framework, which builds upon the model and approach described earlier. In particular, we describe the mechanisms for creating, distributing, and enforcing content-based policies in a distributed CPS system. Our framework is built on top of PADRES [5], an existing rule-based CPS middleware platform implemented by our research group in Java.

4.1   API and Language

Only minor changes to the API are needed to support our policy framework. The `subscribe(msg)`, `advertise(msg)`, and `publish(msg)` methods previously used by clients have simply been extended to accept an optional policy statement argument, resulting in `subscribe(msg, policy)`, `advertise(msg, policy)`, and `publish(msg, policy)` as the new API. For advertisements and subscriptions, `setPolicy(msgID, policy)` also allows for specifying policies after the message has already been issued. There is a factory class that can create commonly used policy statement objects directly, but it is also possible to build a policy statement from either XML specifications or a more compact language shown in Fig. 2. However, our focus in this paper is on developing the policy framework mechanisms rather than providing a specific syntax for writing policies. This language represents the construction of a single self-contained policy statement. Each policy statement contains one or more policy rules enclosed by the On(...) keyword and two mandatory parameters that define policy rule types.

```
1   PolicyStatement {
2     On (
3       [Forward | Insert],
4       [Advertisement | Subscription
5         | Publication | Unsubscription
6         | Unadvertisement]) {
7
8       @matching: [Before | After]?
9       @broker: [Ingress | Egress | Routing]*
10      @attach: [Never | Always | KeepExisting
11                | IfYield]?
12      @yield_attach: [False | True]?
13
14      If <conditions ...> Then <actions ...>
15      Elseif <conditions ...> Then <actions ...>
16      ...
17
18      OnException {
19        If <conditions ...> Then <actions ...>
20        Elseif ...
21      } } }
```

Fig. 2. Policy language

The parameter choices on line **3** specify whether the rule is applicable to messages being forwarded or to messages being inserted into broker routing tables. The parameter choices on lines **4** to **6** specify which type of message the policy rule is applicable to. Lines **8** to **12** show optional qualifiers that further define when and where the policy is applicable. When the rule is applied, the conditions specified on line **14** are evaluated and the actions are executed if the conditions all return true. Subsequent condition clauses are only evaluated if the preceding condition clause fails. Line **18** encloses conditions to evaluate and actions to attempt if an exception occurs when applying the rule. In the following sections, we discuss how this is used to specify policies and control how they are applied.

4.2   Creation and Distribution of Policies

Using the new API, both clients and brokers can create policies either when CPS messages are first issued or by associating policies with filters (advertisements and subscriptions) at any time afterwards. For instance, advertise(msg, policy) attaches a policy to the advertisement when it is issued. The attached policy is routed along with the advertisement and stored by brokers, who associate the policy with the advertisement. Similarly, subscribe(msg, policy) attaches a policy to the subscription that is routed through the overlay and stored by brokers. The policies stored by brokers can also be set using setPolicy(msgID, policy), which updates the policy associated with either an advertisement or subscription. In general, a policy that routes with a message in the overlay is said to be *attached*, while a policy that is stored by a broker and linked to a filter is said to be *associated*. Policies can be attached to any CPS message type but can only be associated with either advertisements or subscriptions.

Table 1 summarizes the available methods for specifying policies applicable to each message type. For example, publication policies (i.e., policies applied

Table 1. Specification methods for policies

Policy \ Message	Adv.	Sub.	Pub.	Unadv.	Unsub.
Adv.	Attached	×	×	×	×
Sub.	On(*)	Attached	×	×	×
Pub.	On(*)	On(*)	Attached	×	×
Unadv.	On(*)	×	×	Attached	×
Unsub.	×	On(*)	×	×	Attached

to publications) can either be specified by policies associated with advertisements and subscriptions using the On(Publication) qualifier or attached to the publication itself, while unsubscription policies can only either be specified by policies associated with subscriptions using the On(Unsubscription) qualifier or attached to the unsubscription itself. Similarly, advertisement policies can only be created and attached to the advertisements they are to be applied to. However, subscription policies can either be attached directly to the subscription or associated with advertisements as On(Subscription) policy rules. In the latter case, the @attach and @yield_attach qualifiers can additionally be used to allow subscriptions to inherit the policy from the advertisement. That is, the subscription policy associated with the advertisement can be attached to the subscription rather than applied normally. These additional qualifiers allow greater control over the specification of default policy attachments.

4.3   Enforcing Applicable Policies

Brokers are solely responsible for interpreting and enforcing the policies applicable to messages they receive. When a policy is enforced by evaluating conditions or executing actions, we say that the policy is being *applied* to a message. In general, if a broker receives a message M with a policy T_M attached to it and M matches a set of filters $\{F_1, \cdots F_n\}$ associated with a set of policies $\{T_1, \cdots, T_n\}$, then the set $\{T_M, T_1, \cdots, T_n\}$ contains all policies potentially applicable to M. However, the applicability of a policy rule to any given message depends on a combination of the policy rule type and the policy rule qualifiers[6]. For instance, a publication matching an advertisement-associated policy that contains only subscription rules will not have any of those rules applied to it. Two qualifiers are currently supported to further specify *when* and *where* a policy rule is applicable.

The @match qualifier specifies whether the rule is applied before or after the message goes through content-based matching. Rule application before matching is supported since some policies may require checking conditions or executing actions before accepting the message for matching. Policies for fast message forwarding that bypass matching altogether or content-independent authorizations are more appropriate for application before matching, for example. However,

---

[6] From here on, we will use the terms "policy rule" and "rule" synonymously.

such policies do not benefit from the advantages of scalability and expressiveness that are possible with rules applied after matching. More specifically, a powerful implication of evaluating rules after matching is that the rules are selectively applied based on message content. We focus on exploring the benefits of post-matching policy rules with our evaluation scenarios in Sec. 5.

The @broker qualifier specifies the broker overlay contexts where the rule is applicable and can be any combination of *ingress*, *egress*, and *routing* as shown in Fig. 1 and discussed in Sec. 3. Ingress rules are evaluated for messages entering the CPS system, egress rules are evaluated for messages leaving the CPS system, and routing rules are evaluated for messages at internal brokers.

Together, the @match and @broker qualifiers give applications significant flexibility in specifying when and where policy rules are applicable.

4.4   Framework Extensibility with Modular Rule Elements

The level of functionality achievable in our framework depends on the conditions and actions supported inside policy rules. In our framework, all conditions and actions are implemented as *rule elements* chained together inside policy rules. Every policy rule contains one or more rule element chains. Applying a policy rule essentially involves traversing its rule element chains, evaluating and exe-

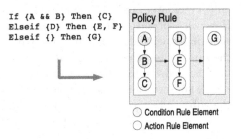

Fig. 3. Policy rule structure

cuting the corresponding conditions and actions as appropriate. Fig. 3 shows an example of how conditions and actions are represented as a policy rule. In this example, the rule elements A, B, C are accessed in order first. Should the conditions corresponding to either rule elements A or B fail for instance, then the next chain consisting of rule elements D, E, F is accessed. Recall that a single policy statement may also contain multiple policy rules, one for each type of message at each interception point. If an exception occurs while traversing the rule elements, compensation policy conditions and actions as specified in the OnException clause shown in Fig. 2 are accessed. Further exceptions during compensation actions are no longer handled by the policy framework itself and instead, a meta-event (as presented in Sec. 5) that describes the exception is generated.

Although we have already implemented a number of rule elements presented in Sec. 5 that cover a wide range of CPS functionality, our framework is designed to be easily extensible with new rule elements in response to emerging application requirements.

5   Evaluation Scenarios

In this section, we evaluate our policy framework by applying it to a number of different scenarios, demonstrating the expressiveness and flexibility achieved using the language presented in Sec. 4. Several of these scenarios represent novel CPS features that become easy to specify and implement using our policy framework. Where appropriate, we also present experimental data resulting from the implementation of these scenarios. We do not include any experimental data for scenarios that are purely functional and instead present only the associated policies. Since we focus on the post-matching model, all policy statements shown are implicitly qualified with @matching: After to avoid repetition in presentation. All experiments presented in this section were run using separate Intel Dual Xeon 3.xGHz processor, 2GB memory systems for each broker or client. We divide our evaluation into two broad scenario categories: CPS semantics and security.

5.1 Specifying CPS Semantic Policies

Since there has been no standardization of CPS implementations, there are still many subtle operational semantics that are open to interpretation by implementers. As such, it is useful to have a flexible CPS system that allows customization of operational semantics according to the needs of applications. The following examples highlight how we can dynamically tune system semantics using policies.

Notification Semantics. Although the semantic of delivering notifications only to interested subscribers is well-established [1,2,3,4,6], the actual content delivered in notifications typically remains an implementation decision. However, different applications may want notifications delivered to them in different forms. Suppose there is a stream of publications of the form $P_i = [(class, event), (a_1, v_{i1}), \ldots, (a_n, v_{in})]$. A subscriber issuing a subscription $S = [(class=event), (a_1 > x_1), \ldots, (a_k > x_k)]$ can optionally associate the policy in Fig. 4 with S. This policy specifies that just before notifications are delivered to the subscriber (at Egress brokers), they are "trimmed" to match attributes in the subscription. In this example, attributes $a_{k+1} \ldots a_n$ would be removed from all P_i since they do not appear in the subscription. The TrimAttributes() action automatically selects attributes for removal based on the subscription, but other possible notification semantic actions include RemoveAttributes(attributeList)

```
PolicyStatement {
  On(Forward,Publication) {
    @broker: Egress
    If {} Then {TrimAttributes()}
} }
```

Fig. 4. Notification policy

and KeepOnlyAttributes(attributeList), which allow a subscriber to remove or keep a specified list of attributes, respectively. Although we expect some performance improvement from removing unnecessary attributes, it is not immediately obvious exactly how much improvement can be achieved because of other factors such as message header overhead.

Fig. 5 shows that the effects of trimming attributes on network traffic are still very significant in our system despite message header overheads. We used three different streams of publications consisting of 10, 20, and 30 attribute publications. A subscription was associated with policies for removing from 0 to all attributes. The solid lines for each stream show the network usage of receiving full publications and the dashed lines show the network usage of delivering the same publications if notification policies are applied. The values shown are averages over 100 publications. Clearly, even removing a small number of unwanted attributes could mean substantial overall network performance improvements when delivering to large numbers of subscribers. Since the infrastructure cannot always predict application workloads, our framework allows applications to help optimize performance by specifying exactly which attributes are relevant and should be delivered.

In addition to improving network performance, notification policies have functional benefits as well. Transformation from one syntax to another is also easily expressed using the same policy by using the appropriate action such as ToXML(). The actions can of course be stacked as well to compose more complicated notification policies such as

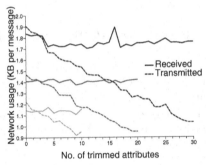

Fig. 5. Trimming notifications

```
Then {TrimAttributes(), ToXML()}
```

that both trims the notification and then converts it to XML syntax. For example, such transformation policies can be used to create proxy brokers between different CPS infrastructures that require different message formats by using the @broker: Routing qualifier and specifying appropriate conditions and actions such as

```
If {AuthenticateReceiver(Domain1)} Then {ToFormat1()}
Elseif {AuthenticateReceiver(Domain2)} Then {ToFormat2()}
```

The important point is that different subscribers may specify different notification policies, thereby receiving different versions of the same event. Note also that no condition has been specified in the policy we show here, but it is easy to imagine how notification semantics can be combined with conditions such as authentication to achieve access control.

Distributed Tracing. Although keeping the infrastructure transparent to clients is an important CPS feature, applications sometimes need information about the infrastructure for monitoring or debugging purposes. Policies are well-suited for specifying this type of message content augmentation on an as-needed basis for applications. For example, consider the policy in Fig. 6.

This policy specifies that at every broker hop, publications are augmented with information about the broker, the load state of the broker, and the total time spent processing the publication. When attached to publications, this policy is applied on a per-publication basis and does not affect other publications that do not have the policy attached. Consequently, this is most useful if tracing is only needed occasionally. Alternatively, the policy can be automatically attached to publications by adding the @attach: Always qualifier and associating the policy with an appropriate advertisement, which would give tracing information to all subscribers by default. Associating the policy with subscriptions would instead allow the augmentation to occur on a per-subscriber basis. The @broker qualifier and If{} conditions can of course also be changed to restrict augmentation to certain brokers. The unique combination of content-based expressiveness, policy language, and policy framework gives applications great flexibility in choosing a suitable tracing semantic.

```
PolicyStatement {
  On(Forward,Publication) {
    @broker: Ingress,Egress,Routing

    If {}
    Then {AugmentBrokerHostInfo(),
          AugmentBrokerLoadIndex(),
          AugmentProcessingTime()}
} }
```

Fig. 6. Tracing policy

The actions shown here place augmented data into a binary payload that is part of the publication, but similar alternative actions can instead extend the publication by placing augmented data into reserved CPS attributes. The second method would allow subscribers to further specify notification semantics on tracing attributes even when advertisement-associated or publication-attached tracing policies are used.

Meta-Events and Triggers. Sometimes events in the CPS system itself can be of interest to clients and brokers. As such, our policy framework enables generating publications based on system events such as matches occurring under certain conditions. For example, consider the policy in Fig. 7. This policy

```
PolicyStatement {
  On(Insert,Subscription) {
    @broker: Ingress

    If {MessageSizeIndex() > 0.8
       && BrokerLoadIndex() > 0.75}
    Then {UninsertMessage(),
      Publish("[class,DropMessage]
              ,[cause,'Broker load']
              ,[message,$Message]")}
  }
```

```
  On(Forward,Subscription) {
    @broker: Ingress

    If {MessageSizeIndex() > 0.8
       && BrokerLoadIndex() > 0.75}
    Then {BlockMessage()}
} }
```

Fig. 7. Meta-event policy

specifies that if a large subscription is injected at a time when the broker is sufficiently loaded, then the subscription is not stored in routing tables (uninserted using the UninsertMessage() action) and also prevented from propagating any further (blocked using the BlockMessage() action). Furthermore, a publication is internally generated by the policy framework regarding this event using the Publish() action. The variable $Message inserts the offending subscription as a string into the generated publication content. Internally generated publications are processed by the same broker that generated it and treated as a normal

publication for matching and routing purposes. Effectively, this policy specifies a simple load resilience scheme where interested subscribers are notified of
dropped subscriptions. The dropped subscription event may be relevant to applications for recovery purposes or to system management services for resource
provisioning.

Note that this policy does not necessarily affect all subscriptions since the application can choose which subscriptions are potentially dropped by associating
this policy with the appropriate advertisements. For instance, associating this
policy with the advertisement $A = [(class = CustomerOrder), (priority < 5)]$
specifies that only subscriptions to low priority customer orders will be dropped
and all other subscriptions will be unaffected by the policy. This kind of policy is
not possible in normal pre-matching policies or generic policy framework layers
without duplicating content-based functionality.

Flooding Semantics. In terms of routing efficiency, there are some situations
in which flooding subscriptions may be preferable to flooding advertisements.
This can be the case if a particular application consists of many publishers and
only a few subscribers interested in content from all publishers or if publishers are
highly mobile while subscribers are mostly stationary. Our CPS system is based
on advertisement flooding by default, but preference for subscription flooding
can be specified using the policy in Fig. 8.

```
PolicyStatement {
  On(Forward,Advertisement) {
    @broker: Ingress,Routing

    If {} Then {BlockMessage()}
  }
  On(Forward,Subscription) {
    @broker: Ingress,Routing

    If {} Then {FloodMessage()}
} }
```

Fig. 8. Flooding policy

When attached to advertisements, this policy prevents the advertisement from propagating beyond a single broker hop using
BlockMessage(). Furthermore, any subscription that matches an advertisement associated
with this policy will be tagged for flooding to all
neighbours. A broker can control which event
schemas are flooded by internally generating
an appropriate advertisement and associating
this policy with it. For example, a group of
brokers can agree to flood infrastructure management subscriptions by internally storing the
advertisement $A = [(class = BrokerManage-$
$ment), \cdots]$ in each of their own routing tables associated with the above policy.
Notice that the enforcement of subscription flooding is left up to the discretion
of brokers and does not occur at brokers that do not similarly store this policy.

We set up the scenario shown in Fig. 9 where subscribers are situated at
different brokers and remain stationary while publishers move from broker to
broker frequently in between issuing publications. This scenario reflects characteristics found in applications where mobile clients need to continuously send location and status updates to home servers, for instance. Fig. 11 shows that under
the normal advertisement flooding scheme, advertisement, unadvertisement, and
subscription messages are continuously routed throughout the network as the
application runs. Subscriptions are routed as a result of the unadvertisements/re-
advertisement process, which triggers removal and re-propagation of subscrip-

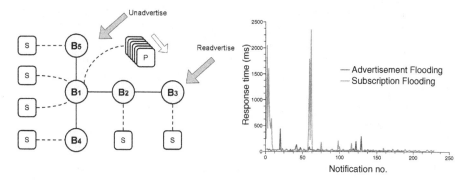

Fig. 9. Highly mobile publishers   **Fig. 10.** Negligible policy overhead

tions. However, if a subscription flooding policy is used, then no additional advertisement or subscription messages need to be routed while the application runs since subscribers remain stationary. Fig. 12 shows that significant network traffic is saved by using subscription flooding. Furthermore, the subscription flooding policy only incurs overhead when the advertisements are initially issued and subscriptions are flooded. Subsequent notification response times are unaffected as Fig. 10 shows.

Of course, there are reverse scenarios (such as subscriber mobility) that favour advertisement flooding instead. However, our purpose is only to show that different application scenarios can benefit significantly from different flooding semantics. With our policy framework, both semantics can be active simultaneously and specified on a per event schema basis.

5.2 Specifying Security Policies

Although security mechanisms are typically orthogonal to the policy framework, security behaviours can still be specified at the CPS level. We implemented a simple security mechanism for use with our policy framework in which authentication and encryption is based on *Trust Group* membership. Trust groups are

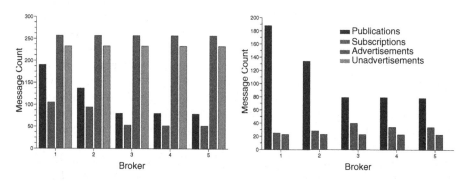

Fig. 11. Normal advertisement flooding   **Fig. 12.** Subscription flooding policy

conceptually similar to secure multicast groups [23]. Each trust group is associated with a shared group secret K_g so that members of the same group are able to perform authentication and encryption within the group. To establish K_g, there must be an out-of-band bootstrapping process to either set up K_g directly or set up public/private keys on the appropriate clients and brokers so that K_g can be exchanged securely. We support both bootstrapping methods since the first has the advantage of simplicity and low overhead while the second method is more flexible.

Authenticated Event Scope. Although advertisements are normally flooded in our CPS system, trust group authentication can be used to limit the visibility of events in the overlay on a per schema basis by issuing advertisements attached with the policy in Fig. 13. This policy specifies that the advertisement must only be sent to brokers belonging to either the `TrustGroup1` or `TrustGroup2` trust groups. If the receiver of the advertisement is successfully authenticated, the advertisement is sent normally and no additional special actions are performed. However, if authentication fails for both groups, the delivery of the advertisement is blocked by the `BlockMessage()` action. Alternatively, the condition

```
If {AuthenticateReceiver(TrustGroup1)
  && AuthenticateReceiver(TrustGroup2)}
```

can be used to specify that only brokers belonging to both trust groups will receive the advertisement. Although authentication is currently based on trust group membership, the same policies can be used to express authentication based on other mechanisms such as public key identities or Role-Based Access Control [12] since the actual authentication process uses out-of-band mechanisms.

```
PolicyStatement {
  On(Forward,Advertisement) {
    @broker: Ingress,Routing

    If {AuthenticateReceiver(
        TrustGroup1)} Then {}
    Elseif {AuthenticateReceiver(
        TrustGroup2)} Then {}
    Elseif {} Then {BlockMessage()}
} }
```

Fig. 13. Authentication

Fig. 14 shows publication processing time when a sender-authentication policy is in place between two brokers (the policy is associated with a subscription). Each step in the plot represents 0, 1, 3, and 5 different trust group authentications required by the policy. For the "Authorization" line, the receiving broker is able to authenticate the sending broker for all five trust groups. Since authentication results are not cached, the authentication protocol must run for every publication, resulting in worst case performance that is proportional to the number of trust groups specified in the policy. For the "Denial" line, the sending broker belongs to no trust groups so that authentication fails on the first attempt regardless of how many trust groups are specified in the policy. However, by caching authentication results, we can avoid running the authentication protocol for every message at the expense of lower responsiveness to trust group membership changes. The "Cached" line shows that since cached entries do not expire simultaneously, performance remains acceptable even when several groups are specified in the policy. Therefore, incurred overhead is due to

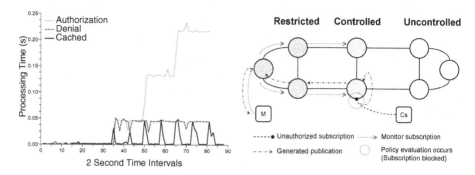

Fig. 14. Authentication processing time   **Fig. 15.** Monitoring subscription attempts

the authentication process itself rather than processing and management performed by the policy framework. Note that we set the expiry time to a low value here in order to observe the effects of authentication cache expiry. Since our focus is on the policy framework and not the authentication mechanism itself, we implemented a protocol similar to CHAP [24] for the purposes of this evaluation. Without the post-matching model, the policy framework would have to duplicate content-based functionality to achieve expressive, fine-grained authentication policies based on content.

Security Zones. Suppose a broker network is divided into restricted, controlled, and uncontrolled security zones as shown in Fig. 15. This setup is not uncommon in organizations separating their intranet (restricted) systems from the Internet (uncontrolled) using a demilitarized zone (DMZ, controlled). To enforce privacy, all attributes may be visible within the restricted zone but some attributes must not appear in the controlled zone. No events from the application should be visible at all in the uncontrolled zone. Furthermore, only authorized clients may subscribe from either zone. These application requirements can be expressed by attaching the policy in Fig. 16 to an advertisement issued from within the restricted zone.

This policy combines the use of authentication, message transformations, and meta-events to enforce privacy across different security zones. Fig. 15 illustrates the resulting meta-event message flow for an event schema using this policy.

Content-Based Firewall. In CPS systems, subscriptions are analogous to firewall "allow" rules on publications while advertisements are analogous to "allow" rules on subscriptions. In this respect, the existing filtering capabilities of CPS systems already provide some firewall functionality. However, consider a stable application in which advertisements have been established and no longer need to change. Subscriptions originating from an "internal" overlay are sent to a neighbouring "external" overlay and attract publications. In order to temporarily block certain publications from entering the internal overlay, the subscriptions used by the application must change. For instance, this may be necessary as a

```
PolicyStatement {
  On(Forward,Advertisement) {
    @broker: Ingress,Routing

    If {AuthenticateReceiver(Restricted)}
      Then {}                                    On(Forward,Publication) {
    Elseif {AuthenticateReceiver(Controlled)}      @broker: Routing (Ingress)
      Then {RemoveAttributes(a, ... ,n)}           @attach: Always  // Routing only
    Elseif {} Then {BlockMessage()}
  }                                                If {AuthenticateReceiver(Restricted)} Then {}
  On(Forward,Subscription) {                       Elseif {AuthenticateReceiver(Controlled)}
    @broker: Ingress                               Then {RemoveAttributes(a, ... ,n)}
                                                   Elseif {} Then {BlockMessage()} } }
    If {AuthenticateSender(AuthorizedSubscribers)}
      Then {}
    Elseif {}
      Then {Publish("[class,UnauthorizedSubscribe],
                    [message,$Message]")}
  }
}
```

Fig. 16. Security Zones policy

reaction to detecting fraudulent publications that suddenly need filtering. Not only would such a change affect subscriptions throughout both overlays, the resulting subscriptions could potentially become a cumbersome mix of filters for attracting wanted publications and filters for fine-grained blocking of unwanted publications. Depending on the subscription language, this could be very difficult or even impossible to express in a single subscription. Similarly, preventing certain subscriptions from exiting the internal overlay would require changing the advertisements that originated from the external overlay. The same issue of expressing "allow" and "deny" filters in a single advertisement exists.

To block publications from entering the internal overlay, we can issue subscriptions from an internal firewall broker B_{if} to an external firewall broker B_{ef} as shown in Fig. 17 with the policy in Fig. 22 attached. This policy blocks forwarding of all publications *strictly* matching the subscription as determined by the `StrictMatch()` condition. A publication strictly matches a subscription if the publication contains exactly the same attributes as the subscription, while a subscrip-

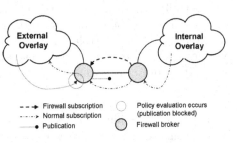

Fig. 17. Content-based firewall setup

tion strictly matches an advertisement if their filters are the same. For example, a subscription $S = [(class = C), (a < 10)]$ is strictly matched by the publication $P_1 = [(class, C), (a, 9)]$ but not $P_2 = [(class, C), (a, 9), (b, 5)]$ even though P_2 normally matches S. Strict matching conditions can be used to achieve content-based firewall rules with more precision if needed but are not required

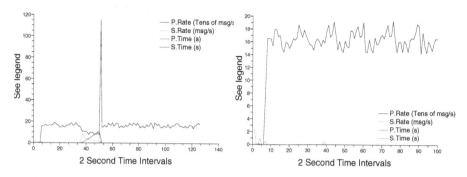

Fig. 18. Individual firewall subscriptions   **Fig. 19.** Merged firewall subscription

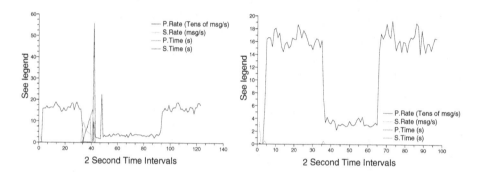

Fig. 20. Individual firewall subscriptions   **Fig. 21.** Merged firewall subscription

in situations where the normal matching semantic is sufficient. The subscription and its associated policy is analogous to a single content-based firewall rule on publications. Note that authenticated event scoping is used to restrict firewall subscriptions and advertisements to the firewall brokers. Similarly, subscriptions are blocked by issuing an advertisement from B_{ef} to B_{if} and attaching the same policy using `On(Subscription)` instead of `On(Publication)`. In Figs. 18 and 20, we issue 100 separate firewall subscriptions to the internal firewall broker that block roughly 80% of the incoming publications overall. The publication rate `P.Rate` remains steady at the external broker (Fig. 18) but is much lower at the internal broker (Fig. 20) when the firewall policies are in effect. The time to process both publications and subscriptions (`P.Time` and `S.Time`, respectively) increases when the 100 firewall subscriptions are received.

When firewall subscriptions are first issued and processed with their policies, broker processing times spike briefly before returning to normal sub-millisecond values. Subsequent removal of the same 100 firewall subscriptions via unsubscription is significantly faster, incurring no noticeable overhead. In Figs. 19

```
PolicyStatement {
  On(Forward,Publication) {
    @broker: Routing

    If {StrictMatch()}
      Then {BlockMessage()}
} }
```

Fig. 22. Firewall policy

and 21, we issue a single subscription merged from the 100 separate firewall subscriptions that block the same amount of traffic. As there is only a single subscription and policy rule to process, Fig. 21 shows that there is no noticeable disruption to broker processing when the policy takes effect and is later removed. The original subscription issued by the application did not need to change in either case. This technique allows us to dynamically specify content-based firewall rules that are totally independent of the filters specified by existing applications. In these experiments, the firewall subscriptions were issued to the internal broker by a normal CPS client, but the authentication policies described earlier can be used to place access control policies on who is able to issue firewall filters. Note that a reverse scenario where publications are blocked from leaving the internal overlay and subscriptions are blocked from entering is also possible.

6   Conclusion and Future Work

In this paper, we have presented a content-based policy framework for distributed CPS systems that supports a novel *post-matching* policy model. Evaluations of our reference implementation show that this model is capable of achieving scalable and expressive policies in distributed CPS systems with little overhead. In particular, we showed that our policy framework enables new features related to both CPS semantics and security such as notification semantics, meta-events, security zoning, and CPS firewalls. By leveraging the capabilities of existing CPS matching algorithms, our policy model allows these features to be specified easily and dynamically. Since our model is based on generic CPS matching concepts, our approach is appropriate across different CPS systems using either advertisement or subscription based semantics.

Although we have addressed many concepts in our policy framework implementation, some future work still remains. In particular, we have not discussed self-management features such as conflict resolution in any detail. Although many conflict resolution strategies are possible [25,21], none are universally applicable across all conflict situations. At the moment, we use our own meta-notification feature to inform the application about policy conflicts and exceptions when they are detected. However, certain conflicts may be resolvable automatically by the system. We have started work in this area by identifying conflict situations amongst authorization and message transformation policies in the CPS context. Also, the policies we presented in this paper are based mostly on authorization and message transformation. There are still other types of policies that need to be explored, such as generic obligation actions [10] involving logging, persisting messages to a database, and other similar actions. The meta-notification feature implemented using our policy framework is work in this direction.

Acknowledgements

This research was funded in part by OCE, NSERC, CA and Sun. We would also like to thank the anonymous reviewers and the members of the Middleware Systems Research Group for their valuable feedback regarding this work.

References

1. Banavar, G., Chandra, T., Mukherjee, B., Nagarajarao, J., Strom, R.E., Sturman, D.C.: An Efficient Multicast Protocol for Content-based Publish-Subscribe Systems. In: ICDCS (1999)
2. Carzaniga, A., Rosenblum, D., Wolf, A.: Design and Evaluation of a Wide-Area Event Notification Service. ACM Transactions on Computer Systems 19(3), 332–383 (2001)
3. Pietzuch, P.R., Bacon, J.M.: Hermes: A Distributed Event-Based Middleware Architecture. In: DEBS (2002)
4. Fiege, L., Mezini, M., Mühl, G., Buchmann, A.P.: Engineering Event-Based Systems with Scopes. In: Magnusson, B. (ed.) ECOOP 2002. LNCS, vol. 2374, Springer, Heidelberg (2002)
5. Fidler, E., Jacobsen, H.A., Li, G., Mankovski, S.: The PADRES Distributed Publish/Subscribe System. In: Feature Interactions in Telecommunications and Software Systems (2005)
6. Aekaterinidis, I., Triantafillou, P.: PastryStrings: A Comprehensive Content-Based Publish/Subscribe DHT Network. In: ICDCS (2006)
7. Cugola, G., Picco, G.P.: REDS: A Reconfigurable Dispatching System. In: International Workshop on Software Engineering and Middleware (2006)
8. Sivaharan, T., Blair, G.S., Coulson, G.: GREEN: A Configurable and Reconfigurable Publish-Subscribe Middleware for Pervasive Computing. OTM Conferences 1, 732–749 (2005)
9. Calo, S., Lobo, J.: A Basis for Comparing Characteristics of Policy Systems. In: POLICY, pp. 183–194. IEEE Computer Society, Washington, DC, USA (2006)
10. Sloman, M.: Policy driven management for distributed systems. Journal of Network and Systems Management 2, 333–360 (1994)
11. Opyrchal, L., Prakash, A., Agrawal, A.: Supporting Privacy Policies in a Publish-Subscribe Substrate for Pervasive Environments. Journal Of Networks 2, 17–26 (2007)
12. Belokosztolszki, A., Eyers, D.M., Pietzuch, P., Bacon, J., Moody, K.: Role-Based Access Control for Publish/Subscribe Middleware Architectures. In: Distributed Event Based Systems (2003)
13. Sturman, D., Banavar, G., Strom, R.: Reflection in the Gryphon Message Brokering System. In: Reflection Workshop at OOPSLA (1998)
14. Strassner, J., Schleimer, S.: Policy Framework Definition Language (1998), http://www3.ietf.org/proceedings/98dec/I-D/draft-ietf-policy-framework-pfdl-00.txt
15. Brownlee, N.: SRL: A Language for Describing Traffic Flows and Specifying Actions for Flow Groups (1999), http://www.rfc-archive.org/getrfc.php?rfc=2723
16. Blunk, L., Damas, J., Parent, F., Robachevsky, A.: Routing Policy Specification Language next generation (RPSLng) (2005), http://www.ietf.org/rfc/rfc4012.txt

17. Stone, G.N., Lundy, B., Xie, G.G.: Network Policy Languages: A Survey and a New Approach. IEEE Networks, 10–21 (January/February 2001)
18. Agrawal, R., Srikant, R., Thomas, D.: Privacy Preserving OLAP. In: SIGMOD (2005)
19. WS-Policy: http://www.w3.org/Submission/WS-Policy/
20. Li, G., Jacobsen, H.A.: Composite subscriptions in content-based publish/subscribe systems. In: Middleware (2005)
21. Aib, I., Agoulmine, N., Fonseca, M.S., Pujolle, G.: Analysis of policy management models and specification languages. Network control and engineering for Qos, security and mobility II 2, 26–50 (2003)
22. Dulay, N., Lupu, E., Sloman, M., Damianou, N.: A policy deployment model for the Ponder language. In: IEEE/IFIP International Symposium on Integrated Network Management (2001)
23. Rafaeli, S., Hutchison, D.: A Survey of Key Management for Secure Group Communication. ACM Computing Surveys 35(3), 309–329 (2003)
24. CHAP: http://www.networksorcery.com/enp/rfc/rfc1994.txt
25. Dunlop, N., Indulska, J., Raymond, K.: Methods for Conflict Resolution in Policy-Based Management Systems. EDOC 00, 98 (2003)

Hybrid Dissemination: Adding Determinism to Probabilistic Multicasting in Large-Scale P2P Systems[*]

Spyros Voulgaris[1] and Maarten van Steen[2]

[1] Dept. of Computer Science, ETH Zurich, Switzerland
spyros@inf.ethz.ch
[2] Dept. of Computer Science, Vrije Universiteit Amsterdam, The Netherlands
steen@few.vu.nl

Abstract. Epidemic protocols have demonstrated remarkable scalability and robustness in disseminating information on internet-scale, dynamic P2P systems. However, popular instances of such protocols suffer from a number of significant drawbacks, such as increased message overhead in push-based systems, or low dissemination speed in pull-based ones.

In this paper we study push-based epidemic dissemination algorithms, in terms of hit ratio, communication overhead, dissemination speed, and resilience to failures and node churn. We devise a hybrid push-based dissemination algorithm, combining probabilistic with deterministic properties, which limits message overhead to an order of magnitude lower than that of the purely probabilistic dissemination model, while retaining strong probabilistic guarantees for complete dissemination of messages. Our extensive experimentation shows that our proposed algorithm outperforms that model both in static and dynamic network scenarios, as well as in the face of large-scale catastrophic failures. Moreover, the proposed algorithm distributes the dissemination load uniformly on all participating nodes.

Keywords: Epidemic/Gossip protocols, Information Dissemination, Peer-to-Peer.

1 Introduction

Large-scale information dissemination constitutes fundamental functionality for a multitude of applications, ranging from file-sharing and web-casting to the massive distribution of software, security patches, and world-wide worm alert notifications. The emergence of new types of applications for large-scale decentralized systems drives the need for efficient, reliable, and scalable information dissemination frameworks.

Early attempts for information dissemination focused on network-layer solutions, leading to a number of IP Multicast protocols. These protocols rely on functionality embedded in routers, that enables the dynamic construction of spanning trees that reach all participating nodes, but generally provide no reliability guarantees. A number of solutions have been proposed on top of IP Multicast, such as SRM [6] and RMTP [13], to improve its reliability. Nevertheless, IP Multicast is not widely deployed on the Internet mainly due to extra complexity and state imposing on routers.

---

[*] Part of this work is funded by the European IST-FP6-15964 project AEOLUS (Algorithmic Principles for Building Efficient Overlay Computers).

R. Cerqueira and R.H. Campbell (Eds.): Middleware 2007, LNCS 4834, pp. 389–409, 2007.

Application-layer multicast forms an alternative class of solutions that has emerged in the recent years. The main advantage of these solutions is that they are very generic, and, therefore, they can be directly deployed over today's network infrastructure. There exist application-layer multicast protocols that provide reliability guarantees [8]. However, many of them do not scale well to a large number of nodes [17].

A class of application-layer multicast has recently emerged [3,2,21], based on the structure of DHTs such as Chord, Pastry, and Tapestry. What is common in these DHTs is that, in their respective overlays, each node is the root of a tree spanning the whole network. These spanning trees are used for message dissemination. Although systems of this class are nearly optimal with respect to message overhead, a single failure along a spanning tree can result in a whole branch missing a message. Failures are disregarded as a whole in [3], where the assumption of reliable communication is made. Scribe [2] provides by default best-effort delivery. Reliability is improved to some extent by imposing TCP connections among nodes, a rather heavy assumption for dynamic, large-scale P2P networks. Finally, Bayeux [21], a system mainly targeted at data streaming, improves on reliability by redundantly disseminating messages across different paths of a spanning tree. However, its design is exposed to scalability problems, as each request to join a group is routed to a single node managing that group.

Gossip-based protocols, such as Bimodal Multicast (*pbcast*) [1] and Directional Gossip [14] form an alternative to broadcasting approaches without sufficient redundancy. Each node forwards a message to a small random subset of the network, and so on. These protocols generally provide only *probabilistic* guarantees for message delivery. However, they are attractive because they are easy to deploy and resilient to node and link failures, due to redundant message deliveries. On the other hand, scalability can suffer if nodes are required to maintain full knowledge of the network, notably when node churn is at stake. Optimizations have been suggested in [1] to overcome such scalability issues.

Other gossiping protocols, such as *lpbcast* [4,5] and [12,7] provision for membership management too. In particular, [7] describes a hybrid dissemination system, that multicasts messages using a tree-based hierarchical structure, and locally switches to gossiping when a large number of failures is detected. These protocols drop the assumption of full knowledge of the network. Each node maintains a small view of the network, consisting of a few links to neighbors, which are used for dissemination. This makes them highly scalable. However, due to their probabilistic nature, a message may fail to reach the whole network even in a fail-free environment. To alleviate this, highly redundant message forwarding is employed.

Excessive redundancy of push-based approaches can be reduced while retaining a high hit ratio, by employing pull-based epidemic techniques: nodes periodically poll other nodes to pull messages they may have missed. However, the periodic nature of pull-based gossiping results in relatively long latency of message dissemination, significantly longer than reactive push-based approaches. We will not consider pull-based techniques in this paper.

Contributions

The contributions of this paper are three-fold. First, we study the algorithm proposed in [12] (which we call RANDCAST), we observe and quantify the excessive message overhead it imposes on the network, and explain why the class of flat, *probabilistic dissemination algorithms* requires high levels of redundancy to disseminate messages to the whole node population.

Second, we reason that imposing some level of *determinism* on probabilistic dissemination algorithms can substantially reduce the dependence on message redundancy, introducing the class of *hybrid (probabilistic/deterministic) dissemination algorithms*. Protocols of this class achieve deterministic dissemination to all nodes in fail-free environments. When failures occur, their reliability degrades gracefully with the number of failures.

Third, we propose RINGCAST, a novel hybrid dissemination algorithm, which achieves complete dissemination of messages (hit ratio 100%) with an order of magnitude lower message overhead compared to RANDCAST. Our extensive experimentation and side by side comparison of the two protocols, show that RINGCAST outperforms RANDCAST in terms of hit ratio, message redundancy, tolerance to node churn, and resilience to (even large-scale) node failures. Moreover, both algorithms distribute the dissemination load uniformly on all participating nodes.

2 Evaluating a Dissemination System

A number of issues are of concern when evaluating or comparing information dissemination systems. It is essential for the rest of this paper to list the metrics used to evaluate the effectiveness and usefulness of a dissemination system.

Hit ratio. This is defined as the ratio of nodes that receive a message over the total node population. It rates the dissemination reliability. Ideally, a reliable dissemination system should always achieve a hit ratio of 100%. In our evaluation (Section 7) we present graphs of the complementary *miss ratio* metric, defined as: $MissRatio = 1 - HitRatio$.

Resilience to failures and churn. For a dissemination system to be meaningful in a real-world dynamic network, it should operate reasonably well in the presence of node or link failures, and node churn. The operation under such conditions is evaluated by means of the hit ratio, described above.

Dissemination speed. The time required for the dissemination of a particular message to complete. The faster a message is disseminated the better. Dissemination speed depends on two principal factors. First, the delay in forwarding messages (processing delay on nodes plus network latency). Second, the number of hops a message takes to reach the last node. In our evaluation we focus on the latter factor.

Message overhead. The overall number of times a message is forwarded during its dissemination. For a message to reach N recipients, it should be forwarded a minimum of N times. In practice, however, messages are forwarded a number of redundant additional times, to sustain churn and failures. Message overhead rates a dissemination system with respect to preserving or wasting network resources.

Load distribution. The distribution of load over nodes, in terms of messages received and messages forwarded. Ideally, load should be evenly distributed among participating nodes.

when node P generates message m,
      or receives m from node Q **do**
    if m not already seen **then**
      $targets \leftarrow$ selectGossipTargets(Q)
      foreach $T \in targets$ **do** send(T, m)
    endif
end

          (a)

function selectGossipTargets(Q)
    $targets \leftarrow view\text{-}\{Q\}$
    return $targets$
end

          (b)

Fig. 1. (a) The generic dissemination algorithm. (b) Gossip target selection for deterministic dissemination (flooding).

In this paper we are interested in reliable dissemination of messages originating at *any* node to *all* participating nodes. We do not focus on optimizing the dissemination of messages with respect to any proximity metric or by building a spanning tree. Also, we do not consider positive or negative acknowledgements, or requests for retransmission of lost messages. Instead, we introduce redundancy in message dissemination and examine its relation to the level of reliability achieved. We investigate the power of epidemics at disseminating messages to all nodes, with a high probability.

3   Deterministic Dissemination

Consider a system consisting of N nodes, and a set of directed links among them. A *message* can originate at any of the participating nodes, and aims at reaching the whole network. A node that generates a new message or receives a message for the first time, forwards it across *all* its outgoing links. If a node receives a message for the second time, it simply ignores it. As an optimization, a message is never forwarded back to the node it was just received from. This basic algorithm is often referred to as *flooding*. Figure 1(a) shows the pseudocode for the dissemination algorithm.

The distinguishing characteristic of flooding is that one can deterministically control dissemination by imposing the appropriate overlay on the nodes. The underlying requirement to guarantee complete dissemination starting from any participating node, is to form a *strongly connected directed graph*[1] including *all* nodes. A multitude of overlays have been proposed for information dissemination by means of flooding, each one demonstrating a different behavior with respect to the metrics listed in the previous section.

Spanning trees or simply *trees* were among the first types of overlays proposed for flooding. Their strong point is that they are optimal with respect to the number of links maintained and, consequently, to the message overhead associated with dissemination. Indeed, in a network consisting of N nodes, the complete dissemination of a message over a tree involves exactly $N - 1$ point-to-point communications. Their main disadvantage, though, is that a single failure of any link or any non-leaf node disconnects the tree prohibiting messages from reaching all nodes. Also, maintaining a valid tree structure, ensuring the graph is connected and yet acyclic, is not a trivial task in the

---

[1] A directed graph in which there is a directed path between any ordered pair of nodes.

presence of failures. For these reasons, trees are not suitable for dynamic environments where failures can happen.

A special type of tree-based overlays for flooding is the *server-based* class (*star graphs*), where all nodes are connected by bidirectional links to a single node acting as a relay server. In these overlays all but the server node are leaf nodes, therefore their failure has no effect on the remaining nodes, but the server becomes a single point of failure. In addition, such overlays demonstrate the worst possible load distribution, the server node being linearly loaded by the number of nodes and number of messages being disseminated, rendering it a non-scalable solution.

On the other end of the spectrum lie *cliques* (*complete graphs*). In such a setting, every node has a complete view of the network. A node broadcasts a message by sending it to every other node in the network. This provides maximum reliability, at the cost of high maintenance costs. Although messages always reach all nodes irrespectively of how many nodes have failed, maintaining this type of overlay is impractical. Maintaining a fully connected graph is expensive in networks larger than a few dozen nodes, notably when the membership changes continuously.

A class of flooding overlays deserving more attention is the one based on *Harary graphs*, introduced by Harary in [9], further studied by Jenkins and Demers [11], and applied by Lin et al. [15] in flooding. A Harary graph of connectivity t is a minimal link graph that is guaranteed to remain connected when up to $t - 1$ nodes or links fail. Its minimum cut, therefore, consists of t links. Moreover, in a Harary graph links are evenly distributed across nodes, each node having either t or $t + 1$ bidirectional links. An example Harary graph of connectivity two is a bidirectional ring, that we will use later in Section 5.1. Such overlays are very appealing for information dissemination in the presence of failures, as they are guaranteed to sustain up to a certain number of failures while imposing the minimum message overhead (for the corresponding reliability guarantees), and this overhead is evenly balanced across all nodes. The maintenance of such graphs, notably of higher connectivity t, can be a complicated and expensive task for large-scale, dynamically changing networks.

4 Probabilistic Dissemination

Acquiring reliability by imposing systematic structure on overlays is infeasible in dynamic networks of massive scale. In this section we take a look at an appealing alternative, *probabilistic dissemination* algorithms, which trade-in deterministic reliability guarantees in return of overlay construction and maintenance simplicity.

In these algorithms, dissemination is not guaranteed by means of a strategic topology, but by increased redundancy in message forwarding. The basic idea is that a node receiving a message forwards it to a number of *random* other nodes. It turns out that if that number is sufficiently high, messages reach all nodes with a high probability [12]. The choice of random nodes to forward messages to can be easily handled by a PEER SAMPLING SERVICE, as described in [10]. The main advantage of probabilistic dissemination algorithms is that they are very simple to implement and inherently tolerant to dynamic environments, at the cost of increased message overhead.

4.1   The RANDCAST Dissemination Algorithm

We consider a system consisting of N nodes. Each node runs the PEER SAMPLING SERVICE, providing it with a small, random, partial view of the network. A *message* can originate at any of the participating nodes, and aims at reaching the whole network. A node that generates a new message or receives a message for the first time, forwards it to (up to) F nodes, called the node's *gossip targets*, chosen randomly from its PEER SAMPLING SERVICE view. F is a system-wide parameter, called the *fanout*. A message is never forwarded back to the node it was just received from. Figure 2 shows the pseudocode for the selection of gossip targets in the RANDCAST dissemination algorithm.

function selectGossipTargets(Q)
    targets ← F random nodes from *view*-$\{Q\}$
    return *targets*
end

Fig. 2. Gossip target selection for the RANDCAST dissemination algorithm

Note that this algorithm is quite efficient at spreading a message to a considerable percentage of the nodes in the network very fast, specifically at exponential speed with base F: A new message progressively reaches F^0 (=1, the message generator), F^1, F^2, ... other nodes. Consequently, a message spreads very fast even for small values of $F \geq 2$. As expected, dissemination slows down when the message is forwarded to nodes that have already received it. However, if the selection of nodes to forward a message to is uniformly random, this slowdown is expected to be negligible until the message has reached a substantial percentage of the network.

Despite its strength at spreading messages fast, RANDCAST is not as efficient at achieving *complete dissemination*, that is, to reach every single node in the network. It is by nature a probabilistic algorithm. Even in the absence of failures, it provides no hard guarantees that a message will reach *all* nodes. It is not hard to see why. By forwarding messages at random, a node has no guarantees that at least one of its incoming links will be chosen to forward the disseminated message. To alleviate this, abundant redundancy should be introduced by means of a large fanout. However, this is not desirable, because message overhead increases proportionally to the fanout, as we will see in the evaluation in Section 7. The RANDCAST dissemination algorithm has been analyzed and evaluated by Kermarrec et al in [12].

In the following section we introduce a novel class of hybrid dissemination algorithms, combining deterministic and probabilistic dissemination. We also present a particular protocol of this class. We defer the evaluation of both protocols until Section 7, where they are compared side by side.

5   Hybrid Dissemination

As we discussed above, although probabilistic protocols are good at spreading messages fast even for small values of F, a large value of F is mandated to reach every single node in the network. This inefficiency can be tackled by introducing some *determinism* in the selection of gossip targets, ensuring any possible dissemination graph is connected and includes all nodes.

Hybrid dissemination protocols aim at combining probabilistic and deterministic behavior. To that end, they establish two types of links among nodes. Random links (*r-links*) contribute to their probabilistic behavior, and deterministic links (*d-links*) bring in determinism. R-links are simply links randomly selected, just like in purely probabilistic dissemination protocols. When presented with a message, a node forwards it across a few r-links. Consequently, messages initially spread to a large portion of the network at close to exponential speed.

However, a message being disseminated should reach every single node in the network. That is, it should be forwarded across at least one incoming link of each node. The basic idea is to establish a set of d-links, and have nodes deterministically forward messages across *all* their outgoing d-links, in addition to a few of their outgoing r-links. If the set of d-links forms an overlay compliant to the deterministic dissemination protocols' requirement, that is, it forms a strongly connected directed graph including all nodes, complete dissemination of messages is guaranteed. In such a graph, each node's indegree is at least 1. Moreover, if we ensure that the graph defined by the d-links has a minimal cut of t, then complete dissemination is guaranteed even in the presence of up to $t - 1$ faulty nodes.

Hybrid protocols effectively decouple the two fundamental goals in information dissemination. On one hand, spreading a message to a large percentage of the nodes fast, and on the other, reaching every single node. The probabilistic component carries out the bulk of the dissemination task, while the deterministic one takes care of the fine-grained details.

What makes hybrid dissemination protocols attractive, is that the set of d-links does not need to form a particularly sophisticated and hard-to-maintain structure. The sole requirement is that the set of d-links forms a strongly connected directed graph over all nodes. A simple structure satisfying this requirement is a ring. In the following section we explore how it can be used as a basis for a practical hybrid dissemination system.

5.1 The RINGCAST Dissemination Algorithm

We introduce RINGCAST, a novel *hybrid dissemination algorithm* that—even with a very low fanout—guarantees complete dissemination in a failure-free environment. In the presence of failures, its performance degrades gracefully, nevertheless still outperforming RANDCAST. Finally, when confronted with continuous churn, RINGCAST proves again more reliable than RANDCAST, excluding nodes that joined the system very recently (for which it performs worse).

As discussed above, hybrid dissemination algorithms maintain two types of links between nodes, namely r-links and d-links. R-links are random links, obtained by a membership management protocols such as the PEER SAMPLING SERVICE [10]. With respect to d-links, RINGCAST organizes nodes in a *global bidirectional ring* structure. A bidirectional ring constitutes a strongly connected graph, as required by deterministic dissemination protocols. Figure 3 illustrates an example RINGCAST overlay, where nodes form a bidirectional ring, and each one has a single outgoing r-link.

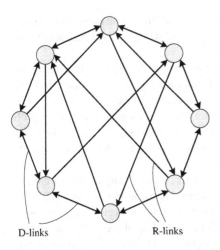

D-links   R-links

Fig. 3. Example of a RINGCAST overlay. Nodes are organized in a bidirectional ring (by means of the *d-links*), and each one has a number (in this case only one) outgoing random links (*r-links*).

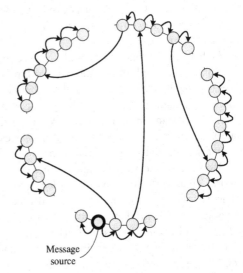

Message source

Fig. 4. Example of a message dissemination in a partitioned ring. For clarity, only a few of the followed r-links are shown.

```
function selectGossipTargets(Q)
      targets ← {}
      if ringNeighbor1 ≠ Q then targets ← targets + {ringNeighbor1}
      if ringNeighbor2 ≠ Q then targets ← targets + {ringNeighbor2}
      targets ← targets + (F−targets.size) random nodes from (view−{Q})
      return targets
end
```

Fig. 5. Gossip target selection for the RINGCAST dissemination algorithm

Just like in the dissemination protocols discussed earlier, a node that generates a new message or receives a message for the first time, forwards it to (up to) F nodes, where F is the system-wide fanout parameter. However, in the case of RINGCAST, a node always forwards a message to its two ring neighbors (sending it across its two outgoing d-links), and across $F - 2$ randomly selected r-links. If the message was received through one of the node's ring neighbors, the node forwards it to the other ring neighbor, and across $F - 1$ random r-links. Figure 5 shows the pseudocode for the selection of gossip targets in the RINGCAST dissemination algorithm.

Note that a bidirectional ring is a Harary graph of connectivity two, that is, its minimal cut is two. Consequently, although no single node failure can break the ring in two disjoined partitions prohibiting complete dissemination to the remaining nodes, such a situation *will* occur if two non-adjacent nodes fail. In most cases, however, this is not a crucial problem for dissemination, as d-links are only one facet of the process. R-links can carry the message to arbitrary nodes, most often bridging the gap between two or more disjoined ring partitions. Effectively, it suffices if any *one* node of an isolated ring partition receives the message, as the message will propagate to the whole partition over the d-links. Figure 4 presents a complete dissemination scenario over a ring split in several partitions. As we will see in the evaluation in Section 7, RINGCAST achieves a high hit ratio (higher comparatively to RANDCAST) even in the presence of many failed nodes.

6 Building the RANDCAST and RINGCAST Overlays

The r-links and d-links are built using epidemic protocols too:

Random links (*R-links*). Several methods may be applied to randomly sample peers in an unstructured peer-to-peer overlay, e.g. by means of the PEER SAMPLING SERVICE [10]. In RINGCAST we use CYCLON [19], an epidemic protocol that is an instance of the PEER SAMPLING SERVICE, and that has shown to produce overlays that strongly resemble random graphs. Omitting certain details, in CYCLON each node maintains a small view of ℓ_{cyc} links to random other nodes. A node periodically gossips with another node, trading *some* of their links with each other. As a result, node views are periodically refreshed by links to random other nodes in the network. At any given moment, the current snapshot of the nodes along with their links resembles a random graph.

Deterministic ring links (*D-links*). Such links are maintained using a proximity-based topology construction epidemic protocol, here we use VICINITY [20]. The basic idea is that nodes maintain short views of the network of length ℓ_{vic}. They periodically gossip to random other nodes, exchanging their views. Upon epidemic view exchanges, a node keeps the ℓ_{vic} links to the closest peers according to a given proximity metric. This way, the neighbor set of each node gradually converges to the closest peers out of the whole node population. Here proximity refers to the distance between—arbitrarily chosen— *sequence IDs*, which determine the organization of nodes in a ring structure. The d-links of a node are the two peers with just higher and just lower sequence ID. Links to a few more peers with gradually higher and lower sequence IDs are not involved in the dissemination protocol, but are useful in maintaining the ring in dynamic conditions.

  Note that both these protocols have a periodic nature. Each node initiates an epidemic view exchange (per protocol) once every T time units (nodes have independent, non-synchronized timers). We refer to T as the *cycle* of the protocol. This will be relevant in Section 7.3, where the churn rate is defined relative to the cycle length.

7 Evaluation

We evaluate the two protocols side by side in three scenarios. First, in a static and failure-free network. Second, in a static network right after a catastrophic failure, that is, after the sudden failure of a large number of nodes. Finally, in a dynamic network under continuous node churn. Evaluation was done with respect to the following criteria, as discussed in Section 2:

1. Hit ratio
2. Dissemination speed
3. Message overhead

We do not explicitly address load balancing, because both protocols are by nature distributing the load across all nodes evenly. A node receiving a message forwards it to F others, just like any other node.

Experiments were carried out using the PeerSim simulator [16]. We tested all scenarios by instantiating a network of 10,000 nodes. Each node was running CYCLON and, in the case of RINGCAST, VICINITY too, as described above, with view length 20 for each protocol ($\ell_{cyc} = \ell_{vic} = 20$). The view lengths are not crucial for the behavior of these algorithms ([20]). Nodes were initially supplied with a certain single contact in their CYCLON views, forming a star topology. VICINITY views were initially empty. After letting the network self-organize (for the record we let it run for 100 cycles, which were more than enough), we started disseminating messages from various nodes picked at random.

We assume a very simple dissemination model, that allows us to study the evolution of disseminations in terms of discrete rounds, that we call *hops*. The generation of a message is marked hop 0. At hop 1, the message reaches F neighbors of the origin node. At hop 2, it further reaches the neighbors' neighbors, and so on. This way, we can evaluate the progress of a dissemination by counting the number of messages sent and the number of new nodes notified per hop.

An implicit assumption underlying our dissemination model is that the processing delay and network latency between all pairs of nodes are the same. Although latencies vary in a real wide-area network, our assumption does not have an effect on the macroscopic behavior of dissemination with respect to the hit ratio. Dissemination relies on nodes forwarding the messages they receive. A node that receives a message for the first time, forwards it to the same number of neighbors picked with the same logic, irrespectively of the time this happens. Consider for instance two scenarios of RANDCAST, executing over the same static overlay (assume gossiping is currently stalled), starting from the same origin and each node picking the same gossip targets in both cases. If pair-wise latencies are different in the two scenarios, the order in which nodes are notified may change, but the exact same set of nodes will have been eventually notified. In the case of RINGCAST, the set of nodes notified may change, but the same macroscopic behavior is maintained.

7.1 Evaluation in a Static Failure-Free Environment

We first evaluate and compare the two protocols side by side by considering a failure-free static environment.

We instantiated a network of 10,000 nodes in PeerSim. Each node was running CYCLON and, in the case of RINGCAST, VICINITY too as described above, with view length 20 for each protocol. Nodes were initially supplied with a given single contact in their CYCLON views, forming a star topology. VICINITY views were initially empty. After letting the network self-organize for 100 cycles, we started posting messages and observing their dissemination.

We ran a number of experiments—not presented here—to investigate the effect of gossiping speed on dissemination. More precisely, we explored the relation between the gossiping period and message forwarding time, that is, the time is takes a node to process a message and forward it to a neighbor. We varied the message forwarding time from zero to several times the gossiping period. We recorded no effect whatsoever on the macroscopic behavior of disseminations. That is, although changing the message forwarding time results in different experiments, with different nodes being reached each time and in a different order, all macroscopic properties, such as the hit ratio, dissemination speed, and message overhead, are preserved. It is not hard to see why. With respect to VICINITY-managed d-links, they are not even altered by gossip exchanges once the optimal sets have been obtained. With respect to CYCLON-managed r-links, these are random links anyway, irrespectively of whether they are being updated fast or are currently fixed. Consequently, forwarding a message along a few of them has an equivalent effect regardless of whether gossiping runs at a high rate or is currently stalled.

Having verified this, we chose to disseminate messages over *fixed* overlays in all experiments presented in this section. This choice was primarily made to limit simulation execution to a reasonable time, considering the large number of experiments we carried out. So, in each experiment, after self-organizing for 100 cycles, the overlay was frozen and only then did disseminations start.

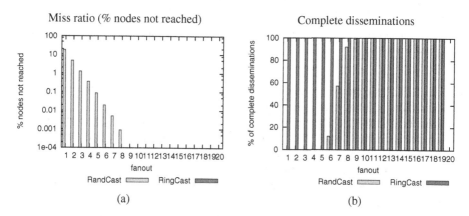

Fig. 6. Dissemination effectiveness as a function of the fanout, for a failure-free static network of 10K nodes. (a) Miss ratio averaged over 100 experiments; (b) Percentage of 100 experiments that resulted in complete dissemination.

For each value of F ranging from 1 to 20, we posted 100 messages from various nodes picked at random, resulting in a total of 2000 experiments for each protocol. Since the hit ratio approaches 100% even for small values of F, it is more meaningful to present the miss ratio instead, in logarithmic scale. Figure 6(a) presents the dissemination miss ratio averaged over 100 experiments for each value of F. RANDCAST and RINGCAST are represented by light and dark bars, respectively. The miss ratio for RANDCAST appears to be dropping exponentially as a function of the fanout F. Note that no dark bars appear in this graph, as the miss ratio for RINGCAST is zero for any

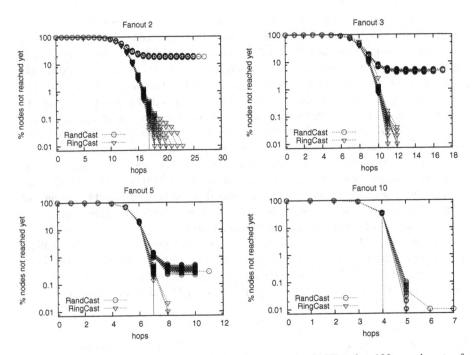

Fig. 7. Dissemination progress in a static failure-free network of 10K nodes. 100 experiments of each protocol are shown.

choice of F. This comes as no surprise, as RINGCAST's operation guarantees complete dissemination in failure-free static networks.

Figure 6(b) shows the percentage of experiments that resulted in a complete dissemination, for each value of F. With respect to RANDCAST, it is interesting to see that the transit from 0% to 100% follows a rather steep curve. For instance, even with a fanout of 5, although the overall hit ratio was above 99.9% (Fig. 6(a)), none of the 100 experiments resulted in a complete dissemination. With a fanout of 7, more than half of the disseminations were complete, while by further increasing the fanout to 11 or higher we get only complete disseminations. As far as RINGCAST is concerned, this graph validates once again that disseminations are always complete, irrespectively of the chosen fanout.

Having seen to what extent messages eventually spread, we now take a closer look at the evolution of dissemination hop by hop. Figure 7 shows the progress of all 100 dissemination for each protocols, for four different fanouts. More specifically, it shows the number of nodes that have not yet been notified, as a function of the hops taken.

Four main observations can be made by examining these graphs. First, for a given fanout, all experiments of a protocol demonstrate very small variations in their progress with respect to the hit ratio and dissemination latency. This is important as it shows that by selecting the appropriate fanout value, we can tune a system's dissemination behavior to a good level of accuracy. Second, we notice a clear—expected—influence of the fanout on dissemination latency. The higher the fanout, the shorter a dissemination's

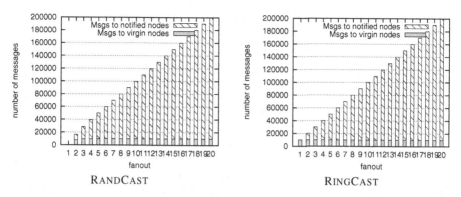

RANDCAST

RINGCAST

Fig. 8. Total number of messages sent, divided in messages sent to not-yet-notified and already notified nodes

duration. Third, we observe that the progress of disseminations for the two protocols is alike for a few initial hops, when the message has not yet reached a significant portion of the network. The protocols differentiate only after a substantial percentage of the nodes (i.e., at least 80%-90%) have been notified. This is a direct effect of the two protocols' operation. By forwarding messages at random, RANDCAST hardly reaches any more non-notified nodes, in an already saturated network. On the contrary, by also forwarding messages along the ring, RINGCAST exhaustively reaches out to every single node. Finally, we see that the higher the fanout the more similarly the two protocols disseminate messages. However, in all cases RINGCAST reaches the last node in fewer hops, demonstrating a lower dissemination latency.

The third metric we are interested in is message overhead. As we already mentioned in Section 4.1, message overhead increases proportionally to the fanout. Indeed, if a node forwards a newly received message to F other nodes and N_{hit} nodes are reached in a dissemination, the total number of messages sent is $F \times N_{hit}$. Figure 8 confirms this assessment. The shaded segments represent the number of messages reaching nodes for the first time (noted as "virgin" nodes). The striped segments represent the number of *redundant messages*, that is, messages reaching already notified nodes, and therefore constitute a waste of network resources. As the network consists of $10K$ nodes, for a given fanout F a complete dissemination involves $F \times 10K$ total messages, out of which $10K$ are messages to "virgin" nodes, and the rest $(F - 1) \times 10K$ are redundant. The two graphs are practically identical except for low fanouts, for which RANDCAST disseminations do not reach all nodes. These graphs are illustrative with respect to the reason the fanout should be kept as low as possible.

7.2 Evaluation After Catastrophic Failure

For a system to be usable in a realistic environment, it has to cope with failures. In this section we explore the behavior of the two protocols in the face of catastrophic failures, that is, when a number of nodes suddenly break down.

We set up the experiments like the ones in the previous section, but before starting the disseminations we kill a randomly chosen portion of the nodes. That is to say, for each experiment we simulate a network of 10,000 nodes, let it self-organize for 100 cycles, and stall gossiping. We subsequently remove a randomly chosen set of the nodes and examine dissemination over the remaining ones.

Unlike failure-free static networks where ongoing gossiping has no influence on dissemination after some point (see Section 7.1), in the face of failures gossiping *does* have an effect, namely a positive one. Following a catastrophic failure, gossiping allows the network reorganize itself, removing links to dead nodes and reestablishing valid ring links. In our experiments gossiping was *not* allowed following the catastrophic failure, exploring the ability of a partially damaged overlay to disseminate messages without giving it the chance to self-heal. This was our deliberate choice, aiming at testing a catastrophic failure's worst-case influence on dissemination.

Figure 9 presents the dissemination effectiveness for both protocols after catastrophic failures killing 1%, 2%, 5%, and 10% of the nodes. Similarly to Figure 6 in the previous section, the graphs on the left show the miss ratio, and the ones on the right the percentage of disseminations that reached all nodes, as a function of the fanout F. One can clearly see that RINGCAST is more effective at disseminating messages in all experiments. A closer look at these graphs shows that as the volume of the catastrophic failure grows larger, the difference between the two protocols' effectiveness decreases. However, even when 10% of the nodes are killed at once, RINGCAST demonstrates an order of magnitude lower miss ratio than RANDCAST. The lower miss ratio of RINGCAST reflects on the significantly higher percentage of complete disseminations for small fanouts.

Figure 10 shows the evolution of disseminations after a catastrophic failure of 5% of the nodes, in accordance to Figure 7 in the previous section. Once again, the relation between the chosen fanout and dissemination latency is verified. We also see that the evolution of disseminations exhibits small variations for a given configuration, like in the case of a failure-free static network.

7.3   Evaluation Under Churn

Apart from catastrophic failures, a system should also be able to deal with node churn, that is, continuous node arrivals and departures. In this section, we examine the behavior of the two protocols under churn.

We evaluate the two protocols against the artificial churn model described here. In each cycle a given percentage (known as the churn rate) of randomly selected nodes are removed, and the same number of new ones join the network. Note that this constitutes a worst case churn scenario, as removed nodes never come back, so dead links never become valid again, and new nodes have to join from scratch. We tested both protocols with a churn rate of 0.2%, which, given a gossiping period of 10 seconds, corresponds to the churn rate observed in the Gnutella traces by Saroiu et al [18].

Unlike experiments on static networks where a small number of cycles sufficed to warm up the respective overlays (Sections 7.1 and 7.2), experiments on dynamic networks required significantly more warm-up cycles. A network of 10,000 nodes was let gossip in the presence of continuous artificial churn, until every node had been removed and reinserted at least once. For all experiments this took several thousand cycles. Then

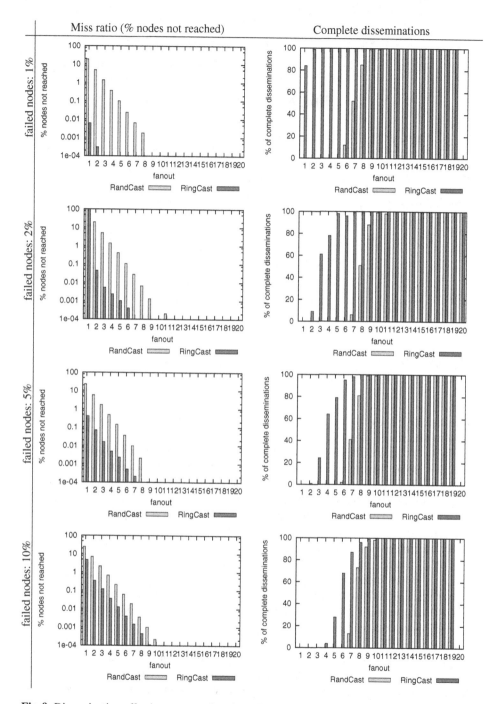

Fig. 9. Dissemination effectiveness as a function of the fanout for static network of 10K nodes, after catastrophic failures of 1%, 2%, 5%, and 10% of the nodes

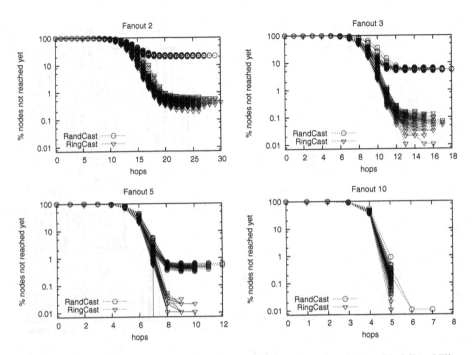

Fig. 10. Dissemination progress in a static network of 10K nodes, after catastrophic failure killing 500 nodes (5%). 100 experiments of each protocol are shown.

the respective network was frozen, and the resulted overlay was tested with respect to dissemination effectiveness.

Figure 11 shows the miss ratio and the percentage of complete disseminations as a function of the fanout. Although RINGCAST results in a lower miss ratio than RAND-CAST for low fanouts (2 to 5), it performs slightly worse for fanouts 6 or higher. It should also be noted that none of the protocols achieves any complete disseminations, except when maximizing the fanout, in which case RANDCAST appears to be performing better again.

By looking at these quantitative graphs alone, one could come to the conclusion that RINGCAST is not any better—if not worse—than RANDCAST when node churn is at stake. A closer, qualitative examination of *which* groups of nodes contribute to each protocol's miss ratio will prove otherwise. As we will see, RINGCAST's miss ratio is almost entirely due to its poor performance at reaching newly joined nodes, while it provides good dissemination guarantees to all older nodes.

Along these lines, we now investigate the relation between a node's *lifetime*, that is, the number of cycles since it joined the network, and its chance of receiving a disseminated message. Figure 12 presents the distribution of node lifetimes after the execution of several thousand cycles, when every node has been removed and reinserted at least once. In fact, Figure 12 plots the exact count of nodes having a given lifetime, aggregated over 100 experiments, in log-log scale. Given that the network consists of 10,000 nodes and the churn rate is 0.2%, at each cycle 20 random nodes are evicted and 20 new

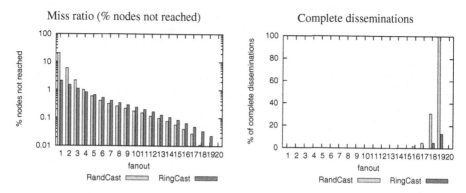

Fig. 11. Dissemination effectiveness as a function of the fanout, in the presence of node churn. In each cycle, a randomly selected 0.2% of the nodes was removed, and replaced by an equal number of newly joined nodes.

are added. Therefore, the number of nodes having a given lifetime cannot exceed 20. For all 100 experiments together, the number of nodes of a given lifetime ranges from 0 to 2000, hence the range of the vertical axis.

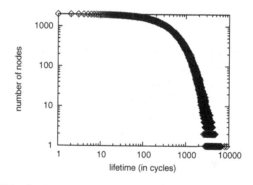

Fig. 12. Distribution of node lifetimes, summed over 100 experiments

The distribution of lifetimes of nodes that *were not notified* during dissemination, is presented in Figure 13. The distributions for two fanouts are shown, 3 (top) and 6 (bottom). It is clear that in all cases newly joined nodes (i.e., ones that joined up to 20 or 30 cycles ago) experience significantly higher miss ratio than other, older nodes. RING-CAST, in particular, results in quite more misses (notice the log scale) than RANDCAST for these nodes. Nevertheless, for nodes that have been in the network for at least 20 or 30 cycles, it demonstrates a substantially lower miss ratio, almost negligible compared to that of RANDCAST. For instance, let us take a look at dissemination with fanout 6. Although RINGCAST appears to have a higher overall miss ratio than RANDCAST (Fig. 11), it hardly suffers any misses for nodes that joined at least 20-30 cycles earlier, contrary to RANDCAST. Its miss ratio is entirely attributed to misses in newly joined nodes.

The implication behind this observation is worth noting. RINGCAST proves to be a better dissemination tool, except for the first few cycles after a node's join. Once a warm-up period of a few cycles has elapsed, a node receives all disseminated messages with very high probability. For a gossiping period of 10 seconds and a view length $\ell_{cyc} = 20$, the warm-up phase amounts to a bit over 3 minutes. In applications where faster node joins is vital, new nodes can gossip at an arbitrarily higher rate for the first few cycles, to complete their warm-up phase correspondingly fast. However, this is a mere optimization and will not be considered further in this paper.

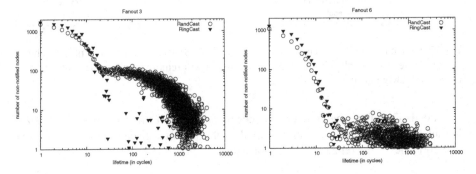

Fig. 13. Distribution of lifetimes of nodes that were not notified, summed over 100 experiments

At this point, it is interesting to understand why new nodes experience more misses, and why this phenomenon is more intense in RINGCAST. Nodes are notified through their incoming links. Their probability of being notified is tightly related to how well they are known by other nodes. A new node joins the network with zero indegree, and gradually increases it. Until a node's indegree reaches the average indegree of the network, it has less chance to receive a message than older, better connected nodes. This shows clearly in the aforementioned graphs (Fig. 13).

More specifically, a new node's r-link indegree increases by one in each of its first few cycles, and takes approximately ℓ_{cyc} (here $\ell_{cyc} = 20$) cycles to stabilize to the average indegree of the network (which is ℓ_{cyc} too). This is a property of CYCLON, which manages r-links. So, for RANDCAST, which depends solely on CYCLON, we observe a steep decrease in misses for nodes of lifetimes 1 through 20, followed by an immediate stabilization thereafter. This is a direct effect of the join process in CYCLON, which takes approximately ℓ_{cyc} cycles to establish the average number of incoming links.

On the other hand, RINGCAST also depends on VICINITY to form the d-links (i.e., the edges of the ring). However, a node does not benefit from incoming VICINITY links until the appropriate incoming d-links are formed, that is, until it eventually becomes known by its two direct ring neighbors. Generally this does not happen instantly, but may require an undefined—yet small—number of cycles. Until then, a newly joined node relies only on its incoming r-links to receive messages. During that phase, it is clear that newly joined nodes have better chances to receive messages in RAND-CAST, where messages are forwarded to F r-links, as opposed to only $F - 2$ r-links in

RINGCAST. This explains why RINGCAST exhibits more misses than RANDCAST for nodes that joined roughly in the last 20 cycles (Fig. 13).

Note that the further curve in misses for lifetimes greater than 100 simply follows the lifetime distribution of the general node population (Fig. 12).

8   Conclusions and Discussion

We explored push-based epidemics for information dissemination in very large-scale systems, focusing on limiting redundant messages while retaining strong probabilistic delivery guarantees. We introduced a new class of push-based epidemic dissemination protocols, which combine probabilistic with deterministic features. The probabilistic component contributes in the exponential spreading of messages, while the deterministic component takes care of the "fine-grained job", making sure that a message reaches every single node. We proposed RINGCAST, a new protocol of this hybrid class, and by extensive experimentation in static, dynamic, and catastrophic failure scenarios performed better than RANDCAST, and at a significantly lower communication cost (message overhead).

Some applications may require higher reliability in dynamic environments. Recall from Section 3 that a bidirectional ring is a Harary graph of minimal cut two. One way to increase reliability, would be to design gossiping protocols that form Harary graphs of higher connectivity. Another, simpler way, is to organize nodes in multiple rings, assigning them a different random ID per ring. In both cases, reliability would be improved at the cost of increased gossip traffic.

Another potential optimization is proximity-based dissemination. Proximity can have many faces, e.g., geographic distance, domain name, network hops, etc. In the protocols examined in this paper, proximity is not taken into consideration. For instance, a message originating in the Netherlands could follow a path such as Netherlands → Australia → Switzerland → Canada → Greece → Uruguay → New Zealand. Obviously, such a path is far from optimal.

A straightforward way to partially deal with domain name proximity in RINGCAST, is to incorporate domain names in the VICINITY similarity function. In this version of RINGCAST, a node forms its ID by reversing its domain name (country domain first) and appending a randomly chosen number. I.e., the ID of a node at the `.inf.ethz.ch` domain of the ETH Zurich could be `ch.ethz.inf.1234`. Without any additional modifications, nodes naturally self-organize in a ring sorted by domain name, and domains sorted by country.

Finally, it should be noted that the protocols discussed in this paper are perfectly suitable for *topic-based publish/subscribe* too. In topic-based pub/sub, a number of *topics* are defined, and each event is associated with one of them. All events associated with a topic should be delivered to all nodes subscribed to that topic. The usage of dissemination protocols such as RANDCAST and RINGCAST for event dissemination is straightforward. Each topic forms its own, separate dissemination overlay. Subscribers join the overlay(s) of the topics of their interest. Finally, events are multicast by disseminating them in the appropriate dissemination overlay.

In this research we have explicitly not considered *pull-based* dissemination. We expect it to significantly improve the efficiency of the protocol in terms of reliability. However, additional issues have to be taken into account, such as the pull frequency, the duration for which nodes maintain old messages, the size of buffers on nodes, etc. Pull-based dissemination is left as future work, as it constitutes a natural extension of our current research.

References

1. Birman, K.P., Hayden, M., Ozkasap, O., Xiao, Z., Budiu, M., Minsky, Y.: Bimodal multicast. ACM Trans. Comp. Syst. 17(2), 41–88 (1999)
2. Castro, M., Druschel, P., Kermarrec, A.-M., Rowstron, A.: SCRIBE: A Large-scale and Decentralized Publish- Subscribe Infrastructure. IEEE JSAC 20(8) (October 2002)
3. El-Ansary, S., Alima, L.O., Brand, P., Haridi, S.: Efficient broadcast in structured p2p networks. In: IPTPS, pp. 304–314 (2003)
4. Eugster, P., Handurukande, S., Guerraoui, R., Kermarrec, A.-M., Kouznetsov, P.: Lightweight Probabilistic Broadcast. In: Int'l Conf. on Dependable Systems and Networks, IEEE Computer Society Press, Los Alamitos (2001)
5. Eugster, P.Th., Guerraoui, R., Handurukande, S.B., Kermarrec, A.-M., Kouznetsov, P.: Lightweight probabilistic broadcast. ACM Trans. Comp. Syst. 21(4), 341–374 (2003)
6. Floyd, S., Van Jacobson, Liu, C.-G., McCanne, S., Zhang, L.: A reliable multicast framework for light-weight sessions and application level framing. IEEE/ACM Trans. Netw. 5(6), 784–803 (1997)
7. Gupta, I., Kermarrec, A.-M., Ganesh, A.J.: Efficient and adaptive epidemic-style protocols for reliable and scalable multicast. IEEE Transactions on Parallel and Distributed Systems 17(7), 593–605 (2006)
8. Hadzilacos, V., Toueg, S.: Fault-tolerant broadcasts and related problems, pp. 97–145. ACM Press/Addison-Wesley Publishing Co., New York, NY, USA (1993)
9. Harary, F.: The maximum connectivity of a graph. In: Proceedings of the National Academy of Sciences, vol. 48, pp. 1142–1146 (1962)
10. Jelasity, M., Guerraoui, R., Kermarrec, A.-M., van Steen, M.: The Peer Sampling Service: Experimental E valuation of Unstructured Gossip-Based Implementations. In: Fifth ACM/IFIP/USENIX International Middleware Conference, Toronto, Canada, pp. 79–98. Springer-Verlag New York, Inc., New York, NY, USA (2004)
11. Jenkins, K., Demers, A.J.: Logarithmic harary graphs. In: ICDCS Workshops, pp. 43–50 (2001)
12. Kermarrec, A.-M., Massoulié, L., Ganesh, A.J.: Probabilistic Reliable Dissemination in Large-S cale Systems. IEEE Trans. Par. Distr. Syst. 14(2), 248–258 (2003)
13. Lin, J.C.-H., Paul, S.: Rmtp: A reliable multicast transport protocol. In: INFOCOM, pp. 1414–1424 (1996)
14. Lin, M.-J., Marzullo, K.: Directional Gossip: Gossip in a Wide Area Network. In: European Dependable Computing Conference, pp. 364–379 (1999)
15. Lin, M.-J., Marzullo, K., Masini, S.: Gossip versus Deterministic Flooding: Low Message Overhead and High Reliability for Broadcasting on Small Networks. In: 14th Int'l Symp. Distributed Computing (DISC), pp. 253–267. University of California at San Diego (2000)
16. PeerSim, no date, http://peersim.sourceforge.net
17. Piantoni, R., Stancescu, C.: Implementing the swiss exchange trading system. In: FTCS 1997. Proceedings of the 27th International Symposium on Fault-Tolerant Computing (FTCS 1997), p. 309. IEEE Computer Society Press, Washington, DC, USA (1997)

18. Saroiu, S., Gummadi, P.K., Gribble, S.D.: Measuring and Analyzing the Characteristics of N apster and Gnutella Hosts. Multimedia Systems Journal 9(2), 170–184 (2003)
19. Voulgaris, S., Gavidia, D., van Steen, M.: Cyclon: Inexpensive membership management for unstructured p2p overlays. Journal of Network and Systems Management 13(2), 197–217 (2005)
20. Voulgaris, S., van Steen, M., Iwanicki, K.: Proactive gossip-based management of semantic overlay networks. Concurrency and Computation: Practice and Experience (to appear)
21. Zhuang, S.Q., Zhao, B.Y., Joseph, A.D., Katz, R.H., Kubiatowicz, J.D.: Bayeux: an architecture for scalable and fault-tolerant wide-area data dissemination. In: NOSSDAV 2001. Proceedings of the 11th international workshop on Network and operating systems support for digital audio and video, Port Jefferson, New York, United States, pp. 11–20. ACM Press, New York (2001)

A Utility-Aware Middleware Architecture for Decentralized Group Communication Applications

Jianjun Zhang[1], Ling Liu[1], Lakshmish Ramaswamy[2], Gong Zhang[1], and Calton Pu[1]

[1] College of Computing, Georgia Institute of Technology, Atlanta, GA 30332, USA
{zhangjj,lingliu,gzhang3,calton}@cc.gatech.edu
[2] Department of Computer Science, University of Georgia, Athens, GA 30602, USA
laks@cs.uga.edu

Abstract. Although unstructured Peer-to-Peer (P2P) networks provide economical platforms for supporting group communication applications, their ad-hoc nature poses significant challenges to the performance of the group communication services. This paper presents the design and implementation of GroupCast − a utility-aware middleware architecture for scalable and efficient P2P group communications. The GroupCast design is characterized by two unique features. First, we present a *utility function* for quantifying the role of unicast links in enhancing the scalability and efficiency of the group communication applications. Second, we develop a utility-aware distributed spanning tree construction algorithm for efficiently propagating group communication messages. It dynamically creates and maintains the group communication channels by optimizing the utility value of the group communication spanning trees. In addition, we also outline a utility-based overlay management protocol for constructing and maintaining low-diameter overlay networks. Our experiments show that the GroupCast system can improve the scalability of wide-area group communication services by one to two orders of magnitude.

Keywords: Peer-to-peer systems, Overlay networks, Utility functions.

1 Introduction

Multi-party group communication applications such as multi-player online games, online community based advertising, real-time conferencing [3], and instant messaging [2] have experienced a surge of popularity in the past few years. The applications are characterized by exchanges of textual or multimedia contents among multiple participants. Decentralized Peer-to-Peer (P2P) networks have evolved as a promising paradigm for providing open and distributed information sharing services by harnessing widely distributed, loosely coupled, and inherently unreliable computer nodes (peers) at the edge of the Internet. The success of Skype [5] has demonstrated both the opportunity and the feasibility of utilizing P2P networks as economical infrastructures for providing wide-area group

R. Cerqueira and R.H. Campbell (Eds.): Middleware 2007, LNCS 4834, pp. 410–428, 2007.
© IFIP International Federation for Information Processing 2007

communication services. However, the overlay networks in Skype are used only for service lookup and control signaling. Under the multi-party conference settings, each node is required to send the payloads directly to other participants of the communication group through its IP unicast links [9]. This places severe limitations on the scalability of multi-party conference calls in Skype.

The natural questions that come up include: *Can P2P overlays be utilized for implementing scalable group communication services over wide-area networks? If so what techniques and system level optimization are critical for enhancing the efficiency and scalability of decentralized wide area group communications?* Although several researchers have explored a related problem in the context of designing application-level multicasting or end-system multicasting (ESM) schemes [20,22] over P2P overlays, surprisingly most of these works are designed to work in conjunction with structured P2P networks, and they rely on the distributed hash table (DHT) abstractions of the P2P network for inter-peer communication and routing [11,21]. However, it is widely recognized that in environments that exhibit high *churn* rates maintaining DHT-based structures imposes severe overheads, which can affect the performance of the applications running on top of these networks to a considerable extent [13]. In contrast, *unstructured P2P networks* like Gnutella [25] are simple to implement, have low maintenance costs, and provide better resilience to network churn caused by peer entries, exits, and failures. To the best of our knowledge, very few group communication applications have been implemented on top of unstructured P2P networks. We hypothesize that common concerns about the non-deterministic nature of communication and service lookup in unstructured overlay networks and their inefficient utilization of the underlying IP network resources are the main reasons for the lack of work in this area.

Designing scalable group communication services on top of unstructured P2P networks poses three main challenges. The first challenge is to translate wide-area group communication application requirements such as communication efficiency and system scalability into the metrics that can be used while designing the communication structures and managing the topologies of the overlay networks. Second, the unstructured P2P networks suffer from heavy messaging overheads and high service lookup latencies. The challenge is to devise low-cost service lookup mechanisms that are effective for both control signaling and communication group management. The resilience of unstructured P2P overlays to network churn is rooted in the fact that they do not use any global control mechanisms for regulating resource distribution and the network topology. The third challenge is to design overlay network management protocols such that the features critical to the performance of group communication applications are incorporated without trading away the inherent randomness of these overlays.

Towards addressing these challenges, this paper presents *GroupCast* - a utility aware decentralized middleware architecture for scalable and efficient P2P group communication applications. In designing the GroupCast system, this paper makes two unique contributions:

- First, we propose a utility function to quantify the usefulness of unicast links to the efficiency of individual communication groups as well as to the scalability of the entire group communication infrastructure. This utility function provides a careful combination of the two most important factors that influence the performance of the system, namely *network proximities of the peers* and *resource availabilities at the end hosts*.
- Second, we design a *utility-aware* mechanism for constructing spanning trees required for disseminating group communication payloads. The objective of this scheme is to optimize the utility-values of the resultant spanning trees. Further, considering the decentralized nature of unstructured P2P networks, this scheme has been designed to operate in a completely distributed fashion, and it does not rely upon any global topological information.

In addition to the above contributions, we also outline a *utility-based* P2P overlay network management protocol that uses the proposed generic utility function for constructing low-diameter unstructured P2P overlays that are comparable to structured P2P network in their scalability and efficiency. This paper presents several experiments to evaluate the utility-aware middleware architecture and its component techniques. The results show that the proposed techniques provide significant scalability and efficiency benefits for the group communication applications.

2   The Basic P2P-Based Group Communication Framework

Spanning tree forms the fundamental structure in most group communication schemes. The spanning tree is an acyclic overlay connecting all the participants of a communication group. The group communication messages (payload) are disseminated through the spanning tree so that they reach all the participants. The various group communication schemes differ in the manner in which they construct and maintain the spanning trees. Our system employs multi-level spanning trees for achieving the scalability needed for supporting group communication in large wide-area networks. The proposed framework includes completely distributed strategies for building and maintaining spanning trees of communication groups.

We introduce a few notations that would be used in the rest of the paper. The P2P network is conceptualized as a directed graph $G < V, E >$, where $V = \{p_0, p_1, p_2, \ldots, p_{N-1}\}$ represents the peers in the network and $E = \{e_0, e_1, \ldots e_{M-1}\}$ denotes the logical links in the network. The spanning tree $T_{Pt} < V_{Pt}, E_{Pt} >$ is defined as a connected, acyclic sub-graph of G, where the participant set $V_{Pt} \subseteq V$ and links set $E_{Pt} \subseteq E$. Each peer is aware of only its immediate neighbors. Further, the network does not have any distributed hash table (DHT) abstractions.

2.1   Constructing a Distributed Spanning Tree

One of the challenges in developing group communication systems is to design a completely distributed scheme for building spanning tree. Several application level multicast (end-system multicast) systems have addressed a very similar problem (the problem of constructing multicast trees). However, as we explain below, none of them are directly applicable for building spanning trees on unstructured P2P networks.

The existing multicast tree construction schemes can be classified into three broad categories. In the first approach, the participants of a multicast group explicitly choose their parents in the multicast tree from a list of candidate nodes [7,18,17]. Due to the complexity of those protocols, there are very few actual implementations of these algorithms. The second approach, which is adopted by systems like Narada [14] and Scattercast [12], constructs the spanning tree in two-steps. The first step constructs a well-connected mesh from the nodes in the network. The second step uses this mesh structure and constructs shortest path spanning trees through well-known distributed algorithms. However, these systems do not scale well, especially when the underlying network experiences considerable churn. The third approach, represented by systems like CAN-multicast [21] and SCRIBE [11], assumes that the nodes of the underlying network are organized as a structured P2P network [20,22]. The multicast tree is constructed using the deterministic routing functionalities of these P2P networks. As we discussed in Section 1, DHT-based structured P2P networks are not suitable for scenarios wherein the peer populations are transient. In short, none of the current multicast tree construction approaches are applicable for the problem at hand.

We have developed completely decentralized scheme for building group communication spanning trees on a generic unstructured P2P network. We leverage techniques such as selective message forwarding for reducing the communication costs of spanning tree construction and maintenance.

2.2   Building the Communication Group

The objective of our communication group construction algorithm is to select the edges or the links in the P2P overlay to form the spanning tree that connects all the group participants. The communication group construction algorithms usually includes the implementation of two functionalities. First, participants should be aware of the existence of the communication group to which they will join. Second, a newly joined participant should be able to setup a connection to the existing nodes in the chosen communication group for sending and receiving the communication payloads.

The first task is usually accomplished by appointing a node as the rendezvous point or the multicast source, and publishing the node's information at a well-known location such as a bulletin board system. Two strategies have been proposed for implementing the second functionality. The first scheme is similar to the DVMRP IP-multicast protocol [16]. Instead of using the IP level network devices such as routers to implement the polling and pruning processes of multicast group management, this strategy uses overlay networks and peers. This strategy is adopted by the Scattercast system [12], in which the source node solely advertises route information and each node in the overlay forwards this advertisement and builds the local routing table entries. To remove loops and to avoid the problem of counting-to-infinity, the full path information is embedded into the forwarded advertisement messages. We refer to this scheme as *Non-Selective Service Announcement*(NSSA) scheme. In the second strategy, the multicast source is mapped to a well-known node serving as the rendezvous point, and the subscribers use this identifier as the keyword in their subscribing requests [11]. The structured system topology and the deterministic routing algorithms decide the series of peers through which each subscription request would be forwarded so that it reaches the rendezvous point or an existing participant in the multicast group. The reverse of this path would be used for forwarding the multicast payloads down from the multicast source.

Two characteristics of our system prevent us from directly reusing these schemes. First, the nature of group communication applications is different from end-system multicast systems. In end-system multicast systems, communication payloads are forwarded in one direction in most of the cases (from the multicast source to all the other nodes), while in group communication systems, each participant may initiate messages in addition to receiving them. Second, the unstructured nature of our P2P overlay prevents us from directly using the reverse of the searching path as the payload communication path.

We have proposed a scheme that combines the advantages of these two schemes, while avoiding their disadvantages. We call our scheme the *Selective Service Announcement* (SSA) scheme. In this scheme, the spanning tree for a communication group is established in three steps.

Step 1 - Choosing Rendezvous Point: First, a peer in the P2P overlay is chosen as the rendezvous point. Unlike the rendezvous point in SCRIBE [11], to which all the multicast payloads are first forwarded, our rendezvous point serves as the source of the group advertisement messages and will behave as a normal node in the communication spanning tree. There are several ways to choose such a rendezvous point. It can be setup as a dedicated server donated by a service provider who injects contents into the communication group. For groups that are setup for applications like online conferences, the first participant can initiate a random walk search to locate a node that has enough access network bandwidth and computational power to act as a rendezvous point.

Step 2 - Advertising: In the second phase, the rendezvous point advertises the group information to the potential participants of the communication group. The flooding scheme used for similar purposes in DVMRP [16] and Scattercast [12] incurs redundant messages in the overlay network. Our SSA scheme alleviates the communication overheads in the following manner. In our scheme, each peer that receives the advertisement message will forward it to a few of its neighbors, rather than flooding the message to all neighboring nodes. Our basic group communication framework uses a very simple approach for selecting neighbors, namely the random strategy. In this algorithm, the rendezvous point and the other nodes receiving the advertisement message randomly select a pre-specified fraction of their neighbors and send them the message. The message propagation terminates when the TTL becomes zero. However, this simple advertisement scheme suffers from two major drawbacks. We discuss these limitations later in the paper and present schemes for mitigating them.

Step 3 - Subscribe: Subscription activities are initiated when a peer p_i decides to join a communication group. Two scenarios need to be considered. First, if the potential service subscriber (peer p_i) has already received and routed the service advertisement, then it is already on the message forwarding path of this communication group. All it needs to do is to start the subscription process by sending the joining message in the reverse direction of incoming SSA message. However, note that the advertisement message might not reach all potential subscribers. In case the subscriber has never received the SSA message, a search method provided by the P2P overlay is triggered to look up the neighborhood of the peer for discovering nodes that might have received the SSA advertisement message.

The search method is implemented as a ripple search in standard Gnutella P2P network, with initial TTL (Time to Live) value set to a very low value. Because our advertisement mechanism would have already *pushed* the service information to different topological regions of the network, a potential subscriber can find a nearby neighbor that has received the SSA message with high probability. Our experiment reports that the average success rate of subscription search is close to 100%, even when the TTL of the search messages are set to 2. Once such a node is discovered, the subscription message is sent to it, which then forwards in the reverse direction of the original SSA message.

2.3   Limitations of the Basic Framework

The basic group communication framework has two important limitations which can affect its efficiency and scalability. The first limitation is the manifestation of the overlay-underlay mismatch problem. Since, in the advertisement phase of the scheme, a node receiving the advertisement forwards the message to a *randomly* chosen subset of neighbors, the resulting tree might not always be efficient in terms of the relative locations of its nodes on the physical network. For example, a node p_i located in New York might have a node p_j located in Australia as one of its children, which in-turn might have a child p_l located in Boston. This has a negative effect on the latencies experienced by the group communication messages. Similarly, the capability (resource availability) of a node p_i in the spanning tree might be completely different from the capabilities of its parents or children. This mismatch among the capacities of the neighbors in the spanning tree can result in high packet losses. This again affects the performance of group communication.

We propose two middleware level techniques for overcoming the above drawbacks, namely a utility-aware spanning tree construction scheme and a utility-aware topology management scheme for the underlying P2P network. While the first technique addresses the question as to *how should the connections in the overlay be utilized for group communication applications?*, the second technique addresses the question of *how the peers should choose and maintain their neighbors in the overlay?* However, it is interesting to observe that these two questions are the manifestations of the same design issue, namely *given a list of nodes, say L, what are the metric(s) that dictate which of these nodes a peer p_i should connect to?* Both these techniques rely upon a unique utility-function, which assigns different preferences (rankings) to each peer in the list L. In the next section, we explain the formulation of the utility function. We then describe how this utility function is utilized in the proposed techniques.

3   The Utility-Aware Middleware for P2P Group Communication

This section focuses on the two main components of the GroupCast design. First, we describe the utility function we use to quantitatively model the critical performance metrics of wide area group communication applications. Second, we discuss how to employ our utility function to optimize the group communication channel construction and maintenance by developing a utility-aware distributed spanning tree construction algorithm that can efficiently propagate group communication messages. Finally, we also outline our utility-based overlay management protocol which provides the capability for constructing and maintaining low-diameter overlay networks to further enhance the performance of the group communication services.

3.1   The Utility Function

The group communication in overlay networks essentially occurs by forwarding the communication payload through unicast IP network links. Hence, the properties of the unicast links interconnecting peers in the P2P overlay largely decide the performance and the efficiency of the group communication system. Our utility function considers the two important factors that determine the performance of unicast links, namely the network proximity of the end-nodes and the similarity between among the capacities of the peers. The network proximity between the end-hosts determines the latency of the unicast link. Similarly, it is known that mismatch between the packet-forwarding workloads and the capacities of peers introduces bottlenecks in the communication overlay and may result in high packet losses. We note that these two factors might sometimes be counteracting. For instance, a peer in the list L which is closest to p_i, might have completely different resource availabilities than p_i. Our utility function provides a careful combination of these two factors based on the utility preference of peer p_i, as well as the desired performance properties of the entire overlay.

Concretely, for each node p_j in the list L (recall that L represents a list on potential nodes from which the peer p_i chooses a subset), we assume that two types of information are available: the node capacity C_j, and the relative distance between peer p_i and peer p_j, denoted by $D(p_i, p_j)$. The capacity of a peer is measured in terms of its accessible network bandwidth, since the performance of a peer in a distributed environment like P2P networks is largely decided by its access network bandwidth available for forwarding communication payloads. The access network bandwidth can be specified by the end user in terms of the number of 64kbps connections the node is willing to support. Alternatively, it can also be estimated by network probing techniques. We use the network coordinates to estimate the relative distance between any two peers. Vivaldi [15] and GNP [1] are some of the techniques proposed for measuring the network coordinates of nodes in wide area networks.

We define two utility-based preference metrics based on the two important performance factors namely network proximity and node capacity. Given a list of peers L, we define the *Distance Preference* of peer p_i to peer $p_j \in L$ as the probability that peer p_i chooses peer p_j out of L, based on the network coordinate distance between them. The closer the peer p_j is to peer p_i, the more likely it is chosen. The *Distance Preference* is computed as indicated in Equation 1.

$$PD_{p_i}(L, p_j) = \frac{\frac{1}{d_{p_i}(L, p_j)} - \alpha}{\sum_{p_k \in L} \frac{1}{p_{d_i}(L, p_k)} - \alpha} \tag{1}$$

where $\alpha \in (-\infty, 1)$ is a tunable parameter that indicates the degree to which p_i's prefers closer peers. Higher values of α indicates that p_i strongly prefers closer peers and vice-versa. We choose $\alpha < 1$ so that there is nonzero preference on each $p_j \in L$. The function $d_{p_i}(L, p_j)$ gives the *normalized distance* between p_i and p_j. $d_{p_i}(L, p_j)$ is defined as follows:

$$d_i(L, j) = \frac{D(p_i, p_j)}{\text{MAX}_{p_k \in L} D(P_i, p_k)} \tag{2}$$

Note that $0 < d_{p_i}(L, p_k) \leq 1$ for each peer p_k in the list L.

Similarly, we define the *Capacity Preference* utility metric of peer p_i with respect to peer p_j as the probability that peer p_i chooses peer p_j out of L based on the node capacity of peer p_j. The goal is to utilize higher capacity nodes to relay group communication messages to larger number of peers. Equation 3 gives the formulation for the *Capacity Preference* utility metric.

$$PC_{p_i}(L, p_j) = \frac{C_{p_j} - \beta}{\sum_{p_k \in L} C_{p_k} - \beta} \tag{3}$$

Here C_{p_j} is the node capacity of the peer p_j. The parameter $\beta \in (-\infty, 1)$ plays a similar role as that of α in equation 1.

While the *Capacity Preference* and *Distance Preference* encapsulate the utility of nodes in L from two different perspectives, we need a means to combine these two utility parameters into a single utility function. In this regard, it is interesting to observe that the peer p_i which wants to select a subset of peers from L should also consider its own resource availability (capacity) while making its choices. If the peer p_i possesses more resources, we would like to use it as a forwarding hub in the overlay network and applications. Such a peer should be connected to those peers that have similar resources and play similar roles in the overlay network, which would make it a member of the "core" of the overlay network. On the contrary, if the resources of peer p_i are limited, it should not be placed into the core as that would easily exhaust its resources. A better choice for such a limited resource peer would be to connect to peers that are physically closer to it and use them to access the overlay network. Hence, the weightage given to the two utility metrics (*Capacity Preference* and *Distance Preference*) depends upon the capacity of peer p_i. Accordingly, we define the combined utility function *Selection Preference* of peer p_i to peer $p_j \in L$ as a weighted combination of *Capacity Preference* and *Distance Preference*.

$$P_{p_i}(L, p_j) = \gamma \cdot PC_{p_i}(L, p_j) + (1 - \gamma) \cdot PD_{p_i}(L, p_j) \tag{4}$$

Here γ is the weightage factor such that $0 \leq \gamma \leq 1$.

The configurable parameters α, β, and γ gives us the flexibility to fine-tune the utility function for different application scenarios. For instance, in an overlay network supporting applications that are sensitive to network proximity, α can be set to higher values and γ to be set to lower values. This would ensure that network proximity is the dominating factor when peers make their choices. On the contrary, for an overlay network that emphasizes more on load balancing, a higher value for β and a higher value for γ would be more preferable.

The values of parameter α, β, and γ can be mathematically derived by using techniques similar to the ones used by Bu and Towlsey [10]. However, these techniques require information about the exact number of peers and the exact distributions of the various system-level parameters. In decentralized environments like P2P networks where global statistical mechanisms are expensive to implement, it is unlikely that such information would be available. The GroupCast system adopts an approximation approach to address this problem. Specifically, we define *Resource Level* r_i as the fraction of peers that have less capacity than peer p_i in the overlay network. r_i can be estimated by sampling a few peers that are known to p_i. We use the resource levels of various peers to set the three parameters as $\alpha = 1 - r_i$, $\beta = r_i$, and $\gamma = r_i^{-ln(r_i)}$. Substituting the values for α, β, γ, PC, and PD into equation 4, we obtain:

$$P_i(L, j) = r_i^{-\ln(r_i)} \cdot \frac{C_j - r_i}{\sum_{k \in L} C_j - r_i} + (1 - r_i^{-\ln(r_i)}) \cdot \frac{\frac{1}{d_i(L,j)} - (1 - r_i)}{\sum_{k \in L} \frac{1}{d_i(L,k)} - (1 - r_i)} \tag{5}$$

We note that this configuration reflects our design rationale. The β and γ parameters assume higher values for peers with higher capacities. Hence, these peers would give preference more powerful peers while choosing a subset from L. In contrast, for peers with less resources α assumes higher values whereas β and γ become small. Thus, for these peers the subset selection is predominantly based upon the network proximities. In other words, the less powerful peers connect to nodes that are closer to them. Further, they avoid peers with large capacities, thereby shielding themselves from getting overloaded.

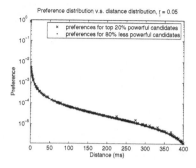
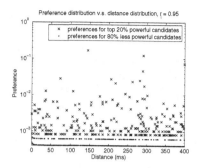

Fig. 1. Selection preference of low capacity peer vs. distance to other peers

Fig. 2. Selection preference of high capacity peer vs. distance to other peers

To evaluate the effectiveness of the selection preference metric, we simulate the selecting process of three peers, using a set of synthetic data. We assign each of them with different resource level value. The one with $r_i = 0.05$ represents a peer with low capacity. Similarly, the one with $r_i = 0.5$ simulates a peer with medium capacity, and the one with $r_i = 0.95$ represents a powerful peer. For each of them, we generated a list of 1×10^3 peers, each of which is assigned a capacity value that follows a zipf distribution with parameter 2.0. We assume that the distance between each candidate peer and the peer evaluating them follows a uniform distribution Unif(0ms, 400ms).

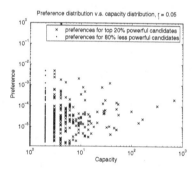
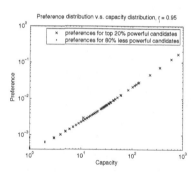

Fig. 3. Selection preference of low capacity peer vs. capacity of other peers

Fig. 4. Selection preference of high capacity peer vs. capacity of other peers

Figure 1 $\sim$ Figure 4 plot the simulation results, which exactly reflects our design rationale. For a weaker peer that has $r_i = 0.05$, the selection preference to other peers is dominantly decided by its distance to them, as plotted in Figure 1 and Figure 3. On the contrary, the selection preference of a powerful peer is largely decided by the node capacity of peers in the candidate set as shown in Figure 2 and Figure 4. For peers that has medium amount of resources, it equally prefers powerful and nearby peers [27].

3.2 Utility-Aware Spanning Tree Construction

In this section, we describe our technique for infusing utility-awareness into spanning tree construction for group communication. The central idea of this technique is to ensure that the edges in the spanning trees have very high utility values, thereby optimizing the overall group communication performance. If the topology of the P2P network and the utility values of all the unicast links in the network were to be available in a centralized location, we could have used one of the several optimization techniques for constructing utility-aware spanning tree. Unfortunately, due to the very nature of P2P systems collecting topological and utility information at a centralized location would be extremely expensive, if not impossible. Therefore, the challenge is to design a completely distributed spanning tree construction technique that is not only effective in ensuring high utility values for the edges in the tree but is also efficient and lightweight.

We observe that the basic spanning tree construction technique that we explained in Section 2 is indeed completely distributed, and it does not rely upon any centralized topological information. Therefore, the question is *whether it is possible to achieve high utility values while retaining the overall spanning tree construction framework?*

Our utility-aware spanning tree construction scheme is based upon the following crucial observation. Of the three phases of the basic spanning tree construction scheme, the advertisement phase has the most significant influence on the structure of the resultant spanning tree. In other words, the advertisement decisions made by various peers more or less determine the structure of the spanning tree. This is because, if a node p_l receiving an advertisement decides to participate in the group being advertised, the very links through which the advertisement was propagated to p_l from the rendezvous node would become a part of the corresponding spanning tree. However, in the basic group communication framework, each peer receiving the advertisement sends it to a randomly selected subset of its neighbors.

From the above observation, we conclude that the most natural way for injecting utility-awareness into the spanning tree construction process is to incorporate it at the advertisement phase. Accordingly, in the utility-based spanning tree construction technique, peer receiving the advertisement forwards it to a subset of its neighbors based on their utility values. Specifically, the probability of a neighbor being included in the subset selected for forwarding the advertisement is directly proportional to its utility value. Thus, a neighbor that has a higher utility value has a higher chance of being included in the subset of nodes to which the advertisement is forwarded.

Specifically, a rendezvous point rp evaluates the utility value of its neighbors using Equation 5. Based on these utility values, it chooses the peers either have similar capacities as rp or are physically close to rp, depending on the capacity of rp. These peers are the ones that are more useful to rp. They receive the advertisement and are likely to be included in the spanning tree.

Upon receiving an SSA message, an arbitrary peer p_k performs two tasks. First, peer p_k uses a local hashing table to check and record if it has already received the same message from any other neighbors. The message will be dropped if it is a duplicated one. Otherwise, it uses a similar mechanism as that of the rendezvous point to select neighbors for further propagating the SSA messages.

In effect, when a peer receives an advertisement, it is more likely that the advertisement traversed a path in which each link had a high utility value. If this peer decides to participate in the group being advertised, the path of the advertisement becomes a part of the corresponding multicast tree. Thus, our scheme seamlessly incorporates utility awareness into the spanning tree construction process.

3.3   Utility-Aware Topology Management

Our utility-aware spanning tree construction algorithm builds the spanning tree from existing connections of the overlay. Thus, the performance of the resultant spanning trees depend upon the topology of the underlying P2P network. With the aim of further enhancing the performance of the GroupCast middleware, we have designed a utility-aware overlay construction mechanism. In this section, we briefly outline the mechanism.

The objective of the utility-aware overlay construction technique is to create P2P networks in which the neighbors of an arbitrary node p_i have reasonably high utility values with respect to p_i. Unlike many P2P networks that are based on the concept of super nodes, our technique inserts both high-capacity and low-capacity peers into the same overlay. Our technique essentially works as follows: When a peer p_i joins the overlay, it gathers the information of a number of existing peers as its neighbor candidates. The new peer calculates the probability of connecting to each candidate by using the utility function defined in Equation 5. These probabilities and the total number of connections that the p_i intends to maintain determine whether p_i would establish a connection with an arbitrary neighbor candidate peer.

Specifically, a joining peer p_i obtains a list of existing peers either using its local cache which contains its P2P network neighbors carried from the last session of activities or by contacting a host cache server. Upon receiving a query request from peer p_i, the host cache sorts its cached entries in the ascending order by their network coordinate distances to peer p_i. From the top of this sorted list, the host cache selects a list of peers BD_i. They are returned to peer p_i together with a list of randomly selected peers BR_i. Starting from the subset B_i of bootstrapping peers received upon its entry, Peer p_i sends a probing message M_{prob} to each peer $p_k \in B_i$. Each peer p_k that receives this probing message sends back a responding message M_{prob_resp}, which is augmented with a list of p_k's P2P network neighbors $Nbr(p_k)$. Peer p_i assembles all the neighbor information contained in the probing replies and compiles them into a candidate list LC_i. For each unique peer $p_j \in LC_i$, peer p_i computes two types of information: (1) The *occurrence frequency* of peer p_j, which records the number of appearances of peer p_j in LC_i, denoted as $f_i(p_j)$. As LC_i serves as a sampling of the peers in the network, $f_i(p_j)$ is the sample of the degree of peer p_j. (2) The estimation of the physical network distance between peer p_i and peer p_j, denoted by $d_i(LC_i, p_j)$, as defined in Equation 2.

Based on these two sets of information, the peer p_i computes the utility value of each peer in LC_i using the equation 6. Depending upon its own its own node capacity, peer p_i selects a certain number of peers from the list LC_i and adds them into its neighbor list ($Nbr(p_i)$). The chances a peer $p_k \in LC_i$ being added to the neighbor list of p_i is directly proportional to p_ks utility values. Concretely, the probability of p_k being selected as a neighbor of p_i is given by the following equation.

$$P_i(LC_i, p_j) = r_i^{-\ln(r_i)} \cdot \frac{f_i(p_j) - r_i}{\sum_{p_k \in LC_i} f_i(p_k) - r_i} +$$

$$(1 - r_i^{-\ln(r_i)}) \cdot \frac{\frac{1}{d_i(LC_i, p_j)} - (1 - r_i)}{\sum_{p_k \in LC_i} \frac{1}{d_i(LC_i, p_k)} - (1 - r_i)} \qquad (6)$$

The peer p_i now sets up its outgoing edges (forwarding connections) to each node in its neighbor list. It then initiates the process to setup the incoming edges (back links to p_i) by sending a backward connection request to each peer $p_k \in Nbr(p_i)$. The request is augmented with the capacity information C_i of peer p_i and its network coordinates. A peer receiving a backward connection request utilizes a similar utility principle to decide whether to accept the request. This ensures that powerful peers are easily accepted by other powerful peers as their neighbors whereas weaker ones are good candidates only when they are close enough. The GroupCast system also includes an epoch-based scheme for maintaining the structure of the P2P overlay even when the network experiences significant churn [27].

4   Experimental Evaluation

We have implemented a discrete event simulation system to evaluate Group-Cast. This system is an extended Java version of p-sim [19] system. We used the Transit-Stub graph model from the GT-ITM topology generator [26] to simulate the underlying IP networks. Peers are randomly attached to the stub domain routers and organized into overlay networks using the algorithm presented in Section 3.3. The capacity of peers is based on the distribution gathered in [23],

Table 1. Capacity distribution of peers

Capacity level	Percentage of peers
1x	20%
10x	45%
100x	30%
1000x	4.9%
10000x	0.1%

as shown in Table 1. We use GNP [1] to assign network coordinate to each peer. Each experiment is repeated over 10 IP network topologies. Each IP network supports 10 overlays, and each overlay network provides service for 10 communication groups.

4.1   Evaluating the GroupCast Service Lookup Mechanism

We begin by evaluating the utility-aware spanning tree construction and group communication mechanisms of the GroupCast system. Most unstructured use either scoped flooding (broadcast) or random walk as their communication paradigm. However, flooding-based mechanisms are expensive in terms of message loads they impose, whereas random walks result in longer delays. The GroupCast system includes a selective service announcement (SSA) mechanism for efficient and low-cost service lookups.

The first experiment evaluates the effectiveness and efficiency of the SSA scheme by simulating the service announcement processes in a number of overlay networks that are generated using either our utility-aware overlay construction mechanism or the centralized PLOD algorithm. In order to gain a better understanding, we compare the SSA mechanism with the non-selective service announcement (NSSA) scheme (see Section 2.1). For each overlay network, we randomly select 10 peers as rendezvous points, and initiate the selective service announcement (SSA) process and the non-selective service announcement (NSSA) process from each of them. For both SSA and NSSA, we first record the fraction of peers in the overlay that have received the service announcement. As we mentioned earlier, when these peers want to subscribe for the group communication service, they can circumvent the service searching process. For peers that have not received the service announcement message, subscription process involves searching its neighborhood for peers that have received the service announcement message. In our simulator, these peers use a ripple flooding search scheme for this purpose with TTL being set to 2. We measure the success rates of service lookups for both SSA and NSSA schemes. We also record the total number of messages generated by these two schemes.

The results in Figure 5 show that the SSA scheme reduces the total number of messages generated in both GroupCast and random power-law overlay networks. The SSA scheme limits the number of subscription messages sent to neighbors that are not likely to be a part of the communication group. This reduces the message load by 63% to 70% when compared with NSSA scheme for the Group-Cast overlay. The reduction is 35% to 44% for the random power-law overlay. We notice that the number of subscription messages of SSA scheme in random power-law overlays is almost negligible. This is because GroupCast overlays have lower cluster coefficient values than the random power-law topologies generated using PLOD. Thus, SSA messages reach fewer peers. The results also show that the SSA scheme performs better for networks with higher connectivity value.

Figure 6 leads to two interesting observations. First, fewer peers in GroupCast receive the SSA messages compared to random power-law topology. Second, all subscribers can locate their services with 100% success rate even when the initial

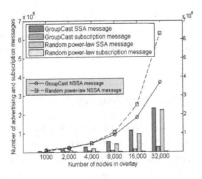
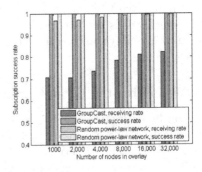

Fig. 5. Message loads of service lookup schemes

Fig. 6. Success rate of service lookup in GroupCast overlay and random power-law overlay with SSA

TTL of the subscription messages is set to *two*. This is essentially because, in the GroupCast overlay, the neighbors of individual peers are likely to have higher utility values. Hence, at each step of the SSA process, more candidate peers meet utility-aware selection criterion. This is also the reason for the relatively large number of service announcement messages in the GroupCast overlay when compared with random power-law network. However, the peers chosen by our utility-aware selection mechanisms are more suitable to the group communication spanning trees and they ensure high subscription success rates even at very small TTL values.

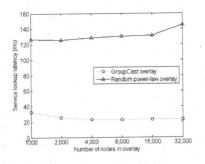
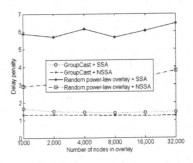

Fig. 7. Latency of service lookup in GroupCast overlay networks and random power-law overlay networks using selective service announcement

Fig. 8. Delay penalty of group communication applications

4.2   Improvement of Application Performance

The second set of experiments studies the effects of the proposed techniques on a group communication application. The group communication application we consider is that of end-system multicasting (ESM). ESM has been proposed as an alternative for IP multicast, which has suffered from lack of wide acceptance and deployment. In this approach, peers form overlay networks and implement multicast functionality. Multicast data are replicated on peers and propagated through unicast edges of the overlay networks. ESM is inherently less efficient than IP multicast, as ESM may send packets with same payload multiple times over the same physical network link. Moreover, the ESM workload distribution among heterogeneous peers affects the overall system performance.

We simulated P2P overlay networks consisting of 1×10^3 to 3.2×10^4 peers. P2P overlay networks are constructed using our utility-aware mechanism as well as the centralized PLOD algorithm. We used the routing weights generated by the GT-ITM package to simulate the IP unicast routing. IP multicast systems are simulated by merging the unicast routes into shortest path trees. We use both SSA and NSSA for service announcement and subscription management.

We quantify the performance of the schemes using *Relative Delay Penalty* and *Link Stress* parameters, which are the two popular metrics for evaluating the efficiency of ESM systems. Relative delay penalty is defined as the ratio of the average ESM delay to the average IP multicast delay. Link stress is defined as the ratio of the number of IP messages generated by an ESM tree to the number of IP messages generated by an IP multicast tree interconnecting the same set of subscribers.

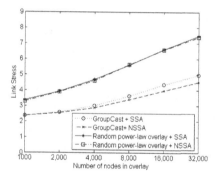

Fig. 9. Link stress of group communication applications

Figure 8 shows the relative delay penalties when multicasting is implemented through various combinations of the two overlay management schemes (utility-aware (GroupCast) and random power-law) and the two spanning tree construction schemes (SSA and NSSA). Figure 9 shows the respective link stress values. The results show that ESM implemented on GroupCast overlays yield significant improvements in terms of both metrics when compared with their counterparts implemented on random power-law networks. The delay penalty of ESM implemented on GroupCast overlay is around 1.5, which is close to the theoretical lower bound of 1. The link stresses of ESM implemented on GroupCast is about two-thirds the link stresses of ESM implemented on top of random power-law network. The improvements are due to the network proximity awareness of the

GroupCast overlay networks. Multicast payloads are forwarded through shorter paths, thus generating fewer IP packets in the underlying IP network.

It is interesting to note that the impact of the SSA scheme on application performance is almost negligible in GroupCast overlay networks, whereas the impact in random power-law networks is significant. We attribute this behavior to the fact that GroupCast overlay networks are already aware of the network proximity of peers. Thus, the peers chosen by the SSA scheme are most likely be the ones that are actually used in the information dissemination spanning tree.

5   Related Work

The work on group communication in P2P networks has mainly focused on structured P2P networks. Researchers have proposed several application-level multicasting schemes for DHT-based structured overlay networks [20,22,24]. However, structured P2P networks have high maintenance costs, especially in highly dynamic environments. In contrast, the GroupCast system does not require any DHT abstractions from the overlay. Instead, Our techniques are completely distributed, and they rely only on local information.

Many distributed group communication systems rely on the services of overlay networks for operation [7,11,14]. Usually, end-hosts in the communication groups use the unicast links of overlay networks to exchange application and management messages. Researchers have explored various techniques to optimize the system performance at the application level with the objective of designing efficient and scalable query processing mechanisms [13].

A popular approach to improving P2P networks is to utilize the rankings of different peers in terms of their node capacity and organize them into different hierarchical layers [4,25]. However, such predetermined hierarchical structures can introduce system vulnerabilities. Further, for efficiency purposes, the supernodes maintain the state information of the normal peers they serve. However, such state information is generally tied to the application, and it is hard to design a supernode overlay layer that can serve as a generic middleware to support different services.

Adaptation mechanisms have been studied in the context of application-layer multicasting [8,28]. Our research is complimentary to these works. These systems can utilize the GroupCast protocols for constructing well-regulated spanning trees. Our protocol can help reduce the number of adaptations by ensuring the efficiency of initial spanning trees. Techniques such as RON [6] have been designed for building generic overlays that are independent of the applications built on top of them. However, unlike these works, the GroupCast system constructs overlay networks that incorporate network proximity information, and it also builds *scale-free* power-law topologies assigning connections according to the peers' capacities.

In short, the work presented in this paper has several unique features and our system addresses a problem that is crucial for the success of several multi-party collaborative applications.

6   Conclusion

This paper presents the design and evaluation of *GroupCast* – a utility-aware decentralized middleware architecture for scalable and efficient wide-area group communications. The GroupCast design incorporates three novel features: (a) A *utility function* that measures the usefulness of unicast links to the scalability and efficiency of the group communication application; (b) A distributed utility-aware scheme for constructing efficient spanning trees for disseminating group communication payloads; and (c) A utility-based overlay management protocol for generating and maintaining low-diameter overlay networks. Our experiments show that GroupCast provides an order of magnitude improvement in the scalability of wide-area group communication applications.

Acknowledgement

This work is partially supported by grants from NSF CSR, NSF SGER, NSF CyberTrust, and grants from IBM SUR and IBM Faculty Award, DoE SciDAC, and AFOSR.

References

1. E. Ng. GNP software (July 2006), http://www.cs.rice.edu/eugeneng/research/gnp/software.html
2. Google Talk (July 2006), www.google.com/talk/
3. Live Meeting (July 2006), http://www.microsoft.com/office/livemeeting
4. Sharman networks LTD. KaZaA media desktop (July 2006), http://www.kazaa.com
5. Skype. (July 2006), http://www.skype.com
6. Andersen, D., Balakrishnan, H., Kaashoek, F., Morris, R.: Resilient overlay networks. In: SOSP. Proceedings of the 18th ACM Symposium on Operating Systems Principles, ACM Press, New York (2001)
7. Banerjee, S., Bhattacharjee, B., Kommareddy, C.: Scalable application layer multicast. In: Proceedings of the 2002 ACM SIGCOMM Conference, ACM Press, New York (2002)
8. Banerjee, S., Kommareddy, C., Kar, K., Bhattacharjee, B., Khuller, S.: Construction of an efficient overlay multicast infrastructure for real-time applications. In: Proceedings of INFOCOM (2003)
9. Baset, S.A., Schulzrinne, H.: An analysis of the skype peer-to-peer internet telephony protocol. Technical Report cucs-039-04, Dept. of Computer Sci., Columbia Univ. (2004)
10. Bu, T., Towsley, D.: On distinguishing between internet power law topology generators. In: IEEE INFOCOM, New York, NY, IEEE, Los Alamitos (2002)
11. Castro, M., Druschel, P., Kermarrec, A., Rowstron, A.: SCRIBE: A large-scale and decentralized application-level multicast infrastructure. IEEE Journal on Selected Areas in communications (JSAC) (2002)
12. Chawathe, Y.: Scattercast: An Architecture for Internet Broadcast Distribution as an Infrastructure Service. PhD thesis, University of California, Berkeley (2000)

13. Chawathe, Y., Ratnasamy, S., Breslau, L., Lanham, N., Shenker, S.: Making Gnutella-like P2P systems scalable. In: ACM SIGCOMM, Karlsruhe, Germany, ACM Press, New York (2003)
14. Chu, Y.-H., Rao, S.G., Zhang, H.: A case for end system multicast. In: ACM SIGMETRICS 2000, pp. 1–12. ACM Press, New York (2000)
15. Dabek, F., Cox, R., Kaashoek, F., Morris, R.: Vivaldi: A decentralized network coordinate system. In: ACM SIGCOMM, Portland, Oregon, USA, ACM Press, New York (2004)
16. Deering, S., Cheriton, D.: Multicast routing in datagram internetworks and extended lans. ACM Transactions on Computer Systems 8(2) (May 1990)
17. Francis, P.: Yoid: Extending the multicast internet architecture (1999)
18. Jannotti, J., Gifford, D.K., Johnson, K.L., Kaashoek, M.F., O'Toole Jr., J.W.: Overcast: Reliable multicasting with an overlay network. In: OSDI. Proceedings of Symposium on Operating System Design and Implementation, pp. 197–212 (2000)
19. Merugu, S., Srinivasan, S., Zegura, E.: p-sim: A simulator for peer-to-peer networks. In: MASCOTS 2003. Proc. of the 11th IEEE Intl. Symp. on Modeling, Analysis, and Simulation of Computer and Telecommunications Systems, IEEE Computer Society Press, Los Alamitos (2004)
20. Ratnasamy, S., Francis, P., Handley, M., Karp, R., Shenker, S.: A scalable content addressable network. In: Proceedings of SIGCOMM, ACM Press, New York (2001)
21. Ratnasamy, S., Handley, M., Karp, R., Shenker, S.: Application-level multicast using content-addressable networks. In: Crowcroft, J., Hofmann, M. (eds.) NGC 2001. LNCS, vol. 2233, Springer, Heidelberg (2001)
22. Rowstron, A., Druschel, P.: Pastry: Scalable, decentralized object location, and routing for large-scale peer-to-peer systems. In: Guerraoui, R. (ed.) Middleware 2001. LNCS, vol. 2218, pp. 329–350. Springer, Heidelberg (2001)
23. Saroiu, S., Gummadi, P., Gribble, S.: A measurement study of Peer-to-Peer file sharing systems. In: Proceedings of MMCN, San Jose, CA (August 2002)
24. Stoica, I., Morris, R., Karger, D., Kaashoek, F., Balakrishnan, H.: Chord: A scalable Peer-To-Peer lookup service for internet applications. In: Proceedings SIGCOMM, pp. 149–160. ACM, New York (2001)
25. WWW. The Gnutella RFC (July 2006), `http://rfc-gnutella.sourceforge.net`
26. Zegura, E.W., Calvert, K.L., Bhattacharjee, S.: How to model an internetwork. In: IEEE Infocom, vol. 2, pp. 594–602. IEEE, Los Alamitos (1996)
27. Zhang, J., Liu, L., Ramaswamy, L., Pu, C.: Scalable and Efficient Peer-to-Peer Group Communication: A Utility-based Approach. Technical report, College of Computing, Georgia Tech. (2006)
28. Zhou, Y., et al.: Adaptive reorganization of conherency-preserving dissemination tree for streaming data. In: ICDE (2006)

Programming Wireless Sensor Networks with the TeenyLIME Middleware

Paolo Costa[1], Luca Mottola[2], Amy L. Murphy[3], and Gian Pietro Picco[4]

[1] Vrije Universiteit, Amsterdam, The Netherlands
costa@cs.vu.nl
[2] Politecnico di Milano, Italy
mottola@elet.polimi.it
[3] ITC-IRST, Povo, Italy, & U. of Lugano, Switzerland
murphy@itc.it
[4] University of Trento, Italy
picco@dit.unitn.it

Abstract. Wireless sensor networks (WSNs) are evolving to support sense-and-react applications, where actuators are physically interspersed with the sensors that trigger them. This solution maximizes localized interactions, improving resource utilization and reducing latency w.r.t. solutions with a centralized sink. Nevertheless, application development becomes more complex: the control logic must be embedded in the network, and coordination among multiple tasks is needed to achieve the application goals.

This paper presents TeenyLIME, a WSN middleware designed to address the above challenges. TeenyLIME provides programmers with the high-level abstraction of a tuple space, enabling data sharing among neighboring devices. These and other WSN-specific constructs simplify the development of a wide range of applications, including sense-and-react ones. TeenyLIME yields simpler, cleaner, and more reusable implementations, at the cost of only a very limited decrease in performance. We support these claims through a source-level, quantitative comparison between implementations based on TeenyLIME and on mainstream approaches, and by analyzing measures of processing overhead and power consumption obtained through cycle-accurate emulation.

Keywords: Wireless sensor and actuator networks, middleware, tuple spaces.

1 Introduction

Wireless sensor networks (WSNs) are a popular technology for monitoring and control applications, where they simplify deployment, maintenance, and ultimately reduce costs. Early WSN efforts were primarily concerned with *sensing* from the environment and reporting to a central data sink [1]. In contrast, an increasing number of applications (e.g., [2,3,4]) now include nodes hosting actuators, able to *react* to external stimuli gathered by nearby sensors and affect the environment under control.

The sense-and-react pattern has a relevant impact on application development. Appropriate programming constructs are required to deal with the increased complexity of specifying how multiple tasks *coordinate* to accomplish the desired global functionality.

R. Cerqueira and R.H. Campbell (Eds.): Middleware 2007, LNCS 4834, pp. 429–449, 2007.

Dedicated abstractions must be provided to describe the *stateful* interactions commonly present in control mechanisms. The ability to locally *react* based on external stimuli is as important as—if not more important than—the ability to gather data. These aspects are discussed in more detail in Section 2, where we both describe a paradigmatic sense-and-react application and illustrate that many of its characteristics are typical of common sense-only applications and lower-level system functionality.

To meet the requirements above we developed TeenyLIME, a WSN middleware whose foundation is the notion of distributed *tuple space* [5], a repository of elementary sequences of typed fields called tuples. This is revisited in TeenyLIME by considering WSN requirements (e.g., resource consumption and reliability) in the programming model. TeenyLIME adopts a minimalist approach: a limited number of powerful operations, with a simple and yet efficient implementation, allow for the development of both application-level and system-level functionality. An overview of TeenyLIME's base concepts and application programming interface (API) is provided in Section 3, while Section 4 illustrates concretely the power of its WSN-specific abstractions by showing them in action in the design of the aforementioned sense-and-react application. Section 5 provides a concise account of the TeenyLIME architecture.

Section 6 evaluates quantitatively TeenyLIME along two dimensions. First, we assess the effectiveness of its *programming model* in different contexts. We examine the implementation of the reference application, whose design we sketched in Section 4, and report about uses of TeenyLIME in sense-only applications and at the system level. We derive code metrics for the TeenyLIME implementations and their counterparts, implemented using plain nesC or the higher-level support provided by Hood [6]. Results indicate that the expressive power of TeenyLIME yields cleaner, simpler, and more compact code. Second, we analyze the TeenyLIME *implementation*. We compare its overhead, in terms of processing time and energy consumption, against existing programming platforms. The results gathered using cycle-accurate emulation demonstrate that the beneficial higher level of abstraction provided by TeenyLIME comes with only a very limited overhead.

Finally, existing node-level abstractions for WSN programming are reviewed in Section 7, before our concluding remarks in Section 8.

A preliminary description of TeenyLIME appeared in a short paper [7]. Here, in addition to a more precise and exhaustive presentation, we illustrate key aspects entirely missing in [7], namely: *i)* a complete TeenyLIME-based design of a sense-and-react application; *ii)* a quantitative, source-level evaluation of the benefits to the programmer; *iii)* a quantitative, cycle-accurate evaluation of the run-time performance.

2   Scenario and Motivation

Sense-and-react applications emerge in many settings, from home automation [3] to road traffic control [4]. As a paradigmatic example, we consider *building monitoring and control*. Modern buildings typically focus on the following functionality:

1. *heating, ventilation, and air conditioning* (HVAC [2]) systems provide fine-grained control of indoor air quality;
2. *emergency control* systems provide guidance and first response, e.g., in case of fire.

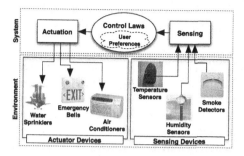

Fig. 1. High-level scheme of a building monitoring and control application

These applications, as with any other embedded control system, feature four main components, illustrated in Figure 1. The *user preferences* represent the high-level system goals, e.g., the desired temperature in the building and the need to limit fire spreading. *Sensing devices* gather data from the environment and monitor relevant variables, in our case, humidity and temperature sensors monitor air quality, while smoke and temperature detectors recognize the presence of a fire. *Actuator devices* perform actions affecting the environment under control: air conditioners adjust the air quality, while water sprinklers and emergency bells are used in case of fire. *Control laws* map the data sensed to the actions performed, to meet the user preferences. In our case, a (simplified) control loop may activate air conditioners when temperature deviates significantly from the user preferences, tuning this action based on the humidity in the same location. Further, it may immediately activate emergency bells when the temperature increases above a safety threshold, but operate water sprinklers only if smoke detectors actually report the presence of fire. Oscillating behaviors must be avoided in all situations.

Application development in these scenarios is complicated not only by the peculiarities of devices, but also by the complexity of their interactions. The many requirements can be grouped into high-level challenges common to several settings:

- *Localized computations* [8] must be privileged, to keep processing close to where sensing or actuation occurs. In sense-and-react applications it is indeed unreasonable to funnel all the sensed data to a single base-station, as this may negatively affect latency and reliability, without any significant advantage [9].
- The system performs *multiple tasks* in parallel. In our example, two control laws coexist: one for air conditioning, the other for handling emergencies. These need to *share data* (e.g., temperature readings) generated by a subset of the sensing devices.
- Differently from sense-only scenarios, sense-and-react applications often require *stateful* coordination, e.g., using current shared conditions (state) to act collaboratively. This, in combination with the use of WSNs for safety critical applications, motivates an explicit account for *reliability* in the programming model.
- *Reactive interactions*, actions that automatically fire based on external conditions, assume a prominent role. In our case, a temperature reading deviating from user preferences triggers an action in both of the two application tasks. *Proactive interactions*, common in many sense-only scenarios, are still needed to gather information and

fine tune the actuation about to occur. For instance, the sprinklers in the building ask for smoke readings before taking any action.

Note how sense-*and-react* scenarios essentially subsume sense-*only* ones. Therefore, the aforementioned requirements represent the most general set of application-level issues WSN developers must cope with. Also, subsets of these requirements must be accounted for at lower levels, below the application. For instance, localization algorithms [10]—often one of the many tasks of object tracking applications [11]—must rely on localized interactions, as most of the approaches in the field base the position estimation on data reported by nearby hosts. Similarly, multi-hop routing mechanisms [12] require reactive interactions to adapt to mutable network conditions, and may also exploit reliable operations to guarantee message delivery [13]. The Teeny-LIME programming model, described next, supports application development without losing the ability to express system-level mechanisms.

3   TeenyLIME: Basic Concepts and API

TeenyLIME is based on the *tuple space* abstraction, originally proposed in Linda [5], and here re-elaborated in the context of WSNs. A tuple space is a repository of data represented as *tuples*, sequences of typed fields such as ⟨"foo", 29⟩. Three core Linda operations allow processes to manipulate the tuple space by creating (**out**), reading (**rd**), and removing (**in**) tuples. Tuple selection with **rd** and **in** is based on matching patterns such as ⟨"foo", ?integer⟩ against the tuple space content. Patterns may use either *actual* or *formal* values, the latter serving as a kind of "wild card" matching any data of a particular type.

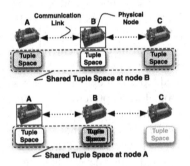

Fig. 2. Tuple space sharing in Teeny-LIME

In Linda, the tuple space is assumed globally accessible to all processes—an undesirable choice in WSNs. Instead, in TeenyLIME each node hosts a tuple space, shared among nodes within direct (one-hop) communication range. *Sharing* means that a node views its local tuple space as containing its own tuples, plus those in the tuple spaces hosted by its neighbors, as shown in Figure 2. Operations span the whole shared tuple space. For instance, a query issued by a node may return a matching tuple found in any tuple space in the one-hop neighborhood—including the local one. Therefore, Teeny-LIME programmers can specify interactions among nodes abstractly, by focusing on the application logic (e.g., reading temperature in the neighborhood) and leaving system configuration issues (e.g., tracking node identity and presence) to the middleware.

The choice to limit sharing to one-hop neighbors is motivated by the fact that interactions with these nodes are the most frequent in WSNs. Whitehouse et al. analyzed 16 publicly available applications to determine the node interactions, and

"All neighborhoods discovered were one-hop neighborhoods [...]" ([6], p.9)

```
interface TupleSpace {
    // Standard tuple space operations
    command TLOpId_t out(bool reliable, TLTarget_t target, tuple *tuple);
    command TLOpId_t rd(bool reliable, TLTarget_t target, tuple *pattern);
    command TLOpId_t in(bool reliable, TLTarget_t target, tuple *pattern);
    // Group operations
    command TLOpId_t rdg(bool reliable, TLTarget_t target, tuple *pattern);
    command TLOpId_t ing(bool reliable, TLTarget_t target, tuple *pattern);
    // Managing reactions
    command TLOpId_t addReaction(bool reliable, TLTarget_t target, tuple *pattern);
    command TLOpId_t removeReaction(TLOpId_t operationID);
    // Returning tuples
    event result_t tupleReady(TLOpId_t operationId, tuple *tuples, uint8_t number);
    // Request to reify a capability tuple
    event result_t reifyCapabilityTuple(tuple *capTuple, tuple *pattern);
}
interface NodeTuple {
    // Request to provide a tuple containing node-level system information
    event tuple* reifyNodeTuple();
}
```

Fig. 3. TeenyLIME API

Interestingly, all neighborhoods were of limited size (at most ten nodes), and were used either directly at the application level to gain access to *nearby* information, or as a building block for lower-level system functionality, e.g., to implement multi-hop routing. These considerations also support our design choice, drawing the foundations for a highly-reusable programming model supported a by lightweight, scalable implementation. Furthermore, it should be noted that the applications considered in [6] were conventional sense-only ones. Sense-and-react applications exacerbate the need for localized interactions [8], and are therefore expected to benefit even more from our design. As a result, the TeenyLIME programming model can be used in many contexts, ranging from sense-and-react to sense-only, and from application-level to system-level.

Figure 3 shows the TeenyLIME API. While in principle the programming model is independent of the node platform, we present here the API in nesC, as our middleware is currently built on top of TinyOS. The interface provides the operations to manipulate TeenyLIME's shared tuple space. The first three operations correspond to the Linda operations discussed earlier, while **rd** and **ing** are variants (as in [14]) that return all matching tuples, instead of a single match.

TeenyLIME operations are asynchronous, allowing the application to continue while the middleware completes the operation execution[1]. This approach blends well with the event-driven concurrency model of nesC. Therefore, all operations are *split-phase* [15]: the operation is issued, and later the `tupleReady` event is signaled when the operation completes. The `tupleReady` event contains an identifier allowing the application to associate the event with its earlier request. Depending on the operation, one or more tuples, indicated by the `number` parameter, may also be contained in the event.

The operations provided in the API deserve further discussion. However, instead of describing them in isolation, in the next section we discuss them "in action", i.e., hand-in-hand with the TeenyLIME-based design of our reference application.

---

[1] In most Linda systems **rd** and **in** are blocking, i.e., do not return until a tuple is matched.

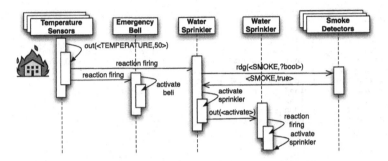

Fig. 4. Sequence of operations to handle a fire. Notified about increased temperature, a node controlling water sprinklers queries the smoke detectors to verify the presence of fire. If necessary, it sends a command activating nearby sprinklers.

4 Application Development with TeenyLIME

As discussed in Section 2, our reference application contains two sub-tasks, one managing the air conditioning system (HVAC) and the other for emergency situations such as fire. Each sub-task involves different types of nodes, e.g., humidity sensors in the HVAC sub-task, and smoke detectors to address fire emergencies. Temperature sensors are instead used in both sub-tasks. For all types of nodes, the application processing has been implemented in a single component sitting entirely on top of the `TupleSpace` interface, which masks completely TinyOS' generic communication layer. An additional component is employed to interact with the sensors/actuators attached to the node.

In the following, we explain the rest of our reference application's design and implementation. We illustrate how we exploit data sharing and related operations, and how interactions among nodes benefit from the WSN-specific API features. Throughout, the reference application is used as a motivation and source of examples for the discussion.

Sharing Application Data through Proactive and Reactive Interactions. In our design, *sensed data* and *actuating commands* take the form of tuples. These are shared across nodes (and components on the same node) to enable coordination of activities as well as data communication. Access to this data can occur *proactively*, e.g., using the rd and in operations. However, TeenyLIME supports also a notion of *reaction*, a code fragment whose execution is automatically triggered upon the appearance of a given tuple anywhere in the shared tuple space. The tuples of interest are identified through pattern matching, and the `tupleReady` event is used to signal a reaction firing. This provides an easy and yet very powerful way to monitor changes in the neighbors' data through the content of the shared tuple space.

Figure 4 uses the fire control sub-task to illustrate how proactive and reactive interactions are used together to trigger notifications, to perform distributed operations for gathering data from neighboring nodes, and to request actuation commands. Notably, similar patterns of interactions recur in both sub-tasks of our application.

Both emergency bells and water sprinklers have a reaction registered on their neighbors, watching for temperature tuples, as shown in the code in Figure 5. Temperature sensors periodically take a sample and pack it in a tuple, which is then stored in the local

```
command result_t StdControl.start() {
  tuple tempTemplate = newTuple(2, actualField_uint16(TEMPERATURE),
                                formalField(TYPE_UINT16_T));
  call TS.addReaction(FALSE, TL_NEIGHBORHOOD, &tempTemplate);
  return SUCCESS;
}
 event result_t TS.tupleReady(TLOpId_t operationId,
                              tuple *tuples, uint8_t number) {
   // Notification triggered ...
 }
```

Fig. 5. TeenyLIME code for an actuator node interested in temperature values

```
command result_t StdControl.start() {
  return call SensingTimer.start (TIMER_REPEAT, SENSING_TIMER);
}
event result_t SensingTimer.fired() {
  return call TemperatureSensor.getData();
}
event result_t TemperatureSensor.dataReady(uint16_t reading){
  tuple temperatureValue = newTuple(2, actualField_uint16(TEMPERATURE),
                                    actualField_uint16(reading));
  call TupleSpace.out(FALSE,TL_LOCAL,&temperatureValue);
  return SUCCESS;
}
```

Fig. 6. TeenyLIME code for a temperature node

tuple space, as shown in Figure 6. Insertion is accomplished using **out** by setting the target parameter to TL_LOCAL, which entails outputting the tuple to the local tuple space. This operation, by virtue of one-hop sharing, automatically triggers all the afore-mentioned reactions[2], which process the tuple contained in the event tupleReady. However, different types of actuator nodes behave differently when high temperatures are detected. The node hosting the emergency bell immediately activates its device. Instead, the water sprinkler node proceeds to verify the presence of fire, as shown in Figure 4. The latter behavior, specified as part of the reaction code, consists of proactively gathering the readings from nearby smoke detectors, using a **rdg** restricted (by setting target to TL_NEIGHBORHOOD) to the union of their tuple spaces. If fire is reported, the water sprinkler node requests activation of nearby sprinklers through a two-step process that relies on reactions as well. The node requesting actuation inserts a tuple representing the command on the nodes where the activation must occur, using **out** with target set to the sprinkler node address. The presence of this tuple triggers a locally-installed reaction delivering the activation tuple to the application, which reads the tuple fields and operates the actuator device accordingly.

Reliable Operations. Since fire detection requires the maximum degree of reliability, its implementation takes advantage of *reliable operations* for guaranteeing correct communication of reactions and query results of the **rdg** operation on smoke detectors and

---

[2] We assume that actuators are interested in all temperature values. We show later how notifications can be triggered only when temperature is above (or below) a given threshold.

of the **out** operations towards actuators. Furthermore, in the HVAC sub-task the system runs the risk of oscillating behavior if multiple nodes controlling air conditioners in the same location (e.g., same floor) independently run the control algorithm. To prevent this, we designed a mechanism to assign a master role to only one of the co-located controller nodes, achieving a sort of distributed mutual exclusion. The master node is identified as the one holding a special token tuple, periodically exchanged among co-located nodes to achieve a form of load-balancing. As a token loss implies no controller acting as the master, strong guarantees on token transfer are imperative. Therefore, the token exchange from the previous to the new master node is accomplished using a reliable **in** operation performed by the latter.

As shown in Figure 3, the selection between unreliable and reliable is done using a flag, available in most operations. The former offers a lightweight form of best-effort communication suitable for state-less applications (e.g., data collection), while the latter offer stronger guarantees to applications requiring stateful interactions.

Sharing System Data. Coordination of activities across heterogeneous nodes sometimes relies on system information, such as the node location or capabilities. In Teeny-LIME, this information is made available in the same way as application data, i.e., as tuples shared among neighboring nodes. In our scenario, these tuples contain a field describing the (logical) location (e.g., a room) where a node is deployed, and the sensor/actuator devices attached. Which data to provide is defined by the application programmer, by specifying the body of the handler for the `reifyNodeTuple` event, shown in Figure 3. This event is signaled periodically by the TeenyLIME run-time, and the execution of the corresponding handler regenerates the tuple with new application-defined values. In our implementation, the local tuple space on every node contains tuples describing each of its neighbors. This is accomplished by appending the neighbor tuple to all outgoing messages; therefore, when the message is overheard by neighbors, they extract the neighbor tuple and insert it locally. This way, it is easy to query the tuple space to obtain information on neighbors with specific capabilities.

Filtering Data. In many WSN applications, including ours, action must be taken only when a sensed value crosses a given threshold. Nodes controlling air conditioners must receive notifications when temperature falls outside a user-defined threshold. Similarly, the nodes controlling water sprinklers and emergency bells described previously only need to receive notifications when temperature rises above a safety threshold. These conditions require a predicate over tuple field values—something that cannot be achieved with the standard Linda matching semantics, which is based on either types or exact values. In TeenyLIME, patterns are extended to support custom matching semantics on a per-field basis. For instance, the requirement concerning safety thresholds can be expressed concisely by using *range matching*, requiring the temperature field to be greater than a given parameter, as in:

```
tuple temperatureTempl = newTuple(2, actualField_uint16(TEMPERATURE),
                                     greaterField(TEMPERATURE_SAFETY));
```

The above uses the default range matching, which the programmer can easily redefine.

Note how the issue is *not* simply one of expressive power, as it deeply affects communication. Without filtering, the programmer can only specify a *generic* pattern matching

```
command result_t StdControl.start(){
  tuple capTSmoke = newCapabilityTuple(2, actualField_uint16(SMOKE),
                                          formalField(TYPE_BOOL));
    call TupleSpace.out(FALSE,TL_LOCAL,&capTSmoke);
    return SUCCESS;
}
event result_t  TupleSpace.reifyCapabilityTuple(tuple *ct, tuple *p){
    return call SmokeDetector.getData(); // Request a reading from the sensor
}
event result_t SmokeDetector.dataReady(uint16_t reading){ // Sensor reading
  tuple smokeValue = newTuple(2, actualField_uint16(SMOKE),
                                   actualField_bool(reading));
    call TS.out(FALSE,TL_LOCAL,&smokeValue);
    return SUCCESS;
}
```

Fig. 7. TeenyLIME code for a smoke detector node

any temperature. All matching, outputted tuples would be transmitted (in our case, each time a new sample is available) and frequently discarded as out of range by the reaction code of the requester in Figure 5, wasting significant communication resources.

Dealing with Short-Lived Data. In some cases, sensor data remain useful only for a limited time after collection. For instance, an emergency bell is not interested in temperature values sensed an hour before. Instead, the same data may be of interest for a component that is periodically run to build a day-long analysis of temperature trends.

In TeenyLIME, time is divided into *epochs* of constant length, and every data tuple is stamped with an application-accessible field containing the current epoch value. Three helper functions allow the application developers to deal with time:

```
setFreshness(pattern,freshness)
getFreshness(tuple)
setExpireIn(tuple,expiration)
```

The first customizes a pattern, similarly to range matching above, to impose the additional constraint to match tuples no more than `freshness` epochs old. If a pattern does not specify freshness, it matches any tuple regardless of its age. The second function returns the number of epochs elapsed since the `tuple` was created. Finally, the third specifies how many epochs the `tuple` is allowed to stay in the tuple space. When the timeout associated to the tuple expires, the tuple is automatically removed.

Generating Data Efficiently. In our application, humidity sensors and smoke detectors need not be monitored continuously: their data is accessed only when actuation is about to occur. However, when a sensed value is requested (e.g., by issuing a **rd**) fresh-enough data must be present in the tuple space. If these data are only seldom utilized, the energy required to keep tuples fresh is mostly wasted. An alternative is to require that the programmer encodes requests to perform sensing in a way similar to actuation commands, enabling the receiving node to perform sensing on-demand and return the result. However, this solution requires extra programming effort, is error-prone, adds processing overhead, and is therefore equally undesirable.

To deal with these (frequent) situations, TeenyLIME provides the ability to output *capability tuples* indicating that a device has the capability to produce data of a given pattern. A code example for a smoke detector is shown in Figure 7. When a query is remotely issued with a pattern matching a capability tuple, the `reifyCapability-Tuple` event is signaled. This reports the pattern included in the query and the matching capability tuple. The application handles this event by taking a fresh reading and outputting the actual data to the tuple space. The sequence of operations is depicted in Figure 8. Note how, from the perspective of the data consumer, nothing changes. Instead, on the side of the data producer, capability tuples enable considerable energy savings as the readings are taken only on-demand, without the need to maintain constantly fresh data in the tuple space.

Interestingly, capability tuples can be generalized to allow *any action* to be taken by the data producer. For example, matching a pattern to a capability tuple may invoke any application function (e.g., computing the average of all temperature tuples), whose results are inserted in the tuple space and returned to the requester.

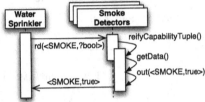

Fig. 8. Processing of capability tuples

5   The TeenyLIME Middleware

The design of TeenyLIME aims at enabling easy customization and extension of the middleware. Therefore, *local* processing, *distributed* processing, and *communication* concerns are fully decoupled, and one aspect can be changed without impact on the rest of the system. Due to space constraints, here we focus only on a few aspects of our architecture, namely, the implementation of *distributed reactions* and *capability tuples*, and the support for *reliable operations*. More details about the current prototype are reported in [16].

The implementation of *remote reactions* currently rely on a *soft-state* approach, to deal with nodes joining or failing. Each node periodically sends a message containing control data for all reactions that should be installed on its neighbors. Upon receipt of this message, a timer associated with installed reactions is refreshed. If and when a timer expires, the corresponding reaction is removed. This may happen either because the registering node became unreachable, or the application deregistered the reaction thus no longer refreshing it. Similar approaches are widely used in WSN, (e.g., in [17]), as they are sufficiently lightweight and effective.

Processing *capability tuples* requires keeping track of the source nodes whose query matched a local capability tuple so that, once the actual tuple is (locally) output by the application, it can be returned to the appropriate node. Due to nesC split-phase operations [15], this processing requires a lot of bookkeeping code. However, we noted that this processing is the same *as if* a reaction (for the same pattern as the query) were installed by a neighbor *before* the application outputs the actual tuple. Our implementation exploits this observation and installs a local reaction for the query pattern before firing the `reifyCapabilityTuple` event. When the node outputs the tuple, this matches the aforementioned reaction and is subsequently, automatically delivered to the intended recipient. The only additional processing required is to remove the reaction right after it fires. This solution only requires 24 nesC lines.

Finally, TeenyLIME poses only a single requirement on the communication layers: the ability to overhear messages for populating the tuple space with neighbor tuples. As a result, many existing solutions (e.g., [18, 19]) can be employed to provide *reliable operations*. Nevertheless, if reliability is only seldom required, the solutions above may be overkill, e.g., because scheduling mechanisms (as in [19]) negatively impact latency. To meet scenarios where reliable operations are rare, our current prototype includes a simple reliability scheme based on explicit acknowledgments. Messages contain a unique identifier, reported in the corresponding acknowledgment when transmission succeeds. Therefore, lost packets are easily recognized and retransmitted upon timeout expiration. Control information is piggybacked on application messages whenever possible, to reduce overhead. Our protocol is not tied to TeenyLIME, and exports the same interface as TinyOS' generic communication layer. Therefore, it can be re-used by plain TinyOS applications demanding reliable communication. More details on its internals and performance can be found in [16].

6 Evaluation

We compare quantitatively TeenyLIME against common alternatives, analyzing its impact on the application source code and on run-time performance.

6.1 Evaluating the Programming Model

Our objective is to assess the effectiveness of TeenyLIME in enabling a flexible design and clean implementations. To the best of our knowledge, there are no programming abstractions expressly designed for application scenarios such as sense-and-react. Therefore, we compare a TeenyLIME-based implementation of our reference application against one implemented directly on top of TinyOS. On the other hand, the applicability of TeenyLIME goes beyond sense-and-react applications, and reaches into system-level mechanisms, below the application layer. We substantiate this claim by reporting about implementations in both TeenyLIME and Hood [6], a programming abstraction designed around similar requirements.

Reference Application. In the TinyOS version of our reference application, each type of node (e.g., temperature sensors or air conditioners) has a component configuration similar to the one mentioned in Section 4, where however TeenyLIME is replaced by the TinyOS GenericComm component[3]. However, the TinyOS-based implementation is far more complex. The reader can informally verify this statement by visually comparing the *excerpt* of TinyOS code for a temperature sensor in Figure 9 against the *complete* (and *much* simpler) TeenyLIME-based equivalent shown earlier in Figure 6. The superior expressive power of TeenyLIME manifests itself in several aspects:

– Developers using plain TinyOS must keep track within the application code of all the potential data consumers. This requires several dedicated functions, such as matchesInterest() in Figure 9. Using TeenyLIME, the same functionality is achieved using *reactions*: no application-level bookkeeping is required.

---

[3] Or with our reliability component if reliable interactions, not supported by TinyOS, are required by the application. We elaborate further on reliability in Section 6.2.

```
bool pendingMsg, pendingReading;
TOS_Msg sendMsg, queueMsg[MAX_QUEUE_SIZE];
uint8_t nextQueueMsg, lastQueueMsg;
nodeInterest interests[MAX_AIR_CONDITIONERS];
void interest(uint16_t node,uint8_t t,uint16_t tShold,uint16_t tStamp){ // ... }
bool isRecipient(struct InterestMsg* msg,uint16_t nodeId) { // ... }
bool matchesInterest(uint16_t reading) { // ... }
bool enqueueMsg(TOS_Msg msg) { // ... }
bool messageWaiting() { // ... }
bool sendQueuedMsg() { // ... }
command result_t StdControl.start() {
  // ... data initialization ...
  return call SensingTimer.start(TIMER_REPEAT, SENSING_TIMER);
}
event result_t SensingTimer.fired() {
  pendingReading = TRUE;
  return call TemperatureSensor.getData();
}
event TOS_MsgPtr ReceiveInterestMsg.receive(TOS_MsgPtr m) {
  struct InterestMsg* payload = (struct InterestMsg*) m->data;
  if (!pendingReading && isRecipient(payload, TOS_LOCAL_ADDRESS))
    interest(payload->sender, payload->type,
             payload->threshold, payload->timestamp);
  return m;
}
event result_t TemperatureSensor.dataReady(uint16_t reading){
  TOS_Msg msg;
  struct DataMsg* payload = (struct DataMsg*) msg->data;
  payload->sender = TOS_LOCAL_ADDRESS;
  payload->type = TEMPERATURE;
  payload->value = reading;
  if (!pendingMsg && matchesInterest(reading)) {
    atomic {
      pendingMsg = TRUE;
      sendMsg = msg;
    }
    if (call SendDataMsg.send(TOS_BCAST_ADDR,
                              sizeof(struct AppMsg),&sendMsg)!= SUCCESS) {
      pendingMsg = FALSE;
    }
  } else if (pendingMsg)
    enqueueMsg(msg);
  pendingReading = FALSE;
  return SUCCESS;
}
event result_t SendDataMsg.sendDone(TOS_MsgPtr msg, result_t success) {
  if (msg == sendMsg) pendingMsg = FALSE;
  if (messageWaiting()) sendQueuedMsg();
  return SUCCESS;
}
```

Fig. 9. A temperature node in our reference application, using plain TinyOS. The processing above is equivalent to the TeenyLIME version in Figure 6.

- Figure 9 contains two separate execution flows: one begins when a message is received (ReceiveInterestMsg.receive), the other when a reading from the sensing device is ready (TemperatureSensor.dataReady). These two flows are not at all evident in the code, due to nesC split-phase operations [15]. Thus, maintenance and debugging are greatly complicated [20]. This problem is significantly alleviated using TeenyLIME, as only the latter execution flow is necessary.

- Distributed processing forces TinyOS programmers to delve into the details of message transmission, parsing, and buffering, therefore mixing communication aspects

Component	Explicit states		Lines of code		% of application data in TeenyLIME
	TeenyLIME	Plain TinyOS	TeenyLIME	Plain TinyOS	
AirConditioner	3	8	93	282	72%
MutualExclusion	(ML × 2)	(ML × 3) + 1	153	205	48%
TemperatureSensor	0	NC + 2	44	107	100%

Fig. 10. Comparing the TeenyLIME-based implementation against plain TinyOS. ML represents the maximum number of different locations the component implementing token exchange handles, NC represents the maximum number of air conditioners around a temperature sensor.

with the application semantics. Instead, the TeenyLIME component in Figure 6 contains only *application-specific* processing related to the actual *data of interest*.

– As a consequence of all the above, TinyOS programmers must manage *state variables* to deal with nearby air conditioners (`interests`), the sensing device (`pendingReading`), and the radio (`pendingMsg`). These can be the source of race conditions [15]. Conversely, in TeenyLIME these aspects are either handled by the middleware, or no longer required.

A good way to assess the complexity of implementations is to analyze them as state machines and count the number of *explicit application states*, as in [6]. These are typically stored in state variables, modified by commands and event handlers to express state transitions. The higher the number of application states, the harder it is to express state transitions [20], and the more complex and error-prone applications become.

Figure 10 reports this and other metrics for the temperature sensor and other components of our sense-and-react application, showing that the advantages of TeenyLIME hold for all the (diverse) tasks of our application. For instance, the plain-TinyOS component implementing the air conditioner control law has 8 explicit application states, whereas the TeenyLIME-based one has only 3. The reduction is due to the aforementioned ability of TeenyLIME to hide communication details, here complemented by the ability to express data filtering as patterns. The former avoids the use of several state variables, while the latter delegates most of the data processing to the middleware. Nicely, the reduction of explicit states in the application code causes the *number of lines of code* to decrease as well, as shown in the second column of Figure 10. Indeed, fewer state transitions, and therefore far less bookkeeping code, are needed.

It is worth noting that the above simplifications are *not* accomplished by *removing* application information. Doing so would indeed affect the application semantics. Rather, they are obtained by *moving* information and related processing from the application components into TeenyLIME. This is not possible using plain TinyOS, as its abstractions provide only message passing and do not explicitly represent *state*. This is instead achieved in TeenyLIME using the tuple space, as its content is *persistent*. For instance, a reading tuple output by a temperature sensor node represents its current state and remains in its tuple space until a new reading becomes available.

To quantify this aspect, the rightmost column in Figure 10 indicates the amount of information that can be moved from the application component into TeenyLIME, expressed as the percentage ratio between the TeenyLIME-based and the TinyOS-based applications. We compute it by looking at the per-component storage of *global variables* concerned with application data. The results confirm the reasoning above, showing that a considerable portion of the application state can be managed inside the middleware. Remarkably, *all* the application data and related processing for a temperature sensor can be moved into the tuple space, as shown by comparing Figure 6 and 9.

The advantages above come at the price of a slight increase in the size of the binary code deployed on the motes. The code of a temperature node occupies 69 Kbytes using plain TinyOS and 80 Kbytes using TeenyLIME (including the middleware itself). These figures increase to 72 Kbytes and 90 Kbytes, respectively, for the air conditioner. We note, however, that the latter is a complex component, and yet it remains well within the limits imposed by commercially available sensor platforms (e.g., 128 Kbytes for MICA2).

Sense-only Applications and System-level Functionality. TeenyLIME provides relevant benefits also to the development of sense-only applications and system-level functionality. We support this statement by illustrating insights obtained by re-implementing some of the applications used in [6] to evaluate Hood, a programming abstraction geared towards sense-only applications and system mechanisms that, like TeenyLIME, focuses on one-hop interactions. Notably, by limiting ourselves to sense-only (instead of sense-and-react) applications, and comparing against Hood on the same applications used for its evaluation, we put ourselves in the most challenging situation.

Specifically, we consider the object tracking application and the multi-hop routing protocol called Mutation Routing, both described in [6]. In these applications, the evaluation using the same *quantitative* metrics considered earlier for plain-TinyOS applications shows that TeenyLIME achieves slight improvements also w.r.t. Hood. For instance, only three explicit application states are needed to implement Mutation Routing, whereas five states are required using Hood. Space constraints prevent us from an in-depth discussion of these aspects, available in [16]. Instead, we draw *qualitative* considerations showing that TeenyLIME yields cleaner and more reusable designs:

- TeenyLIME achieves a *more flexible software architecture* w.r.t. Hood. In object tracking, for instance, three components cooperate on a node to implement the desired processing: a localization algorithm, a tracking mechanism, and a geographical routing protocol. In Hood, the three need to be *wired* together using dedicated nesC interfaces. Therefore, adding a further component (e.g., to log the position of the moving object on external memory) requires modifications in several places. Instead, in TeenyLIME the three components are fully *decoupled*, and exchange data *anonymously* through the local tuple space. Thus, adding a logging component can be easily achieved without affecting the rest of the application.

- TeenyLIME fosters *code re-use* to a great extent. For instance, in Mutation Routing two nodes are appointed the role of source or destination for packets flowing along a multi-hop path. The source (destination) role must be passed between neighboring devices as some physical phenomena moves. In a TeenyLIME-based implementation, this processing can be accomplished by reusing *as is* the component implementing the token-based, mutual exclusion mechanism described in Section 4. Simply, we create a token for each role at system start-up, exchanged based on the presence of the moving target close to a given node. In Hood this functionality is interspersed with message processing, preventing its reuse.

– TeenyLIME's one-hop shared tuple space and associated operations are sufficiently powerful to express *multi-hop mechanisms*. In both Mutation Routing and the geographical routing component of object tracking, messages are easily described as tuples. At each hop, these are output to the tuple space of the next-hop node, where a previously-installed reaction delivers the tuple to the routing component. There, the subsequent forwarding to the next-hop node is determined based on the status of neighboring devices, as reflected by the information locally available in the tuple space. As a result, all the routing decisions are encapsulated in the `tupleReady` event handler. This provides an easy and clean way to implement this functionality that cannot be achieved in Hood due to the absence of abstractions to describe the node state.

The considerations above confirm that TeenyLIME's benefits in terms of better design and simpler code hold not only for the development of application logic in sense-and-react scenario, but also for sense-only applications and system-level functionality.

6.2 Evaluating the Middleware Implementation

To verify that the advantages we identified do not negatively affect the system performance, we extend our evaluation beyond the programming model, into TeenyLIME's implementation. Specifically, a middleware layer may impact the *network overhead* and *execution time*, due to the additional processing w.r.t. a plain TinyOS implementation. As a consequence, the *system lifetime* may decrease as well. The latter is key in WSNs, as nodes are usually battery-powered and must operate unattended for long periods.

To investigate the above concerns, we conducted experiments using Avrora [21], an instruction-level emulator for WSNs equipped with a precise energy model. The latter is based on experimental data relative to MICA2 [22] nodes, a widespread hardware platform for WSNs. This approach allows us to gather realistic, fine-grained statistics regarding the energy consumption of arbitrary nesC code. We consider two benchmarks:

1. The *HVAC* sub-task we illustrated in Section 2, whose TeenyLIME implementation is described in Section 4. We place a variable number of temperature/humidity sensors in the same neighborhood as an air conditioner node. Every 10 seconds, each temperature sensor randomly generates a reading, whose value can deviate from the user preference with a 20% probability. This triggers actuation at the air conditioner controller, which first queries nearby humidity sensors for their most recent reading, and then decides on the specific actions to be taken.
2. A simple application using the token-based, *mutual exclusion* component illustrated in Section 4. A variable number of nodes, in the same neighborhood, express the intention to obtain the token. Every 10 seconds the token is released by the node holding it, and a different, randomly chosen node is selected as the new token holder.

Both applications above involve several TeenyLIME-specific constructs. In the first one, a temperature reading may trigger a remote *reaction* previously installed by the air conditioner, whose pattern contains a dedicated *range field* to express the user preference as a temperature interval. Moreover, humidity values are represented as *capability tuples*. Therefore, the (unreliable) query coming from the air conditioner triggers the execution of the `reifyCapabilityTuple` event on the humidity sensors. These react by locally outputting the actual tuple[4], which is delivered by TeenyLIME to the air conditioner as the result of the initial query. Similarly, in the mutual exclusion application, releasing the token entails outputting a token tuple in the local tuple space, and possibly triggering some previously installed, remote *reaction*. Nodes receiving this notification then perform a *reliable* in operation to obtain the token. Among them, only one succeeds.

The processing above is the same in other scenarios where the data involved have different semantics. For instance, the processing to exchange the token (i.e., a reaction firing followed by a reliable query) is the *same* executed by a water sprinkler in the fire sub-task, shown in Figure 4: only the tuple content changes. In this sense, the meaning of our results extends beyond the benchmark applications we consider here.

For comparison, we consider a plain TinyOS implementation of the same applications. Figure 11 illustrates the component configurations in the two cases. To compare them on common ground when required, we provide TinyOS with reliable communication by using our reliable protocol, mentioned in Section 5.

The emulation settings, in Figure 12, are taken from real MICA2 motes. The larger message size in TeenyLIME is due to the additional control information contained in the tuples. As independent variables, we vary the number of nodes in a neighborhood and the probability ε of losing a message, to investigate TeenyLIME's overhead w.r.t. system scale and network conditions.

Results. In our benchmark applications, TeenyLIME does not generate any increase in the *number* of messages exchanged w.r.t. a TinyOS-based implementation. Therefore, TeenyLIME's overhead in execution time is essentially due to extra *local* processing. In this respect, Figure 13 analyzes the CPU time taken to perform a set of relevant operations in our benchmark applications. The worst case accounts for a 10.08% overhead, which is reasonable given the absolute values involved. We believe these results are due to the generality of TeenyLIME's abstractions. These can capture commonly-used sequences of operations in a natural way, which allows our TeenyLIME implementation to perform close to application-specific mechanisms.

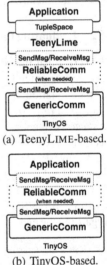

(a) TeenyLIME-based.

(b) TinyOS-based.

Fig. 11.   Component configurations

Parameter Name	Value
MAC Layer	standard TinyOS MAC for CC1000 chip
Initial Energy Budget	≈ 2 AA batteries
Message Size	47 bytes (TinyOS), 104 bytes (TeenyLIME)

Fig. 12. Emulation parameters

---

[4] Gathering of physical readings from the sensor device is assumed to be instantaneous.

Operation	TeenyLIME	Plain TinyOS	Overhead
Notifying the Air Conditioner	2.18ms	1.99ms	9.54%
Sending a Humidity Query	1.97ms	1.85ms	6.48%
Replying to a Humidity Query	2.25ms	2.03ms	10.08%

(a) HVAC.

Operation	TeenyLIME	Plain TinyOS	Overhead
Releasing the Token	2.03ms	1.97ms	3.04%
Sending a Token Notification	2.28ms	2.07ms	8.21%
Requesting the Token	2.09ms	1.92ms	8.85%

(b) Mutual exclusion.

Fig. 13. Execution times in the components of our benchmark applications

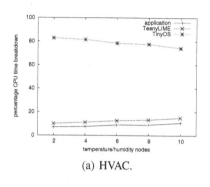

(a) HVAC.

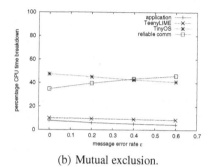

(b) Mutual exclusion.

Fig. 14. CPU time breakdown in TeenyLIME-based implementations

Figure 14 further elaborates on the timing aspects in our TeenyLIME implementations, showing the breakdown of CPU time in the different layers. Figure 14(a) illustrates the aforementioned metric for an air conditioner node in the HVAC application, against the number[5] of temperature/humidity nodes in its neighborhood. TinyOS is responsible for most of the processing, as it handles all hardware interrupts and radio-related functions, triggered quite frequently. The trend of the processing dedicated to the application and to TeenyLIME is due to the number of notifications and query replies received at the air conditioner, that grows with the number of nearby nodes. TeenyLIME engages the CPU at most 15% of the time, when 10 nodes are in reach of the air conditioner. The above metric is not directly affected by the message error rate in the HVAC application, as reliability guarantees are not required.

Conversely, when reliability is required it becomes the dominant factor, and system scale bears little effect on our metrics. Figure 14(b) analyzes the CPU time breakdown in the mutual exclusion application against a varying message error rate, with eight nodes in the neighborhood. The chart indeed shows how the reliability protocol increasingly engages the CPU as communication becomes less reliable. In fact, our reliable protocol runs periodic activities (e.g., checking whether messages not yet acknowledged need a retransmission) that take a time proportional to the number of buffered messages. In absolute values, TeenyLIME execution times remain the same regardless of mutable network conditions. Therefore, its relative contribution decreases as the

---

[5] Half of the nodes in the x-axis are temperature nodes, while the other half are humidity nodes.

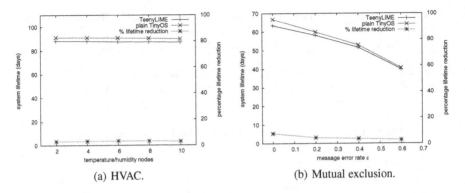

(a) HVAC.   (b) Mutual exclusion.

Fig. 15. System lifetime

reliable protocol is more stressed. This is a result of our design: TeenyLIME and the reliable communication component are fully decoupled, and the processing implemented in the former is independent from the latter.

It is interesting to look at how TeenyLIME affects the overall system lifetime. Figure 15(a) shows the time until the air conditioner node in the (unreliable) HVAC application runs out of power. This metric is only marginally affected by TeenyLIME, whose additional overhead is always under 4%. The chart also illustrates an almost constant behavior w.r.t the number of temperature/humidity nodes. This is expected: reactions and queries are issued in broadcast by the air conditioner, therefore the energy expenditures for communication are independent of the number of neighbors. Conversely, the number of temperature/humidity sensors affects the local processing, as more neighbors correspond to more replies received. Nevertheless, the extra overhead imposed by TeenyLIME has a very limited impact on the overall lifetime. Along the same lines, Figure 15(b) shows the lifetime in the (reliable) mutual exclusion application, measured as when the last node depletes its battery. The trends here are strongly tied to the message error rate: an increasing number of retransmissions are indeed required as communication becomes less reliable. TeenyLIME's overhead, however, is comparable to the HVAC application, and becomes less relevant as the probability of losing a message increases and, consequently, the reliable protocol is involved more.

Finally, we analyzed our reliable protocol, to verify that our results are not biased by an inefficient implementation. Instead, Figure 16 shows that our solution can provide 100% message delivery with a very small number of retransmissions. This performance is in line with alternative reliability mechanisms in the literature [23], and therefore confirms that our reliable protocol is a valid choice in our evaluation.

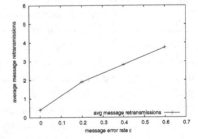

Fig. 16. Performance of TeenyLIME reliable protocol

In conclusion, the trade-offs between the benefits of the programming model and its run-time overhead are reasonable, making TeenyLIME an effective middleware for WSNs.

7 Related Work

TeenyLIME is inspired by LIME [24], which originally introduced the notion of shared tuple spaces in mobile ad hoc networks. However, not only is TeenyLIME's implementation based on entirely different technologies and mechanisms from LIME, but its model and API introduce novel concepts geared expressly towards WSNs, such as range matching, capability tuples, freshness, and explicit control over reliability. Teeny-LIME follows in time another adaptation of LIME to WSNs, called TinyLIME [25]. The two, however, profoundly differ in target scenario, model, and implementation. TinyLIME focuses on mobile data collection and employs the standard LIME middleware to provide data sharing over 802.11 among mobile sinks (the data consumers) that, in turn, gather data from nearby WSN sensor nodes (the data producers). Therefore, intelligence is on sinks: the TinyLIME code deployed on sensors is "dumb" and largely application-agnostic, reporting data to external sinks (its only interlocutor) on request. Instead, TeenyLIME is expressly designed for scenarios where the application intelligence is in the network, built around node-to-node interactions inside the WSN.

The work most closely related to TeenyLIME is Hood [6], a neighborhood abstraction where nodes can share state with selected one-hop neighbors. Selection is based on attributes periodically broadcast by neighbor nodes. Neighborhoods are specified using extensions to the basic nesC constructs, precompiled into plain nesC. Therefore, unlike TeenyLIME, in Hood data sharing is decided at compile-time. Moreover, Hood provides neither the ability to affect the state of another node nor the abstractions to *react* to changes in the shared state. This hampers its use in sense-and-react applications, and in general provides a less expressive programming framework.

In Abstract Regions [26] ⟨*key, value*⟩ pairs are shared among nodes in a region (i.e., a set of topologically-related nodes), and manipulated through read/write operations. Again, there is no way to receive notifications when some given data appears in the system, unlike TeenyLIME. Moreover, although nodes in a region may leverage multi-hop communication, this and other aspects must be coded explicitly by the programmer on a per-region basis, therefore hampering generality and applicability.

Context Shadow [27] exploits multiple tuple spaces, each hosting only locally-sensed information representing a given context. Applications retrieve the data of interest by explicitly connecting to one of them. Similarly, the tuple spaces used in Agilla [28] for coordinating among mobile agents are shared only local to a node. Instead, TeenyLIME enables data sharing in a neighborhood by creating the illusion of a single address space. Moreover, these systems lack WSN-specific tuple space constructs.

8 Conclusions

Developing WSN applications is a difficult task, and sense-and-react applications are the most challenging. This paper presented and evaluated TeenyLIME, a middleware designed for sense-and-react WSN applications, but whose programming constructs are effective in a wide range of applications. TeenyLIME yields simpler, cleaner, and more reusable designs, as we demonstrated quantitatively in non-trivial applications. Moreover, our evaluation with cycle-accurate emulation demonstrated that these benefits are supported by an efficient implementation that introduces low overhead w.r.t. plain-TinyOS implementations. The TeenyLIME middleware is freely available for download at `http://lime.sf.net/teenyLime.html`.

Acknowledgements. The work described in this paper was partially supported by the European Community under the RUNES (IST-004536) and the XtreemOS (IST-033576) projects, and by the Swiss National Science foundation NCCR-MICS (5005-67322).

References

1. Habitat Monitoring on the Great Duck Island, www.greatisland.net
2. Deshpande, A., Guestrin, C., Madden, S.: Resource-aware wireless sensor-actuator networks. IEEE Data Engineering 28(1) (2005)
3. Petriu, E., Georganas, N., Petriu, D., Makrakis, D., Groza, V.: Sensor-based information appliances. IEEE Instrumentation and Measurement Mag. 3, 31–35 (2000)
4. Manzie, C., Watson, H.C., Halgamuge, S.K., Lim, K.: On the potential for improving fuel economy using a traffic flow sensor network. In: Proc. of the Int. Conf. on Intelligent Sensing and Information Processing (2005)
5. Gelernter, D.: Generative communication in Linda. ACM Computing Surveys 7(1) (1985)
6. Whitehouse, K., Sharp, C., Brewer, E., Culler, D.: Hood: A neighborhood abstraction for sensor networks. In: Proc. of 2nd Int. Conf. on Mobile systems, applications, and services (2004)
7. Costa, P., Mottola, L., Murphy, A.L., Picco, G.P.: TeenyLIME: Transiently Shared Tuple Space Middleware for Wireless Sensor Networks. In: Proc. of the 1st Int. Workshop on Middleware for Sensor Networks (MidSens) (2006)
8. Estrin, D., Govindan, R., Heidemann, J., Kumar, S.: Next century challenges: scalable coordination in sensor networks. In: MobiCom. Proc. of the 5th Int. Conf. on Mobile computing and networking (1999)
9. Akyildiz, I.F., Kasimoglu, I.H.: Wireless sensor and actor networks: Research challenges. Ad Hoc Networks Journal 2(4), 351–367 (2004)
10. Whitehouse, K., Culler, D.: Calibration as parameter estimation in sensor networks. In: Proc. of the 1st Int. Wkshp. on Wireless sensor networks and applications (2002)
11. Abdelzaher, T., et al.: Envirotrack: Towards an environmental computing paradigm for distributed sensor networks. In: ICDCS. Proc. of the 24th Int. Conf. on Distributed Computing Systems (2004)
12. Al-Karaki, J.N., Kamal, A.E.: Routing techiniques in wireless sensor networks: a survey. IEEE Wireless Communications 11(6) (2004)
13. Wan, C.Y., Campbell, A.T., Krishnamurthy, L.: Reliable transport for sensor networks: PSFQ—Pump slowly fetch quickly paradigm. Wireless sensor networks (2004)
14. Rowstron, A.: WCL: A coordination language for geographically distributed agents. World Wide Web Journal 1(3), 167–179 (1998)
15. Gay, D., Levis, P., von Behren, R.: The NesC language: A holistic approach to networked embedded systems. In: Proc. of the ACM Conf. on Programming Language Design and Implementation, ACM Press, New York (2003)

16. Costa, P., Mottola, L., Murphy, A.L., Picco, G.P.: Developing Sensor Network Applications Using the TeenyLIME: Middleware. Technical Report DIT-07-059, University of Trento, Italy (2006), Available at dit.unitn.it/~picco/papers/teenylimeTR.pdf
17. Intanagonwiwat, C., et al.: Directed diffusion for wireless sensor networking. IEEE/ACM Trans. Networking 11(1) (2003)
18. van Dam, T., Langendoen, K.: An adaptive energy-efficient MAC protocol for wireless sensor networks. In: SENSYS. Proc. of the 1st Conf. on Networked Sensor Systems (2003)
19. Rajendran, V., Obraczka, K., Garcia-Luna-Aceves, J.J.: Energy-efficient, collision-free medium access control for wireless sensor networks. Wirel. Netw. 12(1) (2006)
20. Kasten, O., Römer, K.: Beyond event handlers: programming wireless sensors with attributed state machines. In: Proc. of the 4th Symp. on Information processing in sensor networks (2005)
21. Titzer, B., Lee, D., Palsberg, J.: Avrora: scalable sensor network simulation with precise timing. In: Proc. of the 4th Int. Symp. on Information processing in sensor networks (2005)
22. Crossbow Technology Inc., http://www.xbow.com
23. Naik, P., Sivalingam, K.M.: A survey of MAC protocols for sensor networks. Wireless sensor networks, 93–107 (2004)
24. Murphy, A.L., Picco, G.P., Roman, G.C.: LIME: A coordination model and middleware supporting mobility of hosts and agents. ACM Trans. on Software Engineering and Methodology (TOSEM) 15(3), 279–328 (2006)
25. Curino, C., Giani, M., Giorgetta, M., Giusti, A., Murphy, A.L., Picco, G.P.: Mobile data collection in sensor networks: The TinyLime middleware. Elsevier Pervasive and Mobile Computing Journal 4(1), 446–469 (2005)
26. Welsh, M., Mainland, G.: Programming sensor networks using abstract regions. In: Proc. of the 1st Symp. on Networked Systems Design and Implementation (2004)
27. Jonsson, M.: Supporting Context Awareness with the Context Shadow Infrastructure. In: Wkshp. on Affordable Wireless Services and Infrastructure (June 2003)
28. Fok, C.L., Roman, G.C., Lu, C.: Rapid development and flexible deployment of adaptive wireless sensor network applications. In: ICDCS. Proc. of the 25th IEEE Int. Conf. on Distributed Computing Systems, IEEE Computer Society Press, Los Alamitos (2005)

Author Index

Lecture Notes in Computer Science

Sublibrary 2: Programming and Software Engineering

For information about Vols. 1– 4192
please contact your bookseller or Springer